BOOK OF MORMON

Scriptural Phrases

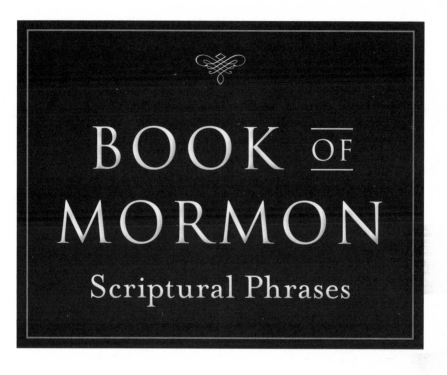

BOOK OF MORMON

Scriptural Phrases

ROGER A. DIBB

DESERET
BOOK
Salt Lake City, Utah

Library of Congress Cataloging-in-Publication Data

Dibb, Roger Alan, 1947– author.
  Book of Mormon scriptural phrases / Roger Alan Dibb.
    pages cm
  Includes bibliographical references.
  ISBN 978-1-62972-107-1 (paperbound)
  1. Book of Mormon—Dictionaries. I. Title.
  BX8627.A1D53 2015
  289.3'2203—dc23   2015012779

Printed in United States of America
Publishers Printing, Salt Lake City, UT

10   9   8   7   6   5   4   3   2   1

To my beloved wife, Ann.

To our children, Sarah, Alan, Mark, and Jeff.

And to our beautiful grandchildren.

I pray that they all may ever prosper and increase.

CONTENTS

ACKNOWLEDGMENTS

I am extremely indebted to Elaine Alger for invaluable assistance in polishing my drafts and providing guidance in style and format. Likewise Catherine Scott was an excellent copy editor in eliminating grammatical and typographical errors from the document. I am grateful to all the staff at Deseret Book for their assistance, particularly Sheri Dew, Lisa Roper, Robert Millet, Derk Koldewyn, Heather Ward, and Rachael Ward. Finally love and thanks to my wife, Ann, for her encouragement.

FOREWORD

For many years, as I have read the scriptures, I have thought that it would be most helpful to have a reference volume that defined the word combinations found in holy writ. Certain multi-word terms have specific scriptural meanings, and we should be aware of those meanings as we read and study the scriptures. These multi-word terms can be called "scriptural phrases."

Often the meaning of two words together in the scriptures contains more—and the combined meaning is different—than just the sum of the two words. For example, *eternal life* in the scriptures means much more than just immortal life forever. *Eternal life* is a scriptural phrase that means exaltation in the celestial kingdom (see Doctrine and Covenants 88:4).

All entries herein are scriptural phrases of two words or more. I have left single words to be defined by the Bible Dictionary and other references.

There are many scriptural phrases that mean no more than the words contained in the phrase. Looking for meaning in scriptural phrases can become obsessive to the point that we begin to "look beyond the mark." For example, in Enos 1:11 we find "my faith began to be unshaken in the Lord." How can it be said more plainly and simply than that? I do not believe there is additional meaning there, but that phrase is a great description of what our faith should look like.

That being said, it became apparent that scriptural phrases that are plain and simple in meaning perhaps should be included in this study because it is important to see the various contexts in which the phrase is used. A good example is the scriptural phrase "in that day" which often precedes prophecy. It is insightful to see the many times and places in the Book of Mormon where this phrase appears. Therefore I have included a good number of the plain and simple scriptural phrases.

My purpose here is not to replace the footnotes found at the bottom of each page in the scriptures—do not overlook a study of the footnotes. One should always look first to the footnotes for a better understanding of the terminology of the scriptures.

My goal while preparing these materials was to keep the explanations short so that one can get right back to the Book of Mormon. I would be loath to divert anyone for very long from reading directly from the pages of the Book of Mormon.

As I have worked on this compilation, I have observed that these scriptural phrases are the language of the scriptures, they are the language of the holy prophets and the language of prophecy, and they truly are the sacred word of the Lord.

Many scriptural phrases are in reality the testimony of gospel principles given by the prophet who wrote them. Those that recur in the Book of Mormon are the witness of two or more holy men, and these witnesses establish the truthfulness of the doctrine and of the book. Some chapters of scripture have many more of these scriptural phrases. For example, Alma 5 and Moroni 7 have a high number of them. As I compiled these phrases, I began to recognize the truth of how really simple the gospel is. Such terms as "faith in Christ," "real intent," and "according to their faith in God" are not complicated principles.

Studying and understanding the scriptures is very much like studying and understanding a new language. Only by constantly immersing oneself in the language or frequently reading the scriptures can we better understand their meaning. A word or phrase dictionary helps, but we must then try out the words and phrases for ourselves to become more proficient in and knowledgeable of the scriptures.

Those who have been in the Church for a number of years might feel that the meaning of some of these scriptural phrases seems obvious. However, I have tried to put myself in the shoes of a youth or recent convert who has not heard many of these scriptural phrases before. Even the most elementary scriptural phrases have been included here.

As Moroni wrote as he readied the plates to seal them up, "And if there be faults they be the faults of a man" (Mormon 8:17). Please overlook the foibles of man. The errors herein—which I am sure still exist—are mine. In the end, the true meaning of the scriptures is given to men and women by the Holy Ghost. We must pray as we read the scriptures that God will bless us with a true understanding. No reference book can take the place of personal prayer when it comes to scripture study.

When one knows the meaning of the terms, then the meaning and intent of the whole passage of scripture becomes more clear and understandable. And when we become familiar with these scriptural phrases, we will then recognize them more often in talks, in classes, and in hymns. They will then enrich our lives and our spiritual worship.

If I were asked why I undertook this study, the answer would be twofold: First, this study has greatly benefited my own understanding of the gospel, and second, as Nephi said in 2 Nephi 4:15, I write "them for the learning and the profit of my children [and grandchildren]."

Finally, this study has strengthened my belief in the truthfulness of the Book of Mormon all the more. I testify that the Book of Mormon is truly the word of God, and contains the gospel of our Lord and Savior, Jesus Christ. This study has confirmed to me that the truths of the gospel are taught in the Book of Mormon. As you look through these pages, you will see over and over again the simple truths of the gospel of Jesus Christ found in the Book of Mormon.

I love the Book of Mormon. The more you read it, the more is revealed unto you. That is a sure promise.

HOW TO USE THIS BOOK

The scriptural phrases included in this book number over 4,200 and are listed alphabetically word by word. As a general rule there are two types of entries found in the pages of this book as illustrated by the following:

EXAMPLE 1

❶ **Firm in the faith of Christ** ❷ (Alma 27:27; 48:13; 57:27; Helaman 6:1; 15:8). ❸ Meaning steadfast in keeping the commandments of God. In other words, immovable in a determination to follow the example of Christ. ❹ *See also:* Exceeding faith; Firm and steadfast (and undaunted); Made strong; Minds are firm; Sure foundation.

❶ Name of the scriptural phrase.

❷ Verses in Book of Mormon where this scriptural phrase is found.

❸ A meaning or explanation of the scriptural phrase.

❹ *See also:* A cross reference to other scriptural phrases found in the book that are similar in meaning or more fully explain the meaning of this scriptural phrase.

EXAMPLE 2

❶ **Firm and steadfast (and un-daunted)** ❷(1 Nephi 2:10; Helaman 15:8; 3 Nephi 6:14). ❸ *See:* Firm in the faith of Christ.

❶ Name of the scriptural phrase.

❷ Verses in Book of Mormon where this scriptural phrase is found.

❸ No meaning is listed. Rather there is a cross reference to "see" a scriptural phrase in the book that has the same or very similar meaning and has a definition for that meaning.

When looking for scriptural phrases in these pages you may have to peel back the outer layers of words to find the core phrase. For example, the phrase "How oft would I have gathered you as a hen gathereth her chickens and ye would not" will be found at the listing "Hen gathereth her chickens." If you do not find what you are looking for at first, peel off the first word or words and likely you will find the remainder of the phrase.

In the interest of brevity and order, some scriptural phrases have been combined. For example, the entry "Bring forth (good) fruit" combines both the phrase "Bring forth fruit" and the phrase "Bring forth good fruit." Since these two phrases have similar meanings they have been combined into one entry.

Along the same lines, the entry "According to his (my/our/the/their/ thy/your) faith" combines several similar phrases ("According to his faith"; "according to my faith"; "according to our faith"; and so on). In these cases, the words or phrases that could replace a particular word or phrase follow alphabetically in parentheses and are separated by slashes.

Phrases which recur far too frequently to cite each instance (such as "And it came to pass") are cited by their first occurrence and then the Latin word *passim,* meaning "recurring throughout."

Items found within brackets [like this] are words added by the author to clarify meaning.

SCRIPTURAL
PHRASES

A

Abasing themselves (Alma 4:13). To humble oneself. *Abase* is defined as "to lower in rank, office, prestige, or esteem" (*Webster's Collegiate Dictionary*, s.v. "abase"). In D&C 101:42, "He that exalteth himself shall be abased, and he that abaseth himself shall be exalted."

Abhor sin (such wickedness) (2 Nephi 9:49; Alma 13:12; 27:28; 37:29). To abhor is to turn away from or avoid with extreme repulsion. *See also:* Hatred against (to) sin; No more desire (disposition) to do evil; Shake at the appearance of sin.

Abide in (upon/with) him (them) (1 Nephi 11:27; Alma 17:9; Mormon 2:26; Ether 12:41). Refers to the Spirit of God (the Holy Ghost) being and remaining with one who is worthy of that sacred presence.

Abide in (with) you forever (Ether 12:41; Moroni 9:26). Meaning the grace of God abide in you forever. Both of these verses are admonishments by the prophet Moroni to seek and be worthy of the grace of God, which is His goodness and divine assistance.

Abide the day of his coming (3 Nephi 24:2). Refers to those that will stand at the Second Coming of the Lord. In other words, those that will be caught up and will not be burned. *Contrast:* Consumed as stubble. *See also:* D&C 61:39; 128:24.

Abominable above all sins save it be the shedding of innocent blood or denying the Holy Ghost (Jacob 2:5, 21, 24; Mosiah 11:2; Alma 39:5). Sexual sin and lusting in one's heart are abominable in the sight of God. So heinous and great are these sins they are subordinate only to the two greatest sins named.

Abominable church (1 Nephi 13:5–6, 8, 26, 28, 32, 34; 14:3, 9, 15, 17; 22:13–14; 2 Nephi 6:12; 28:18). *See:* Great and abominable church.

Abominable in the sight of the Lord (Jacob 2:5; Mosiah 11:2; 23:9). All sin is offensive and repugnant ("abominable") before the Lord.

Abominations of his people (Mosiah 3:7; 28:15; 29:18). Meaning the sins and wickedness of the people. *See also:* Abominable in the sight of the Lord.

Abound(-ing) in good works
(Mosiah 5:15; Alma 7:24; Ether
12:4). Means performing good
works in great quantity. "Let your
light so shine before men, that they
may see your good works, and glorify your Father which is in heaven"
(Matthew 5:16). "If a man bringeth
forth good works he hearkeneth
unto the voice of the good shepherd" (Alma 5:41). "And let us consider one another to provoke unto
love and to good works" (Hebrews
10:24). "All people . . . shall stand
before God, to be judged of their
works, whether they be good or
whether they be evil" (3 Nephi
26:4). *See also:* According to their
(your) works (deeds); Good works;
Judged according to (of) their
works.

Abraham, Isaac, and Jacob
(1 Nephi 17:40; Mosiah 7:19; Alma
5:24; 7:25; Helaman 3:30). Often
referred to as the fathers or the pa-
triarchs. These great prophets were
faithful unto God, strove with
their might to keep God's commandments, sought to further the
Kingdom of God and His work,
and in death have received their exaltation. *See also:* God of Abraham,
God of Isaac, and God of Jacob.

Abused his laws (Mormon 9:3).
Simply means to have broken God's
commandments. Also to have ratio-
nalized away God's laws, trampled
them underfoot, and considered
them a thing of naught.

Acceptable before God (Moroni
7:44). It should be one of our primary desires to be pleasing unto
God, meaning to be meek and contrite and striving to do only that
which is right. *See also:* Stand spotless before me at the last day.

Acceptable time (1 Nephi 21:8).
God's timing is perfect. Though we
might desire a different timing, we
must accept God's timing. *See also:*
Own due time (of the Lord).

According to God's justice
(1 Nephi 14:4; Jacob 6:10; Alma
12:18; 42:13, 23; 50:39; 3 Nephi
6:4, 29; 26:5; Mormon 6:22). God
administers the eternal laws of justice perfectly. Complete justice is
part of God's moral code. Justice
provides that there are consequences
to every action. There is no variation
from the just law of consequences.
God desires to be perfectly just and
at the same time He desires to be
merciful (see Alma 42:15). Thus the
plan of salvation provides an infinite sacrifice so that mercy may sup-
plant the consequences of justice.
See also: All his judgments are just;
Demands of justice; Judgments are
just; Justice of God.

**According to God's (thy abun-
dant) mercy** (1 Nephi 8:8; Alma
18:41; 3 Nephi 26:5; Mormon
6:22). God has infinite love for His
children. Knowing we would each
err and sin, God mercifully provided the plan of salvation that we
might each return to his presence if

we repent and accept the Atonement of Jesus Christ wherein mercy may satisfy the demands of justice. When Enoch described the Lord, he used the phrase "Mercy shall go before thy face and have no end" (Moses 7:31). *See also:* Demands of justice; Great plan of mercy; Infinite mercy; Justice and mercy (of God); Merciful God (Being).

According to God's will (1 Nephi 7:12; 2 Nephi 2:21, 28; 10:22; 25:22; 27:13; Jacob 4:9; 5:14, 75; Words of Mormon 1:7; Mosiah 7:33; Alma 4:14; 12:17; 14:13; 3 Nephi 5:14; 23:4; 28:7; Moroni 1:4; 10:17). Because God is perfect, His will and pleasure are always correct and are to be followed. Also because God only has our best interest as His priority, then we should follow His will. *See also:* Will of God.

According to God's word (1 Nephi 17:31, 54; 2 Nephi 4:14; 31:13; Jacob 2:11; 5:5, 10; Alma 6:8; 7:8; 12:9, 36–37; 17:17; 36:30; 62:51; Helaman 12:15; 3 Nephi 5:22; 29:1; 4 Nephi 1:31). *According* means in conformity, adherence, and observance. Thus God's word must be and always will be fulfilled. "What I the Lord have spoken, I have spoken, and I excuse not myself; and though the heavens and the earth pass away, my word shall not pass away, but shall all be fulfilled, whether by mine own voice or by the voice of my servants, it is the same" (D&C 1:38). *See also:* According to his word; According

to that which had been spoken (he hath sworn); According to the promise(-s) of the Lord; According to the prophecy (prophecies) of the Lord; According to the word of God (the Lord); According to the word(-s) of the angel; Executeth all his words; Fulfil all his (my) promises; Fulfill all things which I have made known unto the children of men; Fulfill all that which I have caused to be spoken by the mouth of my holy prophets; Fulfill his word which he hath declared; Fulfilled the prophecies; Fulfilled the promise; Fulfilled the scriptures; Fulfilled the word(-s) of God (the Lord); Fulfilleth the words which he hath given; Fulfilling of (all) his (the) word(-s/of the Lord); Fulfilling of the prophecies; Fulfilling of the promise; Must be fulfilled; Must come to pass; Promise of the Lord; Promises of the Lord; Promises shall be fulfilled; Scriptures fulfilled; Word of God must be fulfilled; Word of God (prophets/the Lord) has been (was/were) fulfilled (verified); Words fulfilled which he prophesied.

According to his (my/our/the/ their/thy/your) faith (1 Nephi 7:17; 16:28–29; 2 Nephi 26:13; 27:23; Enos 1:18; Jarom 1:4; Mosiah 27:14; Alma 5:12; 7:27; 9:20; 12:30; 13:3; 14:26, 28; 15:10; 18:35; 19:23; 31:38; 37:40; 57:21; 61:17; 3 Nephi 5:14; Mormon 9:37; Ether 12:29; Moroni 7:41; 10:7). It is absolute and sure that God answers prayers and performs miracles based on the faith of the people or an individual—if it be God's will. Faith is the principle by which all things are accomplished. Without faith nothing can be accomplished. For example, a builder who did not have the faith that he could build a house would not be able to build a house, and as a result he would not be a builder of houses. Spiritually it is paramount that we have faith in God. Faith is the first principle of the gospel. Without faith in God there is no spiritual progression nor salvation. Only by faith are miracles brought to pass. There must be obedience to God's commandments, otherwise faith withers and dies. According to or based on the strength of one's faith, God can work in one's life to improve that life. We must strive with faith to do God's will. Most importantly we must pray for our faith to grow, for in the end, great faith is a gift from God to those who seek it. If we desire a gift from God, knowledge from God, assistance from God, comfort from God, or a million other things from God, then we must approach God in faith. Thus that which is received from God is based on our faith, if God so wills it. We must have faith that God will provide what is best for us according to our faith. God is a great rewarder of those who have faith.

According to his will and pleasure (2 Nephi 10:22; Jacob 4:9; 5:14). *See:* According to God's will.

According to his word (1 Nephi 17:31; 2 Nephi 4:14; 31:13; Jacob 5:5; Alma 7:8; 12:36–37; 36:30; 62:51; Helaman 12:15; 3 Nephi 5:22; 29:1; 4 Nephi 1:31). *See:* According to God's word.

According to his works (shall his wages be) (Mosiah 3:24; Mormon 8:19). *See:* According to their (your) works (deeds).

According to that which had been spoken (he hath sworn) (1 Nephi 17:54; 3 Nephi 5:2; 29:8). *See:* According to God's word.

According to the faith and diligence and heed (1 Nephi 16:28; Mosiah 1:16; Alma 7:26; 12:9). In order to obtain eternal reward and exaltation we must do more than just declare belief in Jesus Christ. To truly accept Jesus as our Savior we must also strive with our might to give heed to His commandments and follow His example with diligence. *See also:* Commandments of God (the Father/the Lord); Good works.

According to the flesh (1 Nephi 19:6; 22:2, 18, 27; 2 Nephi 2:8, 27, 29; 9:53; 10:2; 31:7; Alma 7:12–13). Meaning after the manner of mortality. Or in other words, "while they are in the flesh" (2 Nephi 10:15). Also as in "judged according to men in the flesh" (D&C 76:73). This phrase is used in the scriptures in a number of contexts, including: (1) lineage according to the flesh (rightful heirs); (2) men are free according to the flesh (moral agency); and (3) concerning Jesus Christ who: (a) was born of Mary, a mortal mother (after the manner of the flesh); (b) laid down His life according to the flesh (suffered physical death); (c) suffered according to the flesh (took upon him our sins and pains); (d) humbled himself according to the flesh (condescended to earth); and (e) "will take upon him their infirmities, that his bowels may be filled with mercy, according to the flesh, that he may know according to the flesh how to succor his people according to their infirmities" (Alma 7:12). The Christmas carol "What Child Is This" by William C. Dix illustrates this doctrinal point in the lyrics "Hail, Hail the Word made flesh" (see Keyte and Parrott, *Book of Carols*, 161).

According to the (holy) order of God (Alma 5:44; 6:1; 8:4; 13:18). Refers to officiating in the priesthood of God. *See also:* Order of God.

According to the power (and captivity) of Satan (the devil) (Jacob 7:4; Alma 9:28; 12:6, 17). Satan can only gain power over us if we allow him to through our sinning; thus one becomes captive to Satan. *See also:* Power of Satan.

According to the power of God (1 Nephi 17:29; Alma 17:17; 37:28). Meaning done by and through the almighty and omnipotent power of God. *See also:* Power of God.

According to the power of (his) deliverance (1 Nephi 1:20; Alma 4:14; 7:13; 9:28). Jesus Christ is the Great Deliverer. We will be resurrected and can gain salvation through and because of the Atonement of Jesus Christ, who delivers us from physical and spiritual death. *See also:* Atonement of Christ (the Only Begotten Son); Bring(-eth) salvation.

According to the power of justice (Jacob 6:10; Alma 9:28). *See:* Power of justice.

According to the power of the Father (3 Nephi 27:15). God the Father has all power and has given a fulness of His power to His Only Begotten Son, Jesus Christ. There is no power that they have not obtained, and they have the power to do anything they will to do. *See also:* Power of God.

According to the power of the resurrection (Jacob 4:11; Alma 41:2). All persons who have lived on earth will be resurrected by this power, which is the power by which Jesus Christ was resurrected, and thereby He became the first fruits of the Resurrection—in other words, the first of men to be resurrected. *See also:* Power of the resurrection.

According to the promise(-s) of the Lord (Mosiah 1:7; Alma 28:11–12; 4 Nephi 1:11, 49; Moroni 7:41). All the promises of the Lord have been, are now being, and will be fulfilled. *See also:* According to God's word.

According to the prophecy (prophecies) of the Lord (2 Nephi 25:10, 26; Alma 3:27; 4:13, 20; 5:47; 6:8; 8:24; 10:12; 12:7; 13:26; 23:6; 43:2; Helaman 8:20; 15:13; 3 Nephi 1:26; 3:16). Meaning according to the word of God as given through prophets and scriptures. *See also:* According to God's word; Things (which are) to come.

According to the Spirit (1 Nephi 22:1; 2 Nephi 1:6; 2:28; 4:12; 25:4; 28:1; Jarom 1:4; Words of Mormon 1:7; Alma 3:26–27; 4:13, 20; 5:47; 6:8; 7:5, 16, 26; 8:24, 32; 10:12; 11:22; 12:7; 13:26; 18:35; 23:6; 43:2; 45:10; 61:15; Mormon 3:16). Refers to the Spirit of God or the Holy Ghost. Meaning as directed by the Spirit, revealed by the Spirit, prophesied by the Spirit, spoken by the Spirit, confirmed by the Spirit, and testified by the Spirit. The Spirit can work in us in many ways to further the work of the Lord and the salvation of God's people.

According to the testimony of the Holy Spirit which testifieth in me (Alma 7:16, 26). Holy prophets and other righteous individuals testify by the power of the Spirit of God that works in them. Such testimony can have a profound effect on the hearer. *See also:* By the power of the Holy Ghost (Spirit).

According to the will of God (the Lord) (2 Nephi 2:21; 27:13; Alma 14:13; 3 Nephi 5:14; 28:7; Moroni 1:4). *See:* According to God's will.

According to the word of God (the Lord) (1 Nephi 18:4; 2 Nephi 25:3; Jacob 5:10; Jarom 1:10; Words of Mormon 1:11; Mosiah 26:34; Alma 12:22; 17:17; 42:5; 3 Nephi 28:23; 29:7; Mormon 8:16; Ether 1:33). *See:* According to God's word.

According to the word(-s) of the angel (1 Nephi 12:19; 14:27; 19:8, 10; 2 Nephi 6:9; 25:19). The words of holy angels are the words of God delivered by angels and will all be fulfilled and come to pass. *See also:* According to God's word; Angels minister(-ed/appeared/declared/descending) unto him (them).

According to the words of the prophet(-s) (1 Nephi 2:13; 22:23; 2 Nephi 6:14; 25:19; 3 Nephi 1:20; 5:2). *See:* According to the prophecy (prophecies) of the Lord.

According to the words which are written (2 Nephi 2:17; 5:12; 25:22; 29:11; Words of Mormon 1:11). The scriptures contain the word of God as recorded by His prophets. *See also:* According to God's word; Scriptures fulfilled.

According to the workings of the Spirit (of the Lord) which is in me (2 Nephi 1:6; Words of Mormon 1:7). *See:* According to the Spirit; Workings in (of) the Spirit.

According to their (your) deeds (works) (2 Nephi 28:23; 29:11; Mosiah 3:24; 16:10; Alma 3:26;

5:15; 7:27; 9:28; 11:41, 44; 12:8, 12, 30; 13:3; 33:22; 40:21; 41:3; 42:23, 27; Helaman 12:24; 3 Nephi 27:15; Mormon 3:18; 6:21). As explained in the entry "According to his (my/our/the/their/thy/your) faith," blessings from God are predicated upon our faith. However, good works are also required, for "faith without works is dead" (James 2:20, 26). *See also:* Abound(-ing) in good works; Good works; Judged according to (of) their works.

Acknowledge to our everlasting shame (Jacob 6:9; Alma 12:15). If we come to stand before God unrepentant and stained with sin, we will experience and have to admit our great shame. *See also:* Not be ashamed.

Acknowledge your faults (unworthiness) (Alma 38:14; 39:13). One of the first steps of repentance is to acknowledge, admit, and declare our sins before God. Thus in humility and with a contrite and broken heart we seek forgiveness from our Maker. This we must do throughout our lives. If we do not repent of our sins, we will come before God covered and stained with sin and filthiness. *See also:* Acknowledge to our everlasting shame.

Acquainted with grief (Mosiah 14:3, 10). The same phrase found in Isaiah 53:3 which refers to our Savior's experience while in mortality. Many of the prophets were given to know that Jesus, even though He was perfect and without sin, also experienced the sorrows and grief of mortal life. Thus He can relate to the suffering and sorrows that we experience, and He can effectively and perfectly administer empathy, relief, and balm when we turn to Him. *See also:* Alma 7:11–12.

Act for themselves (yourselves) (2 Nephi 2:16, 26; 10:23; Helaman 14:30; 3 Nephi 1:29). "Act for themselves" means to choose for themselves. Each of us has our moral agency to make our own decisions. Thus mortality becomes a probationary state, wherein is the opportunity to "prove them herewith, to see if they will do all things whatsoever the Lord their God shall command them" (Abraham 3:25).

Act or be acted upon (2 Nephi 2:13–14, 26). *See:* To act or to be acted upon.

Adam and Eve (1 Nephi 5:11, 19). Our first parents, formed in the image and likeness of God, and placed on the earth to bring forth the generations of man. Adam and Eve were prominent persons in the premortal life and were faithful unto God in mortality. Adam is also known in the scriptures as Michael the archangel, who was, is, and will be the leader of the armies of heaven in the cause of God.

Administer(-ed) unto him (them) (Alma 15:18; 17:18; 19:33; 22:3, 25; 35:9). To administer the gospel to others is to preach the word, officiate in the ordinances thereof, and to provide spiritual and physical sustenance. Wilford Woodruff said, "When an apostle, or president, bishop or any man holding the priesthood officiates, he administers by the authority of the Lord Jesus Christ; then that priesthood has effect, and all the blessings that a servant of God bestows upon the children of men will take effect both in this life and that which is to come . . . and if I am true to my covenants through this life, I can claim every blessing that has been conferred upon me, because that authority by which they were conferred is ordained of God; and it is that by which the sons of the Most High administer unto the children of men and ordinances of life and salvation; and those official acts will have their effect upon those persons beyond the grave as well as in this life" (*Discourses of Wilford Woodruff*, 70). *See also:* Jacob 2:19; Mosiah 4:16.

Administer(-ing) relief to the sick and the afflicted (Jacob 2:19; Mosiah 4:26). Pure and true religion is to visit the sick, afflicted, the widow and fatherless (see James 1:26). *Administer* means to provide spiritual *and* temporal relief, comfort, assistance, means, and encouragement.

Administering the flesh and blood of Christ (Moroni 4:1; 5:1). Meaning to bless and pass the sacrament of bread and wine or water to the members of the church that they might eat in remembrance of the body of the Son and drink in remembrance of the blood of the Son. Thus they renew their covenants of baptism.

Admonished by the church (Mosiah 26:6). Meaning confronted and called to repentance. In the absence of repentance, made subject to church disciplinary action. The purpose of discipline in the Church is to help individuals overcome and repent from sin and to ensure protection of the innocent from predatory acts and from the spread of sin. It is also to safeguard the honorable name and integrity of Christ's church. Discipline includes restrictions and conditions of repentance.

Admonish(-ed) with the word (Jacob 2:9; Omni 1:13; Mosiah 26:39; Alma 1:7). To admonish is to warn, advise, exhort, caution, and counsel. In these verses the admonishment is done by using the word of God as found in the scriptures and as revealed by prophets.

Admonitions of the Lord (2 Nephi 4:13; Enos 1:1). The warnings and counsels received from God and spoken or otherwise delivered to men by God's servants. *See also:* Admonish(-ed) with the word.

Advocateth the cause of the children of men (Moroni 7:28). Jesus Christ is our advocate with God the Father. Jesus pleads mercy for us and offers salvation to repentant and faithful souls. *See also:* Great Mediator; D&C 45:3; 62:1.

Affairs of the church (Mosiah 26:37; 29:42; Alma 1:28; 46:7; Helaman 3:1). Meaning the responsibility of administering, building up, strengthening, and protecting the Church.

Afflict my soul (1 Nephi 17:47; 2 Nephi 1:16; 4:17, 26–28; 26:7, 10–11; Jacob 2:6, 9; Mosiah 27:29; Alma 26:20; 31:30; 36:12, 14; 46:25; 61:2; Helaman 7:9). The fourth chapter of Second Nephi is sometimes referred to as the Psalm of Nephi, where he glories in the gospel and his God but also anguishes over the frailties and struggles of mortality. He says that temptation and sin disturb his peace and afflict his soul. *Afflict* means to torment or distress. Anguish and anxiety of soul also come from seeing the sin and wrongdoings of others. If we each truly care for our fellowman then it grieves our souls, sorrows our souls, pains our souls to see their wickedness. *See also:* Agony of his soul; Burdeneth my soul; Pain(-ed) my heart (soul); Soul rent with anguish.

After I had received strength (1 Nephi 15:6). After receiving revelation or being in the presence of the Lord, mortals often find themselves physically weak and in need of a space of time to regain normal physical strength. *See also:* Moses 1:10; Joseph Smith–History 1:20, 48.

After much tribulation (Mosiah 23:10; 27:28). "For after much tribulation come the blessings" (D&C 58:4). Tribulations can be a testing of our faith, and include afflictions, sorrow, rudeness, hate, wars, contentions, ignorance, persecution, wickedness, desolation, sickness, weariness, abuse, and much more. "Our mortal life, however, was never meant to be easy or consistently pleasant. Our Heavenly Father, who gives us so much to delight in, also knows that we learn and grow and become refined through hard challenges, heartbreaking sorrows, and difficult choices" (Monson, "Joy in the Journey," 5; paragraphing altered). *See also:* Bear afflictions (with patience).

After the manner of the flesh (1 Nephi 11:18). *See:* According to the flesh.

After the order of his (the) Son (Alma 13:1–2, 7, 9; Helaman 8:18). D&C 107:1–5 says, "There are, in the Church, two priesthoods, namely, the Melchizedek and Aaronic, including the Levitical Priesthood. Why the first is called the Melchizedek Priesthood is because Melchizedek was such a great high priest. Before his day it was called *the Holy Priesthood, after the Order of the Son of God.* But out of respect or reverence to the name of the Supreme Being, to avoid the too frequent repetition of his name, they, the church, in ancient days, called that priesthood after Melchizedek, or the Melchizedek Priesthood. All other authorities or offices in the church are appendages to this priesthood." *See also:* Authority from (of) God; Called after the holy order of God; Called by the order of God; Psalm 110:4; Hebrews 5:6, 10; 6:20; 7:11, 17, 21; D&C 76:57; 107:9, 10, 29, 71, 73, 76; 124:123; Moses 6:67.

After their (they had/they have) faith (Ether 12:6, 7, 12, 17, 18, 30, 31). *See:* According to his (my/our/the/their/thy/your) faith.

Against God (1 Nephi 17:42; 2 Nephi 25:14; Jacob 1:8; Mosiah 2:37; 3:12; 15:26; 16:5; 21:30; 27:11; Alma 3:18; 10:6; 23:7; 30:29; 36:13; 3 Nephi 6:18). Referring to those that revile, fight, or rebel against God.

Against that which is good (2 Nephi 28:16, 20; Helaman 16:22; Moroni 7:12). Satan and his minions constantly strive against all that is good. Because they are evil, it is not in their nature to do otherwise.

Agony of his soul (Helaman 7:6). Meaning sorrow to his being and in his heart. *See also:* Afflict my soul.

Alive in Christ (2 Nephi 25:25; Moroni 8:12, 22). A state of being for which we should all strive. To become alive in Christ, we must obtain greater faith in Christ. Because of the Atonement of Jesus Christ we can be forgiven of our sins and live free of guilt. To be alive in Christ is to be vibrant in our testimony, busily enjoying doing good, and full of joy and hope about our todays and our tomorrows. The scriptures tell us that Jesus is the life of the world. It is the light of Christ that gives life to all living things. As we come unto Christ we obtain more of His light, so that we feel fully animated and thankful unto God for our very being. The opposite is to reject Christ and His gospel, come into subjection to the devil, curse life, experience spiritual death, and sink into despair.

All are alike unto God (2 Nephi 26:33; Moroni 8:17). God is no respecter of persons; all men and women are admonished equally to come unto Christ and be saved. None are barred from salvation if they will accept Christ and keep His commandments. *Compare:* Favored of God. *See also:* All men; All men are privileged the one like unto the other; Denieth none that come unto him; Draw all men unto him (me); Esteemeth all flesh in one; Persuade all men to come unto Christ (repentance); Redeem all those (mankind) who believe on his name.

All eternity to all eternity (Mosiah 3:5; Alma 13:7; Moroni 8:18). *See:* From (all) eternity to all eternity.

All his judgments are just (2 Nephi 1:10; Omni 1:22; Mosiah 16:1; 29:12; Alma 12:15; 14:11). God is the perfect embodiment of being just. He follows strictly the laws of justice. He administers in mercy all justice. He desires to be both just and merciful. God cannot overlook justice; if He did he would cease to be God. *See also:* According to God's justice; Judgments are just.

All his promises shall be fulfilled (Alma 37:17; 3 Nephi 20:46; Mormon 8:22). *See:* According to God's word.

All his (spoken) words shall be fulfilled (1 Nephi 7:13; 2 Nephi 9:17; Mosiah 21:4; Helaman 11:8; 3 Nephi 5:1; 23:10; 29:2; Mormon 8:26; Ether 15:3, 33). *See:* According to God's word.

All is well (2 Nephi 28:21, 25; Helaman 13:28). "Wo be unto him that crieth: All is well!" (2 Nephi 28:25). "All is well" is a flattering phrase used by Satan and his minions to lull people into a false sense of security that there is no work to do, there are no other people who need assistance, wickedness does not need to be weeded out, and the kingdom of God does not need to be built up. Though we might be blessed and prospered by the Lord, we must not believe that nothing else needs to be done.

All kindreds, tongues, and people (1 Nephi 5:18; 11:36; 13:40; 14:11; 22:28; 2 Nephi 30:8; Mosiah 27:25;

3 Nephi 26:4; 28:29). *See:* All ye ends of the earth.

All manner of abominations (iniquity) (1 Nephi 12:23; 22:23; 2 Nephi 9:9; 27:1; Mosiah 11:2; 24:7; 29:36; Alma 1:32; 5:22, 23; 11:20; 13:17; 16:18; 45:12; 47:36; 62:40; Helaman 3:14; 6:23; 7:21; 10:3; 12:5; 13:22, 24; 3 Nephi 6:15–16; 12:11; 16:10; 4 Nephi 1:27, 34; Mormon 8:31, 36; Ether 8:16; 9:10; 11:10; 13:26). The sins listed in the Book of Mormon as "all manner of sins" include but are not limited to robbing, murders, plunder, lyings, whoredoms, oaths of darkness, envying, strifes, malice, persecutions, pride, deceits, smiting, wearing of costly apparel (today costly cars and houses as well), cursing, hypocrisy, mischiefs, priestcrafts, bearing false witness, power seeking, mockings, boasting, stealing, breaking the law, contentions, dissentions, lasciviousness, indolence, reviling, adultery, disturbances, rioting, thieving, drunkenness, secret works, lusts of the flesh, seeking popularity, and being full of idleness.

All men (1 Nephi 10:18; 13:40; 14:23; 2 Nephi 1:10; 2:10, 21, 27; 9:5–6, 13, 15, 21–23, 44; 10:19; 11:6, 8; 26:24, 27–28, 30; 29:7, 11; 31:20; 33:10; Jacob 1:8; Omni 1:25; Mosiah 2:4; 27:3, 31; Alma 1:4; 5:33; 9:28; 21:6; 28:8; 29:5; 30:11; 33:22; 40:11; 48:17, 19; Helaman 12:25; 3 Nephi 11:32; 27:14–15; Mormon 9:13; Ether 3:15; 12:27, 38; 13:2). The plan of salvation encompasses all men, meaning all men, women, and children. All were created by God, all are born into mortality, all are beckoned to repent and come unto Christ. The Atonement of Christ is offered to all, all will stand before God to be judged, and all will receive a reward in the next life according to their works. *See also:* All are alike unto God.

All men are privileged the one like unto the other (2 Nephi 26:28). God is no respecter of persons, and anyone may choose to come unto Christ and seek salvation. *See also:* All are alike unto God.

All my (our/their/thy) sins (Mosiah 27:35; Alma 22:16, 18; 24:11; 36:12–13; Helaman 14:13; 3 Nephi 3:25; 5:3; 27:19; 30:2; Mormon 7:5; Moroni 6:2). To be right before God we must repent of all our sins, not just some of them, not just the ones we have been caught in, not leaving out those we still desire to participate in. True repentance is repentance from *all* our sins. Baptism and other ordinances cannot be effectual and sealed by the Holy Spirit of Promise unless we are truly repentant, humble, and contrite, laying all our sins before God in true and complete penitence. *See also:* All your (our) sins (guilt/iniquities/wickedness).

All power (1 Nephi 9:6; Mosiah 4:9; Alma 12:15; 26:35; Mormon 5:23; Ether 3:4). We believe that God is omnipotent—that is He has all power. There are not any powers that He does not have or has yet to obtain. He has the power to do all that He wills to do. He has the power to command the elements, all worlds, and the very universe. They all obey His word. God's power is supreme, divine, infinite, and unlimited. God's power is in harmony with the nature of eternal existence. *See also:* Power of God; Power of his voice (word).

All-powerful Creator (Jacob 2:5; Alma 44:5). *See:* All power; Created all things; Power of God.

All-searching eye (2 Nephi 9:44; Mosiah 27:31). Because of the infinite power, all-knowing nature, and omnipresence of God, there is nothing that goes without His notice. We cannot keep a secret from God because He knows all our thoughts, actions, and intents. *Compare:* Jacob 2:10, 15. *See also:* In the sight of God (the Lord).

All shall rise from the dead, both the just and the unjust (Alma 11:41; 12:8; 33:22; 40:5, 10). There are two main results of the Resurrection and Atonement of Jesus Christ: (1) all men, women, and children who have lived on earth in mortality will be resurrected, because Jesus was the first fruits of the Resurrection, making it a free gift to all mankind; (2) those who accept the gospel of Jesus Christ accept the saving ordinances of the gospel plan and endeavor with all their heart, might, and mind to live a Christlike life will obtain eternal exalted life—salvation—in God's presence. *See also:* Immortal body.

All that watch for iniquity (2 Nephi 27:31). Those that seek iniquity, do evil, and hearken not unto the Lord their God (see 1 Nephi 22:23). *See also:* D&C 45:50.

All the ends of the earth (Mosiah 12:24; 15:31; Alma 29:7; 3 Nephi 16:20; 20:35; Mormon 3:18; Moroni 10:24). The whole, complete, total, and entire earth, including the very ends and far distant parts. *See also:* All ye ends of the earth.

All the holy prophets (1 Nephi 3:20; 5:13; Jacob 4:4; Mosiah 15:11, 13; Alma 5:24; 30:44; Helaman 8:16; 3 Nephi 1:26; 5:1). The prophets are faithful men called and sent by God to testify of Christ and call mankind to repentance. *See also:* Holy man; Holy prophet(-s/of God); Holy ones of God; Prophet of the Lord God.

All the remainder of our days (Mosiah 5:5). Once we are converted to the gospel of Jesus Christ and have received the saving ordinances, it is required that we serve one another and keep the commandments of God all the remainder of our days. *See also:* Endure(-th) to the end.

All these (many) witnesses (2 Nephi 11:3; 27:14; Jacob 4:6, 13; Mosiah 26:9; Alma 30:45; 34:30, 33). God provides more than just one witness. Many witnesses of His being, of His commandments, and of the validity of Jesus Christ, our Redeemer, are planned and sent by God. *See also:* Testimony of many (two or three).

All things common (3 Nephi 26:19; 4 Nephi 1:3). Refers to those righteous saints that did not withhold goods from the poor. All shared alike the necessities and bounties of what they had (see Acts 2:44). In 4 Nephi 1:25 the people regressed and did no longer have their goods and substance common. *See also:* Common among them; Liberal to all; They were in one.

All things fulfilled (1 Nephi 7:13; 3 Nephi 28:7; Ether 12:3). *See:* Fulfilling of (all) his (the) word(-s/ of the Lord).

All things had (have) become new (3 Nephi 12:47; 15:2–3; Ether 13:9). (1) In 3 Nephi, this phrase describes the Law of Moses that is fulfilled and done away, replaced by Christ's teachings. (2) In Ether, the phrase refers to the Millennium, when the "earth will be renewed and receive its paradisiacal glory" (Articles of Faith 1:10). *See also:* Earth shall (should) pass away; Heavens and the earth should pass away; New heaven and a new earth; Old have passed away and all things have become new; Old things are done (had passed) away and (that) all things had (have) become new.

All things must be a compound in one (2 Nephi 2:11). Meaning no opposites and just one choice. The full context of the verse is "For it must needs be that there is an opposition in all things. If not . . . [then] all things must needs be a compound in one." In other words, if there were not choices between opposites, then there would only be one choice; and if there was only one choice for all of life, then there would be no life. *See also:* Compound in one.

All things that in them are (2 Nephi 2:14; Alma 11:39; 3 Nephi 9:15; Mormon 9:11; Ether 4:7). This phrase is used in the scriptures to emphasize that all things were created or, more correctly, organized by God. God organized the heavens, all of the earth, and absolutely everything that is encompassed or existing within the heavens and the earth.

All things what ye should do (2 Nephi 32:3, 5). If we are true and faithful and follow the promptings of the Holy Ghost, those things necessary for our salvation and those things needed for us to fulfill our mission will be revealed unto us in the Lord's due time and if the Lord determines it expedient or necessary. In D&C 18:18, "Ask the Father in my name in faith, believing that you shall receive, and

you shall have the Holy Ghost, which manifesteth all things which are expedient unto the children of men." And in D&C 75:10, "Calling on the name of the Lord for the Comforter, which shall teach them all things that are expedient for them." Yet, "It is not meet that I should command in all things; for he that is compelled in all things, the same is a slothful and not a wise servant; wherefore he receiveth no reward" (D&C 58:26). President Joseph Fielding Smith said, "The promise is sure that the Lord will not deny the humble petition which is offered, and it may not be expedient in some prayers that the answer be given as requested" (*Answers to Gospel Questions*, 3:84).

All things which are good cometh of God (Alma 5:40; Moroni 7:12, 24). Goodness has its source in God and emanates from His being to fill the immensity of space. God is the fount of all light, truth, love, and righteousness. If we give a gift, it is a reflection of God's goodness and brings glory to God. For truth, any gift we have to give came from God's graciousness and we give because of the goodness of God that is in us. Thus all good gifts come from God. *See also:* Every good gift; Infinite goodness (of God).

All-wise Creator (Mosiah 29:19). We believe that our God knows all things (2 Nephi 9:20), which is to say that God is omniscient— He is all-knowing. Because of that knowledge, He also has all wisdom. *See also:* God knoweth all things; Knoweth all things; Lord knoweth all things; Wisdom in (of) God (the Lord/the Father).

All wisdom (Mosiah 4:9; Alma 26:35). God has all wisdom and knowledge. *See also:* All-wise Creator; Wisdom in (of) God (the Lord/the Father).

All ye ends of the earth (2 Nephi 26:25; 33:10, 13; Alma 5:50; 29:7; 3 Nephi 27:20; Mormon 3:22; Ether 4:18; Moroni 7:34). Refers to all the inhabitants of the earth. All people, all nations, all continents, all kindreds, all tongues, everyone from the north to the south and from the east to the west (2 Nephi 29:11). The gospel will be preached to all these, the elders shall go forth to all these, the voice of the Lord shall be unto all these, the message of the gospel is for all these, the Lord will make bare his holy arm to all these, salvation by coming unto Christ is to all these. The righteous and elect shall come forth from the ends of the earth, for Jesus said, "Repent, and come unto me ye ends of the earth, and be saved" (3 Nephi 9:22). Analogous to the scriptural phrase "the four corners of the earth" (Isaiah 11:12; 2 Nephi 21:12; D&C 124:128). *See also:* All the ends of the earth; Unto the ends of the earth.

All ye Gentiles (3 Nephi 30:2). A salutation calling the Gentiles to repentance. *See also:* All ye ends of the earth; O ye Gentiles.

All your might, mind, and strength (2 Nephi 25:29; Mosiah 2:11, 21; Alma 39:13; Mormon 9:27; Moroni 10:32). Meaning giving our all and holding nothing back. God knows the thoughts and intents of our hearts, thus He knows if we truly are expending all our might, mind, and strength. *See also:* Laboring with his (our) might; Might, mind, and strength; Thoughts and intents of his (the) heart; With all diligence (your [their] might).

All your (our) sins (guilt/iniquities/wickedness) (2 Nephi 9:14; Alma 5:18; 11:43; 12:14; 24:11; Helaman 14:13; 3 Nephi 3:15; 30:2; Mormon 7:5). We must repent of all our sins, not just some of our sins. Otherwise we will remember with shame our unrepented sins when we are brought to be judged before God.

Almighty power of the Lord (Mormon 9:26). Jesus has almighty power given Him by God the Father. "He was crucified, died, and rose again the third day; and ascended into heaven, to sit down on the right hand of the Father, to reign with almighty power according to the will of the Father" (D&C 20:23–24). *See also:* All power; God Almighty; Power of God.

Almighty word (1 Nephi 17:46; Helaman 12:8–21). *See:* Power of his voice (word).

Alpha and Omega (3 Nephi 9:18). One of the names of our Lord, Jesus Christ. "I am Alpha and Omega, the beginning and the end" (see Revelation 1:8, 11; 21:6; 22:13). "Alpha is the first letter of the Greek alphabet, and omega is the last letter, thus verifying that Christ is the member of the Godhead who began the work of bringing 'to pass the immortality and eternal life' (Moses 1:39) of mankind upon this mortal earth and will be the one to conclude the events of this earth's plan of salvation" (Nyman, "'I Am Jesus Christ the Son of God,'" 9). *See also:* D&C 19:1; 38:1; 45:7.

Altar of God (Alma 17:4). When we come before God, it is said we approach the altar of God. The altar of God is the place where God is, and the place from which He rules. *See also:* Altar of stones; Psalm 43:4.

Altar of stones (1 Nephi 2:7). The scriptures anciently specified that altars were to be built of unhewn stones (Exodus 20:24). Altars were "a focal point of religious worship throughout the ages . . . used for prayer, sacrifice and related purposes. . . . Sacred and symbolic meaning is ascribed to the altar. . . . The altar was built that people might kneel by it to communicate and make covenants with their God" (*Encyclopedia of Mormonism,*

1:36–37). Today, sacred altars are found in our latter-day temples, built of polished stone and fine upholstery. The sacrament table is also sometimes referred to as an altar before which we renew our covenants.

Always remember him (me) (3 Nephi 18:7, 11; Moroni 4:3; 5:2). This is one of the promises we make when we are baptized and when we partake of the sacrament. Not only is it a commandment to always remember Him, but it is wisdom on our part to do so, for by so doing we can avoid error and sin. *See also:* Remember the Lord our (their/your) God; In remembrance of my body (blood).

Anchor to the souls of men (Ether 12:4). Having faith in and living the gospel of Jesus Christ is an anchor to our souls. Mormon 5:18 explains, "But now, behold, they are led about by Satan, even as chaff is driven before the wind, or as a vessel is tossed about upon the waves, without sail or anchor, or without anything wherewith to steer her; and even as she is, so are they" (see also Hebrews 6:19). "It holds them steady and calm despite the social turbulence and wickedness that swirls around them. Of course, this faith must be more than just lip service, or it won't be strong enough to withstand the stresses placed upon it by contemporary living. In order for our faith to be meaningful and effective as an anchor to our souls, it must be centered on Jesus Christ" (Ballard, *Our Search for Happiness*, 118).

Ancient (and long dispersed) covenant people (of the Lord) (2 Nephi 29:4, 5; Mormon 8:15). The Jews and the children of Israel are the dispersed and ancient covenant people. *See also:* Covenant which he hath made unto his people who are of the house of Israel; Dispersed of my people [Judah].

And it came to pass (1 Nephi 1:6; *passim*). A conjunctive phrase (a phrase that links different parts of the text) found first in the Book of Mormon at 1 Nephi 1:6, and, according to one scholar, used 1,060 times in total in the Book of Mormon, and also found 396 times in the Bible. This scriptural phrase can have different meanings, such as: (1) "the passage of time"; (2) "because or in consequence of"; (3) "all things promised of God shall come to pass"; (4) "after the trial of our faith"; and (5) referring to some event in our lives whether expected or not (Allred, *And It Came to Pass*, 17, 26, 37, 61, see 71). *See also:* And thus we see.

And thus we see (1 Nephi 16:29; 17:3; Alma 12:21, 22; 24:19, 27; 28:13, 14; 30:60; 42:4, 7, 14; 46:8; 50:19; Helaman 3:28; 6:34, 35, 36, 40; 12:3; Ether 14:25). A scriptural phrase found only in the Book of Mormon which is the preface to phrases which describe the conclusion of, the consequences of, the

outcome of, or the results of some thing or action. "And thus we see" indicates knowledge gained, understanding and reason obtained, and eternal truth that has become apparent. *See also:* And it came to pass.

Angel appeared (Mosiah 27:11, 32; Alma 8:14; 10:7; 17:2; 30:53; 3 Nephi 11:8). Through all the ages, God has sent, does send, and will send messenger angels to warn and instruct His children upon the earth. *See also:* Angels minister(-ed/appeared/declared/descending) unto him (them).

Angel did make (hath made) them known unto me (1 Nephi 14:29; Mosiah 3:2; Alma 11:31; 24:14; 36:5; 40:11). At times special messages and instructions are sent to individuals, often to the prophets. *See also:* Angels minister(-ed/appeared/declared/descending) unto him (them).

Angel fell (fallen) from heaven (from before the presence of the Eternal God) (2 Nephi 2:17; 9:8). Refers to Satan, who because of his rebellion fell from grace and was cast out of heaven to become the father of all evil. *See also:* Revelation 12:7–9; Moses 4:3.

Angel from (of) God (2 Nephi 2:17; 25:19; Mosiah 3:2; 27:15; Alma 10:9). *See:* Angels minister(-ed/appeared/declared/descending) unto him (them).

Angel had (has/hath) spoken (1 Nephi 3:30; 4:3; 14:8; 17:45; Helaman 14:26). Because an angel has spoken it, it has particular importance and should be noted. *See also:* Angels minister(-ed/appeared/ declared/descending) unto him (them).

Angel of light (2 Nephi 9:9; Alma 30:53). The devil and his minions can appear as an angel. *See:* Form of an angel; 2 Corinthians 11:14; D&C 128:20; 129:8.

Angel of the Lord (1 Nephi 3:29; 7:10; 11:34–36; 13:24, 34; 14:29; Mosiah 4:1; 27:11, 18; Alma 8:14, 18; 10:7; Helaman 13:7). A true messenger from God. *See also:* Angels minister(-ed/appeared/ declared/descending) unto him (them).

Angel said (unto me) (1 Nephi 11:14, 21, 26; 12:1, 11, 14, 22; 13:2, 5, 11, 21, 24; 14:8, 20; 15:29; Mosiah 3:2; 27:14; Alma 8:20; 10:7–9; 36:8; Helaman 14:9, 26, 28). *See:* Angel did make (hath made) them known unto me; Angels minister(-ed/appeared/ declared/descending) unto him (them).

Angel spake unto me (him) (1 Nephi 11:19, 30–32; 12:8, 16, 19; 13:1, 8, 40; 14:5, 16, 18; 2 Nephi 10:3; Mosiah 27:17; Alma 36:11). *See:* Angel did make (hath made) them known unto me; Angels minister(-ed/appeared/declared/ descending) unto him (them).

Angel stood before him (me) (1 Nephi 1:11; 3:29; 8:5; 11:14; Mosiah 3:2). It is hard to miss the message if the angel appears right before you. *See also:* Angels minister(-ed/appeared/declared/ descending) unto him (them).

Angels appear (Alma 21:5; Helaman 16:14; Moroni 7:36, 37). *See:* Angels minister(-ed/appeared/ declared/descending) unto him (them).

Angels declare(-d/declaring) (Alma 13:24–25; 38:7; 39:19; Helaman 5:11; 13:7; 16:14). "And thus the Gospel began to be preached, from the beginning, being declared by holy angels sent forth from the presence of God" (Moses 5:58). *See also:* Angels minister(-ed/appeared/declared/ descending) unto him (them).

Angels minister(-ed/appeared/ declared/descending) unto him (them) (1 Nephi 11:30; 16:38; Alma 19:34; Helaman 16:14; 3 Nephi 7:15, 18; 17:24; 19:14; Moroni 7:25). Throughout the history of the world, the righteous have received the visitation of angels (seen and unseen). "The ministering of angels is one of the manifestations of [the] Spirit. . . . 'The word "angel" is used in the scriptures for any heavenly being bearing God's message' (George Q. Cannon, *Gospel Truth* [1987], 54). The scriptures recite numerous instances where an angel appeared personally. . . .

"But the ministering of angels can also be unseen. Angelic messages can be delivered by a voice or merely by thoughts or feelings communicated to the mind. President John Taylor described 'the action of the angels, or messengers of God, upon our minds, so that the heart can conceive . . . revelations from the eternal world' (*Gospel Kingdom* [1987], 31)" (Oaks, "The Aaronic Priesthood and the Sacrament," 38, 39). Additionally, ministering of angels means "divine power for protection, for guidance, for comfort, for strength" (Hinckley, "'Upon You My Fellow Servants'"). *See also:* According to the word(-s) of the angel; Angel appeared; Angel did make (hath made) them known unto me; Angel from (of) God; Angel had (hath/has) spoken; Angel said (unto me); Angel spake unto me (him); Angel stood before him (me); Angels appear; Angels declare(-d/declaring); Angels sent; By the mouth of angels; Conversed with angels; Holy angel(-s); Seen angels; Send his angel; Sent angels; Thus hath the angel spoken; Visit us by angels; Voice of his (the) angels; Word of the angel.

Angels sent (Alma 9:25; 10:10; 12:29; 36:6; 38:7; Helaman 5:11; Moroni 7:22). Through the ages God has sent His angels to deliver the gospel message. *See also:* Angels declare(-d/declaring); Angels minister(-ed/appeared/declared/descending) unto him (them).

Angels to a (the) devil (2 Nephi 9:9; Jacob 3:11). Those who become followers of Satan, both the third who followed him in the premortal life and those here on earth who rebel against God and refuse to repent of their sins.

Anger of the Lord (2 Nephi 15:25; 26:6; Alma 9:18; Helaman 13:30, 39). We believe that God is a God of body, parts, and passions. Anger is one of those passions. Though God is a God of great and perfect love, the scriptures attest that He can and does become angry with the rebellious and non-penitent. The Lord is merciful and slow to anger towards those that humble themselves and repent. *See also:* Anger of the Lord is kindled against them; Fierce anger of the Lord; Fiery indignation; Fulness of his (my) wrath; Fulness of the wrath of God; His fierce anger he will not turn away; In my fierce anger; Provoke him to anger; Turn away thine anger; Visit them (this people) in my anger; Visit them in their iniquities and abominations; Visit them with a sore curse; Wrath of God (the Lord).

Anger of the Lord is kindled against them (2 Nephi 15:25; 26:6; Helaman 13:30). "Kindled" means to start up, arouse, flare up, and to begin to burn. *See also:* Anger of the Lord.

Anguish of soul (1 Nephi 17:47; 2 Nephi 26:7; Mosiah 2:38; 28:4; Alma 8:14; 38:8; Mormon 6:16).

Depending on the context, this phrase means: (1) The pain and sorrow the wicked experience once they realize the horror of their sins. Closely related to the "buffetings of Satan" experienced by those that will not reside on earth during the millennium, but will dwell in spirit prison; (2) "Anguish of soul" is also a term used to describe the tribulations sometimes experienced by the righteous as a part of the test of mortal life. We look forward to a better life in the next existence when we will rest from all such anguish and trials. *See also:* Furnace of affliction; In tribulation(-s).

Another Messiah (2 Nephi 25:16, 18). There is no other or additional Messiah. Only Jesus Christ is the Savior, Redeemer, and King over all. The Jews rejected Jesus Christ as the Messiah and looked for another. The scriptures state that in the last day there shall be many false Christs and false Messiahs. The scriptures also testify there is no other name nor way nor salvation other than Jesus Christ of Nazareth. *See also:* False Christs; None other name; True Messiah.

Answered the ends of the law (2 Nephi 2:7; Moroni 7:28). "Ends of the law" means the results or consequences of the law. "Wherefore, the ends of the law which the Holy One hath given, unto the inflicting of the punishment which is affixed, which punishment that is affixed is in opposition to that of the happiness which is affixed" (2 Nephi 2:10).

Answered upon the heads of your parents (2 Nephi 4:6). *See:* Sins and iniquities shall be answered upon their heads.

Answered upon their own heads (heads of their kings) (Mosiah 29:30–31). *See:* Sins and iniquities shall be answered upon their heads.

Answering the sins of the people upon our own heads (Jacob 1:19). *See:* Sins and iniquities shall be answered upon their heads.

Anti-Christ (Alma 30:6, 12). One who teaches against and wages war in variance to Jesus Christ, the Lord. Also one who teaches there is not or there will be no Christ (e.g., Sherem in Jacob 7). Korihor as described in Alma 30 was an anti-Christ who taught the rationalizations of an anti-Christ. The term is also "used . . . to describe one who would assume the guise of Christ but in reality would be opposed to Christ (1 Jn. 2:18–22; 4:3–6; 2 Jn. 1:7). In a broader sense it is anyone or anything that counterfeits the true gospel or plan of salvation and that openly or secretly is set up in opposition to Christ. The great antichrist is Lucifer, but he has many assistants both as spirit beings and as mortals" (Bible Dictionary, s.v. "antichrist," 609). *See also:* No Christ.

Anxiety for you (2 Nephi 1:16; 6:3; Jacob 1:5; 2:3; 4:18; Mosiah 28:12; Alma 13:27). A trait of just and true individuals, of genuine friends, and good neighbors is to be concerned about the people around them, even to be concerned for all people. Concern for fellowmen is a godly attribute. *See also:* Could not bear that any soul should perish; Desire for the welfare of my brethren; Filled with pain and anguish for the welfare of their souls; Pray continually for them; Weighed down with sorrow; Welfare of my brethren (your souls).

Apostles of the Lamb (1 Nephi 11:34–36; 12:9; 13:26, 39–41; 14:20). *See:* Twelve apostles of the Lamb.

Appear unto them (2 Nephi 26:9; Alma 16:20). Prophecy that Jesus Christ would appear and minister to them at a future date. *See also:* Christ shall (should) come; Coming of Christ.

Appeared unto me in the form of an angel (Alma 30:53). The devil can and will deceive by appearing as an angel and delivering false messages. *See also:* Angel of light; Form of an angel.

Applied your hearts to understanding (Mosiah 1:2; 2:9; 12:27; Alma 17:2; 32:28, 34). Honest seekers of knowledge and discernment will humble themselves, fast and pray, and study the scriptures and

other good books. *See also:* Men of perfect (sound) understanding.

Appointed captains (Alma 2:13, 16; 43:6, 44; 48:5; 49:5, 11, 13, 17, 21, 23, 25; 52:19, 28; 55:23; 56:12; 58:25; 59:12; Helaman 16:6; 3 Nephi 3:17–19). Throughout the ages the appointing of captains over 50, captains over 100, and captains over 1,000 has been an effective means of organizing and directing peoples and armies. Both Moses and Brigham Young used this method (see D&C 136:3, 15).

Appointed priests and teachers (Mosiah 6:3; Alma 45:22–23). *See:* Authority from (of) God; Consecrate(-d) priests (and teachers/ and elders).

Appointed unto men that they must die (Alma 12:27; 40:8). Into mortality we are born, and from mortality we will die. To be born and to die is part of the plan of salvation. Because of the Atonement of Jesus Christ, physical death is overcome in the Resurrection; we will all live again as immortal souls without sickness or death, forever and ever.

Arise from the dust (2 Nephi 1:14, 21, 23; 8:25; 3 Nephi 20:37; Moroni 10:31). A phrase used as a call to repentance and the pursuit of doing good. Shake off the dust of inactivity, throw off the chains of Satan's captivity, rise to the higher and nobler things of God, and be proactive in seeking salvation for ourselves and for our fellowman.

Arm of flesh (2 Nephi 4:34). The scriptures tell us that man should not trust in the arm of flesh (see D&C 1:19). The wisdom and strength of man is nothing when compared to the greatness and power of God. Thus the opposite phrase, the "arm of the Lord" (Isaiah 53:1; Mosiah 14:1; D&C 45:47), is used in the scriptures to denote great power and glory. *See also:* Boast in their own strength.

Arm (of mercy) is extended (towards you in the light of day) (2 Nephi 28:32; Jacob 6:5; Mosiah 1:14; 16:12; Alma 5:33; 19:36; 29:10; 3 Nephi 9:14). The arm of mercy is God's arm reaching out to us. "In the light of day" refers to the time of our probationary state before the "night of darkness," which is when we die physically. *See also:* Hen gathereth her chickens (under her wings); Lengthen out mine arm; Probationary state (time).

Arm of the Lord (revealed) (2 Nephi 8:9; Mosiah 14:1). The arm of the Lord is all-powerful, and the arm of the Lord shines forth in great glory. The arm of the Lord is extended to all that humble themselves and come unto Him. The arm of the Lord is an arm of wonderful and miraculous mercy. The arm of the Lord is like an immense and vengeful sword that will destroy the wicked at the last day. The arm of

the Lord can do infinite good. The arm of the Lord is revealed to the righteous and will be revealed to all at the great day of the Lord.

Armed with righteousness (1 Nephi 14:14). "To be armed with righteousness is to be armed with the power of God and to be worthy of the Lord's protecting care. . . . President Harold B. Lee taught: "By faith in God you can be attuned to the Infinite and by power and wisdom obtained from your Heavenly Father harness the powers of the universe to serve you in your hour of need in the solution of problems too great for your human strength or intelligence' (*Church News*, 15 Aug. 1970, p. 2). With the power of the priesthood, faith, and the guidance of the Holy Spirit, the Saints of the last days will be armed sufficiently to withstand all opposition" (*Book of Mormon Student Manual*, 14; paragraphing altered).

Armor of righteousness (2 Nephi 1:23). Living righteously—that is, keeping the commandments and doing good—shields us from the temptations of the devil (see 1 Nephi 15:24). In Ephesians 6:13–17 we are admonished to "take unto you the whole armour of God" including the "breastplate of righteousness."

Arms of his love (2 Nephi 1:15). The Lord has said, "Be faithful and diligent in keeping the commandments of God, and I will encircle thee in the *arms of my love*" (D&C 6:20; emphasis added). Nothing can compare to the greatness of the overpowering and all-encompassing feeling of love that God can bestow upon someone. This gift can be a minute portion of God's love, the good feeling after doing a good turn for another. On the other end of the spectrum, there are occasions in life when God will bless us with an overpowering feeling of love so great that it is as though it were a consuming of our whole being. "He [God] hath filled me with his love, even unto the consuming of my flesh" (2 Nephi 4:21).

Arouse your (the) faculties (of your souls) (Jacob 3:11; Alma 32:27). An appeal to use all the ability that is within our power, or in other words, with all our heart, might, and mind to seek the word of God, come unto Christ with faith, keep His commandments, and serve our fellowman. *See also:* Arise from the dust.

Arts and cunning of the people (Alma 10:15; Ether 13:16). Refers here to the worldly learning and devices of man, sometimes inspired by the devil, used by men to get gain and wield unrighteous dominion. *See also:* Cunning arts; Cunning of the world.

Arts of the evil one (Helaman 16:21). *See:* Cunning one.

As a lion teareth in pieces (3 Nephi 20:16; 21:12; Mormon 5:24). Refers to the Second Coming of the Lord, when the Gentiles who have had the gospel presented to them in the last days but have not accepted it and have remained in sin will be destroyed in the same manner as a lion who runs rampant and wild through the flock of sheep (unrepentant Gentiles) and tears them to pieces and from which there is no deliverance, because the day of their probation is past. Also found in the Bible in Micah 5:8–9. *See also:* Fulness of the Gentiles.

As a little child (3 Nephi 9:22; 11:37–38). To become as a little child is to be "submissive, meek, humble, patient, full of love, willing to submit to all things which the Lord seeth fit to inflict upon him, even as a child doth submit to his father" (Mosiah 3:19). Jesus said, "Verily I say unto you, Except ye be converted, and become as little children, ye shall not enter into the kingdom of heaven. Whosoever therefore shall humble himself as this little child, the same is greatest in the kingdom of heaven" (Matthew 18:3–4).

As a man speaketh with another (1 Nephi 11:11; Ether 12:39). Meaning literally standing in the presence of Deity, like one speaking to a friend. *Compare:* Exodus 33:11; D&C 50:12; Moses 7:4. *See also:* Face to face.

As he was thus pondering (Helaman 10:3). *See:* Ponder(-ing) in his (mine/your) heart.

As I live, saith the Lord (1 Nephi 21:18). A phrase found often in the Old Testament, but only once in the Book of Mormon, and that occurrence is Nephi quoting Isaiah. It means as surely as, in all reality, and with absolute surety. In other words, it is an oath by the Lord promising outcome and validity.

As long as the earth (world) shall stand (2 Nephi 25:21–22; Moroni 10:19). Meaning as long as the earth is the dwelling place of mortal men and up to the time of the Lord's Second Coming, and perhaps also into the millennium. Thus the promises made by the Lord in these verses shall continue on the earth until the earth becomes celestial and is the abode of those obtaining eternal life.

As many as believed were baptized (and did receive the Holy Ghost) (Mosiah 18:4; Alma 19:35; Helaman 16:5; 3 Nephi 28:18). A true indication of one's belief and a measure of one's repentance upon hearing the gospel is their desire to be baptized.

As many as will believe on his name (in Christ) (2 Nephi 25:14; 30:7; 3 Nephi 9:17). *See:* Believe on his (my/holy) holy name.

As the Lord (God) liveth (and as we live) (1 Nephi 3:15; 4:32; 2 Nephi 9:16; 25:20; 27:31; Omni 1:26; Alma 10:10; 23:6; 44:11; 54:10; Helaman 13:26; 15:17; 3 Nephi 3:15, 21; 5:24, 26; Mormon 8:23; Moroni 7:26). *See:* Made an oath unto us.

As though there had been no redemption made (Mosiah 16:5; Alma 11:41; 12:18; Moroni 7:38). If a person persists in disobedience to God, rebels against God, and will not come unto Christ with humbleness of heart to repent and accept the laws and ordinances of the gospel, then that individual cannot gain salvation and is as though no redemption had been made for him, except he will still be resurrected. Our Savior suffered for all men's sins, but in order for one's sins to be forgiven, one must repent and follow Christ. In other words, for the unrepentant it is as though Christ's suffering for that man's sins is of no avail or benefit.

Ascension (of Christ) into heaven (Mosiah 18:2; Alma 40:20; 3 Nephi 10:18; 11:12). Refers to Jesus Christ's ascension into heaven after his mortal ministry in Jerusalem at the meridian of time as recorded in Acts 1:9–11: "And when he [Jesus] had spoken these things, while they beheld, he was taken up; and a cloud received him out of their sight. And while they looked steadfastly toward heaven as he went up, behold, two men [angels] stood by them in white apparel; which also said, Ye men of Galilee, why stand ye gazing up into heaven? this same Jesus, which is taken up from you into heaven, shall so come in like manner as ye have seen him go into heaven."

Ask in faith (1 Nephi 15:11; 2 Nephi 33:3; Enos 1:15; Mosiah 4:21; Alma 22:16; Moroni 7:26). A prayer without faith has no effect and is rejected by God. If our faith is weak we must pray that our faith be strengthened. "Help thou [O Lord] mine unbelief," is a valid prayer (see Mark 9:24). "It made me shiver. And I about made up my mind to pray, and see if I couldn't try to quit being the kind of boy I was and be better. So I kneeled down. But the words wouldn't come. Why wouldn't they? It warn't no use to try and hide it from Him. Nor from *me*, neither. I knowed very well why they wouldn't come. It was because my heart warn't right; it was because I warn't square; it was because I was playing double. . . . deep down in me I knowed it was a lie, and He knowed it. You can't pray a lie—I found that out" (Twain, *Huckleberry Finn*, 295).

Ask not amiss (2 Nephi 4:35; Helaman 10:5; 3 Nephi 13:8; Mormon 9:28). As we come to know God and learn of his ways, we begin to understand what is proper to ask for in our prayers. *See also:* Thou shall not ask that which is contrary to my will.

Ask the Father in my name (in the name of Christ) (3 Nephi 16:4; 17:3; 18:20; 27:28; Mormon 9:21, 27; Moroni 4:3; 5:2; 7:26). *See:* Pray(-ed) unto the Father in my (the) name (of Christ).

Assemble (assembling) themselves (yourselves) (1 Nephi 20:14; Mosiah 2:9, 27–29; 18:25, 32; 25:4, 15, 21; 27:22; Alma 6:5; 15:17; 21:6, 20; 22:7; Helaman 9:10). Concerning meeting together to worship and learn of God, the Lord said, "Where two or three are gathered together in my name, there am I in the midst of them" (Matthew 18:20; see also D&C 6:32).

At hand (2 Nephi 23:6; Jacob 5:71; Mosiah 7:18; Alma 5:28–29, 31, 36, 50; 7:9; 9:25, 28; 10:20, 23; 60:29; Helaman 5:32; 3 Nephi 1:13–14, 16, 18; 17:1; Ether 4:16). Meaning close or soon to be. *See also:* End draweth nigh; End is nigh at hand; End soon cometh; Hour is close at hand; Is at hand; Kingdom of heaven is nigh (soon) at hand; My time is at hand; Repent ye (repent ye) for the kingdom of heaven is (nigh) at hand; Time is at hand.

At that day (1 Nephi 13:37; 14:17; 15:14–15; 19:11; 2 Nephi 27:12; 28:20; 29:1; 30:18; Alma 5:19, 21; 3 Nephi 16:10; 20:20; 21:20, 26; 27:16; 28:40; 29:4, 7; Mormon 8:33–34). The phraseology of prophecy. Words that precede prophecy of the future as spoken by prophets, seers and revelators.

See also: I would prophesy; Things (which are) to come.

At the last day (1 Nephi 13:37; 16:2; 22:31; 2 Nephi 9:33, 44; 25:18; 33:11, 14; Jacob 1:19; 3:10; Mosiah 17:10; 23:22; 26:28; 27:31; Alma 1:4; 7:21; 13:29; 14:11; 22:6, 15, 18; 24:15–16; 26:6–7; 30:60; 34:39; 36:3, 28; 37:37; 38:5, 15; 39:8; 41:3; 3 Nephi 15:1; 27:5, 6, 20, 22; 28:34, 39; Mormon 2:19; 8:31; Ether 4:10, 19; 5:4, 6; Moroni 7:35, 47). Refers to the day of the Lord's Second Coming. *See also:* Come(-th/coming) in his glory; Day of the Lord; Great and dreadful day of the Lord.

At the right hand of God (Mosiah 5:9; 26:23–24; Alma 5:58; 28:12; Helaman 3:30; Ether 12:4; Moroni 7:27; 9:26). *See:* Inheritance at my right hand.

Atone(-d) for the sins of man (of the world) (Mosiah 3:11, 16; Alma 22:14; 33:22; 34:8; 36:17; 42:15). Through the Atonement of Jesus Christ we can be forgiven of our sins if we repent and come unto Christ. "There is no other name given whereby salvation cometh" (Mosiah 5:8; see also Mosiah 3:17). *See also:* Atonement of Christ (the Only Begotten Son).

Atonement of Christ (the Only Begotten Son) (Jacob 4:11–12; Mosiah 3:19; Alma 13:5; Moroni 7:41). "We believe that through the Atonement of Christ, all mankind may be saved, by obedience to the laws and ordinances of the Gospel" (Articles of Faith 1:3). President Marion G. Romney said, "It took the atonement of Jesus Christ to re-unite the bodies and spirits of men in the Resurrection. And so all the world, believers and non-believers, are indebted to the Redeemer for their certain resurrection, because the Resurrection will be as wide as was the fall, which brought death to every man.

"There is another phase of the atonement which makes me love the Savior even more, and fills my soul with gratitude beyond expression. It is that in addition to atoning for Adam's transgression, thereby bringing about the resurrection, the Savior by his suffering paid the debt for my personal sins. He paid the debt for your personal sins and for the personal sins of every living soul that ever dwelt upon the earth or that ever will dwell in mortality upon the earth. But this he did conditionally. The benefits of this suffering for our individual transgressions will not come to us unconditionally in the same sense that the resurrection will come regardless of what we do. If we partake of the blessings of the atonement as far as our individual transgressions are concerned, we must obey the law. . . .

"When we commit sin, we are estranged from God and rendered unfit to enter into his presence. No unclean thing can enter into his presence. We cannot of ourselves, no matter how we may try, rid ourselves of the stain which is upon us as a result of our own transgressions. That stain must be washed away by the blood of the Redeemer, and he has set up the way by which that stain may be removed. That way is the gospel of Jesus Christ. The gospel requires us to believe in the Redeemer, accept his atonement, repent of our sins, be baptized by immersion for the remission of our sins, receive the gift of the Holy Ghost by the laying on of hands, and continue faithfully to observe, or do the best we can to observe, the principles of the gospel all the days of our lives" (Romney, in Conference Report, October 1953, 35, 36). We must believe with all our hearts that the Atonement of Jesus Christ will save us. "The Atonement will protect and bless you beyond your ability to fully understand" (Cook, "The Lord Is My Light," 66).

Atonement of his blood (Mosiah 3:15; Alma 21:9; 24:13). *See:* Atoning blood of Jesus Christ; Blood of Christ atoneth for their sins.

Atonement satisfieth the demands of his justice (2 Nephi 9:26; Mosiah 15:9; Alma 34:16; 42:15). The eternal law of justice requires that a penalty be applied to every sin. Our Savior, Jesus Christ, suffered for our sins conditionally on our repentance, and thus through His merciful sacrifice, the demands of justice can be met so we do not have to suffer the penalty for our sins.

Atoning blood of Jesus Christ (Mosiah 3:11, 15, 18; 4:2; Helaman 5:9; see also Moroni 10:33). While suffering for our sins, Jesus Christ sweat great drops of blood in pain and agony. "Which suffering caused myself, even God, the greatest of all, to tremble because of pain, and to bleed at every pore" (D&C 19:18). Additionally, his suffering for us included his blood that was spilled upon the cross. These things we remember when we partake of the emblems of the sacrament. The sacrament prayer says, "All those who drink of it, that they may do it in remembrance of the blood of thy Son, which was shed for them" (D&C 20:79; see also Moroni 5:2). It is the blood of Christ that washes away our sins. *See also:* Blood of Christ atoneth for their sins; Cleansed (and made white) by the blood of the Lamb (by the power of the Holy Ghost); Garments cleansed through the blood of the Lamb (made white/washed); Made white in the blood of Christ; Washed white through the blood of Christ.

Author and finisher of their faith (Moroni 6:4). "Jesus [is] the author and the finisher of our faith" (Hebrews 12:2). Meaning Jesus accepted the Father's plan and undertook all the preparations and the carrying out of that plan; thus He is the author of the plan in which is our faith. Also Jesus is the finisher of the plan in that he suffered and died to bring about the Atonement for our benefit. Jesus uttered at his death on the cross, "It is finished" (John 19:30). Additionally at the great coming of the Lord, "Another angel shall sound his trump, which is the seventh angel, saying: It is finished; it is finished! The Lamb of God hath overcome and trodden the wine-press alone" (D&C 88:106). Our faith is that Jesus Christ will complete the plan of the Father to its end and present the finished plan to God the Father for the glory of the Father. *See also:* Beginning and the end; First and the last; I am Alpha and Omega, the beginning and the end.

Author of all sin (Helaman 6:30; 8:28). Satan the devil is the evil one who devises plans and temptations to destroy the souls of men and prevent them from returning to God.

Authority from (of) God (Mosiah 13:6; 18:13, 17–18, 26; 21:33; 23:17; 27:14; Alma 5:3; 17:3; Helaman 11:18; 3 Nephi 11:25; Moroni 8:16, 28). Refers to the priesthood of God, which is the authority to act in God's name and a bestowal of His power. "No man taketh this honour unto himself" (Hebrews 5:4). "We believe that a man must be called of God, by prophecy, and by the laying on of hands by those who are in authority, to preach the Gospel and administer in the ordinances thereof" (Articles of Faith 1:5). *See also:* After the order of his (the) Son; Called after the holy order of God; Called by the order of God.

Authority to preach (Mosiah 18:18; 23:17). *See:* Authority from (of) God; Preach with great power and authority.

Avenge his blood (their wrongs/ themselves) (Alma 54:16, 24; 61:6; 3 Nephi 3:10–11; Mormon 3:9, 14; Ether 14:24). "Vengeance is mine . . . saith the Lord" (Romans 12:19). It is important to protect our freedoms, rights, and privileges, but it is wrong and sinful to seek vengeance. We must forgive yet protect ourselves against further wrong. "Man shall not smite, neither shall he judge; for judgment is mine, saith the Lord, and vengeance is mine also, and I will repay" (Mormon 8:20). *See also:* Defend themselves; Vengeance is mine.

Awake and arouse your faculties (Alma 32:27). *See:* Arouse your (the) faculties (of your souls); Awake from a deep sleep (the slumber of death).

Awake and put on thy strength O Zion (2 Nephi 8:9, 24; 3 Nephi 20:36). Meaning to awake from spiritual sleep and put on the authority of the priesthood. *See also:* Put on (thy) strength O Zion; D&C 113:7–8.

Awake from a deep sleep (the slumber of death) (2 Nephi 1:13; Jacob 3:11). Much of the world lies in spiritual death because they do not keep the commandments of God and they reject the holy prophets. To "awake" from this death is an appeal to have faith in Christ, repent of one's sins, be baptized by immersion, receive the Holy Ghost, and seek eternal life. *See also:* Arise from the dust; 2 Nephi 9:47; Mosiah 2:40; 2:38; Alma 4:3; 5:7; 7:22.

Awake my soul (2 Nephi 4:28). This phrase is found in what is sometimes called the Psalm of Nephi, or also the song or prayer of Nephi. Therein Nephi sorrows and expresses despair because of the wickedness of the world, the temptations all around, the press of evil, and his own weakness before sin. However, Nephi then thinks of his Great God, the blessings and redemption he has received from Him, and the hope and trust he has in Him. These latter things brighten his outlook and give hope and peace concerning the future of his soul. Therefore he exclaims, "Awake my soul!"

Awful chains (2 Nephi 1:13; 28:22). The chains with which Satan ensnares men and women are awful because they are heavy, hard to throw off, and they bring about great fear and anguish. *See also:* Chains of hell.

Awful hell (1 Nephi 15:29, 35; Alma 19:29; 54:7). Hell is not a place we would want to be, for it is truly awful, dreadful, frightful,

and horrible. Those that dwell there experience no peace and rest, but rather weeping and gnashing of teeth. Moses "began to fear, [and] saw the bitterness of hell" before he commanded Satan to depart (see Moses 1:20). Hell is a place of filthiness prepared for those which are filthy still (see 1 Nephi 15:34).

Awful monster the devil (2 Nephi 9:10, 19, 26). The devil or Satan is a fiend, a brute, a demon, a beast, and a villain of the worst kind. In him there is no liking but only hate. He is real and truly exists. He desires all to be miserable like unto himself (see 2 Nephi 2:27).

Awful situation (Mosiah 2:40; Ether 8:24). Those that have accepted sin and do not repent, as well as those that allow sin to exist around them (i.e., allow secret combinations) live in peril of the judgment of God. Their situation is truly awful because they are allowing Satan to take them captive. *See also:* Chains of hell.

Awful state of wickedness (1 Nephi 13:32; 15:35; 2 Nephi 9:27; Mosiah 3:25; Alma 12:13–14; 26:17; 40:14; Helaman 4:25; 6:40; 7:4; 3 Nephi 6:17; Ether 4:15; Moroni 7:38). Those engulfed in sin are not truly happy, but experience hopelessness, misery, a loss of self-respect. They often sink into depravity, curse God, and fight against truth and right. After a time in this state, the Spirit of God abandons them and they no longer have a compass of right versus wrong. Even God's most severe warnings, including famine and wars, do not bring such to repentance. Sad is the case of those who altogether turn from truth and God.

Awful view of their own guilt (Mosiah 3:25). *See:* Bright recollection of all our guilt.

Awoke unto God (Alma 5:7). Means to come to a knowledge of God and live according to God's will. *See also:* Awake from a deep sleep (the slumber of death); Born of God.

Ax is laid at the root of the tree (Alma 5:52). Compares man to a tree or vine who has become corrupted through sin and thus has no place in the kingdom of God. Thus the ax will be used to cut them out at the root, and then they will be cast into the fire. Compare Jacob 5, the allegory of the tame and wild olive trees.

B

Bands of death (Mosiah 15:8–9, 20, 23; 16:7; Alma 4:14; 5:7, 9–10; 7:12; 11:41–42; 22:14). Death, be it physical or spiritual, is a captivity, an imprisonment, and a confinement. Fortunately the great plan of our God, the plan of salvation, provides a release from the bands of physical death through the Resurrection and from the bands of spiritual death via faith in Christ, repentance, forgiveness, and purification through the Atonement. *See also:* Broken (breaketh) the bands of death; Chains of hell; Loose the bands of death; Loosed from this eternal band(-s) of death.

Bands of iniquity (Mosiah 23:12). *See:* Bands of death; Chains of hell.

Bands of thy neck O captive daughter of Zion (2 Nephi 8:25). The Lord provided the meaning of this phrase, saying, "The curses of God upon her, or the remnants of Israel in their scattered condition among the Gentiles" (D&C 113:10). This curse is because of Israel's wickedness and unwillingness to follow the will of God for them.

Baptism by (of/with) water (2 Nephi 31:14, 17; 3 Nephi 7:25).

In D&C 39:6 we read, "And this is my gospel—repentance and baptism by water, and then cometh the baptism of fire and the Holy Ghost, even the Comforter, which showeth all things, and teacheth the peaceable things of the kingdom." In 3 Nephi the Lord commanded, "On this wise shall ye baptize; and there shall be no disputations among you. . . . Behold, ye shall go down and stand in the water, and in my name shall ye baptize them. . . . Having authority given me [been commissioned] of Jesus Christ, I baptize you in the name of the Father, and of the Son, and of the Holy Ghost. Amen. And then shall ye immerse them in the water, and come forth again out of the water" (3 Nephi 11:22–26). "We believe that the first principles and ordinances of the Gospel are: first, Faith in the Lord Jesus Christ; second, Repentance; third, *Baptism by immersion for the remission of sins;* fourth, Laying on of hands for the gift of the Holy Ghost" (Articles of Faith 1:4; emphasis added).

Baptism of fire and of the Holy Ghost (2 Nephi 31:13–14, 17). "Refers to the experience of an individual who receives the ordinance of the laying on of hands for the gift of the Holy Ghost. It is the second in a two-part sequence following baptism by immersion in water through which a repentant person committed to Christ and his gospel is born of God or born again. As Jesus explained to Nicodemus, 'Except a man be born of water and of the Spirit, he cannot enter into the kingdom of God' (John 3:5). . . . The baptism of fire, ministered by the Holy Ghost, is manifested through a set of personal sensations, impressions, and insights that constitute a spiritual witness from deity that one has received a remission of sins (2 Ne. 31:17). The baptism of fire inaugurates the transmission of spiritual gifts to the faithful to assist them throughout life in remaining true to their baptismal covenant (1 Cor. 12; Moro. 10:8–23; D&C 46:10–33)" (*Encyclopedia of Mormonism*, 1:97). Also found in D&C 20:41; 33:11; 39:6. *See also:* Baptize(-d) with fire and the Holy Ghost; Cometh the baptism of fire; Filled as if with fire; Fire and the Holy Ghost; Sanctified by (the reception of) the Holy Ghost; Visit him with fire and with the Holy Ghost.

Baptized as a witness and a testimony (2 Nephi 31:14; Mosiah 18:10; 21:35; 3 Nephi 7:25; 18:11; Moroni 6:2). Baptism is an outward step one takes to signify and commit to God that they desire to become a member of the fold of God and are willing are to live the commandments of God (see Mosiah 18:8–10; D&C 20:37).

Baptized first with water then with fire (Mormon 7:10). Except a man be born of water and of the Spirit, he cannot enter into the kingdom of God. *See also:* Baptism of fire and of the Holy Ghost.

Baptized in my name (2 Nephi 31:12; 3 Nephi 11:23, 37–38; 18:5, 11, 16, 30; 21:6; 27:16, 20; 30:2; Ether 4:18; Moroni 7:34). *See:* Baptized in the name of (the Lord) Jesus.

Baptized in the name of (the Lord) Jesus (2 Nephi 31:11; Mosiah 18:10; 3 Nephi 26:17, 21; 4 Nephi 1:1; Mormon 7:8). We are commanded to do all things in worthiness and in the name of Jesus Christ (see Mormon 9:29; D&C 48:31). Baptism by the proper authority, in the proper manner, and in the name of Jesus Christ is the only baptism recognized by God. The exact words of the baptismal prayer are given in the scriptures (see 3 Nephi 11:25; D&C 20:73).

Baptize(-d) unto repentance (Mosiah 26:22; Alma 5:62; 6:2; 7:14; 8:10; 9:27; 48:19; 49:30; Helaman 3:24; 5:17, 19; 3 Nephi 7:26). Baptism without repentance is null and void (except for eight-year-olds who were before without sin). Baptism is a witness unto God that one has repented of his or her sins and desires now to live the gospel (see 3 Nephi 7:25). The proper steps are faith, repentance, baptism, and receiving the Holy Ghost (see Articles of Faith 1:1).

Baptize(-d) unto the Lord (their God) (Alma 15:12–13; 62:45; Helaman 16:1). When we are baptized it is in remembrance of the Savior and signifies an acceptance of the gospel of Jesus Christ. When baptized, we covenant to take upon us His name, always remember Him, and keep His commandments. *See also:* Mosiah 18:8–10; D&C 20:37.

Baptize(-d) with fire and the Holy Ghost (3 Nephi 9:20; 12:1, 2; 19:13; Mormon 7:10; Ether 12:14). *See:* Baptism of fire and of the Holy Ghost.

Baptize(-d) with water (1 Nephi 10:9–10; 2 Nephi 31:5–6, 8; Mosiah 18:15; 25:18; 3 Nephi 7:24–25; 11:23; 12:1; 19:12–13; Mormon 7:10). *See:* Baptism by (of/with) water.

Baptizing unto repentance (Mosiah 26:22; Alma 5:62; 6:2; 7:14; 8:10; 9:27; 48:19; 49:30; Helaman 3:24; 5:17, 19; 3 Nephi 1:23; 7:26; Moroni 8:11). *See:* Baptize(-d) unto repentance.

Bar of Christ (Alma 11:44; Moroni 10:34). The judgment place before God. *See also:* Bar of God.

Bar of God (Jacob 6:9, 13; Mosiah 16:10; Alma 5:22; 12:12; Moroni 10:27). The place where we will stand before God to be judged.

"And I saw the dead, small and great, stand before God; and the books were opened . . . and the dead were judged out of those things which were written in the books" (Revelation 20:12). The term "bar of God" perhaps has its origin in the legal courts where the prisoner stands at the bar of the court before the judge. The term "the court's pleading bar" has relevance here. Other related phrases include: "the bar of God's tolerance" and "barred from heaven until allowed entrance." In Jacob 6:13 and Moroni 10:34 the righteous will find it to be the "pleasing bar of God." And again in Jacob 6:13 it says the "bar striketh the wicked with awful dread and fear." *See also:* Bar of Christ; Before his (the) bar; Judgment bar; Judgment-seat of Christ (God); Stand before God.

Be (as) stubble (1 Nephi 22:15; 2 Nephi 26:4, 6; 3 Nephi 25:1). *See:* Consumed as stubble.

Be of good cheer (comfort) (Mosiah 24:13, 16; 27:23; Alma 17:31; 3 Nephi 1:13). The gospel of Jesus Christ is a gospel of hope, joy, comfort, and cheer. It is the good news that should give us optimism, confidence, and assurance. No matter how dire our circumstances, if we are true to God, we will have the peace of God to dwell in us, and a bright hope of the future in the presence of God.

Be perfect(-ed) in Christ (Moroni 10:32). The commandment is, "Be ye therefore perfect, even as your Father which is in heaven is perfect" (Matthew 5:48). In this life we will not achieve full godlike perfection, because we are mortal and prone to make mistakes; yet we are commanded to strive to be perfect. What we most certainly must do in this life is become purified, sanctified, and cleansed in and through Christ, meaning having prayed for the Atonement of Christ to be applied to ourselves, we might be forgiven of our sins and able to stand without sin before God at the judgment day.

Be saved (1 Nephi 6:4; 8:3; 13:37, 40; 15:14; 22:17, 31; 2 Nephi 2:9; 6:12; 9:23; 25:13, 20; 28:8; 31:15–16, 21; 33:12; Jacob 6:4; Omni 1:26; Mosiah 3:16; 4:8; 12:33; 13:32; 16:13; Alma 1:4; 5:21, 31; 9:17; 11:37; 20:17; 22:6, 18; 24:16; 31:17; 32:13; 38:9; 41:8; Helaman 5:9; 12:22–23, 25; 13:39; 14:29; 3 Nephi 9:22; 11:33; 12:20; 23:5; 27:6; Mormon 7:3; 9:23; Ether 4:18; 8:26; Moroni 7:34, 36, 38; 8:10, 13; 9:22; 10:21, 26). Meaning to be saved in the kingdom of God. It should be our desire and fondest wish to be saved. To be saved means to be saved from death—both spiritual and physical. The only means by which we can be saved is through the gospel of Jesus Christ; there is no other way. To be saved we must believe on the name of Jesus Christ, repent, be baptized, receive the Holy Ghost, keep the commandments of God, receive the other ordinances of salvation, and endure to the end. By the grace of God and through His mercy, we can be saved after all we can do. To be saved is why we came here to earth. *See also:* Saved in the kingdom of God.

Be their God (1 Nephi 17:40; 2 Nephi 10:4). We should seek for the True and Living God to be our God. This means to seek after His ways and come to know Him personally. *See also:* Turn unto the Lord God.

Be their (your) rearward (3 Nephi 20:42; 21:29). Meaning the Lord will be your rearguard. In Isaiah 52:12 and 58:8, it is promised the Lord God will be thy (your) rearward. In D&C 49:27, we read, "Behold, I will go before you and be your rearward; and I will be in your midst, and you shall not be confounded."

Be unto you a sign (1 Nephi 11:7; 19:10; Jacob 7:14; Helaman 14:4–5; 3 Nephi 21:7). At certain exceptional times, God through his prophets provides notice or warning that a specified event, sign or miraculous occurrence will be given to prove, signify, or mark God's actions. *See also:* Give unto thee (you) a sign; Show unto me (thee/you) a sign; Things (which are) to come.

Be wise (Jacob 6:12; Mosiah 29:8, 10; Mormon 9:28). Be wise rather than foolish. Be prudent and sensible rather than rash and silly. The wise man built his house (his reputation and his eternal reward) upon rock while the foolish man built his house upon sand (see Matthew 7:24–27).

Be ye clean that bear the vessels of the Lord (3 Nephi 20:41). It is a grave and serious sin to officiate in the ordinances of God while unworthy. It is a compounding of sin that condemns the violator and requires severe repentance.

Bear afflictions (with patience) (Alma 26:27; 31:30, 33; 34:40–41). President John Taylor said, "It is necessary then, that we pass through the school of suffering, trial, affliction, and privation, to know ourselves, to know others, and to know our God. . . . [The Savior] had to grapple with the hypocrisy, corruption, weakness, and the imbecility of man; having met with temptation and trial in all its various forms, and [overcame]. . . . He knows how to estimate and put a proper value upon human nature, for he, having been placed in the same position as we are, knows how to bear with our weaknesses and infirmities, and can fully comprehend the depth, power, and strength of the afflictions and trials that man have to cope with in this world" (*Gospel Kingdom*, 120). God knows the afflictions that we each bear and will sustain us if we seek Him in faith: "Ye may know of a surety that I, the Lord God, do visit my people in their afflictions" (Mosiah 24:14). Thus it is our duty to cheerfully face our trials. In an eternal perspective, our afflictions are but a small moment (see D&C 121:7). Someone has said, "In life, trials are mandatory, but misery is optional." *See also:* After much tribulation; Bear with patience; Bore with patience the persecution; Consecrate thine afflictions for thy gain; Console you in your afflictions; Patience and long suffering [of men and women]; Patience in their afflictions (tribulations); Sorrows and afflictions; Suffer with patience these afflictions; Suffered all manner of afflictions; Suffering all manner of afflictions for Christ's sake; Visit my people in their afflictions; Wade (wading) through much tribulation (affliction and sorrows).

Bear false witness against thy neighbor (Mosiah 13:23; Helaman 7:21). Meaning to lie about one's fellowmen. One of the Ten Commandments speaks against this sin (Exodus 20:16). *See also:* False swearers (witness); Lyings and deceivings.

Bear my name (Mosiah 26:18). To "bear my name" means to put on, support, holdup, take upon, carry, and sustain the name of Jesus Christ. In a larger sense it means to proselyte, teach, and minister in the name of Christ. The covenant of baptism and the sacrament includes a commitment to take upon us the name of Jesus. In the final analysis it means one has "been faithful in the testimony of Jesus while . . . in mortality; and . . . offered sacrifice in the similitude of the great sacrifice of the Son of God, and . . . suffered tribulation in [the] Redeemer's name" (D&C 138:12–13).

Bear testimony (2 Nephi 25:28; 27:13; Alma 4:19–20; 7:13, 16, 20; Moroni 7:31). *See:* Bear(-eth) record; Stand as a (bright) testimony against the world (this people/you).

Bear the shame of the world (Jacob 1:8). The Saints of God often endure the ridicule and persecutions of worldly and wicked people. *See also:* Finger of scorn.

Bear their iniquities (Mosiah 14:11). It was for the transgressions of all men and women that Jesus suffered and died. *See also:* Atonement of Christ (the Only Begotten Son).

Bear with patience (Mosiah 24:15; Alma 26:27; 38:4). *See:* Bear afflictions (with patience).

Bear(-eth) record (1 Nephi 10:10; 11:7, 32, 36; 12:7, 18; 13:24; 14:27, 29; Enos 1:20; Helaman 8:14; 3 Nephi 11:15, 32, 35–36; 17:15–16, 25; 18:37, 39; 19:14, 33; 28:11; Ether 4:11; 5:4; 12:41). To give, present, state, and pronounce verbal or written testimony, affirmation, confirmation, and attestation of the truthfulness of the gospel of Jesus Christ, the validity of Jesus Christ, and concerning sacred events and things. *See also:* Bear testimony; Forbidden that I (they) should write (utter/preach).

Because of faith (1 Nephi 1:20; 2:19; 12:10–11; 2 Nephi 3:21; 25:25; Jacob 1:5; Enos 1:8, 12; Mosiah 4:3; 26:15–16; Alma 7:17; 14:15; 19:10; 31:38; 32:42; 44:3; 57:26; 60:26; Helaman 5:47; 6:1; 15:9; 3 Nephi 1:11, 30; 9:20; 17:20; 19:28–29; 27:19; Ether 3:9; 12:8, 20–21, 23; Moroni 7:41). *See:* According to his (your) faith; By faith.

Because of iniquities (iniquity) (1 Nephi 3:29; 17:41; 18:10, 18; 19:9; 2 Nephi 1:7; 4:17; 5:21; 10:5–6; 25:9, 12; 27:5; Jacob 2:23, 35; 3:7; Mosiah 7:20, 24; 10:12; 12:2, 7, 12; 17:16; 21:15; 28:4; 29:18; Alma 15:5; 19:14, 27; 31:1, 31, 33; 40:13; 45:14; 49:3; 53:9; 60:28; 62:2; Helaman 4:14, 23; 5:4; 7:14; 10:3; 11:34; 12:18, 21; 13:23, 30; 14:11; 15:4; 3 Nephi 1:18; 2:19; 9:2; 15:19–20; 21:5; 4 Nephi 1:28; Mormon 1:13, 16; Ether 3:3; 11:15; 14:1; Moroni 10:22). All actions have consequences. Good deeds bring forth good rewards and progression, while bad deeds and sin bring deterioration and punishment. The eternal laws of justice require just consequences. When a person and people descend into sin and iniquity, their moral fiber unwinds and they sink into degradation, depravity, corruption, and disorder. *See also:* Consequences of sin; Justice of God.

Because of pride (1 Nephi 12:19; 2 Nephi 28:12–14; Helaman 4:12; 7:26; Mormon 8:36). *See:* Lifted up in (unto) pride (of their eyes/hearts/ and boasting).

Because of unbelief (2 Nephi 10:2; 32:7; Mosiah 26:3; Alma 45:12; Helaman 15:15, 17; 3 Nephi 1:18; 15:18; 16:4, 7; 19:35; 21:5; Mormon 1:14; 5:15; 9:20; Ether 4:13–14; Moroni 7:37; 10:24). Unbelief blocks us from all gifts from God. Because of unbelief, people cannot be saved, cannot come to a greater knowledge of God, cannot progress in life or in the eternities, cannot experience miracles, cannot have angels minister unto them, cannot obtain the spiritual gifts of God, cannot receive added light, cannot receive a testimony from God, cannot have an increase of hope, cannot feel the unlimited love of God, and cannot receive a fulness of the Father.

Become as a little child (Mosiah 3:18–19; 3 Nephi 9:22; 11:37–38; Moroni 8:10). "Jesus knew that little children are pure and without sin. 'Except ye be converted, and become as little children,' He said, 'ye shall not enter into the kingdom of heaven' (Matthew 18:3). King Benjamin, the great Nephite prophet, explained what it means to become as a little child: 'submissive, meek, humble, patient, full of love, willing to submit to all things which the Lord seeth fit to inflict upon him' (Mosiah 3:19)"

(Morrison, "'For This Cause Came I into the World,'" 27).

Become as God knowing good and evil (2 Nephi 2:18; Alma 12:31; 42:3). The state of knowledge Adam and Eve obtained because they partook of the forbidden fruit. Thus all men and women come into earth life with a conscience knowing good from evil. *See also:* Light of Christ.

Become corrupted (2 Nephi 28:11– 12; Jacob 5:42, 46, 48; Omni 1:17; Helaman 4:22; 5:2). Corrupted means turned from virtue to evil and loss of moral values. Sin leads one into corruption. "My vineyard has become corrupted every whit; and there is none which doeth good save it be a few; and they err in many instances because of priest-crafts, all having corrupt minds" (D&C 33:4).

Become free forever (2 Nephi 2:26). To be free forever is the great promise of living true to the gospel of Jesus Christ. Free forever is free from sin and free to pursue eternal progress and become like God. *See also:* Made free.

Become incorruptible and immortal (2 Nephi 9:13, 15; Mormon 6:21). *See:* Immortal body; Put on incorruption.

Become my sons and my daughters (sons of God) (Mosiah 5:7; 3 Nephi 9:17; Ether 3:14; Moroni 7:26, 48). Meaning being born again and becoming spiritually begotten of God. *See also:* Become the sons of God; Becoming his sons and daughters.

Become popular (1 Nephi 22:23; Alma 1:3). Meaning obtaining worldly popularity and fame, and thus being sustained by worldly honor and praise. There is no safety and salvation in the arm of flesh, rather we should seek protection and guidance through the arm of God. *See also:* Priest and teacher ought to become popular.

Become slippery (Helaman 13:31, 33, 36; Mormon 1:18). The Nephites were given a land of promise as long as they remained faithful. But when they fell into wickedness, the Lord cursed their possessions that they could not hold on to them. *See also:* Curse(-d) the land.

Become subject unto him (2 Nephi 9:5; Moroni 7:30; 9:26). We must of our own free will conform completely to the will of the Lord Jesus Christ. As we do so we will live and serve subject to Him, we will reap the benefits of the Atonement subject to Him, and we will be a part of the great reward hereafter when all things become subject to Him.

Become the sons of God (3 Nephi 9:17; Moroni 7:26, 48). In D&C 11:30, "Verily, verily, I say unto you, that as many as receive me, to them will I give power to become the sons of God, even to them that believe on my name." *Compare:* Moses 6:23. *See also:* Become my sons

and my daughters (sons of God); Becoming his sons and daughters; Spiritually begotten.

Becoming as Gods (Alma 12:31). *See:* Become as God knowing good and evil.

Becoming his sons and daughters (Mosiah 27:25). *See:* Become my sons and my daughters (sons of God); Become the sons of God.

Before his (the) bar (2 Nephi 33:11; Jacob 6:9, 13; Mosiah 16:10; Alma 5:22; 11:44; 12:12; Mormon 9:13; Moroni 10:27, 34). Meaning being brought before God to be judged. *See also:* Bar of God.

Before the throne of God (2 Nephi 28:23; Jacob 3:8). Meaning to stand or be brought before God to be judged. *See also:* Bar of God; Judgment-seat of Christ (God).

Began to be fulfilled (Helaman 16:13–14; 3 Nephi 1:4; 29:1; Ether 15:3). Meaning the prophecies spoken started to really happen, occur, and transpire. *See:* According to God's word.

Began to murmur (1 Nephi 3:31; 16:20; 17:17; Mosiah 21:6; 27:1; Alma 17:28; 19:19). Guard thyself against the insidious and introductory sin of murmuring, for it only leads to greater sin and eventually to destruction. Murmur not against God nor the servants of God, for Satan tempts one to do so. Murmur not, neither grumble nor complain. Rather be of good cheer and pray to God to find a way to accomplish good.

Beginning and the end (Alma 11:39; 3 Nephi 9:18). A descriptor or name of Jesus Christ the Lord. *See also:* Author and finisher of their faith; First and the Last; I am Alpha and Omega, the beginning and the end; D&C 19:1; 38:1.

Beginning to be fulfilled (3 Nephi 29:1). *See:* Began to be fulfilled.

Beginning to labor in sin (2 Nephi 9:51; Jacob 2:5; Mosiah 11:6). Meaning they began to indulge in, participate in, and venture into sin.

Beguiled our first parents (2 Nephi 9:9; Ether 8:25). As Eve said in Genesis 3:13, "The serpent beguiled me, and I did eat [the forbidden fruit]." Satan came tempting Adam and Eve, our first parents, in the Garden of Eden and beguiled them, meaning that he tempted them to partake of that which God commanded that they not partake of. Thus our first parents fell because of transgression and brought mortality into the world. "For as in Adam all die, even so in Christ shall all be made alive" (1 Corinthians 15:22). The fall of Adam and mortality was a necessary part of God's plan and was foreseen by Him, thus the plan also included a Savior, Jesus Christ, to deliver us from the effects of the fall. *See also:* Atonement of Christ (the Only Begotten Son); Plan of salvation.

Beheld (behold) his glory (1 Nephi 11:28; 14:14; 2 Nephi 1:15; 2:4; Alma 5:50; 12:29). Meaning these individuals saw Jesus and His glory. *Compare:* John 1:14; D&C 76:20; 93:11; Moses 1:11, 25. *See also:* Saw Jesus.

Belief in Christ (Alma 46:15; 4 Nephi 1:29). *See:* Believe in Jesus Christ (the Lord); Believest thou.

Belief (believe) in God (Mosiah 4:9; Alma 25:11). *See:* Believest thou; Believest thou that there is a God.

Believe in him (2 Nephi 2:9; 6:14; 26:13; 33:4; Jarom 1:11; Alma 30:9; Ether 3:26). Him being Jesus Christ. *See also:* Believe in Jesus Christ (the Lord); Believest thou.

Believe in his (my/the/their/ these/thy/your) words (1 Nephi 2:16; 11:5; 2 Nephi 30:3; 33:10; Mosiah 5:1–2; 18:3; 28:7; Alma 1:5; 5:11; 14:1; 15:7, 9; 17:29; 18:23; 19:35; 22:11–12; 32:27; 39:11; 45:5; Helaman 6:36; 9:2; 16:2–3, 5–6; 3 Nephi 12:2; 19:21, 23, 28; 21:11; Mormon 9:25; Ether 4:12). To believe in Jesus Christ is to believe His words and the words of His servants sent by Him. *See also:* Believe in Jesus Christ (the Lord); Believed in my (the) words; Believed on his word(-s); Believest thou; Believeth in the word of God.

Believe in his Son (2 Nephi 30:2). *See:* Believe in the Son of God; Believest thou.

Believe in Jesus Christ (the Lord)
(1 Nephi 19:23; 2 Nephi 25:16, 23–24, 28–29; 30:7; 33:10; Jacob 1:8; Mosiah 4:2; Alma 25:6; Mormon 7:5, 10; 9:1; Moroni 7:16). The very belief necessary to obtain salvation, for salvation cometh by no other person or name but by Christ, and by no other way. We must believe that Jesus suffered and died for our sins. Belief in Jesus Christ is the key part of the plan of salvation that will bring us eternal life in the presence of God. *See also:* Atonement of Christ (the Only Begotten Son); Belief in Christ; Believe in the Lord; Believest in the redemption of Christ (Son of the most high God); Believest thou; Believest thou in Jesus Christ who shall come; Believest thou in the power of Christ unto salvation; Believeth in Christ.

Believe in me (2 Nephi 10:7; 3 Nephi 11:32; 12:1, 19; 19:22–23; 20:31). Many places in the scriptures Jesus commands us to "believe in me" and to "follow me." *See also:* Believest thou; Believeth in me.

Believe in my name (Mosiah 26:22; Mormon 9:24–25; Ether 4:18). *See:* Believe on his (my/holy) name; Believest thou.

Believe in the Lord (1 Nephi 19:23; Alma 25:6). Meaning to believe in the Lord, Jesus Christ. *See also:* Believe in Jesus Christ (the Lord); Believest thou.

Believe in the Son of God (1 Nephi 11:6; Alma 33:22; Ether 12:18). In other words, believe that Jesus Christ is the Only Begotten Son of the Father in the flesh. *See also:* Believe in his Son; Believe on the Son of God; Believest in the Son of the most high God; Believest thou; Believest thou that the Son of God shall come to redeem mankind from their sins.

Believe on his (my/holy) name (2 Nephi 25:13–14; Alma 11:40; 19:13, 36; 22:13; 26:35; 32:22; 34:15; Helaman 3:28; 14:2, 12–13; 3 Nephi 9:17; Ether 3:14). It is imperative that we believe on the name of Jesus Christ, for there is no other name by which we can be saved. *See also:* Believe in my name; Believest thou; Believeth on his name; None other name.

Believe on the Son of God (Helaman 14:8). *See:* Believe in the Son of God; Believest thou.

Believe the gospel of Jesus Christ (Mormon 3:21; 5:15; Ether 4:18). To believe in Jesus Christ is to believe in His gospel. *See also:* Believe in Jesus Christ (the Lord); Believest thou.

Believed in my (the) words (1 Nephi 2:17; Alma 14:7; 15:1; 30:57; 3 Nephi 1:16). *See:* Believe in his (my/the/their/these/thy/your) word(-s); Believest thou.

Believed on his word(-s) (Mosiah 18:7; Alma 1:7; 21:12; Helaman

9:39; 16:1, 5). *See:* Believe in his (my/the/their/these/thy/your) word(-s); Believest thou.

Believest in the redemption of Christ (Son of the most high God) (1 Nephi 11:6; Alma 15:8). *See:* Believe in Jesus Christ (the Lord); Believe in the Son of God; Believest thou.

Believest thou (1 Nephi 11:4; Jacob 7:10; Alma 11:24; 15:6; 18:24, 26, 28; 19:9; 21:7; 22:7, 10; 30:35, 37, 41; 45:2, 4; Ether 3:11). The question to ask is, "What do I believe?" Belief is foundational to who we are. Belief is the basis of hope. Belief gives us strength to soldier on. Without any belief, there would be no meaningful existence. We must seek to believe in all that is true and real. Belief in untruth leads to destruction and captivity. Belief in Jesus Christ brings salvation. We must progress in belief, line upon line, until we come to a knowledge of things before unseen. The Articles of Faith outline what we believe. *See also:* Believe in him; Believe in his (my/the/their/these/thy/your) word(-s); Believe in Jesus Christ (the Lord); Believe in me; Believe in the Son of God; Believe on his (my/holy) name.

Believest thou in Jesus Christ who shall come (Alma 45:4). *See:* Believe in Jesus Christ (the Lord); Believest thou.

Believest thou in the power of Christ unto salvation (Alma 15:6).

See: Believe in Jesus Christ (the Lord); Believest thou.

Believest thou that the Son of God shall come to redeem mankind from their sins (Alma 21:7). *See:* Believe in the Son of God; Believest thou.

Believest thou that there is a God (Alma 11:24; 18:24, 26, 28; 22:7; 30:37). Belief in God is foundational to one's spirituality. God does exist, whether one believes He exists or believes He does not exist. We were sent to earth to live by faith. It would not require any faith, nor would it be a test, if God revealed Himself to everyone with no seeking or effort on their part. As Alma points out, we must begin to experiment upon the word [that there is a God] and exercise a particle of faith; ever tending and growing our belief [in God] until we come to a sure knowledge [that God exists] (see Alma 32:26–33). The *Lectures on Faith* says, "Let us here observe, that three things are necessary in order that any rational and intelligent being may exercise faith [belief] in God unto life and salvation: First, the idea that he actually exists. Secondly, a *correct* idea of his character, perfections, and attributes. Thirdly, an actual knowledge that the course of life which he is pursuing is according to [God's] will" (*Lectures on Faith*, 38). *See also:* Belief (believe) in God; Believest thou; Believeth in God; Know God.

Believeth in Christ (Mormon 9:21). *See:* Believe in Jesus Christ (the Lord); Believest thou.

Believeth in God (Ether 12:4). *See:* Believest thou; Believest thou that there is a God.

Believeth in me (3 Nephi 11:33, 35). *See:* Believe in me; Believest thou.

Believeth in the word of God (Alma 32:16). *See:* Believe in his (my/the/their/these/thy/your) word(-s); Believest thou.

Believeth not shall be damned (3 Nephi 11:34; Mormon 9:23; Ether 4:18). To be damned is to be cursed, condemned, and blocked from any progression. To believe in Christ leads to salvation. To not believe is to rebel and reject the Atonement of Christ. Abinadi describes damnation as being delivered up to the devil because they, "having gone according to their own carnal wills and desires; having never called upon the Lord while the arms of mercy were extended towards them; for the arms of mercy were extended towards them, and they would not; they being warned of their iniquities and yet they would not depart from them; and they were commanded to repent and yet they would not repent" (Mosiah 16:12).

Believeth on his name (Alma 5:48; 12:15). *See:* Believe on his (my/holy) name; Believest thou.

Believing that ye shall receive (1 Nephi 15:11; Enos 1:15; Mosiah 4:21; Alma 22:16; 3 Nephi 18:20; Moroni 7:26). Why would one ask if one did not have some hope of receiving from the request? The Lord promised, "Therefore, ask, and ye shall receive; knock, and it shall be opened unto you; for he that asketh, receiveth; and unto him that knocketh, it shall be opened" (3 Nephi 27:29). *See also:* Ask in faith; Moroni 10:4.

Belong to the church (of God) (Mosiah 25:18; 26:38; Alma 1:19, 21, 31–32; 4:9–10; 5:6, 62; 6:2–3; 46:14–15; Helaman 3:33; 4:11; 11:21; 3 Nephi 28:19). Many excuse themselves by saying that religion and churches are of man. To a large extent this is true, except for the true Church of God. When the Lord Jesus was on the earth, He organized His Church (see Ephesians 4:11–16). The true Church of God is on the earth in these latter days (see D&C 115:3–4). Likewise the Church of God was among the Nephites, as documented in these Book of Mormon verses.

Beloved brethren (2 Nephi 6:2; 9:1, 3, 39–41, 44–45, 52; 10:1, 18, 20, 24; 26:1, 23; 30:1, 18; 31:1, 6, 10, 13–14, 16, 19, 21; 32:1, 8; 33:10, 13; Jacob 2:2; 4:2–3, 11, 18; 6:5, 11; Omni 1:26; Alma 5:49–50, 53; 7:1, 17, 22, 26; 9:30; 24:12; 26:9, 26; 32:24; 34:28, 37, 40; 60:10; Helaman 15:1; Moroni 7:2, 14, 27, 29, 35, 39, 40, 46, 48; 10:18–19).

A greeting of the highest order because it involves love. *Beloved* literally means "dearly loved." Jesus was the beloved son of God. All people should be "beloved brethren and sisters." Then we would truly follow the command to "love one another, as I have loved you" (John 15:12).

Beloved by his people (Mosiah 23:6). In other words, loved and highly esteemed by his people.

Beloved disciples (Mormon 1:13, 16). A true disciple loves deeply his teacher and exemplar. We should be beloved disciples of Jesus.

Beloved people (Alma 24:7; 27:30). A greeting like "dear friends." *See also:* Beloved brethren.

Beloved Son (2 Nephi 31:11; 3 Nephi 11:7; 21:20; Moroni 8:2, 9; 9:1, 6, 11). God the Father said, "This is my beloved Son, in whom I am well pleased" (Matthew 17:5). Thus, Beloved Son has become another name for Jesus Christ.

Better for you that ye had not known me (2 Nephi 31:14). If someone receives an elevated witness of Christ and then denies Him, it would be better that they had not known Him. In D&C 132:27 this is described as "blasphemy against the Holy Ghost, which shall not be forgiven in the world nor out of the world[; it] is in that ye . . . assent unto my death." *Assent unto my death* means to agree or concur with the wicked crucifixion of the

innocent Jesus. This is rebellion after having received a sure knowledge of the divinity of Christ. *See also:* Contend no more against the Holy Ghost; Deny the Holy Ghost; Unpardonable sin.

Beyond measure (Mosiah 28:12; 29:40; Alma 31:19; Helaman 3:25). Meaning very great or so large it cannot be measured.

Bind you down to destruction (2 Nephi 1:13; Alma 7:15). *See:* Chains of hell.

Bitter cup (Alma 40:26; 3 Nephi 11:11). Meaning the cup that is filled with the sins and iniquities of the world. "The Savior . . . drank the bitter cup to the dregs [D&C 19:18], and tasted for every man and for every woman; and redeemed the earth and all things upon it. But he was God in the flesh, or he could not have endured it" (Young, *Discourses of Brigham Young*, 176). If we do not repent and come unto Jesus, we will have to drink from the bitter cup of our own sins.

Bitter fountain (Moroni 7:11). Occasionally a source of water is undrinkable, caustic, dank, or foul. Here a bitter fountain is an analogy meaning "a man being evil cannot do that which is good" (Moroni 7:10).

Blameless before God (Mosiah 3:21–22; Alma 5:27; 7:3, 22). "None shall be found blameless before God, except it be little children, only through repentance and faith on the name of the Lord God Omnipotent" (Mosiah 3:21). Thus to be blameless we must invoke the Atonement of Christ to purify us from sin.

Bless thee (and thy house) (2 Nephi 3:3; Alma 3:17; 10:7; Helaman 10:5; 11:16; Ether 1:43). When the Lord says, "I will bless thee," or when a servant of God says, "The Lord will bless thee," it is fortunate indeed for that person or people. We all need and should desire the blessings of God. May we always be worthy of the blessings of God.

Bless thee (them) forever (2 Nephi 3:3; Alma 3:17; 28:8; Helaman 10:5; Mormon 9:37). Blessings from God are wonderful, and the blessings forever from God are impossible to describe in human words. "Eye hath not seen, nor ear heard, neither have entered into the heart of man, the things which God hath prepared for them that love him" (1 Corinthians 2:9).

Blessed are they (those/ye) (1 Nephi 13:37; 2 Nephi 6:12; 28:30; Jacob 6:3; Mosiah 18:30; 26:15–16; 27:37; Alma 26:5; 27:12; 32:8, 13, 16; Helaman 12:23; 13:11, 13; 3 Nephi 9:14; 12:1–11; 16:6; 17:20; 18:10, 12, 14, 34; 27:22; 28:3, 7; Ether 13:10–11). *See:* Blessed art thou.

Blessed art thou (1 Nephi 2:1, 19; 11:6; 2 Nephi 3:25; 4:11; Jacob 5:75;

Mosiah 26:15, 17; Alma 8:15; 19:10, 12; 45:8; 50:20; Helaman 10:4). Meaning great, noble, and loved are you because of your service and faithfulness. This praiseful descriptor is pronounced by both God and man, but is particularly joyous when given from God. *See also:* Blessed are they (those/ye).

Blessed be (is) the name of the Lord (Most High) God (Enos 1:1; Alma 7:4; 19:12; 26:8, 36; 57:35; 3 Nephi 4:32; 11:17). A statement used in praise and thanksgiving to God. *Blessed* denotes holy, divine, sacred, and full of glory.

Blessed his (mine) house (Alma 8:22; 10:11). When ministering to a family or individual—for example, home teaching or priesthood visits—it is sometimes customary to leave a blessing on the home. Such a blessing invites the Spirit to dwell there and also bestows peace, comfort, health, and protection on the occupants of the home.

Blessed of the Lord (1 Nephi 3:8; 16:8; Alma 5:16; Ether 10:28). Meaning the Lord has been especially mindful of and prospered an individual because that person had diligently sought the Lord and emulated the works of the Lord.

Blessed people (1 Nephi 14:2; Jacob 3:6; Alma 50:20). Meaning a people favored of the Lord because of their goodness.

Blessing of God (the Lord) (Alma 10:7, 11; 45:16; 46:10). Blessings from God are a consequence of good and moral living. All good things come from God. When we are so blessed we must recognize it is from God and we must give Him thanks for the blessing.

Blessings poured out (Helaman 3:25; 3 Nephi 10:18). Our all-powerful God is able to open the windows of heaven and pour out blessings according to His will. These blessings are promised to the faithful in the due time of the Lord. Sometimes the blessings are withheld until after the trial of our faith.

Blind(-ed/-eth) the (their/your) eyes (minds) (1 Nephi 12:17; 13:27; 17:30; Mosiah 11:29; Alma 10:25; 48:3; 3 Nephi 2:2). *See:* Blindness of their minds.

Blindness of their minds (1 Nephi 14:7; Jarom 1:3; Alma 13:4; 14:6; 3 Nephi 7:16; Ether 4:15, 15:19). It is the design of Satan to blind our minds and eyes so that we do not see the truth or follow the ways of God. Satan uses the philosophies of men, convoluted rationalizations, and half-truths to cloud the real truth, thus bringing darkness and confused thinking into the minds of men. To compound the problem, when one sins, the Spirit of God withdraws, leaving the sinner without the light of truth. One of the effects of repentance then is to remove the blindness of our minds.

Additionally, consistent prayer and reading of the scriptures has the effect of eliminating this blindness and keeping truth before our eyes. *See also:* Deaf that will not hear . . . blind that will not see, for they shall perish.

Blood come upon our garments (2 Nephi 9:44; Jacob 1:19; Mosiah 2:27; Ether 12:38). *See:* Rid my (our) garments of your (blood and) sins.

Blood of Christ atoneth for their sins (Mosiah 3:11, 16, 18; 4:2; Alma 5:27; 24:13; Moroni 10:33). *See:* Atoning blood of Jesus Christ; Made white in the blood of Christ.

Blood of nobility (Alma 51:21). *See:* Pride of nobility.

Blood of the innocent shall stand as a witness against them (Mosiah 17:10; Alma 14:11; 20:18). Throughout the history of the world, wicked men have murdered innocents. Often people ask why God does not put a stop to such atrocities. We should understand that by not allowing murder, agency would be limited and abridged. Importantly, Alma in Alma 14:8–11 perfectly explains that the murdered innocent are received into the presence of God—paradise —and murders are allowed only during the time of this mortal earth, as an eternal witness against such wicked individuals. These martyrs' blood will condemn the wicked on judgment day.

Blood of the prophets and the saints shall not come up any more unto me against them (2 Nephi 26:3; 28:10; Alma 37:30; 3 Nephi 9:5, 7–9, 11; 10:12). *See:* Blood of the saints (shall cry unto the Lord); Blood would come upon us for vengeance.

Blood of the saints (shall cry unto the Lord) (2 Nephi 26:3; 28:10; 3 Nephi 9:5, 7–9, 11; 10:12; Mormon 8:27, 41; Ether 8:22). In the eternal realms, all deeds are noted and will receive their just consequences. As a general rule, sins can be forgiven after sincere and true repentance and the stain removed from our garments. However, an unpardonable sin is the purposeful murder of innocent individuals. The spilled blood of these innocents will remain as a testimony against these evil murderers and will even cry from the earth for justice and for vengeance, which is the Lord's alone. *See also:* Blood of the prophets and the saints shall not come up any more unto me against them; Blood would come upon us for vengeance.

Blood should not come upon me (2 Nephi 9:22; Jacob 1:19; Mosiah 2:27; Ether 12:38). *See:* Rid my (our) garments of your (blood and) sins.

Blood would come upon us for vengeance (Alma 1:13; 20:18; 37:30; 60:10; Mormon 8:40–41; Ether 8:22, 24). *See:* Blood of the prophets and the saints shall not come up any more unto me against them; Blood of the saints (shall cry unto the Lord).

Blot out their transgressions (Alma 7:13). Before the advent of ballpoint pens, writing was often done with open containers of ink and pens that had to be dipped frequently in the ink. Regularly a spill of ink or inadvertent drops of ink occurred, and thick absorbent blotting paper was used to soak up, clean up, and wipe away such mistakes. In a similar manner, our sins can be cleaned up and wiped away through the Atonement of Jesus Christ, if we sincerely repent. In Psalm 51:1: "Have mercy upon me, O God, according to thy lovingkindness: according unto the multitude of thy tender mercies blot out my transgressions." *See also:* Atonement of Christ (the Only Begotten Son).

Blotted out (Mosiah 26:36; Alma 1:24; 5:57; 6:3; Moroni 6:7). Meaning to remove or erase one's name from among the Saints. "They were not numbered among the people of Christ" (Moroni 6:7). *See also:* Admonished by the church.

Boast in their own strength (Mosiah 11:19; Alma 26:11–12; 38:11; 39:2; Mormon 3:9; 4:8). Pride causes one to boast of their own strength. Compared to the strength of God the strength of men is nothing. "Cursed is he that putteth his trust in the arm of flesh. Yea, cursed is he that putteth his trust in man or maketh flesh his arm" (2 Nephi 4:34). *See also:* Arm of flesh; Left in their own strength; Own strength; Putteth his trust in man, or maketh flesh his arm.

Body of my spirit (Ether 3:16–17). The Lord Jesus Christ appears here to the brother of Jared in His spirit body because He has not yet been born into mortality. Compare also Nephi's explanation of the spirit body of the Holy Ghost in 1 Nephi 11:11.

Bonds of iniquity (Mosiah 23:13; 27:29; Alma 41:11; Mormon 8:31; Moroni 8:14). *See:* Chains of hell.

Book of Ether (Ether 1:2). A history of the Jaredites, who were scattered at the time the Lord confounded the language of the people when they were building the Tower of Babel. The book is an abridgement by Moroni, who included comments of his own as identified in its pages.

Book of life (Alma 5:58). A shortened rendering of the Lamb's or Lord's book of life. "In a figurative sense, the book of life is the complete record of one's life, the sum total of thoughts, words, and deeds written in the soul, of which the Lord will take account in the day of judgment (Rev. 20:12; Alma 12:14). The scriptures also speak of a book of life, or 'the Lamb's book of life,' as 'the record . . . kept in heaven'

(D&C 128:7) in which are written both the names and deeds of the faithful. It is also the heavenly register of those who inherit eternal life (Heb. 12:23; Alma 5:58; D&C 76:68), 'the book of the names of the sanctified, even them of the celestial world' (D&C 88:2; cf. Mal. 3:16–17). . . . Names of faithful Saints may be recorded in the book of life conditionally while they are in mortality . . . but may be 'blotted out' because of unrepented transgression (Rev. 3:5; 22:19; Alma 5:57; D&C 85:5, 11). Ultimately, only the names of those who qualify for eternal life remain written or 'sealed' (*TPJS*, p. 9) in the Lamb's book of life" (*Encyclopedia of Mormonism*, 1:138, 139; paragraphing altered).

Book of remembrance (3 Nephi 24:16). The Lord has commanded his people to keep records including genealogies, records of important events, and sacred writings such as revelations and testimonies, i.e. the command to Nephi to keep records in 1 Nephi 19:1–6; 2 Nephi 5:29–30. Other references to "Book of remembrance" are Malachi 3:16, D&C 85:9, Moses 6:5, 46. President Spencer W. Kimball said, "Those who keep a book of remembrance are more likely to keep the Lord in remembrance in their daily lives. Journals are a way of counting our blessings and of leaving an inventory of these blessings for our posterity" (*Teachings of Spencer W. Kimball*, 349).

Book of the Lamb of God (1 Nephi 13:28, 38). Refers in these verses to the Holy Bible.

Book which doth proceed out of the mouth of the Jews (1 Nephi 13:23–24, 38; 14:23; 2 Nephi 30:3). Meaning the Holy Bible.

Books of Moses (1 Nephi 5:11–13; 19:23). The Brass Plates that Nephi obtained from Laban contained the five books of Moses and a record of the Jews from the beginning down to the commencement of the reign of Zedekiah, king of Judah. The five books of Moses found in our present day Bible—Genesis, Exodus, Leviticus, Numbers and Deuteronomy—are a partial record of the original. Joseph Smith began a translation of the Bible to restore lost content. The Book of Moses in the Pearl of Great Price is an extract from the book of Genesis in Joseph Smith's Translation of the Bible. The Books of Moses and many other hidden and lost scriptures are promised to be revealed in the due time of the Lord. *See also:* Plates of brass.

Bore the sins of many (Mosiah 14:12). Refers to our Savior, who took upon Him the sins of all men, and suffered and bled at every pore, that we would not have to suffer if we repent and come unto Him. *See also:* Atonement of Christ (the Only Begotten Son).

Bore with patience the persecution (Alma 1:25; Alma 53:13). *See:* Bear afflictions (with patience).

Born again (of God) (Mosiah 5:7; 27:25, 28; Alma 5:14, 49; 7:14; 22:15; 36:5, 23–24, 26; 38:6). "Jesus answered and said unto him, Verily, verily, I say unto thee, Except a man be born again, he cannot see the kingdom of God" (John 3:3). To be born again, one must be "born of water and of the Spirit" (John 3:5). To be spiritually born again or born of the spirit is to be "changed from their carnal and fallen state, to a state of righteousness" (Mosiah 27:25). It also means to receive the Lord's image upon their countenance (Alma 5:19) and to become the sons and daughters of God (Mosiah 27:25). Those born again and sanctified by the Holy Ghost will have no more inclination to do evil, but will abhor sin (Alma 13:12) and will experience the pure love of God (Mosiah 4:2–3). Elder Bruce R. McConkie said: "We are born again when we die as pertaining to unrighteousness and when we live as pertaining to the things of the Spirit. But that does not happen in an instant, suddenly. That also is a process. Being born again is a gradual thing, except in a few isolated instances that are so miraculous they get written up in the scriptures. As far as the generality of the members of the Church are concerned, we are born again by degrees, and we are born again to added light and added knowledge and added desires for righteousness as we keep the commandments" ("Jesus Christ and Him Crucified"). *See also:* Moses 6:59–60.

Born of the Spirit (Mosiah 27:24). *See:* Born of God.

Borne our griefs (sins) (and carried our sorrows) (Mosiah 14:4; 15:12). The Savior suffered for our sins and experienced all our griefs so that our sins may be remitted and so he can relieve our griefs and pains (see Alma 7:11–12). *Compare:* Isaiah 53:4. *See also:* Acquainted with grief; Bowels are (may be) filled with compassion (mercy); Bowels of mercy.

Both quick and dead (Moroni 10:34). Jesus Christ is the judge of the quick (the living) and of the dead (see Acts 10:42; 2 Timothy 4:1).

Bound down by the chains of hell (2 Nephi 1:13, 23; Alma 13:30). The chains of hell are heavy and burdensome, and he that has heaped sin upon himself is shackled as if by a great many chains that cannot be escaped from except through repentance and faith on the Lord Jesus Christ. *See also:* Chains of hell.

Bow down before God (2 Nephi 25:29; Alma 22:16–17; 3 Nephi 17:10). A posture of worship, prayer, reverence, honor, humility, praise, respect, veneration, homage, and adoration before God. An example of genuine worship found in D&C

76:21 reports, "And [we] saw the holy angels, and them who are sanctified before his throne, worshiping God, and the Lamb, who worship him forever and ever." *See also:* Bow(-ed) down himself to the earth.

Bow(-ed) down himself to the earth (1 Nephi 21:23; 2 Nephi 6:7; Alma 22:17; 46:13; 3 Nephi 1:11; 19:19, 27; Ether 6:12). To bow down to God in prayer or worship is an act and sign of humility before God. The deeper the bow, even all the way down to the ground, if done in true earnest and sincerity, signifies greater submissiveness, all the time realizing that God knows our heart. *See also:* Bow down before God; Mighty prayer.

Bowels may be (are) filled with mercy (compassion) (Alma 7:12; 3 Nephi 17:6–7). In our day we refer to tender feelings as feelings of the heart. In ancient times feelings of mercy, love, and compassion were described as feelings deep within the abdomen or the bowels. *See also:* Bowels of mercy; Moved with compassion.

Bowels of mercy (Mosiah 15:9; Alma 7:12; 26:37; 34:15; 3 Nephi 17:7). Refers to Christ's compassion and tender feelings toward the suffering of man; also describes the mercy that satisfies for the repentant soul. Jesus Christ "shall go forth, suffering pains and afflictions and temptations of every kind. . . . and he will take upon him their infirmities, that his bowels may be filled with mercy, according to the flesh, that he may know according to the flesh how to succor his people according to their infirmities" (Alma 7:11–12). "That great and last sacrifice will be the Son of God: yea, infinite and eternal; and thus he shall bring salvation to all those who shall believe on his name; this being the intent of this last sacrifice, to bring about the bowels of mercy, which overpowereth justice, and bringeth about means unto men that they may have faith unto repentance" (Taylor, *Mediation and Atonement*, 174). *See also:* Moved with compassion.

Branch of the house (tree) of Israel (1 Nephi 15:12, 16; 19:24; 2 Nephi 3:5; 9:53; Alma 26:36). The house of Israel is likened unto an olive tree from which the Lord has led away ("broken off") from time to time groups of people (i.e., a "righteous branch" and "remnant of Joseph"; see 2 Nephi 10:22; Alma 46:24). Lehi and his family were a branch that ran over the wall (see 1 Nephi 15:12).

Branch which was (who have been) broken off (1 Nephi 15:12; 19:24; 2 Nephi 3:5). *See:* Branch of the house (tree) of Israel.

Brazen serpent (2 Nephi 25:20; Helaman 8:14–15). The serpent that Moses made of brass and placed on a pole. If a man were bitten by the serpents sent by the Lord and then looked upon the brazen serpent, he lived. And if, for lack of faith he did not look upon the brazen serpent, he died (see Numbers 21:9).

Bread and the waters of life (Alma 5:34). Jesus Christ is the bread of life. He that cometh unto Christ and believeth on Him shall never hunger nor never thirst (referring to spiritual nourishment and ultimately to eternal life). *See also:* Fountain of living waters; Living waters.

Break forth into (joy) singing (1 Nephi 21:13; 2 Nephi 24:7; Mosiah 12:23; 15:30; 3 Nephi 4:31; 16:19; 20:34). Because of our Lord Jesus Christ's redemption in our behalf and because of our Heavenly Father's plan of salvation for us, we should wish to sing songs of joy and praise to God and his Son. There are numerous psalms that express the singing of praises to God, the Lord and our Heavenly King.

Breaketh the bands of death (Mosiah 15:8; Alma 22:14). *See:* Bands of death.

Breath of his lips (2 Nephi 21:4; 30:9). Concerning the Second Coming of Christ, President John Taylor described the changes that will take place "to regulate and restore the brute creation to their former state of peace and glory, causing all enmity to cease from off the earth. But this will never be done until there is a general destruction poured out upon man, which will entirely cleanse the earth, and sweep all wickedness from its face. This will be done by the rod of his mouth, and by the breath of his lips; or, in other words, by fire as universal as the flood" (*Government of God*, 114). *See also:* Rod of his mouth and with the breath of his lips.

Bridle all your passions (Alma 38:12). A bridle with reins is placed on a horse to control and direct the horse. Likewise, we must control our passions and desires, resist temptation, and direct ourselves aright. "A youth boiling with hormones will wonder why he should not give full freedom to his sexual desires; and if he is unchecked by customs, morals, or laws, he may ruin his life before he matures sufficiently to understand that sex is a river of fire that must be banked and cooled by a hundred restraints if it is not to consume in chaos both the individual and the group" (Will and Ariel Durrant, *Lessons of History*, 35–36).

Bright recollection of all our guilt (2 Nephi 9:14, 46; Jacob 6:9; Mosiah 2:38; 3:25; Alma 5:18; 11:43; 12:1; 14:6; Mormon 9:3). Meaning a perfect and complete remembrance of all our unrepentant sins. *Compare:* Guilt was swept away; Peace of conscience; Taken away the guilt from our hearts. *See also:* Awful view of their own guilt; Consciousness of (his/your) guilt (filthiness); Harrowed up under a consciousness of his own guilt; Lively sense of his own guilt; Perfect remembrance of all your wickedness; Racked with a consciousness of guilt; Remember your awful guilt; Remembrance of our guilt.

Bring again (forth) Zion (1 Nephi 13:37; Mosiah 12:22; 15:29; 3 Nephi 16:18). This scriptural phrase refers to the latter-day work of building up Zion in the stakes of the Church. It also refers to the return of the City of Enoch and the Second Coming of the Lord. In his landmark address in 1977, Elder Bruce R. McConkie described the bringing again of Zion. "Zion is people; Zion is the saints of God; Zion is those who have been baptized; Zion is those who have received the Holy Ghost; Zion is those who keep the commandments; Zion is the righteous; or in other words, as our revelation recites: 'This is Zion—the pure in heart' (D&C 97:21). . . . Isaiah made particular mention of stakes of Zion (Isaiah 54:2) which would be established in the day of restoration. . . . Stakes of Zion are also being organized at the ends of the earth. In this connection, let us ponder these truths; a stake of Zion is a part of Zion. You cannot create a stake of Zion without creating a part of Zion. . . . To create a stake is like founding a City of Holiness. . . . Scattered Israel in every nation is called to gather to the fold of Christ, to the stakes of Zion" ("Come: Let Israel Build Zion," 117, 118; paragraphing altered).

Concerning future events, Elder McConkie also said, "The scripture says that Enoch 'built a city that was called the City of Holiness, even Zion'; that Zion 'was taken up into heaven' (Moses 7:19). . . . This same Zion which was taken up into heaven shall return during the Millennium, when the Lord brings again Zion; and its inhabitants shall join with the New Jerusalem which shall then be established. (See Moses 7:62–63.) Our Article of Faith says that 'We believe . . . in the restoration of the Ten Tribes.' This . . . will occur when the Lord brings again Zion, according to the promises" (Ibid., 118). Bringing again Zion can also apply to us personally and individually: "Each one of us can build up Zion in our own lives by being pure in heart. . . . Each one of us can extend the borders of Zion by gathering our friends and neighbors into the fold of Israel" (Ibid.). See D&C 113:8, which refers "to those whom God should call in the last days, who should hold the power of priesthood to bring again Zion, and the redemption of Israel." *See also:* Laborer in Zion; Lengthen thy cords and strengthen thy stakes; Seek to bring forth my Zion; Strengthen thy stakes and enlarge thy borders; Welfare of Zion.

Bring forth (good) fruit (Jacob 5:27, 54, 60–61; Alma 13:13; 32:37, 43; 3 Nephi 14:18). The references in Jacob 5 liken good or natural fruit to the bringing forth or harvesting of converts to the gospel. The remaining verses have reference to the fruit of eternal life that is picked from the tree of one's faith and works. See Lehi's dream in 1 Nephi 8:11–12. *See also:* Fruit of the tree of life [Lehi's dream]; Tame olive tree.

Bring souls to repentance (Alma 26:22; 29:9; 36:24; 42:31). Meaning to declare the true gospel of Jesus Christ, including faith in Christ, repentance from sin, and following the straight and narrow path unto salvation.

Bring souls unto me (Jesus/thee) (Alma 31:35; 3 Nephi 28:9, 29). *See:* Bring souls to repentance.

Bring them to a (the) knowledge (Mosiah 28:2; Alma 17:9; 26:24; Helaman 15:6; 3 Nephi 5:23). Meaning to bring individuals to a knowledge of God and of the gospel of Jesus Christ. *See also:* Bring souls to repentance; Come to the knowledge.

Bring them unto repentance (Alma 17:16; 34:15). *See:* Bring souls to repentance.

Bring you down unto repentance (Alma 34:30; 42:29). Hearing the testimony of truth and experiencing the trials of life sometimes brings people to a knowledge of the need to repent and follow a true course to salvation through Jesus Christ.

Bring you into subjection unto him [the devil] (Alma 12:6). It is Satan's objective to take away our freedom by getting us to sin and follow him. Thus we become subject to, controlled, and enslaved by him. *See also:* Captive by (captivity/captivation of/the will of) the devil; Chains of hell; Kingdom of the devil.

Bring(-eth/brought) forth fruit (works which are) meet for repentance (Alma 9:30; 12:15; 13:13; 34:30; Moroni 6:1). Meaning acting in faith and doing works that show one is worthy to receive a forgiveness of sins; preparing one to then go on to baptism and the other ordinances of eternal life. *See also:* Meet for repentance.

Bring(-eth/brought) good tidings (Mosiah 12:21; 15:14, 18; 27:37; Helaman 5:29; 3 Nephi 20:40). The gospel of Jesus Christ is the good tidings or good news. Those that have been blessed with truth are obliged to bring these truths to their friends and neighbors, not hide them under a bushel.

Bring(-eth) salvation (2 Nephi 2:3; 3:15; Alma 34:15; 37:7; 42:26; Helaman 5:11; 14:15). Jesus Christ, our Redeemer and Savior, and His gospel provide salvation to those who repent and follow the Savior's example. Salvation is deliverance from physical and spiritual death.

It is also redemption or cleansing from sin so that we may again enter God's presence. Generally salvation encompasses the effects of the Atonement of Christ, including resurrection to immortal life and, for the faithful who qualify, exaltation in the celestial kingdom. In some scriptures, salvation refers to just the resurrection portion of the Atonement, while exaltation is the word used to denote eternal life in God's presence. *See also:* Salvation of our (their) souls; Salvation of the Lord (our God).

Bringeth to pass the resurrection (Mosiah 15:20, 24; Alma 40:3; 42:23; Helaman 14:16–17; Mormon 7:6; 9:13). It was part of the mission and calling of our Lord Jesus Christ to bring to pass the resurrection of the dead. He was chosen and anointed to this mission. Because Jesus was the only begotten Son of God in the flesh, only He had power to raise His body from the grave, to break the bands of death, and become the first to be resurrected, thus providing the means whereby we also will all be resurrected. *See also:* Resurrection of the body.

Bringeth unto repentance (Alma 12:15; 34:15; Helaman 5:11; 14:18; 15:7; Moroni 8:25). *See:* Bring souls to repentance.

Broad roads (1 Nephi 12:17). Strait is the gate and narrow is the way which leads unto life eternal.

Whereas broad is the path to wander and many are the worldly broadminded philosophies that lead to spiritual destruction.

Broken heart(-s) and (a) contrite spirit(-s) (2 Nephi 2:7; 4:32; Jacob 2:10; 3 Nephi 9:20; 12:19; Mormon 2:14; Ether 4:15; Moroni 6:2). Means to come down to the depths of humility and to be without pride. Indicates that our heart is prepared and we desire to undergo change to the good. To understand that next to God, man is nothing (Moses 1:10). Also means to treat all fellow men as equals and fellow sojourners here on earth and not consider ourselves to be better than them. *See also:* Meek and humble.

Broken (breaketh) the bands of death (Mosiah 15:8–9, 20, 23; 16:7; Alma 4:14; 5:9–10; 22:14). *See:* Bands of death.

Brought (back) into the presence of the Lord (Alma 36:15; Helaman 14:15, 17; Mormon 9:13). Refers to being resurrected and brought back into the presence of the Lord to be judged of our life on earth, for all will be judged of Christ the Lord. *See also:* Brought into the presence of the Lord.

Brought down the wrath of God (Mosiah 7:28; Alma 10:18; Ether 2:11). *See:* Wrath of God (the Lord).

Brought down (to lie) low in the dust (1 Nephi 18:18; 2 Nephi 1:21; 26:15; Alma 28:11). Meaning to

die and be laid in the grave and the mortal flesh returns to the dust from which it sprang. There the spiritless mortal body will remain until the day of resurrection. *See also:* Temporal death.

Brought forth fruit [before baptism] (Alma 12:15; 13:13; 34:30; Moroni 6:1). Meaning that they were worthy of baptism; in other words, presented themselves suitable or proper for baptism. This would include faith in the Lord Jesus Christ, a humble and contrite heart, and repentance of all sins. As stated in Mosiah 18:8–10, fruit meet for baptism also involves being willing to accept the covenants of baptism and serve one another.

Brought forth (good/much) fruit [in building the kingdom] (Jacob 5:17–20, 22–26, 32, 36, 40, 42, 45, 75; Alma 29:15; 32:37, 43; 3 Nephi 14:17–19). Meaning to bring forth many good works, converts unto the gospel of Jesus Christ, and eternal life to the righteous. *See also:* Abound(-ing) in good works.

Brought forth triumphant through the air (Moroni 10:34). Moroni here looks forward to the great day when he will be resurrected. He says "triumphant" because of his faithfulness—he describes victorious, successful, and jubilant feelings. "Through the air" because Moroni died before the Second Coming and will therefore be among the Saints who come through the air to earth with Christ at the Lord's Second Coming. *See also:* Seal you his.

Brought himself under condemnation (Mosiah 26:31; Moroni 9:6). *See:* Under condemnation.

Brought into bondage (Mosiah 7:20; 11:21, 23; 12:2; 23:23; 29:18; Alma 5:5; 44:7). The Lord has sometimes allowed his people to be brought into bondage to humble them and to get them to return unto Him. "They were brought down to humble themselves like unto their brethren, and to fight valiantly for their freedom from bondage" (Alma 51:21). *See also:* Brought out of bondage; Deliver(-ed) out of bondage.

Brought into (to/unto) the everlasting (marvelous) light (2 Nephi 32:4: Alma 26:3, 15; Mormon 8:16). Those that come unto Christ and accept His ways quite literally come into the light of the gospel, which is the light of truth. The earth lies in darkness, but the humble seeker of truth can find everlasting light, the light of Christ. *See also:* Marvelous light of God.

Brought into the presence of the Lord (Ether 3:13). The faith of the brother of Jared was so great that he could not be kept without the veil. Thus he was allowed into the presence of the Lord. *Compare:* Beheld (behold) his glory; Saw Jesus. *See also:* Brought (back) into the presence of the Lord; Could not be kept from within the veil.

Brought low in the dust (1 Nephi 22:23; 2 Nephi 12:12, 17). Meaning made extremely low, without stature, leveled from lofty pride, and reduced to nothingness.

Brought out of bondage (1 Nephi 17:25; Mosiah 12:34; Alma 9:22; 36:28–29). *See:* Deliver(-ed) out of bondage.

Brought out of darkness unto light (2 Nephi 3:5; Alma 37:25; Mormon 8:16). *See:* Brought into the light; Darkness unto light; Marvelous light of God.

Brought out of obscurity (1 Nephi 22:12). *See:* Out of obscurity.

Brought to stand before (the Lamb of) God (1 Nephi 15:33; Mosiah 16:10; Alma 11:43; 12:8; 24:15; 36:15; 40:21; Mormon 9:2, 13). It is the testimony of the scriptures and the holy prophets that all men and women will be brought before God to be judged of their works and judged according to the light and knowledge they had while on earth. *See also:* Bar of God; Stand before God.

Brought to the knowledge (Mosiah 5:4; 27:14; Alma 18:34; 21:17; 23:5–6; 24:27; 37:8–9; Helaman 15:7, 13; 3 Nephi 16:4; 20:13). *See:* Come to the knowledge.

Brought unto repentance (Helaman 12:24; 3 Nephi 7:24;

Ether 7:25). *See:* Bring souls to repentance.

Brought unto salvation (Enos 1:13; Mosiah 5:15; Alma 24:27; 26:15, 20; 34:31; 37:8; Helaman 14:15; 3 Nephi 5:20). Meaning to bring souls unto repentance and to the gospel of Jesus Christ, which leads to salvation. *See also:* Bring(-eth) salvation.

Brought upon him (them) (Mosiah 4:17; Alma 3:19; 39:11; 42:9, 12; 50:21). For every good or bad action there is a consequence. Some consequences are minute and hardly, if at all, perceptible. Other consequences are large and unmistakable. In these verses there were consequences brought upon persons because of sin. *See also:* Consequences of sin.

Bruised for our iniquities (Mosiah 14:5). Meaning Jesus suffered for our sins. Same as Isaiah 53:5.

Build (built up) churches unto themselves (2 Nephi 26:20–21; 28:3; 4 Nephi 1:26, 34, 41; Mormon 8:32–33). *See:* Built up churches to get gain (power/praise of men).

Built up again [Jerusalem] (1 Nephi 10:3; 2 Nephi 25:11; 3 Nephi 20:29, 33, 36, 46; Ether 13:5). Jerusalem has been a troubled city with a troubled history. The children of Israel and the Jews have been scattered from Jerusalem, and it has been prophesied that they will be gathered again, return to their covenant land, and build up again Jerusalem. Three specific times can be readily identified: (1) Shortly after Lehi left, Jerusalem was destroyed. King Cyrus conquered Babylon, and because of a dream decreed the Jews to return to Judah and rebuild the city and the temple. (2) Sixty years after Christ's crucifixion, Jerusalem and the temple were destroyed, and the Jews were scattered. Another gathering has taken place in the establishment of the country of Israel in 1948 by the Balfour agreement. We believe this occurrence to be the direct result of Joseph Smith sending Orson Hyde to Palestine and dedicating it for the return of the Jews. (3) In our day a spiritual gathering of the Jews is beginning, but will grow tremendously when Jesus appears on the Mount of Olives to deliver the Jews at his Second Coming. Then during the Millennium, Jerusalem will be built up again. There will be the New Jerusalem on the American continent, and also the Old Jerusalem will be rebuilt (see Ether 13:11; 2 Nephi 12:3).

Built up churches to get gain (power/praise of men) (1 Nephi 22:23; 2 Nephi 26:20, 29; Alma 30:35; Helaman 7:5, 21; 3 Nephi 29:7; 4 Nephi 1:26; Mormon 8:33). Throughout the history of the world, men have built up their own churches and established their own conjured beliefs for their own personal purposes. The Savior described these false churches, saying, "Their creeds were an abomination in his sight; that those professors were all corrupt; that: 'they draw near to me with their lips, but their hearts are far from me, they teach for doctrines the commandments of men, having a form of godliness, but they deny the power thereof'" (Joseph Smith–History 1:19). In 2 Nephi 28:12, 14, the description is, "Because of pride, and because of false teachers, and false doctrine, their churches have become corrupted . . . and because of pride, and wickedness, and abominations, and whoredoms, they have all gone astray save it be a few, who are the humble followers of Christ." *See also:* Destroy the church; Great and abominable church.

Built upon my gospel (3 Nephi 27:8–11). Jesus explains here that if a church is not built upon His gospel, the true and living gospel of Christ, then it is not His Church.

Built upon my rock (2 Nephi 28:28; Helaman 5:12; 3 Nephi 11:39–40; 14:24–25; 18:12–13). The true gospel or doctrine of Christ is the rock on which we should build. "Behold, verily, verily, I say unto you, this is my gospel; and remember that they shall have faith in me or they can in nowise be saved; and upon this rock I will build my church; yea, upon this rock ye are built, and if ye continue, the gates of hell shall not prevail against you"

(D&C 33:12–13). *See also:* Doctrine of Christ.

Burdeneth my soul (Jacob 2:9). *See:* Afflict my soul.

Burdens may be light (Mosiah 18:8; 24:15; Alma 33:23). We must pray unto God that He will make the burdens of mortal life light, that we may bear them with patience. Also, it is required of us to help others bear their burdens, for it is the mark of a true Christian and a follower of Christ.

Burn as an oven (3 Nephi 25:1). *See:* Burn as stubble; D&C 133:64.

Burn as stubble (1 Nephi 22:15; 2 Nephi 26:4; 3 Nephi 25:1). *See:* Consumed as stubble.

Burnt offerings (1 Nephi 5:9; 7:22; Mosiah 2:3; 3 Nephi 9:19). *See:* Sacrifice(-s) and burnt offerings.

Buy milk and honey, without money and without price (2 Nephi 9:50; 26:25; Alma 1:20). The gospel of Jesus Christ is free and brings spiritual sustenance, satisfaction, and salvation. "Wherefore, do not spend money for that which is of no worth, nor your labor for that which cannot satisfy. Hearken diligently unto me, and remember the words which I have spoken; and come unto the Holy One of Israel, and feast upon that which perisheth not, neither can be corrupted, and let your soul delight in fatness" (2 Nephi 9:51). *See also:* Redeemed without money; Salvation is free.

By faith (1 Nephi 10:17; 2 Nephi 1:10; Ether 12:3, 7, 10–11, 16–17, 20–23; Moroni 7:25–26, 37; 8:25). "Without faith you can do nothing" (D&C 8:10). Faith is the great motivator. Faith is power. By faith all things are possible. By faith all things have been accomplished. After all we can do to strengthen our faith, exceedingly great faith is a gift from God. God desires that we develop great faith, whereas Satan wants to undermine our faith. The opposite of faith is fear. Compare Ether 12:3–23 with Hebrews 11:4–31.

By faith miracles are wrought (Mormon 9:19; Ether 12:16; Moroni 7:37). When there is no faith, miracles cease. God is a God of miracles, and as long as the people have faith and strive to be faithful, then miracles will be upon the earth. *See also:* God of miracles; Mormon 1:13.

By grace that we are saved after all we can do (2 Nephi 25:23). Without the grace of Jesus Christ no man could gain salvation, yet "faith without works is dead" (James 2:26). We must always be grateful for our Savior's Atonement in our behalf. "No flesh . . . can dwell in the presence of God, save it be through the merits, and mercy, and grace of the Holy Messiah" (2 Nephi 2:8). But the scriptures make it abundantly clear that to gain salvation, made possible by our Redeemer, we must keep the commandments of God, serve our fellowmen, and endure to the end.

By his grace (Jacob 4:7; Moroni 10:32). Meaning by the Lord's goodness and divine help, for He is full of grace. *See also:* Full of grace (equity/mercy) and truth; Grace of God.

By his Holy Spirit (1 Nephi 2:17; Alma 5:46; 18:34). The Saints of God are commanded to do much good in the name of Christ and as directed by the Holy Spirit. The Holy Spirit, also known as the Holy Ghost, can manifest truths unto us, direct us, comfort us, and protect us. *See also:* By the Holy Ghost; By the power of the Holy Ghost (Spirit).

By his word (1 Nephi 17:26, 31, 46; Mormon 9:17). The Lord has not done anything except He has done it by His word. In some scriptures, "by his word" means by His actual spoken word or command. In other scriptures, "by his word" means by His Son, Jesus Christ, as defined in John 1:1–5. *See also:* Power of his voice (word).

By small and simple things are great things brought to pass (1 Nephi 16:29; Alma 37:6–7, 41; Ether 3:5). God is quite capable of great miracles and mighty signs and wonders, but for the most part, God accomplishes his purposes by small and simple things and through the efforts of humble and common people. Thus it is by faith we must recognize God's hand in the events of life and the history of this earth. Additionally, we as individuals progress in life by performing small and simple acts of love and service. No one makes one or two huge steps to Christlike character. Rather we progress line upon line and precept upon precept.

By small means (1 Nephi 16:29; Alma 37:6–7, 41). *See:* By small and simple things are great things brought to pass by God.

By the grace of God (2 Nephi 10:24; Moroni 7:2; 10:32–33). *See:* By grace that we are saved after all we can do; By his grace; Grace of God.

By the hand of the Lord (God) (1 Nephi 5:14; 2 Nephi 1:5–6; 5:12; 28:6; Omni 1:16; Mosiah 1:2, 5, 16; 2:11; 28:15; 29:25; Alma 2:28; 9:9, 22; 37:4; 45:19; 46:7, 24; 4 Nephi 1:16; Mormon 6:6; 8:26; Ether 1:1; 2:6; 10:28). The Lord God is all powerful, and by His mighty hand He can accomplish all things. Nothing is impossible with God. *See also:* Deliverance by the hand of the Lord; Hand of God (the Lord); Led by the power of his arm (the hand of God); Power of God; Preserved by the hand of the Lord God; Strengthened by the hand of the Lord.

By the Holy Ghost (1 Nephi 10:11; 2 Nephi 32:2; Alma 13:12; 3 Nephi 15:23; 16:4; 4 Nephi 1:48). *See:* By his Holy Spirit; By the power of the Holy Ghost (Spirit).

By the law no flesh [no man] is justified (2 Nephi 2:5). Salvation does not come by the law alone, but by faith in Christ unto salvation (see Mosiah 13:28). In other words, just keeping the law of God does not justify us or save us; we must accept and apply the Atonement of Christ, which is offered unto us by the grace of Christ. *See also:* Romans 3:20–25; Galatians 2:16; 3:24.

By the mouth of angels (Mosiah 4:11; Alma 13:22, 25–26; 36:5). God sends His angels to instruct men in His word. *See also:* Angels minister(-ed/appeared/declared/descending) unto him (them).

By the mouth of the holy prophets (1 Nephi 3:20; 5:13; 13:41; 2 Nephi 9:2; 25:1; Mosiah 18:19; 25:21; Alma 5:11; 3 Nephi 1:13; Ether 1:39; 15:3). God sends prophets to declare His word. *See also:* Word of God.

By the power of God (1 Nephi 13:19; 2 Nephi 27:10; Enos 1:26; Mosiah 15:3; 23:13; Alma 37:15, 40; Helaman 9:36; Mormon 7:9; 8:16; 9:13; Ether 5:3). God has the power to do all that He wills to do. *See also:* Power of God.

By the power of his holy arm (Jacob 2:25; Enos 1:13; Omni 1:13). *See:* Arm of the Lord (revealed); By the hand of the Lord (God).

By the power of his voice (word) (1 Nephi 17:46; Jacob 4:9; Alma 5:5; Helaman 12:10–12; Mormon 8:24; 9:17). *See:* Power of his voice (word).

By the power of the Father he hath risen (Mormon 7:5). God the Father gave His Son, Jesus Christ, the power to raise His body from the grave (see Mormon 7:5).

By the power of the Holy Ghost (Spirit) (1 Nephi 10:17, 19; 2 Nephi 2:8; 26:13; 28:31; 32:3; 33:1; Jacob 7:12; Alma 7:10; 3 Nephi 7:21; 21:2; 29:6; Moroni 3:4; 6:4, 9; 7:44; 8:7; 10:4–5, 7). Through the power of the Spirit, visions, revelations and knowledge are given, the power of God is manifest unto man, mighty miracles and signs are given, a belief and testimony of truth is given, a forgiveness of sins and fiery cleansing is given, directions on how to proceed are given, and a knowledge of the true and living God is given, to name just a few. *See also:* Power of the Holy Ghost (Spirit).

By the spirit (1 Nephi 3:20; 4:6, 10; 15:12; 19:12; 22:2; 2 Nephi 14:4; Jacob 4:15; Alma 9:21; 19:13; 21:16; 22:1; 24:30; 37:15; 45:19; Helaman 10:16; 3 Nephi 7:22; Moroni 10:9, 17). *See:* By the power of the Holy Ghost (Spirit).

By the words of three, God hath said, I will establish my word (2 Nephi 11:3). *See:* Testimony of many (two or three).

By their works ye shall know them (1 Nephi 15:32; Alma 5:54; 3 Nephi 27:11, 14, 25; 4 Nephi 1:5; Mormon 3:18; Moroni 7:5). We will be judged by our works, whether they be good or bad. Also, men might know of us by our works. It behooves us to associate among those that bring about good works, for there is safety there. *See also:* Abound(-ing) in good works; According to their (your) works (deeds).

By way of command(-ment) (1 Nephi 19:3; Alma 5:62). Simply, God directs by command. Here God has commanded His servants to deliver specific messages.

By way of exhortation (Moroni 10:2). *Exhort* means to encourage, give advice, and give warning. "Strengthen them by the word of exhortation" (D&C 50:37). *See also:* Exhort them (you).

By way of the Gentiles (1 Nephi 15:17). The Book of Mormon was to come forth by way of the Gentiles. "Joseph Smith (through whom the Book of Mormon was revealed) was of the Tribe of Ephraim. At the same time the Prophet was of the Gentiles, meaning that he was a citizen of a Gentile Nation" (McConkie, *Mormon Doctrine*, 311).

C

Call on the name of the Lord (Alma 19:16; 24:21; 3 Nephi 4:30; Ether 2:14–15). Meaning pray in the name of the Lord Jesus Christ. *See also:* Call on (upon) the Father in my name.

Call on (upon) his (holy) name (2 Nephi 22:4; Alma 9:17; 12:30; 13:28; 17:4; 22:16; 34:17; Helaman 3:27). Meaning pray unto God. *See also:* Call on (upon) the Father in my name.

Call on (upon) the Father in my name (3 Nephi 21:27; 27:7, 9; Ether 4:15; Moroni 2:2). The proper pattern of prayer is to (1) address or petition our prayer to God the Father; (2) thank God for our multitude of blessings; (3) humbly ask for needed aid and assistance; and (4) close in the name of Jesus Christ. Thus we are commanded by Jesus in the Lord's Prayer, "After this manner therefore pray ye . . ." (Matthew 6:9; 3 Nephi 13:9). *See also:* In the name of Jesus (Christ/the Lord God); Pray(-ed) unto the Father in my (the) name (of Christ).

Call upon the Lord their God (Mosiah 26:4; Ether 3:2). Meaning pray in the name of the Lord Jesus Christ. *See also:* Call on (upon) the Father in my name.

Call upon the name of the Lord (Ether 2:14–15). Meaning pray in the name of the Lord Jesus Christ. *See also:* Call on (upon) the Father in my name.

Called after the holy order of God (2 Nephi 6:2; Alma 5:44, 49; 6:8; 8:4; 13:6, 8, 11, 18; 43:2; Helaman 8:18; Ether 12:10). *See:* After the order of his (the) Son; Authority from (of) God; Called by the order of God.

Called by a holy calling (his Holy Spirit) (Alma 13:6; 29:13; 18:34). *See:* Called of God (the Holy Spirit).

Called by the order of God (Alma 5:44; 8:4; 13:6, 18; 43:2; Helaman 8:18; Ether 12:10). Meaning called to the priesthood to preach and minister the gospel to men. "We believe that a man must be called of God, by prophecy, and by the laying on of hands by those who are in authority, to preach the Gospel and administer in the ordinances thereof" (Articles of Faith 1:5). *See also:* After the order of his (the) Son; Authority from (of) God; Called after the holy order of God.

Called of God (the Holy Spirit) (2 Nephi 6:2; Alma 18:34; 42:31). To be called through inspiration and revelation by God's anointed. "We believe that a man must be called of God, by prophecy, and by the laying on of hands by those who are in authority, to preach the Gospel and administer in the ordinances thereof" (Articles of Faith 1:5). *See also:* Authority from (of) God; Called by a holy calling (his Holy Spirit); Called to his (the) ministry; His calling unto me.

Called to his (the) ministry (Alma 39:16; 3 Nephi 28:2; Moroni 8:2). *See:* Called of God (the Holy Spirit).

Called with a holy calling (Alma 13:3, 4, 6, 8; 29:13). Prophets, bishops, missionaries, and other church officers are called of God and have holy and sacred callings to preach the word of God and, to the best of their ability, be examples of Christ. *See also:* Authority from (of) God; Called of God (the Holy Spirit).

Calves of the stall (1 Nephi 22:24; 3 Nephi 25:2). Meaning all their needs are provided like young calves that are cared for and raised in a stall; thereby protected, fed, and sheltered. "During the Millennium, when the Lord reigns, children will grow up in an environment of righteousness. No longer will the calves of Abram's herds and the lambs of Jacob's flocks be lost in the deserts of sin; no longer will they forage for food by the wayside and drink water from stagnant pools; no longer will they be pulled down by the evils and designs of conspiring men. In the millennial day, in the household of faith, children will be brought up in the nurture and admonition of the Lord, as calves in the stall, as lambs in the sheepcote [sheepfold]" (McConkie, *Millennial Messiah*, 669).

Came (come) down from (out of) heaven (1 Nephi 11:27; 12:6; Mosiah 3:5; 4:2; Helaman 5:45, 48; 13:13; 3 Nephi 11:8; 17:24; 19:14; 21:25; Ether 13:3). God sends down from heaven messengers and things He sees as necessary, including His Son, Jesus Christ, the Holy Spirit, angels, prophets, power, fire, and anything else He wills according to His great wisdom. *See also:* Come down out of heaven.

Came prophets (1 Nephi 1:4; Alma 37:30; Ether 7:23; 9:28; 11:1, 12, 20). Throughout the ages, God has sent forth prophets to call people to repentance, declare the Savior Jesus Christ, and prophesy of events to come. *See also:* Sent prophets.

Came to the knowledge of their Redeemer (Mosiah 18:30). Salvation is dependent on coming to a true knowledge of Christ. We must come unto Him and keep His commandments. Missionary work is to preach the gospel of Jesus Christ. *See also:* Know God; Knowledge of their Redeemer.

Can in nowise inherit the kingdom of heaven (Mosiah 27:26; Alma 5:51; 9:12; 39:9; 3 Nephi 11:38; Moroni 10:21). There are definite things we must do to inherit the kingdom of heaven, and they include but are not limited to having faith, exercising repentance, being baptized, receiving the Holy Ghost, accepting the ordinances of salvation, becoming as a little child, having a change of heart, having charity, keeping the commandments, and remaining faithful.

Cannot be saved in your sins (Alma 11:37; Moroni 10:26). We cannot receive salvation in the kingdom of heaven while still being stained with sin and rebellion. The Atonement of Christ makes it possible for us to be cleansed and purified so that we may return to God's presence. *See also:* Save them in their sins.

Captive by (captivity/captivation of/the will of) the devil (1 Nephi 14:4, 7; Alma 9:28; 12:11, 17; 40:13; 3 Nephi 18:15; 27:32). They that harden their hearts "are taken captive by the devil, and led by his will down to destruction. Now this is what is meant by the chains of hell" (Alma 12:11). *See also:* Chains of hell; Hold upon the (their/your) hearts.

Captive daughter of Zion (2 Nephi 8:25; Jacob 2:33; 3 Nephi 20:37). The term "captive daughter of Zion" refers to the inhabitants of Jerusalem. In a broader sense it also means any person who has allowed themselves to become captive to sin and the devil.

Carnal and devilish (Mosiah 16:3; Alma 41:13). *See:* Carnal, sensual, and devilish.

Carnal mind (Alma 30:53; 36:4). *See:* Carnally minded.

Carnal nature (Mosiah 16:5; 41:11; 42:10). *See:* Carnal, sensual, and devilish.

Carnal security (2 Nephi 28:21). False security that men of the world often get because of their position, wealth, or other prideful self-assurance. In truth there is no security in carnality. Only through God can we gain true security, which is spiritual security.

Carnal, sensual, and devilish (Alma 42:10). "The Book of Mormon . . . clearly teaches that all men, not just 'incorrigible sinners,' are by nature 'carnal, sensual, and devilish' (Alma 42:10), that through the fall of Adam there was brought upon all mankind a spiritual and temporal death by which men were cut off or separated from God (Alma 42:9). . . . No matter how basically good we may consider the spirits of men to have been in their pre-existent state, the fact is that the Nephite scripture makes clear that, except for the Atonement of Christ, the fall of Adam would have made our spirits, following our temporal death, like unto the devil, and we would have 'become devils, angels to a devil, to be shut out from the presence of our God' (2 Nephi 9:9). Such was the power of the fall. So while man may have been essentially good in his pre-existent state, the fact remains that his acquisition of a mortal body and the effect of Adam's fall upon it make for him a very serious problem. . . . When he [man] is born into this life, he is regarded as innocent, being neither good nor bad, morally speaking. Little children are innocent because they are not accountable nor capable of committing sin (Moroni 8:10). The penalty pronounced upon Adam and his posterity is held in abeyance, as far as little children are concerned, until they grow up and become accountable for their actions before God" (Sperry, *Answers*, 1–2). Mosiah 3:19 says, "For the natural man is an enemy to God, and has been from the fall of Adam, and will be, forever and ever, unless he yields to the enticings of the Holy Spirit, and putteth off the natural man and becometh a saint through the atonement of Christ the Lord." And in Mosiah 27:25–26, "And the Lord said unto me: Marvel not that all mankind, yea, men and women, all nations, kindreds, tongues and people, must be born again: yea, born of God, changed from their carnal and fallen state, to a state of righteousness, being redeemed of God, becoming his sons and daughters; and thus they become

new creatures; and unless they do this, they can in nowise inherit the kingdom of God." Simply put, the only way to overcome our fallen and carnal state is to have faith in Jesus Christ, repent, be baptized by immersion, receive the Holy Ghost, and endure to the end. *See also:* Carnal state; Moses 5:13; 6:49.

Carnal state (Mosiah 4:2; 16:5; 26:4; 27:25; Alma 22:13; 41:11). Being to some degree or other in an ungodly state. Having a nature contrary to the way of God. The carnal state is a fallen state, a sinful state, and an unrepentant and uncleansed state. *See also:* Carnal, sensual, and devilish.

Carnal wills and desires (Mosiah 16:12). *See:* Carnal, sensual, and devilish.

Carnally minded (2 Nephi 9:39). Romans 8:6–9 says, "For to be carnally minded is death; but to be spiritually minded is life and peace. Because the carnal mind is enmity [hostility] against God: for it is not subject to the law of God, neither indeed can be. So then they that are in the flesh cannot please God. But ye are not in the flesh, but in the Spirit, if so be that the Spirit of God dwell in you." *See also:* Carnal, sensual, and devilish.

Carried away captive (1 Nephi 1:13; 10:3; 2 Nephi 1:13; 3:4; 6:8; 25:10; Omni 1:15; Alma 16:4; Ether 7:17). The reference in 2 Nephi 1:13 refers to spiritual captivity by the devil; the other references have reference to physical captivity. Being captive and being freed from bondage are recurring themes in the Book of Mormon. *See also:* Deliver(-ed) out of bondage.

Carried away in God (Alma 19:6). A spiritual, trance-like experience that occurs on occasion to individuals who sincerely desire, have humbly repented, feel the light of Christ, and the love of God to a very high degree. *See also:* Fell to (unto) the earth (as if he were dead).

Carried away in the spirit (in a vision) (1 Nephi 1:8; 11:1, 19, 29; 14:30; 15:1; 2 Nephi 4:25; Alma 19:6; 29:16). Visions occur in different ways. Sometimes the spirit of the person is carried away in understanding and even in location when receiving the vision. Sometimes they are carried away to a very high mountain in spirit or in body. *See also:* Get thee into the mountain; Moses 1:1.

Carried in their arms and upon their shoulders (1 Nephi 21:22; 22:6, 8; 2 Nephi 6:6). Compare with Isaiah 49:22. Refers to the house of Israel—the Jews and descendants of Lehi (Native Americans)—who will be gathered, nourished, aided, and fostered in the last days by the Gentiles and more specifically by the United States of America. *See also:* Kings shall be thy nursing fathers and their queens thy nursing mothers; Nourished by the Gentiles.

Carried our sorrows (Mosiah 14:4). Same as Isaiah 53:4. Jesus, our Savior, not only suffered and paid for our sins, but He also suffered for our sorrows, pains, anguish, sadness, grief, and physical ills. This He did so that He could understand our mortal sorrows and so He could lift these sorrows from us. Thus it is fulfilled that "he descended below all things" (D&C 88:6; see D&C 122:8). *See also:* Healing in his wings; I shall (will) heal them; Alma 31:24.

Cast down (and grieved) because of the wickedness of the people (Alma 31:24; Helaman 10:3). *See:* Tribulation and anguish of soul; Weighed down with sorrow.

Cast in their voices (Mosiah 29:39; Alma 2:6). Meaning to cast their vote or ballot as in a popular election. *See also:* Become popular.

Cast into the fire (Jacob 5:7, 9, 26, 37, 42, 45–47, 49, 58, 66; 6:7; Alma 5:35, 52, 56; 14:18–19; Helaman 14:18; 3 Nephi 27:11, 17; Mormon 8:21). Referring to the wicked, represented symbolically by the tares and the unfruitful branches that are hewn and cut down and destroyed in the fire. *See also:* Burn as stubble; Consumed as stubble.

Cast lots (1 Nephi 3:11). To throw dice, draw straws, or some other method of choice by chance. To cast lots was customary in ancient times, and numerous references to it are also found in the Old Testament.

Cast off (forever/from the presence of the Lord) (1 Nephi 8:36–37; 10:21; 15:33; 17:47; 2 Nephi 7:1; 10:20; 30:2; Jacob 5:7, 9, 26, 73; Mosiah 27:16, 27; 28:4; Alma 22:6, 15; Helaman 12:25; 14:18). *See:* Cut off from the presence of the Lord.

Cast out [the prophets, believers and righteous] (1 Nephi 1:20; 7:14; 11:28; 2 Nephi 26:3; Jacob 7:26; Mosiah 17:3; Alma 8:13, 24; 10:23; 12:4; 14:7; 15:1; 17:20; 20:30; 23:2; 26:29; 32:24; 33:10; 35:6, 8–9; Helaman 13:2, 14, 24–26, 33; 14:10; 3 Nephi 7:14; 8:25; 9:10; 18:23; Ether 8:25; 9:29; 13:13, 15). Means to reject the prophets and their message. Often the wicked have driven the prophets and the righteous from their cities and stoned them, meaning killed them.

Cast out [the wicked] (1 Nephi 15:35; 2 Nephi 25:29; Jacob 5:66, 69, 74; 6:3; Mosiah 16:2; Alma 5:25; 11:2; 30:56; 32:28; 34:29; 40:13, 26; Helaman 12:25; 3 Nephi 12:13; 16:15). *See:* Cut off from the presence of the Lord.

Cast out [unclean spirits] (1 Nephi 11:31; Mosiah 3:6; 3 Nephi 7:19, 22; 14:22; Mormon 9:24). "And he [Jesus] ordained twelve, that they should be with him, and that he might send them forth to preach, and to have power to heal sicknesses, and to cast out devils" (Mark 3:14–15). "And these signs shall follow them that believe; In my name shall they cast out devils" (Mark 16:17). Thus the servants of God who have been given the power and the authority of the holy priesthood can, in the name of Jesus Christ, cast out unclean spirits that sometimes possess (take possession of) the bodies of people.

Cast [not] your pearls before swine (3 Nephi 14:6). Spiritual gifts and sacred events are reserved for the faithful. The wicked and rebellious regard not the light of truth, and trample under their feet like swine into the mire any pearls of great price placed before them. We should be very reserved about sharing personal spiritual experiences. They are in fact personal and specifically tailored by God for us individually. Such experiences should not be broadcast when tempted to do so. They are not for show or to build up one's pride. *Compare:* Matthew 7:6; D&C 41:6. *See also:* Moroni 7:37–38.

Catch (caught) in a snare (2 Nephi 27:32; Mosiah 23:9; Alma 12:6). The devil and his minions set traps and snares to entangle men in sin. Mortals who are not just and true also dig pits and try to cross others for gain and other wicked reasons. *See also:* Chains of hell; Cross his words; Cunning one; Devices of the devil; That they might cross him.

Caught away in the spirit (1 Nephi 11:1). *See:* Carried away in the spirit (in a vision); Acts 8:39; Moses 6:64.

Cause of Christians (Alma 46:15–16; 48:10). Christians are followers of Christ. The cause of Christians is the same as the cause of Jesus Christ. Thus true Christians emulate the life and teachings of Jesus, serve God and fellow beings, and do much good.

Cause of freedom (liberty) (Alma 46:16, 35; 50:39; 51:7, 17; 58:12; 60:16, 30; 61:14; 62:1, 11). Meaning to further freedom and liberty, stand up for freedom, declare liberty, fight for liberty, and even give one's life for liberty. The cause of moral agency (the right to choose) was the very basis for the war in heaven. God declares that if we are faithful and obedient, we will be free forever. *See also:* Defend themselves; Title of liberty; 2 Nephi 2:26.

Cause the lame to walk and the blind to receive their sight, and the deaf to hear (4 Nephi 1:5). The servants of God, through faith, by the power of the priesthood, and in the name of Jesus, can heal those that are not whole. The ministry of Jesus included many examples as recorded in the four gospels and 3 Nephi. *Compare:* D&C 35:9. *See also:* Work(-ing) mighty miracles.

Cease to be God (Alma 42:13, 22–23, 25; Mormon 9:15, 19). God will never cease to be God—this we can be assured of. Certain scriptures state that if God were to be unjust or do other ungodly things, He would cease to be God; but in the same breath these scriptures say He would not, worlds without end, do such things, because such actions are completely contrary to the nature of God and His ways. God's ways are one eternal round, and He does not vary to the left nor to the right.

Ceaseless praises (Mormon 7:7). *See:* Sing ceaseless praises with the choir above unto the Father and unto the Son; Sing praises unto the Lord.

Ceaseth not to be God (Alma 42:23; Mormon 9:19). *See:* Cease to be God.

Chaff before the wind (Alma 37:15; Mormon 5:16, 18). Chaff is the husk that grows about the grain of wheat. After the harvest, the wheat is thrown up into the air to winnow it. The wind blows away the chaff, which is not wanted, and the heavier grain falls in a pile on the floor. Mormon 5:18 says, "But now, behold, they are led about by Satan, even as chaff is driven before the wind, or as a vessel is tossed about upon the waves, without sail or anchor, or without anything wherewith to steer her; and even as she is, so are they."

Chaff that passeth away (2 Nephi 15:24; 26:18; Mosiah 7:30; Alma 37:15; Mormon 5:16, 18). For the most part the chaff is worthless, and it is discarded or destroyed. *See also:* Chaff before the wind.

Chain(-ed) down to an everlasting destruction (Alma 12:6, 17). *See:* Chains of hell; Everlasting destruction.

Chains by (with) which ye are bound (2 Nephi 1:13, 23). *See:* Chains of hell.

Chains of death (Alma 36:18). Both spiritual death and physical death are bondage. Only the Atonement of Jesus Christ can release us from these chains. *See also:* Chains of hell; Temporal death.

Chains of hell (Alma 5:7, 9–10; 12:11; 13:30; 26:14). Each time we follow the enticings of Satan to sin, Satan in effect places a flaxen cord around our necks. As these small threads multiply they become a great rope or an awful chain by which Satan will have made us captive. In 2 Nephi 28:21–22 we are told, "The devil cheateth their souls, and leadeth them away carefully down to hell. . . . Until he grasps them with his awful chains." To repent is to throw off the chains and come unto Christ. There is no other way of being set free from the chains of hell. *See also:* Bands of death; Chains of him that (which) would bind you fast; Moses 7:26.

Chains of him that (which) would bind you fast (2 Nephi 1:13; 9:45). "They chose evil works rather than good; therefore the spirit of the devil did enter into them, and take possession of their house" (Alma 40:13). *See also:* Chains of hell.

Change of heart (Mosiah 5:2, 7; Alma 5:7, 12–14, 26; Helaman 15:7). Meaning to be born again and become a new person no longer having a desire to do evil, but having a desire to do good continually. *See also:* No more desire (disposition) to do evil.

Changed from this mortal to an immortal state (Alma 11:45; 12:20; 41:4; 3 Nephi 28:8, 36). Meaning to be resurrected to an immortal body. *See also:* Immortal state; Resurrection of the body.

Changed in a twinkling of an eye (3 Nephi 28:8). Meaning changed from having a mortal body to an immortal body when resurrected in a moment instantly. *See also:* 1 Corinthians 15:52; D&C 43:32; 63:51; 101:31.

Changeth not (Mormon 9:19; Moroni 8:18). "For I am the Lord, I change not" (3 Nephi 24:6). Our God is an unchanging God, perfect, all-powerful, all-knowing, and that great being we can always count on, forever and forever. *See also:* Same yesterday, today and forever.

Charity never faileth (Moroni 7:46). Charity is the pure love of Christ, which is everlasting (never-failing) and is the same yesterday, today, and forever. *Compare:* 1 Corinthians 13:8.

Charity suffereth long (Moroni 7:45). Meaning charity is a love that endures through thick and thin.

Love that continues against great odds. Love that is faithful and true always. *See also:* Charity never faileth.

Chasten(-ed) him (his people/them) (1 Nephi 16:25, 39; Mosiah 23:21; Helaman 12:3; 15:3; Ether 2:14). Except the Lord chastens His people with all manner of afflictions they will not remember Him. And in Proverbs 3:12, "Whom the Lord loveth he correcteth."

Cheer up your hearts (2 Nephi 10:23). *See:* Be of good cheer (comfort); Lift up their hearts and rejoice.

Cherubim and a (the) flaming sword (Alma 12:21; 42:2–3). A guardian angel with a very frightful and effective weapon to block the way of Adam and Eve from partaking of the tree of life and thus living forever in their sin of partaking of the forbidden fruit. This would have frustrated God's plan, but God's plan will not be thwarted. God's plan requires a probationary time, earth life, "to see if they will do all things whatsoever the Lord their God shall command them" (Abraham 3:25).

Chief judge (Mosiah 29:42, 44; Alma 2:16; 4:17; 8:12; 14:4–5, 14, 23–24, 27; 27:20–21; 30:21, 29–30, 51, 57; 50:37, 39; 51:2, 4, 6, 12–13; 60:1; Helaman 1:5, 13, 21; 6:19; 9:2–4, 10, 12, 23, 41; 10:13; 3 Nephi 1:1; 3:19; 7:1). In Mosiah 29, when the sons of King Mosiah would not be king, Mosiah proposed a system of judges, appointed by the voice of the people. These judges ruled over the people and judged them according to the law. This "reign of the judges" included a chief judge, the idea being that the voice of the greater part of the people would choose just men as judges. "And if the time comes that the voice of the people doth choose iniquity [unjust judges], then is the time that the judgments of God will come upon you" (Mosiah 29:27). Alma the Younger was the first chief judge.

Child of Christ (Moroni 7:19). *See:* Children of Christ; Children of God; Sons (and daughters) of Christ (God).

Child of hell (the devil) (Alma 5:39, 41; 10:28; 11:23; 54:11). A follower of Satan and Satan's evil ways.

Children are alive in Christ (Moroni 8:12, 22). Meaning children under the age of eight (the age of accountability—D&C 68:25, 27) are spiritually alive and whole, and not subject to spiritual death because they are not yet accountable for sin, and because power is not given unto Satan to tempt little children.

Children of Christ (Mosiah 5:7; 7:19; 4 Nephi 1:17; Mormon 9:26). *See:* Sons (and daughters) of Christ (God).

Children of God (Mosiah 18:22; Alma 6:6; 30:42; 3 Nephi 12:9;

4 Nephi 1:39). Often in the Book of Mormon 'children of God' is a reference to the Saints who are members of the Lord's Church. In a larger sense, all mankind are truly the spirit children of God, their spirits being the literal offspring of God. Our desire should be to ascend to a higher level and become the "spiritually begotten" sons and daughters of God. *See also:* Children of Christ; Sons (and daughters) of Christ (God).

Children of Israel (1 Nephi 17:23, 25, 29; Jacob 1:7; Mosiah 7:19; 13:29; 3 Nephi 29:1–2). Meaning the descendants or house of Israel. These are the multitude of people brought out of the land of Egypt by the hand of the Lord and by the prophet Moses, including their descendants. They are a people of promise and a covenant people consisting of the twelve tribes and their posterity. *See also:* House of Israel; Twelve tribes of Israel.

Children of men (1 Nephi 10:17; 11:31; 12:17–18; 14:7; 15:4, 13; 22:2, 16, 22; 2 Nephi 2:9, 21; 9:9; 10:15, 17; 25:8, 17; 26:13–14, 33; 27:11, 13, 21–23; 28:2, 20, 30; 29:1, 7; 30:16, 18; Mosiah 3:5; 4:6; 7:27; Alma 5:50; 13:6; 26:16; Helaman 12:1, 4, 7; 3 Nephi 27:18; Ether 3:28; 12:12, 33; Moroni 7:4, 27, 31, 36–37). The people who live upon the earth. Generally referring to those who have not yet accepted the gospel and have not become the sons and daughters of God

(the saints of the Lamb). *Compare:* Children of God. *See also:* Sons (and daughters) of Christ (God).

Children of the covenant (3 Nephi 20:25–26; 21:11). "As people come to a knowledge of Jesus Christ, receiving the ordinances of salvation and keeping the associated covenants, they become 'the children of the covenant' (3 Nephi 20:26)" (*Gospel Principles*, 247). *See also:* Numbered among the (his) people of Christ (God/the church).

Children of the kingdom of the devil (1 Nephi 14:3; Alma 5:25). Those who have chosen sin and rebellion. Thus they have no place in the kingdom of heaven, but have accepted the devil as their master and home. *See also:* Child of hell (the devil).

Choice land (2 Nephi 10:19; Ether 2:12; 13:2). The Nephites and the Jaredites were promised that the American continent, to which they were brought by God, would be a blessed land above all lands on earth and free from bondage if the people but serve the God of the land. That promise continues in the latter days. *See also:* Land choice above all other lands.

Choirs above (Mosiah 2:28; Mormon 7:7). There exists in heaven great choirs who sing praises to God and His Son. Saints of God have a desire to sing praises to God and look forward to joining the choirs above. "And saw the holy angels, and them who are sanctified before his throne, worshiping [and praising] God, and the Lamb, who worship him forever and ever" (D&C 76:21).

Choose good (or evil) (2 Nephi 17:15; Alma 13:3; Helaman 5:2). The entirety of mortal life is a succession of choices to either choose good or choose evil. Our eternal destiny depends upon our choices. When we err, it is imperative that we repent swiftly and pursue again the straight and narrow way to God. *See also:* Choose life or death.

Choose liberty and eternal life (2 Nephi 2:27). *See:* Choose life or death.

Choose life or death (2 Nephi 2:27–29; 10:23; Helaman 14:31). We have been given the great gift of moral agency to choose. "And they are free to choose liberty and eternal life, through the great Mediator of all men, or to choose captivity and death, according to the captivity and power of the devil" (2 Nephi 2:27). *See also:* Know(-ing) good and (from) evil.

Choose (works of) darkness rather than light (2 Nephi 26:10; Helaman 13:29). Is to choose the ways of Satan, who is the prince of darkness, rather than to choose the light of Christ. *See also:* Children of the kingdom of the devil.

Chosen for the work (Alma 16:15). "We believe that a man must be called of God, by prophecy, and by the laying on of hands by those who are in authority, to preach the Gospel and administer in the ordinances thereof" (Articles of Faith 1:5). *Compare:* D&C 3:9, 10; 112:7. *See also:* Authority from (of) God; Called of God (the Holy Spirit).

Chosen land (Alma 46:17; Ether 13:2). *See:* Land choice above all other lands.

Chosen man of God (Mosiah 7:26; Alma 10:7; Helaman 9:16). Meaning a prophet of God, a servant of the Lord. *See also:* Chosen for the work.

Chosen people (Alma 31:28; Helaman 15:3). Meaning preferred, favored, and elect of God.

Chosen the good part (2 Nephi 2:30). Meaning having chosen good most of one's life and sought consistently to do good. *See also:* Do good; Luke 10:42.

Chosen vessel(-s) of the Lord (Alma 7:10; Moroni 7:31). *Vessel* means here a person, messenger, or representative. "A person into whom some quality (as grace) is infused" (*Merriam-Webster's Collegiate Dictionary*, s.v. "vessel"). *See also:* Chosen man of God.

Christ shall (should) come (2 Nephi 10:3; 11:6; Jacob 1:6; 7:3, 9, 14; Mosiah 3:13; 4:2–3; 7:26; Alma 5:27, 48; 6:8; 30:26, 39; 34:8; 39:15; 45:4; 46:15; Helaman 5:9; 8:22; 13:6; 16:4, 18; 3 Nephi 2:7;

11:10; Moroni 7:23). *See:* Coming of Christ.

Christ their Redeemer (Alma 37:9; 3 Nephi 5:26; 10:10). Jesus Christ is the Redeemer and Savior of mankind, for all those that accept Him and live His gospel. *See also:* Atonement of Christ (the Only Begotten Son); No other name given whereby salvation cometh.

Christ their shepherd (Alma 5:38; Mormon 5:17). Jesus is the Good Shepherd who cares for His flock and rescues the lost sheep. *See also:* Good Shepherd.

Christ's ascension into heaven (Mosiah 18:2; Alma 40:20; 3 Nephi 10:18; 11:12; Moroni 7:27). Throughout the ages the prophets have testified of the coming of Christ in the meridian of time—that He would live and minister among the Jews, that wicked men would crucify Him, and He would rise resurrected. It was also prophesied and came to pass that after He was resurrected He would ascend into heaven. This was particularly noteworthy to the Nephites, because it was also prophesied that after His ascension He would visit the Nephites on the American continent. *See also:* Other sheep.

Church began to be (was) broken up (3 Nephi 6:14). Because of wickedness and rebellion, the church does break up in that the spirit no longer dwells therein, the priesthood becomes ineffective in sinful men, and people begin to depart from the true faith and gospel of Jesus Christ. *See also:* Destroy the church.

Church established (Alma 5:2; 6:1, 8; 8:11; 16:21; 28:1; Helaman 6:3; 3 Nephi 5:12). *See:* Church of Christ; Establish church; D&C 84:2.

Church of Christ (Mosiah 18:17; 3 Nephi 26:21; 28:23; 4 Nephi 1:1, 26, 29; Moroni 6:4). Meaning the Church of Jesus Christ. For Jesus said, "And how be it my church save it be called in my name? For if a church be called in Moses' name then it be Moses' church; or if it be called in the name of a man then it be the church of a man; but if it be called in my name then it is my church, if it so be that they are built upon my gospel" (3 Nephi 27:8). In D&C 115:4, "For thus shall my church be called in the last days, even The Church of Jesus Christ of Latter-day Saints."

Church of God (Mosiah 18:17; 21:30; 25:18, 22–23; 26:38; 27:9, 10, 13; Alma 1:7, 19; 2:4; 4:4–5, 9; 5:3, 5; 8:23; 27:27; 36:6, 9, 11; 62:46; Helaman 3:33; 6:3; Mormon 8:38). *See:* Church of Christ.

Church of the devil (1 Nephi 14:10). "The church of the devil is the world; it is all the carnality and evil to which fallen man is heir; it is every unholy and wicked practice; it is every false religion, every supposed system of salvation which does not actually save and exalt man in the highest heaven of the celestial world. . . . It is 'secret combinations,' oath-bound societies, and the great world force of Godless communism" (McConkie, *Doctrinal New Testament Commentary*, 3:552). See also D&C 18:20 ("Contend against no church, save it be the church of the devil").

Church of the Lamb of God (1 Nephi 14:10, 12, 14). *See:* Church of Christ.

Clapped his hands upon them (Alma 31:36). Clapped his hands can be defined as applied, affixed, or clasped his hands on them. Also brought his hands together on them. *See also:* Laying on his hands.

Clasped in the arms of Jesus (Mormon 5:11). A holy embrace. Also being protected in the arms of Jesus. *See also:* Encircled about (eternally) in (the arms of) his love; Gathered you as a hen gathereth her chickens under her wings.

Clean hands (2 Nephi 25:16; Alma 5:19). Meaning clean from the sins of this world. "Who shall ascend into the hill of the Lord? or who shall stand in his holy place? He that hath clean hands, and a pure heart; who hath not lifted up his soul unto vanity, nor sworn deceitfully. He shall receive the blessing from the Lord" (Psalm 24:3–5).

Cleanse from all unrighteousness (Alma 7:14). Also in 1 John 1:9 and D&C 76:41. Meaning to purify us from sin. *See also:* Cleansed (and made white) by the blood of the Lamb (by the power of the Holy Ghost).

Cleansed (and made white) by the blood of the Lamb (by the power of the Holy Ghost) (Alma 5:21, 24, 27; 3 Nephi 8:1; Mormon 9:6; Moroni 6:4). *See:* Atoning blood of Jesus Christ; Garments cleansed through the blood of the Lamb (made white/washed); Moses 6:59; 7:48.

Clear conscience before God (Mosiah 2:15, 27). Meaning having no unrepented sins and thus able to stand with confidence in the presence of God. *See also:* Peace of conscience; Remorse of conscience.

Cleave unto charity (Moroni 7:46). Meaning to seek after and cling onto with all one's might to this attribute of Christlike love. For if we have not charity then we are nothing (see 1 Corinthians 13:1–2).

Cleave unto every good thing (Moroni 7:28). Meaning to cling, adhere, and attach oneself to all that is good and pure. The Thirteenth Article of Faith says in part, "If there is anything virtuous, lovely, or of good report or praiseworthy, we seek after these things." Also in D&C 98:11, "And I give unto you a commandment, that ye shall forsake all evil and cleave unto all good."

Cleave unto (the Lord their) God (Jacob 6:5; Helaman 4:25). Meaning to remain loyal to, to seek after, to abide with, and to depart not from. *See also:* Come unto Christ.

Clothe the naked (Jacob 2:19; Alma 35:9). It is our duty as Christians to feed the hungry and clothe the naked. King Benjamin taught that we are all beggars before God, and that person who does not assist the poor has "no interest in the kingdom of God." Additionally he taught that in order to retain a "remission of your sins from day to day" we must "impart of [our] substance to the poor." *See also:* Poor and needy; Mosiah 4:16–26.

Clothed with purity (2 Nephi 9:14). Meaning to surround one's self with and act in all purity, cleanliness, honesty, and virtue. *See also:* Robe of righteousness.

Cloud of darkness (Alma 19:6; Helaman 5:28–29, 31, 34, 36, 40–43). The cloud of darkness that settles over the sinner from which one is released to the light of God upon repentance and acceptance of the gospel of Jesus Christ. *See also:* Encircled about with everlasting darkness and destruction; Scales of darkness shall begin to fall from their eyes.

Combinations of Gadianton (the devil) (2 Nephi 26:22; Helaman 3:23; 4 Nephi 1:42). *See:* Gadianton robbers (and murderers); Secret combination(-s).

Combine against righteousness (the people of the Lord) (3 Nephi 6:28–29). "Therefore, fear not, little flock; do good; let earth and hell combine against you, for if ye are built upon my rock, they cannot prevail" (D&C 6:34).

Come forth both small and great (Mormon 9:13). The same terminology used in Revelation 20:12, meaning literally all (with no exceptions) will stand before God and be judged. *Compare:* D&C 128:6; 138:11, 35.

Come forth from the dead (Alma 40:4–5, 21). *See:* Resurrection of the dead.

Come forth out of obscurity (2 Nephi 1:23). *See:* Out of obscurity.

Come in unto the covenant (3 Nephi 21:22). To be converted and receive the covenant of baptism and the other ordinances of the gospel. In our day, the latter days, this is the "new covenant" or the "new and everlasting covenant," also "the new covenant, even the Book of Mormon and the former commandments which I have given" (D&C 84:57). The new covenant "made new by its renewal and confirmation in these latter-days, is our covenant relationship with Jesus Christ. It incorporates the fulness of the gospel (see D&C 66:2; 132:6), which President Joseph Fielding Smith described as 'the sum total of all gospel covenants and obligations.'" (*Doctrines of Salvation*, 1:156). From the foregoing it is evident that the 'new covenant' contained in the Book of Mormon and the former commandments is that central promise of the gospel, rooted in the atonement and resurrection of Jesus Christ, which gives us the assurance of immortality and the opportunity for eternal life if we will repent of our sins and make and keep the gospel covenant with our Savior. By this means, and through his grace, we can realize the fulfillment of the great promise 'that through the Atonement of Christ, all mankind may be saved, by obedience to the laws and ordinances of the Gospel' (Articles of Faith 1:3)" (Oaks, "'Another Testament of Jesus Christ'"). *See also:* Covenant(-ing) with God (him).

Come to the knowledge (1 Nephi 10:14; 15:14; 2 Nephi 6:11; 10:2; Words of Mormon 1:8; Mosiah 4:6, 11; 27:14; Alma 23:15; Mormon 7:5). Meaning coming to a knowledge of their Redeemer and salvation by Him. *See also:* Bring them to a (the) knowledge; Brought to the knowledge.

Come under condemnation (Helaman 14:19; 3 Nephi 18:33). *See:* Under condemnation.

Come unto Christ (Jacob 1:7; Omni 1:26; Moroni 10:30, 32).

This is the very command of God (3 Nephi 27:20), which is to have faith in Christ, repent of all sins, be baptized, keep the commandments of God, serve one another, receive all the ordinances of the gospel, and endure to the end. Thus to come unto Christ is not just conversion to the gospel and baptism, but is a lifetime of living the gospel. "As we commit ourselves to Him [Jesus Christ]—spiritually, physically, and emotionally—He blesses our lives with loving direction. Every decision we make from that time on is affected, because there are certain things a man or woman of Christ simply will not do. Our actions become more disciplined, our relationships become more righteous; even our language becomes more pure as we live a life that is centered on Jesus Christ and His teachings. Simply put, after the spirit of Christ enters our hearts and our souls, we can never be the same again. That doesn't mean we suddenly become perfect. We all fall short of that mark, which is why we're so thankful for the gift of repentance through our faith in Christ. It just means that we're always trying to live up to the responsibility of being a true follower of Christ, not because we fear Him or Heavenly Father but because we love them and want to serve them" (Ballard, *Our Search for Happiness*, 14–15). *See also:* Repent and come unto God (him/me/my Beloved Son); D&C 20:59.

Come unto God (2 Nephi 2:10; 9:45; Omni 1:25; Alma 29:2). *See:* Come unto Christ.

Come unto him (me/thee) (1 Nephi 1:14; 10:18; 13:40; 15:14; 2 Nephi 8:19; 26:25, 33; 28:32; Omni 1:26; Alma 5:34–35; 15:4; 3 Nephi 9:14, 22; 12:3, 19–20, 23–24; 18:25, 32; 21:6, 27; 27:20; 30:2; Mormon 3:2; Ether 4:13–14, 18; 12:27; Moroni 7:34). *See:* Come unto Christ.

Come unto Jesus (Mormon 2:14). *See:* Come unto Christ.

Come unto me ye blessed (Enos 1:27; Alma 5:16). Referring to when the righteous stand before the Lord to be judged and He welcomes them home for their faithfulness. *See also:* Matthew 25:34.

Come unto my Beloved Son (3 Nephi 21:20). *See:* Come unto Christ.

Come unto the Father (Ether 5:5). "Jesus saith unto him, I am the way, the truth, and the life: no man cometh unto the Father, but by me" (John 14:6). *See also:* None other name.

Come unto the fountain of all righteousness (Ether 8:26). Jesus Christ is the fountain of all righteousness. *See also:* Come unto Christ.

Come unto the Gentiles (1 Nephi 15:13; 3 Nephi 16:7; 29:1; Mormon 7:8). It is prophesied in the Book of Mormon that in the latter days the gospel of Jesus Christ, the truth, and the Book of Mormon would come forth among the Gentiles. This prophecy was fulfilled with the restoration of the gospel through Joseph Smith and continues to be fulfilled as the gospel is preached throughout the world. From this preaching many Gentiles and many of the scattered house of Israel shall accept. These include the descendants of Lehi and the scattered Jews. This great preaching will be a fulfillment of the covenant with Abraham and his seed that the blessings of the gospel will come to the world through them. But then the more part of the Gentiles will grow more wicked and reject the gospel, so the gospel will be taken from them. And then the covenant the Lord made with Israel will be fulfilled wherein the Lord will bring the gospel to them. Thus the last shall be the first (the Gentiles in the latter days will hear the gospel first, but they were last at the meridian of time when Jesus and His Apostles first went to the Jews and then to the Gentiles), and thus again the first shall be last (the Jews who were first at the meridian of time will now hear the gospel last in the latter days after it has been preached to the Gentiles and then rejected by the Gentiles).

Come unto the God of Isaac and the God of Jacob (1 Nephi 6:4). We must come unto Jesus, who is Jehovah, the God of Isaac and the

God of Jacob. *See also:* Come unto Christ.

Come unto the Holy One of Israel (2 Nephi 9:51). Jesus Christ is the Holy One of Israel. *See also:* Come unto Christ.

Come unto the Lord (2 Nephi 9:41; Alma 29:10; Mormon 9:27). *See:* Come unto Christ.

Come unto the true fold of God (1 Nephi 15:15; Mosiah 18:8). The true fold of God is the Church of Jesus Christ. *See also:* Come unto Christ.

Come unto thee (1 Nephi 1:14; 3 Nephi 28:2). *See:* Come unto Christ.

Come(-th/coming) in his glory (Jacob 4:4; Alma 5:50; 9:26; 13:24; 3 Nephi 26:3; 28:7). Refers to Christ's Second Coming. At the meridian of time Jesus Christ was born in a humble stable, but at His Second Coming He will come in great glory for all to see. *See also:* Coming of Christ; In power and great glory.

Cometh the baptism of fire (2 Nephi 31:13, 17). *See:* Baptism of fire and of the Holy Ghost; D&C 33:11; 39:6.

Cometh the Son of God (2 Nephi 25:19; Alma 5:48, 50; 7:9; 39:15; Helaman 14:2). *See:* Coming of Christ.

Come(-th) unto repentance (Mormon 7:3). All men and women

must repent. Repentance is a necessary step to salvation. Without sincere repentance no one can hope to dwell again with God. *See also:* Baptize(-d) unto repentance; Bringeth unto repentance; Conditions of repentance; Faith unto repentance; Fruit meet for repentance; Fruit unto repentance; Meet for repentance; Procrastinate not the day of your repentance; Sincere repentance; Truly penitent.

Comfort my (their) soul in Christ (Alma 31:31–32). A valid prayer for the faithful is for peace and comfort. Our Savior promised, "I will not leave you comfortless" (John 14:18). To accept the gospel of Jesus Christ and be a true follower of Him brings peace and comfort to the soul. To know that you are truly living faithfully brings peace, in that no matter the turmoil in the mortal world around us, our souls are saved in the kingdom of God. "Peace I leave with you, my peace I give unto you: not as the world giveth, give I unto you. Let not your heart be troubled, neither let it be afraid" (John 14:27). Additionally, confirmed members of the Church have the constant companionship of the Holy Ghost to comfort them.

Comforted his people (1 Nephi 21:13; Mosiah 7:18; 12:23; 15:30; Alma 17:10; 3 Nephi 16:19; 20:34). The Lord is mighty to save and to comfort. Throughout the ages in times of hardship and grief the Lord has comforted His people if they have humbled themselves before Him. As the future events of this earth unfold the Lord has promised He will comfort His people. And in the end, the Saints of God will be comforted from all their earthly experiences and receive mansions in heaven. *Compare:* Isaiah 49:13; 52:9.

Coming of Christ (2 Nephi 11:4; Words of Mormon 1:2, 4; Mosiah 7:26; 26:2; Alma 18:39; 21:9; 25:15; 30:6; 34:2, 37; 36:17; 39:15; 40:2; 45:4; Helaman 8:22; 14:12; 3 Nephi 2:8; 3:1; 10:15; 4 Nephi 1:21, 48; Mormon 3:4; Moroni 7:22, 25; 10:1). Depending on the context and time this phrase refers to the coming of Christ at the meridian of time or to the Second Coming of Christ at the last day. All must have faith and believe in the coming of Christ, that He came and that He will come again a second time. *See also:* Christ shall (should) come; Come(-th/coming) in his glory; Cometh the Son of God; Coming of our (the) Lord (Messiah/Son of God); Day of his coming; Day of the Lord; Great and dreadful day of the Lord; Jesus Christ shall (should) come; Power and great glory; Prepare the way of the Lord; Son of God (shall) come(-th); That great day; Time of his coming; Who should come.

Coming of our (the) Lord (Messiah/Son of God) (1 Nephi 1:19; 2 Nephi 6:13; Mosiah 4:30; 13:33; 15:11; Alma 16:19; 34:2; 36:17; Helaman 8:13; 14:12;

3 Nephi 25:5; 29:2; Mormon 8:6). *See:* Coming of Christ.

Command in the name of Jesus (1 Nephi 17:48; Jacob 4:6; Alma 44:5). To command in the name of Jesus Christ, our master, employs great power. It is in this manner that devils are cast out, the sick and the lame are healed, and many other great miracles are wrought. However, it must be done by the priesthood of God, by faithful and true servants of God, and according to the will of God.

Commanded of the Lord (1 Nephi 2:3; 4:34; 5:21; 16:9; 17:26; 19:2; Omni 1:13; Mosiah 2:35; 6:6; Helaman 14:9; 3 Nephi 26:12; Mormon 6:6; Ether 4:1, 5). Those commanded of the Lord must carry out those commands at the peril of their salvation. It is a sacred duty to carry out the commands of the Lord. The commands of the Lord must come before all other priorities. We each must be like Nephi in his closing words in 2 Nephi 33:15, "For thus hath the Lord commanded me, and I must obey."

Commanded to write (2 Nephi 33:11; Omni 1:1; 3 Nephi 24:1; 26:12; 30:1; Mormon 8:1; Ether 4:1, 5; 8:26). The Lord in His great wisdom has commanded His revealed word to be recorded as scripture and sacred histories to be kept, for out of the books and what has been written shall men be judged at the last day. "For I command all men

. . . that they shall write the words which I speak unto them; for out of the books which shall be written I will judge the world . . . according to that which is written" (2 Nephi 29:11). *See also:* Write the (these) things (words).

Commandments and his statutes and his judgments (1 Nephi 17:22; 2 Nephi 5:10; Mosiah 6:6; Alma 8:17; 58:40; Helaman 3:20; 15:5). Meaning the laws, decrees, and edicts of God. In Exodus 21:1*a*, judgments are identified as "ordinances." Leviticus 18:4–5 states, "Ye shall do my judgments, and keep mine ordinances, to walk therein: I am the Lord your God. Ye shall therefore keep my statutes, and my judgments." *See also:* Commandments of God (the Father/the Lord).

Commandments of God (the Father/the Lord) (1 Nephi 2:10; 3:5, 16, 21; 4:1, 11, 15, 34; 5:21; 8:38; 15:10; 16:4, 8; 17:3, 15; 19:4; 22:30; 2 Nephi 1:32; 5:10, 19, 31; 9:27; 30:1; 31:7, 10; Jacob 5:72, 74; Omni 1:2; Mosiah 1:4, 7, 11; 2:4, 13, 31, 41; 4:30; 6:3; 10:13; 11:2; 12:33; 13:11; 15:22, 26; 17:20; 26:33; 27:10, 33; 28:11; 29:11, 14, 22, 36, 45; Alma 1:25; 3:11; 5:18, 43; 7:16, 23; 8:15; 9:8, 14; 21:23; 30:3; 31:9; 36:1, 30; 37:13, 15–16, 20, 35; 38:1; 39:1; 46:21, 23; 48:15–16, 25; 49:27; 50:22; 53:21; 60:20, 34; 63:2; Helaman 3:20, 37; 4:21; 5:6, 14; 6:31; 7:4, 7; 8:3; 13:1; 16:12; 3 Nephi 6:14; 12:19; 18:14, 27).

God has given us commandments or laws to protect us and to bless us. We are promised if we live the commandments, then through the grace of God we can gain salvation in the presence of God. *The commandments* is a term that encompasses the Ten Commandments and the other edicts of God. God has said, "For you shall live by every word that proceedeth forth from the mouth of God" (D&C 84:44). The commandments are a strict guide in mortal life that begin to teach us how to live a godly life. *See also:* Commandments and his statutes and his judgments; Judgments and statutes; Obedient to the commandments (of God); Obedient unto the word of the Lord; Observe his judgments and his statutes; Observe to do; Statutes and judgments.

Commit(-ting) whoredoms (2 Nephi 9:36; 26:32; 28:14–15; Jacob 2:23, 33; 3:5; Mosiah 11:2, 6, 20; 12:29; 29:36; Alma 1:32; 30:18; 50:21; Helaman 3:14; 6:23; 3 Nephi 5:3; 16:10; 21:19; 30:2; Mormon 8:31; Ether 8:16; 10:7, 11). Whoredoms are unlawful or sinful sexual practices including fornication, adultery, lasciviousness; they are lewd, base, corrupt, and unworthy pursuits.

Common among them (3 Nephi 26:19; 4 Nephi 1:3, 25). *See:* All things common.

Communion with the Holy Spirit (Jarom 1:4). *Communion* means association, communication, and close relation with. The constant companionship of the Holy Ghost is communion with the Holy Ghost. In the terminology of D&C 45:57, it is to "have taken the Holy Spirit for their guide."

Compound in one (2 Nephi 2:11). *Compound* is defined as composed of or combined together. Thus Lehi says that without opposition in all things, then all would be composed of or made up of only "one." Rather than two or many choices, there would only be one choice. To better understand, try to imagine an existence without choices, without opposites or opposition. Such an existence is impossible, unfeasible, unworkable, and is without life. In the verses that follow, Lehi says such an existence is a "thing of naught" where there would be no creation, no man, and no God. In other words, without opposites and choices there would be left only one thing, and that would be eternal death and nonexistence. If all things were a compound in one, then life would be without choices, which is no life, meaning no existence, and all would be null and void. To have life we must have choices; to always choose the right is to have a God-like life. *See also:* All things must be a compound in one.

Conceived by the power of God (Mosiah 15:3; Alma 7:10). Jesus Christ was conceived by (born of) His father, God the Father, and of His mortal mother, Mary. Mary was a virgin and a "chosen vessel who shall be overshadowed and conceive by the power of the Holy Ghost" (Alma 7:10). *See also:* Matthew 1:20.

Concerning these things (1 Nephi 15:19; 22:29; 2 Nephi 10:20; Jacob 7:5; Mosiah 1:5; 2:34; 13:33; Alma 10:6; 18:20–21; 54:11; 3 Nephi 10:16; 28:24; Ether 12:6, 39). An interesting phrase used in the Book of Mormon and Doctrine and Covenants, but not in the Bible. It refers to greater knowledge, things of God and heaven, the commandments and order of the Church, and special things revealed and yet to be revealed.

Condescension of God (1 Nephi 11:16, 26; 2 Nephi 4:26; 9:53; Jacob 4:7). The willingness of God to leave the glories on high and stoop to man's level for the purpose of providing salvation to men and women. "The condescension of God is the ultimate manifestation of God's love. . . . The word 'condescension' implies 'voluntary descent,' 'submission,' and 'performing acts which strict justice does not require'" (*Encyclopedia of Mormonism,* 1:305; paragraphing altered).

Conditions of repentance (Alma 17:15; 42:13; Helaman 5:11; 14:11). Forgiveness of sins and salvation are only obtained on conditions of repentance, meaning only if one properly and actually repents will our Savior's suffering for our sins take effect. The requirements or steps of repentance include recognition of sin, sorrow for sin, confession of sin, praying for forgiveness of sin, restitution for sin, and forsaking of sin.

Confess(-ed/-ing) his (their) sins (faults) (Mosiah 26:29, 35–36; 27:35; Alma 17:4; 39:13; Helaman 5:17; 16:1, 5; 3 Nephi 1:25). A necessary step of repentance to acknowledge one's sins before God and man. *See also:* Conditions of repentance.

Confessed (confesses) the Christ (Jacob 7:17; Moroni 7:44). Meaning to have stated and expressed belief in Christ.

Confound him (the wise/them/ in all their words) (1 Nephi 2:14; Jacob 7:8; Mosiah 12:19; Alma 32:23; 37:6–7; Helaman 5:17; 9:18). By the power of the Holy Ghost the true and faithful are able to withstand, thwart, leave speechless, and cause to quake those that attempt to fight against God. This is accomplished through humble prayer and by the will of God.

Confounded and could not contend against me (1 Nephi 17:52; 22:22; 2 Nephi 4:22; 7:7). *See:* Confound him (the wise/them/in all their words).

Confounded the language (of the people) (Omni 1:22; Mosiah 28:17; Ether 1:33, 35–36; 3:24). Meaning to mix up and multiply the languages so that instead of just one

language there became many languages. Thus the people attempting to build a tower to heaven could no longer understand one another and began to be divided and scattered into groups, tribes, and nations. Thus their unrighteous tower project was frustrated and blocked.

Consciousness of (his/your) guilt (filthiness) (Alma 12:1; 14:6; Mormon 9:3–4). *See:* Bright recollection of all our guilt.

Consecrate my prayers (2 Nephi 33:4). Meaning to acknowledge, respond, and dedicate his prayers for the benefit of the people.

Consecrate thine afflictions for thy gain (2 Nephi 2:2). The Lord allows trials and afflictions in our lives so that we may gain experience and wisdom. *See also:* Bear afflictions (with patience); D&C 98:3.

Consecrate thy performance unto thee (2 Nephi 32:9). Continuing the verse, "That thy performance may be for the welfare of thy soul." This verse stresses that if we perform anything for or in the name of the Lord we should first pray for guidance, then God will bless us and our efforts.

Consecrate unto thee this land (2 Nephi 3:2). *See:* Consecrated this land.

Consecrated as (the) high priest over the church of God (Alma 4:4; 5:3). Here Alma appears to be anointed and set apart as the highest authority of the Church, analogous to being president of the latter-day Church. *See also:* Authority from (of) God; Consecrated priests; Laying on his hands.

Consecrate(-d) priests (and teachers/and elders) (2 Nephi 5:26; Jacob 1:18; Mosiah 23:17; Alma 4:7; 15:13; 23:4). To *consecrate* means to call, ordain, and set apart. *See also:* Authority from (of) God; Laying on his hands.

Consecrated this land (2 Nephi 1:32; 3:2; 10:19). Meaning to set apart and bless the land for a righteous people to inhabit. *See also:* Land choice above all other lands.

Consequences of sin (2 Nephi 9:48; Jacob 3:12). Every act we commit has a consequence, result, or outcome being either good or bad. Sin brings the consequence of punishment. "I, the Lord, have suffered the affliction to come upon them, wherewith they have been afflicted, in consequence of their transgressions" (D&C 101:2).

Console you in your afflictions (Jacob 3:1; Mosiah 27:33; Helaman 3:35). We must pray that God will support and comfort us in our adversity. *See also:* Bear afflictions (with patience); Visit my people in their afflictions.

Constrained by the Spirit (Holy Ghost) (1 Nephi 4:10; 2 Nephi 28:1; Jacob 2:9; Alma 60:34; Helaman 8:11; 4 Nephi 1:48).

Constrained means to be impelled, thus being obliged and required by the Spirit to act. *See also:* Led by the (Holy) Spirit.

Consult one with another (with the people) (1 Nephi 3:10; Mosiah 22:1). It is wisdom to counsel together, for the knowledge and experience of two or more is greater than that of just one. As the old adage says, "Two heads are better than one."

Consume it on your lusts (Mormon 9:28). Meaning one should not consume, use up, exhaust, and spend one's days, energy, and money on earthly lusts, worldly passions, and physical urges and cravings. One of the tests of life is to learn to control one's physical body, maintain our actions within proper bounds, and shun excessiveness. *See also:* Lusts of the flesh.

Consumed as stubble (1 Nephi 22:15, 23; 2 Nephi 15:24; 26:4, 6; 3 Nephi 25:1). *Stubble* is the stem part of grain plants that remain attached to the ground after the harvest of the grain. In other words, it is the stubble stalk or the stubble straw. Though not agriculturally or ecologically recommended by many today, in prior times the burning of fields of stubble cleared the fields so they could be replanted in the next growing season. Such stubble-clearing fires tended to be large, intense, fierce, and all-consuming. Thus "consumed as stubble" became a very descriptive metaphor for the burning of the wicked at Christ's Second Coming. In D&C 29:9, "For the hour is nigh and the day soon at hand when the earth is ripe; and all the proud and they that do wickedly shall be as stubble; and I will burn them up, saith the Lord of Hosts, that wickedness shall not be upon the earth." *See also:* Be (as) stubble; Burn as stubble; Shall be (as) stubble.

Consuming of my flesh (1 Nephi 17:48; 2 Nephi 4:21). Both the influence of the Spirit and the love of God can be poured out on an individual in such abundance and profusion that one has the experience of being filled to capacity; surrounded and almost consumed by fire; and completely swallowed up in omnipotence and love. Such an experience often leaves one physically weakened for a time thereafter. *Compare:* Joseph Smith–History 1:20; Moses 1:9. *See also:* Encircled about with fire; Filled as if with fire; Well nigh consumeth me.

Contend against the word of the Lord (1 Nephi 17:35; 2 Nephi 29:14; Mosiah 11:29; Alma 1:7; 9:1, 30; 12:13; 21:5; Helaman 10:15; 16:17; Ether 4:8; Moroni 9:4). Many refuse to accept the word of God but instead reject it, fight against it, and harden their hearts towards it. They argue against the word of God and rationalize it away. Such people are in danger of hellfire and damnation.

Contend no more against the Holy Ghost (Alma 34:38; 39:6). Meaning to be unresponsive to and not follow the promptings of the Holy Ghost. As an individual sins and ignores the promptings of the Holy Ghost, those promptings become less and less frequent until one is left alone without heavenly direction. In a more serious sense it means to reject and deny the witness of the Holy Ghost. *See also:* Better for you that ye had not known me; Deny the Holy Ghost; Unpardonable sin.

Contend one with another (1 Nephi 12:19; 2 Nephi 26:32; 28:4; Mosiah 9:13; Alma 1:22; Helaman 1:3–4; 4:11). To *contend* is to clash, fight, argue, dispute, and battle. "Cease to contend one with another; cease to speak evil one of another" (D&C 136:23). *See also:* Spirit of contention.

Contend with him (them) that contendeth with thee (1 Nephi 21:25; 2 Nephi 6:17). These scriptures affirm that God will fight for us and curse those that do evil towards the faithful. *Compare:* Isaiah 49:25.

Contention(-s) among them (the people) (Omni 1:10, 28; Words of Mormon 1:16; Mosiah 1:1; 6:7; 18:21; 19:3; 23:15; 29:21; Alma 2:1; 19:28, 31; 22:22; 25:8; 50:25–26; 51:2, 7; Helaman 1:2, 18; 2:1; 3:1–3, 19; 4:1; 3 Nephi 7:7; 11:29;

4 Nephi 1:13, 15, 18). *See:* Contend one with another.

Contrary to God (Mosiah 27:10; Alma 1:15; 30:7; 41:11; Helaman 6:23; 8:3; 16:12). Means to be against or opposite to the laws, commandments, words, and even the very nature, character, and attributes of God. Contrary to God is rebellion against God. *See also:* Rebel(-led/-ling/-lion) against God.

Contrary to the commandments (Mosiah 27:10; Alma 8:17; Helaman 8:3; 16:12). To think, speak, or act contrary to or counter to the commandments is to be against God and in rebellion against God. *See also:* Contrary to God.

Contrite spirit (2 Nephi 2:7; 4:32; Helaman 8:15; 3 Nephi 9:20; 12:19; Mormon 2:14; Ether 4:15; Moroni 6:2). *Contrite* means repentant, humble, self-effacing, and without pride. *See also:* Broken heart(-s) and (a) contrite spirit(-s).

Conversed with angels (Alma 9:21; 19:34). To speak with angels. *See also:* Angels minister(-ed/appeared/declared/descending) unto him (them).

Converted to (unto) the Lord (Alma 19:16–17, 31; 22:23; 23:3, 6, 8, 13; 24:6; 25:6; 30:58; 53:10; 3 Nephi 1:22; 2:12; 7:21; 28:23; 4 Nephi 1:2). Means to come unto Christ, acknowledge Him as the Savior of mankind, and follow after His ways and commands. *See also:* Baptize(-d) unto the Lord (their God); Come unto Christ.

Converted unto the true faith (3 Nephi 6:14). The true faith is the pure doctrine of Christ as found in the scriptures, and as taught by the authorized servants of the Lord. *See also:* Doctrine of Christ.

Convincing of the Jews that Jesus is the very Christ (1 Nephi 13:39; 2 Nephi 25:18; 26:12). The Jews rejected Jesus Christ as the Savior. The wicked Jews crucified Him because they expected a worldly king that would free them from the bondage of the Romans. It is prophesied that in the latter days the Jews will begin in a small way to recognize and accept Jesus Christ as their true Savior and King. Then at the Second Coming of Christ, when He appears on the Mount of Olives and saves the Jews and Jerusalem from defeat and destruction, the Jews will then recognize the wounds in His hands and feet and will know that Jesus is the Lord their Savior (see Zechariah 13:6; D&C 45:51–52).

Corrupted the (hearts of all the) people (Helaman 4:22; 5:2; Ether 9:6). Meaning to pervert, debase, and deprave the laws, practices, beliefs, and morals of a person, a community, a nation, or a society.

Corruption put on (raised in) incorruption (2 Nephi 2:11; 9:7; Mosiah 16:10; Alma 5:15; 40:2; 41:4). *Corruption* means the mortal body, and *incorruption* means immortality, thus the Resurrection will bring about this change. In other words, the mortal body will put on immortality. *See also:* Immortal body; Put on incorruption; Resurrection of the dead.

Costly apparel (Jacob 2:13; Alma 1:6, 27, 32; 4:6; 5:53; 31:28; Helaman 13:28). Analogous in our present day to costly houses and costly automobiles, also costly jewelry and costly purses. When our desire for these things becomes paramount in our lives, then these things have become our God. Rather, we should seek first the kingdom of God (Jacob 2:18; 3 Nephi 13:33). Often the rich who wear costly apparel look down on and persecute the poor for the "coarseness of their apparel" (Alma 32:2). *See also:* Treasure is their God.

Could not be kept from within the veil (Ether 3:6, 19–20; 12:19–21). The brother of Jared, whose name, revealed to Joseph Smith, was Mahonri Moriancumer (see McConkie, *Mormon Doctrine*, 463–65) had faith so great that the veil that separates this mortal world from the presence of God was taken from off his eyes and he beheld Christ and the many things Christ revealed unto him. "And there were many [others] whose faith was so exceedingly strong, even before Christ came, who could not be kept from within the veil, but truly saw with their eyes the things which they

had beheld with an eye of faith, and they were glad" (Ether 12:19). *See also:* Beheld (behold) his glory.

Could not be restrained because of the Spirit of the Lord which was in him (1 Nephi 17:48, 52–53; 2 Nephi 1:26; Mosiah 13:2–6; Helaman 16:2, 6; Ether 12:2). At times the Spirit is so strong and powerful when a person is preaching the word of God that those listening cannot counter his words, cannot detain or jail him, cannot harm him, and cannot keep him from preaching. *See also:* Could not hit him with their stones.

Could not bear that any human soul should perish (Mosiah 28:3; Alma 48:25). President Howard W. Hunter said, "Any time we experience the blessings of the Atonement in our lives, we cannot help but have concern for the welfare of others. . . . A great indicator of one's personal conversion is the desire to share the gospel with others" (in *Preach My Gospel*, 13). *See also:* Anxiety for you.

Could not find utterance (Mosiah 4:20; Helaman 5:33; 3 Nephi 19:34; 28:14). Some great and wonderful things that are revealed are so marvelous and wonderful that they are beyond what mortal words can describe, or are forbidden by God to be recorded or related until some future time. *See also:* Forbidden that I (they) should write (utter/preach).

Could not hit him with their stones (Mosiah 13:7; Alma 8:31; 17:36; 19:23–24; Helaman 5:26; 10:16; 16:2–3, 6; 3 Nephi 28:19; Mormon 8:24). According to His will, God can protect His servants from harm. *See also:* Could not be restrained because of the Spirit of the Lord which was in him.

Counsel in wisdom (Jacob 4:10; Alma 37:12). The Lord God doth counsel His children in great wisdom because He possesses all wisdom. *See also:* Wisdom in (of) God (the Lord/the Father).

Counsel not the Lord (Jacob 4:10; 5:22). It is vanity and foolishness to think that any man can counsel the Lord; for man is finite and unknowing, whereas God has all power, knowledge, and wisdom.

Counsel with the Lord (2 Nephi 28:30; Alma 29:8; 37:37; Helaman 12:5). Meaning seek the counsel, advice, and wisdom of the Lord. It is not wise to seek counsel and then not follow it.

Counseleth in wisdom and justice (Jacob 4:10). God's wisdom and justice are perfect, absolute, and supreme. Thus it behooves us to counsel with Him because He only gives good counsel. *See also:* Wisdom in (of) God (the Lord/the Father).

Counsels of God (2 Nephi 9:28–29). *See:* Counsel with the Lord.

Countenance did shine upon them (3 Nephi 19:25). Meaning the brilliant, brighter-than-the-light-of-the-sun countenance of God shines throughout the universe and is reflected in the countenance of the righteous. When the countenance of God shines down, it fills that person with warmth, comfort, and love. *See also:* Face shone with exceeding luster; Image of God engraven upon your countenances.

Countenance doth witness against them (2 Nephi 13:9; 3 Nephi 13:16). People have a countenance or appearance about them that often belies or reveals the state of their soul. The Saints of God often have a bright, happy, and shiny countenance. Many have what appears to be a rather neutral countenance, but God knows their real countenance. Those that have chosen darkness and sin often have a sullen, sad, and dark countenance.

Course is one eternal round (1 Nephi 10:19; Alma 7:20; 37:12). One eternal round is the "eternal way of life" (McConkie, *Mortal Messiah*, 1:28). God does not "vary from that which he hath said, therefore his paths are straight, and his course is one eternal round" (D&C 3:2). His "course is one eternal round, the same today as yesterday, and forever" (D&C 35:1). Our Heavenly Father's plan for His children was around for those who went before us, it has come around for us now, and the same plan and same God will be around for the generations and worlds to come.

"From one preexistence to the next he does not vary, his course is one eternal round. . . . *All eternity* being one which would be redundant were it not for the scriptural use of the word *eternity* as applying to the successive and recurring expanses of creative periods" (McConkie, *Promised Messiah*, 166). The same plan, the same truths, and same commandments and ordinances will be available throughout eternity to God's endless children forever and ever. One eternal sequence of creations, one eternal progression for each of God's children, one consistent eternal and true path the same for all. Never stagnant or boringly repetitive because God loves His children perfectly; and thus He makes it His work and His glory. So that we might begin to understand eternity, it could be compared to a grandparent seeing, assisting, and finding great satisfaction in the wonder and joy of new and more grandchildren learning, growing, and excelling, only on a much grander and more perfect scale.

Covenant of my peace (3 Nephi 22:10). Though the earth shall pass away, the kindness and promised peace of the Lord shall never be removed from the people of the Lord. Compare Isaiah 54:10*b*, referencing Malachi 2:5, which says, "My covenant was with him [and each of us] of life and peace." Every promise of the Lord has the weight of a covenant, for they are all predicated upon our faithfulness. "Peace I leave with you, my peace I give unto you" (John 14:27). *See also:* Comfort my (their) soul in Christ; Peace be unto you; They shall have peace with him.

Covenant of peace (Alma 44:14–15, 20; 46:31; 3 Nephi 6:3). Meaning a treaty to not make war. *See also:* Made an oath unto us.

Covenant of the Father (3 Nephi 21:4; Moroni 10:33). *See:* Covenants of the Father.

Covenant people (of the Lord) (1 Nephi 14:14; 15:14; 2 Nephi 6:13, 17; 29:4–5; 30:2; Mormon 3:21; 8:15, 21). The children of Israel, or in other words, the posterity of Abraham, Isaac, and Jacob, are the covenant people of the Lord. This includes all who are adopted into the twelve tribes by conversion and by living the commandments. Additionally, we each should become individuals that personally covenant with God, for this is how we progress in the gospel.

Covenant the Lord made to our father Abraham (1 Nephi 15:18). *See:* Covenant which he made with Abraham.

Covenant to your fathers (3 Nephi 10:7). *See:* Covenant which he made with Abraham.

Covenant which he hath made unto his people who are of the house of Israel (1 Nephi 14:8, 17; 2 Nephi 6:12; 3 Nephi 16:5, 11; 20:12, 29; 21:7; 29:1, 3, 9; Mormon

9:37). The covenant which God made with Abraham applies to all the faithful of the house of Israel. *See also:* Covenant which he made with Abraham.

Covenant which he made with Abraham (1 Nephi 15:18; 22:9; 2 Nephi 29:14; 3 Nephi 20:25–27; Mormon 5:20; Ether 13:11). Known as the Abrahamic covenant. In return for Abraham's faithfulness, the Lord promised Abraham that he would have numberless posterity, that the land of Jerusalem would be their inheritance forever, and that his posterity would be a blessing to all the kindreds of the earth (1 Nephi 15:18), meaning Abraham's seed would administer the gospel and its ordinances unto all people. Additionally, 2 Nephi 29:14 says that God "covenanted with Abraham that I [God] would remember his seed forever." The same covenant made with Abraham is also extended to all the faithful saints of God.

Covenant which I God made unto (with) thy fathers (2 Nephi 3:7, 21; 3 Nephi 20:25; Ether 4:15). *See:* Covenant which he made with Abraham.

Covenant which I made with your father Jacob (3 Nephi 20:22). The Abrahamic Covenant was renewed with Jacob. *See also:* Covenant which he made with Abraham.

Covenant which they made (Alma 46:22). *See:* Made an oath unto us.

Covenant with thee that thou shalt have eternal life (Mosiah 26:20). *See:* Seal you his.

Covenanted with Abraham (1 Nephi 17:40; 2 Nephi 29:14). *See:* Covenant which he made with Abraham.

Covenanted with his (my) people (3 Nephi 15:5; 20:19, 46; 21:4). *See:* Covenant which he hath made unto his people who are of the house of Israel.

Covenanted with their fathers (1 Nephi 17:40; 2 Nephi 10:7). *See:* Covenant which he made with Abraham.

Covenant(-ing) with God (him) (Mosiah 5:8; 6:1; 18:10; 21:31–32; Alma 7:15; 24:18; 46:22). God's people are a covenant-making people. The ordinances of the gospel provide covenant power and promise of salvation. Additionally, it behooves us to make personal covenants with God, promises we individually need to make to overcome weaknesses so we may progress line upon line and precept upon precept. We must covenant with God that we will keep His commandments, serve Him, and endure to end.

Covenants of the Father (1 Nephi 14:8; 22:9; Moroni 7:31; 10:31). *See:* Covenant(-ing) with God (him); Covenant which he made with Abraham.

Covenants of the Lord (1 Nephi 13:26; 2 Nephi 3:5; 9:53). *See:* Covenant(-ing) with God (him).

Covenants of the Lord that he has covenanted with all the house of Israel (1 Nephi 13:23; 14:5; 22:6; 2 Nephi 9:1). The covenant God made with Abraham applies to all the faithful of the house of Israel. *See also:* Covenant which he hath made unto his people who are of the house of Israel; Covenant which he made with Abraham.

Covenants of the Lord which he made unto Joseph (2 Nephi 3:4). The Abrahamic covenant was renewed with Joseph. *See also:* Covenant which he made with Abraham.

Covenants of the Lord with our fathers (1 Nephi 22:6; 2 Nephi 11:5). *See:* Covenant which I God made unto (with) thy fathers.

Covenants which he hath made to his people who are of the house of Israel (1 Nephi 14:8). *See:* Covenant which he hath made unto his people who are of the house of Israel.

Covenants which he made with our (to their/to thy) fathers (1 Nephi 17:40; 19:15; 2 Nephi 3:7). *See:* Covenant which I God made unto (with) thy fathers.

Covenants which I have made unto the children of men (his children) (2 Nephi 6:12; 29:1; Moroni 7:31–32). *See:* Covenant(-ing) with God (him).

Covered thee in the shadow of mine hand (1 Nephi 21:2; 2 Nephi 8:16). Meaning protected by the Lord's hand or sheltered under God's almighty power.

Created (creation of) Adam (Mosiah 28:17; Alma 18:36; 22:12–13; Mormon 9:12; Ether 1:3; Moroni 10:3). All scripture affirms that God created, formed and organized man, even the first man, Adam, and the first woman, Eve. They were formed and organized from the elements, or in the terminology of the scriptures, man was created "from the dust of the ground" (see Moses 3:7; Abraham 5:7). *See also:* Created after the image of God; Created all flesh; Created all men (people); Created all things; Created by the hand of God; Created his children; Created man (after his own image); Created of the dust of the earth; Created our first parents; Created the heavens and the earth and all things that in them are; Created them (you).

Created after the image of God (Mosiah 7:27; Alma 18:34; 22:12; Ether 3:15). *See:* Image of God.

Created all flesh (Jacob 2:21). Meaning God created all men and women, both bond and free, black and white, the great and the small. *See also:* Created all men (people); Created his children.

Created all men (people) (2 Nephi 29:7; Alma 1:4; 18:32; 4 Nephi 1:16; Ether 3:15). *See:* Created all flesh.

Created all things (2 Nephi 2:14–15; Mosiah 4:9; 5:15; Alma 18:28–29; 22:10–11). *See:* Created the heavens and the earth and all things that in them are.

Created by the hand of God (4 Nephi 1:16). Thus personalizing the creation by God. By the power of His hand He was directly, intimately, and concernedly involved in the creation. The Lord chides those that say He did not create them, "For shall the work say of him that made it, he made me not? Or shall the thing framed say of him that framed it, he had no understanding?" (2 Nephi 27:27).

Created his children (1 Nephi 17:36). Our Heavenly Father is the literal father of our spirits, and through His Beloved Son He directed the creation of this earth and our first parents so that we, His children, might have physical bodies.

Created man (after his own image) (2 Nephi 2:15; Jacob 4:9; Mosiah 7:27; Alma 18:34; 22:12; Mormon 9:12, 17; Ether 3:15–16). *See:* Created all flesh; Created his children; Image of God.

Created of the dust of the earth (Mosiah 2:25; Mormon 9:17). The scriptures attest that man was created from the dust or elements of the earth. *See also:* Created (creation of) Adam.

Created our first parents (2 Nephi 2:15). *See:* Created (creation of) Adam.

Created the heavens and the earth and all things that in them are (1 Nephi 17:36; 2 Nephi 2:14; Jacob 4:9; Mosiah 4:2; 3 Nephi 9:15; Mormon 9:11). The phrase used in the scriptures to emphasize that God is the Great Creator and that He truly did create and organize absolutely everything. In fact, there is nothing in the heavens or the earth that He did not create and organize. *See also:* Creation of the world.

Created them (you) (1 Nephi 2:12; Jacob 2:21; Mosiah 2:20–21, 23, 25; 4:12, 21; 26:23; Alma 5:15; Helaman 12:6; Mormon 5:2). *See:* Created all flesh.

Creation of the world (1 Nephi 5:11; 2 Nephi 1:10; 6:3; Alma 18:36; Ether 1:3). "We will go down, for there is space there, and we will take of these materials, and we will make an earth whereon these may dwell; and we will prove them herewith, to see if they will do all things whatsoever the Lord their God shall command them" (Abraham 3:24–25).

Creator of all things (heaven and earth) (Jacob 2:5; Mosiah 3:8; Helaman 14:12). *See:* Created all things; Created the heavens and the earth and all things that in them are.

Cried from the dust (2 Nephi 3:19). *See:* Cry from the dust.

Cried unto God (him) continually (this long time) (Enos 1:15; Alma 34:27; Ether 1:43). *See:* Cried unto God (the Lord); Pray(-eth/-ing) continually (without ceasing).

Cried unto God (the Lord) (1 Nephi 2:18; 17:7; Mosiah 29:20; Alma 15:10; 22:17; 43:49–50; 3 Nephi 1:11–12; Ether 2:18). *See:* Cry unto God (Jesus Christ/the Lord).

Cried unto him in mighty prayer (Enos 1:4; Alma 22:17; 3 Nephi 1:11–12). *See:* Cried unto God (him) continually (this long time); Cry mightily to God (the Father/the Lord).

Cried repentance unto the people (Ether 11:20). *See:* Cry(-ing) repentance unto the people.

Crooked paths (Alma 7:20). "God doth not walk in crooked paths, neither doth he turn to the right hand nor to the left, neither doth he vary from that which he hath said, therefore his paths are straight, and his course is one eternal round" (D&C 3:2). So the principles, doctrines, laws, and commandments of God are the same forever and never vary; and we must become likewise unwavering in following after and living the ways of God.

Cross his words (Mosiah 12:19; Alma 10:16; Helaman 9:19). The wicked described in the Book of Mormon often tried to trick the prophets to trip on their words or to contradict the words which they had spoken. Thus the wicked tried to catch the prophets in a lie, by which they would have cause to put the prophets away (kill them or cast them out or into prison). *See also:* That they might cross him.

Cross yourself in all these things (Alma 39:9). Meaning guard yourself against these things. Perhaps referring to protecting and shielding oneself from the onslaught of the adversary.

Cry from the dust (2 Nephi 3:19–20; Mormon 8:23; Ether 8:24). Refers to the Book of Mormon, a record of an ancient people, which was "brought forth from the earth as the voice of a people speaking from the dust" (Book of Mormon, Testimony of the Prophet Joseph Smith). The symbolism is the gold plates being unburied or coming forth out of the ground. *See also:* Crying from the dead (dust); Spake from the dead; Speak from the dead; Speak from the dust; Speak out of the ground; Speaking out of the dust; Speech shall be low out of the dust; Voice of one crying from the dust.

Cry from the ground for vengeance (2 Nephi 26:3; 28:10; Alma 20:18; 37:30; 3 Nephi 9:11; Mormon 8:40; Ether 8:22, 24). *See:* Blood of the prophets and the saints shall not come up any more unto me against them.

Cry mightily to God (the Father/ the Lord) (Mosiah 9:17; 11:25; 21:10, 14; 24:10; Mormon 9:6). To pray mightily means earnestly, vigorously, with all of one's effort, and with tremendous, genuine zeal. *See also:* Cry unto God (Jesus Christ/ the Lord); Mighty prayer.

Cry of the blood of the saints shall ascend up to God (2 Nephi 26:3; 28:10; Alma 14:11; 20:18; 37:30; 3 Nephi 9:11; Mormon 8:27, 40; Ether 8:22, 24). *See:* Blood of the prophets and the saints shall not come up any more unto me against them; Blood of the saints (shall cry unto the Lord).

Cry unto God (Jesus Christ/the Lord) (1 Nephi 2:16; 17:7; 2 Nephi 4:30, 35; 5:1; 26:7; 33:3; Enos 1:4, 16; Mosiah 11:24; 21:14; 23:28; Alma 18:41; 19:15; 33:5, 8, 11; 34:18, 20–24, 27; 37:30, 36; 38:8; Helaman 5:41–42; 11:3, 8; 13:32; 3 Nephi 3:12, 15; Mormon 8:23, 27, 40; 9:6; Ether 1:34–39; 6:7; 9:34). To pray unto God with real intent and with full energy of heart. *See also:* Cry mightily to God (the Father/the Lord).

Cry unto the people (Alma 5:49; 7:9; 9:25; 10:20; 14:7; 29:1; Helaman 5:37; 14:9; 3 Nephi 7:23; Mormon 3:2–3). *See:* Cry(-ing) repentance unto the people.

Crying from the dead (dust) (2 Nephi 33:13; Moroni 10:27). The closing words of two great prophets testifying that the words they have written will come forth out of the ground (the Book of Mormon) in the latter days. *See also:* Cry from the dust.

Cry(-ing) repentance unto the people (2 Nephi 3:20; Alma 29:1; Helaman 16:4; 3 Nephi 7:23; Mormon 3:3; Ether 9:28; 11:20; 12:3). Meaning preach repentance with emphasis and immediacy.

Cunning and lying craftiness (Mosiah 7:21; 9:10; 10:18). *See:* Cunning of the world.

Cunning arts (1 Nephi 16:38; Alma 10:13, 15; Helaman 16:21; Ether 13:16). Cunning means exhibiting skill, being crafty and artful, being cute, pretty and appealing, also clever and sly, having knowledge, learning and able in magic arts to deceive and lead away. *See also:* Cunning one.

Cunning devices (Alma 10:13; 11:21; 30:42; 46:10). Meaning the crafty or deceiving methods of the devil. *See also:* Cunning arts; Cunning one.

Cunning flattery (Ether 8:2). *See:* Cunning arts.

Cunning man (Mosiah 7:21; 9:10; 10:18; Alma 2:1–2; 46:10; 47:35; 51:27). *See:* Cunning of the world.

Cunning of the devil (3 Nephi 21:10). *See:* Cunning one.

Cunning of the world (Mosiah 24:7; Alma 2:1; Ether 13:16). The cunning of the world is the wisdom of the world that Satan teaches man so that man can gain power, wealth, and worldly honor to put the carnal man above others. The cunning of the world is not the wisdom of God and does not seek the will and glory of God.

Cunning one (2 Nephi 9:28, 39; Helaman 16:21). Satan or the devil is the cunning one who seeks only to ensnare men and women and drag them down to hell. It is good to know that: (1) God's wisdom is greater than the cunning of Satan (3 Nephi 21:10; D&C 10:43); (2) Satan does not know the mind of God, nor can he know the mind of God (Moses 4:6); and (3) God's power is greater than Satan's power. Thus we need not unnecessarily fear the cunning of the devil if we are faithful in keeping the commandments. *See also:* Cunning and lying craftiness; Cunning arts; Cunning devices; Cunning flattery; Cunning man; Cunning of the devil; Cunning of the world; Cunning people (plans/snares and the wiles of the devil/words); Cunning plan of the evil one; Deceived by the devil; Power of Satan.

Cunning people (plans/snares and the wiles of the devil/words) (Mosiah 24:7; Alma 10:15; 28:13; 47:35; Helaman 3:29; Ether 8:2). *See:* Cunning one; Cunning of the world.

Cunning plan of the evil one (2 Nephi 9:28; Helaman 16:21). *See:* Cunning one.

Cup of his fury (of the wrath of God) (2 Nephi 8:17, 22; Mosiah 3:26; 5:5). Jesus drank "out of that bitter cup" when he suffered in the Garden of Gethsemane (3 Nephi 11:11; see D&C 19:18). If we do not repent, we warrant God's wrath; then we will also have to suffer to drink from the cup of his fury (see Alma 40:26). *See also:* Drink out of the cup of the wrath of God.

Curse God (Alma 49:27; Mormon 2:14). "Among the wicked, men shall lift up their voices and curse God and die" (D&C 45:32). As people sink into the depths of depravity and sin, they lose perspective, cease to honor God, and forget the true knowledge of God's love and blessings. Thus they begin to take His name in vain, denounce God, and actually blame Him for their sorrows.

Curse of Adam (Moroni 8:8). The punishment Adam received as a consequence for disobeying God by partaking of the forbidden fruit. Thus Adam brought upon himself death (spiritual death, in that he was cast out of the Garden of Eden and out of God's presence). And at the end of his mortal probation he suffered physical death. "For as in Adam all die, even so in Christ shall all be made alive" (1 Corinthians 15:22). The effect of Adam's transgression extends to all mankind, that we will all die physically. But through Christ we will all be resurrected. Through Christ we also may, by following the proper steps, be born again and be able to return to God's presence. "We believe that men will be punished for their own sins, and not for Adam's transgression" (Articles of Faith 1:2).

Curse of God (Alma 17:15; 23:18). God in His perfect wisdom and justice can name any curse He sees appropriate. In these verses the curse referred to is the dark skin that was placed upon the Lamanites (see 2 Nephi 5:21).

Curse(-d) the land (1 Nephi 17:35; 2 Nephi 1:7; Jacob 2:29; 3:3; Enos 1:10; Alma 37:28, 31; 45:16; Helaman 13:17–19, 23, 30, 35–36; 3 Nephi 3:24; Mormon 1:17–18; Ether 7:23; 9:16, 28; 11:6; 14:1). The Americas are a promised land unto the righteous and a land of liberty, but they will be cursed for those who do wickedly. *See also:* Land choice above all other lands.

Curious workmanship (1 Nephi 16:10; 18:1; Alma 37:39; Ether 10:27). Curious can mean odd, peculiar, extraordinary, wonderful, and remarkable. Thus the Liahona was of workmanship unseen before and not familiar.

Cut off (1 Nephi 2:21; 20:19; 22:19–20; 2 Nephi 1:17, 20; 2:5; 4:4; 5:20; 9:6; 19:14; 20:7; 21:13; 24:22; 27:31; Mosiah 14:8; Alma 9:11, 13–14; 36:30; 37:13; 38:1; 42:6, 7, 9, 11, 14; 50:20; Helaman 12:21; 14:16, 18; 3 Nephi 20:17, 23; 21:11, 13–17, 20; Mormon 3:15; Ether 2:15; 10:11; Moroni 8:14). Most often means cut off from the presence of the Lord. In some cases, it means cut off from among the people or nation or land. To be cut off from God's presence can be for eternity or can be during mortality, thus denied God's spirit and influence. Being cut off from God is a severe result and it should be our strongest desire to avoid such a fate. Rather we should seek to again obtain our Heavenly Father's presence and to be blessed by His spirit while in this life. To obtain God's presence we must be humble and keep His commandments.

Cut off and destroyed forever (2 Nephi 1:17; 2:5; Moroni 8:14). The unrepentant will be cut off from all righteousness and from the presence of God forever.

Cut off as to things pertaining to righteousness (2 Nephi 27:31; Helaman 14:18). *See:* Spiritual death; Death as to things pertaining unto righteousness.

Cut off from among the people (1 Nephi 22:19–20; 2 Nephi 21:13; Mosiah 14:8; 3 Nephi 20:17, 23; 21:11, 13–17, 20). The Lord God will protect His people. At various times in the past He has cut out and cast off the wicked from among His people, and He has promised that He will in the future as well.

Cut off from his (my/thy) presence (2 Nephi 1:20; 4:4; 5:20; Alma 36:30; 37:13; 38:1; 42:14; Helaman 12:21). *See:* Cut off; Spiritual death.

Cut off from the face of the earth (Alma 9:11; 42:6; Mormon 3:15). *See:* Destroy(-ed) them (you) from off the face of the earth.

Cut off from the presence of the Lord (1 Nephi 2:21; 2 Nephi 5:20; 9:6; Alma 9:13–14; 42:7, 9, 11; 50:20; Helaman 14:16; Ether 2:15; 10:11). *See:* Cut off from his (my/thy) presence.

Cuts you to your hearts (Mosiah 13:7). Meaning the truth hurts the wicked deep within them because they know in their heart it is true, and they know that they have lied against God. Nephi said to his brothers Laman and Lemuel, "The guilty taketh the truth to be hard, for it cutteth them to the very center" (1 Nephi 16:2). *See also:* Speakest hard things against us.

Cutteth them to the very center (1 Nephi 16:2). *See:* Cuts you to your hearts.

D

Damnation to the (of his/to your own/upon their) soul(-s) (Mosiah 2:33; 3:18, 25; Alma 9:28; 3 Nephi 18:29; Mormon 8:33). "To be damned means to be stopped, blocked or limited in one's progress. Individuals are damned whenever they are prevented from reaching their full potential as children of God. Damnation is falling short of what one might have enjoyed if one had received and been faithful to the whole law of the gospel. In this sense, all who do not achieve the highest degree of the celestial kingdom are damned, even though they are saved in some degree of glory. . . . In this context, damnation does not necessarily refer to eternal suffering in hell with the devil, for the loss of blessings is in itself a type of hell and damnation. . . . In the scriptures, damnation usually refers to the judgment or condemnation that will be pronounced by Jesus Christ on the wicked at the end of the world (Matt. 25:41–46). 'Damnation' is an English equivalent of the Hebrew *rasha*, which implies being wicked, impious, ungodly, or guilty" (*Encyclopedia of Mormonism*, 1:353). *See also:* Believeth not shall be damned; Damned souls in hell.

Damned souls in hell (Mormon 9:4). *See:* Believeth not shall be damned; Damnation to the (of his/ to your own/upon their) soul(-s).

Danger of hell fire (3 Nephi 12:22; Mormon 8:17, 21). Meaning that one's incorrect actions, without correction, will result in a sore judgment, being in danger of receiving eternal damnation and in danger of being hewn down and cast into the fire. *See also:* Burn as stubble; Hell fire; Matthew 5:22.

Darkest abyss (Mosiah 27:29; Alma 26:3). An *abyss* is commonly defined as a deep hole or bottomless pit. An abyss can also mean a grievous or vast intellectual or spiritual void. These verses refer to the state of a serious sinner who finds himself in a dark and removed place in mind or location. Has semblance to the bottomless pit into which the devil is cast. *See also:* Depths of hell; Revelation 20:1–3.

Darkness unto light (2 Nephi 3:5; 30:17; Alma 5:7; 19:6; 26:3, 15; 37:23, 25–26; Mormon 8:16). Meanings include: bring a person or people out of spiritual darkness unto the light of the gospel, out of the darkness of unbelief unto the light of faith and testimony, having all unrepentant darkness and sin made manifest in the light for all to see, and the Book of Mormon shall be brought out of darkness (out of the earth) unto the light to show forth the word of God. *See also:* 1 Peter 2:9.

Daughter(-s) of Zion (2 Nephi 8:25; 13:16; 14:4; 20:32; 3 Nephi 20:37; Moroni 10:31). Depending on the context, (1) *Daughter of Zion* is a Hebrew term representing Israel, the children of Israel, the inhabitants of Jerusalem, the people of Israel, or those that should be the people of the covenant; or (2), alternately refers to actual women in their immodesty and pride.

Day cometh (1 Nephi 14:17; 19:15; 22:15; 2 Nephi 6:10, 14; 10:7; 12:12; 23:9; 25:12; 26:4, 6; 27:11; Jacob 6:2; Alma 11:41; 45:13; 3 Nephi 25:1; Mormon 6:21; 8:33; Moroni 10:24). A phrase most often used in prophecies concerning the future, meaning at a future time "such and so" will come to pass. *See also:* Things (which are) to come.

Day of grace was passed (Helaman 13:38; Mormon 2:15). "It is possible for people to get so far in the dark through rebellion and wickedness that the spirit of repentance leaves them . . . and they get *beyond the power of repentance* . . . because of their [willful] wickedness and the hardness of their hearts, which the Spirit of the Lord could not penetrate" (Smith, *Doctrines of Salvation,* 2:194–95). *See also:* Everlastingly too late.

Day of his coming (3 Nephi 24:2). *See:* Coming of Christ.

Day of judgment (2 Nephi 9:46; Alma 9:15; Helaman 8:25; Mormon 7:10). *See:* Judgment day.

Day of miracles (Moroni 7:35). Means a day or period when miracles actually take place on earth. *See also:* God of miracles.

Day of my wisdom (Helaman 15:16). Meaning in the day that the Lord sees fit or by His great wisdom He determines it the best time to take place.

Day of probation (2 Nephi 33:9). *See:* Days of probation.

Day of salvation (1 Nephi 21:8; Alma 13:21). The day of deliverance, the day of the promised gathering, and the day for which all must prepare—when salvation comes to the faithful. *See also:* Bring(-eth) salvation; Day of your salvation; 1 Nephi 19:11.

Day of the Lord (cometh/is at hand) (2 Nephi 12:12–13; 23:6, 9; Alma 31:12; 3 Nephi 25:5). Refers to the Second Coming of Christ. *See also:* At hand; Coming of Christ; Day cometh; Great and dreadful day of the Lord.

Day of your salvation (Alma 34:31; Helaman 13:38). Meaning now is the time or day to repent, and do not procrastinate repentance. We must seek salvation during our mortal days of probation before it is too late. *See also:* Everlastingly too late; Alma 13:21.

Day of (your) visitation (2 Nephi 20:3; Mormon 9:2). The Second Coming of the Lord will come suddenly at a time when one thinks not, so we must be prepared. *Compare:* Isaiah 10:3.

Day that cometh shall burn (consume) them (2 Nephi 26:4, 6; 3 Nephi 25:1). *See:* Consumed as stubble.

Days of probation (our lives) (1 Nephi 10:21; 15:31–32; 2 Nephi 2:21, 30; 9:27; 33:9; Helaman 13:38; 16:21; Mormon 9:28). "For behold, this life is the time for men to prepare to meet God; yea, behold the day of this life is the day for men to perform their labors. . . . For after this day of life, which is given us to prepare for eternity, behold, if we do not improve our time while in this life, then cometh the night of darkness wherein there can be no labor performed. . . . For that same spirit which doth possess your bodies at the time that ye go out of this life, that same spirit will have power to possess your body in that eternal world" (Alma 34:32–34). *See also:* Everlastingly too late; Probationary state (time).

Day(-s) of the Gentiles (1 Nephi 13:34; 14:1; 2 Nephi 27:1; 28:32; 3 Nephi 16:7; 28:32). The last days, or in other words the latter days, when the truth will come unto the Gentiles (see 2 Nephi 16:7). The scripture here "is speaking of the day of universal apostasy; of the day in which the gospel is to be restored; of the day preceding the Second Coming, in which evil and iniquity and sorrow will increase" (McConkie, *New Witness*, 435). *See also:* Come unto the Gentiles; Day(-s) of the Gentiles; Fulness of the Gentiles; Gentiles had received the fulness of the gospel; Gentiles shall be blessed.

Days shall not be prolonged (2 Nephi 23:22; Alma 9:18). *See:* Prolong(-ed) their days (existence) in the land.

Deaf hear the words of a book and the eyes of the blind shall see (2 Nephi 27:29). This is a prophecy concerning the coming forth of the Book of Mormon in the latter days. Because of the truths in the Book of Mormon those that were deaf shall hear, and those that were blind shall see. *Compare:* Isaiah 29:18.

Deaf that will not hear . . . blind that will not see, for they shall perish (2 Nephi 9:31–32). There are those that are deaf and blind to the truth, and when it is presented to them they refuse to hear or see. They shall perish and not obtain salvation. *See also:* Blind(-ed/-eth) the (their/your) eyes (minds); Blindness of their minds.

Deafness of their ears (Jarom 1:3). *See:* Deaf that will not hear . . . blind that will not see, for they shall perish.

Deal justly (one with another) (Alma 41:14; 4 Nephi 1:12). Meaning to deal rightly, appropriately, fairly, and as we ourselves would want to be dealt with. The Golden Rule says, "Do unto others as you would have them do unto you." *See also:* Just and true [individuals].

Dealings of the Lord God (1 Nephi 2:12; Mosiah 10:14; Alma 50:19). Meaning the workings, ways, purposes, designs, and intents of God. "This is my work and my glory—to bring to pass the immortality and eternal life of man" (Moses 1:39). *See also:* Doings of the Lord; Work(-s) of the Lord.

Dearly beloved brethren (Alma 26:9; 27:4; 56:2). *See:* Beloved brethren.

Death as to things pertaining unto righteousness (Alma 5:42; 12:16, 32; 40:26; Helaman 14:18). Refers to the second or spiritual death. Because the wicked have chosen wickedness, they will be separated from the presence of God and separated from dwelling in a state and place of all righteousness. *See also:* Cut off as to things pertaining to righteousness.

Death is (was) swallowed up by the victory of (in) Christ (Mosiah 16:8; Alma 22:14; 27:28; Mormon 7:5). Meaning the sting, the pain, and the sorrow of death is no more because it is eliminated and taken away by the Resurrection of Jesus Christ. Jesus, our Savior, came to earth to be crucified and then resurrected by the power of God. Christ was the "firstfruits" of the Resurrection (see 1 Corinthians 15:20, 23), and all mankind who live on earth will be the following fruits of the Resurrection. Each of us will be resurrected to immortal life, receiving a perfected body to live without disease or death through all eternity. This is a free gift to all from our Savior and Redeemer. *See also:* Death should have no sting; Sting of death (is swallowed up in Christ); Swallowed up by the victory of (in) Christ; Victory of Christ (over death); Victory over the grave.

Death of the spirit (2 Nephi 2:29; 9:10). The spirit of man is eternal and cannot cease to exist, but death of the spirit is to be separated from or cast out from God. Death of the spirit or spiritual death is to become captive of the devil (see Alma 34:35). "Spiritual death is hell" (2 Nephi 9:12). *See also:* Spiritual death.

Death of the temporal body (1 Nephi 15:31; 2 Nephi 9:10; Alma 11:45; 40:11). The separation of the body and the spirit (see James 2:26). *See also:* Temporal death.

Death should have no sting (Mosiah 16:7–8; Alma 22:14; Mormon 7:5). Meaning that because of Christ's Resurrection we all will be resurrected and thus the fear and hurt of death is no longer.

Deceived by the devil (Jacob 7:18; Alma 30:53). Satan is the great deceiver, the father of all lies. His only desire is to mislead and beguile men and women to depart from the strait and narrow path that leads back to God. *See also:* Cunning one; Devil hath deceived me (this people); Flattered (flattereth) them away; Wiles of the devil.

Declare good tidings (Mosiah 3:3; Alma 13:22; 39:15–16, 19; Helaman 5:29, 13:7; 16:14). Meaning to speak, preach, and publish the good tidings or good news of the gospel of Jesus Christ. It is truly good news because through Christ we are and can be redeemed from physical and spiritual death. *See also:* Good tidings.

Declare his generation (Mosiah 14:8; 15:10). *See:* Who shall declare his generation.

Declare my (the) word(-s) (Jacob 2:2, 11–12; Enos 1:26; Alma 6:8; 17:12; 21:15; 30:32; 35:15; 37:47; 42:31; 43:1; 45:20; 62:45; Helaman 10:12, 14; 3 Nephi 5:13; Moroni 10:27). Meaning words of Christ,

which is the doctrine of Christ, the gospel of Christ.

Declare(-d) unto thee (them/the people/you) (1 Nephi 1:18; 2:1; 16:1; 20:7; 22:21; 2 Nephi 9:54; Jacob 2:2, 12; 7:2, 7; Mosiah 2:29; 3:3–4; 15:24; 27:37; 29:6; Alma 9:6–7; 13:22, 25; 17:12; 19:33–34; 21:21–22; 29:2; 37:30; 38:7; 49:30; Helaman 5:6; 6:4; 9:16, 30; 10:6, 11–12, 14–15, 17; 13:7; 15:1; 16:14; 3 Nephi 9:10; 11:31; 21:2, 9; Moroni 7:23). Meaning to speak, preach, and publish to individuals and all people. *See also:* Declare my (the) word(-s); Declare the word.

Decrees (of God) are unalterable (Alma 29:4; 41:8). *See:* According to God's word.

Defence of country (freedom/liberty/property/wives and children) (Alma 51:20; 53:13; 60:29; 61:6; 62:5, 9; 3 Nephi 3:2; Ether 14:2). The modern American spelling is *defense. See:* Defend themselves.

Defend his (my/our/their) country (Alma 43:26; 43:47; 48:13; 51:13, 15; 53:18; 56:5; 58:8; 60:28; Helaman 4:7). *See:* Defend themselves.

Defend themselves (Alma 18:16; 24:5; 35:14; 43:23, 26, 30, 47; 48:14, 16; 49:20; 50:1; 52:6; 53:16; 54:13; 58:8; 3 Nephi 3:22; Moroni 2:4). It is natural that we would defend ourselves and our families, yet it would be a sin to too quickly shed the blood of another person. The Lord gave guidance on how to proceed in our defense: "And again, this is the law that I gave unto mine ancients, that they should not go out unto battle against any nation, kindred, tongue, or people, save I, the Lord, commanded them. And if any nation, tongue, or people should proclaim war against them, they should first lift a standard of peace unto that people, nation, or tongue; and if that people did not accept the offering of peace, neither the second nor the third time, they should bring these testimonies before the Lord; then I, the Lord, would give unto them a commandment, and justify them in going out to battle against that nation, tongue, or people. And I, the Lord, would fight their battles" (D&C 98:33–37). *See also:* Cause of freedom (liberty); Defence of country (freedom/liberty/property/wives and children); Defend his (my/our/their) country; Land of liberty; Maintain their liberty; Maintain their rights; Stand fast in that (this) liberty wherewith God hath made them free; Standard of liberty; Support the cause of (their) liberty; Take not up weapons save God shall command you; Title of liberty; Ye shall defend your families even unto bloodshed.

Delight in the chastity of women (Jacob 2:28). God's law is complete abstinence before marriage and absolute fidelity after marriage. Sexual sin is abhorrent to God, whereas being pure and chaste is a joy unto God. *See also:* Abominable above all sins save it be the shedding of innocent blood or denying the Holy Ghost.

Delight in the shedding of blood (Mosiah 11:19; Alma 26:24; 48:23; Mormon 7:4). A landmark point in the digression of men who choose evil and rebel against God. Such men have become numb to the Spirit of God, in fact the Holy Ghost has withdrawn Himself from them because of their wicked ways and their desire to kill. Such was the mindset of the Nephites just before their complete destruction.

Delighteth in his words (plainness/prophecy/righteousness/ the coming of the Lord/the covenants of the Lord/the scriptures/ things of the Lord) (2 Nephi 4:15–16; 9:49; 11:2, 4–6; 25:4–5, 13; 31:3). *Delighteth in* means to cherish, prize, treasure, and to esteem highly. All these verses are attributed to Nephi, who delights in many good things. "If there is anything virtuous, lovely, or of good report or praiseworthy, we seek after these things" (Articles of Faith 1:13).

Delightsome people (2 Nephi 30:6–7; Words of Mormon 1:8; 4 Nephi 1:10; Mormon 5:17; Moroni 9:12). Meaning a pure people who believe in Christ. *Delightsome* is defined as that which gives joy, satisfaction, and gratification. Therefore a delightsome people unto the Lord are a people that cause those emotions in God.

Deliverance by the hand of the Lord (1 Nephi 1:20; Mosiah 9:17; Alma 14:26; 46:7; 56:47; 58:11). *See:* Deliver(-ed/-ing) from enemies; None could deliver them but the Lord.

Deliverance of Jesus Christ (2 Nephi 9:11; Alma 4:14; 7:13; 9:28). The deliverance spoken of here refers to the redemption from temporal and spiritual death because Jesus is our Savior and Redeemer. *See also:* According to the power of (his) deliverance; Great and eternal plan of deliverance from death (of redemption).

Deliver(-ed/-ing) from enemies (2 Nephi 4:31; Omni 1:7; Mosiah 2:4, 31; 9:17; 11:21; Alma 2:28; 9:10; 45:1; 48:16; 49:28; 57:35; 58:10, 37; 60:20; 61:13; 62:50; Helaman 12:2; 3 Nephi 3:25; 4:8, 33; Mormon 3:13). God is all powerful and is mighty to deliver His people from their enemies. We should humbly pray to be delivered from our enemies if it be God's will. *See also:* Defend themselves; Deliver(-ed) out of bondage; Deliverance by the hand of the Lord.

Delivered from (unto) Satan (Alma 15:17; 37:15). Repentance and coming unto Christ will deliver us from Satan, whereas unrepentant wickedness will deliver us unto Satan. *See also:* Deliverance of Jesus Christ; Delivered their souls from death (hell).

Deliver(-ed) out of bondage (Mosiah 7:15, 33; 8:7; 11:23; 21:15, 36; 22:1–2, 4; 23:23; 24:13, 16–17, 21; 25:8, 10, 16; 27:16; 29:20, 40; Alma 5:5; 29:11–12; 36:2, 28–29). The Lord will deliver His people out of bondage. Mosiah 11:23 says, "Except this people repent and turn unto the Lord their God, they shall be brought into bondage; and none shall deliver them, except it be the Lord the Almighty God." This can be an earthly bondage while in this life, and those that do not repent will eventually be in bondage to Satan. *See also:* Brought into bondage; Brought out of bondage; Free(-dom) from bondage; Led out of captivity; Out of bondage; Out of captivity; Yoke of bondage.

Delivered their souls from death (hell) (2 Nephi 11:5; Alma 5:7). The redemption of Jesus Christ delivers souls from death and hell. *See also:* Deliverance of Jesus Christ.

Demands of justice (2 Nephi 9:26; Mosiah 2:38; 15:9; Alma 34:16; 42:15, 24). The eternal laws of justice will require the just consequences for all our actions. The sinner must be punished unless he repents and seeks the redeeming effects of the Atonement of Christ. (See example in Mosiah 4:2). *See also:* According to God's justice; All his judgments are just; Requisite with the justice of God.

Denieth none that come unto him (2 Nephi 26:33). When Christ says come unto me, none are exempted, all are invited, both male and female, black and white, bond and free. *See also:* All are alike unto God.

Deny (denied/denieth/denying) the Christ (God) (2 Nephi 31:14; Jacob 6:8; 7:9; Alma 5:39; 11:25; 30:39; 34:37; 3 Nephi 29:5; 4 Nephi 1:26–27, 29: Mormon 9:3, 8, 26; Ether 4:8; Moroni 1:2–3; 7:17; 8:23, 29; 10:6, 33). To deny is to reject rather than accept, to disbelieve rather than believe, to turn away rather than come unto, to renounce rather than defend, to disown rather than affirm, and to forsake rather than cherish. Jesus Christ and His gospel, doctrine, example, ways, commandments, and Atonement are our only hope. To deny Him is to reject salvation and to instead embrace Satan.

Deny (denieth) gifts (power) of God (2 Nephi 28:26; Jacob 6:8; Moroni 10:7–8, 33). The gifts and power of God are manifest only to them that believe and have faith. To disbelieve, not have faith, and to sin is to eliminate the gifts and power of God from our lives. Thus the wicked and misdirected reject the gifts and power of God because they do not experience them. Rather they must plant the seed of faith (see Alma 32:26–30) and in humility and repentance seek God and His gifts.

Deny him not (2 Nephi 25:28–29). The only way to salvation is to believe in Christ and not deny Him. *See also:* Deny (denied/denieth/denying) the Christ (God).

Deny (not) the power of God (2 Nephi 28:5, 26; Jacob 6:8; 3 Nephi 29:6; Mormon 9:26; Moroni 10:7, 32–33). God has all power to do anything He wills to do. For a person to deny that God has all power does not change that fact that He does have all power. Belief of God's almighty power is an important component to our faith. *See also:* D&C 76:3; Joseph Smith–History 1:19.

Deny the faith (Alma 34:28; 44:4). Meaning to reject the gospel of Jesus Christ and depart from it. "In short, if a man shall do anything which he knows to be wrong, and repenteth not, he cannot enjoy the Holy Spirit, but will walk in darkness and ultimately deny the faith" (*Discourses of Brigham Young*, 85).

Deny the Holy Ghost (2 Nephi 28:4; 31:14; Jacob 6:8; Alma 39:5–6; 3 Nephi 29:6; Moroni 8:28; 10:4–8). "If ye deny the Holy Ghost when it once has had place in you, and ye know that ye deny it, behold, this is a sin which is unpardonable" (Alma 39:6). *See also:* Better for you that ye had not known me;

Contend no more against the Holy Ghost; Unpardonable sin.

Deny the justice of God no more (Alma 42:30). The justice of God is absolute, and He is one hundred percent just. God is not more just toward some and then lenient to others. *See also:* According to God's justice; Judgments are just.

Deny the more parts of the gospel (4 Nephi 1:27). The gospel of Jesus Christ is an all-or-nothing profession; to not accept it all is to not have the real or true thing. To reject parts of the gospel is to be on the road to apostasy. "You cannot approach the gospel as you would a buffet or smorgasbord, choosing here a little and there a little. You must sit down to the whole feast and live the Lord's loving commandments in their fulness" (Wirthlin, "It's Your Choice").

Deny the revelations of God (Helaman 4:12; 3 Nephi 29:6; Mormon 9:7). False creeds reject continuing revelation and say the Bible is all the revelation needed (see 2 Nephi 29:6). "We believe all that God has revealed, all that He does now reveal, and we believe that He will yet reveal many great and important things pertaining to the Kingdom of God" (Articles of Faith 1:9).

Deny the true church of Christ (4 Nephi 1:26). Many believe in Christ to a point, but reject the Church of Jesus Christ. This in fact is a partial rejection of Christ Himself. *See also:* Church of Christ; Deny (denied/denieth/denying) the Christ (God).

Deny the word(-s) of Christ/ God (Jacob 6:8; Alma 11:34, 37; Helaman 8:13; Ether 4:8). Meaning to dispute or reject the words and doctrine of Christ. *See also:* Deny (denied/denieth/denying) the Christ (God); Doctrine of Christ.

Deny them not (1 Nephi 10:22; Alma 30:41; Helaman 8:24; Ether 4:8). Reject not the truth that is presented unto you. Deny them not is a warning, a testimony, and a marker of important things.

Deny yourselves of all ungodliness (3 Nephi 12:30; Moroni 10:32). Meaning to shun and not participate in sin, for all sin is contrary to God and His ways. *See also:* Touch not their unclean things.

Depart from the right way (2 Nephi 4:5; 3 Nephi 6:14; Mormon 9:20). Meaning to diverge not or deviate not from God's way, also known as the way you should go, the strait and narrow way, the rod of iron, the true faith, obedient to the commandments of God, and turn not to the right nor to the left. *See also:* Rod of iron; Strait and narrow course (path).

Depths of hell (1 Nephi 12:16). Compare 1 Nephi 8:32 "Depths of the fountain" of filthy waters. "They have brought upon themselves death; and a hell I have prepared for them, if they repent not" (Moses 6:29). "And, behold, there is a place prepared for them from the beginning, which place is hell" (D&C 29:38). "A place of filthiness prepared for that which is filthy. . . . even that awful hell of which I have spoken, and the devil is the preparator of it; wherefore the final state of the souls of men is to dwell in the kingdom of God, or to be cast out" (1 Nephi 15:34–35). *See also:* Darkest abyss; Down to destruction; Down to hell; Lead(-ing/stealing) away the hearts (souls) to destruction (hell); Place of filthiness prepared for that which is filthy; Place prepared [hell]; Prepared a place of filthiness (fire and brimstone/hell); Prepared for the wicked; Thrust down to hell.

Depths of humility (2 Nephi 9:42; Mosiah 4:11; 21:14; Alma 62:41; Helaman 6:5; 3 Nephi 12:2). To recognize without reservation our sinful and imperfect state before God; and to feel this feeling enough to cause us to repent and come unto Christ and change our ways. Humility is also an acknowledgement that our talents, abilities, all that we have, even our lives, are gifts from God. Of ourselves mortal men and women are nothing (see Moses 1:10). *See also:* In the depth(-s) of humility.

Desire for the welfare of my brethren (Enos 1:9, 11; Mosiah 25:11; Alma 60:10). It is the interest of all good people to be concerned for their fellow men. *See also:* Anxiety for you.

Desire of power (Alma 44:2; 60:16). *See:* Get power.

Desired to do evil (Alma 41:5; 42:28). *See:* All that watch for iniquity; Carnal mind; Carnally minded; Carnal wills and desires.

Desire(-s) of your (their/his) heart(-s) (Mosiah 11:2; 18:10–11; Alma 41:3). Denotes the real intent of a person. A popular saying is, "As a man thinketh, so is he." That which we think and desire in our hearts is known to God and will be weighed in the balance on judgment day. *See also:* Intents of our hearts.

Desire(-s/-ed/-eth) to know (1 Nephi 2:16; 11:1, 10–11; 2 Nephi 5:33; Mosiah 5:1; 8:12; 12:25; 28:12; Alma 16:5; 32:24; 33:1; 40:9). It is important to have knowledge and to use it wisely and for good. Knowledge of truth and of the gospel can protect us from evil and gain us exaltation. The Lord has commanded, "Seek ye diligently and teach one another words of wisdom; yea, seek ye out of the best books words of wisdom; seek learning, even by study and also by faith" (D&C 88:118). *See also:* Greater things; Mysteries of God.

Desirous for gain (power) (Alma 46:4; Ether 9:11). *See:* Get gain; Get power; Vain things of the world.

Desolate places (dwellings/ houses/lands/cities) (1 Nephi 21:19; 2 Nephi 15:9; 16:11; 17:19; 23:9, 22; Alma 16:10–11; Helaman 3:5–6; 14:24; 15:1; 3 Nephi 4:1, 3; 10:7; 22:3). *Desolate* means destroyed, barren, ravaged, deserted, forsaken, sacked, and wasted. Thus is the fate of the dwelling places, the cities, and the lands of the wicked and those that rebel against God. The Lord has said, "For if they do reject these things [the gospel of Jesus Christ] the hour of their judgment is nigh, and their house shall be left unto them desolate" (D&C 84:115).

Despair cometh because of iniquity (Moroni 10:22). Faith brings hope, whereas sin brings despair. Sin defeats self-esteem. Sin eliminates the blessings of God. Sin exposes one to the buffetings of Satan. Thus iniquity and sin brings one despair, depression, discouragement, and hopelessness. *See also:* Take happiness in iniquity (sin); Wickedness never was happiness.

Destroy the church (Mosiah 27:10, 16; Alma 2:4; 26:18; 36:6, 9, 11; 46:10). It is the aim and desire of Satan and his minions—wicked men, apostates, and those who have rebelled against God—to tear down, discredit, and scorn the Church of God. *See also:* Built up churches to get gain (power/praise of men); Build (built up) churches unto themselves; Church began to be (was) broken up; Deny the true church of Christ; Finger of scorn; Persecute the church of God.

Destroy the government (3 Nephi 7:2, 6, 11; 9:9). Those that seek the honor of the world, unrighteous power, and immorally gained riches seek to replace just and orderly government with tyrants, gangs, and anarchy.

Destroy(-ed) them (you) from off the face of the earth (Jarom 1:10; Mosiah 12:8; Alma 9:12, 24; 37:22, 25; Helaman 7:28; Ether 11:12). Concerning the promised land, God has decreed many times that if the people do not repent He will destroy them from off the face of the earth. *See also:* Land choice above all other lands.

Devices of the devil (Alma 11:21; 30:42). Meaning the various temptations of the devil. Satan has many tricks, lies, and rationalizations he uses to lure people away from Christ and the truth. We must guard ourselves in all things to avoid these devices of the devil. *See also:* Cunning one; Wiles of the devil.

Devil and his angels (children) (1 Nephi 14:3; 2 Nephi 9:9, 16, 37; Mosiah 26:27; Alma 30:60; 3 Nephi 9:2; Moroni 7:17). Those that follow the devil and do evil are the children of the devil. His angels are the minions that followed him in rebellion against God in the premortal sphere and now assist Satan in his diabolical work.

Devil cheateth their souls (2 Nephi 28:21). *See:* Devices of the devil.

Devil has got so great hold upon your hearts (Helaman 7:15). The devil actively and successfully deceives the hearts, minds, thoughts, and desires of the people (see 3 Nephi 2:2). *See also:* Satan did get hold (possession) upon the hearts of the people.

Devil has (hath) power over you (them/him) (Mosiah 16:3, 5; Alma 9:28; 28:13; 30:42; 34:35). *See:* Power of Satan; Yield(-ing) themselves (yourselves) unto (the power of) Satan (the devil).

Devil hath deceived me (this people) (Jacob 7:18; Alma 12:4; 30:53; 3 Nephi 2:2). *See:* Cunning one; Deceived by the devil.

Devil is an enemy unto God (Mosiah 4:14; 16:5; Alma 34:23; Moroni 7:12). *See:* Enemy of (to) all righteousness; Enemy of (to/unto) God.

Devil would never have power over (Alma 48:17; Helaman 5:12). *See:* Power of Satan.

Devils and unclean spirits (1 Nephi 11:31; Mosiah 3:6; 3 Nephi 7:19, 22; 14:22; Mormon 9:24). *See:* Cast out [unclean spirits].

Did not sin ignorantly (3 Nephi 6:18). In other words, they knew the commandments of God but ignored them and rebelled against them. *Compare:* Ignorantly sinned.

See also: Not sinned against great knowledge which ye have received.

Did as the Lord commanded (1 Nephi 2:3; 19:1). The commands of God are not casual suggestions, but absolute directives that must be obeyed. Our diligence in obeying God's commandments is an indicator of our love and respect for Him. Great will be our reward and satisfaction if we can say, "I did as I was commanded." *See also:* Commanded of the Lord; 2 Nephi 33:15.

Did that which was good in the sight of the Lord (Alma 63:2; Ether 10:16–17, 19). These verses refer to just men who were leaders of the people and who strived to lead the people and be an example of living the laws of God. *See also:* Just man (men).

Did witness of it (1 Nephi 11:7; Words of Mormon 1:2; Alma 14:9; 30:44; 3 Nephi 7:20; 10:1, 3; 19:14; Mormon 3:16). God has designated witnesses of His word, actions, and existence, and He has commanded them to so witness. *See also:* Testimony of many (two or three).

Die for all men (2 Nephi 2:27; 9:5, 21–22; 26:24, 27; Alma 5:33; 28:8; 33:22; 3 Nephi 27:14–15; Mormon 9:13). Jesus came to the earth to become the Redeemer of all men and women that come unto Him: (1) He died and was resurrected so that all men will also be resurrected; and (2) He suffered for our sins and died so that we may be forgiven and cleansed if we will repent, come unto Him, and follow His ways. *See also:* All are alike unto God; Atonement of Christ (the Only Begotten Son).

Die no more (Alma 11:45). After the Resurrection we will never die again. *See also:* Immortal body; Resurrection of the body.

Die(-th) in their sins (2 Nephi 9:38; Mosiah 15:26; Alma 12:16; Moroni 10:26). To die physically and leave this mortal life *before* repenting of one's sins.

Diligently search (seek[-eth]/ sought) (1 Nephi 2:19; 10:17, 19; Mosiah 1:7; Alma 12:8; 17:2; 40:3, 9; 3 Nephi 23:1; Moroni 7:19). We are commanded to search the scriptures; also to pray that we might know the mind and will of God. "Ask, and it shall be given you; seek, and ye shall find; knock, and it shall be opened unto you: for every one that asketh receiveth; and he that seeketh findeth; and to him that knocketh it shall be opened" (Matthew 7:7–8).

Discern his thoughts (Jacob 2:5; Alma 10:17; 12:3, 7; 18:16, 18, 20; Helaman 9:41; 3 Nephi 28:6). *See:* Know all my (thy) thoughts.

Disciple of Jesus [follower] (3 Nephi 5:13). A disciple is defined as a follower. Thus we all can be disciples. A true disciple lives and teaches strictly the gospel of Jesus Christ.

Disciples of Jesus [twelve special witnesses] (1 Nephi 1:10; 11:29, 34–36; 12:7–10; 13:24, 26, 39–41; 14:20; 3 Nephi 12:1; 13:25; 15:11; 18:1, 10, 17, 26, 36; 19:4, 6–7, 15, 24, 30, 35; 26:17; 27:1, 33; 28:1; 4 Nephi 1:1, 5, 13–14, 30, 37, 46; Mormon 3:18–19; 8:10; 9:22; Moroni 2:1). Twelve Apostles were chosen by Jesus in the land of Jerusalem. Also twelve "ministers" were chosen by Jesus from among the Nephites (see 1 Nephi 12:9–10).

Disciples ordained in their stead (4 Nephi 1:14). Under the direction of God, men are called to fill the vacancies in the twelve. For example, when the vacancy caused by Judas, who betrayed the Lord, was created, it is recorded in Acts 1:24–26, "And they prayed, and said, Thou, Lord, which knowest the hearts of all men, shew whether of these two thou hast chosen, that he may take part of this ministry and apostleship, from which Judas by transgression fell, that he might go to his own place. And they gave forth their lots; and the lot fell upon Matthias; and he was numbered with the eleven apostles." The Fifth Article of Faith states: "We believe that a man must be called of God, by prophecy, and by the laying on of hands by those who are in authority, to preach the Gospel and administer in the ordinances thereof" (Articles of Faith 1:5).

Dispersed of my people [Judah] (2 Nephi 21:12; 3 Nephi 21:26–27;

Mormon 8:15). *See:* Scattered tribes of Israel.

Disputations among the people (them/you) (1 Nephi 15:6; 3 Nephi 8:4; 11:22, 28; 18:34; 27:3; 4 Nephi 1:2; Moroni 8:4–5). To dispute is to engage in argument and make a contest over a matter or principle. After the Savior visited the Nephites on the American Continent, all the people were converted to the Lord "and there were no contentions and disputations among them, and every man did deal justly one with another" (4 Nephi 1:2). The Lord God commanded that "there shall be no disputations among you" (3 Nephi 11:28). *See also:* Spirit of contention.

Dissented from the church (Alma 46:7; 48:24; Helaman 5:35). Meaning those that separated themselves from the Church because they disagreed, opposed, rebelled, disputed, protested, and contended against it. *See also:* Rebel(-led/-ling/-lion) against God.

Divided into classes (Alma 32:2; 4 Nephi 1:26). Classes come about because of the pride of some who believe they are better than others. Thus they segregate themselves from others. *See also:* All are alike unto God; Lifted up in (unto) pride (of their eyes/hearts/and boasting).

Do all things [God can] (1 Nephi 7:12; 17:31; Alma 7:8; Helaman 12:2). God has all power to do all that He wills to do. *See also:* All power; Power of God.

Do all things [people can, with God's help] (1 Nephi 17:50; 2 Nephi 1:10; Alma 20:4; 26:12; 3 Nephi 26:20; Mormon 9:29; Moroni 10:23). "Therefore, dearly beloved brethren, let us cheerfully do all things that lie in our power; and then may we stand still, with the utmost assurance, to see the salvation of God, and for his arm to be revealed" (D&C 123:17).

Do evil or do good (Alma 12:31; 41:7; Helaman 14:31). Moral agency is given by God to man to choose for himself. The Light of Christ is given to all men to know good from evil. Knowledge of good and evil increases or decreases based on how diligent we are in following the light. *See also:* Act for themselves (yourselves); Choose good (or evil); Light of Christ.

Do good (continually) (2 Nephi 33:4, 10; Jacob 2:19; Mosiah 5:2; Alma 12:31; 39:12; 41:7, 14; 63:2; Helaman 12:4; 14:31; 3 Nephi 12:44; Ether 4:11–12; 8:26; Moroni 7:13, 16–17). *See:* Doing good.

Do not (does not) understand them (2 Nephi 32:4; Jacob 7:11; Alma 33:2; Mormon 9:8). To read the scriptures does not mean that one correctly interprets them. It is imperative that the scriptures are read prayerfully and with the assistance of the Holy Ghost to understand them. *See also:* D&C 10:63.

Doctrine of Christ (2 Nephi 31:2, 21; 32:6; Jacob 7:2, 6; 3 Nephi 2:2).

The doctrine of Christ is to "enter in by the way [repentance and baptism], and receive the Holy Ghost, [which] will show unto you all things what ye should do" (2 Nephi 32:5). "They shall come to the knowledge of their Redeemer and the very points of his doctrine, that they may know how to come unto him and be saved" (1 Nephi 15:14). "This is my doctrine, and whoso buildeth upon this buildeth upon my rock, and the gates of hell shall not prevail against them" (3 Nephi 11:39). *See also:* Built upon my rock; Know the truth; Law which ye shall do; Learn doctrine; Only and true doctrine; Points of doctrine; True doctrine; Word of Christ; Word of God.

Doctrine of the Father (2 Nephi 31:21; 3 Nephi 11:32). Same as and uniform with the Doctrine of Christ, for the Father and Son are one, meaning completely united in all things. The Son did and taught all things that the Father commanded Him.

Doing good (Alma 48:16). The Thirteenth Article of Faith says, "We believe in being honest, true, chaste, benevolent, virtuous, and in doing good to all men." (Articles of Faith 1:13). In Acts 10:38 it says that Jesus of Nazareth "went about doing good." This is the example that we must follow. *See also:* Do good.

Doings of abominations (2 Nephi 25:2; Mosiah 12:1; 3 Nephi 30:2). Meaning the extremely sinful activities of the people. *See also:* Abominable in the sight of the Lord; Abominations of his people.

Doings of the Father unto the children of men (3 Nephi 28:7). Refers to what Heavenly Father is doing to bring about the plan of salvation in the lives of His children. Thus He is aware of events here on earth, and ensures that the promised events will transpire. Because of this, all men will be judged in accordance with their choices of right and wrong. The gospel will be taught to the honest in heart, that they might receive the ordinances of salvation. *See also:* Great and eternal purpose(-s).

Doings of the Lord (1 Nephi 19:22; 2 Nephi 22:4; 3 Nephi 29:4–5). *See:* Dealings of the Lord God; Work(-s) of the Lord.

Doubt not but be believing (Mormon 9:27). "Pray always, and be believing, and all things shall work together for your good, if ye walk uprightly" (D&C 90:24). It must be our prayer that our beginning belief will become a great faith. *See also:* Doubting nothing.

Doubting nothing (Mormon 9:21, 25). Meaning to have faith without doubt, without faltering or hesitancy, which is great faith. We must strive for greater faith and pray for sufficient faith to be saved. A great example is the man in Mark 9:24 who pleaded with the Lord, saying, "I believe; help thou mine unbelief." *See also:* Doubt not but be believing.

Down to destruction (1 Nephi 14:3, 7; 2 Nephi 26:10; Enos 1:23; Alma 7:15; 10:18; 12:6, 11, 17, 36; 30:47; 54:9; Helaman 6:25, 28; 3 Nephi 2:19). Generally the terminology of the scriptures is down to hell and up to heaven. Satan seeks the destruction of men's souls so they will dwell eternally down in hell with him as their captor. Hell is the destruction of progression and the destruction of being free forever. *See also:* Depths of hell.

Down to hell (1 Nephi 14:3; 2 Nephi 2:29; 9:34, 36; 24:15; 26:10; 28:15, 21; Alma 30:60; 31:17; Moroni 8:14). *See:* Down to destruction.

Draw all men unto him (me) (2 Nephi 26:24; 3 Nephi 27:14–15). The emphasis here is "all men." Christ suffered and died for *all men* that they might of their own free will and choice come unto Him and be saved. Likewise, by their own free will, they can choose to not come unto Him and to not be redeemed from spiritual death. *See also:* All are alike unto God.

Draw near unto me with their mouth, and with their lips do honor me, but have removed their hearts far from me (2 Nephi 27:25). The word of the Lord as prophesied by Nephi telling of the latter days when the gospel is restored, because the true Church of Jesus Christ was not found on the earth. *See also:* Joseph Smith–History 1:18–19.

Drawn out (in prayer) unto the Lord (Alma 34:27; Helaman 13:22). *Drawn out in prayer* means pleadings, lengthened prayer, or much prayer seeking an answer. *See also:* Mighty prayer.

Dream of a night vision (2 Nephi 27:3). A fleeting and unreal experience that is here for a moment and then gone, like a dream that seems so real while you are having it, but when you awaken it is gone. It seems unreal in hindsight, and it is mostly forgotten. "The Lord of hosts [will] visit the multitude of all the nations of the earth, that fight against Mount Zion, with thunder, and earthquake, and with the flame of devouring fire, and they shall be as the dream of a night vision, they shall pass away from the face of the earth and be as chaff blown to the four winds of heaven, and no place shall be found for them" (Pratt, in *Journal of Discourses*, 2:287). *Compare:* Isaiah 29:7.

Dreamed a dream (1 Nephi 3:2; 8:2). *See:* In a dream.

Drink out of the cup of the wrath of God (2 Nephi 8:22; Mosiah 5:5). Those that rebel against God and knowingly break the commandments will partake of the wrath of God and incur His displeasure.

Quite literally their punishment will be to drink out of the bitter cup themselves. Such people must quickly reverse their course, repent, and come unto God; otherwise their souls will become subject to Satan and experience the anguish of hell. *See also:* Cup of his fury (the wrath of God); Wrath of God (the Lord).

Drink the dregs of a bitter cup (2 Nephi 8:22; Alma 40:26). The dregs are the bitter sediment or residue in the bottom of the cup. The wicked who do not repent will have to suffer for their own sins and drink the bitter dregs. *See:* Psalm 75:8; D&C 19:15.

Drink(-eth) damnation to their souls (Mosiah 2:33; 3:18; 3 Nephi 18:29). Meaning to bring upon themselves damnation. Damnation of the soul is defined as being "stopped, blocked, or limited in one's progress. Individuals are damned whenever they are prevented from reaching their full potential as children of God" (*Encyclopedia of Mormonism*, 1:353). *See also:* Believeth not shall be damned; Damnation to the (of his/ to your own/upon their) soul(-s); Eateth and drinketh damnation to his soul.

Driven to and fro (upon the face of the earth) (2 Nephi 6:11; Mosiah 21:13; Helaman 15:12). God sometimes allows the wicked to be driven to and fro as a punishment and a reminder of their sinful behavior.

Driven to and fro includes being captive, burdened, smitten, and ravished. Sin also causes one to become captive to Satan, who drives one to and fro in a spiritual wasteland. *See also:* Chaff before the wind.

Dross which the refiners do cast out (Alma 34:29). Refers to that which has no worth and is fit only to be cast out into the dump. *See also:* 3 Nephi 24:2.

Drunk damnation to their own souls (Mosiah 3:25). *See:* Drink out of the cup of the wrath of God; Drink the dregs of a bitter cup.

Drunk out of the cup of the wrath of God (Mosiah 3:26). *See:* Drink out of the cup of the wrath of God; Drink the dregs of a bitter cup.

Drunken with iniquity (2 Nephi 27:1, 4). Just as alcohol dulls the senses of the physical body, in a like manner sin and iniquity dull the senses of the spiritual body, so that we respond with a lesser ability to things of the spirit and to anything which is good.

Drunken with their own blood (1 Nephi 21:26; 22:13; 2 Nephi 6:18). Meaning the bloodthirstiness of the wicked will be turned away from the Saints and will afflict the wicked themselves. Thus the wicked will become so caught up in killing that they will turn and kill among themselves and their own wicked forces.

Dust of the earth (Mosiah 2:25; 4:2; Helaman 12:7–8; Mormon 9:17). The first three of these verses proclaim that man is less than the dust of the earth for the reasons stated in each verse. The last verse proclaims that man was created from the dust of the earth. *See also:* D&C 77:12.

Duty to God (Mosiah 13:30; Alma 7:22; 43:46; Helaman 15:5). Every man and woman has a duty to God, meaning they owe God allegiance, gratitude, praise, service, and reverence. We owe this duty because everything we have has been given to us by Him. The only thing we can give in return is to conform our will to His will. This is our duty.

Dwell in the presence of God in his kingdom (1 Nephi 15:33, 35; 2 Nephi 2:8; Mormon 7:7). *See:* Dwell with God (him in glory).

Dwell with God (him in glory) (1 Nephi 10:21; Mosiah 2:41; 15:23; Alma 24:22; 28:12; 36:28; 3 Nephi 28:40; Mormon 9:4; Moroni 8:26). It should be our desire to dwell again with God. The whole purpose of the plan of salvation is to bring us back into the presence of God. "And if thou art faithful unto the end thou shalt have a crown of immortality, and eternal life in the

mansions which I have prepared in the house of my Father" (D&C 81:6).

Dwelleth eternally in the heavens (Moroni 7:28). *See:* Dwell with God (him in glory).

Dwellings shall become desolate (3 Nephi 10:7). *See:* Desolate places (dwellings/houses/lands/cities).

Dwindle(-d) in unbelief (1 Nephi 1:13; 12:22–23; 13:35; 15:13; 2 Nephi 1:10; 26:15, 17, 19; Mosiah 1:5; Alma 45:10, 12; 50:22; Helaman 6:34; 15:11, 15; 3 Nephi 21:5; 4 Nephi 1:34, 38; Mormon 9:20, 35; Ether 4:3). Our spiritual nature and faith must be nourished continually, otherwise we dwindle, regress, diminish, lessen, and waste away spiritually until we are no longer spiritual but have become carnal and devilish. "Thus saith the Lord God: I will give unto the children of men line upon line, precept upon precept, here a little and there a little; and blessed are those who hearken unto my precepts, and lend an ear unto my counsel, for they shall learn wisdom; for unto him that receiveth I will give more; and from them that shall say, We have enough, from them shall be taken away even that which they have" (2 Nephi 28:30).

E

Earth is his footstool (1 Nephi 17:39; 3 Nephi 12:35). A phrase declaring that God rules absolutely over the earth. This meaning is illustrated in Psalm 110:1, where the Lord says to David, "Sit thou at my right hand, until I make thine enemies thy footstool." The glory and might of God over His footstool is indicated in Abraham 2:7–8, "For I am the Lord thy God; I dwell in heaven; the earth is my footstool; I stretch my hand over the sea, and it obeys my voice; I cause the wind and the fire to be my chariot; I say to the mountains—Depart hence—and behold, they are taken away by a whirlwind, in an instant, suddenly. My name is Jehovah, and I know the end from the beginning; therefore my hand shall be over thee."

Earth shall be rolled together as a scroll (Mormon 5:23; 9:2). The transition of the mortal earth to the millennial earth is described in the Tenth Article of Faith: "The earth will be renewed and receive its paradisiacal glory" (Articles of Faith 1:10). The earth will be returned to its configuration when Adam dwelt thereon, before the separate continents were formed during the flood at Noah's time. Thus the continents will all be again rolled together in one landmass, and the oceans will be pushed to the north and the south (see D&C 133:22–24). The prophecy is that in the latter days the earth will be in commotion, or in other words the earth is preparing to be rolled together. The result is we see great earthquakes, volcanoes, and other natural phenomena.

Earth shall shake and tremble (1 Nephi 17:45; 2 Nephi 12:21; 24:16; Mosiah 27:11; Helaman 12:11; 14:21; Mormon 8:24; Ether 4:9). There shall be many earthquakes in the last days. *See also:* Shake the earth.

Earth shall (should) pass away (1 Nephi 17:46; Alma 9:2–3; 3 Nephi 26:3; Ether 13:8). God has decreed that the future of the earth will be a changed earth from what we know it to be now. During the Millennium it will be "renewed and receive its paradisiacal glory" (Articles of Faith 1:10), and after the final judgment the earth will be celestialized as a great transparent globe for celestial individuals to live on (see D&C 130:9).

Earth shook (Alma 14:27; Helaman 5:27, 31–32, 33). God can shake the earth, and His authorized servants who are invested with the priesthood power of God can shake the earth. *See also:* Shook the earth.

Easily beset (2 Nephi 4:18; Alma 7:15). Meaning the sins of the world that so readily—and seemingly without hindrance—overcome, plague, torment, and encompass us.

Easiness of the way (1 Nephi 17:41; Alma 37:46). *See:* Simpleness of the way.

East wind (Mosiah 7:31; 12:6). A scriptural phrase found often in the Old Testament and only twice in the Book of Mormon. To Jerusalem and the ancient tribes of Israel, the imagery of the east wind is a hot, dry wind from the deserts east of them. The east wind brought drought, famine, and pestilence. The Lord punishes wickedness by smiting the people and the land with an "east wind." *See also:* Famine(-s) and pestilence(-s).

Easy to be entreated (Alma 7:23; Helaman 7:7). The word *entreated* is defined as to persuade, appeal to, or invite. True saints are not only humble, meek, and patient, but also easy to be persuaded of God and invited to partake of the fruits of the gospel.

Eateth and drinketh damnation to his soul (Mosiah 2:33; 3 Nephi 18:29). Refers to those that partake of the sacrament unworthily. To do so is the height of hypocrisy before God. We are commanded to repent, prepare to come to church, and renew our covenants through the ordinance of the sacrament. Casual participation without forethought or preparation borders on this sin.

Elders of the church (Alma 4:16; Moroni 3:1). Meaning the General Authorities of the Church or the ruling brethren who have been called of God to oversee the whole Church.

Elements shall melt with fervent heat (3 Nephi 26:3; Mormon 9:2). In that great day when the Savior comes the second time, there shall be a great consuming fire such that the elements shall melt with fervent heat, the mountains shall be brought low and the valleys exalted, the earth shall be wrapped together as a scroll, all things shall become new, and the knowledge and glory of the Lord will dwell upon all the earth.

Encircle me around in the robe of thy righteousness (2 Nephi 4:33; 9:14). *See:* Robe of righteousness.

Encircle you about with his chains (Alma 12:6). *See:* Chains of hell.

Encircled about by the angels of him who hath sought to destroy our souls (Helaman 13:37). *See:* Chains of hell.

Encircled about by (with) the (everlasting) bands (chains) of death (Alma 5:7, 9; 36:18). *See:* Chains of hell.

Encircled about by the pains of hell (Alma 14:6). *See:* Chains of hell.

Encircled about (eternally) in (the arms of) his love (2 Nephi 1:15; Alma 26:15). *See:* Love of God.

Encircled about with everlasting darkness and destruction (Alma 26:15). The presence of Satan, the evil one, is darkness. In Joseph Smith's account of the First Vision, just before the Father and the Son appeared, Joseph experienced, "I had scarcely [begun to pray] when immediately I was seized upon by some power which entirely overcame me, and had such an astonishing influence over me as to bind my tongue so that I could not speak. *Thick darkness gathered around me,* and it seemed to me for a time as if I were doomed to sudden destruction" (Joseph Smith–History 1:15; emphasis added). Outer darkness is the destined non-kingdom of the devil and those who choose to follow him. The opposite of darkness is God's shining light. *See also:* Encircled about with fire.

Encircled about with fire (Helaman 5:23–24, 43–44; 3 Nephi 17:24; 19:14). In numerous places in the scriptures heavenly manifestations are described which include individuals encompassed about by fire that does not consume them. The very presence of God is as fire, and mortals must be changed or quickened to be able to endure God's presence (see Moses 1:11). *See also:* Consuming of my flesh.

End draweth nigh (Jacob 5:47, 62, 64; Alma 13:21). Meaning the end of mortal men's existence on earth. Then comes the Second Coming of Christ, the consuming of all the wicked by fire, and the beginning of the millennial reign of our Lord Jesus. Individually our life, which is our probationary period, draws nigh, and we will each die. *See also:* End is nigh at hand; End soon cometh.

End is nigh at hand (Jacob 5:71; Alma 9:25). Meaning the great day of the Lord is soon to come when Christ will come in the clouds in great glory, the righteous shall be caught up to meet Him, and the wicked shall burn. *See also:* At hand; End draweth nigh; D&C 29:9–11.

End of man (2 Nephi 2:15; 29:9). *See:* End draweth nigh; End of the world.

End of the world (1 Nephi 14:22; 2 Nephi 27:10; Mosiah 4:7). There will be an end of the mortal or telestial earth at the Lord's Second Coming. There will also be an end of the Millenium or terrestrial world when the one thousand years have passed. The earth will then be celestialized to become the eternal abode of those that receive eternal life and exaltation, forever without end.

End soon cometh (Jacob 5:29; 6:2). This has been and is the cry of the prophets throughout the history of the world. *See also:* At hand; End draweth nigh; End is nigh at hand.

Endless damnation (Mosiah 16:11). "In the Great Plan [of Salvation] there is no provision for the eternal damnation of man. At the best, men will be ranged according to their stage of progression—some higher, some lower. In a universe ruled by intelligent beings filled with love for one another, there can be no thought of an endless damnation only as men, by opposition to law, destroy themselves. Endless punishment and eternal punishment, terms often used, of little meaning to the human mind, mean simply God's punishment [see D&C 76:43–48], which is beyond our understanding. Those who refuse to accept truth, or to abide by law, will gradually take less and less part in the work of progression. They will be left behind, while their intelligent fellows, more obedient, will go on. In nature there is no standing still; those who do not advance will retrograde, become weaker and finally wither and be forgotten in their low estate" (Widtsoe, *Rational Theology*, 183). *See also:* Endless torment.

Endless happiness (Mosiah 16:11; Alma 41:4; Mormon 8:38). Meaning life in the kingdom of heaven, which is endless happiness because there is no more death, no more sickness, and no more temptation or evil. For would not that be happiness? *See also:* Eternal happiness; Happiness which hath no end; Never-ending happiness; State of (never-ending) happiness which hath no end.

Endless hell (Moroni 8:13). *See:* Endless torment; Endless damnation.

Endless life (Mosiah 16:9, 11). Meaning immortal life forever and never to die or be sick. *See also:* Immortal body.

Endless misery (and wo) (Alma 9:11; 28:11; 41:4; Helaman 5:12; 7:16; 12:26; Mormon 8:38). *See:* Endless damnation; Endless torment; Pains of hell; Weeping and wailing and gnashing of teeth.

Endless night of darkness (Alma 41:7). *See:* Endless misery (and wo).

Endless sleep (Mormon 9:13). Refers to a hypothetical endless death in the grave, which would have been the case without the Resurrection of Jesus Christ, our Savior, which makes it sure that we will all be resurrected to immortality. *See also:* Immortal body.

Endless state (Alma 12:24). That time is after the resurrection of the dead when we will live forever without death as immortal beings in that place prepared by God according to our faithfulness and works.

Endless torment (2 Nephi 9:19, 26; 28:23; Jacob 6:10; Mosiah 3:25; 28:3; Moroni 8:21). If one's works are evil, and he does not repent, then "they are consigned to an awful view of their own guilt and abominations, which doth cause them to shrink from the presence of the Lord into a state of misery and endless torment, from whence they can no more return; therefore they have drunk damnation to their own souls" (Mosiah 3:25). *See also:* Endless damnation; Endless misery (and wo).

Ends of the atonement (2 Nephi 2:10). Meaning the results, the safety, the purposes, and the promises of the Atonement.

Ends of the earth (1 Nephi 21:6; 2 Nephi 24:2; 26:25; 29:2; 33:10, 13; Mosiah 12:24; 15:31; Alma 5:50; 29:7; 3 Nephi 9:22; 11:41; 16:20; 20:35; 27:20; Mormon 3:18, 22; 9:21, 25; Ether 3:25, 4:18; Moroni 7:34; 10:24). Meaning all the earth, including the farthest parts of the earth. *See also:* All ye ends of the earth.

Ends of the law (2 Nephi 2:7, 10; Moroni 7:28). Meaning the results or consequences of the law, the purpose of the law, the safety of the law, the promises of the law, the blessings of the law, and the course and way of the law. Each of these phrases fit in place of "the ends of the law" and help to explain what the scripture means. *See also:* Consequences of sin.

Endure(-th) to the end (1 Nephi 13:37; 22:31; 2 Nephi 9:24; 31:15–16, 20; 32:13, 15; 33:4; 38:2; Omni 1:26; Alma 32:13, 15; 38:2; 3 Nephi 15:9; 27:6, 16; 27:17; Mormon 9:29; Moroni 8:26). All those who continue faithfully until the end of the physical life that God appoints unto them are promised to be saved unto eternal life. To continue faithfully means to keep the commandments, love God and neighbor, serve and lift fellowmen, and build the Kingdom of God. Enduring to the end includes: remaining faithful, keeping faith in God, patiently putting up with, never giving up, continuing until the goal is obtained, choosing the right consistently, doing good always, living life well, and seeking to be just and true with integrity. *See also:* All the remainder of our days.

Endurance of faith on his name to the end (Moroni 3:3; 8:3). *See:* Endure(-th) to the end.

Endured the crosses of the world (2 Nephi 9:18). *See:* Take up your cross.

Endureth all things (Mosiah 3:19; Alma 7:23; 38:10; 3 Nephi 11:11; Moroni 7:45). We are commanded to endure to the end of our mortal lives. We must endure *all things* that God allows to afflict us. This is possible for us to do because God will not allow afflictions and trials greater than we can individually bear (see 1 Corinthians 10:13). *See also:* Endure(-th) to the end.

Endureth forever (Moroni 7:47). In this context it refers to charity that endureth forever or that charity is an eternal principle that is the same yesterday, today, and forever. Also in each of us charity should remain and continue always and forever.

Enemy of (to) all righteousness (Mosiah 2:37; 4:14; Alma 34:23; Moroni 9:6). Satan the devil is the enemy of all righteousness. Righteousness is not in Satan's nature. *See also:* Enemy of (to/unto) God.

Enemy of (to/unto) God (Mosiah 2:38; 3:19; 16:5; 27:9; Moroni 7:12). The devil or Satan is the enemy of God and has been since he rebelled in the premortal life. 2 Nephi 2:17 says, "He [Satan] became a devil, having sought that which was evil before God." Those that become followers of Satan are his minions, and they also become enemies to God, because they likewise rebel and seek to do evil. They have chosen darkness rather than light, eternal death rather than eternal life. James 4:4 says, "Whosoever therefore will be a friend of the world is the enemy of God." In other words, the carnal man is an enemy to God. *See also:* Devil is an enemy unto God; Rebel(-led/-ling/-lion) against God.

Enemy listeth to carry them (Alma 26:6). Meaning wherever the enemy, Satan, chooses or desires to take them captive. This is the fate of the unrepentant sinner. However, the faithful will be protected from this fate. *See also:* Captive by (captivity/captivation of/the will of) the devil; Led away by the evil one; Taken captive by the devil.

Energy of heart (Moroni 7:48). Meaning putting your whole heart into the effort and dedicating yourself to the cause. *See also:* Energy of my soul.

Energy of my soul (1 Nephi 16:24; Alma 5:43). Meaning to put forth a very great effort. *See also:* Energy of heart.

Enlarge my soul (Alma 32:28). Meaning growth and progression of the soul because of enlightened understanding, increased spirituality, strengthened faith, and greater gratitude towards God.

Enlighten my understanding (Alma 32:28, 34). It is the Spirit of God that brings understanding to us. In D&C 11:11, 13, the Lord says, "I am the light which shineth in darkness, and by my power I give these words unto thee. . . . I will impart unto you of my Spirit, which shall enlighten your mind." *See also:* 2 Nephi 21:2.

Enlightened by the Spirit (Alma 24:30). *See:* Enlighten my understanding.

Ensign to the nations (people)
(2 Nephi 15:26; 21:10, 12). Meaning the restored church and the missionary work to teach the gospel as a light and a standard to the entire world. Shortly after arriving in the Salt Lake Valley in 1847, Brigham Young, Wilford Woodruff, and others hiked to the top of the dome-shaped peak north of the valley. "The summit where they stood was named Ensign Peak out of reference to these great prophetic words of Isaiah: 'And he [speaking of God] will lift up an ensign to the nations from far, and will hiss unto them from the end of the earth: and, behold, they shall come with speed swiftly.' (Isa. 5:26.)

"'And he shall set up an ensign for the nations, and shall assemble the outcasts of Israel, and gather together the dispersed of Judah from the four corners of the earth.' (Isaiah 11:12.)

"There is some evidence to indicate that Wilford Woodruff took from his pocket a bandanna handkerchief and waved it as an ensign or a standard to the nations, that from this place should go the word of the Lord, and to this place should come the people of the earth" (Hinckley, "An Ensign to the Nations," 51–52).

"Ever since the Salt Lake Temple was dedicated, we have interpreted that scripture from Isaiah, repeated again in Micah (see Micah 4:1–2), as applying to this sacred house of the Lord. And of this place, since the day of its dedication, an ever-increasing number from across the world have said in effect, 'Come ye, and let us go up to the mountain of the Lord, to the house of the God of Jacob, that He might teach us of His ways, that we might walk in His paths.'

"I believe and testify that it is the mission of this Church to stand as an ensign to the nations and a light to the world" (Hinckley, "An Ensign to the Nations, a Light to the World," 82).

"Centuries before and at the time The Church of Jesus Christ of Latter-day Saints was organized it was prophesied that it would become a world church and that the gospel would be preached to all people. Isaiah prophesied in these words: 'And it shall come to pass in that day, that the Lord shall set his hand again the second time to recover the remnant of his people.' . . . 'And he shall set up an ensign [the Church] for the nations' (Isa. 11:11–12)" (Tanner, "Christ's Worldwide Church," 2). *See also:* Set up my standard to the people.

Ensnare the hearts of men (Alma 28:13). Meaning Satan and his minions trap and bind down the hearts and souls of men and women when they sin. *See also:* Satan did get hold (possession) upon the hearts of the people.

Enter in (into/by) the (narrow/strait) gate (way/path) (1 Nephi 8:20; 2 Nephi 9:41; 31:18–19; 32:1, 5; 33:9; Jacob 6:11; 3 Nephi 14:13,

14; 27:33). *See:* Gate by which ye should enter; Strait and narrow course (path).

Enter into a covenant (Mosiah 5:5; Alma 7:15; 46:20, 35; 62:16; 3 Nephi 5:4–5; 6:28, 29). Meaning to become a party to a contract, promise, or oath. Unto such a covenant our word should be our bond. The covenant can be with other men or with God. A covenant with God is a particularly serious promise. *See also:* Covenant(-ing) with God (him); Made an oath unto us.

Enter into his (my/the) rest (of the Lord/of God) (Jacob 1:7; Alma 12:34–37; 13:6, 12–13, 16, 29; 16:17; 57:36; 60:13; 3 Nephi 27:19; Moroni 7:3). Often we harbor great concern, we experience anxiety, we worry and have apprehensions about matters most unsettling to the human mind and body. To wish for and seek rest from these matters is common. Peace and rest from worldly and other cares is a gift from God—a gift given to the Saints at times in this life and promised in the next life. The gospel of Jesus Christ teaches us that the faithful and righteous will find peace and rest with our Redeemer when we die. We will experience rest from earthly cares and a peace that is sublime. *See also:* Find rest (to their souls); In him I shall rest; Know that in him I shall rest; My soul did rest; Place of my rest; Rest from all afflictions (care/sorrow/troubles); Rest in paradise; Rest of the Lord (their God); Rest to

their souls; State of rest and peace; Ye shall find rest.

Enter [not] into temptation (Alma 31:10; 3 Nephi 18:18). *See:* Yield to no temptation.

Entered into a covenant of peace (Alma 43:11; 44:15, 20; 46:31, 35; 53:15–16; 62:17; 3 Nephi 6:3). We read how the Nephites allowed the Lamanite prisoners of war to go free if they made a covenant of peace after they had been captured. In today's world that seems foreign to us because we do not trust the word or promise of enemies or even neighbors. But in the Book of Mormon times, an oath or covenant was honored and adhered to. *See also:* Made an oath unto us.

Entered into a covenant with God (Mosiah 5:8; 6:1–2; 18:10, 13; 21:31, 32; Alma 7:15). *See:* Covenant(-ing) with God (him).

Enticeth to do good (2 Nephi 2:16; Moroni 7:13). God, holy angels, prophets, and saints invite men to do that which is good continually. This is the example of Jesus unto us. *See also:* Do good.

Enticeth to sin (2 Nephi 2:16; 9:39; Helaman 6:26; 7:16; Moroni 7:12). The devil invites men only to sin. It is not in the nature of Satan to do otherwise. *See also:* Yield to no temptation.

Enticings of the Holy Spirit (Mosiah 3:19). *See:* Enticeth to do good; All things what ye should do.

Envyings and strifes (2 Nephi 26:21; Alma 16:18; 3 Nephi 21:19; 30:2). Meaning clashes, discord, ill will, jealousy, quarrels, malice, and rivalry. Satan is the author of these bad behaviors. *See also:* Spirit of contention.

Equal chance (grounds) (Mosiah 29:38; Alma 30:11). Meaning equal and alike before the law.

Equity and justice in my hands (Alma 10:21). God's judgment is fair and just. None can call God's justice incorrect. His judgment is perfect and pure. *See also:* Judgments are just.

Errand from the Lord (Jacob 1:17). *See:* Called of God (the Holy Spirit).

Erred in spirit (2 Nephi 27:35). Gone astray by teaching incorrect and corrupted doctrines.

Establish church (Mosiah 25:19; 26:17; 27:13; Alma 1:6, 28; 4:4; 5:2–3, 5; 6:1, 4, 8; 8:1, 11; 15:13, 17; 16:15, 21; 19:35; 20:1; 21:22; 23:4; 28:1; 29:11, 13; 45:22; 62:46; Helaman 6:3; 3 Nephi 5:12; 21:22). The Lord said in D&C 10:53, 55: "If this generation harden not their hearts, I will establish my church among them. . . . Therefore, whosoever belongeth to my church need not fear, for such shall inherit the kingdom of heaven." And in D&C 10:69, "And now behold, whosoever is of my church, and endureth of my church [endureth in perseverance] to the end, him will I establish upon my rock, and the gates of hell shall not prevail against them."

Establish his (my/the) word(-s) (1 Nephi 13:41; 2 Nephi 11:3; 27:14; Alma 12:1; 17:11; 29:13). Meaning to preach, teach, and testify of the word of God. *See also:* Doctrine of Christ; Word of God; Word of the Lord.

Established in one (1 Nephi 13:41). Declared and verified as one true doctrine. *See also:* Gathered in one.

Esteem his neighbor as himself (Mosiah 27:4; 29:5; Alma 1:26). The Lord said, "Let every man esteem his brother as himself" (D&C 38:24). Also, "Love thy neighbor as thyself" (D&C 59:6). The golden rule is to do unto others as you would have them do unto you.

Esteem it as of great worth (1 Nephi 19:7; 2 Nephi 33:3; Alma 50:38). Meaning to honor, respect, reverence, treasure, and value words, records, and things of God.

Esteem them as (things of) naught (1 Nephi 19:7; 2 Nephi 33:2). Meaning to consider the things of God as having no value. *See also:* Thing of naught.

Esteemed by their brethren as dross (Alma 32:3). Dross means having no worth and fit only to be cast out. Thus the proud look down on their brethren, falsely judging them as worthless individuals, and individuals they do not want to associate with.

Esteemed him as naught (afflicted) (Mosiah 14:3–4; Ether 13:13). Speaking of how many will despise and reject Christ and His prophets.

Esteemed him highly (as great) (2 Nephi 3:7; Mosiah 29:40; Helaman 11:18). The people thought highly of him.

Esteemeth all flesh in one (1 Nephi 17:35; Mosiah 23:7). God is no respecter of persons or people. "All men are privileged the one like unto the other, and none are forbidden" (2 Nephi 26:28). "He inviteth them all to come unto him and partake of his goodness; and he denieth none that come unto him, black and white, bond and free, male and female; and he remembereth the heathen; and all are alike unto God, both Jew and Gentile" (2 Nephi 26:33). *See also:* All are alike unto God.

Eternal as the life of the soul (Alma 42:16). Our intelligence and spirit existed before mortality and our soul (spirit and resurrected body) will exist into all eternity hereafter.

Eternal band of death (Mormon 9:13). The bands of temporal death would have been eternal or forever had not Christ loosed the bands of death. *See also:* Bands of death.

Eternal death (2 Nephi 2:29). Speaking here of spiritual death and becoming captive to Satan, which would have been eternal or forever had not Christ provided a way to escape this death. *See also:* Everlasting death.

Eternal despair (Alma 26:19). *See:* Eternal torment.

Eternal destruction of both soul and body (1 Nephi 14:7; 2 Nephi 1:22). *See:* Eternal band of death; Eternal death.

Eternal Father (1 Nephi 11:21; 13:40; Mosiah 16:15; Alma 11:38; Moroni 4:3; 5:2; 10:4, 31). The name that describes in some contexts God the Father and in others Jesus Christ. Refer to these references to see examples of both. *See also:* Eternal Father of heaven and of earth.

Eternal Father of heaven and of earth (Mosiah 15:4; Alma 11:39; Mormon 6:22). A name for Jesus Christ, who is the Father of heaven and earth because He is the creator of both, and everything that in them are.

Eternal God (1 Nephi 12:18; 2 Nephi 9:8; 26:12; Alma 11:44; 34:9; Ether 8:23). Our majestic and almighty God is not only all powerful, all knowing, and all present by His Spirit, He is also endless, ceaseless, everlasting, infinite, and neverending. Thus we can have complete and absolute faith in and reliance on Him. This description applies to both God the Father and His Son, Jesus Christ.

Eternal gulf of misery and woe (2 Nephi 1:13; Alma 26:20; Helaman 3:29; 5:12). Meaning hell. *See also:* Eternal torment; Hell fire.

Eternal happiness (Alma 3:26). *See:* Endless happiness; Plan of happiness.

Eternal Head (Helaman 13:38). Jesus Christ is our head. He is the head of the gospel, the head of His church, the head of the priesthood, and the head or author of our redemption.

Eternal Judge (Moroni 10:34). Jesus Christ is the Eternal Judge, for in John 5:22–23 we learn, "For the Father judgeth no man, but hath committed all judgment unto the Son: That all men should honour the Son, even as they honour the Father."

Eternal kingdom of God (2 Nephi 10:25). *See:* Kingdom of God; Kingdom of heaven.

Eternal life (2 Nephi 2:27–28; 10:23; 31:18, 20; Jacob 6:11; Enos 1:3; Mosiah 5:15; 15:23–24, 25; 18:9, 13; 26:20; 28:7; Alma 1:4; 5:28; 7:16; 11:40; 13:29; 22:15; Helaman 5:8; 3 Nephi 9:14; 15:9; Moroni 9:25). Eternal life or life eternal is the scriptural phrase used to denote the highest degree of life hereafter. In short it is life in the eternities to come like unto God's life. Eternal life (also called eternal lives) means more than life eternally or immortality. The Resurrection

and immortality are free gifts from God to all who come to earth (Alma 11:42–45). Eternal life is more than just immortality; it is exaltation in the highest degree of the celestial kingdom. It is synonymous with the terms eternal increase and the continuation of seeds forever and ever as promised to Abraham and his faithful posterity. In the words of President Spencer W. Kimball, "Immortality is to live forever in an assigned kingdom. Eternal life is to gain exaltation in the highest heaven and live in the family unit" ("An Eternal Hope in Christ," 72). *See also:* Life eternal; Moses 1:38; D&C 29:43; 132:24; 138:51.

Eternal misery (Alma 3:26). *See:* Endless misery (and wo); Endless torment; Eternal torment.

Eternal plan of deliverance (2 Nephi 11:5). Meaning deliverance from physical and spiritual death. Christ is the great deliverer. *See also:* Great and eternal plan of deliverance from death (of redemption); Plan of salvation.

Eternal punishment (Jacob 7:18; Alma 42:16). Punishment is an eternal component that has ever been and will ever be, for the purpose of justly providing consequences for sin. God desires that we avoid the consequences of sin and has provided a means for our escape of consequences if we sincerely seek repentance. *See also:* Endless misery (and wo); Endless torment; Eternal torment.

Eternal purposes (of the Lord) (2 Nephi 2:12, 15; Alma 37:7; 42:26; Mormon 5:14; 8:22). *See: Great and eternal purpose(-s).*

Eternal round (1 Nephi 10:19; Alma 7:20; 37:12). *See:* Course is one eternal round.

Eternal salvation (Alma 25:16). *See:* Life eternal.

Eternal torment (Mosiah 27:29; Alma 36:12). Refers to the anguish of soul experienced by the wicked. Eternal because it has always existed and will always exist as the punishment of the wicked. Alma the Younger experienced this torment *for a time* after the angel of God reprimanded him. During that time Alma was harrowed up by the memory of his many sins. *See also:* Endless misery (and wo); Endless torment.

Eternal word (2 Nephi 9:16). Meaning God's word, which will always stand and will never be forgotten or changed. *See also:* According to God's word.

Eternal world (Alma 3:26; 34:34; 48:23). The worlds, kingdoms, and life before and after mortality.

Everlasting burning (Mosiah 27:28). *See:* Hell fire.

Everlasting chains (2 Nephi 28:19; Alma 36:18). *See:* Chains of hell.

Everlasting damnation (Mosiah 2:33; Helaman 12:26; 3 Nephi 26:5). *See:* Everlasting death.

Everlasting darkness (Alma 26:15). To be cut off or cast out from the light of God. *See:* Everlasting death.

Everlasting death (2 Nephi 10:23, 25; Alma 12:32). To be eternally cut off from the presence of God. This is the second death or spiritual death. It is the opposite of eternal life. *See also:* Spiritual death.

Everlasting decree of God (Ether 2:10). The words of God shall never pass away, but shall all be fulfilled and shall come to pass. *See also:* According to God's word.

Everlasting destruction (Alma 5:7; 12:6, 17, 36; 26:15; 27:4; Helaman 6:40; 8:26; 3 Nephi 4:33; Ether 14:25). *See:* Everlasting death.

Everlasting farewell (2 Nephi 33:14). A separation forever, after the final judgment, of the faithful saints of God from those that reject the Savior Jesus Christ and His redemption.

Everlasting fire (prepared for the devil and his angels) (2 Nephi 9:16; Mosiah 26:27). *See:* Hell fire.

Everlasting God (1 Nephi 11:32; 15:15; 2 Nephi 4:35; Helaman 12:8; Moroni 10:28). *See:* Eternal God.

Everlasting gulf (of death and) of misery (2 Nephi 1:13; Alma 26:20; Helaman 3:29; 5:12). Meaning hell. *See:* Hell fire.

Everlasting hatred against sin and iniquity (Alma 37:32). Meaning to abhor sin now and forever. *See also:* Abhor sin (such wickedness).

Everlasting hell (Helaman 6:28). *See:* Endless misery (and wo); Endless torment; Eternal torment; Hell fire.

Everlasting kingdom of the Lamb (1 Nephi 13:37). *See:* Kingdom of heaven.

Everlasting life (Alma 19:6; 32:41; 33:23; Helaman 12:26; 14:8; 3 Nephi 5:13; 26:5). *See:* Eternal life; Life eternal.

Everlasting light (Alma 26:15). Jesus Christ is our everlasting light, and all light and life radiate from Him. *See also:* Marvelous light of God.

Everlasting misery (Helaman 7:16). *See:* Endless misery (and wo); Endless torment; Eternal torment.

Everlasting power (Alma 36:29). God's omnipotent power, which is the same yesterday, today, and forever. *See also:* Power of Christ (the Lamb of God/the Lord); Power of God.

Everlasting punishment (Mosiah 2:33; 27:31). *See:* Endless misery (and wo); Endless torment; Eternal torment; Hell fire.

Everlasting salvation (Mosiah 5:15; Alma 26:15). *See:* Eternal life; Life eternal.

Everlasting shame (Alma 12:15). Unrepentant sin is the shame and remorse that never ends. *See also:* Not be ashamed.

Everlasting to everlasting (Moroni 7:22). Meaning forever and forever; the same yesterday, today, and forever; without beginning of days or end of years. *See also:* Course is one eternal round; I am the same yesterday, today and forever.

Everlasting word (Alma 5:7). *See:* According to God's word; Eternal word.

Everlastingly too late (Helaman 13:38). Now is the time, meaning during mortality is the day of our probation. We must not put off repenting and coming unto Christ. *See also:* Day of grace was passed; Day of probation; Day of your salvation; Now is the time to repent, for the day of salvation draweth nigh; Procrastinate [not] the day of your repentance; Procrastinated the day of your salvation; Wasteth the days of his probation.

Every form of godliness (Moroni 7:30). To strive with all our might to become like our Heavenly Father and Jesus in their godly characteristics. "Add to your faith virtue; and to virtue knowledge; and to knowledge temperance; and to temperance patience; and to patience godliness" (2 Peter 1:5–6).

Every good gift (Moroni 7:10; 10:18, 30). "Every good gift and every perfect gift is from above, and cometh down from the Father of lights, with whom is no variableness, neither shadow of turning" (James 1:17). *See also:* All things which are good cometh of God; Gifts of God; Good gift.

Every knee shall bow (Mosiah 27:31). The Lord God hath spoken it, so it will assuredly be that every person will bow their knee before the Lord and be judged of their life in mortality. *See also:* D&C 88:104.

Every nation, kindred, tongue, and (or) people (1 Nephi 19:17; 2 Nephi 26:13; Mosiah 3:13, 20; 15:28; 16:1; Alma 9:20; 37:4; 45:16). Meaning everyone without exception, no one excluded.

Every tongue confess (Mosiah 27:31). "For it is written, As I live, saith the Lord, every knee shall bow to me, and every tongue shall confess to God. So then every one of us shall give account of himself to God" (Romans 14:11–12).

Every whit (1 Nephi 4:19; Alma 34:14; 3 Nephi 1:20, 25; 8:1; Ether 15:3). *Whit* is defined as a small part or minutest bit of something. Thus "every whit" means including absolutely every part of something, no matter the size or significance.

Every word (which proceeded forth out of the mouth of God) (1 Nephi 17:35; Alma 57:21; Moroni 7:25). "And Jesus answered him, saying, It is written, That man shall not live by bread alone, but by every word of God" (Luke 4:4).

Evil cometh of the devil (Omni 1:25; Alma 5:40; Moroni 7:12). It is not in the nature of Satan to do good. Does a bitter fountain bring forth good water? The answer is an emphatic no. Satan is the father of all lies and continually stirreth men up to do iniquity.

Evil doings (Mosiah 11:29; 12:1; 3 Nephi 30:2; Mormon 2:8). *See:* All manner of abominations (iniquity); Doings of abominations.

Evil one (2 Nephi 4:27; 9:28; Alma 46:8; Helaman 8:28; 12:4; 16:21; Mormon 1:19). Meaning Satan or the devil, the father of all lies and evil thoughts, he whose only purpose is to promote evil, fight against God, and enslave mankind.

Evil spirit (2 Nephi 32:8; Mosiah 2:32, 37; 4:14). Satan is the evil spirit. *See also:* Evil one.

Evil works (Mosiah 3:24; 16:10; Alma 5:41; 9:28; 11:44; 12:32; 13:3; 40:13, 26; 41:4; 3 Nephi 26:4; 27:14; Mormon 3:20). The works, activities, and purposes of Satan and his followers, including the deeds and acts of those who do not keep the commandments, who rebel against God, and who follow the temptations of the devil. *See also:* Evil doings.

Example of our Savior (the Son) (2 Nephi 31:9, 16; 3 Nephi 18:16; Mormon 7:10). Jesus Christ is our exemplar in all things. From these verses it is abundantly clear that we are to look to His example and do likewise. In numerous places in the four gospels, Jesus admonished the people to "follow me." "My sheep hear my voice, and I know them, and they follow me" (John 10:27).

Exceeding faith (2 Nephi 3:24; Jacob 3:1; Mosiah 4:3; 26:15–16; Alma 13:3, 10; 19:10; 57:26; 60:26; Ether 3:9). There appears to be, and it has been seen, that there are degrees of faith—from no faith through weak faith up to strong and exceeding faith. *See also:* According to his (my/our/the/their/thy/your) faith.

Exceedingly great faith (Alma 13:3; Ether 12:19; Moroni 10:11). *See:* Exceeding faith.

Exceeding(-ly) great joy (1 Nephi 8:12; Mosiah 3:13; 4:11, 20; 5:4; 21:24; 25:8; Alma 7:4; 17:2; 27:18; 36:20, 24–25; 45:1; 57:36; 62:1; Helaman 3:32; 3 Nephi 12:12). In this mortal world we are meant to understand opposites: good and bad; pleasure and pain; health and sickness; happiness and sadness; joy and misery. Thus we are glad when we experience earthly happiness. On a higher plain we are sometimes blessed to experience immense joy that is borne by the Spirit when we sense spiritual things. Closely related is the peerless joy that comes from envelopment in God's love. "Be faithful and diligent in keeping the commandments of God, and I will encircle thee in the arms of my love" (D&C 6:20).

Exceedingly humble (Alma 62:49; 3 Nephi 6:13). Extremely and genuinely humble before God. *See also:* Humble themselves (yourselves) before God (the Lord).

Exceedingly sorrowful (1 Nephi 3:14; 16:20; 17:19; Alma 19:28; 20:29; 31:2, 31; 35:15; 59:11; 62:27; Helaman 6:20; 3 Nephi 1:10; 3:26; Ether 8:7). Two words used together curiously only in the Book of Mormon and not found in the other standard works. The sins and wrongs of this world bring sorrow. *Contrast:* Exceeding(-ly) great joy.

Execute judgment (in righteousness) (1 Nephi 22:21; 3 Nephi 29:9; Ether 7:1, 11, 24, 27; 9:21; 11:20). The first two references are about the Lord Jesus Christ, who shall perform judgment, being a perfect being without error in His judgment. The references in Ether are concerning kings who attempted and appear to have succeeded in performing their kingly ruling duties in all fairness and exactness. *See also:* Judgment of God.

Execute vengeance (Mosiah 17:19; 3 Nephi 21:21). Punishments are promised to those who disobey and sin. *See also:* Execute judgment (in righteousness); Sword of vengeance.

Executeth all his words (2 Nephi 9:17). All that God says will come to pass will in fact come to pass. *See also:* According to God's word.

Except they should have charity they were nothing (cannot inherit the kingdom of God) (2 Nephi 26:30; Ether 12:34; Moroni 10:21). "Charity is the pure love of Christ" (Moroni 7:47). We must strive to possess charity, for as we do, God will grant us and bestow upon us greater and perhaps even perfect charity.

Except ye repent (Jacob 3:3–4; Alma 5:51; 8:29; 9:12, 15; 10:23; 39:8; 54:6–7; 60:24; Helaman 7:28; 8:12, 26; 10:11, 14; 13:10; 15:2, 14; 3 Nephi 3:15). Humble repentance is absolutely necessary to salvation. Without repentance and baptism, the other ordinances of salvation and good works are null and hypocritical. No man or woman is without the need of repentance, though the degree of repentance may vary, some needing sore and mighty repentance. Depending on the sin, repentance may take a few days, whereas other sins may take years to repent from. The command of God is to repent and come unto Him, and so we must.

Exercise faith (1 Nephi 7:12; Alma 5:15; 32:27; 33:1; 34:17; 37:41; Ether 4:7; Moroni 7:25). When one exercises their physical muscles, the muscles of their body grow stronger. It is the same with faith. As we show forth faith in God and His ways by keeping God's commandments, our faith grows stronger. Exercising faith in Christ unto the end brings salvation unto man.

Exercise power over them (Mosiah 27:9; Alma 12:5; 4 Nephi 1:30). *See:* Captive by (captivity/captivation of/ the will of) the devil; Power of the devil (evil one).

Exercise the power of God (Alma 8:31; 14:10). Men invested with the priesthood, which is the true power of God, can perform many miracles and do anything according to the will of God. Every priesthood holder by faith and worthiness can exercise the power of God. Some extraordinary servants of God receive the promise given to Nephi in Helaman 10:5, "I will make thee mighty in word and in deed, in faith and in words; yea, even that all things shall be done unto thee according to thy word, for thou shall not ask that which is contrary to my will." *See also:* Power of God.

Exercise their faith (and diligence) (1 Nephi 7:12; Alma 5:15; 32:27; 33:1; 34:17; 37:41; Ether 4:7; Moroni 7:25). Faith is manifest or shown by repenting, accepting the ordinances, keeping the commandments, and serving our fellow man. Diligence means the application of the word of God with zeal. This describes how we must develop and use our faith for the glory of God.

Exhausting of his strength (Alma 27:17, 19). *See:* Fell to (unto) the earth (as if he were dead); Overcome with the Spirit.

Exhort them (you) (1 Nephi 7:21; 8:37; 15:25; 16:4; 17:15; 2 Nephi 6:3; Mosiah 23:27; 25:16; Alma 21:23; 34:3, 39–40; Helaman 6:4; Moroni 6:9; 10:3–4, 7–8, 18–9, 27, 30). To *exhort* is to encourage, admonish, urge, caution or warn, and to advise strongly. One of the greatest gospel talents is to be able to motivate our brothers and sisters to live the gospel of Jesus Christ. It is our duty to warn our neighbor and assist in bringing them unto Christ.

Exhorting them (the people) (1 Nephi 10:2; Jarom 1:11; Omni 1:25; Mosiah 27:33; Ether 12:3). *See:* Exhort them (you).

Exhorting with all long suffering (Jarom 1:11). *See:* Exhort them (you).

Expedient for (in/unto) me (1 Nephi 10:15; 2 Nephi 9:48; Moroni 7:33; 10:23). *Expedient* means that which is important, necessary, and advisable.

Expound all (these) things (Alma 12:9; 21:10; 22:14; 3 Nephi 26:1, 3). Meaning to explain, interpret, describe, and clarify the things of God.

Expound unto him (them) the scriptures (Alma 18:38; 22:13). Meaning to explain and lay open the scriptures to one's understanding.

Expounded all the scriptures in one (3 Nephi 23:6, 14). Jesus expounded, meaning explained, all the scriptures in one by demonstrating how all the scriptures bear a united witness of Him.

Extending the arm of mercy towards them (Jacob 6:5; Mosiah 1:14; 16:12; 29:20; Alma 5:33; 19:36; 29:10; 3 Nephi 9:14). *See:* Arm (of mercy) is extended (towards you in the light of day).

Eye for an eye (3 Nephi 12:38). Under the law of ancient Israel, a person who wronged another was to receive the same harm, as penalty, as the harm he did to another. These laws were given as a guide to the judges under the Law of Moses (see Leviticus 24:17–22). Jesus, however, taught a new and higher law, which requires us to turn the other cheek and give also our cloak. *Compare:* Matthew 5:38–41.

Eye hath not seen (3 Nephi 17:16). *Compare:* 1 Corinthians 2:9; D&C 76:10. *See:* Unspeakable things.

Eye of faith (Alma 5:15; 32:40; Ether 12:19). Faith is things hoped for but not seen. However, when faith is exceedingly strong, the confidence of things is as near real and so vividly visualized in faith that they are known and fathomed with the eye of faith but not the physical eye. To see with the eye of faith is a gift of God.

Eye single to his glory (3 Nephi 13:22; Mormon 8:15). To banish earthly and carnal desires from ourselves and replace them instead with the purposes and will of God.

Eye to eye (Mosiah 12:22; 15:29; Mosiah 16:1; Alma 36:26; 3 Nephi 16:18; 20:32). Meaning shall be as He is. In other contexts this means to have seen and been in the company or presence of. In still other contexts this means men will begin to see eye to eye without enmity and hate towards one another. Additionally they will not contend as to doctrine. Has a similar meaning to "face to face." *See also:* Face to face; Shall see eye to eye.

F

Face of the earth (1 Nephi 1:11; 10:12–13; 12:4–5; 13:39; 14:12–14; 22:3, 18; Jacob 4:9; Mosiah 7:27; 12:8; 13:34; 27:6; 28:17; Alma 5:16, 17; 7:9; 9:11–12, 24; 13:22; 16:11; 28:11; 29:2; 30:44; 37:22, 25; 42:6; 54:12; Helaman 3:8, 16; 6:20; 7:28; 11:13; 14:21–22, 27; 15:12; 3 Nephi 1:17; 5:24; 8:12, 17–19; 9:1; 10:9; 16:4; 19:6; 20:13; 26:3; 28:16; Mormon 3:15; 6:15; 8:31; Ether 1:33, 43; 6:13, 18; 9:30, 35; 11:6–7, 12; 13:17; Moroni 7:36). Meaning on the surface of the earth; also meaning here on this earth, not in heaven or otherwise, and sometimes inferring on all or over all the earth.

Face shone with exceeding luster (Mosiah 13:5; Helaman 5:36). When the Spirit rests upon one in great abundance or when one is in the presence of heavenly beings, the shining brightness of heaven sometimes transfers to their countenance, and they themselves radiate a bright radiance. Another example is when Moses came down from speaking to the Lord on the mount, his face shone so that the people were afraid to come near him (see Exodus 34:29–35). *See also:* Light of the glory of God.

Face to face (2 Nephi 33:11; Alma 38:7; Ether 12:39). To be in the very presence of, to talk as one man does to another, to see the face of. Also to agree and to see things as the same, particularly eternal things. Enos said, "I rejoice in the day when my mortal shall put on immortality, and shall stand before him [Jesus the Redeemer]; then shall I see his face with pleasure" (Enos 1:27). *See also:* Moses 1:1, 31; 7:4; Abraham 3:11.

Fair and delightsome people (2 Nephi 5:21; 4 Nephi 1:10). *See:* Delightsome people.

Fair daughters of this people (Jacob 2:32; Mosiah 19:13; 3 Nephi 2:16; 8:25; 9:2; Mormon 6:19; Ether 7:4; 13:17). The fair daughters represent the bud and blossom of a people. They represent the pure, the clean, the honorable, virtuous and principled, even the promise of the future. "O ye fair ones" in the Book of Mormon represents a lament of what the fathers, mothers, sons, and daughters could have been, but they set aside righteousness and were no longer fair and delightsome. *See also:* Delightsome people.

Faith and repentance (Alma 12:30; 13:10; 22:14; Helaman 6:4; 15:7). The first principles and ordinances of the gospel are faith, repentance, baptism, and the gift of the Holy Ghost (see Articles of Faith 1:4). Faith and repentance are the first steps towards salvation. *See also:* Faith in Christ; Cometh unto repentance.

Faith began to be (becometh) unshaken (2 Nephi 31:19; Enos 1:11; Jacob 4:6; Mormon 9:28). Faith that cannot be dismissed, dissuaded, diminished, or discouraged.

Faith had not been vain (3 Nephi 1:6, 8). All those who live by faith in Christ have a hope that their belief and works will truly be rewarded by a just God.

Faith, hope, and charity (Alma 7:24; Ether 12:28; Moroni 7:1; 8:14; 10:20). Hope encompasses faith and both increase or expand together. The very essence of faith is love or charity. "Except men shall have [faith, hope, and] charity they cannot inherit that place which thou hast prepared in the mansions of thy Father" (Ether 12:34). *See also:* 1 Corinthians 13:1–13.

Faith in Christ (2 Nephi 33:7; Jacob 7:3; Enos 1:8; Alma 25:16; 44:3; Helaman 5:41; 15:9; Moroni 7:25, 32, 39; 10:4). "Having faith in Christ includes having a firm belief that He is the Only Begotten Son of God and the Savior and Redeemer of the world. We recognize that we can return to live with our Heavenly Father only by relying on His Son's grace and mercy. When we have faith in Christ, we accept and apply His Atonement and His teachings. We trust Him and what He says. We know that He has the power to keep His promises. Heavenly Father blesses those who have faith to obey His Son.

"Faith in Christ leads to action. It leads to sincere and lasting repentance. Having faith causes us to try as hard as we can to learn about and become more like our Savior. We want to learn what His commandments are and then obey them. Even though we will still make mistakes, we show our love for Him by striving to keep His commandments and avoid sin" (*Preach My Gospel*, 61–62). *See also:* Faith in God; Faith in him (his name); Faith in me (my Well Beloved/the Holy One of Israel/the Lamb of God/the redemption of him); Faith in the tradition of their fathers.

Faith in God (Enos 1:20; Mosiah 25:22; Alma 37:40; Ether 12:20). *See:* Faith in Christ.

Faith in him (his name) (1 Nephi 7:12; 12:11; 2 Nephi 26:13; 31:19; Jacob 4:11; Alma 46:41; 58:11; Ether 12:7; Moroni 7:26, 28, 38, 39, 41). *See:* Faith in Christ.

Faith in me (my Well Beloved/ the Holy One of Israel/the Lamb of God/the redemption of him) (1 Nephi 12:10; 2 Nephi 9:23; Alma

5:15; Helaman 5:47; 3 Nephi 9:20; Ether 4:7; 12:27; Moroni 7:33–34). *See:* Faith in Christ.

Faith in the tradition of their fathers (3 Nephi 1:11). This verse refers to the righteous traditions of their fathers, which include living by the principles of the gospel. *Compare:* Mosiah 26:1. *See also:* Traditions of our (their/your) fathers.

Faith is not to have a perfect knowledge of things (Alma 32:21, 26). Faith grows until it becomes a perfect knowledge, and once it is a perfect knowledge it is no longer faith. In other words, we have faith in the things of God, and our faith in those things grows, until because of our great faith in them, God reveals unto us a perfect knowledge of those things. An example is the brother of Jared who, "having this perfect knowledge of God, he could not be kept from within the veil; therefore he saw Jesus; and [Jesus] did minister unto him" (Ether 3:20).

Faith is things which are hoped for and not seen (Ether 12:6). A good beginning definition of what faith is. *Compare:* Hebrews 11:1.

Faith is vain (Alma 34:28; Moroni 7:44). The professed or false faith of hypocrites, unrepentant sinners, deceivers, and predators is useless and unavailing.

Faith of Christ (Alma 27:27; 46:27, 41; 48:13; Helaman 3:35). *See:* Faith in Christ.

Faith on his (the) name (of Jesus Christ) (Mosiah 3:9, 21; 5:7; Alma 9:27; Mormon 9:37; Moroni 3:3; 8:3). *See:* Faith in Christ; Faith on his (the) name (of Jesus Christ); None other name.

Faith on the Lamb of God (the Lord/the Son of God) (1 Nephi 10:17; Mosiah 3:12; 18:7, 20; 25:15; Alma 7:14; 13:29; 37:33; Helaman 13:6; 15:7; 3 Nephi 7:16, 18). *See:* Faith in Christ.

Faith on the words (Mosiah 21:30; 26:15–16; Alma 32:26–27; 33:1; 3 Nephi 19:28). To obtain faith in Christ we must first hear the words of Christ. In Alma's discourse on faith, he says, "But behold, if ye will awake and arouse your faculties, even to an experiment upon my words" (Alma 32:27).

Faith unto eternal salvation (Alma 25:16). "True faith, faith unto salvation, is centered on the Lord Jesus Christ, faith in His doctrines and teachings, faith in the prophetic guidance of the Lord's anointed, faith in the capacity to discover hidden characteristics and traits that can transform life" (Scott, "Transforming Power of Faith and Character," 43). *See also:* 1 Peter 1:5.

Faith unto repentance (Alma 34:15–17; Helaman 15:7; Ether 12:3). True faith motivates one to do something and to move forward. Thus to believe in Christ is to believe in His command to repent and come unto Him. *See also:* Cometh unto repentance; Faith and repentance; Alma 7:14; 9:27.

Faithful in Christ (Moroni 9:25). *See:* Faith in Christ; Ephesians 1:1.

Faithful in keeping the commandments (1 Nephi 3:16, 21; 4:1; Mosiah 10:13; Alma 8:15; 39:1; 48:15; 50:22). Faith in Christ is not a true and real faith in Christ (or is only a very weak and fading faith) if we do not keep the commandments of Christ.

Faithful to (until/unto) the end (Mosiah 2:41; Alma 5:13; 3 Nephi 27:19). "If thou wilt do good, yea, and hold out faithful to the end, thou shalt be saved in the kingdom of God, which is the greatest of all the gifts of God; for there is no gift greater than the gift of salvation" (D&C 6:13). *See also:* Endure(-th) to the end.

Faithful unto my name (Alma 46:15; Ether 4:19). Encompasses the same covenants we make in the sacrament prayers, namely, take upon us the name of Jesus; always remember Him; and keep His commandments. *See also:* Faith in Christ.

Faithful unto the Lord (1 Nephi 7:12–13; Alma 44:4; 48:7; Ether 1:38). If we truly love the Lord we will be faithful unto Him. *See also:* Faith in Christ.

Faithfulness the girdle of his reins (2 Nephi 21:5; 30:11). Also in Isaiah 11:5. The righteous shall be clothed in majestic faithfulness like a sash around their waist. *See also:* Girdle of his (their) loins; Robe of righteousness.

Faithfulness unto God (Alma 38:2). Best described in Alma 63:2, which says, "He was a just man, and he did walk uprightly before God; and he did observe to do good continually, to keep the commandments of the Lord his God."

Fall down at his feet and worship him (1 Nephi 11:24; 3 Nephi 11:17). Those who know the Lord and thus recognize Him and realize His power, position, and redeeming sacrifice will automatically and without hesitation fall down at His feet and worship Him. *See also:* Every knee shall bow.

Fall into the pit which they digged (1 Nephi 22:14). "No weapon formed against them [the people of the Lord] shall prosper; that he who diggeth a pit for them shall fall into the same himself" (D&C 109:25).

Fall into transgression (Enos 1:13; Jarom 1:10; Mosiah 1:13; Alma 9:19, 23; 10:19; 37:27; 44:4; 45:12; 46:21–22; 3 Nephi 6:5). Some go to great lengths or heights to find wickedness, some suddenly make a wrong turn into sin, some are not careful and inadvertently fall off the strait and narrow path, and yet others make a great leap off into transgression. Before the actual sin is committed it is most often mentally entertained or premeditated. Seriously large sins are most often preceded by lesser sins that lead up to that serious transgression. We must take the Holy Ghost to be our guide so that we are guided safely away from sin.

Fall of Adam (Mosiah 3:19, 26; 4:7; Alma 12:22; Helaman 14:16). Meaning Adam's fall or descent to mortal status because he partook of the forbidden fruit. "As in Adam all die, even so in Christ shall all be made alive" (1 Corinthians 15:22). Because of the fall of Adam all men are mortal and enter the earth to a probationary state. However, the Second Article of Faith says, "We believe that men will be punished for their own sins, and not for Adam's transgression." *See also:* Fallen man.

Fall of man (2 Nephi 2:4; Alma 18:36; 22:13; Mormon 9:12). *See:* Fallen man; Fall of Adam.

Fall to the earth (Helaman 14:7). *See:* Fell to (unto) the earth (as if he were dead).

Fallen and lost (Alma 34:9). *See:* Fallen man; Lost and fallen state.

Fallen man (2 Nephi 9:6; Mosiah 3:16; Alma 12:22; 22:12, 14; 42:6). Refers to the mortal state that men and women find themselves in here upon the earth, which mortal and fallible existence came into being because Adam and Eve partook of the forbidden fruit. It was part of the great plan of God that man would fall and then require a Savior and Redeemer. All must come unto Christ in order to be redeemed from this fallen state. *See also:* Fall of Adam; Fall of man; Fallen state.

Fallen people (Alma 9:30, 32; 12:22; 30:25). People as a nation or society can fall into sin and disorder, thus causing the disruption, collapse, and the end to strong nations and ordered society. Such nations and societies find themselves regressing rather than progressing, losing the knowledge and enlightenment they once had.

Fallen state (1 Nephi 10:6; 2 Nephi 25:17; Mosiah 4:5; 16:4–5; 27:25; Alma 42:12). *See:* Fallen man.

Fallen to the earth (Mosiah 4:1; Alma 19:16–17; Helaman 9:5, 7; 3 Nephi 4:8; Ether 3:7). *See:* Fell to (unto) the earth (as if he were dead).

False Christs (Words of Mormon 1:15). Beware of false Christs who will even show great signs and wonders, yet deceive. There is in reality only one true Christ. Salvation can only come through Him who is Jesus Christ. We must take the Holy Spirit to be our guide so that we are not deceived. *Compare:* Matthew 24:24; Mark 13:22; Joseph Smith–Matthew 1:22.

False doctrines (2 Nephi 3:12; 28:9, 12, 15; Alma 1:16). Erroneous and untrue beliefs, forms and systems of religion, and philosophies practiced among men, including any contrary or counterfeit tenets. Thus all doctrines not included in the Doctrine of Christ are by exclusion false doctrines. Satan and his followers teach false doctrines to lead the children of men astray. Most often false doctrines are a half-truth which include a lie, thus they may sound correct, but in reality are not true. "The Savior of mankind described Himself as being in the world but not of the world. (See John 17:14; D&C 49:5.) We also can be in the world but not of the world as we reject false concepts and false teachings and remain true to that which God has commanded" (Monson, "Priesthood Power," 67). *See also:* D&C 46:7; Joseph Smith–History 1:19.

False Messiah (2 Nephi 25:18). *See:* False Christs.

False prophets (Words of Mormon 1:16; Helaman 13:26; 3 Nephi 14:15; 4 Nephi 1:34). Men who profess to be prophets but who do not follow all the ways of God nor speak by the power of the Holy Ghost. Rather they teach what has been taught to them by the devil. They draw near to God with their lips, but their hearts are far from the true God. Their teachings are a mixture of scripture and the philosophies of men. They lure followers with the use of sophistries, clever language, and worldly lures.

False swearers (witness) (Mosiah 13:23; Helaman 7:21; 3 Nephi 24:5). People with ungodly motives and those recruited by wicked men to trap the unwary. "Thou shalt not bear false witness against thy neighbor" is one of the Ten Commandments (Exodus 20:16). *See also:* Lyings and deceivings.

Familiar spirit (2 Nephi 26:16). Has an accustomed ring of truth. The Holy Ghost has the power to prick or quicken our spirits when truth is presented to us.

Famine(-s) and pestilence(-s) (2 Nephi 6:15; 10:6; Mosiah 12:4; Alma 10:22–23; 45:11; Helaman 10:6; 11:14–15; 12:3; 13:9; Ether 11:7). Through the centuries, God has often used famine (food shortage mainly from drought) and pestilence (devastating disease) to humble people unto repentance. Only after people see that there is nothing they can do or have power over will they turn to God for deliverance. *See also:* He doth visit them with death, terror, famine and pestilence; Pestilence of earthquakes (famine/tempest/the sword).

Fasted (and prayed) many days (Mosiah 27:23; Alma 5:46; 8:26; 10:7; 30:2). *See:* Fast(-ed much) and pray(-ed much/oft).

Fast(-ed much) and pray(-ed much/oft) (Mosiah 27:22; Alma

17:3, 9; 28:6; 45:1; Helaman 3:35; Moroni 6:5). Fasting with prayer is an added expression of our faith. Thus fasting adds sincerity, effectiveness, and power to prayer. When the disciples were unable to cast out an evil spirit but then Jesus did, the disciples asked Jesus why they could not cast out the evil spirit. Jesus responded that this kind goeth not out but by prayer and fasting. Fasting puts the desires and wants of the body in subjection to the spirit. *See also:* Fasted (and prayed) many days; Fasting and (mighty) prayer.

Fasting and (mighty) prayer (Alma 6:6; 28:6; 30:2; 3 Nephi 27:1; 4 Nephi 1:12). *See:* Fast(-ed much) and pray(-ed much/oft); Mighty prayer.

Father and I are one (3 Nephi 11:27; 20:35; 28:10). God the Father and His Son Jesus Christ are physically two separate beings, yet they are completely united as one in purpose, doctrine, fidelity, and declaration. When Joseph Smith saw the Father and the Son in the Sacred Grove, he saw "two Personages" (Joseph Smith–History 1:17). Thus they are in reality distinct individuals, but the vastness and extent of their unity is striking and majestic. *See also:* Father and the Son and the Holy Ghost which is one God.

Father and the Son and the Holy Ghost (2 Nephi 31:18, 21; Alma 11:44; 3 Nephi 11:25, 27; Mormon 7:7; Ether 5:4). God the Father, God the Son, and God the Holy Ghost make up the Godhead. "We believe in God, the Eternal Father, and in His Son, Jesus Christ, and in the Holy Ghost" (Articles of Faith 1:1). "The Father has a body of flesh and bones as tangible as man's; the Son also; but the Holy Ghost has not a body of flesh and bones, but is a personage of Spirit. Were it not so, the Holy Ghost could not dwell in us" (D&C 130:22).

Father and the Son and the Holy Ghost which is one God (2 Nephi 31:21; Alma 11:44; 3 Nephi 11:27, 36). This phrase "should not be understood to mean that the members of the Godhead are the same physical personage. Rather, they are three separate, distinct individuals who are agreed in one (see 1 John 5:7–8).

"With reference to John 17:11, 20–23, Joseph Smith taught, 'I want to read the text to you myself—"I am agreed with the Father and the Father is agreed with me, and we are agreed as one." The Greek shows that it should be agreed. "Father, I pray for them which Thou hast given me out of the world, and not for those alone, but for them also which shall believe on me through their word, that they all may be agreed with us . . . and all come to dwell in unity."' [*Teachings of the Prophet Joseph Smith*, p. 372]" (*Book of Mormon Student Manual*, 3). *See also:* Father and I are one; D&C 20:28.

Father of all lies (2 Nephi 2:18; 9:9; Ether 8:25). Satan, who is the devil, is the father of all lies (see Moses 4:4). All his temptations and precepts are filled with lies. He has been the perpetrator of lies since the foundation of the earth. When we lie or tell a fib, we are following after Satan and his ways. Each lie we make puts us further and further into subjection to the devil (2 Nephi 28:21–23). The opposite being is God, who is a "God of truth, and canst not lie" (Ether 3:12).

Father of contention (3 Nephi 11:29). Satan is the father of contention and all other bad behaviors. *See also:* Spirit of contention.

Father of heaven and earth (2 Nephi 25:12; Mosiah 3:8; 15:4; Alma 11:39; Helaman 14:12; 16:18; Ether 4:7). Another name and descriptor for Jesus Christ. He is the Father of heaven and earth because He was the creator of heaven and earth, being directed in organizing the earth by God the Father (see Mosiah 4:2).

Father who is in heaven (Jacob 7:22; 3 Nephi 12:16, 45, 48; 13:1, 9; 14:11, 21). When Jesus gave us the pattern of prayer he prayed, "Our Father which art in heaven" (see Luke 11:2; 3 Nephi 13:9) referring to that father who is our Heavenly Father, the Father of our spirits. All the men, women, and children on earth are His spirit children, and we dwelt with Him before we came to earth. "Furthermore we have had fathers of our flesh which corrected us, and we gave them reverence: shall we not much rather be in subjection unto the Father of spirits, and live?" (Hebrews 12:9).

Favored of God (1 Nephi 17:35). *See:* Favored of the Lord.

Favored of the Lord (1 Nephi 1:1; 3:6; Mosiah 1:13; 10:13; Alma 9:20; 27:30; 48:20; 56:19; Ether 1:34; 10:13). "He that is righteous is favored of God" (1 Nephi 17:35). God loves all His children, but He sorrows over those that choose wickedness, for no unclean thing can dwell in the presence of God. It is false doctrine that God's love is unconditional regardless of what we do. God reserves His greatest love and blessings for those of His children that keep His commandments. His Beloved Son did everything according to the will of the Father and was thus the Beloved Son. *See also:* Highly favored (of the Lord).

Fear and tremble (1 Nephi 16:27; 22:23; 2 Nephi 1:25; Mosiah 15:26; Alma 1:4). The righteous fear and tremble for their wicked brethren. The wicked should fear and tremble concerning their fate if they do not repent. "Wherefore, verily I say, let the wicked take heed, and let the rebellious fear and tremble; and let the unbelieving hold their lips, for the day of wrath shall come upon them as a whirlwind, and all flesh shall know that I am God" (D&C 63:6).

Fear came upon them (Alma 19:24; 27:23; Helaman 5:28; 9:5). When the might and power of God is manifested to people it almost certainly causes fear to come over those that witness it. *See also:* Fear and tremble; Fear of the Lord.

Fear God (2 Nephi 27:34; 28:8; Alma 34:37; 39:12; 60:28; 3 Nephi 4:10). *See:* Fear of the Lord.

Fear my name (3 Nephi 25:2). *See:* Fear of the Lord.

Fear not (me) (2 Nephi 8:7; 17:4; Alma 7:15; 61:21; Helaman 5:26; 3 Nephi 22:4; 24:5; Moroni 8:16). We need not fear God or man if we are keeping the commandments of the Lord. For if we are true and faithful to God's commands, we will have peace of mind and we will be assured that all will be right with us in the end if not in the present also.

Fear of God (Alma 39:12). *See:* Fear of the Lord.

Fear of the Lord (1 Nephi 3:6; 2 Nephi 12:10, 19, 21; 21:2–3; Enos 1:23; Mosiah 4:1; 29:30; Alma 19:15; 36:7). Many places in the scriptures say we should fear God. Often the concern is expressed that we should not have to fear a loving God. The Bible Dictionary says, "Care should be taken to distinguish between two different uses of this word [fear]. The 'fear of the Lord' is frequently spoken of as part of man's duty (e.g. Ps. 111:10; Eccl. 12:13; Isa. 11:2–3; Luke 1:50); it is also described as 'godly fear' (Heb. 12:28). In such passages fear is equivalent to reverence, awe, worship, and is therefore an essential part of the attitude of mind in which we ought to stand toward the All-holy God. On the other hand fear is spoken of as something unworthy of a child of God, something that 'perfect love casteth out' (1 Jn. 4:18). The first effect of Adam's sin was that he was afraid (Gen. 3:10). Sin destroys that feeling of confidence God's child should feel in a loving Father and produces instead a feeling of shame and guilt. Ever since the Fall God has been teaching men not to fear, but with penitence to ask forgiveness in full confidence of receiving it" (Bible Dictionary, s.v. "fear," 672).

Feared the judgments of God (2 Nephi 1:17; Mosiah 17:11; Mosiah 26:13; Alma 53:15). Why are men obedient to God? Each must examine themselves and become determined to serve the Lord for specific reasons. One reason men decide to do the will of God is they do not want to offend God by doing wrong or they do not want to incur the wrath of God's judgments. Perhaps obedience purely for the sake of obedience is an appropriate reason. The best reason may be because we honor, respect, and love God. *See also:* Fear of the Lord.

Feared the Lord (3 Nephi 24:16; Ether 3:8). *See:* Fear of the Lord.

Feast upon his love (Jacob 3:2). To experience God's love is one of the greatest gifts of God. Our goal is to return to God's presence, and thereby eternally dwell in His radiant love. "Be faithful and diligent in keeping the commandments of God, and I will encircle thee in the arms of my love" (D&C 6:20). *See also:* Encircled about (eternally) in (the arms of) his love.

Feast upon that which perisheth not (2 Nephi 9:51). The word of God can bring true lasting and spiritual sustenance, gratification, and delight. Whereas, the things of this world will all eventually pass away. "Lay not up for yourselves treasures upon earth, where moth and rust doth corrupt, and where thieves break through and steal: But lay up for yourselves treasures in heaven, where neither moth nor rust doth corrupt" (Matthew 6:19–20). *See also:* Feast upon his love; Feast (-ing) upon the (pleasing) word(-s) of Christ (God).

Feast upon this fruit (Alma 32:42). Meaning the fruit that comes from a mature faith, which represents the blessings of the gospel and the love of God, until one gains eternal life, and will never hunger or thirst again. *See also:* Fruit of the tree of life [Lehi's dream].

Feast(-ing) upon the (pleasing) word(-s) of Christ (God) (2 Nephi 31:20; 32:3; Jacob 2:9). Meaning to read the scriptures with joy and to obtain great satisfaction by hearkening to the words of the prophets. Only by so doing can one gain eternal life.

Feed his sheep (1 Nephi 22:25). Meaning spiritual food or nourishment of one's spirit. *See also:* Bread and the waters of life; Nourished by the good word of God.

Feed the hungry (Jacob 2:19). Meaning temporal or physical food to nourish the physical body. It is sinful to not share our food with the needy and hungry. *See also:* Poor and needy.

Feel the prints of the nails in my hands (3 Nephi 11:14–15). To have a witness, as these Nephites on the American continent had, is to receive a testimony of the divinity of Jesus Christ. Doubting Thomas in the New Testament said, "Except I shall see in his hands the print of the nails, and put my finger into the print of the nails, and thrust my hand into his side, I will not believe" (John 20:25). Soon thereafter Jesus appeared again to his disciples, including Thomas, and Jesus said, "Reach hither thy finger, and behold my hands; and reach hither thy hand, and thrust it into my side: and be not faithless, but believing" (John 20:27). Even though Jesus is a resurrected being, the prints of the nails remain, for how long we do not know, as a proof that He was slain for the sins of the world. Zechariah 13:6 says,

"And one shall say unto him, What are these wounds in thine hands? Then he shall answer, Those with which I was wounded in the house of my friends." At Christ's Second Coming, the prints of the nails will again be witnessed by many.

Feelings are exceedingly tender and chaste and delicate (Jacob 2:7). Those who are innocent and not sullied by earthly evils.

Fell to (unto) the earth (as if he were dead) (Jacob 7:15, 21; Mosiah 27:12, 18; Alma 18:42; 19:14, 16; 27:17; 36:7, 10–11; Helaman 9:4, 14; 3 Nephi 1:16–17; 11:12). After—and sometimes during—significant spiritual experiences, individuals sink and drop to the ground because they are so astounded and stunned, they are so completely spiritually overwhelmed, or their physical body is so weakened and exhausted by the experience. *See also:* Fallen to the earth; Fell to (unto) the earth (as if he were dead); Overcome with the Spirit; Moses 1:9–10; Joseph Smith–History 17:18.

Fellow beings (Mosiah 2:17; 8:18). Meaning our fellowmen, our neighbors, even all of mankind on earth. We are commanded to love our fellow beings and be of service to them. *See also:* D&C 81:4.

Field is ripe (Alma 26:5). Symbolic of a field of ripe grain ready to be harvested. The likeness being that there are many souls ready who

are honest and true and are looking for the truth of the gospel. We are the harvesters to preach repentance and baptism unto Christ. "For behold the field is white already to harvest; and lo, he that thrusteth in his sickle with his might, the same layeth up in store that he perisheth not, but bringeth salvation to his soul" (see D&C 4:4; 6:3; 11:3; 12:3; 14:3; 31:4–5; 33:3, 7).

Fierce anger of the Lord (2 Nephi 23:9, 13; Mosiah 12:1; Alma 8:29; 9:12, 18; 10:23; Helaman 11:12; 13:10). *See:* Anger of the Lord; Fiery indignation.

Fiery darts of the adversary (wicked) (1 Nephi 15:24). A phrase found three other places in the standard works: Ephesians 6:16; D&C 3:8; 27:17. The fiery darts of Satan include: temptations laid to trip us, sins that wound our soul, lies that sever our resolve, and hate that blinds our vision. We must hold to the rod of iron (word of God) and put on the armour of God (faith) in order to withstand Satan.

Fiery flying serpents (1 Nephi 17:41). The Book of Mormon prophet Nephi recounts when serpents came among the children of Israel at Moses' time. They were "snakes marked with flamelike spots, or whose bite caused acute inflammation (Num. 21:6). The Lord sent these upon the children of Israel to 'straiten them,' and He prepared a way that those who were bitten might be healed by looking at the serpent of brass that Moses raised up before them, which was a symbol of the Redeemer being lifted up upon the cross (John 3:14–15)" (Bible Dictionary, s.v. "fiery serpents," 674). Many looked and were saved, while others had not the faith to look and perished.

Fiery indignation (Alma 40:14). A description of the wrath of God towards unrepentant sinners. *Indignation* means anger and wrath. God cannot look upon sin with the least degree of allowance. His anger towards sin is forceful, fierce, and as scorching as a very hot fire. *See also:* Anger of the Lord; Fierce anger of the Lord.

Fight against God (2 Nephi 25:14; Alma 23:7). The fight between good and evil, between God and Satan, began in the War in Heaven in premortal life. It has continued throughout the history of the world, and it goes on today. After a great last battle just before the final judgment, this fight will finally end. Satan and his followers will be cast out into outer darkness, where they will forever be separated from those who receive a reward of glory: celestial, terrestrial, or telestial. Compare "Who's on the Lord's Side, Who?" (*Hymns,* no. 260) and "Choose you this day whom ye will serve . . . As for me and my house, we will serve the Lord" (Joshua 24:15).

Fight(-eth/-ing) against Zion (1 Nephi 22:14, 19; 2 Nephi 6:12–13; 10:13, 16; 27:3). Those that fight against Zion will in the due time of the Lord be cut off, destroyed, and cast out with Satan.

Fight for their wives, and their children, and their homes (Mosiah 20:11; Mormon 2:23). *See:* Defend themselves.

Filled as if with fire (Helaman 5:45; 3 Nephi 19:13). Being born of the Spirit is also referred to as born of fire. The presence of the Holy Ghost is so intense that it is as if one would be consumed by fire: a purifying fire that purges one of sin. This is not a hurtful or terrifying fire, but the fire of truth, godly love, and great glory and light. *See also:* Baptism of fire and of the Holy Ghost; Consuming of my flesh.

Filled (filleth) with hope and perfect love (Moroni 7:48; 8:26). Describes the feelings that accompany being filled with the Spirit. *See also:* Filled with the Holy Ghost.

Filled my soul with exceedingly great joy (1 Nephi 8:12; Alma 29:10; 36:20). *See:* Filled with joy.

Filled with charity (Moroni 8:17). *See:* Filled with love.

Filled with desire (3 Nephi 19:24). *See:* Filled as if with fire; Filled with joy.

Filled with joy (1 Nephi 5:1; 8:12; Mosiah 3:4; 4:3, 20; 21:24, 28; 25:8; Alma 4:14; 19:30; 22:15;

29:10; 36:20, 24; 57:36; 62:1; Helaman 5:44; 3 Nephi 17:17). The inexpressible joy experienced by those who are born again and are filled with the Holy Ghost and the love of God. *See also:* Mosiah 4:20.

Filled with love (2 Nephi 4:21; Mosiah 2:4; 4:12; Alma 38:12; Moroni 7:48; 8:17). Charity, the pure love of Christ in its fullest measure, is a gift from God. "It endureth forever; and whoso is found possessed of it at the last day, it shall be well with him. Wherefore, my beloved brethren, pray unto the Father with all the energy of heart that ye may be filled with this love, which he hath bestowed upon all who are true followers of his Son, Jesus Christ; that ye may become the sons of God" (Moroni 7:48).

Filled with pain and anguish for the welfare of their souls (Mosiah 25:11). *See:* Anxiety for you.

Filled with the Holy Ghost (Alma 8:30; 31:36; 36:24; Helaman 5:45; 3 Nephi 12:6; 19:13; 26:17; 30:2). "Plainly, such expressions as being filled with the Holy Ghost, and His falling upon persons, having reference to the powers and influences that emanate from God, and which are characteristic of Him; for the Holy Ghost may in this way operate simultaneously upon many persons even though they be widely separated, whereas the actual person of the Holy Ghost cannot be in more than one place at a time. Yet we read that through the power of the Spirit, the Father and the Son operate in their creative acts and in their general dealings with the human family. The Holy Ghost may be regarded as the minister of the Godhead, carrying into effect the decision of the Supreme Council" (Talmage, *Articles of Faith*, 145). Being filled with the Holy Ghost brings blessings, powers, and knowledge in immensely varied and vast ways, including: to pronounce prophecy; to see visions; to cast out devils and heal the sick; to bear testimony with power; to rebuff evil and contention; to resist and detect deceivers; to understand the mysteries of God; to know the mind and will of God; to be guided in the way of happiness and eternal life; to minister with love and wisdom; to taste exceeding joy and peace; and many, many more.

Filled with the Holy Spirit (Alma 31:36; Helaman 5:45). *See:* Filled with the Holy Ghost.

Filled with the power of God (1 Nephi 2:14; 17:48). The power of God can be manifest through righteous servants of God. *See also:* Filled with the Holy Ghost.

Filled with the Spirit (of God/the Lord) (1 Nephi 1:12; 2:14; 5:17; 2 Nephi 25:4; Mosiah 18:14; Alma 18:16; 3 Nephi 20:9). *See:* Filled with the Holy Ghost.

Filled with the spirit of prophecy (2 Nephi 25:4). *See:* Spirit of prophecy (and revelation).

Filthy shall be filthy still (remain in filthiness) (1 Nephi 15:33; 2 Nephi 9:16; Alma 7:21; Mormon 9:14). Referring to the fact that unrepentant sinners will be filthy still after death. When we die we will not suddenly become something that we were not while we lived. *See also:* D&C 88:35, 102.

Find mercy (Mosiah 4:2; Alma 32:13; 38:8). To receive a forgiveness of sins when we repent, we must pray unto God for His mercy in forgiving us and wiping our sins clean from us.

Find pasture (1 Nephi 22:25). *See:* Good Shepherd; John 10:9.

Find peace to my soul (Alma 38:8). While mortal, we live in a world of turmoil, sin, hate, and hunger; all of which is anything but peaceful and restful. In this verse, Alma the Younger is praying to God for relief from the pain and anguish of his sins. In a larger sense, all good people are seeking peace from a troubled world. *See also:* Peace of God rest upon you; Peace to my soul; Sit down in peace; State of rest and peace; They shall have peace with him.

Find rest (to their souls) (Alma 37:34; 3 Nephi 28:3). *See:* Enter into his (my/the) rest (of the Lord/ of God).

Fine steel (1 Nephi 16:18). A bow made of steel is also mentioned three times in the Bible (2 Samuel 22:35; Job 20:24; Psalm 18:34). It appears that Nephi was very familiar with, even expert in, metallurgy, which was cutting-edge technology in his day. Evidences of this are: his comments about Laban's sword (1 Nephi 4:9); he made plates on which to record the proceedings of his people (1 Nephi 1:17); he made tools to construct a ship (1 Nephi 17:9, 10, 16); and he made swords after the pattern of Laban's sword (2 Nephi 5:14). *See also:* Precious steel.

Fine things of the world (4 Nephi 1:24; Ether 9:17). "But before ye seek for riches, seek ye for the kingdom of God. And after ye have obtained a hope in Christ ye shall obtain riches, if ye seek them; and ye will seek them for the intent to do good—to clothe the naked, and to feed the hungry, and to liberate the captive, and administer relief to the sick and the afflicted" (Jacob 2:18–19). *See also:* Vain things of the world.

Finger of scorn (1 Nephi 8:33). Brigham Young said, "I am satisfied that it will not do for the Lord to make this people popular. Why? Because all hell would want to be in the Church. The people must be kept where the finger of scorn can be pointed at them. Although it is admitted that we are honest, industrious, truthful, virtuous, self-denying, and, as a community, possess every moral excellence, yet we must be looked upon as ignorant and unworthy, . . . and be hated by the world. What is the reason of this? Christ and Baal cannot become friends. When I see this people grow and spread and prosper, I feel that there is more danger than when they are in poverty. Being driven from city to city or into the mountains is nothing compared to the danger of our becoming rich and being hailed by outsiders as a first-class community. I am afraid of only one thing. What is that? That we will not live our religion, and that we will partially slide a little from the path" (*Discourses of Brigham Young*, 434). President Ezra Taft Benson prophetically said: "Opposition has been and will be the lot of the Saints of the kingdom in any age. The finger of scorn has been pointed at us in the past, and we may expect it in the future. . . . The seed planted and watered in 1830 has now matured to a fully grown tree for all to see. Some will seek the refuge of its shade in the heat of the day, but none will be neutral in their appraisal of its fruit" ("A Marvelous Work and a Wonder," 33). *See also:* Destroy the church.

Fire and the Holy Ghost (2 Nephi 31:13, 17; 3 Nephi 9:20; 11:35; 12:1–2; 19:13; Mormon 7:10; Ether 12:14). *See:* Baptism of fire and of the Holy Ghost.

Firm and steadfast (and undaunted) (1 Nephi 2:10; Alma 57:20; Helaman 15:8; 3 Nephi 6:14). *See:* Firm in the faith of Christ.

Firm in the faith of Christ (Alma 27:27; 48:13; 57:27; Helaman 6:1; 15:8; 3 Nephi 6:14; Moroni 7:30). Meaning steadfast in keeping the commandments of God. In other words, immovable in a determination to follow the example of Christ. *See also:* Exceeding faith; Firm and steadfast (and undaunted); Made strong; Minds are firm; Sure foundation.

Firmness of mind (Jacob 3:1). *See:* Firm in the faith of Christ.

Firmness unshaken (Mormon 9:28). *See:* Firm in the faith of Christ.

First and the last (1 Nephi 20:12; Alma 11:39). A name to describe the Lord Jesus Christ and declaring that He is eternal. He is the first because He is the firstborn of God's spirit children and gained preeminence before the world was. He is the last because He will come in glory to end the mortal existence. Furthermore, described by the words in Hebrews 12:2, "Jesus [is] the author and finisher of our faith." *See also:* Author and finisher of their faith; Beginning and the end; I am Alpha and Omega, the beginning and the end.

First fruits of repentance is baptism (Moroni 8:25). Meaning the immediate outcome of true repentance is a desire to be baptized.

First parents (1 Nephi 5:11; 2 Nephi 2:15; 9:9; Jacob 4:3; Omni 1:22; Mosiah 16:3; Alma 12:21, 26; 42:2, 7; Helaman 5:6; 6:26; Ether 8:25). Adam and Eve are generally referred to as our first parents. However, there are other first parents, such as Lehi and Sariah, plus others. *See also:* Jacob 4:3; Omni 1:22; Helaman 5:6.

First provocation (Jacob 1:7; Alma 12:36). "This is a reference to the refusal of the ancient Israelites, under Moses, to receive the further light and knowledge which the Lawgiver sought to give them, including the fulness of the blessings of the priesthood and thus the privilege of coming into the divine presence" (McConkie and Millet, *Doctrinal Commentary on the Book of Mormon*, 3:91; see also D&C 84:19–24). The reference in Alma points to the Israelites who hardened their hearts and thus damned their progression in the wilderness. Alma admonishes his listeners to repent and harden not their hearts so that they may have claim on the mercy of the Lord, receive forgiveness, and enter into the rest of the Lord (see Alma 12:34–35). The footnote (36*c*) also points to the first provocation of Adam and Eve, which resulted in the "first judgment," in this case the fall to mortality, which would result in an endless damnation if it were not for the infinite Atonement to save repentant mankind from that fate.

First resurrection (Mosiah 15:21–22, 24, 26; 18:9; Alma 40:16–17). Refers to the resurrection of those judged as righteous and their coming forth from their graves before all others. "The resurrection of all the prophets, and all those that have believed in their words, or all those that have kept the commandments of God" (Mosiah 15:22). This resurrection will occur before and at the onset of the millennium, and those resurrected first will dwell with Christ during the millennium. The heathen nations, or those that had not the law, will also come forth at the millennium. "It shall be tolerable for them" (D&C 45:54; see also Revelation 20:6; Alma 40:20; D&C 76:64). An example of the first resurrection was in Jerusalem at Christ's resurrection: "And the graves were opened; and many bodies of the saints which slept arose, and came out of the graves after his resurrection, and went into the holy city, and appeared unto many" (Matthew 27:52–53). The same thing happened among the Nephites. *See also:* Helaman 14:25; 3 Nephi 23:7–13.

First shall be last and last shall be first (1 Nephi 13:42; Jacob 5:63; Ether 13:12). *See:* Come unto the Gentiles; Last shall be first, and the first shall be last.

Firstfruits (of Christ) unto God (2 Nephi 2:9; Jacob 4:11). Jesus Christ and the righteous followers of Christ are all the firstfruits unto

God. Christ was the firstfruits of the Resurrection, being the first resurrected. Also those coming forth in the "first resurrection" can be referred to as firstfruits of Christ unto God. *See also:* First resurrection.

Firstlings of their flocks (Mosiah 2:3). The Nephites observed the law of Moses and offered sacrifice of the firstlings of the flocks. The prophet Jacob wrote, "We knew of Christ, and we had a hope of his glory. . . . Behold [we] believed in Christ and worshiped the Father in his name. . . . And for this intent we keep the law of Moses, it pointing our souls to him [Jesus]" (Jacob 4:4–5). Thus the sacrifice of the firstlings was a symbol of Christ's sacrifice. *Compare:* Firstfruits (of Christ) unto God. *See also:* Law of Moses.

Fit to be numbered among the people of his church (Moroni 7:39). In the prior verse, Moroni 7:38, "For no man can be saved, according to the words of Christ, save they shall have faith in his name." Thus to be suitable, proper, and qualified members of the Church we must have faith in Christ. Other qualifications include being worthy, humble, striving, serving, and full of love.

Flame ascendeth up forever and ever (2 Nephi 9:16; Mosiah 2:38; Alma 12:17). *See:* Unquenchable fire.

Flame of unquenchable fire (Mormon 9:5). *See:* Unquenchable fire.

Flaming fire (1 Nephi 15:30; 2 Nephi 14:5; Helaman 5:44). Meaning a blazing, brilliant, and exceedingly intense fire.

Flaming sword (Alma 12:21; 42:2–3). *See:* Cherubim and a (the) flaming sword.

Flattered (flattereth) them away (2 Nephi 28:22; Alma 17:31; 46:5; 3 Nephi 7:12). By using enticing, vain, lying, and false complimentary words, evil men and Satan deceive many and draw people away from the straight and narrow path to salvation. *See also:* Deceived by the devil.

Flattering words (Jacob 7:2; Mosiah 11:7; 26:6; Alma 30:47; 46:7, 10; 50:35; Helaman 13:28; 3 Nephi 1:29). *See:* Flattered (flattereth) them away.

Flaxen cord (2 Nephi 26:22). When we sin, Satan is thus enabled to slip a thin and ever so fragile flaxen thread around our neck. Even though that thin thread could easily be broken through the process of repentance, many are willing to remain in sin and follow where Satan leads them with that fragile cord. As more sins are committed and not repented of, Satan slips more and more thin flaxen threads around our necks until the accumulation of those threads becomes a strong rope that binds us down. Satan then controls us, unless we repent of all the sins that make up that strong rope. *See also:* Chains of hell.

Flesh and blood (Mosiah 7:27; Ether 3:6, 8–9). This is the term used in the scriptures to refer to the mortal body. This is in contrast to the term "flesh and bone" used in the scriptures to refer to an immortal, resurrected body, such as God's body (see D&C 130:22). Because of the blood, man is mortal and subject to mortal conditions. In other words, blood is what makes man mortal.

Flesh and blood of Christ (3 Nephi 18:28–30; Moroni 4:1). The bread and water administered in the sacrament are the emblems of the flesh and blood of Christ, and remind us of His suffering in the flesh and His spilt blood as He paid for our sins. Each of us must repent so that His sacrifice becomes beneficial to us individually. *See also:* D&C 20:40.

Flesh becoming subject to the Spirit (Mosiah 15:5). Describes how Jesus obtained a fulness of the Father by living a sinless life and doing only the will of the Father. It is the mortal struggle to control this physical body and train it to live the higher law of the gospel of Jesus Christ. Jesus was our example of doing always the will of the Father and living by the Spirit. We must put off the carnal man and yield ourselves to the Spirit so that we may become spiritually born again. *See also:* Spiritually begotten.

Fold of God (1 Nephi 15:15; 2 Nephi 9:2; Mosiah 18:8; Alma 26:4). Means being among the true followers of Jesus Christ. Also refers to Christ's true Church. *See also:* Church of Christ; Numbered among his (my) sheep.

Follow Christ (me) (2 Nephi 31:12–13; Moroni 7:11). Meaning follow in the footsteps and paths of truth that Jesus trod, also do the work and keep the commandments of the Lord. *See also:* Come unto Christ.

Followers of Christ (2 Nephi 28:14; Alma 4:15; Helaman 6:5, 39; Moroni 7:3, 48). *See:* Follow Christ (me).

Following the example of the Son of the living God (2 Nephi 31:13, 16; Mormon 7:10). *See:* Follow Christ (me).

Foolish and blind guides (Helaman 13:29). Refers to those who teach and uphold foolish and vain doctrines. *See:* Foolish and vain.

Foolish and vain (2 Nephi 28:9; Alma 30:13; 39:11; Helaman 12:4; 16:22; 3 Nephi 2:2). Not being led by the Spirit of God, man begins to imagine, suppose, and assume doctrines, hopes, and ideas that are contrary to the revelations of God and have little or no basis in truth. *See also:* Foolish imaginations.

Foolish imaginations (1 Nephi 2:11; 17:20). *See:* Foolish and vain.

Foolish traditions (things) (Alma 8:11; 21:8; 30:13–14, 23, 27; 31:17; 3 Nephi 2:2). The religious traditions, beliefs, commandments, and ordinances of the prophets and true believers were referred to as such by wicked and false teachers and leaders who tried to dissuade those who followed the true religion of Christ. Thus the false teachers attempted to say that the commandments and statutes of God were not necessary. *See also:* Traditions of our (their/your) fathers.

Foolishness of men (2 Nephi 9:28; 26:10). Because of pride, riches, and supposed knowledge, worldly men set aside the things of God to their own destruction. *See also:* Foolish and vain.

Fools before God (2 Nephi 9:42). In this reference, the Lord is condemning those who are puffed up because of their chances for learning and their wealth. It is only when people consider themselves fools before God, as they confess their weakness and spiritual ineptitude, and acknowledge that without the Lord they can accomplish nothing and are nothing, then they can be saved. *See also:* Foolish and vain.

For a standard (1 Nephi 22:6; 2 Nephi 29:2). *See:* Ensign to the nations (people).

For a wise purpose (1 Nephi 9:5; Words of Mormon 1:7; Alma 37:2, 12, 14, 18). God possesses all knowledge and wisdom, thus His ways are wise. He directs the affairs of His children for a good and wise purpose with infinite foreknowledge. *See also:* Wisdom in (of) God (the Lord/the Father).

For Christ's sake (Jacob 1:4; Alma 4:13). Meaning for the sake, benefit, object, and purpose of upholding and advancing the cause of Christ, His teachings, the will of God, and the progress of the Church and kingdom.

For he (the Lord God) hath spoken it (2 Nephi 9:16, 24; 10:9; Mosiah 2:41; 12:12; Alma 5:32, 52; 34:8; Mormon 8:26; Ether 4:19; 10:28). Meaning having great import because the Lord has spoken, revealed, and directed it to be so. God does not trifle with man or His creations. If God has spoken it, we must take notice and obey.

For the righteous' sake (Alma 45:15; 46:10; 62:40; Helaman 13:14). Often the Lord has spared the destruction of a people who had become wicked because of the righteous few that dwelled among those people. The classic example where this might have been true is Sodom and Gomorrah, which God said he would spare if only ten righteous people could be found in the city, but they could not be found (see Genesis 18:23–33; 19:29).

For this end (2 Nephi 11:4; 25:25). Meaning for this purpose.

For this intent (Jacob 4:4–5; Helaman 14:11; 15:4; Mormon 5:14; 8:6). Meaning for this reason.

Forbidden because of unworthiness (4 Nephi 1:27). Refers to offering sacraments and ordinances to those who are not humble and have not repented. Thus they are not worthy of them, and it is damning to them. *See also:* Partake of my flesh and blood unworthily.

Forbidden fruit (2 Nephi 2:15, 18–19; Mosiah 3:26; Alma 12:22; Helaman 6:26). When Adam and Eve were placed in the Garden of Eden, they were given two commandments: (1) Multiply and replenish the earth; and (2) partake not of the fruit of the tree of knowledge of good and evil, the forbidden fruit. Satan came tempting, trying to thwart the plan of God, and Satan got Adam and Eve to partake of the forbidden fruit. As a result, Adam and Eve could now discern between good and evil, they became mortal, and they were cast out of the Garden of Eden. This was according to the plan of God, for this is how man was introduced to mortality. Thus the spirit children of the Father could come to earth and gain physical bodies and dwell in their probationary state.

Forbidden of the Lord (2 Nephi 26:30; Mormon 8:18; Ether 8:19). The Lord God has given commandments, both "thou shalls" and "thou shall nots." God in His great wisdom knows those things that are harmful and not good for man, and thus certain things are forbidden of the Lord.

Forbidden that I (they) should write (utter/preach) (1 Nephi 14:28; 3 Nephi 26:11, 16; 27:23; 28:14, 25; Mormon 1:16–17; 5:9; Ether 4:1; 5:1; 13:13). On occasion there are spiritual manifestations too sacred to be recorded. Sometimes prophets are shown more than they are allowed to share through prophecy. Some of these events are so elevated in nature and so near to God, even though they are seen and heard by man, it is impossible with man's finite language to write them. In these cases God will directly or through the Spirit forbid their utterance or recording. *See also:* Could not find utterance; Lord forbade; Not lawful to be written; Shalt not write; Should not write; Spirit stopped (stoppeth mine) utterance; Stoppeth utterance; Unspeakable things.

Foreknowledge of God (Alma 13:3, 7). God has planned all things relating to the plan of salvation and the existence of His children. Because of His infinite knowledge He can foresee the events of this earth. Thus He directs the affairs of men (and nations; see D&C 117:6) to bring about His purposes. No unhallowed hand can stay the powers of heaven. Thus all the words of God must be fulfilled, otherwise God would cease to be God, but God ceaseth not to be God (Alma 42:23).

Foretold them by the prophets (2 Nephi 25:9). The prophets, by the power of God, have the ability to prophesy, foretell, and warn of consequences.

Forever and ever (1 Nephi 15:30; 2 Nephi 9:16; Jacob 6:10; Mosiah 2:24, 38; 3:19, 27; Alma 12:17; 37:31). "God, even the Father, reigns upon his throne forever and ever" (D&C 76:92). God's existence is forever and ever, meaning eternal, having no beginning and no end. God's existence is one eternal round and will be forever and ever. To Him there is no end. His glory, might, and power are forever and ever. We should seek to dwell in His glorious presence forever and ever.

Forget(-test/-ting/forgotten) the Lord their God (2 Nephi 8:13; Alma 46:8; 47:36; Helaman 7:20; 11:36; 12:2). "Beware that thou forget not the Lord thy God" (Deuteronomy 8:11). To forget the Lord is to forget who we really are (children of God), to forget His commandments given to guide us to peace and safety, and to forget who our great benefactor is, who has given us everything. The baptismal covenant renewed in the sacrament each week includes the promise we make to always remember Him. Additionally, we are admonished in the scriptures to pray often, even

daily, to give thanks and seek assistance from our great God. *See also:* Forsake the Lord [not]; Remember the Lord our (their/your) God.

Form of a dove (1 Nephi 11:27; 2 Nephi 31:8). Also known as the sign of the dove. "A prearranged means by which John the Baptist would recognize the Messiah at Jesus' baptism (John 1:32–34). The sign of the dove was instituted before the creation of the world, a witness for the Holy Ghost, and the devil cannot come in the sign of a dove . . . Though we usually associate the sign of the dove with John the Baptist . . . we learn that it was manifested to Abraham also [see Abr., fac. 2, fig. 7]. We suppose that it has been similarly made known to other prophets on occasion since the time of Adam" (Bible Dictionary, s.v. "dove, sign of," 658).

Form of a man [God/Jesus Christ] (Mosiah 13:34). Meaning Jehovah, the great God of the Old Testament, would come down and take upon Himself a mortal body, minister to the people, and suffer pain and death so that He could redeem mankind. *See also:* Manifest himself in the flesh.

Form of a man [the Holy Ghost] (1 Nephi 11:11). In this reference, Nephi sees the spirit body of the Holy Ghost. D&C 130:22 says, "The Holy Ghost has not a body of flesh and bones, but is a personage of Spirit. Were it not so, the

Holy Ghost could not dwell in us."
Compare: Body of my spirit.

Form of an angel (Alma 30:53).
The devil can appear as an angel
to deceive, or as stated in 2 Nephi
9:9, Satan can appear as an "angel
of light." The Lord has given us the
means by which to detect such de-
ception in D&C 129:1–9. *See also:*
Angel of light.

Forsake the Lord [not] (Alma
46:21). *Forsake* means to turn away
from, abandon, quit, desert, or
leave. "They that forsake the Lord
shall be consumed" (Isaiah 1:28).
See also: Forget(-test/-ting/forgotten)
the Lord their God.

Forsake your sins (Mosiah 4:10;
Alma 39:9; 3 Nephi 5:3). One of
the steps of repentance is to forsake
one's sins. There has not been true
repentance if one returns and com-
mits the same sins again. "By this ye
may know if a man repenteth of his
sins—behold, he will confess them
and forsake them" (D&C 58:43).
See also: Conditions of repentance.

Forswear thyself (thou shalt not)
(3 Nephi 12:33). Anciently people
would swear by the earth, the heavens, their head, or some other object, things which the individual
swearer had little or no control
over. Rather, Jesus commands us
to simply keep our promises. *See
also:* Swear before (by) the heavens;
Swear not at all; Matthew 5:33–37;
James 5:12.

**Found spotless (pure, fair, and
white)** (Jacob 1:19; Alma 12:14;
Mormon 9:6). *See:* Stand spotless
before me at the last day.

Foundation of the world (1 Nephi
10:18; 2 Nephi 9:18; 27:10; Mosiah
4:6–7; 15:19; 18:13; Alma 12:25,
30; 13:3, 5, 7; 18:39; 22:13; 42:26;
Helaman 5:47; 3 Nephi 1:14; Ether
3:14; 4:14–15, 19; Moroni 8:12).
In every occurrence in the Book of
Mormon, this phrase is part of the
phrase "from the foundation of the
world," meaning from the time of
planning for, the time of preparing
for, and the time of the actual organization of this earth.

Founder of peace (Mosiah 15:18).
Another name for Jesus Christ.
Just as love and light emanate from
Christ, so is He the fountain of and
source of all peace, the Prince of
Peace.

Fountain of all righteousness
(1 Nephi 2:9; Ether 8:26; 12:28).
A descriptor of Jesus Christ. He is
the fountain of all righteousness.
Everything that is good, just, and
true comes from Him. The opposite is Satan, who is the fountain of
all lies and evil. *See also:* All things
which are good cometh of God.

Fountain of living waters (1 Nephi
11:25). Jesus Christ is the bread of
life (John 6:35, 48) and the well or
fountain of living water springing
up unto eternal life (John 7:37–39;
Jeremiah 2:13; 17:13). Living water
is the word of God, which can be

obtained without money and which brings life eternal (John 4:9–14). Saints can also become fountains of living water (springing up and flowing). *See also:* Bread and the waters of life; Living waters; Isaiah 58:11; D&C 121:45–46.

Four quarters of the earth (1 Nephi 19:16; 22:25; 3 Nephi 5:24, 26; 16:5; Ether 13:11). Meaning all parts of the earth: north, east, south, and west. *See also:* All ye ends of the earth.

Frame has no strength (1 Nephi 17:47). *See:* Overcome with the Spirit.

Free according to the flesh (2 Nephi 2:27). All men and women have been given their moral agency. Those that use this agency to seek truth and good become more free to do additional and greater things, while those that rebel and do evil will in time become bound down by the chains of the devil, thus forfeiting much or all of their freedom. *See also:* Free forever.

Free forever (2 Nephi 2:26). In the great plan of salvation, having as its basis moral agency, we may choose salvation and freedom through Jesus Christ or we may choose damnation and the captivity of Satan (see Helaman 12:26). John 8:32 says, "Ye shall know the truth and the truth shall make you free." Thus if we follow Christ and keep the commandments we will come to know the truth and become free

forever—"[free] from the bondage of sin, [free] from the chains of hell" (McConkie, *Promised Messiah*, 242)—free from the evil influence of Satan, free to progress in light and truth, free to obtain exaltation and glory, and free to advance towards godhood. We must always be champions and emissaries of this great freedom. *See also:* Made free.

Free with your substance (Jacob 2:17). *See:* Impart of their substance.

Free(-dom) from bondage (Alma 43:48–49; 48:11; 51:21; 62:5; Ether 2:12). *See:* Deliver(-ed) out of bondage; Promised land; Title of liberty.

From (all) eternity to all eternity (Mosiah 3:5; Alma 13:7; Moroni 8:18). Meaning without beginning of days or end of years; having always existed and always will exist. Used most often in the scriptures as a descriptor of the Lord. Also the priesthood is from eternity to all eternity (Alma 13:7), and intelligence, or the light of truth, is likewise from eternity to all eternity (see D&C 93:29). *See also:* Without beginning of days (or end of years).

From generation to generation (2 Nephi 8:8; 9:2; 23:20; 25:9, 16, 21–22; Jacob 1:31; Words of Mormon 1:10–11; Mosiah 28:14; Helaman 6:30; 4 Nephi 1:48; Moroni 10:28). *See:* Generation to (another) generation.

From the beginning (1 Nephi 9:6; 12:18; 20:3, 5, 7; 2 Nephi 11:4; 27:7;

Jacob 5:74; Mosiah 3:8; 28:14; Alma 5:25; 18:32; Alma 37:3; Helaman 6:29; 14:12; 3 Nephi 9:15; 11:11; 26:3; Ether 8:15, 19, 25; 13:2). Meaning from the beginning of man, from the beginning of the earth's creation, or from the beginning counsels in heaven, depending on the context. There have been many beginnings and many ends. The most familiar is the beginning and the end of our mortal existence. In each of our eternal existences there will yet be many millions of beginnings and endings. "For no matter where we are or what our circumstances, an eternity of beginnings and an eternity of endings stretch out before us" (Uchtdorf, "Always in the Middle," 5).

From the creation of Adam (Alma 22:12–13; Moroni 10:3). *See:* From the beginning.

From the creation of the world (2 Nephi 1:10; 6:3). *See:* From the beginning.

From the dust (2 Nephi 1:14, 21, 23; 3:19–20; 8:25; 33:13; 20:37; Mormon 8:23; Ether 8:24; Moroni 10:31). *See:* Arise from the dust; Cry from the dust; Shake thyself from the dust.

From the foundation of the world (1 Nephi 10:18; 2 Nephi 9:18; 27:10; Mosiah 4:6–7; 15:19; 18:13; Alma 12:25, 30; 13:3, 5, 7; 18:39; 22:13; 42:26; Helaman 5:47; 3 Nephi 1:14; Ether 3:14; 4:14–15, 19; Moroni 8:12). Refers to the span of time

since the world was organized by God, and appears to include the time of planning the creation of the world.

Fruit meet for repentance (Alma 12:15; 13:13; 34:30). *See:* Brought forth fruit [before baptism].

Fruit of my loins (2 Nephi 3:4, 6, 14). *See:* Seed of thy loins.

Fruit of the loins of Joseph (Jacob 2:25). Joseph the son of Jacob received certain promises from the Lord, the same as those promised to Abraham. "Fruit of the loins" refers to one's posterity, and Joseph was promised a vast posterity. This included a righteous posterity which would run over the wall, meaning posterity that would leave Jerusalem and settle elsewhere in the world. This refers to Lehi and his posterity that were led by the Lord to the Americas. Lehi learned from the plates of brass that he was a descendant of Joseph (see 1 Nephi 5:14).

Fruit of the loins of Judah (2 Nephi 3:12). Meaning the posterity of the tribe of Judah, which brought forth the Bible.

Fruit of the tree of life [Garden of Eden] (Alma 12:21, 23; 42:3). We are told of two of the trees that existed in the Garden of Eden. One bore the forbidden fruit that was the fruit of the tree of knowledge of good and evil. When Adam and Eve partook of this fruit they learned of good and evil and they became mortal. The other tree was the tree of life, which if Adam and Eve partook of the fruit thereof they would immediately become immortal, thus frustrating the plan of redemption and negating the need for a redeemer. Therefore God placed cherubim and a flaming sword before the tree of life so that Adam and Eve could not partake thereof, and Adam and Eve were cast out of the Garden of Eden to experience mortality and learn to rely with faith on the Redeemer. *See also:* Forbidden fruit; Fruit of the tree of life [Lehi's dream].

Fruit of the tree of life [Lehi's dream] (1 Nephi 15:36; 2 Nephi 2:15; Alma 5:34, 62; 32:40). Meaning the blessings of the gospel in their fullest, even eternal life. In Lehi's dream he described this fruit as "desirable to make one happy . . . it was most sweet, above all that I ever before tasted, [it] was white, to exceed all the whiteness that I had ever seen. And as I partook of the fruit thereof it filled my soul with exceedingly great joy; wherefore, I began to be desirous that my family should partake of it also" (1 Nephi 8:10–12). When Nephi explained Lehi's dream to his brothers, he said that the fruit of the tree of life is "most precious and most desirable above all other fruits; yea, and it is the greatest of all the gifts of God" (1 Nephi 15:36). In D&C 14:7 we learn that this greatest gift of God is in fact eternal life. Finally, Alma

said, "The fruit thereof, which is most precious, which is sweet above all that is sweet, and which is white above all that is white, yea, and pure above all that is pure; and ye shall feast upon this fruit even until ye are filled, that ye hunger not, neither shall ye thirst" (Alma 32:42). *See also:* Fruit of the tree of life [Garden of Eden].

Fruit of thy loins (2 Nephi 3:7, 11–12, 18–19, 21). *See:* Seed of thy loins.

Fruit unto repentance (Alma 12:15; 13:13; 34:30). *See:* Brought forth fruit [before baptism].

Fruitful field shall be esteemed as a forest (2 Nephi 27:28). The full rendering is "Lebanon shall be turned into a fruitful field; and the fruitful field shall be esteemed as a forest." Meaning under God's blessing, after the coming forth of the Book of Mormon, that land (Palestine) which was arid and unfertile will become a fruitful garden blessed with abundant vegetation, foliage, and trees. *See also:* Lebanon shall be turned into a fruitful field.

Fruit(-s) of my (our/their) labors (Alma 26:31; 29:17; 36:25; 40:26). Refers to converts to the gospel of Jesus Christ because of preaching and the testimony of the Spirit. See the parable of the vineyard, which talks about bringing forth good fruit (see Jacob 5). *See also:* Fruit(-s) of my (our/their) labors.

Fulfil all his (my) promises (2 Nephi 10:17; Alma 37:17). A person can count completely and one hundred percent on God's promise. *See also:* According to God's word.

Fulfil all righteousness (2 Nephi 31:5–6). The most familiar use of this phrase was by Jesus when He came to John the Baptist to be baptized: "And Jesus answering said unto him, Suffer it to be so now: for thus it becometh us to fulfill all righteousness" (Matthew 3:15). The meaning being to fulfill the will of the Father and submit to the ordinances of righteousness and salvation.

Fulfil the law (3 Nephi 15:5). Jesus Christ came at the meridian of time to, among other things, fulfill the law of Moses. The entirety of the law of Moses was to point the people to a recognition, remembrance, acceptance, and reverence for the sacrifice of the Savior, Jesus Christ. Once that sacrifice was concluded, the law that pointed the people's minds forward to that event was now complete and fulfilled. Thereafter the new law of Christ was given to love one another and the ordinances that are symbolic of and remind us of our Savior and Redeemer. *See also:* Law of Moses; Alma 34:13–15.

Fulfill all that which I have caused to be spoken by the mouth of my holy prophets (3 Nephi 1:13). *See:* According to God's word; According to the prophecy (prophecies) of the Lord.

Fulfill all things which I have made known unto the children of men (3 Nephi 1:14). *See:* According to God's word.

Fulfill and to do the work of the covenants of the Father (Moroni 7:31). Meaning to help bring about the promises of our Heavenly Father, which is to assist in the accomplishment and realization of God's covenants to Abraham and his seed by bringing the gospel of Christ and salvation to mankind.

Fulfill his word which he hath declared (1 Nephi 20:14). *See:* According to God's word.

Fulfill the covenant (3 Nephi 16:5). Meaning to bring to fruition or completion the promises made to the people of the house of Israel (the Abrahamic covenant); the preaching of the gospel of Jesus Christ to them and the gathering of them as prophesied. *See also:* Covenant which he made with Abraham.

Fulfilled all the commandments (laws) of the Lord (1 Nephi 16:8; 17:3; 2 Nephi 9:17). The emphasis here being on the word *all*. We must keep *all* the commandments and laws of God, not just the ones we find convenient.

Fulfilled all things which the Lord hath spoken (1 Nephi 7:13; Ether 12:3). *See:* According to God's word.

Fulfilled the covenant (1 Nephi 15:18; 2 Nephi 10:15; 3 Nephi 5:25; 15:18; 20:12, 25, 27, 46; 21:4; 29:1; Mormon 5:20; Ether 13:11; Moroni 10:31). Referring to the Abrahamic covenant. *See also:* Covenant which he made with Abraham.

Fulfilled the law [of Moses] (2 Nephi 25:24, 27, 30; Alma 25:15; 30:3; 34:13; 3 Nephi 1:25; 9:17; 12:18–19, 46; 15:4, 5; Ether 12:11). *See:* Fulfil the law; Law of Moses.

Fulfilled the promise (2 Nephi 3:14; 25:21; Mosiah 7:32; Alma 37:17; Mormon 8:22). *See:* According to God's word.

Fulfilled the prophecies (2 Nephi 25:7; Words of Mormon 1:4; Mosiah 20:21; Alma 13:26; 45:9, 14; Helaman 16:14; 3 Nephi 1:4–6, 15; 5:1, 14; 15:6; 16:17; 20:11–12; 23:10; 29:2). *See:* According to God's word; According to the prophecy (prophecies) of the Lord.

Fulfilled the scriptures (3 Nephi 9:16; 10:11; Mormon 8:33). *See:* According to God's word.

Fulfilled the word(-s) of God (the Lord) (1 Nephi 7:13; 2 Nephi 5:19; 5:20; Mosiah 21:4; Alma 3:14; 5:57–58; 7:11; 37:24, 26; Helaman 11:8; 16:13; 3 Nephi 28:7; Ether 15:3, 33). *See:* According to God's word.

Fulfilleth the covenant which he made to Abraham (3 Nephi 20:27). *See:* Fulfilled the covenant.

Fulfilleth the words which he hath given (3 Nephi 27:18). *See:* According to God's word.

Fulfilling of (all) his (the) word(-s/ of the Lord) (1 Nephi 9:6; 10:13; 18:11; Alma 3:18; 37:16; 50:19; 60:16; Helaman 12:26; Mormon 1:19; Moroni 8:29). *See:* According to God's word.

Fulfilling of the (his) covenant (3 Nephi 5:25; 10:7; 20:12, 22; 21:7; 29:9; Mormon 5:14; Ether 13:11). *See:* Fulfilled the covenant.

Fulfilling of the promise (2 Nephi 3:14; 31:18). *See:* According to God's word.

Fulfilling of the prophecies (3 Nephi 10:14; Ether 13:21; Moroni 8:29; 10:28). *See:* According to God's word.

Full of darkness (3 Nephi 13:23). "Their hearts are corrupt, and full of wickedness and abominations; and they love darkness rather than light, because their deeds are evil" (D&C 10:21). Light and truth chase away darkness. Men and women must choose either light or darkness. *See also:* Works of darkness.

Full of grace (equity/mercy) and truth (2 Nephi 2:6; Alma 5:48; 9:26; 13:9). A description reserved for Christ and God the Father. These two divine Gods are full of divine and flawless characteristics such that there is not room left for improvement; or, in other words, they are full of perfection. Thus they are full of grace and truth and all things excellent, and they are completely absent of anything not commendable. In summary they are beings of all godliness and all god-like characteristics. "Full of grace and truth" could well be a name title of God, for He is in fact synonymous with all grace and truth. *See also:* John 1:14; D&C 66:12; 84:102; 93:11; Moses 1:6, 32; 5:7; 6:52; 7:11.

Full of (his) glory (2 Nephi 16:3; Helaman 5:44). Meaning filled with light, power, truth, and the approval of God; even the countenance and majesty of God. We must strive to increase the glory of God and bring the gospel to His children, for by so doing God will then endow us with glory. This is how Jesus gained His glory. *See also:* Full of the knowledge of the Lord.

Full of light (3 Nephi 13:22). Having no part dark and an eye single to the glory of God. Same as being full of truth. *See also:* Marvelous light of God.

Full of love (Mosiah 3:19; Alma 13:21). Void of hate and enmity. Meaning to exemplify and radiate the love of God. "No one can assist in this work except he shall be humble and full of love, having faith, hope, and charity, being temperate in all things, whatsoever shall be entrusted to his care" (D&C 12:8).

Full of the knowledge of the Lord (2 Nephi 21:9; 30:15). Refers to the Millennium, when the love and knowledge of Jesus Christ will cover the earth such that it affects for good the way all the earth's inhabitants act. *See also:* Isaiah 11:9.

Full of the Spirit of God (1 Nephi 17:47). *See:* Filled with the Holy Ghost.

Full purpose of heart (2 Nephi 31:13; Jacob 6:5; Mosiah 7:33; 3 Nephi 10:6; 12:24; 18:32). With true intent and with all possible energy. Giving one's self completely and prayerfully seeking the assistance of God. "Pray and go" is the saying, not hesitating. *See also:* Energy of heart; Energy of my soul.

Fuller's soap (3 Nephi 24:2). Fuller's soap was a caustic alkali- or lye-based soap used to clean and whiten wool. The profession of a fuller was to wash, beat, and rewash fabrics to clean them and make them fuller (fluffier and having body). The symbolism is that Christ will purify and whiten us like the fuller's soap. On the Mount of Transfiguration the robe of Jesus was described, "And his raiment became shining, exceeding white as snow; so as no fuller on earth can white them" (Mark 9:3).

Fully ripe (in iniquity) (2 Nephi 28:16; Alma 37:28, 31; 45:16; Ether 2:15). Being completely immersed, enthralled, and preoccupied with sin. Having every intent to do evil. *See also:* Ripe(-ned) in iniquity.

Fulness of his (my) wrath (1 Nephi 22:17; 2 Nephi 1:17; Ether 2:8–9;

9:20; 14:25). *See:* Fulness of the wrath of God.

Fulness of his own time (2 Nephi 11:7). *See:* Own due time (of the Lord).

Fulness of iniquity (Ether 2:10). *See:* Fully ripe (in iniquity).

Fulness of joy (3 Nephi 27:30–31; 28:10). *See:* Joy is (shall be/was) full.

Fulness of my (the) gospel (1 Nephi 10:14; 13:24; 15:13; 3 Nephi 16:7, 10, 12; 20:28, 30). Meaning the fulness of the blessings of the gospel. This includes all the true doctrine of Christ, all the saving ordinances, all the gifts of the Holy Ghost, and all the priesthood powers pertaining thereto.

Fulness of the Gentiles (1 Nephi 10:14; 15:13; 3 Nephi 16:4, 7). Meaning after the Gentiles have received a fulness of the gospel. In the phrase, "the last shall be first," in the latter days the Gentiles shall receive the gospel first and then it will go to the Jews. The Jews will receive it from the converted Gentiles.

Fulness of the wrath of God (1 Nephi 17:35; 22:16–17; 2 Nephi 1:17; Ether 2:8–9, 11, 20; 14:25). *Fulness* means all that is possible and available. *See also:* Fulness of his wrath; Wrath of God (the Lord).

Fulness of time (2 Nephi 2:3, 26; 11:7). Refers to the meridian of time when Jesus would come to dwell amongst men in the flesh. In the 11:7 reference, it is rendered, "In the fulness of his own time," meaning in God's own due time. It is a fulness because the law of Moses was brought to a finish and the prophecies concerning the coming of Jesus were fulfilled in their fulness. Compare Galatians 4:4–5. We are also familiar with the Doctrine and Covenants scriptural phrase, "dispensation of the fulness of times," meaning the latter days.

Furnace of affliction (1 Nephi 20:10). "The Lord uses adversity to bring about His purposes and to help us learn valuable lessons. . . . Learning often becomes more acute and precise and has greater depth when brought about by adversity. . . . [Job] suffered enormous grief. Still, he continued to trust in the Lord (see Job 13:15). . . . We can then find comfort in the Lord's great promise: 'After much tribulation . . . cometh the blessing' (D&C 103:12)" (Brough, "Adversity, the Great Teacher," 9–11).

G

Gadianton robbers (and murderers) (Helaman 3:23; 6:18, 37; 7:4, 25; 8:1, 28; 11:10, 26; 3 Nephi 1:27, 29; 2:11–12, 18; 3:9, 15; 4 Nephi 1:42, 46; Mormon 1:18; 2:27–28). Called Gadianton because of "one [named] Gadianton, who was exceedingly expert in many words, and also in his craft, to carry on the secret work of murder and of robbery" (Helaman 2:4). "And he was upheld by his band, who had entered into a covenant that no one should know his wickedness" (Helaman 2:3), therefore he became the leader of that band. *See also:* Secret combination(-s).

Gainsaying people (Jacob 6:4). *Gainsay* means to deny. Thus a gainsaying people deny the Christ, deny His gospel, and deny truth.

Gall of bitterness (Mosiah 27:29; Alma 36:18; 41:11; Mormon 8:31; Moroni 8:14). Literally immersed in a bitter and hateful liquid. This is symbolic of the mental state that Alma the Younger found himself in after being chastised by an angel for his sins. He then realized his awful sinful state before God. Sometimes described that it would be better to be banished and extinct or covered by rocks than to face God in one's sins. Compare "bitterness of hell" in Moses 1:20. *See also:* Nakedness before God.

Garden of Eden (2 Nephi 2:19, 22; 8:3; Alma 12:21; 42:2). The garden place of beauty, tranquility, and bounty prepared by God for Adam and Eve to first be placed upon the newly organized earth. Here Adam and Eve lived in innocence and without knowledge of their former premortal life. After partaking of the forbidden fruit, the fruit of the tree of knowledge of good and evil, they were cast out of the garden into the lone and dreary world. There they experienced choosing right over wrong, and brought forth the family of man. *See also:* Forbidden fruit; Fruit of the tree of life [Garden of Eden].

Garments are not spotted with your blood (Jacob 1:19; Mosiah 2:28; Mormon 9:35; Ether 12:38). Those that minister the gospel unto the children of men have a duty to proceed with all diligence. To not give forth their best efforts would make them to some extent responsible for the blood and sins of their generation. In other words, if we do not magnify our callings in preaching repentance, then the blood and sins of those we should have warned would stain us and become part of our own guilt. *See also:* Rid my (our) garments of your (blood and) sins.

Garments are spotless (Alma 5:24; 7:25). *See:* Garments cleansed through the blood of the Lamb (made white/washed).

Garments cleansed through the blood of the Lamb (made white/ washed) (1 Nephi 12:10–11; Alma 5:21, 24, 27; 13:11–12; 34:36; Ether 13:10; 3 Nephi 27:19). Because of the Atonement of Christ, our garments can be washed white through the blood of the Lamb. Our Savior shed His blood in suffering for our sins so that we do not have to suffer and we can be made clean of sin through faith on His name, repentance, baptism, good works, and sanctification and purification by the Holy Ghost.

Garments must be purified (Alma 5:21). *See:* Garments cleansed through the blood of the Lamb (made white/washed).

Garments shall be made clean (Ether 12:37). "Thou hast been faithful; wherefore thy garments shall be made clean" (D&C 135:5). *See:* Garments cleansed through the blood of the Lamb (made white/ washed).

Garments spotless (Jacob 1:19; Alma 5:24; 7:25; 13:12). "If we are faithful in Christ, we shall rid our garments of the blood of all men, and be found spotless before the judgment-seat of Christ, and shall dwell with him eternally in the heavens" (Book of Mormon, Testimony of Three Witnesses). *See also:* Rid my (our) garments of your (blood and) sins.

Garments stained with blood and all manner of filthiness (Alma 5:22). A figurative description of a sinful, wicked, and unrepentant person.

Gate by which ye should enter (2 Nephi 31:9, 17). Verse 17 says: "The gate by which ye should enter is repentance and baptism by water; and then cometh a remission of your sins by fire and by the Holy Ghost." *See also:* Enter in (into/by) the (narrow/strait) gate (way/path); Strait and narrow course (path).

Gate of heaven (Helaman 3:28). In the secular world, sometimes referred to as the pearly gates. "The keeper of the gate is the Holy One of Israel (Jesus); and he employeth no servant there; and there is none other way save it be by the gate" (2 Nephi 9:41). Often referred to as the narrow gate (see 2 Nephi 31:9). The gate to the path that leads to heaven is repentance and baptism (see 2 Nephi 31:17) but thereafter requires enduring to the end. Most importantly, the gate of heaven is open to all who come unto Christ (see D&C 132:22). *See also:* Gate by which ye should enter; Gates of thy righteousness.

Gates of hell (2 Nephi 4:32; 3 Nephi 11:39–40; 18:13). "The gates of hell: the power and policy of Satan and his instruments." (Webster, *American Dictionary, 1828*). In some of these Book of Mormon verses it is as though the gates of hell can reach out and grab you or prevail against you. Thus it is a sure thing the gates of hell shall receive the wicked and unrepentant. The gate to hell is wide, and broad is the way which leadeth to destruction (see 3 Nephi 14:13). *See also:* D&C 21:6.

Gates of thy righteousness (2 Nephi 4:32). In Psalm 118:19–20, the psalmist prays, "Open to me the gates of righteousness; I will go into them, and I will praise the Lord. This gate of the Lord, into which the righteous shall enter." *See also:* Gate of heaven.

Gather in the house of Israel (1 Nephi 19:16; 2 Nephi 21:12; 30:7; 3 Nephi 5:24; 16:5; 21:1). The promise of the Lord is to gather again the tribes of Israel from their long dispersion in which the Lord scattered them among the nations because of their wickedness. *See also:* Gather them in from the four quarters of the earth; Gathered home to the lands of their inheritance; Gathered in from their long dispersion; Gathered together again;

Gathered together to the lands of their inheritance.

Gather them in from the four quarters of the earth (1 Nephi 19:16; 22:25; 2 Nephi 21:12; 3 Nephi 5:24, 26; 16:5; 20:13; Ether 13:11). *See:* Gather in the house of Israel.

Gather together my sheep (Mosiah 26:20). In the metaphor where the Lord Jesus is the Good Shepherd, He calls to His sheep, they know His voice, and He gathers them into His fold wherein there is peace, safety, and green pasture. *See also:* Gathereth his children; Good Shepherd.

Gathered home to the lands of their inheritance (2 Nephi 9:2; 29:14; 3 Nephi 5:26; 21:28). "The physical gathering of Israel means that the covenant people will be 'gathered home to the lands of their inheritance, and shall be established in all their lands of promise' (2 Nephi 9:2). The tribes of Ephraim and Manasseh will be gathered in the Americas. The tribe of Judah will return to the city of Jerusalem and the area surrounding it. The ten lost tribes will receive from the tribe of Ephraim their promised blessings (see D&C 133:26–34)" (*Gospel Principles*, 248). *See also:* Gather in the house of Israel.

Gathered in from their long dispersion (2 Nephi 10:8; 21:1; 3 Nephi 21:1). *See:* Gather in the house of Israel.

Gathered in one (2 Nephi 29:14). The Lord has promised that His word, His people's records, and scriptures will be gathered together in one in His own due time. *Compare:* Ezekiel 37:16–19. *See also:* Established in one.

Gathered into the garners (Alma 26:5). Meaning the Saints will be gathered together in safe places prepared by the Lord. The garners are the storage facilities or silos for preserving grain. The symbolism is the grain of the harvest is gathered in.

Gathered together again (1 Nephi 10:14; 2 Nephi 6:11). *See:* Gather in the house of Israel.

Gathered together to the lands of their inheritance (1 Nephi 22:12; 2 Nephi 6:11). "'The gathering of Israel is one of the fundamental principles of the restored gospel of Jesus Christ. The Lord gathers His people when they accept Him and keep His commandments. The spirit of gathering is an integral part of the restoration of all things in this, the Dispensation of the Fulness of Times.' . . . The Lord gathers His people to worship (Mosiah 18:25), to build up the Church (D&C 101:63–64), for a defense (D&C 115:6) and to receive counsel and instruction (Mosiah 18:7). . . . The primary places of gathering [are] into the Lord's restored Church (D&C 101:64–65), into holy temples (Alma 26:5–6), into stakes of Zion (D&C 109:59) and into families (Mosiah 2:5). . . . The blessings of gathering [are] blessings of edification (Ephesians 4:12–13), preservation (Moses 7:61) and strength (D&C 82:14)" (Bednar, "Marvelous Miracle").

Gathered you as a hen gathereth her chickens under her wings (3 Nephi 10:4–6). *See:* Hen gathereth her chickens (under her wings).

Gathereth his children (1 Nephi 22:25). *See:* Gather together my sheep.

Gave power (2 Nephi 25:20; Mosiah 25:19; Alma 25:6; Helaman 8:11–12; 3 Nephi 11:22; 18:37). Meaning to give the priesthood or the power of God to perform the saving ordinances, administer the gospel, and perform mighty miracles. *See also:* Authority from (of) God; Articles of Faith 1:5.

Gave thanks to (unto) God (the Lord) (1 Nephi 2:7; 5:9; Mosiah 8:19; 24:22; Alma 8:22; 45:1). It is most ungracious to pray and not give many thanks unto God, for truly every good gift that we have received we have received from Him. Prayers entirely of thanks are a praise unto God, and uplift the heart of the one who so prays. We will give thanks unto God forever and ever.

Gave up the ghost (Jacob 7:20). Meaning gave up his spirit, or the separating of the spirit from the physical body, which is temporal death.

Genealogy of his (my/our) fathers (1 Nephi 3:3, 12; 5:14, 16; 6:1; 19:2; Jarom 1:1; Omni 1:1, 18; Alma 37:3). God has commanded that records be kept (see 1 Nephi 19:1–2). In Moses we read that Adam kept a genealogy record: "Now this prophecy Adam spake, as he was moved upon by the Holy Ghost, and a genealogy was kept of the children of God. And this was the book of the generations of Adam" (Moses 6:8).

Generation to (another) generation (1 Nephi 19:4; 2 Nephi 8:8; 9:2; 23:20; 25:9, 16, 21–22; Jacob 1:3; Words of Mormon 1:10–11; Mosiah 28:14, 20; Alma 37:4; 63:13; Helaman 3:16; 6:30; 4 Nephi 1:48; Moroni 10:28). God our Father is concerned about families and generations. Thus He desires to provide blessings for multiple generations, or from generation to generation. Alternately, when the people are wicked, consequences endure for many generations. Thus the wicked are cursed and scourged from generation to generation. *See also:* Visiting the iniquities of the fathers upon the children unto the third and fourth generations.

Gentiles had received the fulness of the gospel (1 Nephi 10:14; 15:13; 3 Nephi 16:10). In the timetable of the Lord, during the last days the gospel of Jesus Christ will be taught first to the Gentiles (defined as the non-Jews, which includes the scattered ten tribes). *See also:* Fulness of the Gentiles; Gentiles shall be blessed.

Gentiles shall be blessed (1 Nephi 22:9; 2 Nephi 6:12; 10:10, 18; 3 Nephi 16:6, 13; 20:27). In the last days the Gentiles will be instrumental in the work of the Lord. The United States of America will be brought forth by the Gentiles and blessed of the Lord. Many Gentiles will accept the gospel and be numbered among the house of Israel. These faithful Gentiles will help carry forth the gospel to the world. But many Gentiles will also not accept the gospel. And when they no longer will accept the gospel it will signal the fulness of the Gentiles. *See also:* Fulness of the Gentiles; Gentiles had received the fulness of the gospel.

Get gain (1 Nephi 22:23; 2 Nephi 26:20, 29; 27:16; Alma 10:32; 11:20; 30:35; Helaman 6:8, 17; 7:5, 21; 3 Nephi 29:7; 4 Nephi 1:26; Mormon 8:14; 8:33, 40; Ether 8:22–23; 10:22; 11:15). It is evil to get gain for selfish and prideful purposes. When a society emphasizes getting gain, and getting gain only, it is a society in decline. Rather a society should build for the future, provide plenty for all, improve conditions commonly, and ensure better things for succeeding generations. *See also:* Fine things of the world.

Get hold upon their hearts (Helaman 6:30; 4 Nephi 1:28). Satan attempts to gain control over the feelings, intents, and desires of the hearts of men and women. Thus he can then rule over them, they become subject to him, and they grow miserable like unto him. *See also:* Satan did get hold (possession) upon the hearts of the people.

Get power (1 Nephi 22:23; Ether 8:22–23; 11:15). Throughout the ages men have not sought the will of God, but instead have sought power over their fellowmen, sought the riches of the world, and sought the honor, fame, and glory of the world. *See also:* Desire of power; Seek for power.

Get thee into the mountain (1 Nephi 17:7). We learn from the scriptures that God has often spoken to His prophets in the high mountains, perhaps because the tops of mountains are far from worldly things. The temples of God today provide the same type of sacred place where prophets and saints of God can go to seek inspiration from on high. *See also:* Carried away in the spirit (in a vision); High mountain; Go into the mount oft; Mountain of the Lord(-'s house).

Get thou up into (go up to) the temple (Jacob 2:1, 11; Mosiah 1:18). To deliver or hear the message of God.

Gift and power of God (the Lamb) (1 Nephi 13:35; Omni 1:20). By the gift and power of God the purposes of the Lord shall be brought to pass, for with God all things are possible. *See also:* Power of God; Matthew 19:26; Mark 9:23; 10:27.

Gift and power of the Holy Ghost (1 Nephi 13:37) The gift and power of the Holy Ghost has equal power with the gift and power of God, because the power of the Holy Ghost is given of God. *See also:* Gift and power of God (the Lamb); Power of the Holy Ghost (Spirit).

Gift from God (Mosiah 8:13–14; 21:28). *See:* Gifts of God.

Gift of his calling unto me (Moroni 7:2). It is a great honor and gift to humbly and worthily serve God, preach His gospel, and provide the ordinances thereof. *See also:* Gifts and callings of God.

Gift of the Holy Ghost (2 Nephi 28:26; Jacob 6:8; Alma 9:21). The gift of God to those who truly repent, are baptized, and receive this gift by the laying on of hands by those in authority and holding the true priesthood of God. It is to have the constant companionship of the Holy Ghost, the third member of the Godhead, as long as one is worthy. We should be very grateful for the gift of the Holy Ghost. *See also:* Power of the Holy Ghost (Spirit); 1 Nephi 10:17; 13:37.

Gifts and callings of God (Moroni 3:4). Those ordained to offices in the priesthood (deacon, teacher, priest, elder, high priest, etc.) in effect have a calling from God (see duties of the various offices in the priesthood in D&C 20). The callings of the priesthood have responsibilities and gifts pertaining thereto. *See also:* D&C 20:27, 60.

Gifts of God (1 Nephi 10:17; 15:36; Mosiah 8:13–14; 21:28; Alma 9:21; Moroni 10:8, 24–25). All good gifts come from God and include the gifts of the Spirit as listed in Articles of Faith 1:7; 1 Corinthians 12:8–11; Moroni 10:8–18; and D&C 46:8–30. Concerning these gifts, the scripture says, "All have not every gift given unto them; for there are many gifts, and to every man [and woman] is given a gift by the Spirit of God" (D&C 46:11). We are also endowed with other gifts or talents, such as music, athletics, academic, speaking, mechanics, etc. The parable of the talents found in Matthew 25 is instructive about how we should develop our gifts. Elder Paul V. Johnson has said, "The Lord has blessed you with a unique set of gifts. They have been given to you for a reason. Do not complain because you do not have someone else's gifts. Find your own. Explore them. Develop them. Bless others with them. This will bring you great joy" ("All These Gifts Come from God"). *See also:* Every good gift; Given by the Spirit of God; Spiritual gifts.

Girdle of his reins (2 Nephi 21:5; 30:11). One's reins are his loins or waist. *See also:* Girdle of his (their) loins.

Girdle of his (their) loins (2 Nephi 15:27; 21:5; 30:11). A wide belt or sash worn around the lower waist, from which often hangs a sword. Additionally the girdle is often worn as a protection, a comfort, and a bolster. Symbolically, the Lord wears a girdle of the faithful and the righteous. "For as the girdle cleaveth to the loins of a man, so have I caused to cleave unto me the whole house of Israel" (Jeremiah 13:11).

Give ear unto his counsels (2 Nephi 9:29; Helaman 12:5). *Give ear* means listen to and has the additional bidding to follow and do as God counsels, commands, and instructs. *See also:* Counsel with the Lord.

Give ear unto my words (2 Nephi 4:3; 8:4; 9:40; 25:4; Alma 36:1; 38:1). "Whether by mine own voice or by the voice of my servants, it is the same" (D&C 1:38). Thus we should listen to and follow the advice of the prophets who are God's servants. *See also:* Give ear unto his counsels.

Give heed (1 Nephi 15:25; 16:3; Alma 37:43–44; 39:10; 45:23–24; 3 Nephi 12:1; 23:4; Moroni 8:21). Observe closely, obey, and be warned. *See also:* Give ear unto his counsels; Give ear unto my words; Take heed.

Give me strength (1 Nephi 7:17; Alma 31:30). We should pray for strength as we navigate mortality and fend off the advances of Satan. We should add these words to our prayer language. *See also:* Give us strength.

Give power (2 Nephi 3:11; 3:17; 26:16; Helaman 10:7; 3 Nephi 11:21; 18:5; 21:11). *See:* Gave power; Give unto you power.

Give thanks in all things (Mosiah 26:39). Meaning to give thanks to God while involved in or doing all righteous things. *See also:* Give thanks unto the Lord their God.

Give thanks to his holy name (Alma 26:8). "See that ye do all things in worthiness, and do it in the name of Jesus Christ" (Mormon 9:29). *See also:* Give thanks unto the Lord their God.

Give thanks unto God (forever) (Mosiah 25:10; Alma 26:37; Mormon 9:31). It is to God we must give thanks, for all good things come from Him. In truth we will be giving thanks unto Him forever, for providing the plan of salvation and the opportunity of eternal life. *See also:* Give thanks unto the Lord their God.

Give thanks unto his holy name (2 Nephi 9:52). Give thanks unto God, and praise His name, for He is indeed holy. *See also:* Give thanks unto the Lord their God.

Give thanks unto the Lord their God (1 Nephi 7:22; 16:32; Mosiah 2:4; 18:23). Our Lord Jesus Christ has provided redemption from physical death, and the opportunity for exaltation and eternal life. For this we are forever thankful. *See also:* Give thanks in all things; Give thanks to his holy name; Give thanks unto God (forever); Give thanks unto his holy name.

Give the Holy Ghost (2 Nephi 31:12; 3 Nephi 18:37; 19:21; Moroni 2:2). Only the true servants of God who administer the true priesthood or power of God can give the Holy Ghost. *See also:* Gift and power of the Holy Ghost; Receive(-d) the Holy Ghost; Acts 8:17–21.

Give thee for a light (1 Nephi 21:6; 3 Nephi 12:14). We are commanded to be a light and example unto the world. "Let your light so shine before men, that they may see your good works, and glorify your Father which is in heaven" (Matthew 5:16).

Give unto thee (you) a sign (2 Nephi 17:14; Alma 30:49; Helaman 14:2–3, 14; 3 Nephi 21:1–2). God gives signs to warn people and to signal predicted events. God can give signs and wonders at His will, but it is evil for us to seek a sign. "A wicked and adulterous generation seeketh after a sign" (Matthew 16:4). *See also:* Shall be a sign unto you.

Give unto you a prophecy (2 Nephi 25:4, 7; Jacob 6:1). Meaning God is speaking to men through His prophets by the power of the Holy Ghost.

See also: I would prophesy; Spirit of prophecy (and revelation).

Give unto you power (2 Nephi 3:11, 17; Alma 31:35; Helaman 10:7; 3 Nephi 11:21; 12:1; 18:5, 37; Moroni 2:2). Meaning to give the priesthood or the power of God to preach salvation, perform the saving ordinances, and administer the gospel. *See also:* Authority from (of) God; Gave power; Articles of Faith 1:5.

Give up the ghost (Jacob 7:21). *See:* Gave up the ghost.

Give us strength (1 Nephi 7:17; Alma 14:26; 58:10). *See:* Lord did strengthen them.

Given by the Spirit of God (Moroni 10:8–9). Meaning the gifts of the Spirit or the gifts of the Holy Ghost. *See also:* Gifts of God; 1 Corinthians 12:8; D&C 46:11, 13, 15–17.

Given to know (Alma 7:4; 12:7, 9–10; 26:22; 42:65; Helaman 9:36; 14:31; 3 Nephi 7:15; Moroni 7:15–16). Meaning to be given to know the mysteries of God by revelation and given to know right from wrong by the Spirit of Christ.

Given us a portion of his Spirit (Alma 24:8). *See:* Portion of his spirit.

Giveth utterance (2 Nephi 1:27; 28:4). Meaning the Holy Ghost will give one the words to speak. "And it shall come to pass, that if you shall ask the Father in my name, in faith believing, you shall receive the Holy Ghost, which giveth utterance" (D&C 14:8). "First seek to obtain my word, and then shall your tongue be loosed; then, if you desire, you shall have my Spirit and my word, yea, the power of God unto the convincing of men" (D&C 11:21). "For it shall be given you in the very hour, yea, in the very moment, what ye shall say" (D&C 100:6). *Compare:* Stoppeth utterance.

Glad tidings (of great joy/of salvation/to my soul) (Mosiah 3:3; Alma 13:22; 39:15–16, 19; Helaman 13:7; 16:14; 3 Nephi 1:26). The gospel of Jesus Christ is the glad tidings. In Christ we can be redeemed from physical death and redeemed from our sins so that we can again stand in the presence of God and be filled with His love, peace, and joy.

Glorified the Father (3 Nephi 9:15; 11:7, 11; 23:9; Ether 12:8). In all things Jesus did the will of the Father for the purpose of glorifying the Father. Jesus was the perfect example of goodness for the purpose of bringing glory to the Father. Jesus provided the redemption of man for the purpose of bringing glory to the Father. And by so glorifying the Father, Jesus glorified Himself. Therein is the principle of progression. As we keep the commandments, serve our fellowmen, and strive to do the will of the Father, we glorify God; and in so doing we bring a portion of glory to ourselves. We cannot gain glory without giving glory to or glorifying God. This is a major element in the process of becoming like our Father in Heaven.

Glorify God (Helaman 11:18; Ether 12:4). To glorify God is to praise, honor, worship, reverence, and exalt God. We glorify God when we do His will. We glorify God when we advance and promote His work and His plan. We must always give glory to the Father and His Son, even forever and forever. We must gain a great desire to glorify God, and to, in fact, act on that desire.

Glorify him forever (Jacob 2:21). *See:* Glorify God.

Glorify my name in the flesh (Ether 3:21). Refers to when Jesus was lifted upon the cross (Ether 4:1), and then finished His work (His sacrifice) unto the children of men, by which He glorified the Father and in so doing glorified Himself. *See also:* Glorified the Father.

Glorify the name of your God (2 Nephi 6:4). *See:* Glorify God.

Glorify your Father who is in heaven (3 Nephi 12:16). *See:* Glorify God.

Glory in his day (Ether 9:22). Meaning to rejoice in the coming of the Lord Jesus.

Glory in my Jesus (2 Nephi 33:6). *See:* Glory in the Lord.

Glory in the Lord (Alma 26:16). Paul explains this best in 2 Corinthians 10:17, "But he that glorieth, let him glory in the Lord." We should praise, honor, and rejoice aloud and in humble prayer our great and marvelous Savior and Redeemer, Jesus Christ.

Glory of God (2 Nephi 1:25; 27:16; Mosiah 4:11; 27:22; Alma 19:6; 60:36; Mormon 9:5). The glory of God is God's divine nature. Great and marvelous is God's glory.

Glory of the world (2 Nephi 27:16; Alma 60:32; Helaman 7:5; Ether 8:7). Meaning the honor and praise of men. To be seeking the glory of men is sinful; for you cannot serve both God and mammon (worldly wealth; see Matthew 6:24). God and Babel (the world) are enemies and cannot both dwell in the hearts of men or women.

Glory of Zion shall be a defence (2 Nephi 14:5). The word *defence* should be rendered a canopy or a covering. Zion will be a place of refuge and safety. *See also:* D&C 45:66–70.

Go before them (you) (3 Nephi 20:42; 21:29; Ether 1:42; 2:5). God will go before His people and lead them. He will also be in their midst and protect them (D&C 49:27). *See also:* Be their (your) rearward.

Go down to hell (2 Nephi 26:10; Moroni 8:14). *See:* Depths of hell; Down to hell.

Go forth from (unto) the Gentiles (1 Nephi 13:25–26, 29, 34–35, 38–39; 2 Nephi 21:5–6, 11; 30:3; 3 Nephi 23:4; Mormon 5:15; Ether 4:6). *See:* Days of the Gentiles.

Go forth in power [Christ will] (Mosiah 3:5; 13:34). Prophecies that Jesus would come down to mortality and with power work many mighty miracles.

Go forth in power [servants of the Lord] (Jacob 6:2). The true servants of God are given power through the Holy Ghost to preach the word and minister unto the people.

Go forth into the water and did baptize them (Mosiah 25:18). Proper baptism is to go down and stand in the water and be baptized by immersion (see 3 Nephi 11:22–27). *See also:* Baptism by (of/with) water.

Go into the mount oft (1 Nephi 18:3). In many places in the scriptures, where there were not temples, prophets got into the mountain to speak to God. Thus "mountain of the Lord's house" (see 2 Nephi 12:2–3) refers to the temple. Nephi said, "I, Nephi, did go into the mount oft, and I did pray oft unto the Lord; wherefore the Lord showed unto me great things" (1 Nephi 18:3). We are fortunate as Latter-day Saints to be able to go to the temple oft, to pray to the Lord, and to receive inspiration. *See also:* Get thee into the mountain; Into (unto) the mountain; Ether 3:1; 4:1.

Go no more out (Alma 7:25; 29:17; 34:36; Helaman 3:30; 3 Nephi 28:40). Those that inherit the kingdom of heaven will sit down and go no more out. This means their mortal probation is finished and they no longer have to experience the temptations of Satan, but are safely within heaven.

Go the way of all the earth (2 Nephi 1:14; Mosiah 1:9; Alma 1:1; 62:37; Helaman 1:2). All earthly things crumble, rust, rot, and deteriorate. Our mortal bodies are no exception: "For from dust thou art, and unto dust shalt thou return" (Genesis 3:19). Thus to "go the way of all the earth" is for the body to die and return to dust.

God Almighty (1 Nephi 1:14; 2 Nephi 9:46; 28:15; 3 Nephi 4:32). A name-title that describes both God the Father and God the Son because they both have all power and might. *See also:* Power of God.

God can (could) not lie (Enos 1:6; Ether 3:12). Or more correctly, God will not and will never lie. *See also:* God of truth; Titus 1:2; D&C 62:6.

God ceaseth not to be God (Alma 42:23; Mormon 9:19). *See:* Cease to be God.

God created all things (2 Nephi 2:14; Mosiah 3:8; 4:2; 5:15; 7:27;

Alma 18:28; 30:44; Helaman 14:12; 3 Nephi 9:15; Mormon 9:11; Ether 4:7). *See:* Created the heavens and the earth and all things that in them are.

God delights in the chastity of women (Jacob 2:28). *See:* Delight in the chastity of women.

God has (have) mercy on him (me/them/us) (Alma 15:10; 19:29; 24:14; 36:18). *See:* Have mercy on me (them/this man/this people/you).

God hath given (2 Nephi 2:26; 7:4; 26:30; Jacob 2:20; Mosiah 1:10; Helaman 14:30; Mormon 5:14). Question not what God hath given, for He is the all-wise giver. *See also:* All things which are good cometh of God; Every good gift; Gift from God.

God is merciful (Alma 12:15; 26:35; 32:22; 41:13; Helaman 3:27). *See:* Merciful God (Being).

God is mindful of every people (Alma 26:37; Moroni 8:3). All the people of the earth are God's children, and He has provided the plan of salvation for all people. Likewise, the Atonement of Christ is universal and available to every people. "Know ye not that there are more nations than one? Know ye not that I, the Lord your God, have created all men, and that I remember those who are upon the isles of the sea; and that I rule in the heavens above and in the earth beneath; and I bring forth my word unto the children of men, yea, even upon all the nations of the earth?" (2 Nephi 29:7).

God is not a partial God (Moroni 8:18). *Partial* means to be biased, prejudiced, unfair, and unjust. God is none of these. "But the wisdom that is from above is first pure, then peaceable, gentle, and easy to be intreated, full of mercy and good fruits, without partiality, and without hypocrisy" (James 3:17). The greatest blessings of God are available to anyone who humbles themselves and comes unto Christ. *See also:* All men.

God is powerful (Alma 37:16). *See:* All power; Power of God.

God is (shall be) my strength (1 Nephi 21:5; 2 Nephi 22:2; Alma 26:12). *See:* In the strength of our God (the Lord).

God knoweth all the times which are appointed unto man (Alma 40:4–5, 10). This phrase, as used in these scriptures, refers to the times designated for the Resurrection and judgment of men. *See also:* Appointed unto men that they must die.

God knoweth all things (2 Nephi 2:14; 9:20; Alma 26:35; 40:5, 10; Mormon 8:17; Moroni 7:22). God is omniscient; He is all knowing. He has all knowledge, and there is no knowledge that He has not yet obtained. God's greatness and majesty is because He knows all things. *See also:* All-wise Creator; Knoweth all things; Lord knoweth all things; Wisdom in (of) God (the Lord/the Father).

God of Abraham, God of Isaac, and God of Jacob (1 Nephi 6:4; 19:10; Mosiah 7:19; 23:23; Alma 29:11; 36:2; 3 Nephi 4:30; Mormon 9:11). Meaning the true and living God. Description and name for Jehovah, Jesus Christ, who is the God of the Old Testament. Jesus Christ as well as God the Father continue to be our Gods today.

God of Israel (1 Nephi 5:9–10; 19:7, 13; 20:1–2; 2 Nephi 9:44; 27:34; 3 Nephi 11:14; 20:42). Meaning He is the God of the children of Israel, His chosen people. He has declared Himself their God and desires that they obey and worship Him so that He may bless them. Yet the children of Israel have often turned away from their true God to follow after false gods. Israel is prophesied to return to the God of Israel and be gathered in according to the promises of the Lord. *See also:* Holy One of Israel.

God of miracles (2 Nephi 27:23; 28:6; Mormon 9:10–11, 15, 19). We believe that God is a God of miracles. One of the witnesses that He is God is that He is a God of miracles. He has in the past performed miracles, He does now perform miracles, and He will always in the future perform miracles, because He is an unchanging God, being the same yesterday, today, and forever. God ceaseth not to be a God of miracles because He ceases not to be God. If miracles dwindle among men, it is because the people "dwindle in unbelief, and depart from the right way, and know not the God in whom they should trust" (Mormon 9:20). We must have great faith in the miracles of God. God provides miracles for the following purposes: To introduce Himself and bring people unto Him; to show love and compassion; to further His work on earth and in heaven; to build and confirm faith; to teach; to prove His divinity and power; to glorify His name; to witness that He has power over all things—even power to provide the Atonement; and to fulfill that which was foreordained and prophesied to come to pass. *See also:* By faith miracles are wrought; Many (mighty) miracles; Mighty miracles; Miracles wrought among them; Work(-ing) mighty miracles; Wrought miracle(-s).

God of the whole earth (3 Nephi 11:14; 22:5). One of the descriptors and names of the Lord Jesus Christ. We believe that He is the God of the whole earth, because He is the creator of the earth, and "there is no other name given whereby salvation cometh" (Mosiah 5:8). The Godhead consists of the Father, the Son, and the Holy Ghost. Other gods named by men are: (1) references to the True God but mistaken in their understanding of His true identity; or (2) they are references to "gods" that do not in reality exist.

God of truth (Ether 3:12). God the Father and Jesus Christ deal only in truth and never deal in untruths. *See also:* Truth which is in (of) Christ (God); Deuteronomy 32:4; Psalm 31:5; Isaiah 65:16.

God raise up [a prophet] (1 Nephi 10:4; 22:20; 2 Nephi 3:6; 20:23). The prophet referred to in 2 Nephi 3:6 is Joseph Smith. The prophet referred to in the other three scriptures is Jesus Christ.

God shall smite him (thee/you) (1 Nephi 17:48; 2 Nephi 30:9; Jacob 7:14; Mosiah 13:3; Alma 30:47; Helaman 10:10; Moroni 9:21). God has all power, including the ability to hew down the wicked. Jacob 2:15 says, "O that he would show you that he can pierce you, and with one glance of his eye he can smite you to the dust."

God sitting upon his throne (1 Nephi 1:8; Alma 36:22). The scriptures mention often that God has a throne from which He rules. A throne is a symbol of power, majesty, and supremeness. *See also:* Throne is high in the heavens; Throne of God.

God whom I fear (Alma 60:28). *See:* Fear of the Lord.

Going before them (1 Nephi 17:30). *See:* Go before them (you).

Gone astray (2 Nephi 12:5; 28:14; Mosiah 14:6; Alma 5:37; 13:17; 30:53). Meaning to have let go of the rod of iron and departed from the strait and narrow path. Not keeping the commandments of God and turning away from God.

Gone away from mine ordinances (3 Nephi 24:7). The ordinances are important and necessary steps to salvation. For example, "Except a man be born of water and of the Spirit [baptism and receiving the Holy Ghost], he cannot see the kingdom of God" (John 3:5). Ordinances remind us of Christ, recommit us to faithfulness, and sanctify us.

Gone out of the way (2 Nephi 28:11). *See:* Gone astray.

Gone the way of all the earth (Alma 1:1; 62:37; Helaman 1:2). *See:* Go the way of all the earth.

Good cometh from (of) God (Alma 4:40; Ether 4:12; Moroni 7:12, 16, 24). The scriptures say in many places that all good things come from God. *See also:* All things which are good cometh of God.

Good fruit (Jacob 5:26–27, 33, 36, 40, 42, 45–46, 54, 60; Alma 5:36, 52; 3 Nephi 14:17–19). *See:* Good works.

Good gift (Moroni 7:10; 10:18, 30). *See:* Every good gift.

Good Shepherd (Alma 5:38–39, 41, 57, 60; Helaman 7:18). Jesus Christ is the Good Shepherd, and we are His sheep. He desires to bring us into the fold of God. We must strive to be worthy to be numbered among His sheep. He is the great example of going out from the fold to find and bring back the ones who have strayed (see the parable of the lost sheep in Luke 15:4–7). *See also:* Christ their shepherd; Gather together my sheep; I know my sheep; In him they shall find pasture; My sheep; Numbered among his (my) sheep; Numbereth his sheep; One fold and one shepherd; Other sheep; Sheep of the Good Shepherd; Voice of the Good Shepherd.

Good tidings (Mosiah 12:21; 15:14, 18; 27:37; Helaman 5:29; 3 Nephi 20:40). Refers to the gospel and message of Jesus Christ; in other words, the "good news" is the gospel. That good news is that because of the Atonement of Jesus Christ all mankind may be saved and find peace and great joy. *See also:* Gospel of (Jesus) Christ.

Good word of God (Jacob 6:7; Moroni 6:4). All the words of God are good and perfect, and there is no evil therein. *See also:* Word of God.

Good works (Mosiah 5:15; Alma 5:41–42; 7:24, 27; 13:3; 26:22; 37:34; Helaman 12:24; 3 Nephi 12:16; Ether 12:4). A requirement for exaltation and the privilege to sit on the right hand of God. Doing good works was the pattern set by Jesus (see Acts 10:38). *See also:* Abound(-ing) in good works; According to their (your) works (deeds); Judged according to (of) their works.

Goodness of God (1 Nephi 1:1; 5:4; 2 Nephi 9:10; 33:14; Jacob 1:7; Mosiah 4:5–6; 5:3; 25:10; 27:22; Alma 12:32; 24:7; 57:25, 36; 60:11; Helaman 12:1; 3 Nephi 4:33; Mormon 2:13). God is full of goodness, He is the example of goodness, and His goodness is infinite and eternal. It is the invitation of God to come and partake of His goodness. *See also:* Infinite goodness (of God).

Goodness of the Lord (2 Nephi 4:17). The Lord Jesus is full of goodness, mercy, and love. He is the pattern of goodness that all should follow. *See also:* Goodness of God; Infinite goodness (of God).

Gospel of (Jesus) Christ (2 Nephi 30:5; Jacob 7:6; 3 Nephi 28:23; 4 Nephi 1:38; Mormon 3:21; 7:8; 9:8; Ether 4:3). The gospel of Jesus Christ is the good news of Christ; it is the doctrine of Christ (Jacob 7:6); it is the Resurrection of Christ; it is the light and life of Christ; it is the truth, the works, the mercy, and the grace of Christ; it is the love of Christ; it is the Church of Christ; it is the goodness and gentleness of Christ; it is the power of Christ unto salvation; it is the law of Christ; and it is the gift of Christ. *See also:* Good tidings.

Gospel of the Lamb (the Lord/the Messiah/their Redeemer) (1 Nephi 13:24, 26, 29, 32, 34; 15:13, 14). *See:* Gospel of (Jesus) Christ.

Grace divine (2 Nephi 10:25). *See:* Grace of God.

Grace for grace (Helaman 12:24). As we give grace (kindness and assistance) to our fellowmen and as we emulate the grace of the Savior, we will be blessed with the infinite grace of God. It is a step-by-step process or pattern throughout our life. *See also:* Grace of God; John 1:16; D&C 93:12, 20.

Grace of God (2 Nephi 10:24; Mosiah 18:16, 26; 27:5; Ether 12:41; Moroni 7:2; 9:26; 10:32, 33). Grace will deliver us, after all that we can do (see 2 Nephi 25:23). "The main idea of the word [grace] is divine means of help or strength, given through the bounteous mercy and love of Jesus Christ. It is through the grace of the Lord Jesus, made possible by his atoning sacrifice, that mankind will be raised in immortality, every person receiving his body from the grave in a condition of everlasting life. It is likewise through the grace of the Lord that individuals, through faith in the Atonement of Jesus Christ and repentance of their sins, receive strength and assistance to do good works that they otherwise would not be able to maintain if left to their own means. This grace is an enabling power that allows men and women to lay hold on eternal life and exaltation after they have expended their own best efforts. Divine grace is needed by every soul in consequence of the Fall of Adam and also because of man's weaknesses and shortcomings. However, grace cannot suffice without total effort on the part of the recipient. Hence the explanation, 'It is by grace that we are saved, after all we can do" (2 Nephi 25:23). It is truly the grace of Jesus Christ that makes salvation possible" (Bible Dictionary, s.v. "grace," 697). *See also:* By his grace; By the grace of God; His grace (is) sufficient for you; My grace is sufficient.

Grant unto him the office of being high priest (Alma 4:18). *See:* Granted unto them power; High priests.

Grant unto them (us/you) (See following list). The Lord grants unto the children of men all that He sees fit that they should have (see Alma 29:8). The list of possible grants from the Lord is infinite. Some examples found in the Book of Mormon are:

- Grant unto thee according to thy desire (Enos 1:12);
- Grant unto you whatsoever ye ask that is right (Mosiah 4:21);
- Grant unto you eternal life (Mosiah 18:13);
- Grant an inheritance at my right hand (Alma 5:58);
- Grant that he might baptize them unto repentance (Alma 8:10);
- Grant unto the children of men to know the mysteries of God (Alma 12:9);
- Grant unto you repentance (Alma 13:30);

- Grant unto them a portion of his Spirit (Alma 17:9);
- Grant unto all nations to teach his word (Alma 29:8);
- Grant that it may be done according to my words (Alma 29:17);
- Grant unto these that they may sit down in the kingdom of God (Alma 29:17);
- Grant unto me that I may have strength and patience (Alma 31:31);
- Grant unto them that they may have strength (Alma 31:33);
- Grant unto us that we may have success in bringing them unto thee (Alma 31:34);
- Grant unto you that your burdens may be light (Alma 33:23);
- Grant unto you that ye may begin to exercise faith unto repentance (Alma 34:17);
- Grant unto you even according to my words (Alma 42:31);
- Grant unto us great faith (Alma 58:11);
- Not grant strength [unto the unrighteous] (Helaman 7:22);
- Grant that men might be brought unto repentance (Helaman 12:24); and
- Grant that their prayers may be answered (Mormon 9:37).

Granted salvation unto his people (Mosiah 15:18). *See:* Bring(-eth) salvation.

Granted unto them according to their prayers (Alma 25:17;

Mormon 9:21, 37). The Lord has promised that the prayers of the those who pray in faith and ask not amiss will be answered liberally (see 2 Nephi 4:35).

Granted unto them liberty (Mosiah 29:39; Alma 46:10). The freedoms of liberty are foundational to the living of the gospel. We should strive to support religious freedoms so that we can practice our religious beliefs and secure the same for others. This is assuming one's religious beliefs do not impinge on the rights of others.

Granted unto them power (Alma 14:28). *See:* Authority from (of) God.

Granted unto us that we might repent (Alma 24:10; 42:4, 22; Mormon 3:3). An important element of the plan of salvation is a time allowed for men and women to repent and turn unto God. If no allowance was made and one was punished immediately for one's errors, there would not be moral agency, which God has guaranteed. Additionally, time to recognize we need to repent is a step of repentance and requires us to accept Christ as our Savior, which is mandatory for salvation.

Granted unto you your lives (Mosiah 2:23). Meaning God has given us life on earth according to His will that we may take part in the plan of salvation.

Grasp of justice (Alma 42:14; 3 Nephi 6:29). The grasp of justice and the consequences of our actions are sure. None can escape justice except through the merciful Atonement. *See also:* Atonement of Christ (the Only Begotten Son); Demands of justice.

Grasp of this awful monster (2 Nephi 9:10; 28:22). The grasp or clutch of physical and spiritual death. Death is an awful monster, but it is overcome by the Atonement of Jesus Christ. *See also:* Chains of hell; Spiritual death; Temporal death.

Grasp(-s) them with his everlasting (awful) chains (2 Nephi 28:19, 22). *See:* Chains of hell.

Grasped with death (2 Nephi 28:23). *See:* Grasp of this awful monster.

Grave hath (shall have) no victory (Mosiah 16:7–8; Alma 22:14; 27:28; Mormon 7:5). Because of the Resurrection of Jesus Christ, all will be resurrected to immortal life. Thus death is overcome and has no victory or no final rule over man. *See also:* Death is (was) swallowed up in the victory of (in) Christ.

Grave must deliver up its captive bodies (2 Nephi 9:12). Death is referred to as a prison from which our bodies will be released by the resurrection brought about by Jesus Christ. *See also:* Resurrection of the body.

Graves shall be opened (Helaman 14:25). This is prophecy and assurance of the Resurrection. *See also:* Resurrection of the body.

Great and abominable church (1 Nephi 13:6, 8, 26, 28; 14:3, 9, 15, 17; 22:13–14; 2 Nephi 6:12; 28:18). "All churches which are built up to get gain, and all those who are built up to get power over the flesh, and those who are built up to become popular in the eyes of the world, and those who seek the lusts of the flesh and the things of the world, and to do all manner of iniquity; yea, in fine, all those who belong to the kingdom of the devil" (1 Nephi 22:23). Jesus said, "Many will say to me in that day, Lord, Lord, have we not prophesied in thy name? and in thy name have cast out devils? and in thy name done many wonderful works? And then will I profess unto them, I never knew you: depart from me, ye that work iniquity" (Matthew 7:22–23). "Because of pride, and because of false teachers, and false doctrine, their churches have become corrupted, and their churches are lifted up; because of pride they are puffed up. They rob the poor because of their fine sanctuaries; they rob the poor because of their fine clothing; and they persecute the meek and the poor in heart, because in their pride they are puffed up. They wear stiff necks and high heads; yea, and because of pride, and wickedness, and abominations, and whoredoms, they have all gone astray save it be a few, who are the humble followers of Christ; nevertheless, they are led, that in many instances they do err because they are taught by the precepts of men" (2 Nephi 28:12–14). *See also:* Abominable church; Great whore; Mother of abominations; Mother of harlots; Whore of all the earth.

Great and coming day (3 Nephi 28:31). Refers to the judgment day. *See also:* Great and judgment day.

Great and dreadful day of the Lord (3 Nephi 25:5). The Second Coming, when Jesus comes again in glory. It will be a great day for the righteous and a dreadful day for the wicked. *Compare:* D&C 110:16.

Great and Eternal Head (Helaman 13:38). One of the titles of our God, which can apply to or pertain to our Father in Heaven and/or our Lord Jesus Christ.

Great and eternal plan of deliverance from death (of redemption) (2 Nephi 11:5; Alma 34:16). God's plan of salvation and happiness for His children contains the means to overcome spiritual and physical death so that we can return to God's presence through the grace and mercy of the Father and the Son. *See also:* Plan of salvation.

Great and eternal purpose(-s) (2 Nephi 2:12, 15; Alma 37:7; 42:26; Mormon 5:14; 8:22). All of God's purposes and designs are great and eternal. There are none

that are substandard. We, God's children, are at the center of all that God does. "For behold, this is my work and my glory—to bring to pass the immortality and eternal life of man" (Moses 1:39).

Great and judgment day (2 Nephi 9:22). The day when men and women will be judged and receive a reward for faith and works or be cast off because of wickedness. *See also:* Judgment day.

Great and last day (2 Nephi 2:26; 33:12; Words of Mormon 1:11; Helaman 12:25; 3 Nephi 26:4; Mormon 9:6). Meaning the day of judgment. *See also:* Great and judgment day; Last day.

Great and last sacrifice (Alma 34:10, 13–14). The sacrifice of Jesus Christ for our sins was the great and last sacrifice. There is no sacrifice greater, for it was eternal in scope. And it is the last sacrifice because the sacrifices under the law of Moses came to an end with the sacrifice of Jesus. "And ye shall offer up unto me no more the shedding of blood; yea, your sacrifices and your burnt offerings shall be done away, for I will accept none of your sacrifices and your burnt offerings. And ye shall offer for a sacrifice unto me a broken heart and a contrite spirit" (3 Nephi 9:19–20).

Great and marvelous thing(-s) (1 Nephi 1:14; Alma 9:6; Helaman 16:20; 3 Nephi 5:8; 11:1; 17:16–17; 26:14; Mormon 8:34; Ether 4:15;

11:20; 12:5). Great and marvelous things include but are not limited to: the things of God; the things of heaven and earth; God's dealings with man; and the things that are prophesied that will come to pass. *See also:* Great and marvelous work(-s/of the Lord).

Great and marvelous words (and prophecies) (3 Nephi 3:16; 19:34; Ether 13:13). Referring to the words of God and His prophets. *See also:* Word of God.

Great and marvelous work(-s/ of the Lord) (1 Nephi 1:14; 14:7; 2 Nephi 1:10; 4:17; Jacob 4:8; Alma 26:15; Helaman 16:16; 3 Nephi 11:1; 21:9; 28:31, 32; 4 Nephi 1:5). "Great and marvelous" are, if you will, codified adjectives used by the prophets to identify the things of God. Such works include miracles and revelations from God. In fact, the phrase includes all the wonderful things of God, including the creation and the direction of things on earth to bring about His purposes. Often in the Book of Mormon, "great and marvelous work" has specific reference to the bringing forth of the gospel of Jesus Christ and the establishment of the kingdom of God on earth in the latter days. This work encompasses the perfecting of the Saints, the great missionary program, the redemption of the dead, and caring for the poor and needy. *See also:* Marvelous work and a wonder.

Great (large) and spacious building (1 Nephi 8:26, 31; 11:35–36; 12:18). "Represents the pride of the world [and] was shown 'in the air, high above the earth' (1 Nephi 8:26). When a building is in the air it has no foundation. How is this related to pride? Notice how often the description 'lifted up in pride' is used in the scriptures (see 2 Nephi 26:20, Jacob 1:16, Mosiah 11:5, Alma 1:6, Helaman 3:34, 3 Nephi 6:10, Mormon 8:28). The great and spacious building is also related to 'high-mindedness' or being 'high-minded' (D&C 90:17; see also Romans 11:20, 1 Timothy 6:17), and those with pride are spoken of as being brought 'down' (Isaiah 25:11, Ezekiel 30:6)" (*Book of Mormon Student Manual*, 10). Those who resided in the great and spacious building wore costly apparel and pointed a finger of scorn at those who humbly pressed forward along the iron rod. See the spacious buildings built by wicked kings in Mosiah 11:8–9 and Ether 10:5.

Great and terrible day (2 Nephi 26:3; 3 Nephi 8:24–25). These verses have reference to the terrible destruction that took place on the American continent just before the appearance of Christ here after His Resurrection. Those that were wicked were destroyed at that time.

Great and terrible gulf (1 Nephi 12:18). Meaning hell as explained by Nephi in 1 Nephi 15:26–29. *See also:* Gulf of misery.

Great and terrible judgments (1 Nephi 12:5). The judgment and destruction of the wicked on the American Continent just before the appearance of Christ after His Resurrection. *See also:* Great and terrible day.

Great are the promises of the Lord (2 Nephi 10:9, 21). "Eye hath not seen, nor ear heard, neither have entered into the heart of man, the things which God hath prepared [has promised] for them that love him" (1 Corinthians 2:9). *See also:* Promises of the Lord.

Great day (2 Nephi 33:13; Mormon 9:2). Meaning the great day of judgment. *See also:* Judgment day.

Great day when the earth shall be rolled together as a scroll (Mormon 5:23; 9:2). Refers to the great day of the Lord's coming, when the righteous will be caught up to meet Christ, the wicked will burn as stubble, and the continents will be brought back together by God with the seas pushed to the north and to the south. Thus the earth will be renewed and receive its paradisiacal glory (see Articles of Faith 1:10), which is the condition like the Garden of Eden. The millennial reign of our Lord Jesus will then begin.

Great hold upon the hearts of the people (Alma 8:9; 10:25; 27:12; Helaman 6:31; 7:15; 16:23). Describes the control that Satan gains over the desires and intents of men's hearts when men have sinned and thus relinquished themselves to Satan. *See also:* Satan did get hold (possession) upon the hearts of the people; D&C 10:20.

Great is my joy (Alma 7:17; 26:35, 37; 29:16; 3 Nephi 27:30). *See:* My joy is full (great).

Great Jehovah (Moroni 10:34). The Great Jehovah is Jesus Christ. This verse, in the last sentence in the Book of Mormon, is one of only two occurrences of the Lord's name Jehovah found in the Book of Mormon. The other is in 2 Nephi 22:2, where it is "Lord Jehovah."

Great Mediator (2 Nephi 2:27–28). One of the names for our Lord, Jesus Christ, because He is the mediator between us and God the Father. He pleads our case to the Father and He is our advocate with the Father (D&C 45:3–5). He atoned for our sins so that we may return to the Father if we repent. Also we pray to and worship the Father in His name. See D&C 76:69 and 107:19, where Jesus is referred to as the Mediator of the new covenant.

Great plan of mercy (2 Nephi 9:6; 11:5; Alma 12:33; 34:16; 42:13, 15, 31). Before the foundations of this world were laid, the effects of mercy were planned to satisfy the demands of justice. All of us have sinned and are therefore condemned. God must be and desires to be just in executing the law. Yet at the same time, He loves us and He desires to be fully merciful unto us. Therefore, the Atonement was put in place to raise us from the dead, and to cleanse us from our sins if we repent, so we can stand before God purified, and so justice will have no claim on us. Oh how wise and beautiful is God's plan of mercy. *See also:* Merciful God (Being); Plan of salvation.

Great plan of the Eternal God (2 Nephi 9:6, 13; 11:5; Jacob 6:8; Alma 24:14; 34:9, 16, 31; 42:5, 8, 31). For truly it is great. *See also:* Plan of salvation.

Great power (1 Nephi 17:51; Mosiah 8:16; Alma 14:20; 18:2–3, 8; 19:15, 24; 25:6; 26:16; Helaman 5:17–18; 6:5; 8:13; 11:18; Ether 3:5; 12:31). God has great power, even all power. God can give a portion of that power to men, both physical and spiritual power, so that righteous men may accomplish the will and purposes of God. *See also:* Minister with power and great authority.

Great Spirit (Alma 18:2–5, 11, 18, 26, 28; 19:25, 27; 22:9–11). This term, by the tradition of the Lamanites, was their name for God.

Great things the Lord hath done (1 Nephi 7:11; 16:29; 18:3; 2 Nephi 1:1; 4:26; Mosiah 27:16; Alma 62:50; Ether 4:14; 6:30; 7:27). We must always remember and give thanks for the great things God has done for us, His children. In 1 Samuel 12:24, "Only fear the Lord, and serve him in truth with all your heart: for consider how great things he hath done for you." The Lord God created this world for us, gave us life and light, provided an Atonement, and will yet provide many more great things for the faithful.

Great whore (1 Nephi 14:10, 12; 22:13–14; 2 Nephi 28:18). The great whore is the great and abominable church, which has adulterated the doctrine, had carnal relations with every sin, and persecuted the true and humble followers of Christ. *See also:* Great and abominable church.

Great works (Ether 3:18). *See:* Great and marvelous work(-s/of the Lord).

Great worth (1 Nephi 5:21; 13:23; 19:7; 22:8; 2 Nephi 3:7; 25:8; 28:2; 33:3; Mormon 8:14). The word of God is of great worth unto the children of men, for to live by the word of God brings peace of mind in this life and salvation in the hereafter.

Greater things (Helaman 14:28; 3 Nephi 26:9–10, 14; Mormon 8:12; Ether 4:4, 8, 13). Great and marvelous are the things promised to those that keep the commandments in faith (see 1 Corinthians 2:9–10). If we accept and live small principles, then God will reveal greater. First we live on milk, and then we can endure meat (see 1 Corinthians 3:2; D&C 19:22). Those that believe in and live the commandments shall have greater things given unto them, whereas those that do not believe and do not keep the commandments shall lose that which they have and greater things shall be withheld from them. *See also:* Mysteries of God.

Greatest of all the gifts of God (1 Nephi 15:36). Meaning eternal life is the greatest gift of God. *See also:* D&C 6:13; 14:7.

Grieveth my soul (2 Nephi 4:17; 26:11; Jacob 2:6). To grieve is to be extremely sad and grief stricken. It grieves the faithful to see others sin and wander into spiritual darkness, because of their love and concern for their fellowmen and their eternal welfare.

Grind upon the face(-s) of the poor (2 Nephi 13:15; 26:20). In this world, our earthly existence, wicked men falsely gain authority (political and religious) so that they can extract money and exert power over their fellow beings, most often over the humble, meek, and poor. In effect they trample, crush, and oppress the poor.

Grow in knowledge of God (Mosiah 4:12; Helaman 6:34). *See:* Know God.

Grow up as calves in the stall (3 Nephi 25:2). *See:* Calves of the stall.

Grow up unto the Lord (Helaman 3:21). Meaning to mature and progress in becoming more like God. "And that they may grow up in thee, and receive a fulness of the Holy Ghost, and be organized according to thy laws, and be prepared to obtain every needful thing" (D&C 109:15). It is important that little children grow up and mature in the light of the gospel, being taught in their youth the right way to go. "Train up a child in the way he should go: and when he is old, he will not depart from it" (Proverbs 22:6).

Guilt was swept away (Enos 1:6; Alma 24:10). To have our guilt swept away is the great blessing of repentance and forgiveness of our sins through the Atonement of Christ. A particularly wonderful gift is to have God pronounce that "all your sins are forgiven" (see example in D&C 112:3). *See also:* Peace of conscience; Taken away the guilt from our hearts.

Gulf of misery (2 Nephi 1:13; Alma 26:20; Helaman 3:29; 5:12). That expanse of place prepared for the wicked. *See also:* Great and terrible gulf.

H

Hand of God (the Lord) (1 Nephi 5:14; 2 Nephi 1:5–6, 10, 12; 8:17; 28:6; 30:6; Mosiah 1:2, 5, 16; 2:11; 28:15; 29:25; Alma 2:28; 9:9, 22–23; 37:4; 45:19; 46:7, 24; 3 Nephi 3:2; 29:9; 4 Nephi 1:16; Mormon 6:6; 8:8, 26; Ether 1:1; 2:6; 10:28). The mighty hand of God is capable of doing all things. By His hand people are blessed, preserved, led in safety, protected, supported, sheltered, brought out of bondage, prepared, fed, provided miracles, delivered, gifted, strengthened, prospered, and much more.

Hand of providence (Jacob 2:13). *Providence* is often used as a synonym meaning God. *See also:* Hand of God (the Lord).

Hand shortened (2 Nephi 7:2). Meaning hand pulled back, which is the opposite of hand extended or reaching out to help and save. *See also:* Lengthen out mine arm.

Handed down (1 Nephi 19:4; 2 Nephi 25:21; Words of Mormon 1:10–11; Mosiah 28:14, 20; Alma 23:5; 30:14; 31:16; 37:4; 63:13; Helaman 3:16; 16:20; 3 Nephi 3:9; 4 Nephi 1:48; Mormon 6:6; 9:32; Ether 8:15). It is important that good things are handed down from one generation to another, from fathers and mothers to sons and daughters, for the learning, assistance, and direction of succeeding generations. In the Book of Mormon those things that are mentioned as being handed down are: sacred records (scriptures), histories, writings, the seer stones (Urim and Thummim), prophecies, righteous traditions, genealogies, language, and other sacred things. Unfortunately wickedness can also be handed down from generation to generation, such as secret oaths, wicked traditions, and works of darkness. *See also:* Traditions of our (their/your) fathers.

Happiness in sin (doing iniquity) (Alma 41:11; Helaman 13:38; Mormon 2:13). Many try to find happiness in sin and iniquity, but it cannot be found there. *See also:* Despair cometh because of iniquity; Take happiness in iniquity (sin); Wickedness never was happiness.

Happiness which hath no end (Mosiah 2:41; Mormon 7:7). The blessing obtained by those that receive salvation. *See also:* Eternal happiness.

Happiness which is affixed (2 Nephi 2:10). Happiness, peace, and joy are the blessings of righteousness. Thus there are happy consequences to all our righteous actions. We reap what we sow. *Compare:* Punishment that (which) is affixed. *See also:* Alma 42:16.

Hard-hearted (Alma 9:5, 31; 15:15). *See:* Harden(-ed) his (our/the/their/your) heart(-s) against the Lord.

Hard in their (your) hearts (1 Nephi 7:8; 15:3; 17:46; Jacob 1:15; 3 Nephi 2:1). *See:* Harden(-ed) his (our/the/their/your) heart(-s) against the Lord.

Harden not our (their/your) hearts (1 Nephi 14:2; Jacob 6:5–6; Alma 12:33, 37; 34:31; 3 Nephi 21:22). *See:* Harden(-ed) his (our/the/their/your) heart(-s) against the Lord.

Harden(-ed) his (our/the/their/your) heart(-s) against the Lord (1 Nephi 13:27; 15:11; 16:22; 17:30, 41–42; 22:5, 18; 2 Nephi 5:21; 6:10; 25:10, 27; 33:2; Mosiah 3:15; 10:14; 11:29; Alma 10:6; 12:10, 13; 21:12; 23:14; 48:3; Helaman 7:18; 10:15; 12:2; 13:12; 16:22; 3 Nephi 1:22; 2:1; 4 Nephi 1:31, 34; Mormon 3:3; Ether 8:25; 11:13; Moroni 9:4). To reject the things of the Lord and rebel against God. Sin and lyings have the effect of hardening the hearts of men. They "forget the Lord their God, and [did] trample under their feet the Holy One" (Helaman 12:2). They receive not the word of their God, "wherefore, they cast many things away which are written and esteem them as things of naught" (2 Nephi 33:2). "Satan did stir them up to do iniquity continually; yea, he did go about spreading rumors and contentions upon all the face of the land, that he might harden the hearts of the people against that which is good" (Helaman 16:22). "And now because of their unbelief they could not understand the word of God; and their hearts were hardened" (Mosiah 26:3). See the difference between Nephi and his brothers Laman and Lemuel in 1 Nephi 15:7–11. No heart is as hard as the heart of him or her that has known the truth and then has rebelled and turned from it. *Compare:* Soften my (our/the/their) heart(-s). *See also:* Devil has got so great hold upon your hearts.

Hardened and impenitent (Alma 47:36; Helaman 6:2). Impenitent means unwilling to repent and having no sorrow for sin. Also uncaring of the consequences of wrongdoing. *See also:* Harden(-ed) his (our/the/their/your) heart(-s) against the Lord.

Hardened in iniquity (Helaman 16:12). *See:* Harden(-ed) his (our/the/their/your) heart(-s) against the Lord.

Hardness of their (your) heart(-s) (1 Nephi 14:7; 15:4; 2 Nephi 1:17; 25:12; Jarom 1:3; Alma 13:4; 14:11;

Helaman 13:8; 3 Nephi 7:16; Mormon 1:17; 3:12; Ether 4:15; 15:19). *See:* Harden(-ed) his (our/the/their/your) heart(-s) against the Lord.

Harrow up his (your) mind (souls) (2 Nephi 9:47; Alma 15:3; 39:7; Mormon 5:8). *See:* Bright recollection of all our guilt; Harrowed up by the memory of all my (many) sins.

Harrowed up by the memory of all my (many) sins (Alma 36:12, 17, 19). *See:* Bright recollection of all our guilt.

Harrowed up under a consciousness of his own guilt (Alma 14:6). *See:* Bright recollection of all our guilt; Harrowed up by the memory of all my (many) sins.

Has been spoken (Mosiah 2:34–36; 5:5, 21; Alma 12:24–25; 40:19, 22, 24; 41:1, 10; Helaman 16:16, 18). The word of God, the prophecies of the prophets, and the scriptures all have been spoken to teach, direct, and warn men to keep them in the path to eternal life.

Hast (have) beheld (1 Nephi 11:7; 13:24; 14:5; 2 Nephi 1:15; 2:3–4; 4:25; 26:2). The prophets and other righteous individuals have beheld the glory of God and have beheld the things that are to come, which is prophecy.

Hated of all men (1 Nephi 22:5; 3 Nephi 16:9). A prophecy concerning the Jews, which came to pass because they did not keep the commandments and because they crucified the Lord Jesus.

Hatred against (to) sin (Alma 26:34; 37:32). *See:* Abhor sin (such wickedness).

Have (has) angels ceased to minister (God ceased to be God/miracles ceased) (Mormon 9:15; Moroni 7:27, 29, 35–38). *See:* God of miracles.

Have his (my) Spirit to be with them (you) (3 Nephi 18:7, 11; Moroni 4:3; 5:2). This is God's promise to those who receive the gift of the Holy Ghost after baptism, if they are worthy of it. This is also God's promise to men and women in the sacramental covenant as found in the sacrament prayers when we renew our covenants of baptism.

Have hope (1 Nephi 19:24; Jacob 2:19; 4:4; Alma 7:24; 32:21; 34:41; Ether 12:9, 32; Moroni 7:3, 40–43, 48; 10:21–22). Faith and hope cannot be separated but go hand in hand. We have faith that certain things are so, and because of that faith we have hope of greater and promised things. For example, we live the commandments by faith. In so doing we have hope of a reward at God's hand for doing His will. *See also:* Hope in Christ; Hope(-s) of glory; Obtain a hope; Perfect brightness of hope; That we (ye) may have hope.

Have mercy on me (them/this man/this people/you) (1 Nephi 8:8; 21:13; 2 Nephi 24:1; Mosiah 4:2; Alma 2:30; 3:14; 12:33; 15:10; 18:41; 19:29; 34:17; 36:18; 41:14; 3 Nephi 22:8; Ether 11:8). These words, or very similar, are the words we each must utter in deep humility to our God and our Savior in order to receive a remission of our sins and be born of God. Lehi prayed these words after traveling many hours in darkness during his vision of the tree of life (see 1 Nephi 8:8). Likewise, Alma the Younger, while in the gall of bitterness, cried for mercy in Alma 36:18. The people of King Benjamin cried for mercy in Mosiah 4:2. Psalm 51:1 says, "Have mercy upon me, O God, according to thy lovingkindness: according unto the multitude of thy tender mercies blot out my transgressions."

Having authority (from God) (Mosiah 18:13, 18; 3 Nephi 11:25; Moroni 8:16). Meaning the same as "by the power of the priesthood in me vested." *See also:* Authority from (of) God.

He doth (immediately) bless (nourish/prosper) you (1 Nephi 17:3; Mosiah 2:22, 24; Alma 34:31, 38; Helaman 12:2). When we keep the commandments the Lord blesses us in the many ways listed in these verses. The scriptures make it clear that many blessings for keeping the commandments will come in the hereafter. If there was an immediate and obvious response, our moral agency would be abridged. Yet King Benjamin says the Lord blesses us immediately. An immediate blessing does happen but is less obvious, and not at all obvious to the unbeliever. King Benjamin says one of these blessings is the sustaining and preserving of our breath and lives. Other less obvious but immediate blessings include: peace of mind, hope, joy, faith, and continence.

He doth not dwell in unholy temples (Alma 7:21). When we sin the Spirit cannot dwell with us. "Know ye not that ye are the temple of God, and that the Spirit of God dwelleth in you? If any man defile the temple of God, him shall God destroy; for the temple of God is holy, which temple ye are" (1 Corinthians 3:16–17).

He doth visit them with death, terror, famine, and pestilence (Helaman 12:3). Because the Lord's people are hard-hearted and turn from their God, He often must visit them with famine and pestilence to humble them and get them to turn back to Him. *See also:* Famine(-s) and pestilence(-s); Pestilence of earthquakes (famine/tempest/the sword).

He doth work righteousness forever (Alma 26:8). God turneth neither to the right nor to the left in deviation from His righteous ways.

He has all power to save (Alma 12:15). Because Christ suffered and provided atonement for all men, the

Father has given Jesus power to save in the kingdom of heaven all those that meet the requirements of salvation, which include faith in Christ, baptism, gift of the Holy Ghost, other saving ordinances, and faithfulness to the end. *See also:* Mighty to save; None other name.

He has borne our griefs and carried our sorrows (Mosiah 14:4). We must be assured that our Savior, Jesus Christ, understands our griefs and sorrows because He came to earth to experience and witness mortality. The scriptures confirm that "he descended below all things, in that he comprehended all things" (D&C 88:6). *Compare:* Matthew 8:17. *See also:* Alma 7:12.

He has borne their sins (Mosiah 15:12). "Who his own self bare our sins in his own body on the tree [the cross]" (1 Peter 2:24). "He is the propitiation for our sins: and not for ours only, but also for the sins of the whole world" (1 John 2:2). *See also:* He was bruised for our iniquities; He was wounded for our transgressions.

He hath no form nor comeliness (Mosiah 14:2). Our Lord Jesus came to the earth at the meridian of time in a mortal body of ordinary appearance, rather than as a person of great beauty. He came not as a king, but as a common man born in a stable. Though He was a God, He did not come that first time in great glory, and He eschewed wealth and worldly popularity. Mosiah 14:2 and Isaiah 53:2 go on to say, "When we shall see him there is no beauty that we should desire him." Our hymn "O God, The Eternal Father" states, "With no apparent beauty, / That man should him desire" (*Hymns*, no. 175).

He himself should be oppressed and afflicted (Mosiah 13:35; 14:7). The prophets were given to know that Jesus Christ would experience earthly sorrows and trials. *See also:* Acquainted with grief; Man of sorrows; Suffereth the pains of all men; Take upon him their infirmities; Alma 7:11–13.

He numbereth his sheep (1 Nephi 22:25; Alma 26:37). *See:* Good Shepherd.

He shall heal them (2 Nephi 26:9). *See:* Healing in his wings.

He shall rise again (from the dead) (1 Nephi 10:11; 2 Nephi 25:13; Alma 33:22; Helaman 14:20). Prophecies concerning the Resurrection of Jesus. *See also:* Resurrection of Christ (Holy One of Israel).

He was bruised for our iniquities (Mosiah 14:5, 10). *See:* He has borne their sins; Isaiah 53:5.

He was wounded for our transgressions (Mosiah 14:5). *See:* He has borne their sins; Isaiah 53:5.

He will remember the covenant he hath made (Mormon 8:23). *See:*

Remember(-ed/-est) his (my/the) covenant(-s/promises).

Head of their corner (Jacob 4:17). Jesus Christ is the sure foundation and the cornerstone (see Ephesians 2:20), the stone upon which we should build our lives and our eternal salvation. *See also:* Built upon my rock; Rock of our Redeemer; Helaman 5:12.

Heal him according to his faith which is in Christ (Alma 15:10; 3 Nephi 17:8). *See:* According to his (my/our/the/their/thy/your) faith; Heal the sick.

Heal the sick (4 Nephi 1:5). President Gordon B. Hinckley, in an October 1988 general conference address, quoted James 5:14 and said: "That power to heal the sick is still among us. It is the power of the priesthood of God. It is the authority held by the elders of this Church.

"We welcome and praise and utilize the marvelous procedures of modern medicine which have done so much to alleviate human suffering and lengthen human life. All of us are indebted to the dedicated men and women of science and medicine who have conquered so much of disease, who have mitigated pain, who have stayed the hand of death. I cannot say enough of gratitude for them.

"Yet they are the first to admit the limitations of their knowledge and the imperfection of their skills in dealing with many matters of life and death. The mighty Creator of the heavens and the earth and all that in them are has given to His servants a divine power that sometimes transcends all the powers and knowledge of men. I venture to say that there is scarcely a faithful elder within the sound of my voice who could not recount instances in which this healing power has been made manifest in behalf of the sick. It is the healing power of Christ" ("The Healing Power of Christ," 54).

Heal them (2 Nephi 26:9; Alma 33:20; 3 Nephi 17:7, 9; 18:32). *See:* Heal the sick; Healing in his wings.

Healed of diseases (infirmities/ sickness) (1 Nephi 11:31; 3 Nephi 7:22; 17:9–10; 26:15). Jesus and His authorized servants have all power to heal the sick and afflicted. *See also:* Heal the sick; Mighty miracles.

Healeth the wounded soul (Jacob 2:8). The wounded soul is the same as the broken-hearted. Our Savior, Jesus Christ, has power to bind up the wounded and heal the broken heart. *See also:* Healing in his wings; Alma 7:11–12.

Healing in his wings (2 Nephi 25:13; 3 Nephi 25:2). Meaning the Atonement whereby Jesus Christ provided for the redemption of man to rescue us from death, sin, and worldly sorrow and pain. In other words, Jesus rose with healing in His wings so that we can be healed, a healing from sin and death. This refers to the fruits of the Atonement, which are the resurrection of all men and the salvation of those who are worthy of exaltation. Both of these are made possible by the redemptive power of Jesus Christ. *See also:* Carried our sorrows; I shall (will) heal them.

Hear the word(-s) of God (Jesus Christ/the Lord) (2 Nephi 10:14; Jacob 2:8, 27; Mosiah 18:32; 25:20; Alma 1:26; 6:5; 16:14; 3 Nephi 30:1; 4 Nephi 1:12). No other words would be as important to hear as the words of the Lord. *See also:* Hearken to the word of God (the Lord).

Hear the words of the book (2 Nephi 27:29). Prophecy that the Book of Mormon will be heard in the last days. *See also:* Words of the book.

Hear the words of the prophet (1 Nephi 19:24; 22:20; Jacob 5:2; Mosiah 1:18; 2:1, 6–9; 4:4; 18:3, 6–7; Alma 16:14; 21:10–11; 36:3; Helaman 13:39; 14:11). An invitation, even a command, to hear the word of God as delivered by His servants. *See also:* Hear the word(-s) of God (Jesus Christ/the Lord).

Heard a voice from the Father (2 Nephi 31:15; 3 Nephi 11:6). Two examples of when God the Father introduced or witnessed of His son, Jesus Christ.

Heard the voice of the Lord (1 Nephi 17:45; 2 Nephi 16:8; Jacob 7:5; 3 Nephi 15:24). On these occasions the revelation received was directly from the Lord's voice.

Hearken to the word of God (the Lord) (1 Nephi 15:24; Jacob 2:27; Helaman 7:7). To *hearken* is to hear and heed. God has given us His word as a guide and a command for our wellbeing. Why then would a person not heed that which was given for their wellbeing, unless they rebel and bring upon themselves destruction. *See also:* Hearken unto God (the Lord); Hearken unto his (my/the/their) words; Hearken unto his (the) commandments; Hearken unto his voice; Hearken unto my precepts; Hearken unto the counsels of God; Hearken unto the Spirit; Hearken unto the voice of the Lord their God.

Hearken unto God (the Lord) (1 Nephi 7:9; 14:1; 15:24; 2 Nephi 9:29; Omni 1:12–13; Mosiah 16:2; 20:21; Alma 5:37–38; Helaman 7:7; 10:13; 12:23; 13:21; Mormon 9:27; Ether 11:13). *See:* Hearken to the word of God (the Lord).

Hearken unto his (my/the/their) words (1 Nephi 2:18; 4:32; 8:37; 17:22; 19:7; 2 Nephi 1:12; 2:28; 3:23, 25; 5:6, 20, 25; 9:51; 25:4; 26:8; 33:10; Jacob 3:11; 5:2; Mosiah 2:9; 7:25; 20:21; Alma 8:9; 13:27; 18:22; 20:30; 35:3; 46:1; 48:19; 50:32; Helaman 4:3; 7:7, 23; 10:13, 15, 18; 11:13–14; 12:4; 13:21; 3 Nephi 21:22; 23:5; 28:34; 30:1; Mormon 9:27; Ether 11:13).

Hearken does not only mean to listen but also to follow the counsel of the words given. We must hold fast to the words of God and use them as our guide. Those that hearken not to the word of the Lord will be lost, cut off, and destroyed (see 1 Nephi 19:7; 2 Nephi 9:28). *See also:* Hearken to the word of God (the Lord).

Hearken unto his (the) commandments (1 Nephi 4:11; 2 Nephi 2:28). *See:* Hearken to the word of God (the Lord).

Hearken unto his voice (2 Nephi 1:28; 9:21). *See:* Hearken to the word of God (the Lord).

Hearken unto my precepts (2 Nephi 28:30–31). *Precepts* are rules, principles, doctrines, decrees, and ordinances. The precepts of God are paramount to our safety and salvation. *See also:* Hearken to the word of God (the Lord).

Hearken unto the counsels of God (2 Nephi 9:29). *See:* Counsel with the Lord; Give ear unto his counsels; Hearken to the word of God (the Lord).

Hearken unto the Spirit (2 Nephi 32:8). The promptings of the Spirit are given to lead us to truth, peace, and safety. One must learn to recognize the Spirit and follow its promptings. By so doing we become better and more adept at recognizing the Spirit. If we ignore the promptings of the Spirit we start to become deaf to its promptings and

eventually the Spirit will withdraw from us. "Put your trust in that Spirit which leadeth to do good— yea, to do justly, to walk humbly, to judge righteously; and this is my Spirit" (D&C 11:12). *See also:* D&C 45:57.

Hearken unto the voice of the Lord their God (2 Nephi 9:21; Omni 1:12–13; Mosiah 16:2; Alma 5:37–38, 60; Helaman 7:18; 12:23; 3 Nephi 16:15). *See:* Hearken to the word of God (the Lord).

Hearken(-ed) not (1 Nephi 2:18; 4:11; 19:7; 2 Nephi 1:28–29; 5:20, 25; 9:28; Mosiah 7:25; 16:2; 20:21; Alma 5:37–38; 8:9; 20:30; 35:3; 46:1; 51:3; Helaman 4:3; 7:18; 10:13, 15, 18; 3 Nephi 3:12; 16:15; 28:34; Ether 11:7, 13). Turned their backs to, turned away from, would not listen, did not follow counsel, kept not the commandments, and ignored the words and counsel presented to them.

Heart did swell (Alma 32:28; 33:23; 48:12). Meaning the feelings of love and compassion did fill and expand the heart. *See also:* Bowels of mercy; Moved with compassion.

Heart did (was filled with) sorrow (2 Nephi 1:17, 21; 4:26; Alma 31:2; Helaman 7:6, 14; Mormon 2:19, 27; Ether 15:2). The prophets and righteous followers of Christ have often sorrowed because of the wickedness of the people. Such is the appropriate response of one who is concerned about his fellowmen. *See also:* Anxiety for you.

Heart had (was) swollen (within him/within them) (Alma 17:29; 19:13; 24:24; Helaman 7:6). *See:* Heart did swell.

Heart is broken and my spirit is contrite (2 Nephi 4:32). *See:* Broken heart(-s) and (a) contrite spirit(-s).

Heart pondereth (2 Nephi 4:15–16). Meaning to consider carefully deep within oneself. A spiritual meditation which invites the enlightenment of the Spirit of God. We must take time to ponder, especially after prayer.

Heart took (did take) courage (Alma 15:4; 62:1; Helaman 1:22). Meaning to have a renewed bravery and valiancy in a worthy cause. *See also:* Hearts took courage.

Heart was filled [with joy and rejoicing] (1 Nephi 1:15; Alma 62:1; Mormon 2:12). *See:* Fulness of joy; Joy is (shall be/was) full. Contrast: Heart was grieved (sorrowful).

Heart was grieved (sorrowful) (2 Nephi 1:17; 4:17, 26; Alma 31:2, 24; 35:15; Helaman 7:6, 14; Mormon 2:19, 27; Ether 15:2). *See:* Heart did (was filled with) sorrow.

Hearts are (had been) changed (Mosiah 5:7; Alma 19:33). *See:* Change of heart.

Hearts are drawn out (Alma 34:27; Helaman 13:22). Meaning to consider upon, ponder, pray, and wait upon the Lord God for a length of time.

Hearts knit together (Mosiah 18:21). We must come to a unity with God and man. The key to unity is a concern for and active participation in improving the welfare of our fellow beings.

Hearts may be purified (Mosiah 4:2). Because of the Atonement of Christ we can be purified and cleansed of all our sins. For this blessing we must pray in all sincerity to be purified and be true followers of Jesus Christ. *Compare:* 3 Nephi 19:28, 29; Moroni 7:48. *See also:* Change of heart; Holy without spot.

Hearts of (the children of) men (1 Nephi 11:22; 12:17; 13:27; 22:15; 2 Nephi 28:20; 30:18; 33:1; Mosiah 3:6; Alma 13:24; 28:13; 48:17; Helaman 6:30; 12:1; 3 Nephi 2:2; 11:29–30; 17:17; Mormon 4:5; Ether 8:25–26). The premortal war in heaven continues today, and the battleground is over the hearts of men. Satan rages in the hearts of men, strives to harden the hearts of men, and attempts to ensnare the hearts of men. Whereas on the good side, God invites men to turn their hearts to Him, to purify their hearts, and to fill their hearts with love and joyfulness.

Hearts of understanding (Mosiah 12:27). God gives us humble and understanding hearts to know the truth and follow in the path of righteousness.

Hearts took courage (Alma 17:12; Helaman 5:24). *See:* Heart took (did take) courage.

Hearts were hardened (Mosiah 26:3; Alma 1:24; 9:30; 12:13). *See:* Harden(-ed) his (our/the/their/your) heart(-s) against the Lord.

Hearts were set upon riches (Alma 17:14). *See:* Set their (your) hearts upon riches; Vain things of the world.

Heavenly Father (Mosiah 2:34; 3 Nephi 13:14, 26, 32). He who is our magnificent, glorious, and all-powerful Father in Heaven. He is the Father of our spirits, who loves us and has provided the plan of salvation for our benefit and progression. He is God the first and the chief member (president) of the Godhead. He is the God of Jesus Christ. Both Christ and the Holy Ghost do the Father's will. Their will is as one and is united. The Father is our God forever and ever. He is a perfected being of flesh and bone, and we are created in His image. He is all powerful, all knowing, and His presence is everywhere by the power of His Spirit. He is infinite, while we mortals are nothing in comparison. We have the privilege of worshipping Him forever. All that we have that is good has come from Him.

Heavenly gift (4 Nephi 1:3; Ether 12:8). In this context a heavenly gift means salvation or exaltation in the kingdom of heaven. *See also:* Gifts of God.

Heavenly King (Mosiah 2:19). Jesus Christ is our heavenly King. He is the King of Kings, Lord of Lords, the ruler of all that He has created.

Heavens and the earth should pass away (1 Nephi 17:46; Alma 9:2–3; 3 Nephi 26:3; Ether 13:8). All things mortal shall pass away, for their mortal probation shall be completed. The heavens and earth as we know them will one day be no more, and there shall be a new earth. During the Millennium the earth shall receive (be renewed to) its paradisiacal glory (see Articles of Faith 1:10) and be as it was when Adam dwelt upon the earth. Eventually the earth will receive its celestial glory and the Lord will state that the earth has faithfully fulfilled its mortal mission and purpose (see D&C 88:25–26).

Heavens are (were) opened (1 Nephi 1:8; 11:14, 27, 30; 12:6; Helaman 5:48; 3 Nephi 17:24; 28:13; Ether 4:9). Refers to visions from heaven. "In the scriptures, the word [heaven] . . . is used in two basic ways. First, it refers to the place where God lives, which is the ultimate home of the faithful (see Mosiah 2:41). Second, it refers to the expanse around the earth (see Genesis 1:1)" (*True to the Faith*, 80). Many have seen the heavens open, peered into heaven, and had revealed unto them great and marvelous things.

Hell fire (3 Nephi 12:22; Mormon 8:17). To suffer the burnings of hell. *See also:* Danger of hell fire; Endless torment; Eternal torment; Everlasting burning; Lake of fire and brimstone; Pains of hell; Torment as a lake of fire and brimstone; Unquenchable fire.

Hell must deliver up its captive spirits (2 Nephi 9:12). The hell referred to here is spirit prison, where the wicked dwell after death until the Resurrection. Thus the spirit prison will release the spirits therein when the Resurrection for them comes, and they will then stand before God to be judged.

Hell which hath no end (1 Nephi 14:3; 15:30; 2 Nephi 9:16). *See:* Eternal torment.

Hen gathereth her chickens (under her wings) (3 Nephi 10:4–6). Just as the sheep know the shepherd's voice, so the young chickens know the call of the mother hen, who calls to her chickens to provide nourishment and protection. "Listen to the voice of Jesus Christ . . . who will gather his people even as a hen gathereth her chickens under her wings, even as many as will hearken to my voice and humble themselves before me, and call upon me in mighty prayer" (D&C 29:1–2). *Compare:* Matthew 23:37.

Hewn down and cast into the fire (Jacob 5:42, 46; 5:66; 6:7; Alma 5:35, 52, 56; Helaman 14:18; 3 Nephi 14:19; 27:11, 17; Mormon 8:21). The fate of the wicked at the last day. The scriptures testify that the wicked shall burn as stubble. *See also:* Consumed as stubble.

Hid up because of unbelief (Ether 4:13). The greater aspects of the gospel, the wonderful promises of the Lord, and the weightier mysteries of God are not presented by the Lord to the unbeliever. "Give not that which is holy unto the dogs, neither cast ye your pearls before swine, lest they trample them under their feet, and turn again and rend you" (Matthew 7:6; 3 Nephi 14:6). *See also:* Hid(-e/them) up unto the Lord.

Hid up treasures (Helaman 12:18; 13:18–20; Mormon 1:18). Treasure, meaning wealth, hid up in the earth by wicked men will be cursed and not found again. The exception is treasure hid up unto the Lord by good men to be used for righteous purposes.

Hide their iniquities (sins/wickedness) and their abominations from before my face (3 Nephi 9:5, 7–8, 15). In the destruction that took place just before Christ appeared to the inhabitants of the American continents, the Lord buried in the earth and the seas the wicked to conceal their wickedness from His sight. *See also:* Blood of the prophets and the saints shall not come up any more unto me against them.

Hid(-e/them) up unto the Lord (2 Nephi 27:22; 4 Nephi 1:48–49; Mormon 4:23; 5:12; 8:4, 14; Ether 4:3; 15:11). Many scriptures and sacred items "are sealed up to come forth in their purity according to the truth which is in the Lamb, in the own due time of the Lord" (1 Nephi 14:26). *See also:* Hid up because of unbelief; Hide(-th) up the records in the earth; Seal (them) up.

Hide us from his presence (Alma 12:14). When we are brought before God to be judged, if our works have been wickedness, then we will not dare to look up at God because of our awful guilt. In that pitiful state we would rather the rocks and mountains fall upon us to cover us up so we do not have to bear being in God's presence for the pain of guiltiness that will be within us. *Compare:* Revelation 6:16. *See also:* Not be ashamed.

Hide(-th) up the records in the earth (4 Nephi 1:48–49; Mormon 8:4, 14; Ether 4:3; 15:11). *See:* Hid(-e/them) up unto the Lord.

High birth (Alma 51:8). Meaning born into the higher, wealthier, or ruling classes. *See also:* Pride of nobility.

High heads (2 Nephi 28:14; Jacob 2:13). A term referring to people lifted up in pride. Holding one's head high often indicates one thinks himself above others, wanting to hold oneself superior to the common folk, and not willing to bow the head in reverence and humility. *See also:* Lifted up in (unto) pride (of their eyes/hearts/and boasting).

High mountain (1 Nephi 11:1). *See:* Get thee into the mountain; Matthew 17:1; Mark 9:2; Revelation 21:10; Moses 1:1.

High priest (over the church/ people) (Mosiah 23:16; 26:7; 29:42; Alma 4:4, 18; 5:3; 8:11, 23; 13:14; 16:5; 30:20). The first elder of the Church having charge concerning all the affairs of the Church. *See also:* After the order of his (the) Son; Consecrated as (the) high priest over the church of God; High priesthood (of the holy order of God); High priests; Holy calling; Holy order (of God); Office of being high priest over the church.

High priesthood forever (Alma 13:14). The priesthood, or power of God, is eternal. It has always existed and will always exist. Alma 13:7 says, "This high priesthood being after the order of his Son, which order was from the foundation of the world; or in other words, being without beginning of days or end of years, being prepared from eternity to all eternity." *See also:* High priesthood (of the holy order of God).

High priesthood (of the holy order of God) (Alma 4:20; 13:6–8, 10, 14, 18). Meaning the

Melchizedek Priesthood. Joseph Fielding Smith said, "The Nephites did not officiate under the authority of the Aaronic Priesthood. They were not descendants of Aaron, and there were no Levites among them. . . . The *Book of Mormon* tells us definitely, in many places, that the priesthood which they held and under which they officiated was the Priesthood after the *holy order,* the order of the Son of God. This higher priesthood can officiate in every ordinance of the gospel, and Jacob and Joseph, for instance, were consecrated priests and teachers after this order" (*Doctrines of Salvation,* 3:87). *See also:* High priest (over the church/people).

High priests (Alma 13:9–10; 46:6, 38; Helaman 3:25). An office in the Melchizedek (the higher) priesthood holding authority to administer spiritual blessings of the Church. *See also:* High priest (over the church/people).

Highly favored (of the Lord) (1 Nephi 1:1; Mosiah 1:13; Alma 9:20; 13:23; 27:30; 48:20; Ether 1:34). *See:* Favored of the Lord.

Highways shall be exalted (1 Nephi 21:11). At the gathering of Israel from their long dispersion, the Lord will provide great avenues of return. *Compare:* Isaiah 35:8–10. *See also:* Gather in the house of Israel; Gathered home to the lands of their inheritance; Isaiah 49:11.

Him that bringeth good tidings (Mosiah 12:21; 15:18; 3 Nephi 20:40). Also in Isaiah 52:7. The "good tidings" is the gospel of Jesus Christ, also known as the good news. "Him that bringeth" are those that preach, teach, and declare the true gospel.

Him that framed it (2 Nephi 27:27). Jesus Christ is the framer, meaning the builder and organizer of the planet earth, all things that are in it, and the heavens that surround it. *See also:* All things that in them are; D&C 20:17.

Him shall ye witness (1 Nephi 11:7). Herein Nephi receives his prophetic call to witness that Jesus is the Christ. Nephi is one of many witnesses of Christ in the Book of Mormon. *See also:* Testimony of many (two or three).

Him who created all flesh (things) (Jacob 2:21; Mosiah 5:15). *See:* Created all flesh; Created the heavens and the earth and all things that in them are.

Him who created you (Mosiah 2:21, 25; 4:12; Alma 5:15). God created, or more correctly organized, man from the elements of the earth and put man's spirit in his physical body to become a living soul. *See also:* Created (creation of) Adam.

Him who is mighty to save (2 Nephi 31:19; Alma 34:18). A title or name for our Savior, Jesus Christ.

By the power of the redemption which He brought about, He can save us if we are willing.

Him will I forgive (receive) (Mosiah 26:21–22; 3 Nephi 9:14, 22). Whosoever will come unto Christ, that person will the Lord receive.

His calling unto me (Alma 29:13; Moroni 7:2; 8:1). *See:* Called of God (the Holy Spirit).

His fierce anger he will not turn away (Alma 9:12; 10:23). God's anger will not be turned away unless we humble ourselves and repent. *See also:* Anger of the Lord.

His grace (is) sufficient for you (Ether 12:26–27; Moroni 10:32). This is an assurance that the suffering and Atonement of Christ is more than enough to provide remission of our sins and to provide solace to the downtrodden. *See also:* Grace of God; My grace is sufficient.

His holy will (Moroni 7:2). The will of God is eternally holy and never otherwise. *See:* Will of God.

His judgments are just (Omni 1:22; Mosiah 16:1; Alma 12:15). God's judgments are perfectly just, fair, accurate, and true. *See also:* Judgments are just.

His paths are straight (Alma 7:19; 37:12). Alma 7:20 says, "He [God] cannot walk in crooked paths; neither doth he vary from that which he hath said; neither hath he a shadow of turning from the right to the left, or from that which is right to that which is wrong." *See also:* Strait and narrow course (path); D&C 3:2.

His righteousness (Alma 7:4; 19:34; 3 Nephi 13:33). Refers to the righteous ways of God which we must seek to follow.

His rod (1 Nephi 17:41). *See:* Rod of his mouth and with the breath of his lips.

His ways (2 Nephi 1:19; 12:3; Jacob 4:8; Mosiah 23:14). We must learn of God's ways, for His ways are perfect. "Now therefore hearken unto me, O ye children: for blessed are they that keep my ways" (Proverbs 8:32). "Love the Lord your God, to walk in all his ways, and to cleave unto him" (Deuteronomy 11:22). *See also:* Strait and narrow course (path).

Hiss and a byword (1 Nephi 19:14; 3 Nephi 16:9). Because the house of Israel, and more particularly the Jews, rejected the Lord and turned to wickedness, it is prophesied they would be scattered, hated of all nations, verbally cursed, and mistreated. Here to "hiss" is to sneer. A "byword" means a scornful name. *See also:* Scattered tribes of Israel.

Hiss (forth) unto them (2 Nephi 15:26; 29:2–3; Moroni 10:28). Meaning signal or call unto them. See also Isaiah 5:26 and Zechariah

10:8 ("I will hiss for [to call] them, and gather them").

Hold guiltless (3 Nephi 27:16). Remove the condemnation caused by one's transgressions. The Lord, through His Atonement, will cleanse those who repent and come unto Him. Thus they will no longer feel guilt, but can lift up their heads being sanctified.

Hold out faithful to the end (Mosiah 2:41). *See:* Endure(-th) to the end.

Hold upon the (their/your) hearts (Alma 8:9; 10:25; 27:12; Helaman 6:30–31; 7:15; 16:23; 4 Nephi 1:28). *See:* Satan did get hold (possession) upon the hearts of the people.

Holiness of God (Jesus Christ) (2 Nephi 2:10; 9:20; 3 Nephi 26:5; Mormon 9:5). Our Lord is completely righteous and pure. He lived a sinless life. He did, does, and will do only the will of His Father. He does only good. His paths do not vary from being entirely holy and virtuous.

Holiness of heart (Mosiah 18:12; 3 Nephi 4:29). Meaning having a good and righteous heart, pure intent, an eye single to God, being without guile, not having ulterior or evil motives, but having a desire to do good to all.

Holy and just God (Mormon 9:4). God the Father and God the Son are both perfectly and fully holy and without the slightest deficiency. It is important that our testimonies concerning them include this knowledge and belief. *See also:* Holiness of God (Jesus Christ); Holy one of Israel; Judgments are just.

Holy angel(-s) (Alma 18:30; 36:5–6; 3 Nephi 27:30). A true messenger from God, as opposed to the devil or his minions appearing as an angel of light. The phrase "holy angels" is usually used in the context that the word of God is proclaimed by holy angels or holy angels will come with Jesus at the great and last day. *See also:* Angels minister(-ed/appeared/declared/descending) unto him (them); Form of an angel.

Holy calling (Alma 13:3, 4–6, 8; 29:13; Moroni 7:2). In Alma 13, the scriptural phrase "holy calling" refers to receiving the high priesthood (Melchizedek priesthood), more specifically the office of high priest in that priesthood. In Alma 29, "holy calling" refers to being called to preach the word of God to the inhabitants of the earth. Thus prophets, Apostles, missionaries, bishops, priesthood leaders, and others are called with a holy calling. *See also:* Timothy 1:9.

Holy church of God (Mormon 8:38). Refers to and is another name for the true and only Church of Jesus Christ (The Church of Jesus Christ of Latter-day Saints, in this dispensation). All other churches may have some part of the true gospel and doctrine of Christ but are otherwise deficient; most notably deficient in not possessing proper priesthood authority and not having full access to the workings of the Spirit. *See also:* Church of Christ; Church of God.

Holy city (of/unto the Lord) (1 Nephi 20:2; 2 Nephi 8:24; 3 Nephi 20:36; Ether 13:5, 8). Generally refers to Jerusalem. In times to come it will be the heavenly city wherein the King of Kings, Jesus Christ, resides. President David O. McKay relates: "I then fell asleep, and beheld in vision something infinitely sublime. In the distance I beheld a beautiful white city. Though far away, yet I seemed to realize that trees with luscious fruit, shrubbery with gorgeously tinted leaves, and flowers in perfect bloom abounded everywhere. The clear sky above seemed to reflect these beautiful shades of color. I then saw a great concourse of people approaching the city. Each one wore a white flowing robe, and a white headdress. Instantly my attention seemed centered upon their Leader, and though I could see only the profile of his features and his body, I recognized him at once as my Savior! The tint and radiance of his countenance were glorious to behold! There was a peace about him which seemed sublime—it was divine!

"The city, I understood, was His. It was the City Eternal; and the people following him were to abide there in peace and eternal happiness.

"But who were they?

"As if the Savior read my thoughts, he answered by pointing to a semicircle that then appeared above them, and on which were written in gold the words:

"*These Are They Who Have Overcome The World—Who Have Truly Been Born Again!*" (David O. McKay, *Cherished Experiences,* 102).

Holy Ghost beareth record of the Father and the Son (1 Nephi 12:18; 2 Nephi 31:18; 3 Nephi 11:32; 16:6; 28:11; Ether 12:41). The number one role and mission of the Holy Ghost is to witness of God the Father and His Only Begotten Son, Jesus Christ. *See also:* D&C 20:27; 42:17; Moses 1:24; 5:9; 7:11.

Holy Ghost did fall upon them (1 Nephi 12:7; 3 Nephi 19:13; Moroni 2:3). Meaning the Holy Ghost came upon them, descended upon them, was poured out upon them; which is received so that men might lead, instruct, and comfort those searching for the truth.

Holy Ghost giveth authority that I should speak these things (1 Nephi 10:22). The Holy Ghost can prompt servants of God to teach doctrine and testify of the same. *Contrast:* Forbidden that I (they) should write (utter/preach).

Holy Ghost manifest the word of God unto me (Moroni 8:9). One of the missions of the Holy Ghost is to teach, instruct, reveal, disclose, impart, and bring to remembrance.

Holy Ghost may have place in their hearts (Moroni 7:32). We must give place in our hearts to the Holy Ghost; or in other words, take the Holy Ghost as our guide (see D&C 45:57). To be worthy of having the Holy Ghost with us we must repent, receive the ordinances of the gospel, and strive with our might to be faithful.

Holy judgment of God (2 Nephi 9:15). God's judgments are holy, righteous, and pure. *See also:* Judgments are just.

Holy land (Enos 1:10). *See:* Precious land(-s).

Holy man (Words of Mormon 1:17; Alma 10:7, 9). A man who "speak[s] the word of God with power and with authority" (Words of Mormon 1:17). *See also:* Holy prophet(-s/of God).

Holy Messiah (2 Nephi 2:6, 8). Another name for Jesus Christ, meaning the divine anointed one.

Holy mountain (2 Nephi 21:9; 30:15). Joel 3:17 identifies Zion as God's holy mountain.

Holy One (1 Nephi 21:7; 2 Nephi 2:10; 9:41; 20:17; Alma 5:52–53; Helaman 12:2; Mormon 9:14). Another name for Jesus Christ. *See also:* Holy One of Israel.

Holy One of Israel (1 Nephi 19:14–15; 20:17; 22:5, 18, 21, 24, 26, 28; 2 Nephi 1:10; 3:2; 6:9–10, 15; 9:11–12, 15, 18–19, 23–26, 40–41, 51; 15:19, 24; 20:20; 22:6; 25:29; 27:30; 28:5; 30:2; 31:13; Omni 1:25–26; 3 Nephi 22:5). Another name or title for Jesus Christ, documented in 2 Nephi 25:29. *See also:* Holy One.

Holy One of Jacob (2 Nephi 27:34). Meaning Jehovah (Jesus Christ), the God of Jacob. Abraham's son was Isaac, whose son was Jacob. The Lord changed Jacob's name to Israel. *See also:* Holy One of Israel.

Holy ones of God (Alma 10:17; 3 Nephi 5:14). Refers to the prophets of God. *See also:* Holy man; Holy prophet(-s/of God).

Holy order (of God) (2 Nephi 6:2; Alma 4:20; 5:44, 54; 6:8; 7:22; 8:4; 13:1, 6, 8, 10–11, 18; 43:2; 49:30; Ether 12:10). Refers to the priesthood of God, more specifically, the higher or Melchizedek priesthood. Concerning the priesthood, Joseph Smith said, "Every [person] who has a calling to minister to the inhabitants of the world was ordained to that very purpose in the Grand Council of heaven before this world was. I suppose I was ordained to this very office in that Grand Council" (*Teachings of the Prophet Joseph Smith,* 365). Additionally, President Spencer W. Kimball said, "Remember, in the world before we came here, faithful women were given certain assignments while faithful men were foreordained to certain priesthood tasks. While we do not now remember the particulars, this does not alter the glorious reality of what we were once agreed to" (*Teachings of Spencer W. Kimball*, 316). The use of the word "order" is emphasized by D&C 132:18, "For my house is a house of order, saith the Lord God." *See also:* After the order of his (the) Son; High priesthood (of the holy order of God); Alma 13.

Holy prophet(-s/of God) (1 Nephi 3:20; 5:13; 13:23; 2 Nephi 9:2; Jacob 4:4; Words of Mormon 1:16; Mosiah 2:34; 3:13, 15; 15:11, 13; 18:19; Alma 5:11, 24; 7:25; 8:20; 20:15; 30:14, 22, 44; Helaman 8:16; 15:7; 3 Nephi 1:13, 26; 5:1; 10:14; 29:2). The true prophets of God are most often referred to in the Book of Mormon as holy prophets. They are the true messengers of God.

Holy sanctuary of the Lord (Ether 13:3). Refers in this verse to the New Jerusalem, the city of the Lord, and more specifically the temple that will be within the city of New Jerusalem, which city is to be established in the Americas in the latter days, and will be joined by the city of Enoch at the onset of the Millennium.

Holy scriptures (Alma 14:8; 18:36; 34:30; 37:3; Helaman 15:7). The written word of God given to men by the holy prophets as they are inspired or commanded by God, angels, and the Holy Ghost. There have been many books of scripture throughout the ages, and in these the latter days we are blessed to have four: the Bible, the Book of Mormon, the Doctrine and Covenants, and the Pearl of Great Price. President Spencer W. Kimball said, "I find that when I get casual in my relationships with divinity and when it seems that no divine ear is listening and no divine voice is speaking, that I am far, far away. If I immerse myself in the scriptures the distance narrows and the spirituality returns" (*Teachings of Spencer W. Kimball*, 135). The Apostle Paul said, "All scripture is given by inspiration of God, and is profitable for doctrine, for reproof, for correction, for instruction in righteousness" (2 Timothy 3:16).

Holy Spirit (1 Nephi 2:17; 2 Nephi 2:28; 33:2; Jacob 6:8; Jarom 1:4; Mosiah 3:19; Alma 5:46, 54; 7:16; 11:44; 13:28; 18:34; 31:36; Helaman 5:45; Moroni 8:23). Meaning the third member of the Godhead, the Godhead consisting of God the Father, God the Son, and the Holy Ghost also known as the Holy Spirit. It is the mission of the Holy Ghost to testify of the verity of the Father and the Son; also to teach, comfort, inspire, direct, strengthen, and sanctify. "The Holy Ghost has not a body of flesh and bones, but is a personage of Spirit. Were it not so, the Holy Ghost could not dwell in us" (D&C 130:22).

Holy without spot (Moroni 10:33). Meaning to be spotless, without stain or filth, having been purified by the blood of the Lamb Jesus. In other words, having one's garments washed and made white by the Atonement of Christ. *See also:* Garments cleansed through the blood of the Lamb (made white/washed).

Holy works (Alma 12:30). Meaning doing good works and acting in the service of God. *See also:* Good works.

Holy writ (Alma 37:5). A scriptural phrase that describes the scriptures. *See also:* Holy scriptures.

Honest and upright in all things (Alma 27:27). To act justly, always choosing the right, and being unbending in our integrity and virtue. This we must each do no matter the circumstances, the consequences, and even if threatened with death. Our word should be our bond, meaning our promise is always kept.

Honor thy father and thy mother that thy days may be long upon the land which the Lord thy God shall give thee (1 Nephi 17:55; Mosiah 13:20). The fifth of the Ten Commandments (see Exodus 20:12). "This is a commandment that remains binding even when we are grown. We should always find ways to honor our parents" (*True to the Faith*, 177).

Hope and views of Christ (Alma 27:28). *See:* Hope in Christ.

Hope cometh of faith (Alma 25:16; 32:21; 58:11; Ether 12:4, 8–9; Moroni 7:41–42). Because we have faith in the gospel, we have hope of wonderful things past, present, and future. "For without faith there cannot be any hope" (Moroni 7:42). As our faith grows, so also grows our hope.

Hope for a better world (Ether 12:4). Mortal life has its ups and downs; it is not perfect. Here we experience opposites, such as good and evil, joy and misery (see 2 Nephi 2:11). Thus we learn to distinguish and choose the good over the bad. Because of the evil and wickedness that exists in the world, we hope for a better world, a utopia, a Shangri-La, or a heaven that is without evil. This is exactly what is promised in the kingdom of heaven.

Hope for salvation (Alma 5:10; 25:16). The very hope of the gospel of Jesus Christ, for we believe that through Christ our Savior and Redeemer we can gain salvation. *See also:* Hope in Christ.

Hope for things which are not seen (Alma 32:21; Ether 12:8). A basic and simple definition of faith. "Faith is the substance of things hoped for, the evidence of things not seen" (Hebrews 11:1).

Hope in Christ (2 Nephi 31:20; 33:9; Jacob 2:19; 4:4, 11; Alma

25:16; 27:28; 30:13; Moroni 7:3, 41, 48; 9:25). Because of our Savior and Redeemer, Jesus Christ, we have hope in the redemption and Atonement of Christ that will bring the Resurrection and exaltation. Hope is a gift of the Spirit. Those that exhibit great hope have godlike love, cheer, faith, and countenances. The opposite is the despair that comes to the natural man who does not follow the enticings of the Spirit. *See also:* 1 Corinthians 15:19.

Hope of his glory (Jacob 4:4; Moroni 9:25). Of the First Vision, Joseph Smith said, concerning God the Father and His Son, Jesus Christ, they were "two Personages, whose brightness and *glory* defy all description" (Joseph Smith–History 1:17; emphasis added). All the holy prophets have testified of the glory of the Lord, and we have faith and hope in those testimonies. We believe that the resurrected Lord has great glory, magnificence, grandeur, splendor, brilliance, and power. That glory gives us hope, and because of our faith in it we believe He can bring about our resurrection and exaltation.

Hope through the atonement of Christ (Moroni 7:41). *See:* Hope in Christ.

Hope(-s) of glory (Jacob 4:11; Alma 22:14). Our desire should be to be resurrected to a body of glory, even a celestial body (D&C 88:28–29), and exalted to a kingdom of glory, even the celestial kingdom (see D&C 76:51–70). In Abraham 3:26, we learn that "they who keep their second estate shall have glory added upon their heads for ever and ever." *See also:* Full of (his) glory.

Hopeth all things (Moroni 7:45). We hope for all things good, and we hope for all things that have been promised in the word of God. *See also:* 1 Corinthians 13:7; Articles of Faith 1:13.

Hosanna to the Lord (the Most High God) (1 Nephi 11:6; 3 Nephi 4:32; 11:17). A shout, declaration, and exclamation of praise, reverence, and honor to the glory and majesty of God. We will forever so praise Him for His grace, mercy, and love for us.

Hour is close at hand (Alma 5:29). The foretold event, the great judgment or the Second Coming of Christ, may be only hours, months, or a few short years away. For any of us the end of our mortal existence may be just around the corner. In the time of God, earthly time is but a moment, so any future earthly event is truly close at hand. None of us knows the time of our judgment so we must act, prepare as though it truly is soon, and be prepared for any event. *See also:* At hand.

House of Israel (1 Nephi 13:23; 14:2, 5, 17, 26; 15:12, 14, 16; 19:10–11, 16; 2 Nephi 3:5, 9; 6:5; 25:4; 29:1, 12, 14; 33:13; Jacob 6:1, 4; 3 Nephi 10:5; 16:7–9, 11–15; 17:14;

20:21, 25, 27; 23:2; 30:2; Mormon 3:17; 4:12; 5:10–11, 14; 7:2; 8:21; Ether 4:14–15; 13:4–5, 10; Moroni 10:31). The house of Israel consists of the descendants of the twelve sons of Jacob, whose name was changed by the Lord to Israel. The house of Israel also consists of those who are adopted into the house of Israel. The adopted are any who embrace the gospel of Jesus Christ. *See also:* House of Jacob; Twelve tribes of Israel.

House of Israel shall no more be confounded (1 Nephi 14:2; 15:20; Moroni 10:31). *See:* No more be confounded; D&C 35:25.

House of Jacob (1 Nephi 20:1; 2 Nephi 12:5–6; 18:17; 20:20; 24:1; 27:33; 3 Nephi 5:21, 25; 20:16; 21:2; 4 Nephi 1:49; Mormon 5:12). The Lord gave Jacob the name of Israel (see Genesis 32:27–28). *See also:* House of Israel.

House of the God of Jacob (2 Nephi 12:3). Any of the latter-day temples.

How beautiful upon the mountains (1 Nephi 13:37; Mosiah 12:21; 15:15–18; 3 Nephi 20:40). How blessed, radiant, splendid, and marvelous are the teachers of the true gospel. Humble converts who were seeking the truth feel thusly about those that introduced them to the gospel of Jesus Christ. The missionaries of the Church must strive to model these descriptions.

How great things the Father hath laid up for you (Ether 4:14). *See:* How great things the Lord had done.

How great things the Lord had done (1 Nephi 7:11; 2 Nephi 1:1; Mosiah 27:16; Alma 62:50; Ether 6:30). The Lord God has done great and wonderful things for His people, particularly for the faithful. A recurring theme in the Book of Mormon is an admonishment to remember what the Lord has done. We must be grateful and give thanks to the Lord for all the many things He has done for us. *See also:* How great things the Father hath laid up for you; Remember, remember.

How merciful (and just) are all the dealings of the Lord (2 Nephi 1:3; Alma 50:19; Moroni 10:3). *See:* Judgments are just; Merciful God (Being).

How merciful God (the Lord) hath been (is) (2 Nephi 1:3; Jacob 6:4; Alma 24:15; 50:19; Moroni 10:3). *See:* Merciful God (Being).

Humble and penitent before God (3 Nephi 6:13). *Penitent* means remorseful and repentant. *See also:* Humble themselves (yourselves) before God (the Lord).

Humble followers of Christ (God) (2 Nephi 28:14; Alma 4:15; Helaman 6:5, 39). If we truly humble ourselves before God we become followers of Christ, we keep the commandments, and we do the will of God. If we do not these things we have not become "sufficiently humble" (Alma 5:27) nor "truly humble" (Alma 32:14).

Humble seekers of happiness (Alma 27:18). Humility is a prerequisite to true joy from above. Saints of the Lord Jesus Christ desire the peace and happiness the gospel promises. *See also:* Exceeding(-ly) great joy.

Humble servant of God (Alma 8:19). If he were not humble he would not be a true servant of God. All those called to serve must cultivate with their might to always be humble in their dealings and to give all glory to God. "And now, O ye priests, this commandment is for you. If ye will not . . . give glory unto my name, saith the Lord of hosts, I will even send a curse upon you" (Malachi 2:1–2).

Humble themselves and become as little children (Mosiah 3:18; Moroni 8:10). King Benjamin explains becoming as a little child as being "submissive, meek, humble, patient, full of love, willing to submit to all things which the Lord seeth fit to inflict upon [you], even as a child doth submit to his father" (Mosiah 3:19).

Humble themselves (yourselves) before God (the Lord) (1 Nephi 13:16; 15:20; 16:5, 32; 18:4; Mosiah 4:10–11; 29:20; Alma 5:54; 6:3; 7:3; 13:13, 28; 15:17; 32:14–16, 25; 34:19; 37:33; 48:20; 51:21;

62:41, 49; Helaman 11:9; 3 Nephi 6:13; Mormon 5:24; Ether 6:12; 12:27). "To be humble is to recognize gratefully your dependence on the Lord—to understand that you have constant need for his support. Humility is an acknowledgment that your talents and abilities are gifts from God. It is not a sign of weakness, timidity, or fear; it is an indication that you know where your true strength lies. You can be both humble and fearless. You can be both humble and courageous.

"Jesus Christ is our greatest example of humility. During His mortal ministry, He always acknowledged that His strength came because of His dependence on His Father. He said: 'I can of mine own self do nothing . . . I seek not mine own will, but the will of the Father which hath sent me' (John 5:30).

"The Lord will strengthen you as you humble yourself before Him. James taught: 'God resisteth the proud, but giveth grace unto the humble. . . . Humble yourselves in the sight of the Lord, and He shall lift you up' (James 4:6, 10)" (*True to the Faith*, 86–87). *See also:* Humble and penitent before God; Humble followers of Christ (God); Humble seekers of happiness; Humble servant of God; Humble themselves and become as little children; Humble themselves (yourselves) even to the depths of humility; Humble themselves (yourselves) even to the dust; Humble themselves (yourselves) before God (the Lord).

Humble themselves (yourselves) even to the depths of humility (Mosiah 4:11; 21:14). *See:* Humble themselves (yourselves) before God (the Lord); In the depth(-s) of humility.

Humble themselves (yourselves) even to the dust (Mosiah 21:13; Alma 34:38). Dust signifies worthlessness and lies lowest to the ground. Thus to humble oneself as the dust means to recognize our nothingness and low stature. *See also:* Humble themselves (yourselves) before God (the Lord).

Hundredth part (Jacob 3:13; Words of Mormon 1:5; Helaman 3:14; 3 Nephi 5:8; 26:6; Ether 15:33). The records of the Nephites cannot contain even a very small fraction of all that transpired. However, the prophet writers attempted to include the most important, the most beneficial, the most significantly spiritual and doctrinal of all they witnessed.

Hunger and thirst after righteousness (3 Nephi 12:6). Meaning to truly desire the things of God. Also to seek to do good works. The Lord loves him that follows after righteousness (see Proverbs 15:9). For example, Abraham stated, "Having been myself a follower of righteousness, desiring . . . to be a greater follower of righteousness" (Abraham 1:2).

I

I AM (1 Nephi 17:53; 20:12; 21:23; 2 Nephi 6:7; 10:7; 27:23; 29:8–9, 14; Mosiah 11:22; 12:3, 24; 26:26; Helaman 10:6; 3 Nephi 9:15, 18; 11:10–11, 14, 21, 27; 12:1–2, 17; 15:5, 9; 16:4; 17:2, 14; 18:16, 24; 19:22; 20:19, 23, 31, 39; 24:6; 27:27; 28:1, 4, 10; Ether 3:14; 4:8, 12). Jesus Christ is the Great I Am. D&C 39:1 says, "Hearken and listen to the voice of him who is from all eternity to all eternity, the Great I Am, even Jesus Christ" (see also D&C 29:1; 38:1). The *I am* name-title is used in the following ways: I am the Lord thy God, I am Alpha and Omega, the beginning and the end, I am the first and the last, I am he who liveth, I am he who was slain, I am your advocate with the father, I am with you to bless you and deliver you forever, I am with you even unto the end, I am God, I am the true light, keep my commandments and ye shall see my face and know that I am, then shall ye know that ye have seen me and that I am. "And God said unto Moses, I AM THAT I AM: and he said, Thus shalt thou say unto the children of Israel, I AM hath sent me unto you" (Exodus 3:14). Footnote *b* in John 8:58 says, "The term I Am used here in the Greek is identical with the Septuagint usage in Exodus 3:14 which identifies Jehovah." Our hymn "Jesus, Once of Humble Birth" says, "The Lord, the great I Am" (*Hymns*, no. 196). *See also:* Beginning and the end; First and the last.

I am able to do mine own work (2 Nephi 27:20–21). Meaning that the Lord God does not need anyone else's help to accomplish His purposes. He is all powerful and all-knowing and can do all that is necessary. Yet the Lord employs servants to act in His name, which has the effect of testing men's faith.

I am Alpha and Omega, the beginning and the end (3 Nephi 9:18). The first and last letters of the Greek alphabet are respectively Alpha and Omega. "Thus saith the Lord your God, even Jesus Christ, the Great I AM, Alpha and Omega, the beginning and the end" (D&C 38:1). This title indicates the eternal nature of the Lord, and that He is the start and the finisher of man's salvation. *See also:* Author and finisher of their faith; Beginning and the end; First and the last.

I am God (2 Nephi 27:23; 29:8, 14; Helaman 10:6). Declaration by God that He is the ruler supreme, He is the lawgiver, He is the creator, He will give judgment, and is all else that being God connotes; there is no other god beside Him. It is hard to conceive of any other declaration that would be more noteworthy to a listener.

I am (he that gave) the law (3 Nephi 15:5, 9). In verse 5, the Savior speaks of the law of Moses, which was fulfilled and had an end with the completion of the Lord's mortal ministry. Verse 9 refers to the commandments and ordinances of the gospel we are to follow today. "And after Christ shall have risen from the dead he shall show himself unto you, my children, and my beloved brethren; and the words which he shall speak unto you shall be the law which ye shall do" (2 Nephi 26:1). *See also:* Law of Moses.

I am in the Father and the Father in me (3 Nephi 9:15; 11:27). A descriptive phrase to describe the oneness of the purposes and ways of God the Father and His Son, Jesus Christ. *See also:* Father and I are one; Father and the Son and the Holy Ghost which is one God.

I am nothing (remember your nothingness) (Mosiah 4:5, 11; Alma 26:12; Helaman 12:7). After Moses spoke with God, Moses said, "Now for this cause I know that man is nothing, which thing I never had supposed" (Moses 1:10). Man's nothingness is a stark contrast to God's infinite greatness, knowledge and power. *See also:* Humble themselves (yourselves) even to the dust.

I am the Father (and the Son) (Mosiah 15:2–3; Mormon 9:12; Ether 3:14; 4:12). A phrase Jesus uses to describe Himself. He is the Father of the creation of all things and the Son because He is the only begotten of God the Father in the flesh. For an excellent detailed description of how Jesus can have both the titles of the Father and the Son, see "The Father and the Son," *Ensign*, April 2002. Yet it must be noted that God the Eternal Father (Elohim) is a separate being and truly the father of Jesus Christ (Jehovah), who is a separate being from the Father, as witnessed in Joseph Smith's First Vision (see Joseph Smith–History 1:17).

I am the first and I am also the last (1 Nephi 20:12; Alma 11:39). Refers to Jesus Christ. *See also:* Author and finisher of their faith; Beginning and the end; First and the last; I am Alpha and Omega, the beginning and the end; Isaiah 44:6; 48:12; Revelation 1:11, 17; 2:8; 22:13; D&C 110:4.

I am the light (3 Nephi 8:16, 24). "Then spake Jesus again unto them, saying, I am the light of the world: he that followeth me shall not walk in darkness, but shall have the light of life" (John 8:12). Meaning they shall gain eternal life. *See also:* I am the light and the life (and the truth) of the world; Marvelous light of God.

I am the light and the life (and the truth) of the world (3 Nephi 9:18; 11:11; Ether 4:12). A description, even a name for the Lord, Jesus Christ. All light, life, and truth emanate from God the Father and from God the Son. Jesus is the life of the world because He gave life as the creator, and by His omnipresence (His everywhere-present influence) He sustains all life, and because He is the Savior and Redeemer He will provide the life of the Resurrection and the life of spiritual rebirth. *See also:* I am the light; I am the light and the life (and the truth) of the world; Marvelous light of God.

I am the Lord (thy God) (1 Nephi 17:53; 21:23; 2 Nephi 6:7; 8:15; Mosiah 11:22; 12:3, 34; 26:26; 3 Nephi 24:6). The same meaning as "I am God," specifically identifying the Lord Jesus Christ, however.

I am the same that leadeth men to all good (Ether 4:12). Meaning I am that God who giveth all good, and there is no other like unto me.

I am the same yesterday, today and forever (2 Nephi 27:23; 29:9). *See:* Same yesterday, today and forever.

I believe (1 Nephi 11:5; Alma 15:7, 9; 18:29, 33; 19:9; 22:11; 45:3, 5). To believe is to have knowledge of truth and faith in the same. To say "I believe" is to declare one's position and express testimony. To instruct with the words "I believe" or "I testify" is to add personal feeling and invite the witness of the Holy Ghost. The words "I believe" carry power with them. "I believe" can be the beginning of greater things and can eventually lead to a perfect knowledge and life eternal.

I came unto my own (3 Nephi 9:16). Meaning that Jesus Christ was born mortally amongst His people, the house of Israel. Jesus came unto His own and they largely rejected Him.

I do know (Alma 5:45–46; 7:8; 34:8; 36:3, 26, 30; 40:9). When we bear testimony in fast and testimony meeting, we say: I have faith, I believe, or I know. Some might argue that these are different levels of testimony, yet they are all based on receiving or experiencing spiritual manifestations. A good way to understand when someone says, "I know the Book of Mormon is true," is to realize that they are saying, "I know I had a spiritual manifestation that the Book of Mormon is true." In the case of a vision, doubters will argue: How do you know it was a vision from God, rather than just an imagination of your mind? Joseph Smith said of the First Vision, "I had seen a vision; I knew it, and I knew that God knew it, and I could not deny it" (Joseph Smith–History 1:25).

I give unto you a prophecy (2 Nephi 25:4). *See:* I would prophesy.

I have seen (1 Nephi 8:2–3; 2 Nephi 1:4; 4:16, 26; 11:2–3; 25:13; 26:7, 10; 31:17; Alma 10:5; 19:13; 36:26; 38:7; 3 Nephi 28:26; Mormon 8:11; Ether 12:39). Prophet, seers, and righteous men and women have seen visions, things of the future and of heaven. Also they have seen angels and even their Savior Jesus Christ. It is the mission of prophets and seers to prophesy and testify of those things God reveals unto them. Righteous individuals are promised knowledge and the mysteries of God to be revealed to them as they progress towards exaltation. *See also:* D&C 93:1.

I have somewhat to prophesy (Alma 45:9). *See:* I would prophesy.

I know all their works (2 Nephi 27:27). The wicked falsely believe they can hide their evil works, but the all-knowing God and the all-seeing eye of God knows of their wicked deeds and will judge them appropriately. *See also:* Evil works.

I know my sheep (3 Nephi 18:31). The Lord knows who the true and faithful are. *See also:* Good Shepherd.

I make an end (1 Nephi 14:30; 2 Nephi 30:18; Jacob 2:22; 3:14; 7:27; Omni 1:3, 9, 11, 30; 3 Nephi 5:19; 10:19; Mormon 8:13). As many of the prophets approached the end of their writings that were included in the Book of Mormon, they wrote some of their most powerful messages, they testified of the truth, they left a warning, they bid farewell, and they affirmed that they kept a record as commanded. Often the final pages and chapters of each prophet's writings are extraordinarily packed with important and marvelous doctrines.

I proceed with mine own prophecy (2 Nephi 25:7). *See:* I would prophesy.

I rule in the heavens above and in the earth beneath (2 Nephi 29:7). God's statement that He rules over all; also found in Abraham 3:21. God oversees and directs all the creations of His vast universe. He is the supreme ruler and there is none higher.

I shall (will) heal them (3 Nephi 17:7; 18:32). The promise of the Savior to those that repent and come unto Him. The healing refers to the cleansing from sin the Savior can provide through the Atonement. The Atonement heals men and women's weaknesses, mortal nature, sins, and fears. *See also:* He shall heal them; Healing in his wings.

I tell you by the spirit of prophecy (Alma 37:15). *See:* I would prophesy.

I the Lord thy God am a jealous God (Mosiah 11:22; 13:13). God is a God of body, parts, and passions. One of the Ten Commandments is, "Thou shalt have no other gods before me. Thou shalt not make unto thee any graven image, or any likeness of anything that is in heaven above, or that is in the earth beneath, or that is in the water under the earth. Thou shalt not bow down thyself to them, nor serve them: for I the Lord thy God am a jealous God" (Exodus 20:3–5).

I was with the Father from the beginning (3 Nephi 9:15). "The beginning" here refers to the time when this earth was planned and created for us to inhabit and have for our mortal probation.

I will be merciful unto them (1 Nephi 13:33–34; 2 Nephi 23:22; 28:32). The Lord is constantly extending His arm of mercy to us that we may come unto Him. *See also:* Merciful God (Being).

I will be their rearward (3 Nephi 20:42; 21:29). Meaning being your protection from threats from behind you. Also meaning assisting and comforting those in the rear struggling to keep up.

I will believe (Alma 18:23; 22:7, 11). Sometimes described as taking the step of faith into the dark. The Lord tested the brother of Jared in this regard with the question, "Believest thou the words which I *shall* speak?" (Ether 3:11; emphasis added).

I will bless thee forever (Helaman 10:5). Equivalent to God pronouncing the assurance of eternal life upon one. *See also:* Eternal life; Seal you his.

I will contend with them that contendeth with thee (1 Nephi 21:25; 2 Nephi 6:17). *See:* I will go before thee (them); I will go with thee.

I will forgive (Mosiah 26:22, 29–30; Ether 2:15). That person who believes in the Lord, Jesus Christ, repents sincerely of his sins, and is baptized unto repentance is promised by the Lord that He will forgive his or her sins. Further, the Lord will continue to forgive throughout life if one will again repent. However, one should not find oneself in the constant circle of sin-repent-sin-repent-sin-repent, for the Lord has said, "Go, and sin no more" (John 8:11). Repetitious sinning is evidence of insincerity, which is to mock God, and that person's insincere repenting each time avails nothing except condemnation.

I will go before thee (them) (3 Nephi 21:29; Ether 1:42). In D&C 84:88, the Lord says, "I will go before your face. I will be on your right hand and on your left, and my Spirit shall be in your hearts, and mine angels round about you, to bear you up." *See also:* I will contend with them that contendeth with thee; I will go with thee.

I will go with thee (Mosiah 24:17). Assurance that God will assist in one's calling and mission. *See also:* I will go before thee (them); I will be their rearward.

I will receive him (them/you) (Mosiah 26:21; Alma 5:33; 3 Nephi 9:14, 22; 12:24). The Lord has promised He will receive and accept all those who humble themselves, repent, come unto Him, and heed His voice. These the Lord will claim as His own, and He will number them in His fold.

I will show unto the children of men (the world/them/thee/you) (2 Nephi 27:21, 23, 27–28; 29:14; 3 Nephi 16:12; 21:10; Ether 3:27; 4:13; 12:27–28). In these verses God assures us that He is able, has power, is constant, is all knowing, is truly the creator, His word will be fulfilled, will gather His people, will fight for His people, His wisdom is greater than the cunning of the devil, He can reveal mysteries, and He can make the weak strong. In short, we can trust in Him, and our trust will be rewarded and validated for us to see.

I would prophesy (2 Nephi 1:6; 25:4, 7, 13; 26:14; 30:3; Enos 1:26; Jacob 6:1; Mosiah 13:26; Alma 8:24–25; 36:17; 37:15; 45:9;

Helaman 14:9). A preface before revelation given from God through His servants the prophets. When we hear or read such words, it would be very prudent to take heed of what is said. If we are living to be worthy of the companionship of the Holy Ghost, we will be prompted as to the validity of the prophecy. *See also:* At that day; Give unto you a prophecy; I give unto you a prophecy; I have somewhat to prophesy; I proceed with mine own prophecy; I tell you by the spirit of prophecy; In that day.

Idol gods (1 Nephi 20:5; Mormon 4:14). An idol is a false god, often an image, a symbol, or an object that is worshipped. Sometimes a mere notion or concept is worshipped. In ancient times, and in some cultures today, idol gods are a figure or statue carved, cast, or otherwise formed out of wood, silver, gold, ivory, or some other (usually precious) material. Idol gods can also be money, possessions, power, fame, sports, houses, cars, and other worldly things. False gods or idols have no power to elevate a man to the heavens. Only the worship of the true and living God will provide salvation. *See also:* Know God; True and living (and only) God; Worship God.

Idolatrous man (people) (Mosiah 9:12; 11:7; 27:8). A man or a group of people who worship idol gods. *See also:* Idol gods.

Idolatry (idolatries) of the people (Enos 1:20; Mosiah 11:6; Alma 1:32; 50:21; 3 Nephi 30:2; Mormon 5:15; Ether 7:23, 26). The practice of worshipping idol gods. *See also:* Idol gods.

Idols of their gold and their silver (2 Nephi 12:20; Helaman 6:31). *See:* Idol gods.

If they (ye) will repent (1 Nephi 22:28; 2 Nephi 28:32; Alma 12:33; 22:6; 34:31; Helaman 13:11, 13; 14:13; 3 Nephi 10:6; 16:13; 21:22). Salvation is predicated, among other things, upon our repentance. To come unto Christ we must repent. "We believe that the first principles and ordinances of the Gospel are: first, Faith in the Lord Jesus Christ; second, Repentance; third, Baptism by immersion for the remission of sins; fourth, Laying on of hands for the gift of the Holy Ghost" (Articles of Faith 1:4).

If thou eat thou shalt surely die (Alma 12:23). When God placed Adam and Eve in the Garden of Eden, He gave them two commandments: (1) multiply and replenish the earth; and (2) do not partake of the fruit of the tree of knowledge of good and evil. Satan came tempting and persuaded Eve to partake of the fruit, and then Adam partook. True to His promise concerning the consequences of eating the fruit, Heavenly Father cast Adam and Eve out of the garden and out of God's presence, thereby suffering spiritual death in separation from God. In addition, by partaking, Adam and Eve became mortal, and at the end of their mortal lives they died physically. *See also:* Spiritual death; Temporal death; Genesis 2:17; Moses 3:17.

If ye have faith (Alma 32:21; Ether 12:9, 27; Moroni 7:33, 38, 42; 10:23). "If ye have faith as a grain of mustard seed, ye shall say unto this mountain, Remove hence to yonder place; and it shall remove; and nothing shall be impossible unto you" (Matthew 17:20). God will bless, protect, comfort, and empower those that have pure and genuine faith in Him. *See also:* Remove mountains.

If ye will keep my commandments ye shall prosper in the land (1 Nephi 2:20; 4:14; 2 Nephi 1:9, 20; 4:4; Jarom 1:9; Omni 1:6; Mosiah 1:7; 2:22, 31; Alma 9:13; 36:1, 30; 37:13; 38:1; 48:15, 25; 50:20; Helaman 3:20). The promise or covenant that God made with Lehi concerning the promised land. This promise was renewed and continued through all the generations of Lehi's family and extends even to us today. *See also:* Land choice above all other lands.

Ignorantly sinned (Mosiah 3:11). Meaning those who have not received the law and are therefore without the law. Some might say they did not know a behavior was wrong, but God knows all the intents of our hearts. To rebel and sin against that which you know is wrong and damnable before God. 3 Nephi 6:18 describes the opposite of ignorantly sinning: "Now they did not sin ignorantly, for they knew the will of God concerning them, for it had been taught unto them; therefore they did willfully rebel against God." *See also:* State of ignorance.

Illuminated by the light of the everlasting word (Alma 5:7). The everlasting word is the word of God, which is truth and light. When we receive the word of God it illuminates, edifies, and enlightens the mind to new, higher, and marvelous knowledge. *See also:* Marvelous light of God.

Image of God (Mosiah 7:27; Alma 18:34; 22:12). Genesis 1:27 says, "So God created man in his own image, in the image of God created he him; male and female created he them." *Image of God* means figure, likeness, form, and semblance of God. Thus we are in His image and likeness. 2 Corinthians 4:4 tells us, "Christ . . . is the image of God." Further, Jesus is in the "express" image of the Father, meaning in the precise or exact image of the Father.

Image of God engraven upon your countenances (Alma 5:14, 19). Refers to one's personal countenance. The righteous have a countenance of purity and light, whereas the wicked acquire a countenance

that is dark and sullen. We are commanded of God to live righteously and come to know God. The promise, if we do, is to have God's image in our countenance. Thus we are following the command to be as He is, having a countenance of light and glory. *See also:* Light of the glory of God.

Imaginations of his heart (1 Nephi 2:11; 17:20). *See:* Visionary man.

Imagine up foolish and vain things in their hearts (Helaman 16:22; 3 Nephi 2:2). To conceive of and invent that which is "wrought by men and by the power of the devil" (3 Nephi 2:2). Also called secret meditations. That which is truly in our heart is the measure of our character. Are there evil thoughts hidden there, or do we have a virtuous heart? *Compare:* Moses 8:22. *See also:* Devil has got so great hold upon your hearts.

Immediate goodness of God (Mosiah 25:10). If we keep the commandments of God, He will bless us in this life; if we are faithful unto the end, He will bless us with eternal life in the next life. The blessings in this life are often only recognized, after introspection, by the humble and sincere. Most often these "immediate blessings" are blessings of the Spirit, including peace of mind, the love of God, divine guidance, understanding, and protection against evil. If immediate blessings were showy and included great worldly riches, they would tend to eliminate moral agency and the faith required in this life. King Benjamin said, "And behold, even at this [very] time, ye have been calling on his name, and begging for a remission of your sins. And has he suffered that ye have begged in vain? Nay; he has poured out his Spirit upon you [now], and has caused that your hearts should be filled with joy" (Mosiah 4:20).

Immortal body (Alma 11:45). Means the resurrected body that will never again die or be sick. *See also:* All shall rise from the dead, both the just and the unjust; Become incorruptible and immortal; Change(-d) from this mortal to an immortal state; Corruption put on (raised in) incorruption; Endless life; Immortal soul; Immortal state; Incorruptible bodies; Mortal body raised in immortality; Mortal shall put on immortality; No more corruption; Perfect form (frame); Put on incorruption; Put on immortality; Raised in (to) immortality; Restored to its (their) perfect (proper) form (frame/order); Resurrection of the body; Resurrection of the dead.

Immortal soul(-s) (Mosiah 2:38; Alma 12:20; Helaman 3:30). Means the resurrected body. "The spirit and the [physical] body are the soul of man. And the resurrection from the dead is the redemption of the soul" (D&C 88:15–16). *See also:* Immortal body.

Immortal spirit (Mosiah 2:28). Man's spirit that dwells within his body is eternal—it existed before this life and will exist after this life forever.

Immortal state (Alma 12:20; 3 Nephi 28:15). The condition of the resurrected body. *See also:* Immortal body.

Impart of their substance (Mosiah 4:17, 21, 26; 18:27–28; Alma 1:27; 4:13; 34:28). Meaning to give to the poor. We are commanded by God to share the bounty He gives us with those in need. This is a very real part of the test of mortal probation. See the parable of the rich man and the beggar named Lazarus in Luke 16:19–30. *See also:* Free with your substance; Poor and needy; Succor(-ing) those who stand in need of their (your) succor.

Impossible for him to deny his word (Alma 11:34, 37). The Lord has stated, "What I have said unto you must needs be" (D&C 101:93) and, "Even as I have said, it shall come to pass" (D&C 101:10). Also, "What I the Lord have spoken, I have spoken, and I excuse not myself; and though the heavens and the earth pass away, my word shall not pass away, but shall all be fulfilled" (D&C 1:38). *See also:* Executeth all his words; Word of God must be fulfilled; D&C 39:16.

In a dream (1 Nephi 2:1–2; 3:2; 8:2, 4; 15:21; Ether 9:3). One of the channels of revelations from God to man. An example found in the New Testament is after the wise men visited, "Being warned of God in a dream that they [the wise men] should not return to Herod, they departed into their own country another way" (Matthew 2:12). Other channels of revelation include: visions, appearance of angels, words spoken aloud or in one's mind, inspiration, and promptings. *See also:* Dreamed a dream; In a vision.

In a state of innocence (2 Nephi 2:23). The state or condition that Adam and Eve lived in *before* they partook of the fruit of the tree of knowledge of good and evil. *See also:* Garden of Eden.

In a state to act (Alma 12:31). The state or condition that Adam and Eve found themselves in *after* partaking of the fruit of the tree of knowledge of good and evil. It was part of the plan of salvation that man experience opposites, such as virtue and vice, exercising agency by acting on every choice. *See also:* Act for themselves (yourselves); Choose life or death.

In a vision (1 Nephi 1:8; 5:4; 8:36; 10:17; 2 Nephi 1:4; Alma 8:20). A vision is a visual revelation from God to man. Authentic visions from God are given to individuals for themselves or their church calling. For example, a vision to a prophet is for God's people, to a bishop is for his ward, to a man or woman is for themselves or their family.

Drug-induced hallucinations and other psychological aberrations are not visions from God. *See also:* I have seen; In a dream; Saw in a vision; Seen a vision.

In all my holy mountain (2 Nephi 21:9; 30:15). Signifies the place where the Lord Jesus Christ will rule. In these verses it refers to the earth during the millennium. *See also:* Holy mountain.

In an acceptable time (1 Nephi 21:8). Meaning in that time acceptable to or determined as appropriate by God. *See also:* Own due time (of the Lord).

In behalf of his (the) people (1 Nephi 1:5; Mosiah 20:25; 3 Nephi 1:11). True leaders, fellow citizens, and Christlike individuals do all they can in behalf of their fellowmen. *See also:* Anxiety for you.

In him I shall rest (Enos 1:27). Enos talks here of becoming old and that he will soon die. "I soon go to the place of my rest." *See also:* Enter into his (my/the) rest (of the Lord/of God).

In him there is no variableness neither shadow of changing (Mormon 9:9). God is an unchanging God, meaning we can always count on His righteousness and concern for us, His children. *See also:* Shadow of changing (turning); James 1:17.

In him they shall find pasture (1 Nephi 22:25). Meaning that in coming unto Jesus Christ, man will find refuge from the world. The word *pasture* here refers to a place of plenty and safety. *Compare:* 1 Nephi 21:9–10. *See also:* Good Shepherd.

In his glory and in his power and in his might, majesty, and dominion (Alma 5:50; 12:15). *See:* Come(-th/coming) in his glory.

In his heart (2 Nephi 20:7; Alma 5:12; 47:4; Helaman 10:3; 3 Nephi 12:28; Ether 15:2). In the heart are one's true intentions. What we ponder, plan, believe, and love is in our heart or deep within us. It cannot be seen by men, unless aided by God; for God knows all the intents of our hearts. *See also:* Intents of our hearts.

In his own due time (Enos 1:16; 3 Nephi 5:25; Mormon 5:12). *See:* Own due time (of the Lord).

In his (thy) name (2 Nephi 9:23–24; 25:16; Jacob 4:5; Alma 19:4; 3 Nephi 27:2; Mormon 8:24; Ether 12:31; Moroni 7:26, 38). The command is, "I say unto you, all things must be done in the name of Christ, whatsoever you do in the Spirit" (D&C 46:31). Meaning all our righteous acts should be done in the name of Jesus Christ, for by so doing we invoke the power and blessing of God on our actions. *See also:* In my name; In the name of Jesus (Christ/the Lord God).

In me hath the Father glorified his name (3 Nephi 9:15; 11:11;

Ether 12:8). Jesus Christ has always emphasized that all glory belongs to the Father, and what He, Jesus, did was for the glory of the Father.

In me is the law of Moses fulfilled (3 Nephi 9:17; 12:18; 12:46; 15:5). *See:* Law of Moses.

In mine (my) wisdom (2 Nephi 3:19; 27:22; 3 Nephi 21:10). God knows all things, has all understanding, and has all wisdom. There is nothing that He does not know, and thus we can have complete faith and confidence in Him. It would be prudent to seek His wisdom rather than go it on our own to discover the correct paths to take. *See also:* Wisdom in (of) God (the Lord/the Father).

In mine own due time (2 Nephi 27:21; 3 Nephi 20:29; Ether 3:27). *See:* Own due time (of the Lord).

In my fierce anger (Mosiah 12:1; Helaman 13:10). *See:* Anger of the Lord.

In my name (2 Nephi 31:12; Mosiah 26:18, 20, 22, 24; 3 Nephi 11:23, 27, 37, 38; 16:4; 17:3; 18:5, 11, 16, 19–21, 23, 30; 20:31; 21:6, 27; 27:7–9, 16, 20, 28; 30:2; Mormon 9:24, 25; Ether 4:15, 18; Moroni 2:2; 7:26, 34). *See:* In his (thy) name; In the name of Jesus (Christ/the Lord God); Pray(-ed) unto the Father in my (the) name (of Christ).

In nowise be cast out (2 Nephi 25:29; Mormon 9:29). The promise of the Lord to the faithful that they will not be cast out of the kingdom of heaven. *See also:* Cast out.

In our bodies we shall see God (2 Nephi 9:4). Testimony that we shall all be resurrected and stand before God to be judged of the works we did on earth. *Compare:* Job 19:26.

In power and great glory (1 Nephi 11:28; 22:24; 2 Nephi 6:14; 33:11; Moroni 7:35). Refers to the Second Coming of the Lord. *See also:* Coming of Christ.

In remembrance of my body (blood) (3 Nephi 18:7, 11; Moroni 4:3; 5:2). The promises we make in the sacrament prayer. "With torn and broken bread, we signify that we remember the physical body of Jesus Christ—a body that was buffeted with pains, afflictions, and temptations of every kind (see Alma 7:11), a body that bore a burden of anguish sufficient to bleed at every pore (see Luke 22:44; Mosiah 3:7; D&C 19:18), a body whose flesh was torn and whose heart was broken in crucifixion (see Psalm 22:16; John 19:33–34; 20:25–27; 3 Nephi 11:14; D&C 6:37; Talmage, *Jesus the Christ* [1916], 669). We signify our belief that while that same body was laid to rest in death, it was raised again to life from the grave, never again to know disease, decay, or death (see Matthew 28:6; Luke 24:6, 39; John 20:20; D&C 76:22–24). And in taking the bread to ourselves, we acknowledge that, like Christ's mortal body, our bodies will be released from the bonds of death, rise triumphantly from the grave, and be restored to our eternal spirits. . . .

"With a small cup of water, we signify that we remember the blood Jesus spilled and the spiritual suffering He endured for all mankind. We remember the agony that caused great drops of blood to fall in Gethsemane (see Luke 22:44; Mosiah 3:7; D&C 19:18). We remember the bruising and scourging He endured at the hands of His captors (see Isaiah 53:5; Matthew 26:67; 27:26, 29–30; Mark 14:65; 15:15, 19; Luke 22:63–65; John 19:1; Mosiah 15:5). We remember the blood He spilled from His hands, feet and side while at Calvary (see Matthew 27:35; Mark 15:15; Luke 23:33; John 19:16, 33–34). And we remember His personal reflection on His suffering: 'How sore you know not, how exquisite you know not, yea, how hard to bear you know not' (D&C 19:15). In taking the water to ourselves, we acknowledge that His blood and suffering atoned for our sins and that He will remit our sins as we embrace and accept the principles and ordinances of His gospel" (Hamula, "The Sacrament and the Atonement," 83–84).

In spirit and in truth (Alma 34:38; 43:10). *See:* Worship in spirit and truth.

In that day (1 Nephi 2:23; 13:34; 14:1; 2 Nephi 3:13; 12:11, 17, 20; 13:7, 18; 14:1–2; 15:30; 17:18, 21, 23; 20:20, 27; 21:10–11; 22:1, 4; 24:3–4; 25:8; 27:29; 28:3, 16; Mosiah 17:18; Alma 5:16–17; Helaman 13:20, 32–33; 14:20; 3 Nephi 14:22; 20:39; 21:9, 14; 24:17; 27:32; Ether 4:7). A prepositional phrase that most often comes before prophecy. *See also:* At that day; Things (which are) to come.

In the beginning (Mosiah 7:27; Alma 18:34; Ether 3:15). These three scriptures have reference to the time of the creation of man's physical body on this earth. The Bible begins with the words "In the beginning God created the heaven and the earth" (Genesis 1:1). This means the beginning of this earth, for there is no beginning to eternity, which has always been and always will be.

In the depth(-s) of humility (2 Nephi 9:42; Mosiah 4:11; 21:14; Alma 62:41; Helaman 6:5; 3 Nephi 12:2). *In the depths* means at the lowest part, even at the very base, with no elevation or rise of pride. For if there exists the smallest part of pride, then we are not truly and fully humble. *See also:* Meek and humble.

In the form of a dove (1 Nephi 11:11, 27; 2 Nephi 31:8). *See:* Form of a dove.

In the midst of fire (Helaman 5:23, 44; 3 Nephi 17:24). *See:* Encircled about with fire.

In the mouth of three (many) witnesses (2 Nephi 27:14; Ether 5:4). *See:* Testimony of many (two or three).

In the name of God (Alma 30:49). In D&C 1:20, "In the name of God the Lord, even the Savior of the world." *See also:* In the name of Jesus (Christ/the Lord God).

In the name of his Son (Alma 12:33). *See:* In the name of Jesus (Christ/the Lord God).

In the name of Jesus (Christ/the Lord God) (2 Nephi 32:9; 33:12; Jacob 4:6; Enos 1:15; Mosiah 18:10; Alma 30:49; 3 Nephi 7:19–20; 8:1; 19:6–8; 26:17, 21; 27:1; 28:30; 4 Nephi 1:1, 5; Mormon 7:8; 9:6, 21, 27, 29; Ether 5:5; Moroni 3:2–3; 4:2–3; 5:2; 8:3; 10:4). Moses 5:8 says, "Wherefore, thou shalt do all that thou doest in the name of the Son, and thou shalt repent and call upon God in the name of the Son forevermore." *Compare:* Acts 3:6. *See also:* Pray(-ed) unto the Father in my (the) name (of Christ).

In the name of my Beloved Son (2 Nephi 31:11). *See:* In the name of Jesus (Christ/the Lord God).

In the name of the all-powerful God (Almighty) (1 Nephi 17:48; Alma 44:5). *See:* In the name of Jesus (Christ/the Lord God).

In the name of the Father, and of the Son, and of the Holy Ghost (3 Nephi 11:25). The sacrament prayers and the baptismal prayer are set prayers, meaning the prayers of those ordinances are to use specific words. This phrase is part of the baptismal prayer and is found in 3 Nephi wherein the Lord, Jesus Christ, instructs the Nephites how to baptize, "On this wise shall ye baptize them" (3 Nephi 11:23). *See also:* D&C 20:72–74; D&C 68:8.

In the name of the Lord (Mosiah 18:10). *See:* In the name of Jesus (Christ/the Lord God).

In the sight of God (the Lord) (2 Nephi 3:24; Jacob 3:24; Mosiah 3:22; 11:2; 23:9; 26:13; Alma 39:5; Helaman 3:20; Ether 8:18; 10:5, 16–17, 19). As many of these verses declare, we should always do that which is right in the sight of God. We should be ashamed to know that we have done wrong in the sight of God. Our actions would be better when we come to understand that our infinite God knows of all our actions, can see anything or any event He desires to see, and is aware of all that transpires in His vast universe by the power of His omnipresent spirit. *See also:* All-searching eye.

In the strength of our God (the Lord) (Words of Mormon 1:14; Mosiah 9:17; 10:10; Alma 20:4; 46:20; 60:16; 61:17–18; 3 Nephi 4:10). Meaning to receive strength and capacity from the Lord. The Lord strengthens His people to face their adversities, if His people will have faith in Him and keep His commandments. "The Apostle Paul taught . . . how to protect themselves from evil, 'Put on the whole armor of God.' . . .

"As you put on the armor of God, you will protect yourself and strengthen your loved ones. Consider the example of the Nephites, who were frequently attacked by powerful enemies. Every time the Nephites went up to battle 'in the strength of the Lord,' they prevailed. . . . As you rely on the strength of the Lord, granted through His atoning sacrifice, you too can be victorious. You can receive the peace, security, and happiness of being firmly grounded in the gospel of Jesus Christ" (*Let Virtue Garnish Thy Thoughts*, 12). *See also:* Give me strength; Lord did strengthen them; Strength in (of) the Lord; Wilt thou give me strength; Helaman 7:22–23.

In thy seed shall all the kindreds of the earth be blessed (1 Nephi 15:18; 22:9; 3 Nephi 20:25, 27). One of the promises made to Abraham in the Abrahamic covenant (Genesis 22:18), meaning that the seed of Abraham would carry the gospel to the whole earth and minister among all the peoples of the earth. *See also:* Children of the covenant.

In tribulation(-s) (2 Nephi 2:1; Jacob 7:26; Mosiah 23:10; 27:28, 32; Alma 8:14; 15:18; 53:13; 56:2, 7; 60:26). Often we must carry out our duty, do good, and serve others while at the same time being persecuted and while enduring great hardships. This tests our resolve to do the will of God and teaches us patience. *See also:* Furnace of affliction.

Inasmuch as ye shall keep my (the) commandments (of God) ye shall prosper in the land (1 Nephi 2:20; 4:14; 17:13; 2 Nephi 1:9, 20; 4:4; Jarom 1:9; Omni 1:6; Alma 9:13; 36:1, 30; 38:1; 50:20). The Lord's promise to Lehi and his posterity concerning the land of promise, the American continent. The promise was renewed to the Book of Mormon peoples throughout the generations and was repeated often as a persuasion to be obedient to God. The Book of Mormon is a testimony that God kept this promise when the people were righteous. Likewise, the people lost the blessing of the Lord when they forgot their God and sinned. *See also:* Land choice above all other lands.

Incomprehensible joy (Alma 28:8). Joy beyond description and without end. Man hath not seen nor heard nor imagined how great and incomprehensible are the things that God has prepared for them that love Him and keep His commandments (see 1 Corinthians 2:9). *See also:* Filled with joy; Filled with love.

Incorrect traditions (Alma 3:8; 37:9). *See:* Traditions of the Lamanites.

Incorruptible and immortal (2 Nephi 9:13). *See:* Incorruptible bodies.

Incorruptible bodies (Mormon 6:21). Meaning immortal, everlasting, and perfected bodies that are not susceptible to disease, sickness, or death. Such will be our bodies upon the Resurrection, which gift is from Christ who was the first fruits of the Resurrection. *See also:* Immortal body.

Indebted unto him (your Heavenly Father) (Mosiah 2:23–24, 34). God has given us so much that it would be impossible to repay Him. He created us and gave us life, He blesses us as we keep His commandments, He has provided this bountiful earth, the plan of salvation, His gift to us will be the Resurrection, and He has made possible exaltation in the celestial kingdom. It is impossible to list all that God has done for us. Because of these things we should give thanks, praise Him forever, and dedicate ourselves to doing His will.

Indulge themselves in sorceries (wicked practices) (Jacob 1:15; Alma 1:32). *Indulge* means to allow, permit, yield to, wallow in, and revel in. Thus such people leave the safety of keeping the commandments, begin to experiment with sin, and then eventually embrace sin. *See also:* Sorceries and witchcrafts and magics.

Industrious people (2 Nephi 5:17; Mosiah 23:5; Alma 23:18; Ether 10:22). Meaning a hardworking, busy, and diligent people. The opposite of being a lazy and indolent people.

Inequality of man (Alma 28:13). Refers to the various standings of men before God. At first, all men and women come into life as innocent children, but then their accountable actions divide them. 1 Nephi 17:35 says, "Behold, the Lord esteemeth all flesh in one; he that is righteous is favored of God. But behold, this people had rejected every word of God, and they were ripe in iniquity; and the fulness of the wrath of God was upon them."

Infinite and eternal (Alma 34:10, 14). These two verses have reference to the all-encompassing and everlasting nature of the atoning sacrifice of Jesus Christ for all mankind. *See also:* Infinite atonement.

Infinite atonement (2 Nephi 9:7; 25:16; Alma 34:12). Christ's atoning sacrifice for all men and women is broader and more expansive in its effect than mortals have the capacity to understand or fathom. Elder Russell M. Nelson said: "His Atonement is infinite—without an end (see 2 Nephi 9:7; 25:16; Alma 34:10, 12, 14). It was also infinite in that all humankind would be saved from never-ending death. It was infinite in terms of His immense suffering. It was infinite in time, putting an end to the preceding prototype of animal sacrifice. It was infinite in scope—it was to be done once for all (see Hebrews 10:10).

And the mercy of the Atonement extends not only to an infinite number of people, but also to an infinite number of worlds created by Him (see D&C 76:24; Moses 1:33). It was infinite beyond any human scale of measurement or mortal comprehension.

"Jesus was the only one who could offer such an infinite atonement, since He was born of a mortal mother and an immortal Father. Because of that unique birthright, Jesus was [and is] an infinite Being" ("The Atonement," 35). Jesus Christ, our Savior and Redeemer, provided the Atonement that is infinite in nature in that it is not restricted by time, not limited to this earth, wrought by an infinite being, applies to the infinite suffering of all, and applies to an infinite number of beings. Truly it is infinite.

Infinite goodness (of God) (2 Nephi 1:10; Mosiah 5:3; Helaman 12:1; Moroni 8:3). God's goodness (that is His rightness, generosity, excellence, and love toward us) is endless, eternal, boundless, limitless, and immense. The goodness of God leads man to repentance (see Romans 2:4). The Lord does not limit a man to not partake of his goodness (see 2 Nephi 26:28). God's goodness towards us includes great long-suffering and lovingkindness. The Atonement is the ultimate manifestation of God's goodness. We must always be grateful for and give thanks for God's goodness. *See* *also:* All things which are good cometh of God; Goodness of God; Goodness of the Lord; Know of the goodness of God; Partake of his goodness; Partake of the goodness of God; Supreme goodness of God.

Infinite mercy (Mosiah 28:4). God possesses all possible mercy and is the perfect example of complete mercy. He loves us, His children, and wishes to apply mercy to its fullest extent to each of our individual situations. However, His mercy is tempered by His desire and need to also apply justice to our individual situations. Fortunately, the Atonement of Jesus Christ allows mercy to triumph over justice, if we will have faith in Christ, sincerely repent of our sins, and strive with our might to do what is right.

Inhabitants of the earth (1 Nephi 1:14; 2 Nephi 2:8; 28:16, 17; 3 Nephi 9:1; Ether 3:25). God's work concerns *all* the inhabitants of the earth. All are invited to come unto Christ and be saved.

Inherit the earth (3 Nephi 12:5). Blessed are the meek, for they shall inherit the earth. The meek are not the weak, but are "gentle, forgiving, or benevolent" (see footnote *a* in Matthew 5:5). To inherit the earth means to possess it and live on it forever and ever. D&C 77:1 says, "What is the sea of glass spoken of by John [the Revelator] 4th chapter, and 6th verse of the Revelation? It is the earth in its sanctified, immortal,

and eternal state." Then in D&C 88:18–20 we learn the earth will "be prepared for the celestial glory; for after it hath filled the measure of its creation, it shall be crowned with glory, even with the presence of God the Father; that bodies who are of the celestial kingdom may possess it forever and ever; for, for this intent was it made and created."

Inherit the kingdom of God (heaven) (2 Nephi 9:18; Mosiah 27:26; Alma 5:51; 7:14; 9:12; 11:37; 39:9; 40:26; 41:4; 3 Nephi 11:33, 38). This is the great goal of mortal life—to prove ourselves worthy to again dwell with God. If we were always mindful of this goal, our decisions would always be good and not sometimes evil.

Inheritance at my right hand (Alma 5:58). Christ sits on His throne in the heavens at the right hand of the throne of God the Father (Hebrews 1:3; D&C 20:24). We seek to obtain salvation and be exalted at the right hand of Jesus. *See also:* Mosiah 5:9; 26:23–24; Alma 5:58; 28:12; Helaman 3:30; Ether 12:4.

Iniquities and abominations (Mosiah 7:20; 12:1, 7; 28:15; 29:18, 36; 3 Nephi 9:5). These are other words for sin.

Inquire(-d) of the Lord (1 Nephi 15:3, 8; 16:24; Jacob 2:11; Mosiah 26:13; 28:6; Alma 16:6; 27:7, 10–11; 40:3, 9; 43:23; Ether 1:38; Moroni 8:7). "It is the privilege and the right of every member of the Church to receive revelation and to enjoy the gifts of the Spirit. When we are confirmed members of the Church, we receive the gift of the Holy Ghost, which is the right to the constant companionship of that member of the Godhead, based on faithfulness. The actual enjoyment of this gift depends upon personal worthiness. 'God shall give unto you knowledge by his Holy Spirit,' the revelation says to the Saints, 'yea, by the unspeakable gift of the Holy Ghost. . . .' (D&C 121:26.)

"Speaking of the revelations received by his father, Nephi said: '. . . he truly spake many great things which were hard to be understood, save a man inquire of the Lord. . . .'

"Of these same revelations, Laman and Lemuel said: '. . . we cannot understand the words which our father hath spoken. . . .'

"Nephi asked: 'Have ye inquired of the Lord?'

"They replied, 'We have not; for the Lord maketh no such thing known unto us.'

"Then Nephi came forth with this glorious pronouncement: 'How is it that ye do not keep the commandments of the Lord? How is it that ye will perish, because of the hardness of your hearts?

"'Do ye not remember the things which the Lord hath said?—If ye will not harden your hearts, and ask me in faith, believing that ye shall receive, with diligence in

keeping my commandments, surely these things shall be made known unto you.' (1 Ne. 15:3, 7–11.)" (McConkie, "The Lord's People Receive Revelation," 78). Joseph Smith said, "The Holy Ghost is a revelator." And, "No man can receive the Holy Ghost without receiving revelations" (*Teachings of the Prophet Joseph Smith*, 328).

Inspired from heaven (3 Nephi 6:20). Inspiration is a form of revelation where words or thoughts come into our mind. *See also:* Inquire(-d) of the Lord.

Inspired of God (Moroni 7:13). *See:* Inspired from heaven.

Instructed of the Lord (1 Nephi 17:18; 2 Nephi 18:11). *See:* Inquire(-d) of the Lord.

Instrument in his (the/thy) hands (of God) (2 Nephi 1:24; 3:24; Mosiah 23:10; 27:36; Alma 1:8; 2:30; 17:9, 11; 26:3, 15; 29:9; 35:14). To be an instrument means to be a tool, a servant, or a faithful agent. In order to be an instrument in the hands of the Lord, we must have faith in Him, we must trust in Him, and we must do His will. "Is there any more beautiful experience than to feel the influence of the Lord working in our lives; to know that He is there, close by; to feel that He magnifies and enhances our natural abilities, thereby making us tools in His hands? I firmly believe that there is much more joy and satisfaction in saying, 'It is the Lord who did it through me,' rather than in saying, 'I did it all by myself'" (Caussé, "'For When I Am Weak, Then Am I Strong'").

Intents of our hearts (Mosiah 5:13; Alma 12:7; 18:32; 21:6; Moroni 7:9; 10:4). God knows the intents of our hearts, and the intents of our hearts cannot be hidden from Him. He knows our thoughts, our fears, and our hopes. Thus we should confess to God the evil intents of our hearts and repent of them. And we must pray that the righteous intents of our hearts will come to pass.

Interposition of their all-wise Creator (Mosiah 29:19). Meaning God has assisted them by intervening, mediating, and interceding on behalf of the people.

Interpret languages (engravings) (Omni 1:20; Mosiah 8:6, 11; 21:28; Ether 3:22). The translation of languages by the use of interpreters, also known as the Urim and Thummim. *See also:* Two stones.

Interpretation thereof (Mormon 9:34; Ether 4:5). Meaning the interpreters. *See also:* Prepared means for the interpretation thereof; Two stones.

Interpreters were prepared (preserved) (Mosiah 8:13, 19; 28:20; Alma 37:21, 24; Ether 4:5). *See:* Two stones.

Into (unto) the mountain (1 Nephi 11:1; 16:30; 17:7; Ether 3:1). Prophets and men of God have often gone up into the mount to commune with God. Before temples these were often sacred places and were as a "sacred grove" unto those that sought God. *Compare:* Genesis 12:8; Exodus 3:1; 19:3; Isaiah 56:7; Micah 4:1, 2; Mark 9:2; Revelation 21:10; Moses 1:1. *See also:* The mount.

Inviteth (and enticeth) to do good (Moroni 7:13, 16). God invites and entices all men to do good. The Spirit of Christ or the Light of Christ that all men and women are born with invites and entices to do good. Also the Holy Ghost can be a companion and dwell with man to direct and invite to do good. These invitations and enticings will always be good and are a key to discerning between good and evil.

Inward vessel shall be cleansed first (Alma 60:23–24). These verses refer to a government that is corrupt and not united within, and thus will fail if not corrected. Individuals are often the same way, masquerading as upright and honest people but within have evil intentions and sin. To be right with God we must have pure and undefiled hearts and minds. *Compare:* Matthew 23:25–28.

Is at hand (2 Nephi 23:6; Mosiah 7:18; Alma 5:31, 36; Alma 7:9; 9:28; 10:20; Helaman 5:32; 3 Nephi 1:13–14; 17:1; Ether 4:16). Footnote *b* in Matthew 4:17 indicates an alternate translation from the Greek is "has come." Also meaning very near or soon, not far off, or at the door. Or as in Mosiah 7:18, "the time is at hand, or is not far distant." *See also:* At hand.

Is just (and true) (2 Nephi 1:10; Mosiah 3:18; 4:12, 25; 27:31; Alma 12:15; 18:34; 29:8; 34:11; 41:13; Moroni 10:6). God is perfectly just, and deals only in that which is just and true. *See also:* Judgments are just.

Islands (isles) of the sea (1 Nephi 19:12, 16; 21:1, 8; 22:4; 2 Nephi 8:5; 10:8, 21; 21:11; 29:7, 11). Meaning all the nations of the earth. "Sir Isaac Newton observes that to the Hebrews the continents of Asia and Africa were 'the earth' because they had access to them by land, while the parts of the earth to which they sailed over the sea were 'the isles of the sea'" (Reynolds and Sjodahl, *Commentary on the Book of Mormon*, 1:214). In 2 Nephi 10:20, Jacob refers to the promised land thusly, "We are upon an isle of the sea." *See also:* All ye ends of the earth.

It is written (Alma 6:8; 3 Nephi 12:27, 33, 38, 43). It has sometimes been said, "As it is written, so shall it be." In ancient times this phrase usually had reference to what was written by God and what was written by kings. Thus the command was to be followed. When considered, "if it is written," then it must have importance and permanence. Those requiring precedence look for what is written. Thus besides religions, governments, lawyers, and many other professions look to what is written. Historians and students of literature are particularly fond of the phrase "it is written." The occurrences of this scriptural phrase found in 3 Nephi have reference to the Ten Commandments and therefore have the ultimate import as to "it is written."

J

Jealous God (Mosiah 11:22; 13:13). *See:* I the Lord thy God am a jealous God.

Jesus Christ (2 Nephi 25:19–20; 30:5; Mosiah 3:8, 12; 4:2–3, 14; Alma 5:48; 6:8; 9:28; 36:17; 37:9, 33; 38:8; 45:4, 10; 46:39; Helaman 3:28; 5:9; 13:6; 14:12; 3 Nephi 5:13, 20, 26; 7:16, 18, 21; 9:15; 10:10; 11:2, 10, 25; 20:31; 21:11; 29:7; 30:1; Mormon 3:14, 21; 7:5; 8:35; 9:5, 12–13, 18, 22, 29, 37; Ether 2:12; 3:14; 4:7–8; 12:22, 41; Moroni 3:3; 4:3; 5:2; 7:2, 48; 8:2; 9:26). The name of our Lord, Savior, and Redeemer whom the entirety of the Book of Mormon is about and testifies of. The subtitle of the Book of Mormon is *Another Testament of Jesus Christ.* The title page of the Book of Mormon states in part that the purpose of the book is "to the convincing of the Jew and Gentile that Jesus is the Christ, the Eternal God, manifesting himself unto all nations." All the holy prophets have testified that Jesus is the Christ, the Savior and Redeemer of the world. The Book of Mormon prophets frequently admonish the reader to come unto Jesus and be saved, and that there is no other name by which man can gain salvation.

His name, Jesus Christ, is first declared in the Book of Mormon in 2 Nephi 25:19, though he is referred to on the first page of the Book of Mormon, ceaselessly throughout the book, and on the last page of the book. These verses in the Book of Mormon testify that Jesus is the Only Begotten of the Father in the flesh; He is the very Son of God; His mother would be Mary; He is the creator; He will come among men; He is full of grace, mercy, and truth; He will redeem His people and atone for their sins; we must have faith in Him and cry unto Him for mercy; He will succor his people; there will be signs of His coming; He will gather his people; we must pray and do all things in His name; He is the great I AM; we must praise Him forever; He has won victory over the grave; He will perform mighty miracles; He was prepared from the beginning; we must seek this Jesus and do His holy will; His love and mercy will be bestowed on His followers; He is ever mindful of us; He sits on the right hand of the Father; and that through faithfulness, we can become His spiritually begotten sons and daughters.

Jesus Christ, even the Father and the Son (Mosiah 15:2; Mormon 9:12; Ether 3:14). *See:* I am the Father (and the Son).

Jesus Christ (Messiah/Son of God) shall come (2 Nephi 26:3; Jacob 7:9, 14; Mosiah 3:5; 4:2; 15:1; Alma 5:48; 9:26; 11:32, 35, 40; 19:13; 21:7; 30:26, 39; 34:8; 39:15; 45:4; Helaman 5:9; 13:6; 16:18; 3 Nephi 11:10; 28:7, 8; Mormon 9:2). *See:* Coming of Christ.

Jesus Christ the Son of God (2 Nephi 25:19; Mosiah 3:8; 4:2; 5:48; Alma 6:8; 36:17–18; Helaman 3:28; 14:12; 3 Nephi 5:13, 26; 9:15; 20:31; Mormon 7:5; 9:22, 29; Ether 4:7). Jesus Christ truly is the Son of God: (1) Jesus was the firstborn of the spirit children of God (D&C 93:21); and (2) Jesus was the Only Begotten of the Father in the flesh, meaning His mortal mother was Mary, and the father of His mortal body was God the Father (John 1:14; John 3:16; D&C 76:13, 23). "Through His mother, Mary, He received many of the frailties of mortality essential to His preordained and much-prophesied mission to suffer and die for the sins of all mankind. Through His Eternal Father He received certain powers of immortality, which gave Him the ability to live a sinless life and to eventually conquer death—for Himself and for us" (Ballard, *Our Search for Happiness*, 9–10). *See also:* Jesus Christ; Only Begotten of the Father; Only Begotten Son.

Jesus Christ their redeemer (Alma 37:9; Helaman 5:12; 3 Nephi 5:26; 10:10; Moroni 8:8). These scriptures state and testify that Jesus Christ is the redeemer, the Savior of mankind. *See also:* Jesus Christ.

Jesus groaned within himself (3 Nephi 17:14). In 2 Corinthians 5:2, 4, Paul says that we "groan, earnestly desiring" and we "groan, being burdened." In other words, to "groan within" is to express deep-felt and intense emotion and desires. *See also:* John 11:33, 38.

Jesus is the (very) Christ (2 Nephi 26:12; Mormon 3:21; 5:14; Moroni 7:44). *See:* Jesus Christ.

Jerusalem of old (Ether 13:8, 11). Meaning the Jerusalem from which Lehi and his family came out and in which Jesus ministered during His mortal life. As compared to the New Jerusalem that shall be established upon the American continent in the last days and during the millennium. From these two world capitals will come the word and the law. And the inhabitants will be those whose garments are white through the blood of the Lamb.

Jews are (were) scattered (1 Nephi 13:39; 2 Nephi 25:15; 30:7). *See:* Scattered tribes of Israel.

Jot and (nor/or) tittle (Alma 34:13; 3 Nephi 1:25; 12:18). Every bit and part, every small detailed item, all things nothing missing, even little things. Meaning all things will be fulfilled, even the smallest, most seemingly insignificant element. *See also:* According to God's word.

Joy is (shall be/was) full (1 Nephi 5:7; 2 Nephi 9:18; Alma 26:11, 30; 27:17; 29:13–14; 3 Nephi 17:20; 28:10). In a figurative sense, we say of good things that one's glass is full to the top and overflowing. In John 15:10–11, "If ye keep my commandments, ye shall abide in my love; even as I have kept my Father's commandments, and abide in his love. These things have I spoken unto you, that my joy might remain in you, and that your joy might be full." *See also:* Fulness of joy.

Joy of Christ (his Son/his God) (Alma 27:17; 31:38; 33:23). *See:* Consuming of my flesh; Swallowed up in the joy of Christ (his God).

Joy of the saints (Enos 1:3). Men and women are that they might have joy. Living the gospel brings true joy. Those things that will bring joy into our lives are testimony, gratitude, faith, and peace. It is important to know that joy and hardship are not mutually exclusive. In other words, to have joy does not mean that we will not experience hardship. There is great joy in knowing we are doing God's will.

Joy which is unspeakable and full of glory (Helaman 5:44). *Compare:* 1 Peter 1:8. *See:* Fulness of joy; Joy is (shall be/was) full.

Joyous to the soul (1 Nephi 11:23). *See:* Soul did rejoice.

Judge of both quick and dead (Moroni 10:34). Jesus is the judge of those who are quickened by the spirit and those that are spiritually dead, both the righteous and the evil. *See also:* Acts 10:42; 2 Timothy 4:1; 1 Peter 4:5.

Judge righteous judgment (Mosiah 29:29, 43). We should seek to have judges who judge righteous judgment, meaning to judge based on what is right and just. The opposite is evil judgment, done from the point of view to obtain selfish ends and to hurt the innocent.

Judge righteously (Alma 41:14; 50:39). It is critical that we each make our daily judgments righteously and that we mingle with those that judge righteously. In the end only the just and true will gain salvation. *See also:* Just and true [individuals].

Judge the world (2 Nephi 29:11; Mosiah 3:10; 3 Nephi 27:16). Jesus Christ shall judge the world, or, in other words, all those who have lived on earth.

Judged according to (of) my deeds (Alma 5:15; 36:15). *See:* Judged according to (of) their works.

Judged according to (of) their works (1 Nephi 15:32–33; 2 Nephi 9:44; 28:23; 29:11; Mosiah 3:24; 16:10; Alma 11:41, 44; 12:8, 12; 33:22; 40:21; 41:3; 42:23; 3 Nephi

26:4; 27:14, 15, 25; Mormon 3:18, 20; 6:21; 8:19). Those who teach that all that is required of man to gain salvation is to declare their belief in Christ have not read nor understood the scriptures and the prophets. Over and over in many places the Lord has declared in the scriptures the requirement of good works to obtain salvation. We will all one day stand before God to be judged of our works and our deeds, whether they be good or whether they be evil. We must realize that no one will escape the consequences of their own deeds. *See also:* Abound(-ing) in good works; According to their (your) works (deeds); Good works.

Judged at the great and last day (for the day shall come) (1 Nephi 15:32; 2 Nephi 9:44; Words of Mormon 1:11; Mosiah 3:24; 27:31; Alma 11:41; 24:15; 33:22; 41:3; 3 Nephi 26:4; Mormon 6:21). *See:* Judgment day.

Judgment bar (2 Nephi 33:11, 15). The judgment place before God where all will be judged according to the good or evil deeds they did in life. As all have sinned to some degree, it behooves us to repent of our misdeeds so that we may stand before the judgment bar clean and washed from our sins. *See also:* Bar of God; Judgment-seat of Christ (God).

Judgment day (2 Nephi 9:22, 46; Mosiah 3:24; Alma 9:15; 33:22;

Helaman 8:25; 3 Nephi 28:32, 40; Mormon 7:7, 10). Elder Bruce R. McConkie summarizes the various judgment days: (1) "Whenever the judgments of God are poured out upon men, it is a *day of judgment*" [i.e., the flood of Noah, Sodom and Gomorrah, Christ's coming to the Nephites, etc.]; (2) "Death itself is an initial *day of judgment*" [see Alma 40:12–14]; (3) "Christ's Second Coming will be a *day of judgment*" [wherein the righteous will be caught up and the wicked burned]; and (4) "After [the Millennium and after] all men have been resurrected the day of the great *final judgment* will come. Every living soul shall then stand before God, the books will be opened, and the dead will be judged out of those things written in the books, according to their works. (Rev. 20:11–15.) 'And it shall come to pass,' Jacob said, 'that when all men shall have passed from this first death unto life, insomuch as they have become immortal, they must appear before the judgment-seat of the Holy One of Israel; and then cometh the judgment, and then must they be judged according to the holy judgment of God.' (2 Nephi 9:15–16.)" (*Mormon Doctrine*, 401–4).

"Prepare your souls for that glorious day when justice shall be administered unto the righteous, even the day of judgment, that ye may not shrink with awful fear; that ye may not remember your awful guilt in perfectness, and be constrained to exclaim: Holy, holy are thy judgments, O Lord God Almighty—but I know my guilt; I transgressed thy law, and my transgressions are mine; and the devil hath obtained me, that I am a prey to his awful misery" (2 Nephi 9:46). *See also:* Day of judgment; Great and judgment day; Judged at the great and last day; Last and judgment day.

Judgment is mine, saith the Lord (Mormon 8:20). No mortal can see or understand all the facets of another person's life well enough to qualify as an impartial, just, and merciful judge. Only God has that capability. Thus we are commanded to judge not that ye be not judged and condemn not that ye shall not be condemned. *See also:* Vengeance is mine.

Judgment of God (2 Nephi 9:15; 3 Nephi 12:21). The judgment of God is just and true. Only God knows the intents of our hearts and the circumstances of our lives. It is important to believe and know that God's judgment is correct, for He is both just and merciful. We must seek to cleanse our soul through the Atonement of Jesus Christ, our Savior and Redeemer, for no unclean thing can dwell with God, and none would be comfortable in receiving an eternal reward that we did not earn nor that we had not prepared ourselves for. In D&C 88:32 this is described as "that which they are willing to receive, because they were not willing

to enjoy that which they might have received." *See also:* Judgment of the Holy One; Judgments are just.

Judgment of the Holy One (1 Nephi 22:21; 2 Nephi 6:10; 9:15; Mormon 9:14). Jesus Christ is the Holy One, and the scriptures attest that he will be our judge. *See also:* Judgment of God.

Judgment-seat [of the Nephite rulers] (Alma 1:2; 4:17–18, 20; 7:2–3; 8:12; 30:33; 50:37, 39; 51:5, 7; 61:4, 9; 62:2, 8, 44; Helaman 1:2–4, 6, 9; 2:1–2, 5–6, 7–9; 3:20, 37; 5:1, 4; 6:15, 19; 8:27; 9:1, 3, 7, 14). In Book of Mormon terminology, the throne of the ruler or chief judge is most often referred to as the judgment-seat.

Judgment-seat of Christ (God) (1 Nephi 10:21; 2 Nephi 9:15; 33:7; 3 Nephi 28:31; Mormon 3:20, 22; 6:21; 7:6; Ether 12:38; Moroni 8:21). The judgment place before God. Used interchangeably with the terms *Judgment bar* and *Bar of God*. *See also:* Bar of God; Judgment bar.

Judgment which ye judge ye shall also be judged (3 Nephi 14:2; Moroni 7:18). The severity or degree of mercy by which we judge will determine the severity or mercy by which we shall be judged. We are commanded to forgive that we may likewise be forgiven. It is best to leave judgment to God, who knows all things.

Judgments and statutes (2 Nephi 5:10; Mosiah 6:6). *See:* Statutes and judgments.

Judgments are just (2 Nephi 1:10; Omni 1:22; Mosiah 16:1; 29:12; Alma 12:15; 14:11). The judgments of God are always just. There is no exception to this truth. We must believe this fact with all our hearts; and trust in God to correctly judge each of us and all humanity. *See also:* According to God's justice; All his judgments are just; Execute judgment (in righteousness); His judgments are just; Holy and just God; How merciful (and just) are all the dealings of God; Is just; Judgment of God; Judgment of him that is just; Judgments of God are always just; Just God; Justice of God; Justice of the Father; Requisite with the justice of God; Righteous judgment; Sword of his justice.

Judgments must speedily come unto you (2 Nephi 28:16; Jacob 2:14; 3:4; Enos 1:23; Alma 5:56; 30:57). If people procrastinate the day of their repentance and do not speedily humble themselves and repent, then the warning is that the judgment and curse of God will speedily, quickly, suddenly, and with great force come upon the unrepentant.

Judgments of God (the Father/the Lord) (1 Nephi 12:5; 17:22; 18:15; 2 Nephi 1:10, 16; 6:10; 25:3, 6; Mosiah 17:11; 29:12, 27; Alma 4:3; 37:30; 58:9; 60:14; Helaman 4:23; 14:11; 3 Nephi 16:9; Mormon 4:5; 5:2). *See:* Judgments are just.

Judgments of God are always just (2 Nephi 1:10; Omni 1:22; Mosiah 16:1; 29:12; Alma 12:15; 14:11). *See:* Judgments are just.

Judgments of him that is just (2 Nephi 1:10; Omni 1:22; Mosiah 16:1; 29:12; Alma 12:15; 14:11). *See:* Judgments are just.

Just and holy men (Alma 3:6; 13:26; 20:15). Often refers to prophets and also righteous men who are close to the Spirit of God. It behooves each of us to become as such, so that we may take the Holy Spirit for our guide. *See also:* Just and true [individuals]; Just man (men).

Just and true [individuals] (Mosiah 2:35). Those who will become heirs to eternal life. To be just means to be honest, correct, fair, lawful, impartial, equitable, and based in fact. To be true means to be true to your faith, true to your beliefs, true to the gospel, true to God, and true to family, friends, and fellowmen. D&C 76:50–53 describes those who will inherit the celestial kingdom, saying they "who shall come forth in the resurrection of the just— . . . who received the testimony of Jesus, and believed on his name and were baptized . . . that by keeping the commandments they might be washed and cleansed from all their sins, and receive the Holy Spirit by the laying on of the hands . . .

and [they] who overcome by faith, and are sealed by the Holy Spirit of promise, which the Father sheds forth upon all those who are *just and true*" (emphasis added). As we strive to be just and true, our motto could be found in D&C 11:12, "And now, verily, verily, I say unto thee, put your trust in that Spirit which leadeth to do good—yea, to do justly, to walk humbly, to judge righteously; and this is my Spirit." *See also:* Deal justly; Judge righteously; Just and true [things]; Just men; D&C 138:12.

Just and true [things] (1 Nephi 14:23; Mosiah 2:35; 4:12; Alma 18:34; 29:8; 3 Nephi 5:18; Moroni 10:6). "Whatsoever thing is good is just and true" (Moroni 10:6).

Just God (2 Nephi 1:10, 22; 26:7; Mosiah 2:28; Alma 29:4; 42:15; 57:26; Mormon 9:4). Not only is God completely just, but "Just God" is one of His names or titles. *See also:* Judgments are just.

Just man (men) (Enos 1:1; Omni 1:25; Mosiah 2:4; 19:17; 23:8, 17; 29:13; Alma 3:6; 13:26; 20:15; 63:2; 3 Nephi 3:12; 8:1). *See:* Just and true [individuals].

Just will be your condemnation (Mosiah 4:22; 16:1; 27:31). *See:* Judgments are just.

Justice and equity (Alma 10:21; Helaman 3:20, 37; 3 Nephi 6:4). Righteous rulers and judges are said to rule with justice and equity. It is a similitude of God who rules with all justice and equity. His justice guarantees and requires that the consequences of our actions are allotted to us. His equity ensures that no one receives undue reward or punishment, for God is no respecter of persons (see Acts 10:34).

Justice and mercy (of God) (2 Nephi 2:12; 11:5; Jacob 4:10; Mosiah 3:26; 5:15; 15:9; Alma 26:20; 34:15–16; 41:14; 42:13, 15, 21–25, 30; 3 Nephi 26:5; Mormon 6:22). *See:* According to God's justice; According to God's (thy abundant) mercy.

Justice claimeth the creature and executeth the law (Alma 42:22). "Justice continueth its course and claimeth its own; judgment goeth before the face of him who sitteth upon the throne and governeth and executeth all things" (D&C 88:40). *See also:* Justice when it has its claim.

Justice could not be destroyed (Alma 12:32; 42:13, 22–23). Justice is an eternal principle that cannot be eliminated or done away with. Without justice all would be chaos. Justice demands that a consequence be delivered for every action. God is the great administrator of the laws of justice. He would cease to be God if He did not administer justice. Yet God desires to be merciful to His children, whom He loves, thus the plan of salvation was put in place. *See also:* Justice of God.

Justice exerciseth all his demands (Mosiah 15:27; Alma 42:24). Without exception, justice comes into play. Justice demands a consequence for our every sin with no exception other than the Atonement.

Justice of God (the Father) (1 Nephi 12:18; 14:4; 15:30; 2 Nephi 2:12; 9:17; Mosiah 2:38; Alma 41:2–3; 42:1, 14, 30; 54:6; 61:12; 3 Nephi 20:20; 27:17; 28:35; Ether 8:23; Mormon 6:22). God not only must be fully and completely just, but He desires to be totally just, otherwise the scriptures tell us He would cease to be God (Alma 42:22). *See also:* According to God's justice; Judgments are just; Alma 42:15.

Justice when it has its claim (Mosiah 15:27). The eternally existent law of justice, which God precisely maintains, requires that the consequences of all people's actions are strictly meted out. Yet God loves us, His children, and has provided a way that the claim of justice can be avoided through the Atonement of Jesus Christ. *See also:* Infinite mercy; Justice claimeth the creature and executeth the law.

K

Keep his commandments (1 Nephi 15:25; 2 Nephi 1:9; Jacob 2:21; Mosiah 2:22; 6:1, 6; 18:10; 21:31–32; 29:43; Alma 7:15; 25:14; 48:25; Helaman 15:5; Moroni 4:3). There are a host of terms in the scriptures that essentially mean the same as commandments. They include: judgments, statutes, decrees, laws, precepts, ordinances, and principles. *See also:* Keep my commandments; Keep the commandments (of God).

Keep his commandments and his statutes (Alma 25:14; Helaman 6:34; 15:5). A statute is a divinely declared law, decree, or rule. *See also:* Keep his commandments; Keep the judgments and the statutes.

Keep his statutes, and his judgments (1 Nephi 17:22; 2 Nephi 1:16; 5:10; Mosiah 6:6; Alma 8:17; 58:40; Helaman 3:20; 15:5; 3 Nephi 25:4). *See:* Keep the judgments and the statutes.

Keep my commandments (1 Nephi 2:20, 22; 4:14; 17:13; 2 Nephi 1:20; 4:4; 31:14; Jacob 2:29; Jarom 1:9; Omni 1:6; Mosiah 13:14; Alma 9:13; 37:13; 45:6; 50:20; Helaman 10:4; 3 Nephi 12:20; 15:10; 18:14). The scriptures and the prophets of God constantly admonish us to keep God's commandments. Commandments are the commands, edicts, laws, and decrees of God concerning man. If we desire to be one with the will of God, then we will strictly obey God's commandments with no variance. "Keep my commandments continually, and a crown of righteousness thou shalt receive" (D&C 25:15). *See also:* Keep his commandments; Keep the commandments (of God).

Keep the commandments (of God) (1 Nephi 4:15; 8:38; 15:10; 16:4; 17:3, 15; 2 Nephi 1:32; 3:2; 30:1; 31:10; Jarom 1:10; Mosiah 1:7; 2:4, 13, 31, 41; 11:2; 12:33; 27:33; Alma 30:3; 31:9; 36:1, 30; 37:16, 35; 38:1; 46:23; 48:25; 53:21; 60:34; 63:2; Helaman 3:37; 5:6; 7:7; 13:1; 3 Nephi 6:14). To keep the commandments is to follow God's instructions on how to live life and how to gain true happiness. If we strive with our might and pray to God for help, He will strengthen us so that we will be able to keep the commandments. Sometimes the blessings of keeping the commandments are not immediately apparent—it is a test of our faith. If we keep the commandments the

Lord's promises are sure. To keep the commandments is the best protection against Satan. Keep the commandments and we will obtain peace and safety. We must keep the commandments in order for our testimonies to grow and strengthen. Do not be deceived to not keep the commandments. We must keep the commandments in order to honor our covenants. We must keep the commandments so we can see and understand the mysteries of God. "As spirit children of our Heavenly Father, we do have the potential to incorporate Christlike attributes into our life and character. The Savior invites us to learn His gospel by living His teachings. To follow Him is to apply correct principles and then witness for ourselves the blessings that follow. This process is very complex and very simple at the same time. Ancient and modern prophets described it in three words: 'Keep the commandments'—nothing more, nothing less" (Uchtdorf, "Developing Christlike Attributes," 8; emphasis added). See also: Keep his commandments; Keep my commandments.

Keep the judgments and the statutes (2 Nephi 5:10; Mosiah 6:6; Alma 25:14; 31:9; 58:40; Helaman 3:20; 6:34; 15:5). Judgments are divinely pronounced laws, decrees, and rules from God. The terms *judgments* and *statutes* are principally found in the scriptures relating to the law of Moses. Yet there is some use of these two terms after the Resurrection of Christ. In the scriptures there are a number of synonyms (words having the same or near meaning), including commandments, decrees, judgments, laws, ordinances, precepts, principles, and statutes. See also: Keep his commandments and his statutes; Keep his statutes, and his judgments.

Keep them in the right way (Moroni 6:4). See: Right way(-s of the Lord).

Keeper of the gate (2 Nephi 9:41). Later in this verse, "the Lord God is his name," or in other words, Jesus Christ is the keeper of the gate to the kingdom of heaven and "he employeth no servant there." Thus we can be assured that the judge of our lives is just, true, and merciful.

Keeping his (my/the) commandments (1 Nephi 2:10; 3:16, 21; 4:1, 34; 15:11; 2 Nephi 31:7; Enos 1:10; Mosiah 1:11; 4:6; 10:13; 23:14; Alma 1:25; 7:23; 8:15; 21:23; 37:20; 38:2; 39:1; 48:15–16; 50:22; Helaman 5:14). See: Keep his commandments.

Kept and preserved (2 Nephi 25:21; Omni 1:6; Mosiah 1:5; 2:11, 20; 7:20; 28:11, 15; Alma 9:22; 37:4). God not only created us, but also by His omnipotent power and by His omnipresent influence, He sustains us and all life day by day and minute by minute. God "is preserving you from day to day, by lending you breath, that ye may live and move and do according to your own will, and even supporting you from one moment to another" (Mosiah 2:21). Additionally God keeps and preserves scriptures, nations, kings, and much else in order to bring about His purposes.

Kill the prophets (2 Nephi 26:5). Evil men kill the prophets because the prophets testify and prophesy of their wickedness. *See also:* Murdered the prophets; Stone(-d) the prophets.

Kindle a flame of unquenchable fire upon you (Mormon 9:5). *See:* Unquenchable fire.

King of all the earth (Alma 5:50). Jesus Christ is King of all the earth.

King of Heaven (2 Nephi 10:14; Alma 5:50). Another name for Jesus Christ.

Kingdom of God (1 Nephi 15:33–35; 2 Nephi 9:18, 23; 10:23; 25:13; 28:8; 31:21; Jacob 2:18; 6:4; Mosiah 4:18; 15:11; 18:18; 27:26; Alma 5:24; 7:19, 21; 9:12; 12:8; 29:17; 39:9; 40:25–26; 41:4; 3 Nephi 9:22; 11:33, 38; 13:33; 4 Nephi 1:17; Ether 5:5; 15:34; Moroni 9:6; 10:21, 26). The kingdom of God and the kingdom of heaven "are used in various combinations and with varying meanings. Generally speaking, the kingdom of God on the earth is the Church. It is a preparation for the greater kingdom—the celestial or kingdom of heaven. This is the manner in which these terms are used in D&C 65. However, kingdom of heaven is sometimes used in scripture to mean the Church (as in Matt. 3:2; 4:17; 13; and 25:1–13), meaning that the true church on the earth is the path to heaven and is the kingdom of heaven on earth. The Church of Jesus Christ of Latter-day Saints is the kingdom of God on the earth but is at the present limited to an ecclesiastical kingdom. During the millennial era, the kingdom of God will be both political and ecclesiastical (see Dan. 7:18, 22, 27; Rev. 11:15; JST, Rev. 12:1–3, 7; D&C 65) and will have worldwide jurisdiction" (Bible Dictionary, s.v. "Kingdom of heaven or kingdom of God," 721). *See also:* Kingdom of heaven.

Kingdom of heaven (Alma 5:25, 28, 50–51; 7:9, 14, 25; 9:25; 10:20; 11:37; Helaman 3:30; 5:32; 3 Nephi 12:3, 10, 20; 14:21). As a rule the kingdom of heaven means the realm of God in heaven and the kingdom of God means the Church of God on earth. In D&C 65:2 we read, "The keys of the kingdom of God are committed unto man on earth, and from thence shall the gospel roll forth unto the ends of the earth." And verse six says, "Wherefore, may the kingdom of God go forth, that the kingdom of heaven may come." Often the kingdom of heaven is referred to as the place the righteous and faithful will inherit (D&C 6:37 and 10:55). However, sometimes these two terms are used interchangeably in the scriptures. *See also:* Kingdom of God.

Kingdom of heaven is nigh (soon) at hand (Alma 5:28, 50; 7:9; 9:25; 10:20; Helaman 5:32). The words "at hand" in the scriptures generally means soon to be or about to come to pass. Often in the scriptures it says to people of all ages "repent for the kingdom of heaven/coming of the Lord is at hand." On a personal level we do not know the day when we will die and need to be prepared to stand before God. In other words, we must not procrastinate the day of repentance. On a grander level, in eternal terms and in God's timing, the end of the world truly is at hand, and we must hasten our preparation. In Alma 5:29–31, "Prepare quickly, for the hour is close at hand, and [ye] knoweth not when the time shall come . . . and the time is at hand that [all] must repent or [ye] cannot be saved!" *See also:* At hand.

Kingdom of my (the) Father (3 Nephi 28:8, 10, 40). Refers to the hereafter and the kingdom in which the righteous shall dwell with the Father and the Son.

Kingdom of the devil (1 Nephi 22:22–23; 2 Nephi 28:19; Alma 5:25; 41:4). Satan, or the destroyer, has a kingdom also, which is a kingdom of darkness. Therein reside the souls of those who have subjected themselves to the devil through sin and rebellion. The scriptures tell us that those who reside there are given

to weeping and wailing and gnashing of teeth (Alma 40:13). D&C 76:25–38 describes this awful place and those that will go there. *See also:* Everlasting damnation.

Kingdom of the Lamb (1 Nephi 13:37). Jesus Christ is the Lamb of God. Therefore this phrase refers to the kingdom hereafter where the righteous "shall dwell in the presence of God and his Christ forever and ever." For "they are Christ's, and Christ is God's" [the Father's] (D&C 76:59, 62).

Kings shall be thy nursing fathers and their queens thy nursing mothers (1 Nephi 21:23; 2 Nephi 6:7; 10:9). In the last days the gospel of Jesus Christ shall come forth among the Gentiles (the latter-day restoration), which shall be of great worth unto the tribes of Israel and the descendants of Lehi. In the words of Nephi, "it is likened unto their being nourished by the Gentiles [kings and queens] and [their] being carried in their arms and upon their shoulders" (1 Nephi 22:8).

Kiss his [Christ's] feet (3 Nephi 11:19; 17:10). An ultimate sign of humble submission and love.

Knew not God (the Lord) (1 Nephi 2:12; Mosiah 24:5; Alma 3:18; 6:6; 9:5). To gain salvation we must come to know God. Yet there are many people who do not know God, either because they refuse to learn of Him or because they have not yet heard. *See also:* Know God.

Knew that God could not lie (Enos 1:6; 3:12). God is a God of truth, and there is nothing but truth in Him. To understand the true nature of God is to know that all truth has God as its source.

Knew the thoughts and intents of his heart (Alma 10:17; 12:7). God knows all the thoughts and intents of our hearts, and sometimes this power of perception is given to the servants of God. *See also:* Know all my (thy) thoughts.

Knit together in unity (Mosiah 18:21). *See:* Hearts knit together.

Knock and it shall be opened unto you (2 Nephi 9:42; 32:4; 3 Nephi 14:7–8; 27:29). He who asks in prayer shall receive, and he who knocks at the door, it shall be opened, and the individual will be brought into the light of God. This is the promise of the Lord Jesus (see Matthew 7:7; Luke 11:9). "What man is there of you, whom if his son ask bread, will he give him a stone? Or if he ask a fish, will he give him a serpent? If ye then, being evil, know how to give good gifts unto your children, how much more shall your Father which is in heaven give good things to them that ask him?" (Matthew 7:9–11). God truly will give answers to the sincere and humble seeker in God's own due time.

Know all my (thy) thoughts (Jacob 2:5; Alma 10:17; 12:3, 7; 18:16, 18, 20; Helaman 9:41; 3 Nephi 28:6).

God knows all the thoughts and intents of our hearts, and sometimes this power of perception is given to the servants of God. *See also:* Discern his thoughts; Knew the thoughts and intents of his heart; Know of their designs; Know the thoughts and intents of his (our) heart(-s); Perceived his (the/their) thoughts; Tell you concerning your thoughts; Thoughts are made known.

Know and bear record (3 Nephi 11:15; 17:25; Ether 4:11). Often individuals experience and witness sacred spiritual things, which they not only see but also testify that these things are true. *See also:* Bear(-eth) record; Forbidden that I (they) should write (utter/preach).

Know concerning the covenants of the Lord (2 Nephi 9:1; 3 Nephi 21:7; 29:1; Mormon 7:10; Ether 4:15). It is important that the people of the world know of the covenants God has made with man—more particularly the covenant God has made with the house of Israel, and how that covenant affects them. *See also:* Covenant which he made with Abraham; Fulfilled the covenant.

Know God (1 Nephi 22:25; Mosiah 26:24; 3 Nephi 5:26; Mormon 8:10; 9:20; Moroni 10:7). The scriptures tell us that in order to gain eternal life we must come to know God (see John 17:3; D&C 132:22–25). "If they *know me* they shall come forth, and shall have a place eternally at my right hand. And it shall come to pass that when the second trump shall sound then shall they that *never knew me* come forth and shall stand before me. And then shall they know that I am the Lord their God, that I am their Redeemer; but they would not be redeemed. And then I will confess unto them that I never knew them; and they shall depart into everlasting fire prepared for the devil and his angels" (Mosiah 26:24–27; emphasis added).

Know(-ing) good and (from) evil (2 Nephi 2:5, 18, 26, 28; 17:15–16; Mosiah 16:3; Alma 12:31; 29:5; 42:3; Helaman 14:31; Moroni 7:15, 16, 19). It is a necessary step in our progression to know good and evil, which is to differentiate between good and evil and to learn to always choose the good. Adam and Eve introduced to mankind this opportunity and privilege by partaking of the forbidden fruit.

Know him (1 Nephi 22:25). *See:* Know God.

Know how to be saved (1 Nephi 15:14; 2 Nephi 25:23; 31:16; Mosiah 12:33; Alma 5:21; 9:17; 22:18; Mormon 7:3; 9:22). These verses list some of the things we must do to come unto Christ and be saved. They include:

- Come to a knowledge of their Redeemer;
- Learn of the doctrine of Christ;
- Follow the Savior's example;
- Endure to the end;
- Keep the commandments;

- Have garments washed white;
- Call on Jesus' name;
- Give away all our sins;
- Come to know God;
- Repent and turn unto God; and
- After all we can do, we are saved by God's grace.

Know not God (Mormon 9:20). *See:* Knew not God (the Lord).

Know of a (their) surety (1 Nephi 5:8; 17:55; 2 Nephi 25:7; Mosiah 1:6; 7:14; 17:9; 24:14; Alma 5:45; 30:15; 32:17, 26; Helaman 9:2; 14:4; 3 Nephi 11:15; Ether 5:3). We can know of a surety of those things that are true by revelation and by the Holy Ghost. *See also:* Know the truth; D&C 5:12, 25.

Know of Christ (2 Nephi 25:26; 31:13; Jacob 4:4; Mosiah 5:9; 3 Nephi 7:15; 28:33; Ether 12:39). *See:* Know their Redeemer.

Know of greater things (3 Nephi 26:9–10; Mormon 8:12; Ether 4:4, 8, 13). *See:* Know of the mysteries (these things).

Know of myself (yourselves/that they are true) (Alma 5:45–46, 48; 36:4; 38:6; Helaman 7:29; 15:8). *See:* Know the truth.

Know of the coming of Christ (2 Nephi 9:5; Jacob 4:4; Alma 13:25; 30:26; 34:2, 8; Helaman 14:12; 16:5; 3 Nephi 29:2). We must know and have a testimony that Christ will come again. *See* *also:* Christ shall (should) come; Coming of Christ.

Know of the goodness of God (1 Nephi 5:4; Mosiah 27:22). *See:* Infinite goodness (of God); Known the goodness of God.

Know of the mysteries (these things) (1 Nephi 2:16; 10:17; Mosiah 1:5; 12:25; Alma 5:45; 12:9–11; 26:22; 37:4; 40:3). The scriptures and revelations are given to man so that man may know the mysteries of God. The knowledge of God and His ways are given to the true seeker who is worthy according to the will of God. *See also:* Greater things; Mysteries of God.

Know of their designs (Alma 10:17). *See:* Know the thoughts and intents of his (our) heart(-s).

Know of things to come (2 Nephi 9:4; Words of Mormon 1:4, 7; Mosiah 8:17; Alma 5:45; 21:8; 30:13). Those of the world do not believe anyone can know of things to come in the future. Yet the scriptures have declared of things to come, and they in fact did come to pass. And there is much yet prophesied to happen that has not yet happened. God's plan of salvation includes much detail concerning the future including the Second Coming, the millennium, and the judgment day. *See also:* According to God's word; I would prophesy; Spirit of prophecy (and revelation); Things (which are) to come.

Know that he be (is) their God (2 Nephi 10:4; Ether 3:18; Moroni 10:7). *See:* Know that I am (the Lord thy God).

Know that I am (the Lord thy God) (1 Nephi 17:53; 21:23, 26; 2 Nephi 6:7, 18; Mosiah 11:22; 12:30; 24:14; 26:26; 3 Nephi 11:14; 12:1–2; 20:39). Concerning God: (1) all things denote and testify there is a God; (2) we must learn who the true and living God is; and (3) we must know of His will concerning us and submit to that will. *See also:* Know God.

Know that I (the Lord) am God (1 Nephi 17:14; 2 Nephi 29:8; 3 Nephi 11:14). *See:* Know that I am (the Lord thy God).

Know that in him I shall rest (Enos 1:27). *See:* Enter into his (my/ the) rest (of the Lord/of God).

Know that the Lord God hath power to do all things (1 Nephi 9:6; Alma 7:8; Mormon 5:23). *See:* All power; Power of God.

Know that the Lord is God (Savior and Redeemer) (1 Nephi 17:14; 22:12; 2 Nephi 6:15). *See:* Know their Redeemer.

Know the decrees of God (Ether 2:11). Meaning to know God's commandments and His will concerning us.

Know the interpretation thereof (1 Nephi 11:11). Each of us can, like Nephi did, ask to know the meaning of spiritual things. Also like

Alma, "Behold, I say unto you they are made known unto me by the Holy Spirit of God. Behold, I have fasted and prayed many days that I might know these things of myself. And now I do know of myself that they are true; for the Lord God hath made them manifest unto me by his Holy Spirit; and this is the spirit of revelation which is in me" (Alma 5:46). *See also:* Diligently search (seek[-eth]/sought); Inquire(-d) of the Lord; Knock and it shall be opened unto you.

Know the mysteries of God (1 Nephi 2:16; Alma 12:9–10; 26:22; 37:4). *See:* Know of the mysteries (these things).

Know the thoughts and intents of his (our) heart(-s) (Jacob 2:5; Mosiah 24:12; Alma 10:17; 12:7; Helaman 9:41; 3 Nephi 28:6). God knows all the thoughts and intents of our hearts, and sometimes this power of perception is given to the servants of God. *See also:* Know all my (thy) thoughts.

Know the true God (Mormon 8:10). *See:* Know God.

Know the truth (Mosiah 5:2; Alma 24:19; Helaman 7:29; Moroni 10:5). It is imperative that we seek for truth, and cast aside all that is false. For the Lord said, "Ye shall know the truth, and the truth shall make you free" (John 8:32). Only the truth can bless our lives, and the truth is found in the gospel of Jesus Christ. In order to learn of the truth of the gospel we must live its principles. "If any man will do his will, he shall know of the doctrine, whether it be of God" (John 7:17). If we struggle with a commandment within the gospel, we must live that commandment and pray in order to gain a testimony of its truthfulness. Finally there is the great promise of truth found in the Book of Mormon, "And when ye shall receive these things, I would exhort you that ye would ask God, the Eternal Father, in the name of Christ, if these things are not true; and if ye shall ask with a sincere heart, with real intent, having faith in Christ, he will manifest the truth of it unto you, by the power of the Holy Ghost. And by the power of the Holy Ghost ye may *know the truth of all things*" (Moroni 10:4–5; emphasis added). *See also:* Know of a (their) surety; Know of myself (yourselves/that they are true); Know they are true.

Know their Redeemer (1 Nephi 22:12; 2 Nephi 6:18; Mosiah 26:26; 3 Nephi 5:26). One of the most important things in mortal life, besides always choosing the right, is to come to know and follow our Savior and Redeemer, Jesus Christ. The Atonement of Jesus Christ on behalf of all mankind is the key to and at the very center of the plan of salvation. We must accept and worship Jesus as our Savior and Redeemer. And we must follow in His footsteps, keep the commandments, and endure to the end. For "at the name of Jesus every knee should bow, of things in heaven, and things in earth, and things under the earth; and that every tongue should confess that Jesus Christ is Lord, to the glory of God the Father" (Philippians 2:10–11). *See also:* Know God; Know of Christ; Know that the Lord is God (Savior and Redeemer).

Know there is a God (Alma 30:39, 48). *See:* Know that I am (the Lord thy God).

Know they are true (Alma 5:46; 10:10; 12:37; 30:24; 34:8; Helaman 7:29; Ether 4:11; 5:3). *See:* Know the truth.

Know ye not (1 Nephi 3:29; 2 Nephi 29:7–8; 31:7; Jacob 6:9; Mosiah 12:30; Alma 14:19; 39:5; Mormon 5:23). An exclamation suggesting that we should know and understand the truths that follow in the verse.

Knowest of things to come (Alma 21:8). *See:* Know of things to come.

Knowest thou the thoughts of my heart (Alma 18:20). *See:* Know all my (thy) thoughts.

Knoweth a thing (it) (Alma 32:18). *See:* Perfect knowledge.

Knoweth all things (1 Nephi 9:6; 2 Nephi 2:24; 9:20; Words of Mormon 1:7; Alma 7:13; Mormon 8:17). Referring to God who knows all things. *See also:* All-wise Creator; God knoweth all things; Lord knoweth all things; Wisdom in (of) God (the Lord/the Father).

Knowledge of Christ (2 Nephi 30:5; Jacob 4:12; Words of Mormon 1:8; Alma 37:9; Mormon 9:36). *See:* Know their Redeemer.

Knowledge of God (Words of Mormon 1:8; Mosiah 18:26; Alma 37:8; 39:6; Helaman 6:34; Ether 3:20). *See:* Know God.

Knowledge of Jesus Christ (2 Nephi 30:5). *See:* Know their Redeemer.

Knowledge of the covenants (2 Nephi 3:7, 12). *See:* Covenant which he made with Abraham.

Knowledge of the Lord (their God) (1 Nephi 10:14; 2 Nephi 21:9; 30:15; Mosiah 3:20; 27:36; 28:2; Alma 23:5; 37:9; 47:36; 3 Nephi 5:23; 19:13; 20:13; 29:13). *See:* Know God; Know their Redeemer.

Knowledge of the truth (Jacob 7:24; Mosiah 27:14, 36; Alma 17:2, 4, 9; 21:17; 23:6, 15; 24:27; 26:24; 37:19; Helaman 15:6–7, 11). Comes with a knowledge of the gospel of Jesus Christ and of our Redeemer. God is full of grace, mercy, and truth. To know God is to come to a knowledge of truth. *See also:* Know the truth; True knowledge.

Knowledge of their fathers (1 Nephi 15:14; 2 Nephi 3:12; 30:5; Jacob 4:2). Refers to the seed of Lehi, that in generations to come they will know that they are descendants of the house of Israel and that they came out of Jerusalem many generations before.

Knowledge of their Redeemer (1 Nephi 10:14; 15:14; 21:26; 22:12; 2 Nephi 6:11; 10:2; Mosiah 18:30; 27:36; Alma 37:10; Helaman 15:13; 3 Nephi 16:4). *See:* Know their Redeemer.

Knowledge of things pertaining to righteousness (Alma 24:30). Talking about people who once had a testimony of the truth borne to them by the Holy Ghost.

Knowledge unto salvation (Alma 24:27; 37:8; 3 Nephi 5:20). Without a knowledge of the gospel and a knowledge that we are in compliance with the gospel, there is no salvation. Key to knowledge unto salvation is a knowledge of and acceptance of the redemption of Jesus Christ in our behalf. Knowledge of the true gospel includes the principles and ordinances necessary for salvation.

Known of his goodness and tasted of his love (Mosiah 4:11).

See: Tasted of God's love and goodness.

Known the goodness of God (1 Nephi 5:4; Mosiah 27:22). It is sweet to come to know the goodness of God. God will shower goodness upon the repentant and humble who seek Him in His own due time. Thus we must also be patient as God teaches us. Even adversity can become sweet through God. *See also:* Infinite goodness (of God).

Known unto God were all their cries and all their sufferings (Alma 60:10). Our God knows everything about each of us. He knows our cares, our circumstances, our pain, and all there is about our lives. *See also:* Bear afflictions (with patience); Alma 7:11–12; Exodus 3:9; Psalm 9:12; Philippians 4:6.

Knows all thy thoughts (Alma 18:32). Many places in the scriptures affirm that God knows even our deepest thoughts. *See also:* Know all my (thy) thoughts; Know the thoughts and intents of his (our) heart(-s).

L

Labor in the spirit (Enos 1:10; Alma 8:10; 17:5). Meaning to strive much to obtain a spiritual manifestation from God. We seek for a testimony, we desire knowledge that God is mindful of us, we pray for answers to gospel questions, and so on. Compare the wrestle Jacob had with a messenger of God found in Genesis 32:24–30. *See also:* Labored much in the spirit; Struggling in the spirit.

Labor with their own hands for their support (Mosiah 2:14; 18:24; 27:4, 5). The Lord's church is a church of lay ministry. Paid ministry often introduces pride and false doctrine. The Book of Mormon prophesies that in the latter days many false churches would be built up to get gain and power (see 2 Nephi 26:20). D&C 52:39 reads, "Let the residue of the elders watch over the churches, and declare the word in the regions round about them; and let them labor with their own hand that there be no idolatry nor wickedness practiced." *Contrast:* Mosiah 11:1–7. *See also:* Laborer in Zion; Preach up unto themselves their own wisdom and their own learning; Teachers who sell yourselves for that which will canker.

Labor(-ed) diligently (exceedingly/without ceasing) (2 Nephi 25:23; Jacob 1:7; 4:3; 5:61; 6:3; 7:3; Jarom 1:11; Alma 29:14–15; 36:24; Moroni 8:6; 9:6). Meaning to work hard, exert much energy, and strive mightily to accomplish in a tireless, persistent, unfailing, and steady manner. *See also:* Laboring with his (our) might.

Labor(-ed) in the vineyard(-s) of the Lord (Jacob 5:5, 16, 29, 61–62, 71–72, 74; 6:3; Alma 28:14). The Lord of the vineyard is Christ. The servants of the Lord are His prophets and other chosen servants that preach the gospel of Jesus Christ. The vineyard is the earth and all the people therein who must be called to repentance and bring forth good fruit. See also 2 Nephi 15:1–7, wherein the vineyard is the house of Israel.

Labored much in the spirit (Enos 1:12; Alma 8:10). *See:* Labor in the spirit; Struggling in the spirit.

Laborer in Zion (2 Nephi 26:30–31). The laborer in Zion is one who strives to build up the kingdom of God. "Thou art called to labor in my vineyard, and to build up my church, and to bring forth Zion"

(D&C 39:13). However, if the laborer practices priestcrafts (labors for money) they shall perish. *See also:* Not suffer the laborer in Zion to perish.

Laboring with his (our) might (Jacob 1:19; 5:75; Words of Mormon 1:18). *See:* All your might, mind, and strength; Labored diligently (exceedingly/without ceasing).

Laid down my life and have taken it up again (3 Nephi 9:22). Jesus said, "I lay down my life, that I might take it again. No man taketh it from me, but I lay it down of myself" (John 10:17–18). Jesus Christ, having the powers of God because of His Father (God the Father) could not have His life taken from Him except He allow it. Because He had a mortal mother He could suffer death, and thus He literally gave up His life on the cross. But God the Father gave Jesus, the Son of God, the power to take up His life again and be resurrected. Thus He became the first to be resurrected on earth and made it possible that all men and women will be resurrected.

Laid from the foundation of the world (Alma 12:25; Ether 4:14). *See:* Prepared from the beginning (foundation of the world).

Laid his (their) hands upon them (Moroni 2:1, 3; 3:2). The "laying on of hands" is the "procedure used from the earliest times in the manner of blessing, conferring the Holy Ghost, and ordaining to the priesthood. . . . Such procedure is in accord with the revealed will of the Lord and is not a mere formality. In latter-day revelation the laying on of hands is discussed by the Lord as follows: 'I will lay my hand upon you by the hand of my servant Sidney Rigdon, and you shall receive my Spirit . . .' (D&C 36:2). The laying on of hands also formed part of the ritual of sacrifice under the law of Moses (Ex. 29:10, 15, 19; Lev. 1:4; 3:2, 8, 13; 4:4; 8:14)" (Bible Dictionary, s.v. "laying on of hands," 723). The method includes first laying hands upon the recipient's head, then the priesthood holder acting as voice performs the ordinance and bestows the blessing. Articles of Faith 1:5 says, "We believe that a man must be called of God, by prophecy, and by the laying on of hands by those who are in authority, to preach the Gospel and administer in the ordinances thereof." *See also:* Lay hands on; Laying on his hands.

Laid the foundation of the earth (1 Nephi 20:13). Compare with "Hearken, O ye people of my church, to whom the kingdom has been given; hearken ye and give ear to him who laid the foundation of the earth, who made the heavens and all the hosts thereof, and by whom all things were made which live, and move, and have a being" (D&C 45:1).

Lake of fire and brimstone (2 Nephi 9:16, 19, 26; 28:23; Jacob 3:11, 6:10; Mosiah 3:27; Alma 12:17; 14:14). The fate of the wicked who do not repent and thus experience the second death (Jacob 3:11) are cast out from God's presence forever. Such will experience endless torment (Jacob 6:10). "And their torment is as a lake of fire and brimstone, whose flames are unquenchable, and whose smoke ascendeth up forever and ever" (Mosiah 3:27). Joseph Fielding Smith said, "This fire and brimstone, we are informed, is a representation of the torment which shall be suffered by the wicked. It is not actual fire, but it is the *torment of the mind*" (*Doctrines of Salvation*, 2:224). Joseph Smith said, "A man is his own tormenter and his own condemner. Hence the saying, They shall go into the lake that burns with fire and brimstone. The torment of disappointment in the mind of man is as exquisite as a lake burning with fire and brimstone. I say, so is the torment of man" (*Teachings of the Prophet Joseph Smith*, 357). *See also:* Hell fire; D&C 63:17; 76:36.

Lamb of God (1 Nephi 10:10; 11:21, 27, 31–32; 12:6, 10–11, 18; 13:24, 28–29, 33–34, 38, 40; 14:1–3, 6–7, 10, 12–14, 25; 2 Nephi 31:4–6; 33:14; Alma 7:14; Mormon 9:2–3). 1 Nephi 13:40 says, "The Lamb of God is the Son of the Eternal Father, and the Savior of the world; and that all men must come unto him, or they cannot be saved." The term *Lamb of God* is a similitude and likeness. "Jesus Christ is the Lamb of God in the sense that he is the Son of God and he offered himself as the sacrifice for the sins of man by the shedding of his blood. From the days of Adam, the righteous saints were instructed to offer up the firstlings of the flocks (including lambs) as a sacrifice to God, to remind them that in the meridian of time the 'lamb without blemish and without spot: who verily was foreordained before the foundation of the world' (1 Peter 1:19) would be offered up as the last, infinite, eternal sacrifice. That Lamb, of course, was the sinless Jesus Christ, who was and is also the Firstborn Son of God in the spirit" (Ludlow, *Companion to Your Study of the Doctrine and Covenants*, 2:163).

Lamb to the slaughter (Mosiah 14:7). A variation of the title *Lamb of God* because He will be sacrificed and killed for us.

Land choice above all other lands (1 Nephi 2:20; 13:30; 2 Nephi 1:5; 10:19; Jacob 5:43; Ether 1:38, 42; 2:7, 10, 12, 15; 9:20; 10:28; 13:2). Refers to the land to which God led Lehi and his party, and the same land to which God led the Jaredites. Also refers to the United States of America in the last days. God promised peace and prosperity to its inhabitants if they would remember Him and keep His commandments.

See also: Choice land; Chosen land; If ye will keep my commandments ye shall prosper in the land; Inasmuch as ye shall keep my (the) commandments (of God) ye shall prosper in the land; Land is consecrated; Land of inheritance; Land of promise; Precious land(-s).

Land is consecrated (2 Nephi 1:7, 32). *Consecrated* in the scriptures means set apart for sacred use. *See also:* Land choice above all other lands.

Land of inheritance (1 Nephi 2:4, 11; 3:16, 33; 5:2; 10:3; 13:15, 30; 17:21; 2 Nephi 1:5, 8–9; 3:2; 10:10, 19–20; 25:11; Jacob 3:4; Omni 1:27; Mosiah 9:1; 10:13; Alma 21:18; 22:28; 27:22; 34:14; 35:14; 54:12–13; 3 Nephi 15:13; 16:16; 20:14, 29, 33, 46; 21:22, 28; Mormon 3:17; 5:14; Ether 1:38; 2:15; 7:16; 9:13; 13:8, 21). Land received as a bequest from either forebears or from God. *See also:* Land choice above all other lands.

Land of Jerusalem (1 Nephi 2:11; 3:9–10; 5:6; 7:2, 7; 16:35; 17:14, 20, 22; 18:24; 2 Nephi 1:1, 3, 9, 30; 25:11; Jacob 2:25, 31–32; Omni 1:6; Mosiah 1:11; 2:4; 7:20; 10:12; Alma 3:11; 9:22; 10:3; 22:9; 24:1; 36:29; Helaman 5:6; 7:7; 8:21; 16:19; 3 Nephi 5:20; 16:1; 20:29; Mormon 3:18–19; Ether 13:7). Meaning most often the city of Jerusalem and surrounding settlements of the Jews in Palestine. However, in the case of Alma 21 and 24, a location in the Americas named by the Lamanites after the name of Jerusalem in the Old World. "The Nephite use of the phrase 'land of Jerusalem' was perfectly normal usage in ancient times. That is to say, an important city X in Palestine would be called the 'land of X,' an expression which referred to the city in question and the adjacent territory under its control. When, therefore, the Nephites said that the Son of God would be born 'at Jerusalem . . . the land of our forefathers,' they did not necessarily mean that Jesus would be born in the city of Jerusalem proper. He could have been born in territory adjacent to Jerusalem but under its control. In this case part of the territory adjacent was the little town or village of Bethlehem, only five miles from Jerusalem" (Sperry, *Answers*, 131–32).

Land of liberty (2 Nephi 1:7; 10:11; Mosiah 29:32; Alma 46:17). A land where every man may enjoy his rights and privileges, where every man might bear his part, where everyone should have an equal chance, where every man will be held accountable for his deeds, and where all will treat one like unto another. These are the principles proposed by Mosiah when he convinced the people to relinquish their desire for a king and instead appoint judges by the voice of the people (see Mosiah 29).

Land of promise (1 Nephi 2:20; 4:14; 5:5, 22; 7:1, 13; 10:13; 12:1, 4;

13:14; 17:33, 42; 18:25; 2 Nephi 1:3, 5, 9–10, 24; 24:2; Jacob 2:12; Alma 37:45; 48:25; Ether 2:7–9). *See:* Land choice above all other lands.

Lands of his (our/their/thine/your) inheritance (1 Nephi 2:4, 11; 3:16, 22; 5:2; 10:3; 13:30; 17:21; 22:12; 2 Nephi 1:5, 9; 6:11; 9:2; 10:7–8, 10, 19–20; 25:11; Jacob 3:4; Omni 1:27; Words of Mormon 1:14; Mosiah 9:1; 10:13; Alma 21:18; 22:28; 27:22; 35:14; 54:12–13; 3 Nephi 15:13; 20:29, 33, 46; 21:28; 29:1; Mormon 2:27–28; 3:17; 5:14; Ether 7:16; 9:13; 13:8). *See:* Land of inheritance.

Language of Mosiah (Nephi/Nephites) (Omni 1:18; Mosiah 9:1; 24:4). *See:* Language of the Egyptians.

Language of my (our) father(-s) (1 Nephi 1:2; 3:19; Mosiah 1:2). *See:* Language of the Egyptians.

Language of the Egyptians (1 Nephi 1:2; Mosiah 1:4; Mormon 9:32–34). Nephi said, "I make a record in the language of my father, which consists of the learning of the Jews and the language of the Egyptians" (1 Nephi 1:2). The brass plates, also known as the plates of Laban, were written in Egyptian (see Mosiah 1:4). Were it not for the brass plates the people would have lost the knowledge contained therein and the language of the Egyptians would have become lost or corrupted (see Mosiah 1:3).

Mormon 9:32–34 states, "We have written this record according to our knowledge, in the characters which are called among us the reformed Egyptian, being handed down and altered by us, according to our manner of speech. And if our plates had been sufficiently large we should have written in Hebrew; but the Hebrew hath been altered by us also; and if we could have written in Hebrew, behold, ye would have had no imperfection in our record. But the Lord knoweth the things which we have written, and also that none other people knoweth our language; and because that none other people knoweth our language, therefore he hath prepared means for the interpretation thereof." *See also:* Prepared means for the interpretation thereof.

Large and spacious building (1 Nephi 11:35; 12:18). *See:* Great (large) and spacious building.

Large(-r) plates (Introduction, the Book of Mormon; Jacob 3:13). Also known as the other plates. These plates "were occupied mostly by a secular history of the peoples concerned" (A Brief Explanation about the Book of Mormon, the Book of Mormon). *See also:* Other plates; 1 Nephi 9:2–4; Jacob 1:3.

Last and judgment day (Mosiah 27:31; Alma 33:22). *See:* Judgment day; Last day.

Last day (1 Nephi 13:37; 16:2; 2 Nephi 9:33, 44; 25:18; 33:11, 14; Mosiah 17:10; 26:28; 27:31; Alma

7:21; 14:11; 22:6, 15, 18; 24:15–16; 26:6–7; 30:60; 34:39; 36:3, 28; 38:15; 39:8; 41:3; 3 Nephi 15:1; 27:5; 28:39; Mormon 8:31; Ether 4:10, 19; 5:3–4, 6; Moroni 7:35, 47). A term used in the scriptures to describe the day or time that Christ will come at His Second Coming in great glory. The day when the righteous will be caught up to meet Him and the wicked will be burned as stubble. Can also refer to the day of judgment. "The day that we shall be brought to stand before him to be judged" (Alma 24:15).

Last days (2 Nephi 12:2; 25:8; 26:14; 27:1). *See:* Latter day(-s/times).

Last death (Alma 12:36). *See:* Second death; D&C 29:41.

Last provocation (Alma 12:36). Refers to the manner and habit of sinning and hard-heartedness of one arriving at the end of his probation unwilling to yield unto God, thus resulting in an eternal fate of spiritual death and separation from God. *See also:* First provocation.

Last shall be first, and the first shall be last (1 Nephi 13:42; Jacob 5:63; Ether 13:12). "In his first advent in the meridian of time, Christ and His message would be declared unto all nations, first to the Jews and then to the Gentiles. In His second coming in the last days, He would reverse that order, His appearance and message first going to the Gentiles and then to the

Jews" (Holland, *Christ and the New Covenant*, 40–41). *See also:* First shall be last and last shall be first.

Latter day(-s/times) (1 Nephi 15:13, 18–19; 2 Nephi 3:5, 12; Helaman 15:12; 3 Nephi 16:7). Refers to the days of the dispensation of the fulness of times that began with Joseph Smith's First Vision and will end with the Second Coming of the Lord, which will be the beginning of the Millennium.

Laughed us to scorn (Alma 26:23). *See:* Finger of scorn.

Law and the prophets (2 Nephi 25:28; 3 Nephi 12:17; 14:12; 15:10). Refers to the law of Moses. *See:* Law of Moses.

Law (is) fulfilled (2 Nephi 9:17; 25:24, 27, 30; Alma 25:15; 30:3; 34:13; 3 Nephi 1:25; 9:17; 12:18–19, 46; 15:4–5, 8; Ether 12:11). Meaning the law of Moses being fulfilled. *See:* Law of Moses.

Law must be fulfilled (2 Nephi 9:17). For so it was prophesied. *See:* Law (is) fulfilled.

Law of circumcision (Moroni 8:8). "The token of the Abrahamic covenant during Old Testament dispensations. Those who received it thenceforth enjoyed the privileges and undertook the responsibilities of the covenant. It symbolized some aspects of separation or dedication (1) to God, to whom Israel belonged; (2) from the world, the uncircumcised with whom Israel might not mix; (3) from sin (Deut. 10:16; 30:6; Jer. 4.4; 9:25–26; Ezek. 44:7)" (Bible Dictionary, s.v. "circumcision," 646).

Law of Moses (1 Nephi 4:15; 17:22; 2 Nephi 5:10; 11:4; 25:24; Jacob 4:5; Jarom 1:5, 11; Mosiah 2:3; 3:14–15; 12:28–29, 31; 13:27–28; 16:14; 24:5; Alma 24:15–16; 25:15–16; 30:3; 34:13; Helaman 13:1; 15:5; 3 Nephi 1:24; 9:17; 15:2; 25:4; 4 Nephi 1:12; Ether 12:11). "The name assigned to the whole collection of written laws given through Moses to the house of Israel, as a replacement of the higher law that they had failed to obey. The law of Moses consisted of many ceremonies, rituals, and symbols, to remind the people frequently of their duties and responsibilities. It included a law of carnal commandments and performances, added to the basic laws of the gospel. Faith, repentance, baptism in water, and remission of sins were part of the law, as were also the Ten Commandments. Although inferior to the fulness of the gospel, there were many provisions in the law of Moses of high ethical and moral value that were equal to the divine laws of any dispensation. The law of carnal commandments and much of the ceremonial law were fulfilled at the death and resurrection of Jesus Christ. The law functioned under the Aaronic Priesthood and was a preparatory gospel to bring its adherents to Christ. . . . The law as

given through Moses was a good law, although adapted to a lower spiritual capacity than is required for obedience to the gospel in its fulness. However, the Jewish leaders had added many unauthorized provisions, ceremonies, and prohibitions to the original law, until it became extremely burdensome. These innovations were known as the 'traditions of the elders.' By New Testament times among the Jews the law had become so altered it had lost much of its spiritual meaning. It is this form of the law that is so harshly spoken against by Jesus and by Paul (see Matt. 15:1–9; Mark 7:1–13; Gal. 2:16–21). There is no evidence that the law of Moses had become as altered among the Nephites as among the Jews, and this may partially explain why the Nephites had less trouble in giving it up when the Savior came" (Bible Dictionary, s.v. "Law of Moses," 722–23).

Alternately, the following is a description of the law of Moses using Book of Mormon scriptures:

The law of Moses was given to the children of Israel because they were a stiffnecked people (see Mosiah 3:14).

The law of Moses was given to point the people towards Christ (see Jacob 4:5).

It was a law of performances and ordinances given to keep the people in remembrance of the Lord (see Mosiah 13:30–31).

When Jesus finished His mission in mortality and provided the Atonement, it was then that the law of Moses was fulfilled. "In me is the law of Moses fulfilled. . . . And ye shall offer up unto me no more the shedding of blood; yea, your sacrifices and your burnt offerings shall be done away. . . . And ye shall offer for a sacrifice unto me a broken heart and a contrite spirit. And whoso cometh unto me with a broken heart and a contrite spirit, him will I baptize with fire and with the Holy Ghost" (3 Nephi 9:17, 19–20).

"Behold, I say unto you that the law is fulfilled that was given unto Moses. Behold, I am he that gave the law, and I am he who covenanted with my people Israel; therefore, the law in me is fulfilled, for I have come to fulfil the law; therefore it hath an end" (3 Nephi 15:4–5).

Law of performances (Mosiah 13:30). Refers to the law of Moses. *See also:* Law of Moses.

Law shall be fulfilled (2 Nephi 25:24, 30). *See:* Law (is) fulfilled.

Law which ye shall do (2 Nephi 26:1). In this verse, Nephi explains that when Jesus Christ comes "the words which he shall speak" shall be what we should do. This new law is to love God and our fellowmen. If we love God we will keep His commandments (John 14:15). Also we must love one another as He has loved us (John 13:34). In D&C

88:21 it is the "law of Christ." *See also:* Doctrine of Christ.

Laws of God (Mosiah 2:33; 4:14; 29:13; Alma 60:33; Helaman 6:23). "None shall be exempted from the justice and the laws of God" (D&C 107:84). If we keep the laws (commandments of God) we are promised that we will be prospered, whereas if we do not keep the commandments we will be cut off from God's presence. God desires for us happiness, progression, safety, and peace, all of which only come from obedience.

Lay a snare (2 Nephi 27:32). Meaning to set a trap or a lure to entangle someone. *See also:* Catch (caught) in a snare.

Lay hands on (Mormon 9:24; Moroni 2:2). The procedure of placing hands on one's head to heal them, to confer the Holy Ghost, to bestow the priesthood, or to pronounce a blessing. *See also:* Laid his (their) hands upon them; Laying on his hands.

Lay hold on (upon) every good thing (Moroni 7:19–21, 25; 10:30). To *lay hold* is to grasp, seize, grip tightly, even to reach out and hold fast. "Seek good and not evil, that ye may live" (Amos 5:14). "If there is anything virtuous, lovely, or of good report or praiseworthy, we seek after these things" (Articles of Faith 1:13).

Lay hold upon the gospel of Christ (word of God) (Helaman 3:29; Mormon 7:8). The word of God and the gospel of Christ are very good things, even the best of things. *See also:* Lay hold on (upon) every good thing.

Laying on his hands (Alma 6:1). The priesthood is given by the laying on of hands. Articles of Faith 1:5 states, "We believe that a man must be called of God, by prophecy, and by the laying on of hands by those who are in authority, to preach the Gospel and administer in the ordinances thereof." Also after baptism by immersion in water comes the baptism of the Spirit by the "laying on of hands for the gift of the Holy Ghost" (Articles of Faith 1:4). *See also:* Laid his (their) hands upon them; Lay hands on.

Lead away captive the daughters (Jacob 2:33). Meaning to tempt, entice, and seduce women and lead them away into evil, corrupt, and amoral ways such as adultery and fornication.

Lead(-ing/stealing) away the hearts (souls) to destruction (hell) (1 Nephi 12:17; 14:3; 15:24; 2 Nephi 28:21; Jacob 7:3; Mosiah 27:9; Alma 10:25, 30; 27:12; 28:13; 30:16, 18, 27, 45, 55; 31:1, 17, 22; 39:4, 11–13; 46:10; 47:30; 48:1–2; 51:9; 61:4; Helaman 6:21, 28, 30–31; 7:15; 16:23; 3 Nephi 2:2; 6:16; 11:29–30; 14:13; 4 Nephi 1:28; Mormon 4:5; Ether 8:26; 9:6;

15:19). In the heart lies the true intent of men and women. It is the determination and design of Satan to lead men and women away from God and from God's ways down to hell and destruction. *See also:* Satan did get hold (possession) upon the hearts of the people.

Leadeth thee by the way (to do good/unto life [eternal]) (1 Nephi 20:17; 3 Nephi 14:14; Ether 4:12). The Lord Jesus Christ and the path He has marked leads to all that is good and also to eternal life. *Compare:* Psalm 23:2–3.

Learn doctrine (2 Nephi 27:35). Only the true doctrine of Christ can save us. *See also:* Doctrine of Christ.

Learn wisdom (2 Nephi 28:30; Mosiah 2:17; Alma 32:11–12; 37:35; 38:9). God possesses all wisdom. Wisdom is a gift from God that is bestowed upon those that seeketh such in worthiness. King Solomon of the Old Testament was given great wisdom. "And God gave Solomon wisdom and understanding exceeding much" (1 Kings 4:29). Solomon later turned to idols, transgressed, and lost his high standing. *See also:* Wisdom in (of) God (the Lord/the Father).

Learning (things) of the Jews (1 Nephi 1:2; 2 Nephi 25:5). Meaning the customs, traditions, laws, common thinking, general beliefs, economy, and history of the Jews. Nephi indicates he understands the Jews because he lived among them, whereas his children and people he is talking to have not. If one lives in a culture or a nation, then that person becomes knowledgeable of what that people are like. *See also:* Manner of the (things of the) Jews.

Least degree of allowance (Alma 45:16). The Lord cannot look upon sin with the least degree of allowance. Sin is completely and absolutely out of the question and not accepted by God. Yet He knows that by our human, carnal nature we will inevitably sin, thus a Savior was provided and the way was made for us to repent and become clean again. *See also:* No unclean thing can enter (inherit) the kingdom of God (heaven); D&C 1:31–32; 19:20.

Leave a blessing (2 Nephi 1:28; 4:5–6, 9). Lehi here leaves a blessing upon the various members of his posterity. Those things promised in these blessings were doubtless prompted by the Holy Ghost and included prophecy, cautions, admonition, counsel, and love.

Leave them neither root nor branch (3 Nephi 25:1). To be without a family tree. "Means the opposite of turning the 'heart of the fathers to the children, and the heart of the children to their fathers' (3 Nephi 25:6). The righteous will be joined in eternal families while the wicked will be cut off from their fathers and grandfathers

(their roots) and also cut off from their children and grandchildren (their branches)" (Valletta, *Book of Mormon for Latter-day Saint Families*, 564).

Lebanon shall be turned into a fruitful field (2 Nephi 27:28). One of the promises of God and prophecies of the prophets that is yet to be fulfilled. It means that by the power of God the land will become exceedingly fertile and productive. This prophecy appears to be unfolding in the working of these lands by the people of the country of modern-day Israel. *See also:* Fruitful field shall be esteemed as a forest.

Led away [by other men into wickedness] (Jacob 7:7; Alma 3:10; 31:17; 36:14; 46:6, 10; 61:4; Helaman 13:29; 3 Nephi 1:29; 4 Nephi 1:34). *See:* Led away by temptation; Led away by the evil one; Yield to no temptation.

Led away by temptation (Alma 34:39; 3 Nephi 18:25). *See:* Led away by the evil one; Led away [by other men into wickedness]; Yield to no temptation.

Led away by the evil one (Alma 12:11; 39:11; 40:13; 46:8; 3 Nephi 18:15; 27:32). *See:* Led away [by other men into wickedness]; Yield to no temptation.

Led away [scattered] (1 Nephi 17:43; 22:4–5; 2 Nephi 1:5; 10:20, 22; 29:12; Jacob 2:25, 32; Omni

1:6; 3 Nephi 15:15; 21:26; 27:32).
See: Scattered tribes of Israel.

Led by the (Holy) Spirit (1 Nephi 4:6; Jacob 4:15; Omni 1:13; Alma 13:28; 21:16; 22:1; Moroni 6:9). The Holy Ghost is a testator, a teacher, a comforter, and a guide. The Holy Ghost puts thoughts and feelings in our minds and frequently warns us. The five wise virgins were those that took "the Holy Spirit for their guide" (D&C 45:57). *See also:* Filled with the Holy Ghost; Power of the Holy Ghost (Spirit).

Led by the power of his arm (the hand of God) (2 Nephi 1:5; Jacob 2:25; Omni 1:13; Alma 9:9; 36:28). *See:* Hand of God (the Lord); Power of his (holy) arm.

Led out of captivity (1 Nephi 5:15; 17:23–24; 19:10; Alma 36:28). *See:* Deliver(-ed) out of bondage.

Led up as calves of the stall (1 Nephi 22:24). *See:* Calves of the stall.

Left hand of God (Mosiah 5:10, 12). "When the Son of man [Jesus the Lord] shall come in his glory, and all the holy angels with him, then shall he sit upon the throne of his glory. And before him shall be gathered all nations: and he shall separate them one from another, as a shepherd divideth his sheep from the goats: and he shall set the sheep on his right hand, but the goats on the left. Then shall the King say unto them on his right hand,

Come, ye blessed of my Father, inherit the kingdom prepared for you from the foundation of the world . . . Then shall he say also unto them on the left hand, Depart from me, ye cursed, into everlasting fire, prepared for the devil and his angels" (Matthew 25:31–34, 41).

Left in their own strength (Helaman 4:13; Mormon 2:26). *See:* Boast in their own strength.

Left to ourselves that the Spirit of the Lord did not abide in us (Helaman 4:24; Mormon 2:26). Because of the wickedness of the people the Spirit of the Lord no longer dwelt with the people.

Left (unto you) desolate (1 Nephi 21:21; Alma 16:10; Helaman 15:1; 3 Nephi 4:1, 3; 8:14). *Desolate* means without friends or family, empty, alone, deserted, lonely, and cheerless. The wicked and their lands will be abandoned and desolate.

Lend an ear to my counsel (2 Nephi 28:30). *See:* Give ear unto my words.

Lengthen out mine arm (2 Nephi 28:32). Meaning the Lord will stretch forth His holy arm to assist and save His penitent and humble Saints. Compare D&C 35:8, "For I am God, and mine arm is not shortened; and I will show miracles, signs, and wonders, unto all those who believe on my name." *See also:* Arm (of mercy) is extended (towards you in the light of day); Extending the arm of mercy towards them; Mine arm is lengthened out; Mine arm of mercy is extended towards you.

Lengthen out their days (Helaman 7:24). "And if thou wilt walk in my ways, to keep my statutes and my commandments, as thy father David did walk, then I will lengthen thy days" (1 Kings 3:14).

Lengthen thy cords and strengthen thy stakes (3 Nephi 22:2). *See:* Bring again (forth) Zion; Strengthen thy stakes and enlarge thy borders.

Less than the dust of the earth (Mosiah 4:2; Helaman 12:7). Man is less than the dust of the earth because the dust of the earth immediately obeys God's every command, but men resist and rebel against the commands of God. We must seek God's assistance to overcome this tendency and strive always to do only the will of God. We stay in contact with God's will through prayer, studying the scriptures, and unselfishly serving our fellow man.

Let us be faithful (unto the Lord) (1 Nephi 3:16; 4:1; 7:12; Ether 1:38). After we have entered the gate, which is baptism, we must endure faithfully to the end, otherwise we cannot gain salvation.

Let your light so shine (3 Nephi 12:16; 18:24). Be an example even as Jesus was. Live a good and honest life so that others will recognize goodness, truth, humble service, love, and a glowing countenance. They will then have much good to say and praise to give of goodness, truth, and God.

Let your soul delight in fatness (2 Nephi 9:51). This is the filling of our spirits with the word of God to overflowing, even a spiritual feast that is joyous and satisfying. "Labor not for the meat which perisheth, but for the meat which endureth unto everlasting life, which the Son of man shall give unto you. . . . I am the bread of life: he that cometh to me shall never hunger; and he that believeth on me shall never thirst" (John 6:27, 35).

Liberal to all (Alma 1:30). Meaning generous in sharing this earth's goods with all those around them, particularly sharing with the poor and needy. *See also:* All things common; Poor and needy.

Liberal unto all (Alma 6:5). Meaning here that the word of God is free and available to all. None are forbidden to come unto Christ.

Lick up the dust of their (thy) feet (1 Nephi 21:23; 2 Nephi 6:7, 13). A sign of being humble and subservient. Those who have bowed down low, even with their face to the ground.

Lied before (unto) God (Jacob 7:19; Alma 11:25; 12:3). It is generally supposed that there are variations to lies, from the "little white lie" up to the bold-faced lie. Yet all lies are lies and are sinful before God. Further, God knows our every lie. However, certain lies are particularly grievous before God, and those are lies in contempt and disregard of God. These include lies of rebellion against God, lies against a higher knowledge of God, lies to deceive and lead people away from God, and lies against a knowledge of God but made to obtain earthly honor, power, and riches.

Life and light of the world (Alma 38:9). "Behold, I am Jesus Christ, the Son of God. I am the life and the light of the world" (D&C 11:28). *See also:* Light and the life (and truth) of the world.

Life, and that eternally (Ether 3:14). *See:* Eternal life.

Life eternal (1 Nephi 14:7; 2 Nephi 9:39; 33:4; Helaman 8:15; Ether 3:14; Moroni 7:41). *See:* Eternal life; Know God; John 17:3.

Life which is in Christ (2 Nephi 25:27). This should be the very goal of our lives here on earth. It is life eternal. Jesus said, "I am come that they might have life, and that they might have it more abundantly" (John 10:10). *See also:* Eternal life.

Lift their cries to the Lord their God (3 Nephi 4:8). *See:* Cry unto God (Jesus Christ/the Lord).

Lift themselves up in the pride of their hearts (Mormon 8:36). *See:*

Lifted up in (unto) pride (of their eyes/hearts/and boasting).

Lift up mine hand (1 Nephi 21:22; 2 Nephi 6:6). Meaning to give them a hand, promote, and champion them, to cause them to prosper and flourish.

Lift up their hearts and rejoice (2 Nephi 9:52; 11:8). The opposite of drooping, sad, and downtrodden hearts. A knowledge of God and His plan of salvation for men is reason to lift up our countenance and praise God and all creation. *See also:* Cheer up your hearts.

Lift up their (your) eyes to heaven (2 Nephi 8:6; Helaman 5:36). Meaning to raise up our eyes to heaven in communion and praise.

Lift up your head(-s) (2 Nephi 9:3; Jacob 3:2; Mosiah 7:18–19; 24:13; Alma 1:4; 30:18, 23; 3 Nephi 1:13). "In 2 Nephi 9:3, Jacob states that he has spoken 'these things that ye may rejoice, and lift up your heads forever.' Later, in 10:20, Jacob ends his discourse in the following manner: 'And now, my beloved brethren . . . let us remember him, and lay aside our sins, and not hang down our heads, for we are not cast off.' While we associate the bowed head with humility, in the ancient Near East it was commonly used to demonstrate the utter power over another. Depictions of successful battle often presented captives with bowed heads, bound together. Thus, the act of lifting the head was associated with release from captivity and deliverance" (Belnap, "'I Will Contend with Them,'" 32). *See also:* Luke 21:28; D&C 110:5.

Lifted their voices in the praises of their God (Mosiah 24:22). Meaning to praise God in heaven above and not embarrassingly so or without confidence. *See also:* Praise(-d/praising) God; Raise their voices to God.

Lifted up at the last day (1 Nephi 13:37; 16:2; Mosiah 23:22; Alma 13:29; 36:3; 37:37; 38:5; 3 Nephi 27:22; Mormon 2:19; Ether 4:19). Meaning to be saved at the last day. *See also:* Last day.

Lifted up by the power of God (1 Nephi 13:30). God hath power to uplift, elevate, raise, hold up, and exalt those whom He chooses, usually the more faithful. In this case God will champion the Gentiles in the last days.

Lifted up his hand (1 Nephi 22:6). *See:* Lift up mine hand.

Lifted up his voice to heaven and cried (Alma 31:26). Prayed with great emphasis. *See also:* Cry unto God (Jesus Christ/the Lord).

Lifted up in their hearts (one above another) (Alma 4:8; 45:24; Helaman 6:17). *See:* Lifted up in (unto) pride (of their eyes/hearts/and boasting).

Lifted up in (unto) pride (of their eyes/hearts/and boasting) (2 Nephi 26:20; 28:12; Jacob 1:16; 2:13; Mosiah 11:5, 19; Alma 1:6, 32; 4:6, 8; 6:3; 7:6; 31:25–26; 38:11; 62:49; Helaman 3:34; 7:26; 12:5; 16:10; 3 Nephi 6:10, 13; 16:10; 4 Nephi 1:24; Mormon 8:28). The false illusions of pride reside in the heart or mind. Personal elevation of pride in one's own feelings, imagination, and thoughts. *Compare:* Moses 8:22. *See also:* Pride of their (your) eyes; Pride of their (your) hearts; Puffed up.

Lifted up to dwell in the kingdom prepared for him (Ether 4:19). God hath prepared great mansions and kingdoms for the eternal habitation of the faithful. *See also:* Lifted up at the last day.

Lifted up unto boastings (Alma 31:25; 3 Nephi 6:10). Boasting is defined as to brag about oneself, swagger in imagined greatness, pretend to be larger than what is real, and broadcast false importance. Humility is the required and preferred characteristic. *See also:* Lifted up in (unto) pride (of their eyes/hearts/and boasting).

Lifted up upon the cross (1 Nephi 11:33; 19:10; Helaman 8:14; 3 Nephi 27:14–15; 28:6; Ether 4:1). Also Moses 7:55. A particularly cruel, slow death, placed high for all to see and be warned. It is interesting to wonder if death by crucifixion had ever been practiced before Roman times, yet the holy prophets were given to see that the Savior of the world would be slain in this awful way.

Lifting themselves up with their pride (Alma 4:12). *See:* Lifted up in (unto) pride (of their eyes/hearts/ and boasting).

Light and knowledge (Alma 9:19, 23; 39:6; 45:12). Increased light and knowledge should be our goal. All light and knowledge emanate from God the Father and His Son. A fulness of light and knowledge reside in them. Light and knowledge is one of the sources of their great power. "And if a person gains more knowledge and intelligence in this life through his diligence and obedience than another, he will have so much the advantage in the world to come" (D&C 130:19).

Light and the life (and truth) of the world (Mosiah 16:9; 3 Nephi 9:18; 11:11; Ether 4:12). Jesus Christ is the light and life of the world. He is the light that is endless (Mosiah 16:9). From Him emanates all truth and light. Also He is the great creator that gave life to all that are here on earth; He is the first fruits of the Resurrection by whom we will all be resurrected to immortal life. He has provided the Atonement, which allows a redemption from our sins such that we can have life eternal in the presence of God. *See also:* Light of Christ; Marvelous light of God.

Light in the wilderness (1 Nephi 17:13). Symbolically and in reality Jehovah was a light in the wilderness to the Israelites. "Yet thou in thy manifold mercies forsookest them not in the wilderness: the pillar of the cloud departed not from them by day, to lead them in the way; neither the pillar of fire by night, to shew them light, and the way wherein they should go" (Nehemiah 9:19). Likewise, Jesus Christ is our light in the wilderness of the wicked world. He has beckoned us to follow Him and thus shows us the way. *See also:* Marvelous light of God.

Light of Christ (Alma 28:14; Moroni 7:18–19). "The phrase 'light of Christ' does not appear in the Bible, although the principles that apply to it are frequently mentioned therein. The precise phrase is found in Alma 28:14, Moro. 7:18, and D&C 88:7. Biblical phrases that are sometimes synonymous to the term 'light of Christ' are 'spirit of the Lord' and 'light of life' (see, for example, John 1:4; 8:12). The 'spirit of the Lord,' however, sometimes is used with reference to the Holy Ghost, and so must not be taken in every case as having reference to the light of Christ.

"The light of Christ is just what the words imply: enlightenment, knowledge, and an uplifting, ennobling, persevering influence that come upon mankind because of Jesus Christ. For instance, Christ is 'the true light that lighteth every man that cometh into the world' (D&C 93:2; see John 1:9). The light of Christ fills the 'immensity of space' and is the means by which Christ is able to be 'in all things, and is through all things, and is round about all things.' It 'giveth life to all things' and is 'the law by which all things are governed.' It is also 'the light that quickeneth' man's understanding (see D&C 88:6–13, 41). In this manner, the light of Christ is related to man's conscience and tells him right from wrong (Moro. 7:12–19).

"The light of Christ should not be confused with the personage of the Holy Ghost, for the light of Christ is not a personage at all. Its influence is preliminary to and preparatory to one's receiving the Holy Ghost. The light of Christ will lead the honest soul who 'hearkeneth to the voice' to find the true gospel and the true Church and thereby receive the Holy Ghost (see D&C 84:46–48)" (Bible Dictionary, s.v. "light of Christ," 725). *See also:* Marvelous light of God.

Light of everlasting life (word) (Alma 5:7; 19:6). Jesus Christ is the light of everlasting life, and from Him emanates all light, life, and truth. This light expands to fill the whole universe and sustains all living things therein. *See also:* Marvelous light of God.

Light of his countenance did shine upon them (3 Nephi 19:25). *See:* Countenance did shine upon them; Light of the glory of God.

Light of the body (3 Nephi 13:22–23). "The Savior Jesus Christ promises those who follow Him: 'Your whole bodies shall be filled with light, and there shall be no darkness in you' (D&C 88:67; see also 3 Nephi 13:22–23). Fill your life with truth, righteousness, peace, and faith. As you fill your life with goodness, there will be no room for pornography and other sources of spiritual darkness. Elder Robert D. Hales observed, 'Light and darkness cannot occupy the same space at the same time. Light dispels darkness. When light is present, darkness is vanquished and must depart. More importantly, darkness cannot conquer light unless the light is diminished or departs' (in Conference Report, Apr. 2002, 80–81; or *Ensign*, May 2002, 70).

"You fill your life with light as you pray and study the scriptures with real intent, seeking to know, understand, and follow the Lord. . . .

"Attending church meetings and partaking of the sacrament, keeping the Sabbath day holy, fasting and paying tithing will help you keep yourself free of the darkness of the world (see D&C 59:9)" (*Let Virtue Garnish Thy Thoughts*, 2).

Light of the glory of God (Alma 19:6). Our marvelous, magnificent, and all-powerful God is the embodiment of all glory, and from Him shines forth brilliant and radiant light. Joseph Smith's description of the First Vision says, "I saw a pillar of light exactly over my head, above the brightness of the sun. . . . When the light rested upon me I saw two Personages, whose brightness and glory defy all description" (Joseph Smith–History 1:16–17). *See also:* Face shone with exceeding luster; Image of God engraven upon your countenances; Light of his countenance did shine upon them; Luster was above that of the sun at noon-day.

Light to the Gentiles (1 Nephi 21:6). The gospel is a light to the Gentiles. It is like a lighthouse for lost ships or like a light in the center of a darkened room, to which the people of the world can come and find peace and truth. *See also:* Light in the wilderness.

Light unto them (forever) (1 Nephi 17:30; 2 Nephi 10:14; Alma 9:19). The Lord God is our light, lighting the way we should go. His example is our light, His teachings are our light, and His truth is our light. "I am the light of the world: he that followeth me shall not walk in darkness, but shall have the light of life" (John 8:12). *See also:* Marvelous light of God.

Line upon line, precept upon precept (2 Nephi 28:30). Progression in life is not one big giant step, but is a succession of small steps. We do not come to understand all there is to know about God's plan and the gospel in one day nor in a one-hour class. Rather, small revelations from above and the daily experiences of life give us knowledge and wisdom. Thus we learn the lessons of life one line of knowledge at a time and one principle of truth at a time. Then, looking back on our lives, we see the multitude of small steps and little bits of knowledge add up to the total of our lives. "Wherefore, be not weary in well-doing, for ye are laying the foundation of a great work. And out of small things proceedeth that which is great" (D&C 64:33). "These should then be attended to with great earnestness. Let no man count them as small things; for there is much which lieth in futurity, pertaining to the saints, which depends upon these things" (D&C 123:14–15).

List(-eth) to obey (Mosiah 2:32–33, 37; Alma 3:27). *Listeth* means to lean towards one, be counted among, or to choose; thus one chooses to obey God; or in the opposite to lean towards obeying the evil spirit.

Live in thanksgiving daily (Alma 34:38). *See:* Thanksgiving to God.

Live unto the Lord their God (Alma 48:10). Meaning to live before God, keeping His commandments, according to their good conscience.

Lively sense of his own guilt (Mosiah 2:38). *See:* Bright recollection of all our guilt.

Living God (1 Nephi 17:30; 2 Nephi 31:16; Alma 5:13; 7:6; 11:25–26, 27; 43:10; 3 Nephi 30:1; Mormon 5:14; 9:28–29). A scriptural phrase used in the scriptures to denote the only real and true God. False gods and idols are dead gods and are unable to pass eternal life onto us. It is our duty to know that God lives and to serve Him.

Living soul (Alma 16:9; 3 Nephi 5:1). The physical body and the spirit of man united constitute the living soul. D&C 88:15 says, "And the spirit and the body are the soul of man."

Living waters (1 Nephi 11:25). Revelations or the word and love of God are the water springing up unto eternal life. Jesus is the source of living waters. To gain eternal life we must come unto Christ, who is the fountain of living waters. *See also:* Bread and the waters of life; Fountain of living waters.

Long suffering (of the Lord) towards the children of men (1 Nephi 19:9; Mosiah 4:6, 11; Alma 5:6; 9:11, 26; 26:16; 42:30; Mormon 2:12; 9:25). Meaning that in spite of the wickedness and errant ways of God's children here on earth, God patiently and lovingly calls to the people to repent and come unto Him before it is too late and the end is come.

Look forward to a redemption (remission) of sins (Alma 5:15; 7:6; 13:2, 16; 30:16). This is the very promise of the gospel of Jesus Christ, for only in Christ can we be redeemed. *See also:* Atonement of Christ (the Only Begotten Son).

Look forward unto Christ (2 Nephi 25:24, 27; 26:8; Jarom 1:11; Alma 13:2, 16; 25:15). Meaning to believe in Jesus Christ, looking forward to His coming, and anticipating our redemption and resurrection provided by Christ.

Look forward with one eye (Mosiah 18:21). Meaning to be united in outlook, all believing the same truths, rather than having conflicting views. Or, in other words, with an eye single to the glory of God.

Look to (the Lord your) God (and live) (Alma 5:19; 37:47; 38:2). To have faith in and obey God.

Look unto my God (the Lord) (1 Nephi 15:3; 18:16; 2 Nephi 8:1; Jacob 3:1; 3 Nephi 15:9; Mormon 8:33). To have faith in and obey God. *See also:* Look forward unto Christ.

Look up to God (Alma 5:19; 12:14). At the judgment day we will look up to God, who will judge us. *See also:* Bar of God.

Looking beyond the mark (Jacob 4:14). Meaning to look beyond the plain truths of the gospel, imagining things that are not. "To '[look] *beyond the mark*' is to look for things that are truer than true. The scriptures speak for themselves and are true. Alma warns of this problem: '*Behold, the scriptures are before you; if ye will wrest them it shall be to your own destruction*' (Alma 13:20).

"To *wrest* is to 'pull, force, or move by violent wringing or twisting movement.' Be careful that you do not look beyond the simple truths of the scriptures and delve into self-interpretation" (Tingey, "The Virtue of the Word of God").

Loose his (their) tongue(-s) (2 Nephi 3:17; 3 Nephi 26:14). A gift sometimes given from God to be able to speak the principles of the gospel effectively and fluently; being given the knowledge and words to speak. The Lord said in D&C 100:5–6, "Therefore, verily I say unto you, lift up your voices unto this people; speak the thoughts that I shall put into your hearts, and you shall not be confounded before men; for it shall be given you in the very hour, yea, in the very moment, what ye shall say."

Loose the bands of death (Alma 5:10; 7:12; 11:41–42; 22:14). *See:* Bands of death; Loosed from this eternal band(-s) of death.

Loose thyself from the bands of thy neck (2 Nephi 8:25; 3 Nephi 20:37). The Lord gave the meaning of this phrase in D&C 113:10, "We are to understand that the scattered remnants are exhorted to return to the Lord from whence they have fallen; which if they do, the promise of the Lord is that he will speak to

them, or give them revelation. . . . The bands of her neck are the curses of God upon her, or the remnants of Israel in their scattered condition among the Gentiles."

Loose yourselves from the pains of hell (Jacob 3:11). The consequences of sin are pain, anguish, sorrow, and tragedy. We must repent and come unto Christ to loose ourselves from these consequences of sin. *See also:* Pains of hell.

Loosed from the pains of hell (Alma 5:9; 26:13). Sin brings man down into the depths of misery and wo, which the scriptures call the "pains of hell." *See also:* Pains of hell.

Loosed from this eternal band(-s) of death (Alma 5:10; Mormon 9:13). The Atonement of Christ looses—or frees—us from the bonds or ties of death, both temporal and spiritual. In other words, we will be resurrected and can be purified from our sins because of the redemption of Christ. *See also:* Bands of death.

Loose(-d) his (their) tongue(-s) (2 Nephi 3:17; 7:4; 31:13–14; 32:2; 3 Nephi 26:14). *See:* Tongue of angels.

Loosed our brethren from the chains of hell (Alma 5:9–10; 26:14; Mormon 9:13). By accepting the gospel, coming unto Christ, and following Him for the remainder of our days we will be freed from the chains of hell. *See also:* Chains of hell; Loosed from this eternal band(-s) of death.

Lord comfort(-ed) us (1 Nephi 21:13; 2 Nephi 8:3; Mosiah 12:23; 15:30; 24:13, 16; Alma 17:10; 26:27; 31:31–32; 3 Nephi 16:19; Ether 12:29). *Comfort* means to console, encourage, ease, calm, relieve, soothe, revitalize, revive, bolster, and refresh; thus providing relief, solace, and peace to those in need of comfort. The Lord is mighty to comfort us and in understanding because he descended below all things so that he could succor us. *See also:* Comfort my (their) soul in Christ; Comforted his people.

Lord commanded him (me/us) (1 Nephi 2:2–3; 3:2, 4; 7:2, 44; 9:1, 5; 19:1; 2 Nephi 33:15; Mosiah 2:30; 3:23, 27; 11:20, 25; 12:1; Alma 29:9; Helaman 4:22; 14:9–10; 3 Nephi 11:20; 26:12; Mormon 3:16; Ether 2:5, 18, 21–22; 3:28; 4:1, 5; 12:22). When the Lord God commands, we must obey. See the excellent example by Nephi in his closing words at the end of his record: "For thus hath the Lord commanded me, and I must obey. Amen" (2 Nephi 33:15). *See also:* Commanded of the Lord; Did as the Lord commanded.

Lord did hear my (their) cries (Mosiah 10:13; 21:15; 23:10; Alma 2:28; Ether 1:40). These verses record examples of when the Lord heard and answered the prayers of individuals. We should record those times God hears our cry, so that we can ever remember them and share them with posterity. *See also:* Cry mightily to God (the Father/the Lord); Mighty prayer.

Lord did (shall/will) bless him (thee/them/us/you) (1 Nephi 16:39; 17:35; 2 Nephi 3:3; Mosiah 10:22; Alma 7:25; 21:17; 28:8; 38:15; 46:20; 62:51; Helaman 11:16; 12:1; 15:10; 4 Nephi 1:18; Mormon 8:14; 9:37). "Pray always, and I will pour out my Spirit upon you, and great shall be your blessing—yea, even more than if you should obtain treasures of earth" (D&C 19:38). *See also:* Blessed are they (those/ye); Blessing of God (the Lord); Pour(-ed/-ing) out his blessings.

Lord did soften my (the) heart(-s) (1 Nephi 2:16; 7:5, 19; 18:20; 2 Nephi 10:18; Mosiah 21:15; 23:29; Alma 24:8). We must pray that the Lord will soften our own hearts and the hearts of others so that we all may be teachable, humble, understanding, and willing to do the will of God. See the example of Nephi, who prayed that his own heart would be softened (1 Nephi 2:16), and the many examples of praying for neighbors and enemies that their hearts would be softened (Mosiah 23:28). *See also:* Soften my (our/the/their) heart(-s).

Lord did strengthen them (Mosiah 23:2; 24:15; Alma 2:18; 2:28; 15:18; 61:21). The Lord God has the power to strengthen mortal men: physical strength to fight and accomplish, physical strength to endure, strengthening of faith and will, strength against Satan's temptations, and any other strength God sees man should need to be blessed with. Thus we should pray often for strength. *See also:* In the strength of our God (the Lord).

Lord did (would) warn me (them) (2 Nephi 5:5; Alma 48:15). According to His perfect will, the Lord has at times warned people of danger. *See also:* Warned of the Lord.

Lord doth (will) counsel in wisdom (2 Nephi 28:30; Alma 29:8; 37:37). The word from God or the counsel of God contains all possible wisdom and is absolute truth. The counsel of God overrides all other counsel and must be followed without exception. *See also:* Wisdom in (of) God (the Lord/the Father).

Lord forbade (3 Nephi 26:11; 28:25). *See:* Forbidden that I (they) should write (utter/preach).

Lord God hath spoken it (2 Nephi 9:16, 24; 10:9; Mosiah 2:41; 12:12; Alma 5:32, 52; 34:8; Mormon 8:26; Ether 4:19; 10:28). We can trust in it if the Lord has spoken it. *See also:* According to the word of God (the Lord); Thus saith our God (the Lord).

Lord had compassion upon him (them/you) (Mosiah 15:9; 3 Nephi 17:6, 7; Ether 1:35, 37, 40). Compassion means forgiveness, tenderness, pity, mercy, and kindness. Might we frequently pray, "Lord have compassion on us, for as thou knowest we are mortal, which causes us to have weakness. Have compassion on our plight, forgive our weakness, and redeem our souls." *See also:* Bowels of mercy; Moved with compassion.

Lord had (has) shown (unto) him (me/them) (1 Nephi 1:15, 18; 11:9; 14:26; 17:9; 18:2; 2 Nephi 6:8–9; 10:2; 31:17; Helaman 5:26; 8:18; 10:2; 15:15; 3 Nephi 10:18; 18:7; 26:15; Mormon 8:34–35; Ether 3:26; 5:3; 8:23; 12:8). The Lord has revealed many great and wonderful things to His prophets and to the faithful Saints. *See also:* Spirit of revelation.

Lord had (hath) said (1 Nephi 15:11; 2 Nephi 3:16–17; Mosiah 7:29; 27:13; Alma 19:23; 27:13; 34:36; 43:46; Mormon 5:9; Ether 3:25). *See:* Lord God hath spoken it.

Lord hath chosen him (them) (1 Nephi 1:20; 3:29; Mosiah 7:26; Alma 7:10; 10:7; Helaman 15:3; 3 Nephi 28:36; Moroni 7:31). In the great plan of salvation God has chosen individuals and peoples to represent Him, to preach the gospel of Jesus Christ, and to perform certain labors. *See also:* Chosen for the work; Chosen man of God; Twelve apostles of the Lamb; Twelve disciples of the Lamb.

Lord hath comforted his people (1 Nephi 21:13; Mosiah 12:23; 15:30; 3 Nephi 16:19). *See:* Lord comforted us; 3 Nephi 20:34.

Lord hath commanded me (1 Nephi 3:2, 4; 9:5; 19:1; 2 Nephi 33:15; Mosiah 2:30; 3:23, 27; 11:20, 25; 12:1; Alma 29:9; Helaman 14:9–10; 3 Nephi 26:12; Mormon 3:16; Ether 2:18, 22; 4:5; 12:22). *See:* Lord commanded him (me/us).

Lord hath made bare his holy arm (Mosiah 12:24; 15:31; 3 Nephi 16:20). A phrase used to describe when the Lord reveals His glory, His power, His word, and His light. *See also:* Made bare his holy arm.

Lord in (his great) mercy (2 Nephi 4:26; Mosiah 27:28; Alma 7:2; 38:7, 14). In other words the Lord acting in all mercy. The Lord Jesus and God the Father possess all possible mercy. *See also:* Merciful God (Being).

Lord is faithful (1 Nephi 21:7). Faithful, meaning the Lord God is constant, devoted, true, and unfailing.

Lord is (was) able (1 Nephi 4:3; 7:12; 11:1; 2 Nephi 27:20; Enos 1:15; 3:5; Alma 7:8). We must have faith to know that the Lord God is able to do all that He desires to do, for the Lord God has all power. He is able to do His own work, not needing help from anyone. Yet He desires the help of His Saints on earth for their own learning, growth, development, and blessing. We must have faith to know that the Lord God is able to do all that He desires to do. *See also:* Power of God.

Lord is (was/will be) merciful (1 Nephi 1:14; 8:37; 13:34; 19:20; 2 Nephi 1:3; 4:7; 6:11; 9:6; 10:2; 28:32; Jacob 3:6; Mosiah 24:21; Alma 9:16–17; 29:10; 50:19; Helaman 3:27; 7:24; 15:12; Mormon 2:12; Ether 3:3; 9:2; 13:7; Moroni 10:3). *See:* Lord in (his great) mercy; Merciful God (Being).

Lord is (was) with thee (1 Nephi 17:55; Alma 38:4). These faithful servants merited having the Lord's presence, power, assistance, and deliverance to aid them in their work of the kingdom.

Lord Jehovah (2 Nephi 22:2). *See:* Great Jehovah; Jesus Christ.

Lord Jesus Christ (Mosiah 3:12; Alma 37:33; 38:8; 46:39; Helaman 13:6; 3 Nephi 7:16, 18; 10:10; Mormon 9:37; Ether 12:41; Moroni 6:6; 7:2; 8:2; 9:26). Jesus Christ is the Lord of lords, and King of kings (see Revelation 17:14). *See also:* Jesus Christ; Lord Jehovah.

Lord knoweth all things (1 Nephi 9:6; Words of Mormon 1:7; Mosiah 4:9). *See:* All-wise Creator; God knoweth all things; Knoweth all things; Lord knoweth all things; Wisdom in (of) God (the Lord/the Father).

Lord of Hosts (1 Nephi 20:2; 2 Nephi 8:15; 12:12; 13:1; 15:7, 9, 16, 24; 16:3, 5; 18:13, 18; 19:7, 13, 19; 20:16, 26, 33; 23:4, 13, 22–23; 24:24, 27; 26:4–6; 27:2, 27–28; 28:17, 32; Jacob 2:28–29, 30, 32–33; Helaman 13:17–18, 32; 3 Nephi 22:5; 24:1, 5, 7, 10–12, 14, 17; 25:1, 3). Another name and title for Jesus Christ. Truly He is the Lord and King of all the Hosts of Heaven and all the hosts of men. Found elsewhere in the scriptures as "Lord of Sabaoth" (e.g., James 5:4 and D&C 88:2). *Sabaoth* in Hebrew is *tzava'ot*, meaning "hosts" (see Bible Dictionary, s.v. "Sabaoth," 764).

Lord of the harvest (Alma 26:7). The Lord Jesus Christ is the Lord of the harvest. At the last day He will gather up the wheat (the Saints) from among the tares (the wicked). The harvest also refers to missionary work: "The harvest truly is great, but the labourers are few: pray ye therefore the Lord of the harvest, that he would send forth labourers into his harvest" (Luke 10:2) and "He that reapeth receiveth wages and gathereth fruit unto life eternal" (John 4:36).

Lord Omnipotent (Mosiah 3:5, 17–18, 21; 5:2, 15). A name or title for our Lord Jesus Christ. *Omnipotent* means to have all power. We believe, and the scriptures teach in many places, that God has all power and can do all things that He desires. *See also:* All power; Power of God.

Lord reigneth (1 Nephi 22:26; Mosiah 3:5; 12:21; 15:14; 27:37; 3 Nephi 20:40). John the Revelator testified, "And I heard as it were the voice of a great multitude, and as the voice of many waters, and as the voice of mighty thunderings, saying, Alleluia: for the Lord God omnipotent reigneth" (Revelation 19:6). The Lord reigneth, meaning ruleth, over all.

Lord remembereth (2 Nephi 10:22; 26:33; Jacob 6:4; Mosiah 27:30; 3 Nephi 29:8). The Lord God remembers all His peoples, all His creations, all His promises, and all His words. *See also:* According to God's word.

Lord said unto me (1 Nephi 17:53; 2 Nephi 3:16, 18; 5:25, 30; 18:1; Enos 1:12, 15, 18; Mosiah 12:2; 27:25; Ether 4:6; 12:37). These are great passages wherein the Lord is speaking unto His prophets and conveying information, promises, and prophecy. *See also:* Lord had (hath) said; Lord spake unto.

Lord shall bring (establish) again Zion (Mosiah 12:22; 15:29; 16:18; 3 Nephi 21:1). *See:* Bring again (forth) Zion.

Lord shall comfort Zion (2 Nephi 8:3). Meaning the Lord shall restore and bless Zion. *See also:* Lord comfort(-ed) us.

Lord showeth all things to him (them) (1 Nephi 14:26; 2 Nephi 27:10; Alma 9:20; Ether 3:26; 4:7;

12:21; 13:2). God has revealed many things, even He can reveal all things that seemeth Him good. By our faith He will continue to reveal much. *See also:* According to his (your) faith.

Lord spake it and it was done (2 Nephi 5:23). The commands of God are always accomplished. *See also:* According to God's word.

Lord spake unto (1 Nephi 2:1, 19; 7:1; 11:35, 36; 13:34; 16:9; 17:8; 2 Nephi 5:23; 17:10; 18:5, 11; 3 Nephi 11:13; Ether 12:26; 15:33). The Lord has spoken, does now speak, and will always speak to His prophets. *See also:* Lord said unto me.

Lord stay his hand (Alma 10:23; Moroni 9:14). Meaning the Lord God will hold back His hand from destroying the wicked because of the righteous that live among them.

Lord their God (1 Nephi 7:21–22; 16:22; 17:30, 53; 2 Nephi 26:32; Mosiah 2:4; 11:21–23, 25; 13:29; 17:15; 18:23, 25; 23:23, 27; 24:5, 12, 21; 26:4, 26; 27:22; 28:2; Alma 9:19; 13:12; 16:17; 21:22; 29:10; 37:9, 30; 43:49; 45:1; 46:8, 21; 47:36; 48:7, 10; 49:28; 50:39; 55:31; 58:40; 60:13; 62:45, 49, 51; Helaman 4:25; 11:4, 7, 34, 36; 12:2, 5–6, 23; 3 Nephi 3:25; 4:8; 5:23; 7:14; 20:13; Mormon 3:3; 5:14; Ether 6:4). The title *Lord* in the scriptures generally refers to Jesus Christ, who is the Lord Jehovah. Jesus Christ is God the Son, while

Heavenly Father is God the Father. *See also:* Jesus Christ.

Lord the(-ir) Redeemer (1 Nephi 10:14; 17:30; 19:18, 23; 21:7; 22:12; 2 Nephi 1:10; Mosiah 26:26; Alma 28:8; 3 Nephi 10:10). The Lord Jesus Christ is the Redeemer and Savior of mankind. Through His atoning sacrifice He has redeemed all men, women, and children from physical death by the resurrection to immortality. His redemption can also restore us from our sins, if we come unto Him, repent, accept the ordinances, and live faithfully.

Lord will consecrate (2 Nephi 3:2; 10:19; 32:9; 33:4). *Consecrate* means to bless and set apart, designate, commission, or appoint for holy purposes.

Lord will go before you, and the God of Israel will be your rearward (3 Nephi 20:42; 21:29). The Lord will prepare the way, He will lead the righteous, and He will also protect them from behind.

Lord will set his hand (2 Nephi 21:11; 25:17; Jacob 6:2). "Set His hand" means to prepare the way for and to accomplish His purposes. Thus the Lord causes His desires and word to be fulfilled. In these three verses He will by His almighty hand cause that scattered Israel will again be gathered and restored in the last days.

Lord worketh in many ways (Alma 24:27). Because of the Lord's great power and complete knowledge, He can accomplish His work in many ways.

Lord worketh not in darkness (secret combinations) (2 Nephi 26:23; Alma 37:22; Ether 8:19). Secret works of darkness are an abomination unto the Lord. Rather the Lord does all His works in the light, for He is the very light. *See also:* Marvelous light of God; Secret combination(-s); Works of darkness.

Lose thy soul (Alma 20:18). Meaning his soul would not be saved in the eternities, for murder of innocent blood cannot be forgiven. "The murderer 'shall not have forgiveness in this world, nor in the world to come' (D&C 42:18).

"In LDS doctrine, murder is second in seriousness only to the unpardonable sin of blasphemy against the Holy Ghost. And even that sin involves a kind of murderous treachery in that one who previously had obtained an absolute witness of Jesus' divinity (*TPJS*, p. 358) in effect 'crucifies [Christ]' afresh or 'assent[s] unto [his] death' (D&C 76:35; 132:27). . . .

"Moreover, because 'man cannot restore life,' and restoration or restitution is a necessary step for repentance, obtaining forgiveness for murder is impossible (Kimball, [*Miracle of Forgiveness*], 1969, p. 129; D&C 42:18–19). . . .

"The Church defines 'murder' as the deliberate and unjustified taking of human life. . . . In the final analysis, only God, who can discern the thoughts of the heart, can judge whether a particular killing is an unforgivable murder or not. . . .

"Only the Lord has power to give life or to authorize it to be taken" (*Encyclopedia of Mormonism*, 2:970, 971).

Lost and fallen people (Alma 9:30, 32; 12:22). *See:* Fallen people.

Lost and fallen state (1 Nephi 10:6; 2 Nephi 25:17; Mosiah 16:4; Alma 34:9; 42:6). *See:* Fallen man.

Lost forever (Alma 42:6). Or in the words of 2 Nephi 9:7, "remained to an endless duration." Thus *lost forever* means they became as fallen man, cut off eternally from the presence of God, never to be resurrected and restored to God's presence were it not for the merciful plan of salvation. *See also:* Fallen man.

Lost tribes of Israel (1 Nephi 22:4; 2 Nephi 29:13; 3 Nephi 17:4; 21:26). Refers to the tribes of Israel that have been scattered to the four corners of the world and led away by the Lord to other lands. Sometimes referred to as the ten lost tribes. The Lord knows their whereabouts and has said He will remember them. They are "not lost to the Father, for he knoweth whither he hath taken them" (3 Nephi 17:4).

Love God (Moroni 7:13; 10:32). To love God is a commandment, even the foremost commandment.

Love of God (1 Nephi 11:22, 25; Mosiah 4:12; Alma 13:29; 4 Nephi 1:15). God's love is perfect and eternal. Contrary to what some say, God's love is not unconditional, for God reserves His greatest love for those who keep His commandments. 1 Nephi 17:35 says, "He that is righteous is favored of God." A fulness of the love of God is a gift promised to those who qualify through faith in Christ, repentance, and by keeping the commandments. In Lehi's dream the tree symbolized the love of God. "The love of God, which sheddeth itself abroad in the hearts of the children of men; wherefore, it is the most desirable above all things" (1 Nephi 11:22). God loves us, is concerned about us, and is mindful of us. "Cast all your care upon him [God]; for he careth for you" (1 Peter 5:7). Nothing "shall be able to separate us from the love of God, which is in Christ Jesus our Lord" (Romans 8:39).

Love of God and of all men (2 Nephi 31:20; Jacob 7:23; Mosiah 2:4; Mormon 3:12). When Jesus was asked which is the great commandment in the law, "Jesus said unto him, Thou shalt love the Lord thy God with all thy heart, and with all thy soul, and with all thy mind. This is the first and great commandment. And the second is like unto it, Thou shalt love thy neighbor as thyself. On these two commandments hang all the law and the prophets" (Matthew 22:37–40).

Love the truth (2 Nephi 9:40). We must love the truth and no other doctrine, for therein we may find salvation and be made free (see John 8:32).

Lowliness of heart (1 Nephi 2:19; Alma 32:12; Moroni 8:26). To be humble and contrite of heart is a requirement of true repentance, a requirement to be a true saint of the Lord Jesus Christ, and a requirement to gain entrance to the kingdom of heaven. *Compare:* Puffed up. *See also:* Lowly in heart; Meek and humble; Poor in heart.

Lowly in heart (Alma 32:8; 37:33–34; Moroni 7:44). Meaning meek, humble, and contrite. *See also:* Lowliness of heart; Poor in heart.

Lucre which doth corrupt the soul (Mosiah 29:40; Alma 11:24). The word *lucre* is defined as money and gain of money. The scriptures say that the love of money is the root of all evil (see 1 Timothy 6:10). Seeking and obtaining money with obsession results in the sin of pride. *See also:* Seek not after riches; Mormon 8:37.

Lust after her (it) (1 Nephi 3:25; 3 Nephi 12:28). "He that looketh upon a woman to lust after her shall deny the faith, and shall not have the Spirit; and if he repents not he shall be cast out" (D&C 42:23). Concerning lusting after money and other things, the commandment states "Thou shalt not covet" (Exodus 20:17).

Luster was above that of the sun at noon-day (1 Nephi 1:9). Refers to the brilliant and exceeding brightness that surrounds and emanates from the presence of the Father and His Son. *See also:* Light of the glory of God; Shone with exceeding luster.

Lusts of the flesh (1 Nephi 22:23). "Abstain from fleshly lusts, which war against the soul" (1 Peter 2:11). Lusts of the flesh are part and parcel to mortality, and part of the test of mortality is to overcome them. The lusts of the flesh include craving desires for worldly things such as power, fame, and riches. Chief among lusts of the flesh are unbridled sexual appetites and lasciviousness. Lusts of the flesh are also any other pleasurable physical indulgences that are sinful. *See also:* Consume it on your lusts.

Lusts of your eyes (Alma 39:9). Means to look upon something and greatly desire it. *See also:* Lust after her (it).

Lying spirit (Alma 30:42). The lying spirit is the spirit of the devil. *See also:* Father of all lies.

Lyings and deceivings (Alma 16:18; 3 Nephi 1:22; 21:19; 30:2). "Thou shalt not bear false witness" is one of the Ten Commandments (Exodus 20:16). It is wickedness to lie or deceive. Satan, his minions, and wicked men go about lying, deceiving, and prompting people to do the same. *See also:* False swearers (witness); Father of all lies.

M

Made alive in Christ (2 Nephi 25:25). "For as in Adam all die, even so in Christ shall all be made alive" (1 Corinthians 15:22). *Made alive in Christ* not only refers to the Resurrection but to a high level of life, a fulness of life, and life eternal. *See also:* Alive in Christ.

Made an oath unto us (1 Nephi 4:33, 35, 37; Mosiah 19:25–26; 20:14, 22, 24; 21:3; Alma 44:8, 11; 48:13; 49:13, 17, 27; 50:39; 53:11, 14; 3 Nephi 3:8; Mormon 5:1). There are various places in the Book of Mormon where an oath, promise, or covenant is made among men or people, and they were honor-bound to keep these oaths. "The oath is the one thing that is most sacred and inviolable among the desert people and their descendants: 'Hardly will an Arab break his oath, even if his life be in jeopardy,' for 'there is nothing stronger, and nothing more sacred than the oath among the nomads,' and even the city Arabs, if it be exacted under special conditions. 'The taking of an oath is a holy thing with Bedouins,' says one authority, 'Woe to him who swears falsely; his social standing will be damaged and his reputation ruined. No one will receive his testimony, and he must also pay a money fine.'

"But not every oath will do. To be most binding and solemn an oath should be by the *life* of something, even if it be but a blade of grass. The only oath more awful than that 'by my life' or . . . 'by the life of my head,' is the . . . 'by the life of God,' or 'as the Lord Liveth.' . . .

"So we see that the only way that Nephi could possibly have pacified the struggling Zoram in an instant was to utter the one oath that no man would dream of breaking, the most solemn of all oaths to the Semite: 'As the Lord liveth, and as I live!' (Nibley, *An Approach to the Book of Mormon*, 104–5). *See also:* As the Lord (God) liveth (and as we live); Covenant of peace; Enter into a covenant; Entered into a covenant of peace; Swear before (by) the heavens; Swear unto him by the God of heaven and also by the heavens; Swear unto you with an oath; Swearing with an oath [men so swearing]; Sworn with an oath; Take(-n) an oath; Took an oath; With an oath.

Made bare his holy arm (Mosiah 12:24; 15:31; 3 Nephi 16:20; 20:35). This phrase means that God will reveal His power and majesty. It means to bring the judgments of God, which are just and holy, down upon the wicked and unrepentant. *See also:* Make bare his arm.

Made free (Mosiah 5:8; 23:13; Alma 58:40–41; 61:9, 21; Helaman 14:30; 15:8; 4 Nephi 1:3). Jesus Christ is He who has made it possible for us to be made free. By accepting His gospel and living steadfast in the faith, we are made free. *See also:* Free forever; Spirit of freedom; Under this head ye are made free.

Made intercession for the transgressors (Mosiah 14:12). *Intercession* means to plead on behalf of. Christ pleads on our behalf to apply mercy and forgiveness to all those that repent and come unto Christ. *Compare:* Isaiah 53:12. *See also:* Atonement of Christ (the Only Begotten Son).

Made known unto me (them/us/ you) (1 Nephi 13:41; 15:11; 22:2; 2 Nephi 10:2; 30:16; Mosiah 3:2; 8:17; Alma 5:46; 7:20; 9:20; 12:3, 30, 32; 13:23, 26; 18:39; 24:14; 36:5; 37:11, 26; 39:18; 40:11; 45:9; Helaman 16:5; 3 Nephi 1:14, 25; 16:7; 21:2–3; Mormon 5:8; Ether 8:20). God does not leave His children in the dark, not knowing the principles and ordinances of the gospel necessary for salvation. He has made known things by various ways and means, including scriptures, prophets, the Holy Ghost, and angels. *See also:* Angels minister(-ed/appeared/declared/ descending) unto him (them).

Made manifest (2 Nephi 3:5; 10:2; 30:17; Jacob 1:5; 7:12; Mosiah 8:17; Alma 37:21; 3 Nephi 26:9; 28:37; Mormon 9:31; Ether 4:2, 4, 14, 16). God makes manifest, reveals, and makes known all those things He sees as necessary and helpful to His children on earth. He has promised that in the future all things will be made manifest unto the faithful. He has also sworn that the secret and wicked acts of evil men will be made manifest, and the wicked will be punished for them if they do not repent. *See also:* Made known unto me (them/us/you); Mysteries of God.

Made strong (2 Nephi 3:13; 33:4; Ether 12:37). God has the power and the ability to strengthen and make strong all those individuals and things that He wills. *See also:* Make him (thee/them) mighty.

Made us clean (Alma 24:15; Ether 12:37). Through the atoning blood of our Savior, we can be made clean from our sins if we repent and come unto Christ. The people of King Benjamin prayed, "O have mercy, and apply the atoning blood of Christ that we may receive forgiveness of our sins, and our hearts may be purified; for we believe in Jesus Christ" (Mosiah 4:2). *See also:* Atoning blood of Jesus Christ.

Made white in the blood of the Lamb (1 Nephi 12:10–11; Alma 5:24, 27; 13:11–12; 34:36; Mormon 9:6). *See:* Atoning blood of Jesus Christ; Garments cleansed through the blood of the Lamb (made white/washed).

Magnify his holy name (2 Nephi 25:13). To enlarge or make great the honor and glory of God. Psalm 34:3 says, "O magnify the Lord with me, and let us exalt his name together."

Magnify mine (our) office (Jacob 1:19; 2:2). "President Thomas S. Monson put it this way for us, 'What does it mean to magnify [your] calling? It means to build it up in dignity . . . , to enlarge and strengthen it to let the light of heaven shine through it to the view of other men. And how does one magnify a calling? Simply by performing the service that pertains to it.' ['Priesthood Power,' *Ensign*, Nov. 1999, 51]" (Eyring, "Serve with the Spirit," 62).

Maintain their liberty (Alma 46:28; 48:10; 51:7; 58:12; 3 Nephi 2:12). It is right that people maintain, preserve, and uphold their liberty and freedoms. *See also:* Defend themselves; Land of liberty.

Maintain their rights (Alma 46:20; 51:6; 54:24; 3 Nephi 2:12). *See:* Defend themselves; Maintain their liberty.

Make a mock of his brother (Alma 5:30). It is an amplified attitude of pride to belittle others, and it is a grave sin. *See also:* Mock him (it/them).

Make a mock of the great plan of redemption (Jacob 6:8; Helaman 4:12). The wicked fight that which is truth and right by belittling and mocking it. They deny that there is a plan, or that portions of the plan are necessary, or that Jesus is the Redeemer. *See also:* Mock him (it/them).

Make an instrument of thee in my hands (Alma 17:11). *See:* Instrument in his (the/thy) hands (of God).

Make bare his arm (1 Nephi 22:10–11). In these contexts it means to bring about God's purposes and to proclaim the gospel to the earth. *See also:* Made bare his holy arm.

Make game of the Jews (3 Nephi 29:8). Refers to the persecution, hatred, rejection, and evil speaking of the Jews. *See also:* Hiss and a byword.

Make him (thee/them) mighty (1 Nephi 1:20; 17:32; 2 Nephi 3:17; Helaman 10:5; 3 Nephi 20:27). The Lord God has the power to make men and nations mighty in word and deed. *See also:* Made strong; Make strong.

Make intercession for the children of men (2 Nephi 2:9; Mosiah 15:8). *Intercession* means to act or mediate between two parties in order to bring about a reconciliation.

Thus Jesus Christ's Atonement intercedes in man's favor based upon man's faith and repentance to purify man that he may again enter the presence of God the Father. *See also:* Great Mediator; D&C 45:3–5.

Make (making) his (my) paths straight (1 Nephi 10:8; 2 Nephi 4:33; Alma 7:19). Make *His* paths straight refers to the Savior Jesus Christ and means to make oneself or a people ready to receive the Lord. Thus John the Baptist taught a preparatory message. The footnotes to these verses refer to Isaiah 40:3–4, "Prepare ye the way of the Lord, make straight in the desert a highway for our God. Every valley shall be exalted, and every mountain and hill shall be made low; and the crooked shall be made straight, and the rough places plain." This scripture gives light to the words "make straight" and also refers to the Second Coming. Secondly, in 2 Nephi 4:33, make *my* path straight refers to the prayer of the faithful wherein they petition the Lord for a less difficult and more clearly marked path to walk in life—the path that is the straight and narrow way to God. *See also:* Prepare (ye) the way of the Lord; Strait and narrow course (path).

Make strong (2 Nephi 3:21; Ether 12:27). *See:* Made strong.

Make thee (them) mighty (1 Nephi 1:20; 17:32; 2 Nephi 3:17; Helaman 10:5; 3 Nephi 20:27).

God has the ability and power to make us mighty beyond mortal ability. *See also:* Made strong; Make strong.

Make these things manifest (Alma 10:10). *See:* Made manifest.

Make up my jewels (3 Nephi 24:17). "Jewels are precious things. Thus the jewels of the Lord are the things which are precious to him—his righteous (obedient) sons and daughters.

""This is an expression . . . where "jewels" refers to the people of God, and where the meaning seems to be that when God segregates His people from the world, His power, as that of a monarch wearing a crown of jewels, will be made manifest to all men.' (Smith and Sjodahl, *DCC*, p. 358.)" (Ludlow, *A Companion to Your Study of the Doctrine and Covenants*, 1:324). Also found in Malachi 3:17; D&C 60:4; 101:3.

Maketh flesh his arm (2 Nephi 4:34; 28:31). "Thus saith the Lord; cursed be the man that trusteth in man, and maketh flesh his arm, and whose heart departeth from the Lord" (Jeremiah 17:5). We must not trust in the arm of flesh or men, rather we must trust in the mighty arm of God. *See also:* Arm of flesh.

Maketh these things known unto me (Alma 38:6). The things of God are revealed through revelation. When we have no faith in revelation, "The Lord maketh no such thing known unto us" (1 Nephi 15:9).

Man had fallen (Alma 22:12, 14). *See:* Fallen man.

Man of God (Mosiah 7:26; 23:14; Alma 2:30; 10:7; Helaman 3:29; 11:8, 18). One who keeps the laws and ordinances of God and does righteous works.

Man of no small reputation (perfect understanding) (Alma 10:4; 48:11). Referring to men who have done well in the sight of God and man. Someone has said "Your front yard is your personality, and your backyard is your character." 1 Samuel 16:7 says, "For man looketh on the outward appearance, but the Lord looketh on the heart."

Man of sorrows (Mosiah 14:3). A description of Jesus Christ, meaning He is familiar with and has experienced the earthly sorrows of men. *See also:* Acquainted with grief; Alma 7:11–12; Isaiah 53:3.

Manifest by the Spirit (1 Nephi 22:2; Jarom 1:4; Alma 5:46; Mormon 3:20). Meaning revealed and made known by the Holy Ghost. *See also:* Manifested unto me by his angel (Holy Spirit).

Manifest himself in the flesh (2 Nephi 6:9; 25:12; 32:6; Enos 1:8). Meaning that God Himself, Jesus Christ, will come down to earth at the meridian of time, take upon Himself a body of flesh, and minister among men. *See also:* Form of a man [God/Jesus Christ]; Take upon him flesh and blood; Take upon him the form (image) of man.

Manifest himself unto them in power and great glory (2 Nephi 6:14). *See:* Coming of Christ; In power and great glory.

Manifest himself unto them in word, and also in power, in very deed (1 Nephi 13:42; 14:1). In the latter days if the Gentiles will accept the gospel of Jesus Christ, He will manifest Himself unto them. They will have true doctrine, they will have the priesthood, and they will see the kingdom of God roll forth as a great stone cut out of the mountain.

Manifest in very deed (Ether 4:16). Refers to the prophecies of John the Revelator, which prophecies will begin to be revealed and fulfilled when the Book of Mormon comes forth. Prophecies of John the Beloved as recorded in the book of Revelation were manifest and made known by the Prophet Joseph Smith, an example of which is found in D&C 77.

Manifested unto me by his angel (Holy Spirit) (1 Nephi 2:17; Jacob 4:13; 7:12; Alma 5:46; 10:10; 3 Nephi 28:37; Mormon 3:20). Meaning revealed by the power of the Holy Ghost. *See also:* Manifest by the Spirit.

Manifestation of the Spirit (1 Nephi 2:17; 22:2; Mosiah 5:3;

Alma 5:47; 7:17; Mormon 3:16, 20; Ether 4:11; Moroni 10:4, 8). One of the principal roles of the Holy Ghost is to be a revelator to men and women on earth. "And behold, there were divers ways that he did manifest things unto the children of men" (Moroni 7:24). "Believe and repent of your sins and be baptized in the name of Jesus Christ, the Son of God, even as our fathers, and ye shall receive the Holy Ghost, that ye may have all things made manifest" (Moses 8:24).

Manner of happiness (2 Nephi 5:27). After the many trials and tribulations Nephi and his people had experienced, and after they had split off away from Laman and Lemuel, Nephi established a righteous people who kept the commandments and served God. Thus Nephi and his people began to experience some peace, prosperity, and happiness. They had joy and happiness amid their afflictions, and they were grateful for it. *See also:* Find peace to my soul.

Manner of the (things of the) Jews (2 Nephi 25:1–2, 5–6; Alma 11:4; 16:13). Meaning the traditions, measures, buildings, regions, wickedness, and prophecies of the Jews in Jerusalem. *See also:* Learning (things) of the Jews.

Mansions of my (thy) Father (Enos 1:27; Ether 12:32, 34, 37). The places of abode prepared for the righteous in heaven. *See also:* Kingdom of heaven.

Many (mighty) miracles (1 Nephi 17:51; Mosiah 15:6; Alma 26:12; 37:40; Helaman 16:23; 3 Nephi 7:20; 8:1; 4 Nephi 1:29; Mormon 9:18). *See:* God of miracles.

Many (more) witnesses (2 Nephi 11:3; 27:14; Jacob 4:6; Mosiah 26:9; Alma 30:45; 34:30, 33). Often in the scriptures God has declared that His word would be established in the mouths of two or three witnesses. "Wherefore, by the words of three, God hath said, I will establish my word. Nevertheless, God sendeth more witnesses, and he proveth all his words" (2 Nephi 11:3). *See also:* Testimony of many (two or three).

Many plain and precious things (1 Nephi 13:26, 28–29, 34–35, 40). Refers to that which has been omitted from the Bible as we have it today. The Prophet Joseph Smith said, "I believe the Bible as it read when it came from the pen of the original writers. Ignorant translators, careless transcribers, or designing and corrupt priests have committed many errors" (*Teachings of the Prophet Joseph Smith*, 327).

Many prophecies of the holy prophets (1 Nephi 5:13; 13:23; 19:1; 2 Nephi 4:2; Words of Mormon 1:4; Helaman 6:14; 3 Nephi 10:14). *See:* According to God's word; Prophecies of the holy prophets; Prophecies which had been spoken; Spirit of prophecy (and revelation).

Many prophets (1 Nephi 1:4; Enos 1:22; Helaman 8:19; Ether 11:1, 12, 20). The Lord sends many prophets to call people to repentance and to testify of Jesus Christ.

Marred because of them (3 Nephi 20:44; 21:10). The first verse refers to Isaiah's prophecy (Isaiah 52:12–15) about the Savior's crucifixion and the cruel way His physical body was put to death. *Marred* meaning spoiled, damaged, and harmed. Yet the Lord arose from the dead, triumphant over death and sin. The second verse refers to Joseph Smith who would also be marred or martyred.

Marvel not (Jacob 4:12; Mosiah 27:25; Helaman 5:49; 3 Nephi 15:3). Meaning question or doubt not, but have faith.

Marvelous are the works of the Lord (1 Nephi 1:14; Jacob 4:8; Mosiah 8:20). The Lord God can perform miracles, wonders, acts both great and small, and accomplish anything He desires. Some of His works are miraculous and others are unnoticed by man. All are for the purpose to bring to pass the immortality and eternal life of man (see Moses 1:39). *See also:* Marvelous things (works).

Marvelous light of God (Mosiah 27:29; Alma 19:6; 26:3; 36:20). Light is of God, and all light emanates from God. The light of God shows us the way. Light is truth, and we can progress towards and be blessed to be full of light. Jesus is the light of the world (see John 8:12), and he that followeth Him shall not walk in darkness. Light brings joy to our souls. *See also:* Brought into (to/unto) the everlasting (marvelous) light; Brought out of darkness unto light; Everlasting light; Full of light; I am the light; Illuminated by the light of the everlasting word; Light and the life (and truth) of the world; Light in the wilderness; Light of Christ; Light of everlasting life (word); Light unto them (forever); Walk in the light of the Lord.

Marvelous power of God (Mosiah 1:13; Alma 10:5; 57:26). God's power is indeed marvelous, remarkable, wonderful, extraordinary, and superb, especially in comparison to man's finite, weak, and feeble power. *See also:* All power; Power of God.

Marvelous things (works) (1 Nephi 1:14, 18; 2 Nephi 1:10; 4:17; Alma 9:5–6; 37:41; Helaman 9:2; 16:16; 3 Nephi 17:16–17; 26:14, 16; 28:31, 33; Mormon 7:9; 8:34; 9:16; Ether 4:15; 11:20; 12:5). *See:* Marvelous are the works of the Lord.

Marvelous work and a wonder (1 Nephi 14:7; 22:8; 2 Nephi 25:17; 27:26; 29:1; Alma 26:15; 3 Nephi 21:9; 28:32). This refers to the restoration of the true gospel of Jesus Christ in the latter days.

Master of sin (Mosiah 4:14). Meaning the devil who is Satan, who is the master of all evil.

Matchless (miraculous) power (1 Nephi 17:42; Mosiah 1:13; 2:11; 4:6; Alma 9:11; 49:28; 57:26; Helaman 4:25). God's power is marvelous and wonderful to behold, and no other has the great and complete power that God has, therefore He is matchless (without peer) in His power. *See also:* Marvelous power of God.

May (must/shall) be fulfilled (1 Nephi 7:13; 15:18; 17:3; 2 Nephi 9:17; 10:15; 25:7, 21, 24, 30; Mosiah 21:4; Alma 5:57–58; 7:11; 13:26; 30:3; 34:13; 37:24; 45:14; Helaman 11:8; 16:13–14; 3 Nephi 1:4–5, 25; 5:1, 14, 25; 15:6; 16:17; 20:11–12, 46; 21:4; 28:7, 29; 29:1, 2; Mormon 8:22, 33; Moroni 10:31). *See:* According to God's word.

Meek and humble (Mosiah 3:19; Alma 13:28; 37:33; Helaman 6:39). Meaning humble, mild, gentle, peaceful, submissive, lowly, and modest. *See also:* Broken heart(-s) and (a) contrite spirit(-s); Contrite spirit; In the depth(-s) of humility; Lowliness of heart; Meekness and lowliness of heart.

Meek and lowly in (of) heart (Alma 37:33, 34; Moroni 7:43). *See:* Meek and humble; Meekness and lowliness of heart.

Meek of the earth (2 Nephi 21:4; 30:9; 3 Nephi 12:5). The Lord has decreed that the meek of the earth shall inherit it (Matthew 5:5; 3 Nephi 12:5).

Meekness and lowliness of heart (1 Nephi 2:19; Alma 32:12; Moroni 8:26). Our Savior, Jesus Christ, is the personification of meekness and lowliness of heart. In D&C 19:23 the Lord says, "Learn of me and listen to my words; walk in the meekness of my Spirit, and you shall have peace in me." The gospel of Jesus Christ can be lived and enjoyed by the meekest and lowliest of heart, and the proud must come down into humility to have the blessings of the gospel. Happiness and peace only come from a contrite acceptance of Jesus Christ and by submitting to His will for us. *See also:* Meek and humble; Meek and lowly in (of) heart.

Meet for repentance (Alma 5:54; 9:30; 12:15; 13:13). Footnote *a* in Matthew 3:8 defines "meet" as "appropriate to or worthy of." Thus we must bring forth faith and works or actions that are appropriate to, worthy of, exemplary of, and deserving of repentance. *See also:* Bring(-eth/brought) forth fruit (works which are) meet for repentance.

Men of God (Alma 48:18). Those that keep the commandments, do the will of God, and have strived to gain the approval of God.

Men of perfect (sound) understanding (Mosiah 1:2; Alma 17:2; 48:11). The Spirit imparts to us a sound and perfect understanding which is the understanding of God and is a gift from God. True and just men begin to ascend unto a more God-like understanding. Sinful men begin to lose sound understanding until after much sinning they have little or no righteous understanding. The popular TV show *World's Dumbest Criminals* is an example where sinning causes the loss of even common sense. Keeping the commandments entitles us to the constant companionship of the Holy Ghost to guide our lives aright. Thus it shows that keeping the commandments enhances our common sense as well as our understanding.

Mercies and long-suffering of the Lord (Mormon 2:12). *See:* Merciful God (Being).

Mercies of Christ (God/the Father/ the Holy One of Israel/the Lord/ thy Son) (1 Nephi 1:20; 2 Nephi 1:2; 9:25; Alma 26:28; 33:16; 34:38; 3 Nephi 16:9; 22:7; Mormon 2:12; Ether 6:12; Moroni 8:19–20, 23). *See:* Merciful God (Being).

Merciful arm (Alma 29:10). Not only is the arm of God powerful and great, it offers mercy and assistance. The Lord says, "I shall lengthen out mine arm unto them from day to day . . . for mine arm is lengthened out all the day long" (2 Nephi 28:32). *See also:* Arm (of mercy) is extended (towards you

in the light of day); Merciful God (Being).

Merciful for that which is merciful (Alma 41:13–14; 3 Nephi 12:7). Those that are merciful to their fellowmen will be blessed with an added measure of mercy from God. One of the Beatitudes says, "Blessed are the merciful: for they shall obtain mercy" (Matthew 5:7).

Merciful God (Being) (1 Nephi 1:14; 2 Nephi 10:20; Alma 26:17, 35; 33:4; 42:15; 50:19). God the Father and His Son, Jesus Christ, are merciful beings. Because of their great mercy they will freely and gladly forgive us our sins if we humbly repent. God is "full of mercy" and desires to exercise that mercy in our behalf if we will again only humble ourselves, believe in Him, and repent. His arm of mercy is extended to man all the day long. *See also:* According to God's (thy abundant) mercy; According to thy abundant mercy; Arm (of mercy) is extended (towards you in the light of day); God is merciful; Great plan of mercy; How merciful (and just) are all the dealings of the Lord; How merciful God (the Lord) hath been (is); I will be merciful unto them; Lord in (his great) mercy; Lord is (was/will be) merciful; Mercies of Christ (God/the Father/ the Holy One of Israel/the Lord/thy Son); Merciful arm; Merciful is our God; Merciful unto them (us/you); Thou art merciful.

Merciful is our God (Jacob 6:4; Alma 24:15). *See:* Merciful God (Being).

Merciful plan of the great Creator (2 Nephi 9:6). *See:* Great plan of mercy.

Merciful unto them (us/you) (1 Nephi 8:37; 13:33–34; 19:20; 2 Nephi 1:3; 4:7; 6:11; 10:2; 23:22; 28:32; Jacob 3:6; 6:4; Jarom 1:3; Mosiah 24:21; Alma 9:16–17; 12:15; 24:14–15; 26:35; 32:22; 33:5, 8–9, 11; 50:19; Helaman 3:27; 7:24; 15:12; 3 Nephi 5:21; Mormon 2:12; Ether 3:3; 9:2; 13:7; Moroni 10:3). These are the many examples of where God and Christ have been merciful to men and women. *See also:* Merciful God (Being).

Mercy and grace of God (2 Nephi 2:8; 9:8, 53; Alma 5:48). *See:* Full of grace (equity/mercy) and truth; Grace of God; Merciful God (Being).

Mercy and justice of God (2 Nephi 2:12; 3 Nephi 26:5). *See:* Justice and mercy (of God); Merciful God (Being).

Mercy and long-suffering toward the children of men (Alma 5:6; 9:11, 26; 26:16; 42:30; Moroni 9:25). *Long-suffering towards men* means to put up with and endure the sinfulness of men and women. God knows well the human mortal state and what it entails, thus He will wait a little longer for us to repent. But we must not procrastinate,

for His coming is nigh, even at the doors. *See also:* Merciful God (Being).

Mercy and power of God (Alma 5:4). In mortal men and women these two characteristics are rarely found together. Yet God is coexistent in His having great mercy and great power. *See also:* Full of grace (equity/mercy) and truth; Merciful God (Being); All power; Power of God.

Mercy claimeth the penitent (Alma 42:22–24). Mercy saves us from justice and the consequences of our sins if we repent. *See also:* Merciful God (Being).

Merits of Christ (him who is mighty to save/his son/the Holy Messiah) (2 Nephi 2:8; 31:19; Alma 24:10; Moroni 6:4). *See:* Relying upon the merits of Christ.

Messenger of the covenant (3 Nephi 24:1). Another name or title for Jesus Christ. He is the messenger of the covenant that brings salvation. Thus as in D&C 93:8 a similar name for Jesus is the Messenger of Salvation. The Father said unto Malachi that He would "send the messenger of the covenant" (Malachi 3:1) to bring the good news of salvation (the covenant of the Father) and to work out the Atonement of man.

Messiah shall (who should) come (1 Nephi 10:11, 17; 2 Nephi

26:3; Jarom 1:11). *See:* Christ shall (should) come; Coming of Christ.

Might, mind, and strength (2 Nephi 25:29; Mosiah 2:11; Alma 39:13; Moroni 10:32). *See:* All your might, mind, and strength.

Mightier than all the earth (1 Nephi 4:1). The Lord God is the creator of all the earth and everything therein, therefore He has power over all the earth and everything therein. The power of all the men, nations, and armies of earth are puny compared to the mighty power of our God. He could destroy them all with one sweep of His arm, and at His Second Coming He will destroy all wickedness from the earth with fire. *See also:* Power of God.

Mighty change wrought in his (their/your) heart (Mosiah 5:2; Alma 5:12–14). A life-altering transformation brought about in one's heart, mind, spirit, and soul. It is a change from carnality to goodness. *See also:* Change of heart.

Mighty God (2 Nephi 6:17; 19:6; 20:21). *Mighty* as in powerful and strong, being strong without peer. *See also:* Power of God.

Mighty in judgment (Ether 7:8). Meaning great and fully capable with perfect judgment. *See also:* Judgments are just.

Mighty in word (2 Nephi 3:24; Helaman 10:5; Ether 12:23). A gift from God caused by being filled with the Holy Ghost such that one's words carry great power and cannot be refuted. *Compare:* Mighty in writing. *See also:* Spake (speak/taught) with power and authority from God.

Mighty in writing (Ether 12:23–24). A gift from God. Evidently the brother of Jared was mighty in writing, "For thou [God] madest him that the things which he wrote were mighty even as thou [God] art, unto the overpowering of man to read them" (Ether 12:24).

Mighty miracles (2 Nephi 10:4; 26:13; Mosiah 3:5; 8:18; 15:6; Alma 26:12; 4 Nephi 1:13, 30; Mormon 9:18; Moroni 10:12). Such miracles include "healing the sick, raising the dead, causing the lame to walk, the blind to receive their sight, and the deaf to hear, and curing all manner of diseases"; also "cast out devils" (Mosiah 3:5–6).

Mighty one of Israel (Jacob) (1 Nephi 21:26; 22:12; 2 Nephi 6:18). One of the many great names for Jesus Christ. *Compare:* Isaiah 1:24; 30:29; 49:26; 60:16.

Mighty power (Mosiah 8:16; 13:34; 23:24; Alma 17:36; 56:56). God has mighty, extraordinary, and unlimited power. On occasion God grants men unusual and greater than normal power. *See also:* All power; Power of God.

Mighty prayer (2 Nephi 4:24; Enos 1:4; Alma 6:6; 8:10; 3 Nephi 27:1;

Moroni 2:2). Suggests sincere and powerful prayer that is directed by the Spirit and thus is according to the will of God. *See also:* Bow(-ed) down himself to the earth; Cried unto him in mighty prayer; Cry mightily to God (the Father/the Lord); Drawn out (in prayer) unto the Lord; Much fasting and prayer; Pour(-ed/-ing) out his soul in prayer unto God; Pray(-ed) mightily; Prayed with many long strugglings.

Mighty to save (2 Nephi 31:19; Alma 7:14; 34:18). Meaning having the power to save and completely capable of saving us. *See also:* He has all power to save; Infinite atonement; Save the world from sin.

Mighty wonders (2 Nephi 3:24; 26:13). *Wonders* is another word for miracles. *See also:* Mighty miracles.

Mighty works (Alma 19:4; Helaman 15:15, 17). The miracles, signs, and wonders of God. In the New Testament it speaks of the mighty works that Jesus did. Mighty works are done by the power of the priesthood and are performed by righteous followers of Christ, not for show but to bring about the kingdom of God. *See also:* Mighty miracles.

Minds are firm (Jacob 3:2; Alma 57:27; Moroni 7:30). Meaning firm in the faith and having a determination to choose the right. Also unshaken, having a testimony founded on strong faith. Minds able

to withstand temptation and tribulation. *See also:* Firm in the faith of Christ.

Mine ancient covenant people (2 Nephi 29:4–5). *See:* Ancient (and long dispersed) covenant people; Children of Israel; Covenant people (of the Lord).

Mine arm is lengthened out (2 Nephi 28:32). God has promised that He will reach far out and down from heaven to aid, assist, and bless His penitent and humble children. *See also:* Lengthen out mine arm.

Mine arm of mercy is extended towards you (Jacob 6:5; Alma 19:36; 29:10; 3 Nephi 9:14). *See:* Lengthen out mine arm; Merciful God (Being).

Mine eyes hath beheld (2 Nephi 4:25; 16:5; 25:5). The prophets have been shown many great and marvelous things in vision, and because of what they have seen they testify that God lives and reveals to man according to His will.

Mine own due time (2 Nephi 27:21; 3 Nephi 20:29; Ether 3:27). *See:* Own due time (of the Lord).

Mine own pleasure (2 Nephi 29:9). Pleasure here means according to God's desires and wants, which are perfect. *See also:* According to God's will; According to his will and pleasure.

Mine own purpose (Jacob 5:36, 53–54). God has His purposes (which are not the same as man's purposes), and God will accomplish His purposes with His perfect knowledge and great power. "For my thoughts are not your thoughts, neither are your ways my ways, saith the Lord" (Isaiah 55:8).

Mine own wisdom (2 Nephi 27:22). *See:* Wisdom in (of) God (the Lord/ the Father).

Minister one to another (3 Nephi 26:19). *See:* Minister unto him (them).

Minister unto him (them) (1 Nephi 11:30; 13:35; Alma 22:23; 35:7, 9; 3 Nephi 7:18; 17:24; 18:30; 19:14– 15; 23:9, 11; 26:14; Ether 3:18, 20; Moroni 7:30). Angels and the servants of God minister spiritually and physically to the needs and righteous desires of men and women. *See also:* Administer(-ed) unto him (them).

Minister unto the (this) people (Helaman 5:50; 3 Nephi 13:25; 19:7; 28:18, 29). *See:* Minister unto him (them).

Minister with power and great authority (3 Nephi 7:17). The true servants of God are given great power to minister to and teach the people. *See also:* Authority from (of) God; Command in the name of Jesus; Go forth in power [servants of the Lord]; Great power; Power and authority from (of) God; Preach with great power and authority; Spake (speak/taught) with power and authority from God; Speak with power; Taught (teach) with power and authority of God; With power and authority.

Ministered unto (1 Nephi 15:14; 16:38; 2 Nephi 4:24; Jacob 7:5; Helaman 5:48; 3 Nephi 19:2, 7, 15; 28:26; Mormon 8:11; Ether 3:18). Meaning to have been taught, visited, comforted, preached to, blessed, healed, and instructed by messengers from God or servants called of God. *See also:* Minister unto him (them).

Ministering of angels (2 Nephi 4:24; Jacob 7:5, 17; Omni 1:25; 3 Nephi 19:15; Moroni 7:25). "The ministering of angels [is] the very power of heavenly beings to guide you, to protect you, to bless you" (Hinckley, "Priesthood of Aaron," 45).

Ministering spirits (Moroni 10:14). *See:* Ministering of angels.

Ministering unto the people (1 Nephi 11:28; 3 Nephi 10:19). Witness that Jesus ministered unto the people. He was the perfect example of how to minister in love, in power, and with the perfect blessing.

Miracles wrought among them (1 Nephi 17:51; 2 Nephi 10:4; 28:6; Alma 26:12; 37:40; Helaman 16:23; 3 Nephi 1:4; 21:5; 28:31–32; 29:7; 4 Nephi 1:5, 13, 29; Mormon 7:9; 9:16–19; Ether 12:15–16, 18; Moroni 7:37). Meaning miracles accomplished and revealed to men. *See also:* God of miracles.

Miserable forever (2 Nephi 2:5, 18; Alma 12:26; 42:11; Mormon 9:4). *See:* Eternal torment.

Misery of the soul (Alma 40:15). *See:* Endless misery (and wo).

Misery which never dies (Mormon 8:38). *See:* Endless misery (and wo); Eternal torment.

Mist(-s) of darkness [during the great destruction by God] (1 Nephi 12:4–5; 3 Nephi 8:22). It is the darkness that covered the land for three days while the Savior lay in the tomb, and this darkness was so dark that no light could penetrate it.

Mist(-s) of darkness [in Lehi's dream] (1 Nephi 8:23–24; 12:17). Defined in Lehi's dream as being the temptations of the devil. In other words, the worldly temptations and interests that divert men and women from the path that leads back to God. *See also:* Yield to no temptation.

Mock him (it/them) (1 Nephi 1:19; Jacob 6:8; Alma 5:30; 14:22; 21:10; Helaman 4:12; 13:24; Ether 7:24; 12:23, 25–26). It is ungodly and evil to mock, belittle, ridicule, scorn, and treat with contempt, for such contention is not of God but is of Satan. Rather, saints should lift up, assist with patience, praise all that is good, and bear with humility the trials of mortality. *See also:* Spirit of contention.

Mockery before God (Moroni 8:9, 23). Because little children are innocent and without sin before God, it is mockery/a farce/a belittlement of the sacred ordinance of baptism to say little children require it. *See also:* Make a mock of the great plan of redemption.

More excellent hope (Ether 12:32). The more excellent hope, more than any other hope, is a hope and faith in Christ. *See also:* Hope and views of Christ; Hope for salvation; Hope in Christ; Hope through the atonement of Christ.

More excellent way (Ether 12:11). The more excellent way, more than any other way, is to come unto Christ, follow Him, and live His gospel completely. Jesus said, "I am the way, the truth, and the life: no man cometh unto the Father but by me" (John 14:6).

More righteous part of the people who were saved (3 Nephi 10:12). *See:* Spared because ye were more righteous than they.

More than man can suffer (Mosiah 3:7). "For behold, I, God, have suffered these things for all, that they might not suffer if they would repent; but if they would not repent they must suffer even as I; which suffering caused myself, even God, the greatest of all, to tremble because of pain, and to bleed at every pore, and to suffer both body and spirit—and would that I might not drink the bitter cup, and shrink—nevertheless, glory be to the Father, and I partook and finished my preparations unto the children of men" (D&C 19:16–19).

More than one witness (Alma 10:12). *See:* Testimony of many (two or three).

Mortal body (Mosiah 4:6; 18:13; Alma 5:15; 11:45; 40:11). Meaning this physical, temporal body of flesh and blood. *See also:* Temporal body; Flesh and blood.

Mortal body raised in immortality (Alma 5:15; 11:45). Refers to the Resurrection from death brought about by the Resurrection and redemption of Jesus Christ. *See also:* Immortal body.

Mortal shall put on immortality (Enos 1:27; Mosiah 16:10; Alma 40:2; Mormon 6:21). Affirming that there will be a resurrection for all men and women who have lived on the earth. For then we will become immortal, to live forever. *See also:* Immortal body.

Most abominable (1 Nephi 13:5, 26; Alma 39:5; Ether 8:18). Meaning most wicked, abhorrent, offensive, contemptible, and despicable. *See also:* Abominable above all sins save it be the shedding of innocent blood or denying the Holy Ghost; Abominable in the sight of the Lord; Doings of abominations; Sin appeareth (was very) abominable.

Most High God (1 Nephi 11:6; Alma 26:14; 3 Nephi 4:32; 11:17). As can be seen in these verses, this is

a title that can apply equally to God the Father or to Jesus Christ.

Mother of abominations (1 Nephi 14:9, 10, 13, 16). Another name for the great and abominable church, because it participates in all manner of wickedness. *Compare:* Revelation 17:5; D&C 88:94. *See also:* Great and abominable church.

Mother of harlots (1 Nephi 13:34; 14:16–17). Another name for the great and abominable church, because it participates in all manner of wickedness. In Revelation 17:5, Babylon the great is referred to as "the mother of harlots and abominations of the earth." *Babylon* is the word used figuratively to represent the evil of the world. "Babylon was known as the center of iniquity, carnality, and worldliness. Everything connected with it was in opposition to all righteousness and had the effect of leading men downward to the destruction of their souls" (McConkie, *Mormon Doctrine*, 69). *See also:* Great and abominable church.

Mount Zion (2 Nephi 14:5; 18:18; 20:12; 27:3). "These are they who are come unto Mount Zion, and unto the city of the living God, the heavenly place, the holiest of all" (D&C 76:66).

Mountain of the Lord(-'s house) (2 Nephi 12:2–3). Refers to the temple. The holy habitation of the Lord God, even where He dwells, and where saints may come and approach Him to learn of His ways. "Many biblical passages refer to the temple not as built on a hill or mountain, but as the hill or mountain of the Lord. . . . 'It was His dwelling place, a place of effectual fervent prayer, and the place from which He, God, Himself would answer His people and dwell among them. . . . God's earthly temple paralleled a heavenly temple'" (Skinner, "Seeing God in His Temple"). *See also:* Get thee into the mountain; Psalm 48:1; Isaiah 2:3; 30:29; Jeremiah 31:23; Ezekiel 20:40; Daniel 9:20; Micah 4:1–2; Zechariah 8:3.

Mourning and howling (lamentation/prayer/sorrow/wailing/weeping) (Mosiah 21:9; Alma 28:4; 30:2; Helaman 7:15; 3 Nephi 8:23; 10:10; Mormon 2:11–12). In these verses the people are mourning and expressing great sorrow because of the death and destruction among them. Also there is mourning by the righteous because of the wickedness among the people. "And now surely this was a sorrowful day; yea, a time of solemnity, and a time for much fasting and prayer" (Alma 28:6).

Moved with compassion (Alma 27:4; 53:13). Meaning to deeply feel compassion, empathy, mercy, sympathy, and tenderness. *See also:* Bowels are (may be) filled with compassion (mercy); Bowels of mercy; Heart did swell; Lord had compassion upon him (them/you).

Much fasting and prayer (Alma 17:3; 28:6). Fasting intensifies prayer. Much fasting and prayer is perhaps an indication of our earnestness and faith. If we give up with only a small amount of fasting and prayer, maybe we gave up hope and had no faith in results. Enos fasted and prayed all day and into the night (Enos 1:4). *See also:* Mighty prayer.

Much tribulation (2 Nephi 2:1; Mosiah 27:10, 32; Alma 8:14). *See:* Bear afflictions (with patience).

Multitude of his tender mercies (1 Nephi 8:8; Ether 6:12). God possesses all possible mercy towards His children, but that mercy is tempered by justice. *See also:* Justice of God; Tender mercies of the Lord.

Multitude of the promises (4 Nephi 1:11). *See:* Promises of the Lord.

Multitude of their terrible ones (2 Nephi 26:18). Refers to the armies of the world.

Murdered the prophets (Alma 37:30; 3 Nephi 7:6; Ether 8:25). *See:* Kill the prophets.

Murmur against the Lord (1 Nephi 16:20; 18:16). To *murmur* is to complain, protest, gripe, criticize, and whine. It is bad enough to participate in these negative emotions and actions, but to do so against God is a most serious sin. If not corrected very soon one will find oneself on the road to apostasy. *See also:* Began to murmur.

Murmur because of the truth (1 Nephi 16:3). *See:* Began to murmur; Murmur against the Lord.

Must be fulfilled (1 Nephi 7:13; 17:3; 2 Nephi 9:17; Alma 5:58; 3 Nephi 1:25; 5:1; Mormon 8:33). The word of God must be fulfilled, and not one word of what He has spoken will pass away and not come to pass. *See also:* According to God's word.

Must come to pass (1 Nephi 17:43; 19:12; 2 Nephi 28:1; 31:1; Jacob 6:1; Words of Mormon 1:4; 3 Nephi 28:31, 33; Mormon 5:8). Every word of God will with perfect certainty be fulfilled. A strict and absolute accounting of God's word is maintained. None of His words are without merit, and all His words must be obeyed. *See also:* According to God's word.

Must obey (2 Nephi 1:27; 33:15). In reality we all must obey, otherwise we will suffer the consequences. The more we come to understand the plan of God, and as our faith and testimony increase, the more we readily and consistently comprehend that we must obey. We obey because we love God and desire His blessing.

My calling to the ministry (Jacob 2:3; Alma 29:13; Moroni 7:2; 8:1). *See:* His calling unto me.

My church (Mosiah 26:22, 28; 27:13; 3 Nephi 18:5, 16; 27:8, 21; Mormon 3:2). The Lord affirms His Church, thus we know God has a church on earth, and He directs that church. These verses indicate that the members of the Church are His sheep, that baptism into the Church is necessary, the sacrament is administered in the Church, we are to pray in church, the name of the Church is stated, what works are to be done in the Church, and that we are to build up the Church. *See also:* Church of Christ; True church (of Christ).

My grace is sufficient (Ether 12:26–27). The meek and the humble will receive of the grace of the Lord. And that grace is fully capable to bless them. *See also:* Grace of God.

My heart doth magnify his holy name (2 Nephi 25:13). In Luke 1:46 it reads, "My soul doth magnify the Lord." *Magnify* means to enlarge, increase, amplify, add to, and augment. Thus Nephi glories in his God and desires to make known the knowledge of the Lord to all the world.

My holy mountain (2 Nephi 21:9; 30:15). *See:* Holy mountain.

My joy is full (great) (Alma 7:17; 26:11, 35, 37; 29:13, 16; 3 Nephi 17:20; 27:30). *See:* Filled with joy.

My own received me not (3 Nephi 9:16). Meaning the Jews, amongst whom Jesus was born in mortality, did not accept Him as the Savior and King.

My people who are of the covenant (2 Nephi 29:5; Mosiah 24:13; 3 Nephi 15:8; 16:11; 20:22, 29, 46; 21:7, 11). *See:* Ancient (and long dispersed) covenant people; Covenant people (of the Lord).

My rock and my salvation (1 Nephi 13:36; 15:15; 2 Nephi 4:35). Jesus is our rock and our salvation. Those that have faith in Jesus can thus exclaim, "He is my rock and my salvation." Jesus is our rock because He is the sure foundation for our life. Jesus is our salvation because He provided for our redemption. *See also:* Built upon my rock; Rock of my (their/your) salvation.

My sheep (Mosiah 26:20–21; 3 Nephi 15:24; 16:3; 18:31). The Lord's sheep are known to Him, and they are numbered unto Him. Additionally, the Lord's sheep know His voice, and they follow Him. *See also:* Good Shepherd.

My soul delighteth (2 Nephi 4:15–16; 11:2, 4–6; 25:4–5, 13; 31:3). *Delighteth* means to cherish, treasure, prize, value, and enjoy. Thus Nephi delighted in many things, including the scriptures; the things of God; the words of Isaiah; the coming of Christ; the Lord's grace, justice, power, and mercy; and in prophecy and truth. *See also:* Isaiah 42:1; D&C 25:12.

My soul did rest (Enos 1:17). *See:* Enter into his (my/the) rest (of the Lord/of God).

My soul hungered (Enos 1:4). Meaning the soul sought after spiritual knowledge, sustenance, and assurance. *See:* Feasting upon the word of Christ.

My soul is filled with joy (1 Nephi 1:15; 8:12; Alma 29:10; 36:20). *See:* Filled with joy.

My time is at hand (3 Nephi 17:1). In this occurrence it means that the time is soon that He must leave them. *See also:* At hand.

My will (Jacob 5:75; Helaman 10:4–5; 15:17). God's will is the one and only true will. We must seek to know and do God's will. We must not ask contrary to God's will. If we do not the will of God, we will be damned.

My wisdom is greater than the cunning of the devil (3 Nephi 21:10). God has assured us that He has more power, knowledge, and wisdom than Satan (see 1 John 3:8). Also we are assured that in the end the devil and his minions will be banished to outer darkness, and they will no longer be allowed access to us. *See also:* Power of Satan; D&C 10:43; 29:28–29; 88:114.

Mysteries of God (1 Nephi 1:1; 2:16; 10:19; Jacob 4:8; Mosiah 1:3, 5; 2:9; Alma 10:5; 12:9–11; 26:22; 37:4; 40:3). The knowledge of God and of eternal things promised to those who seek them in righteousness. The mysteries of God include the ways of God, the precepts of God, the commandments of God, and the nature of God. In order to "be ye perfect" even as God, we must know what God is like so that we can pattern ourselves after Him. Alma 12:10–11 says, "He that will harden his heart, the same receiveth the lesser portion of the word; and he that will not harden his heart, to him is given the greater portion of the word, until it is given unto him to know the mysteries of God until he know them in full. And they that will harden their hearts, to them is given the lesser portion of the word until they know nothing concerning his mysteries" (see also Joseph Smith–History 1:74; D&C 76:7–10).

Elder John Taylor commented, "We know in part, and see in part, and comprehend in part; and many of the things of God are hid from our view, both things that are past, things that are present, and things that are to come. Hence the world in general sit in judgment upon the actions of God that are passing among them, they make use of the weak judgment that God has given them to scan the designs of God, to unravel the mysteries that are past, and things that are still hid, forgetting that no man knows the things of God but by the Spirit of God; forgetting that the wisdom of this world is foolishness with God; forgetting that no man in and of himself is competent to unravel the designs and know the purposes of Jehovah, whether in relation to the past, present, or future; and hence, forgetting this, they fall into all kinds of blunders; they blunder over things that are contained in the Scriptures, some of which are a representation of the follies and weaknesses of men, and some of them perhaps may be the wisdom and the intelligence of God, that are as far above their wisdom and intelligence as the heavens are above the earth" (*Journal of Discourses*, 1:369–70).

Note also the warning in Alma 12:9, "It is given unto many to know the mysteries of God; nevertheless they are laid under a strict command that they shall not impart only according to the portion of his word which he doth grant unto the children of men." *See also:* Greater things.

Mysterious and marvelous power of the Lord (Jacob 4:8; Alma 10:5). *See:* Marvelous power of God; Mysteries of God.

N

Name by which he is (ye are/ye shall be) called (Mosiah 1:11–12; 5:8–9, 12, 14; 25:23; 26:18, 24; Alma 5:38–39; 46:15; 3 Nephi 27:5; Moroni 4:3). Believers and followers of Christ shall be called Christians. However, in this world there are Christians and then there are "Christians." True Christians are those who faithfully live after the pattern of Christ. In the sacrament prayer we promise to take upon us the name of Christ, and then we promise to always remember Him and to keep His commandments. Thus when we take upon us His name we become "of Christ," meaning true followers of Christ, the people of Christ, and the spiritually begotten sons and daughters of Christ (see Mosiah 27:25). To be called His people, we "are willing to bear one another's burdens, that they may be light; yea, and are willing to mourn with those that mourn; yea, and comfort those that stand in need of comfort, and to stand as witnesses of God at all times and in all things, and in all places that ye may be in, even until death" (Mosiah 18:8–9). In latter-day revelation those who truly take upon them the name of Christ are valiant in the testimony of Christ (see D&C 76:79). They have overcome the world (see D&C 76:53, 60). They are the "just, who had been faithful in the testimony of Jesus while they lived in mortality; and who had offered sacrifice in the similitude of the great sacrifice of the Son of God, and had suffered tribulation in their Redeemer's name" (D&C 138:12–13). If we are not willing to do these things, then we have not truly taken upon us His name.

Name(-s) shall be (were) blotted out (Mosiah 1:12; 5:11; 26:36; Alma 1:24; 5:57; 6:3, 7). *See:* Blotted out.

Nakedness before God (2 Nephi 9:14; Mormon 9:5). Conveys the idea of extreme embarrassment for having to face God in our sins. No unclean thing can dwell in the presence of God. Yet if one were unrepentant at the judgment bar, being filthy and stained with sin, one would be ashamed, even mortified. Much better to be clothed in purity. *Contrast:* Not be ashamed; Robe of righteousness.

Narrow gate (2 Nephi 33:9). *See:* Narrowness of the gate.

Narrow is the course (path/way) (1 Nephi 8:20; 2 Nephi 9:41; 31:18–19; Jacob 6:11; Helaman 3:29; 3 Nephi 14:14; 27:33). *Narrow* suggests confined, meaning confined to keeping strictly the commandments of God. "Ye shall observe to do therefore as the Lord your God hath commanded you: ye shall not turn aside to the right hand or to the left. Ye shall walk in all the ways which the Lord your God hath commanded you" (Deuteronomy 5:32–33). We must not turn off the narrow way onto the many broad paths that entice us, "For wide is the gate, and broad is the way, that leadeth to destruction, and many there be which go in thereat; because strait is the gate, and narrow is the way, which leadeth unto life [eternal], and few there be that find it" (Matthew 7:13–14).

Narrowness of the gate (2 Nephi 31:9). "The gate by which ye should enter is repentance and baptism by water; and then cometh a remission of your sins by fire and by the Holy Ghost" (2 Nephi 31:17). There is no other way, and thus the gate is limited and narrow—limited to those who truly humble themselves and sincerely repent. *See also:* Strait is the gate (path).

Nations that fight against apostles of the Lamb (of God) (Mount Zion) (1 Nephi 11:36; 14:13; 2 Nephi 27:3). Great shall be the eventual destruction of all they who fight against Christ and His people.

Natural branches (of the olive tree) (1 Nephi 10:14; 15:7, 13; Jacob 5:13–14, 19–20, 30, 38–39, 52, 54, 60, 67–68, 73). These represent portions of the house of Israel which have been broken off and scattered throughout the world. For example, they have been grafted into other (wild) trees in the vineyard. *See also:* Scattered tribes of Israel.

Natural frame (Alma 19:6; 41:4). Refers to our physical body. *See also:* Perfect form (frame).

Natural fruit (Jacob 5:17, 61, 64, 68, 73–74, 75). Natural fruit or good fruit symbolizes faithful lives, good works, and saved souls.

Natural man (Mosiah 3:19; Alma 26:21). "By 'natural man' is meant man who is subject to the penalty placed upon Adam, unlike little children in this respect, and who, aware that salvation comes only through the atoning blood of Jesus Christ, does not yield to the requirements of the gospel, 'to the enticings of the Holy Spirit,' in order to become a new man in Christ. He remains the 'old man' (Rom. 6:6), cut off by reason of Adam's fall 'from the presence of the Lord' (2 Nephi 9:6). All men, regardless of how ethical or just they may appear to be on the surface, are in this fallen state unless, after proper teaching, they are 'born of the spirit' and become 'redeemed of the Lord'" (Sperry, *Answers*, 3–4). *See also:* Carnal, sensual, and devilish.

Neck is an iron sinew and thy brow brass (1 Nephi 20:4). Meaning obstinate, rebellious, and unwilling to bow the head before God. *See also:* Stiffnecked people.

Needy and the naked (Jacob 2:19; Mosiah 4:14, 26; 18:28; Alma 1:30; 4:12; 34:28; Helaman 4:12; Mormon 8:39). We are unworthy servants and not fit for the kingdom of heaven even if we keep all the commandments but turn away and not assist the needy and the naked. *See also:* Clothe the naked; Poor and needy.

Neither root nor branch (3 Nephi 25:1). *See:* Leave them neither root nor branch.

Never die (Alma 11:45; 12:20). Refers to our resurrected bodies in that our bodies become immortal and incorruptible, to never die again. Additionally, our bodies will never again experience physical pain, sickness, or any type of physical handicap. "The soul shall be restored to the body, and the body to the soul; yea, and every limb and joint shall be restored to its body; yea, even a hair of the head shall not be lost; but all things shall be restored to their proper and perfect frame" (Alma 40:23).

Never-ending happiness (Mosiah 2:41; Alma 28:12). *See:* Endless happiness.

Never-ending torment (Mosiah 2:39; 5:5). *See:* Endless torment.

Never have I showed myself unto man who whom I have created (Ether 3:15). "It is true that the Savior appeared to the prophets before the flood, but it is evident that he did not reveal himself in the fulness as he did to the Brother of Jared. . . . It is a reasonable conclusion for us to reach, and fully in accordance with the facts, that the Lord had never before revealed himself so completely and in such a manner. We may truly believe that very few of the ancient prophets at any time actually beheld the full person of the Lord" (Joseph Fielding Smith, *Answers to Gospel Questions*, 2:124–25).

Never taste of death (3 Nephi 28:7, 25). *See:* Not taste of death.

New creatures (Mosiah 27:26). In order to be received into the kingdom of heaven we must become new creatures, born again, born of God, spiritually begotten sons and daughters of God, even saints unto God. *See also:* Born of God; Mosiah 3:19.

New earth (Ether 13:9). *See:* New heaven and a new earth.

New heaven and a new earth (Ether 13:9). After the Lord's Second Coming, when all the wicked will be destroyed by fire and the elements will melt with fervent heat, the earth will be renewed and restored. During the Millennium, "the earth will be renewed and receive its paradisiacal glory" (Articles of Faith 1:10). *Paradisiacal* meaning the glory of the earth when Adam and Eve were first placed in the Garden of Eden, before the fall of man. Yet another transformation of the earth will take place after the millennium, and the earth, having filled the measure of its creation, will become as a sea of glass like unto a Urim and Thummim, and those worthy of the celestial kingdom will dwell thereon (see D&C 88:25–26; 130:7–9). *See also:* Revelation 21:1–2; D&C 29:23–24.

New Jerusalem (3 Nephi 20:22; 21:23–24; Ether 13:3–6, 10). Isaiah prophesied of the future when there would be two world capitals: "Out of Zion [the City of Zion or the New Jerusalem] shall go forth the law, and the word of the Lord from Jerusalem [meaning the old Jerusalem]" (Isaiah 2:3). The Tenth Article of Faith confirms this by saying: "We believe in the literal gathering of Israel and in the restoration of the Ten Tribes; that Zion (the New Jerusalem) will be built upon the American continent." During the Millennium the old Jerusalem will be built up again and will be the gathering place for the Ten Tribes and the Jews. The New Jerusalem will be built on the American continent by the remnant of the seed of Joseph. The City of Enoch will come down out of heaven and be part of the New Jerusalem. The location of the New Jerusalem was revealed to Joseph Smith as Independence, Missouri (see D&C 57:1–3).

New star (Helaman 14:5; 3 Nephi 1:21). This was the sign of Jesus Christ's birth, seen by the wise men in the old world (See Matthew 2:1–2), and also shown to the Nephites and Lamanites on the American continent.

New tongue (2 Nephi 31:14). *See:* Tongue of angels.

Night cometh (Alma 34:33; 41:5; 3 Nephi 27:33). After the day of life, our probationary earth life, then cometh the night, or death of the physical body.

Night of darkness (Alma 34:33; 41:7). *See:* Night cometh.

No Christ (2 Nephi 11:7; Jacob 7:2, 9; Alma 30:12, 22; 31:16, 29; 34:5). Or anti-Christ, one who professes and teaches there was no Christ, there is no Christ, and there will be no Christ. This is the doctrine of Satan. *See also:* Anti-Christ.

No contention (Mosiah 1:1; 6:7; 18:21; 23:15; Helaman 3:1–2; 4 Nephi 1:13, 15, 18). Jesus said, "He that hath the spirit of contention is not of me, but is of the devil, who is the father of contention, and he stirreth up the hearts of men to contend with anger, one with another" (3 Nephi 11:29). *See also:* No contentions (and disputations among them); Spirit of contention.

No contentions (and disputations among them) (Mosiah 28:2; 29:14; Alma 4:1; 16:1; 3 Nephi 1:24;

4 Nephi 1:2). *See:* No contention; Spirit of contention.

No form nor comeliness (Mosiah 14:2). *See:* He hath no form nor comeliness.

No law given (2 Nephi 9:25; Alma 42:19–21). A discussion of the relation between the law and consequences or punishment. *See also:* State of ignorance; Romans 4:15.

No longer be kept without the veil (Ether 3:6, 19–20; 12:19–21). Exceeding faith grows until it becomes a perfect knowledge. The brother of Jared and others had faith unto knowledge such that they could not be kept without the veil and thus they saw with their eyes what before they saw by faith. *Compare:* Know God. *See also:* Moses 1:5.

No man knoweth of his ways save it be revealed unto him (Jacob 4:8). How is it that misled men are continually convening conferences (for example, the Nicene Creed council) to determine the nature of God by committee, when in reality, God is not discovered by committee, but by revelation? We are blessed to live when the gospel has been restored and so much about God was revealed unto the Prophet Joseph Smith. Ultimately each of us must come to know God and gain a personal testimony by inspiration and revelation. *See also:* Know God.

No more authority than one man (Alma 9:6). *See:* Testimony of one man; Testimony of many (two or three).

No more be confounded (1 Nephi 14:2; 15:20; 22:5, 7; Ether 13:8; Moroni 10:31). *Confounded* means to be confused, to be bothered, and to be scattered. The promise to the Jews and to the house of Israel is that the time will come when they will no longer be confounded, but will become a blessed and protected people.

No more corruption (Alma 11:45; 12:18). After the resurrection of the body, the bodies of men and women will be immortal and incorruptible, meaning no longer subject to any illness, decay, death, or any other mortal malady. *See also:* Immortal body; Put on incorruption.

No more desire (disposition) to do evil (Mosiah 5:2; Alma 13:12; 19:33). Consider the following explanation, "Can you imagine not ever wanting to do anything wrong again? My guess is that there have been many times when you have been a part of an inspiring meeting or engaged in fervent prayer and the Spirit of the Lord came upon you and you found yourself expressing either aloud or to yourself, 'I don't ever want to do anything wrong again. I just want to be good.'

"That is what the people of Benjamin were experiencing. Do we have any evidence to suggest that these people never sinned again? Certainly not. We would suppose that though their lives were changed dramatically, they still would be subject to temptation and as humans prone to make mistakes. No, they sinned again, *but they didn't want to!* Herein is the difference between the natural man or woman and the spiritual man or woman: the former wants to do wrong, whereas the latter wants to do right; their hearts are pointed in different directions. It isn't just that the people of Benjamin suddenly became more disciplined in their deeds, but rather they acquired a new *disposition*, an attitude that pointed them toward the righteous life" (Millet, *Coming to Know Christ*, 53–54). *See also:* Abhor sin (such wickedness); Change of heart.

No other head whereby ye can be made free (Mosiah 5:8). Meaning Christ is our Head, Master, and Savior, and is the only one who can free us from the effects of sin by His redemption. *See also:* None other name; Under this head ye are made free.

No other name given whereby salvation cometh (Mosiah 3:17; 5:8). *See:* None other name.

No other way or means (whereby man can be saved, only in and through Christ) (Alma 38:9; Helaman 5:9). *See:* None other name.

No peace unto the wicked (2 Nephi 20:22). Peace is promised by the Savior for the righteous and not for the wicked. Rather, the wicked will suffer turmoil and anguish, which is the opposite of peace. *Compare:* Find peace to my soul.

No tongue can speak (3 Nephi 17:17; 19:32). *See:* Unspeakable things.

No unclean thing can dwell with God (1 Nephi 10:21). *See:* No unclean thing can enter (inherit) the kingdom of God (heaven).

No unclean thing can enter (inherit) the kingdom of God (heaven) (1 Nephi 15:34; Alma 7:21; 11:37; 40:26; 3 Nephi 27:19). God has declared it often that no unclean thing can dwell in his presence (e.g., Moses 6:57). Since all have sinned, we must come unto Christ and be cleansed and purified by His Atonement in order to dwell with God hereafter. *See also:* Unclean thing.

No variableness neither shadow of changing (Mormon 9:9). Also found in James 1:17. *See also:* In him there is no variableness neither shadow of changing; Shadow of changing (turning).

None are forbidden (2 Nephi 26:28). *See:* All are alike unto God.

None can stay it [the hand of the Lord] (Mormon 8:26). Meaning none can stop it or keep it from happening. *Compare:* Daniel 4:35; D&C 1:5. *See also:* Stay his hand.

None could deliver them but the Lord (Mosiah 23:23; 24:21; Alma 36:2). *Bondage* in these verses refers to physical bondage and servitude to enemies. More importantly, bondage to sin and Satan is much more prevalent, and only the Lord Jesus Christ can deliver us from spiritual bondage. *See also:* Deliver(-ed) out of bondage.

None other name (2 Nephi 25:20; 31:21). "There is none other name given under heaven save it be this Jesus Christ, of which I have spoken, whereby man can be saved" (2 Nephi 25:20). *See also:* No other head whereby ye can be made free; No other name given whereby salvation cometh; No other way or means (whereby man can be saved, only in and through Christ); None other salvation (way); Acts 4:12; D&C 18:23.

None other salvation (way) (2 Nephi 9:41; 31:21; Mosiah 4:8). *See:* None other name.

Not be ashamed (1 Nephi 21:23; 2 Nephi 6:7, 13; 7:7; 3 Nephi 22:4). To know that we have done righteous acts and repented of all our sins would assure us to not be ashamed when we stand before God to be judged. However, if we have sought to do wickedness and not repented of our sins we will shrink before God. *See also:* Acknowledge to our everlasting shame; Everlasting shame; Hide us from his presence; Nakedness before God; Shrink from the presence of the Lord.

Not be kept from within the veil (Ether 3:6, 19–20; 12:19, 21). *See:* No longer be kept without the veil.

Not dare to look up to our God (Alma 12:14). *See:* Look up to God; Not be ashamed.

Not lawful to be written (3 Nephi 26:18). *See:* Forbidden that I (they) should write (utter/preach).

Not numbered among my (the) people (Mosiah 26:32, 36; Alma 5:57; 6:3; 3 Nephi 18:31; Moroni 6:7). The names of the wicked shall not be numbered among the names of the righteous. The names of those who refuse to repent shall not be numbered among the names of the members of God's Church. *See also:* Blotted out.

Not perish (1 Nephi 16:39; 17:5; 22:19; 2 Nephi 1:28; 26:8; Jacob 5:53; Omni 1:7; Mosiah 7:19; 21:17; Alma 24:14; 61:16; Ether 2:20). The righteous and the faithful shall not perish is the promise of the Lord. God is concerned that we not perish spiritually, and He is also concerned about our physical well-being. All good people likewise hope and pray and work that their fellow beings perish not. *See also:* Perish not; Shall not perish.

Not sinned against great knowledge which ye have received (Helaman 7:24). *Compare:* Ignorantly sinned. *See:* Did not sin ignorantly.

Not suffer the laborer in Zion to perish (2 Nephi 26:30). Zion is the pure in heart who practice charity in all things. He who is willing to work and who is not idle shall be fed and clothed by the Saints who reside in Zion.

Not taste of death (3 Nephi 28:7, 25, 38; Ether 12:17). "Therefore, that they might not taste of death there was a change wrought upon their bodies, that they might not suffer pain nor sorrow save it were for the sins of the world" (3 Nephi 28:38; D&C 7:1–8). This is the promise given to the three Nephite disciples who desired to tarry on earth and help build the kingdom of God until the Second Coming of Christ. This is like the promise given to John the Beloved of Christ's Apostles in Jerusalem (see 3 Nephi 28:6). *See also:* Three disciples of Christ.

Not without a shadow (Alma 37:43). *See:* Type(-s) and shadow(-s).

Nothingness of men (Helaman 4:5, 11; 12:7). Compared to the greatness of God, man is nothing (see Moses 1:10). God has all power, all knowledge, and infinite presence. We must not allow pride to make us believe we are anything great. Yet man's spirit has the spark of divinity, which God can make into something, probably long after this earth life. *See also:* Less than the dust of the earth.

Nourish them with things pertaining to righteousness (Mosiah 23:18). Keeping the commandments and living according to righteousness nourishes, supports, and sustains one's testimony and desire to follow the Savior. *See also:* Nourished by the good word of God; Jacob 5; Alma 32:37–41; Alma 33:23.

Nourished by the Gentiles (1 Nephi 22:8). *See:* Carried in their arms and upon their shoulders; Kings shall be thy nursing fathers and their queens thy nursing mothers; Nursed by the Gentiles.

Nourished by the good word of God (Jacob 6:7; Moroni 6:4). The word of God consists of the scriptures, the words of living prophets, and the word received by revelation from above. This means not only to receive the word of God but to live the word of God so one can progress in the gospel and strengthen testimony. Thus they are nourished and become strong. *See also:* Nourish them with things pertaining to righteousness.

Now I know (1 Nephi 5:8; Alma 5:46; 18:4; Ether 12:34). An exclamation of having received knowledge, gaining realization, and obtaining testimony. God has commanded us to seek diligently knowledge and words of wisdom (see D&C 88:63, 118; 109:7).

Now is the time to repent, for the day of salvation draweth nigh (Alma 13:21; 34:31). This is the message of all the holy prophets throughout the ages. We should not procrastinate the day of our repentance. *See also:* Everlastingly too late.

Numbered among his (my) sheep (Helaman 15:13; 3 Nephi 15:24; 16:3; 18:31). Meaning to be among the fold of God. There is one fold and one shepherd. *See also:* Good Shepherd; Numbered among (with) my people; Numbered among the (his) people of Christ (God/the church); Numbered among the people of the first covenant; Numbered among the remnant of the seed of Joseph who were of the house of Israel; Numbered among this the remnant of Jacob.

Numbered among the (his) people of Christ (God/the church) (Mosiah 26:36; Alma 27:27; Moroni 6:4, 7; 7:39). It is good to be numbered among the true followers of Christ and be members of Christ's Church. Therein is found fellowship, nourishing in the word of God, opportunity to serve and be served, meeting together to renew covenants and pray together, and thus assisting one another in striving for righteousness and eternal life.

Numbered among the house of Israel (1 Nephi 14:2; 2 Nephi 10:18; 3 Nephi 30:2). Being numbered among God's chosen people to receive all the blessings promised them. Those who are of direct lineage—the scattered of Israel who are converted, restored, or gathered to be numbered among the house of Israel as prophesied—shall be joined by the Gentiles who accept the gospel and are adopted into the house of Israel. *See also:* Covenant people (of the Lord); House of Israel.

Numbered among the names of the righteous (Alma 5:57; 6:3). Meaning being numbered among those written in the book of life, or those who shall obtain eternal life. *Compare:* Blotted out. *See also:* Book of life.

Numbered among the people of the first covenant (Mormon 7:10). Meaning to be numbered among the elect of God; having become a covenant people, a chosen people who live a covenant life. These are they who live up to all the gospel covenants, baptism through temple ordinances. They become a royal lineage. Through their faithfulness God fulfills His covenant, and these obtain their eternal exaltation.

Numbered among the remnant of the seed of Joseph who were of the house of Israel (Ether 13:10). *See:* Numbered among the house of Israel.

Numbered among this the remnant of Jacob (3 Nephi 21:22). *See:* Numbered among the house of Israel.

Numbered among (with) my people (Mosiah 26:32; 3 Nephi 16:13; 18:31; 21:6; 30:2). *See:*

Numbered among his (my) sheep; Numbered among the house of Israel; Numbered among the (his) people of Christ (God/the church).

Numbered with those of the first resurrection (Mosiah 18:9). *See:* First resurrection.

Numbered with those whom the Father hath given me (3 Nephi 15:24). These words are very similar to "them which thou hast given me" found in the Savior's great intercessory prayer (see John 17:9). "In [this] fervent prayer offered just prior to [Christ's] entrance into Gethsemane, Jesus Christ supplicated His Father in behalf of those whom the Father had given unto Him, specifically the Apostles, and, more generally, all who would accept and abide in the gospel through the ministry of the Apostles" ("The Father and the Son," *Ensign*, April 2002, 14). A review of John 17 indicates these are: they who kept the word of God; they who come unto Christ; they who receive Jesus as their Savior and King; they who bear testimony of Christ, that He is the Son of God; and they who strive to be one with the Father and the Son. *See also:* John 6:37; D&C 27:14.

Numbereth his people (Alma 26:37). *See:* Numbereth his sheep.

Numbereth his sheep (1 Nephi 22:25). The Savior, who is the Good Shepherd, knows His sheep, and His sheep know Him. He will gather His sheep from the four quarters of the earth; they are not lost to Him. When one of His sheep has strayed He will go out to bring back the one. "Now my brethren, we see that God is mindful of every people, whatsoever land they may be in; yea, he numbereth his people, and his bowels of mercy are over all the earth" (Alma 26:37). *See also:* Good Shepherd.

Nursed by the Gentiles (1 Nephi 22:6; 2 Nephi 10:9). *See:* Carried in their arms and upon their shoulders; Kings shall be thy nursing fathers and their queens thy nursing mothers; Nourished by the Gentiles.

Nurture and admonition of the Lord (Enos 1:1). Meaning to feed, care for, train, educate, exhort, and counsel children in the ways of the Lord. *See also:* Ephesians 6:4.

O

O God, receive my soul (Mosiah 17:19). These words are Abinadi's, his final utterance. Compare Luke 23:46 where on the cross Jesus said, "Father, into thy hands I commend my spirit." In Acts 7:59 the martyr Stephen said as he was stoned to death, "Lord Jesus, receive my spirit."

O God, the Eternal Father (Moroni 4:3; 5:2). These are the opening words of the sacrament prayers as recorded in the Book of Mormon. We are taught to begin all our prayers by addressing our Heavenly Father. The Lord's Prayer was given as an example of how to pray and begins by addressing "Our Father which art in heaven" (Matthew 6:9; Luke 11:2).

O house of Israel (Jacob) (1 Nephi 20:1; 21:1, 12, 15; 22:14; 2 Nephi 3:9, 13; 7:2, 4; 12:5; Jacob 5:2–3; 3 Nephi 10:6–7; 16:7, 11–13, 15; 20:12, 21, 27; 21:1, 4, 6, 20; Ether 4:14–15; Moroni 10:31). Refers to Jacob, whose name was changed to *Israel* by God, and includes all of his posterity. In other words, the twelve tribes of Israel.

O Lord (1 Nephi 1:14; 7:17; 2 Nephi 4:30–34; 9:46; 12:6; 22:1; Jacob 7:14; Mosiah 18:12; Alma 2:30; 14:26; 15:10; 18:41; 31:26, 30–32, 34–35; 33:7, 16; 38:14; Helaman 11:4, 10–16; 13:37; Ether 2:18–19, 22; 3:2–5; 12:29). "O Lord" in these verses is the addressee, the person prayed to, who is Jehovah, the God of the Old Testament, and the God to whom the Nephites prayed before Christ appeared on the American continent. In 3 Nephi 18:16 Jesus says, "And as I have prayed among you even so shall ye pray." *See also:* O God, the Eternal Father.

O ye Gentiles (2 Nephi 29:5; 3 Nephi 30:1; Mormon 5:22; Ether 2:11; 4:13; 8:23). A salutation calling the Gentiles to repentance. *See also:* All ye Gentiles.

O ye house of Israel (1 Nephi 21:1; Jacob 5:2; 3 Nephi 10:5, 6; Ether 4:14). *See:* O house of Israel (Jacob).

Oath and sacred ordinance (Alma 13:8; 50:39). Those who are called and set apart to minister or rule have a sacred and holy responsibility to do so righteously, faithfully, and with all their might.

Oath(-s) (after the manner) of the ancients (Alma 37:27; Helaman 6:21, 25–26, 30; 4 Nephi 1:42;

Ether 8:15–16, 20; 9:5; 10:33). *See:* Secret combination(-s).

Obedient to the commandments (of God) (1 Nephi 22:30–31; 2 Nephi 5:31; 31:7; Jacob 2:4; 4:5; Mosiah 5:5; Alma 47:3). Obedience is a principle that if followed brings peace and safety. "The Prophet Joseph Smith taught that obedience to the commandments leads to blessings from God. He said: 'There is a law, irrevocably decreed in heaven before the foundations of this world, upon which all blessings are predicated—and when we obtain any blessing from God, it is by obedience to that law upon which it is predicated' (D&C 130:20–21). . . .

"Our obedience to the commandments is an expression of our love for Heavenly Father and Jesus Christ. The Savior said, 'If ye love me, keep my commandments' (John 14:15). He later declared: 'If ye keep my commandments, ye shall abide in my love; even as I have kept my Father's commandments, and abide in his love' (John 15:10)" (*True to the Faith*, 109). *See also:* Commandments of God (the Father/the Lord).

Obedient unto the word of the Lord (1 Nephi 2:3; Jacob 2:4). Meaning obedient to the commandments of God. *See also:* Commandments of God (the Father/the Lord); Obedient to the commandments (of God).

Observe his judgments and his statutes (2 Nephi 1:16; 5:10; Mosiah 6:6; Alma 25:14; 31:9; 58:40; Helaman 3:20; 15:5). Judgments and statutes are words meaning commandments, laws, and rules of God. *See also:* Commandments and his statutes and his judgments.

Observe the sabbath day to keep it holy (Jarom 1:5; Mosiah 13:16; 18:23). One of the Ten Commandments, which commandment is almost entirely forgotten in this modern day *See also:* Exodus 20:8; D&C 68:29.

Observe to do (2 Nephi 32:6; Mosiah 13:25; Alma 5:61; 63:2; Helaman 15:17; 3 Nephi 18:6). *See:* Commandments of God (the Father/the Lord); Observe his judgments and his statutes.

Obtain a hope (Jacob 2:19; 4:4, 6, 11; Moroni 7:3). By faith and obedience we obtain a hope in Christ's redemption. By obedience we obtain a promise that we will merit the mercy of God and be forgiven. *See also:* Have hope.

Obtained a land of promise (1 Nephi 5:5; 2 Nephi 1:3, 5). *See:* Land choice above all other lands.

Obtained a (the) promise (2 Nephi 1:9; 3:5, 14; Ether 12:17, 21–22). Righteous men, through faith and supplication unto the Lord, have received various and specific promises. There are also promises of the Lord that apply to all His children, chiefly redemption, if they follow the path outlined by God. *See also:* Promises which I have made (the Lord had made unto them).

Of God (1 Nephi 1:1; *passim*). The scriptures abound in descriptions and titles of God. We should be aware of and thankful for all that is of God. By reviewing the following list from the Book of Mormon, we begin to see a small part of all that God is and all that He has done for us. God is explained more fully by each of these scriptural phrases ending in the words "of God."

Altar of God
Angel(-s) of God
Appointed of God
Authority of God
Bar of God
Blessed name of God
Blessings of God
Boast of my God
Born of God
Called of God
Callings of God
Cause of God
Children of God
Chosen of God
Church of God
Commanded of God
Commandments of God
Commands of God
Condemned of God
Condescension of God
Counsels of God
Curse of God
Decrees of God
Delivered of God
Displeasure of God

Doctrine of God
Enemy of God
Existence of God
Favored of God
Fear of God
Finger of God
Fold of God
Followers of God
Foreknowledge of God
Gift(-s) of God
Given of God
Glory of God
Good cometh of God
Goodness of God
Grace of God
Greatness of God
Hand of God
High priests of God
Holy name of God
Holy ones of God
Holy order of God
Image of God
In the sight of God
Inquire of God
Inspiration of God
Inspired of God
Judged of God
Judgment-seat of God
Judgment(-s) of God
Justice of God
Kingdom of God
Knowledge of God
Known of God
Lamb of God
Law(-s) of God
Left hand of God
Light of God
Love of God
Man (Men) of God
Marvelous work of God
Mercies (Mercy) of God
Miracles of God

Mouth of God
Mysteries of God
Name of God
Nature of God
Ordained of God
Order of God
Ordinances of God
Paradise of God
Peace of God
People of God
Plan of God
Power of God
Presence of God
Promises of God
Prophet of God
Redeemed of God
Redemption of God
Remembrance of God
Rest of God
Restoration of God
Revelations of God
Right hand of God
Right way of God
Saints of God
Salvation of God
Sent of God
Servant of God
Service of God
Similitude of God
Smitten of God
Sons of God
Spirit of God
Stars of God
Strength of God
The Son of God
Things of God
Throne of God
Tribunal of God
True faith of God
Trump of God
Truth of God
Voice of God

Will of God
Wisdom of God
Witnesses of God
Word(-s) of God
Wrath of God

Offer sacrifice (1 Nephi 2:7; 5:9; 7:22; Mosiah 2:3; 3 Nephi 9:19–20). "Soon after Adam and Eve were cast out of the Garden of Eden, the Lord gave them the law of sacrifices, which included offering the first-lings of their flocks in a similitude of the sacrifice that would be made of the Only Begotten Son of God (Moses 5:4–8). Thereafter, when-ever there were true believers on the earth, with priesthood author-ity, sacrifices were offered in that manner and for that purpose. This continued until the death of Jesus Christ, which ended the shedding of blood as a gospel ordinance. It is now replaced in the Church by the sacrament of the bread and water, in remembrance of the offering of Jesus Christ" (Bible Dictionary, s.v. "sac-rifices," 765–66). The law of Moses, which the Nephites observed un-til Christ's appearance unto them, included the offering of sacrifices (see 2 Nephi 11:4, 25:24; Jacob 4:5; Alma 25:15–16). Thereafter the Savior instructed them to offer in-stead a sacrifice of a broken heart and a contrite spirit (see 3 Nephi 9:20). *See also:* Law of Moses.

Offer unto the Lord an offering in righteousness (3 Nephi 24:3). As part of the restoration of all things, the sons of Levi will offer sacrifice, just before or at the beginning of the Millennium, as also prophesied by John the Baptist when the Aaronic Priesthood was restored (see D&C 13). *See also:* D&C 84:31; 128:24.

Offer your whole souls as an offering unto him (Omni 1:26). Meaning to present or give one's whole being to the worship and service of the Lord, even all of one's heart, might, and mind. This includes the offering of a broken heart and a contrite spirit.

Office of being high priest over the church (Mosiah 29:42; Alma 4:18). *See:* Consecrated as (the) high priest over the church of God.

Office of my calling (Jacob 2:3). Refers to the responsibilities and duties of the servants of God. *Compare:* D&C 25:5; 124:103, 135. *See also:* Called of God (the Holy Spirit); Called with a holy calling; His calling unto me; My calling to the ministry.

Old have passed away and all things have become new (Ether 13:9). Refers to the Millennium when the "earth will be renewed and receive its paradisiacal glory" (Articles of Faith 1:10). *See also:* Earth shall (should) pass away; Heavens and the earth should pass away; New heaven and a new earth; D&C 29:24; 63:49; 101:25.

Old things are done (had passed) away and (that) all things (had) have become new (3 Nephi 12:47;

15:2–3). Meaning the law of Moses is fulfilled and no longer applicable but is replaced by the new law of Christ. *See also:* Fulfilled the law [of Moses]; In me is the law of Moses fulfilled; Law (is) fulfilled; Law of Moses.

Olive tree (1 Nephi 10:12, 14; 15:7, 12, 16; Jacob 5:3–4, 7, 9–10, 14, 34, 46; 6:1). In the Book of Mormon the house of Israel is compared or likened to an olive tree. Lehi and his family were of the lineage of Joseph, "whose branches run over the wall" (Genesis 49:22). Also "the house of Israel, that they should be compared like unto an olive-tree, whose branches should be broken off and should be scattered upon all the face of the earth" (1 Nephi 10:12). The allegory of the tame and wild olive trees found in Jacob 5 needs to be read over and over to understand the prophecy, symbolism, and meaning of the olive tree as a metaphor.

One baptism (Mosiah 18:21). Having reference here to unity and one faith, one doctrine, one church, and one baptism. An examination of the many churches on earth and their many and varied beliefs even on how to baptize shows the propensity of man to differ. *Compare:* Ephesians 4:5.

One by one (3 Nephi 11:15; 17:21; 18:36; 28:1; Ether 3:6). President Howard W. Hunter noted, "I have always been impressed that the Lord deals with us personally, individually. We do many things in groups in the Church, . . . but so many of the . . . most important things . . . are done individually. We bless babies one at a time, even if they are twins or triplets. We baptize and confirm children one at a time. We take the sacrament, are ordained to the priesthood, or move through the ordinances of the temple as individuals—as one person developing a relationship with our Father in Heaven. . . . Heaven's emphasis is on each individual, on every single person" (Howard W. Hunter, "Eternal Investments").

One church (1 Nephi 14:10; Mosiah 25:22). There is only one true Church of God. "This church . . . the only true and living church upon the face of the whole earth" (D&C 1:30). "For thus shall my church be called in the last days, even The Church of Jesus Christ of Latter-day Saints" (D&C 115:4). "And how be it my church save it be called in my name? For if a church be called in Moses' name then it be Moses' church; or if it be called in the name of a man then it be the church of a man; but if it be called in my name then it is my church, if it so be that they are built upon my gospel" (3 Nephi 27:8).

One Eternal God (Alma 11:44). A name for the Godhead, consisting of God the Father, God the Son, and God the Holy Ghost. *See also:* One God.

One eternal round (1 Nephi 10:19; Alma 7:20; 37:12). Referring to things eternal. Just as a ring has no beginning and has no end but is one eternal round, thus God pursues one eternal course eternally and forever. *See also:* Course is one eternal round.

One faith and one baptism (Mosiah 18:21). *See:* One baptism.

One fold and one shepherd (1 Nephi 22:25; 3 Nephi 15:17, 21; 16:3). There are many churches of the Good Shepherd but only one true Church of Jesus Christ. *See also:* Good Shepherd; One church.

One God (2 Nephi 31:21; Mosiah 15:4–5; Mormon 7:7). God the Father, Jesus Christ, and the Holy Ghost are one in purpose, in attributes, in perfection, in power, and in majestic presence. Though they are separate beings, they together are referred to as one God because of the unity in their ways and purposes.

One God and one Shepherd over all the earth (1 Nephi 13:41). *See:* One fold and one shepherd.

One jot or tittle (Alma 34:13; 3 Nephi 1:25; 12:18). A *jot* is a small bit or fragment. A *tittle* is a small part of writing or one small point made in a discourse. Scripturally, every jot and tittle—not one being missed—shall all come to pass. *See also:* According to God's word.

One Messiah (2 Nephi 25:18). The Jews looked for a different messiah or deliverer, one who would free them from the Romans, thus they did not recognize the true and only Messiah, Jesus Christ. Jesus warned, "Then if any man shall say unto you, Lo, here is Christ, or there; believe it not. For there shall arise false Christs, and false prophets, and shall shew great signs and wonders; insomuch that, if it were possible, they shall deceive the very elect" (Matthew 24:23–24).

Only and true doctrine (2 Nephi 31:21). *See:* Doctrine of Christ; One baptism.

Only Begotten of the Father (2 Nephi 25:12; Alma 5:48; 9:26; 13:9). Meaning Jesus Christ, who is the Only Begotten of the Father in the flesh, or the only person who has lived on this earth whose father of the physical body is God the Father. *See also:* Jesus Christ the Son of God.

Only Begotten Son (Jacob 4:5, 11; Alma 12:33–34; 13:5). *See:* Only Begotten of the Father.

Only in and through Christ ye can be saved (Mosiah 3:17; 16:13; Alma 38:9; Helaman 5:9). *See:* No other name given whereby salvation cometh.

Open rebellion against God (Mosiah 2:37; Alma 3:18; Mormon 2:15). A state of mind none should find themselves in, for it is a person who knows right from wrong but deliberately chooses the evil.

Thus being in defiance against God, choosing to side with Satan, past feeling of things that are right, just, or of the Spirit, unconcerned about and even wishing for the consequences of sin. *See also:* Rebel(-led/ -ling/-lion) against God.

Open the scriptures unto them (Alma 21:9; 41:1). Meaning to explain, clarify, unfold, and interpret the scriptures. This is the very calling of a true teacher and the mission of the Holy Ghost. "Then opened he [Jesus] their understanding, that they might understand the scriptures" (Luke 24:45).

Open their (your) ears to hear (Mosiah 2:9; 3 Nephi 11:5). Symbolically meaning to unplug, remove the obstruction, and cease to resist hearing the word of God, to further strive to understand the truth.

Opposition in all things (2 Nephi 2:11). The plan of salvation, God's plan of happiness, has as an integral part opposites to all choices. Thus mortal man experiences good and bad, happiness and sadness, and many other opposites. By that experience man learns to prize the good, which understanding he would never have had without experiencing pain or sorrow. *See also:* Choose good (or evil).

Ordain priests (and teachers/and elders) (Mosiah 18:18; 25:19; Alma 6:1; 13:1; Moroni 3:1, 4). To bestow the priesthood upon men and designate them to offices within the priesthood. *See also:* Authority from (of) God.

Ordained after the manner of his holy order (2 Nephi 6:2; Alma 13:1, 6, 8, 10; 49:30). Meaning ordained unto the priesthood, which is the holy order of God. *See also:* After the order of his (the) Son; Holy order (of God).

Ordained of God (1 Nephi 12:7). Nephi sees in vision Christ's appearance to his posterity on the American continent, and that He chose and ordained twelve here also to minister unto the people (see 3 Nephi 11:22; 12:1). This is similar to His ordaining of the Twelve Apostles in Jerusalem (see Mark 3:14–19; Luke 9:1–2; John 15:16).

Ordained unto this ministry (3 Nephi 7:25). Men ordained and given power to preach the gospel and baptize those who repent and come unto Christ. *See also:* Ordain priests (and teachers/and elders).

Order after which I am called (2 Nephi 6:2; Alma 5:44, 49; 6:8; 8:4; 13:6, 8, 11; 43:2; Helaman 8:18; Ether 12:10). *See:* Holy order (of God); Holy prophet(-s/of God); After the order of his (the) Son.

Order and faith of (profession of) Nehor (Alma 14:16, 18; 15:15; 16:11; 24:29). False doctrine. These people believed that God will save all men regardless of their actions, therefore they did not believe in the

repentance of sin, the need for good works, or the necessity of a Savior. *See also:* Order of the Nehors.

Order of God (Alma 4:20; 5:44, 54; 6:1; 7:22; 8:4; 13:6, 18; 43:2; 49:30; Helaman 8:18; Ether 12:10). Meaning the holy order of God or the priesthood of God. *See also:* After the order of his (the) Son; Holy order (of God).

Order of the church (Alma 6:4; 8:1; 46:38). Meaning to establish branches [wards] of the Church, including ordaining priesthood leaders therein and seeing that they meet oft, pray together, and administer the sacrament to the members. *See also:* Church established; Establish church.

Order of the Nehors (Alma 21:4; 24:28). False doctrine. *See also:* Order and faith of (profession of) Nehor.

Ordinances and performances (2 Nephi 25:30; Mosiah 13:30; Alma 30:23; 4 Nephi 1:12). Refers to the law of Moses, which was observed strictly by the Nephites from day to day to keep them in remembrance of the Lord and their duty towards Him. This was done until the coming of Christ among them, when the law of Moses was fulfilled and replaced by the higher law of love and obedience taught by Jesus. *See also:* Law of Moses.

Ordinances of God (2 Nephi 25:30; Alma 30:3). These two

scriptures have reference to the law of Moses, which law was to be kept until it was fulfilled at the death of Christ. *See also:* Law of Moses.

Other plates (1 Nephi 9:4; 19:4; 2 Nephi 4:14; 5:30, 33; Jacob 1:3; 7:26; Jarom 1:14; Words of Mormon 1:10). Generally refers to a record of the history of kings, and concerning their wars and contentions. *See also:* 1 Nephi 9:1–6; Jacob 1:1–3.

Other sheep (3 Nephi 15:17, 21; 16:1). In John 10:16 the Savior said, "And other sheep I have, which are not of this fold: them also I must bring, and they shall hear my voice; and there shall be one fold, and one shepherd." Jesus explained to the Nephites that "ye are they of whom I said: Other sheep I have which are not of this fold" (3 Nephi 15:21). Further, He said there were still other sheep in other lands besides the Nephites and the people of Jerusalem. *See also:* Good Shepherd.

Other tribes (2 Nephi 29:12; 3 Nephi 15:15, 20; 16:4). Refers to the other groups of the children of Israel that have been scattered, led away, and taken captive by the power of God. They shall all eventually be gathered again according to the promises of the Lord. *See also:* Gather in the house of Israel; Scattered tribes of Israel.

Out of bondage (1 Nephi 17:24–25; 19:10; Mosiah 7:33; 8:7; 21:15; 22:1–2, 4; 24:13, 16–17, 21; 25:8, 16; 29:20; Alma 1:8; 5:5;

9:22; 29:11–12; 36:28–29). *See:* Deliver(-ed) out of bondage.

Out of captivity (1 Nephi 4:2; 5:15; 10:3; 13:13, 16, 19, 29–30; 22:12; 2 Nephi 3:5; Alma 36:28, 29; 60:20). *See:* Deliver(-ed) out of bondage.

Out of darkness (1 Nephi 22:12; 2 Nephi 3:5; 27:29; Alma 37:25–26; Mormon 8:16). To not accept the gospel of Jesus Christ means "ye are not brought into the light, but must perish in the dark" (2 Nephi 32:4). *See also:* Out of obscurity.

Out of obscurity (1 Nephi 22:12; 2 Nephi 1:23; 27:29). *Obscurity* means oblivion, remoteness, uncertainty, and nothingness. Thus those that come to the gospel of Jesus Christ come out of and come in from the cold, from uncertainty, from nothingness, and from darkness in to the light of the gospel. *See also:* Out of darkness.

Out of the books which shall be written shall the world be judged (2 Nephi 29:11; 3 Nephi 27:25–26). "Wherefore, he [the Lord] shall bring forth his words unto them, which words shall judge them at the last day" (2 Nephi 25:18). "Do you know that the time is coming when *we are going to be judged out of the books that are written?* Therefore we should make these records accurate; we should be sure of the steps we take. We are going to be judged out of the things written in books, out of the revelations of God, out of the temple records, out of those things which the Lord has commanded us to keep and have on file concerning the records of the people [records of the Church]. There will be other records, of course, because if we happen to make mistakes there will be the record in heaven which is a perfect record" (Smith, *Doctrines of Salvation*, 2:200). *See also:* Book of life.

Outcasts of Israel (2 Nephi 21:12). Refers to the tribes of Israel that have been scattered throughout the world, but will be gathered back together in the Lord's own due time. *See also:* Scattered tribes of Israel.

Outer darkness (Alma 40:13). The place of no light or happiness, where the wicked await judgment, which is spirit prison. Also after the final judgment it is the kingdom of no glory where Satan reigns. "Behold, and lo, there are none to deliver you; for ye obeyed not my voice when I called to you out of the heavens; ye believed not my servants, and when they were sent unto you ye received them not. Wherefore, they sealed up the testimony and bound up the law, and ye were delivered over unto darkness. These shall go away into outer darkness, where there is weeping, and wailing, and gnashing of teeth. Behold the Lord your God hath spoken it. Amen" (D&C 133:71–74).

Outward performances (Alma 25:15). Refers to the many duties, rituals, and sacrifices included in the law of Moses. *See also:* Law of Moses.

Over all [God is] (1 Nephi 1:14, 20; 11:6; 13:41; Jacob 4:10; Alma 26:37; 37:12). 1 Nephi 11:6 reads, "For he is God over all the earth, yea, even above all." Meaning over all His works, over all creation. By His power and by His all-present presence and Spirit, God is not only over all, but He is also in all, through all, and He can search all things (see D&C 63:59). God is supreme, and all things are subject to Him and obey His command. He knows all things—there is nothing that He does not know.

Overcome his natural frame (Alma 19:6). *See:* Overcome with the Spirit.

Overcome that they fell to the earth (Jacob 7:21). *See:* Overcome with the Spirit.

Overcome with the Spirit (1 Nephi 1:7, 8). 1 Nephi 17:47 reads, "Behold I am full of the Spirit of God, insomuch that my [natural or physical] frame has no strength." When one experiences great spiritual experiences or testifies by the power of the Spirit, it often leaves the physical body weakened for a time before the body gains back its normal strength. *See also:* Alma 27:17; Moses 1:9–10; Joseph Smith–History 1:20.

Overpowered with joy (Alma 19:14; 27:17; 3 Nephi 17:18). *See:*

Fulness of joy; Joy is (shall be/was) full.

Own due time (of the Lord) (1 Nephi 10:3; 14:26; 2 Nephi 27:10, 21; Enos 1:16; 3 Nephi 5:25; 20:29: Mormon 5:12; Ether 3:24, 27). The Lord God has His time-table as to the events to take place on this earth. He has made various promises of events to take place, but at the time that He determines in His great wisdom. We must be patient, for God's timing is perfect.

Own strength (Mosiah 10:11; 11:19; Alma 26:11; Helaman 4:13; 16:15; Mormon 3:9; 4:8). *See:* Boast in their own strength.

Own wisdom (2 Nephi 26:20; Alma 26:11; 38:11; Helaman 16:15). Meaning man's puny, extremely small, and very finite knowledge and understanding. *See also:* Understanding of men.

P

Pain and anguish of my soul (2 Nephi 26:7; Mosiah 2:38; 3:7; 25:11; Alma 38:8). *See:* Anguish of soul.

Pain(-ed) my heart (soul) (1 Nephi 17:47; Alma 13:27; 14:10; 31:30). *See:* Afflict my soul; Pain and anguish of my soul.

Pained no more (Mosiah 27:29; Alma 36:19–21). These are the two places in the Book of Mormon where Alma the younger describes the mighty change that took place in his heart when he was born again. Before the mighty change he experienced great pain and anguish because of his sins. Once he appealed unto Jesus for a remission of his sins, Alma was no longer pained and instead experienced the exceeding and sweet joy of forgiveness.

Pains of a damned soul (Alma 36:16). *See:* Pains of hell.

Pains of hell (Jacob 3:11; Alma 14:6; 26:13; 36:13). The anguish, lack of peace, and gnashing of teeth that the wicked do and will experience because of their unrepented sins. *See also:* Eternal torment.

Pains of my soul (2 Nephi 26:10). *See:* Anguish of soul.

Pains of the Jews (2 Nephi 29:4). The Jews have not had it easy. They have toiled to keep the law of Moses, they have been conquered and scattered, and they are hated and persecuted. *See also:* Hiss and a byword; Make game of the Jews.

Paradise of God (2 Nephi 9:13; 4 Nephi 1:14; Moroni 10:34). The place in the spirit world to where the good and just go at death (see Alma 40:12, 14). When Jesus hung on the cross he said to the penitent thief beside him, "Today shalt thou be with me in paradise" (Luke 23:43).

Partake not of the sacrament of Christ (my flesh and blood) unworthily (3 Nephi 18:28; Mormon 9:29). Just as we must repent before we are baptized, so also must we repent each time before we partake of the sacrament, which is when we renew our baptismal covenants. If we do not, partaking of the sacrament unworthily condemns us. It is akin to mockery and rebellion against God. In most cases, partaking of the sacrament unworthily is done to appear righteous before men, but ignores the true purpose, which is to repent, approach God humbly, and recommit to fully living the gospel.

Partake of his goodness (2 Nephi 26:28, 33; 33:14; Jacob 1:7). *See:* Infinite goodness (of God).

Partake of his salvation (2 Nephi 26:24, 27; Omni 1:26). Meaning to come unto Christ and obtain and secure salvation. "Yea, come unto him, and offer your whole souls as an offering unto him, and continue in fasting and praying, and endure to the end; and as the Lord liveth ye will be saved" (Omni 1:26). *See also:* Partake of the waters of life freely.

Partake of my flesh and blood unworthily (3 Nephi 18:28–29). Compare 1 Corinthians 11:29. *See:* Partake not of the sacrament of Christ (my flesh and blood) unworthily.

Partake of the fruit (1 Nephi 8:11–12, 15–18, 24; 2 Nephi 2:18; Alma 5:34, 62; 12:21; 42:3; Helaman 6:26). Meaning to eat of the fruit of the tree. Depending on the verse it refers to the tree of knowledge of good and evil (the forbidden fruit in the Garden of Eden) or the tree of life, which was the tree in Lehi's dream and is also the tree that God placed cherubim and a flaming sword to guard so that Adam would not partake of it prematurely.

Partake of the goodness of God (2 Nephi 33:14; Jacob 1:7). *See:* Infinite goodness (of God).

Partake of the waters of life freely (Alma 42:27). Meaning to acquire the words of salvation through Jesus Christ without restriction and without cost. *See also:* Living waters; Partake of his salvation.

Partakers of salvation (Moroni 8:17). Refers to little children, who are automatic partakers of salvation with no action required on their part. They are incapable of sin, therefore they are already redeemed.

Partakers of the (heavenly) gift (4 Nephi 1:3; Ether 12:8–9). To enjoy the many gifts of the spirit and blessings from God because of one's righteous manner of living. Nephi, one of the disciples of Christ, saw that the people were blessed with these things (4 Nephi 1:5). Mormon saw that these gifts were later taken away because of the wickedness of the people (Mormon 1:14). Eternal life is also a heavenly gift.

Partial God (Moroni 8:18). *See:* God is not a partial God.

Past feeling (1 Nephi 17:45; Moroni 9:20). Meaning one can no longer feel the promptings of the Holy Ghost because one's sins have caused the Spirit to withdraw from them. *See also:* Ephesians 4:19.

Paths are straight (Alma 37:12). Meaning God's paths are straight. "For God doth not walk in crooked paths, neither doth he turn to the right hand nor to the left, neither doth he vary from that which he hath said, therefore his paths are straight, and his course is one eternal round" (D&C 3:2). *See also:* Make (making) his (my) paths straight.

Paths of righteousness (1 Nephi 16:5; Alma 7:19). Meaning walking in the path of keeping the commandments, which leads to eternal life. *See also:* Rod of iron; Straight course (path) to eternal bliss; Strait and narrow course (path).

Patience and long suffering [of God] (Mosiah 4:6; 9:26). *See:* Long suffering (of the Lord) towards the children of men.

Patience and long suffering [of men and women] (Alma 7:23; 32:43; 38:3). *See:* Bear afflictions (with patience).

Patience in their afflictions (tribulations) (Alma 26:27; 31:31; 34:3, 40–41; 60:26). *See:* Bear afflictions (with patience).

Patient in long-suffering (Alma 13:28; 17:11; 20:29; 26:28). *See:* Bear afflictions (with patience).

Peace be unto you (Helaman 5:47). The pleasant voice of God, who is the only true giver of peace. Sometimes this salutation comes through heavenly messengers sent from God. *See also:* Peace of God rest upon you.

Peace of conscience (Mosiah 4:3). The blessed state of those who seek and receive a remission of sins through the Atonement of Jesus Christ. Their conscience is no longer pricked by knowledge of their guilt because their sins and the guilt have been swept away. *Contrast:* Remorse of conscience. *See also:* Clear conscience before God; Guilt was swept away; Peace of God rest upon you; Taken away the guilt from our hearts.

Peace of God rest upon you (Alma 7:27). Jesus Christ is the Prince of Peace, and He will bring peace: peace among peoples, and peace of mind and heart to individuals through His Atonement. *See also:* Find peace to my soul; Peace be unto you; Peace of conscience.

Peace to my soul (Alma 38:8; 58:11).

Sweet is the peace the gospel brings
To seeking minds and true.
With light refulgent on its wings,
It clears the human view.

Its laws and precepts are divine
And show a Father's care.
Transcendent love and mercy shine
In each injunction there.

Faithless tradition flees its pow'r,
And unbelief gives way.
The gloomy clouds, which used to
*   low'r,*
Submit to reason's sway.

May we who know the sacred
*   Name*
From every sin depart.
Then will the Spirit's constant
*   flame*
Preserve us pure in heart.

*Ere long the tempter's power will
    cease,
And sin no more annoy.
No wrangling sects disturb our
    peace,
Or mar our heartfelt joy.*

*That which we have in part
    received
Will be in part no more,
For he in whom we all believe
To us will all restore.*

*In patience, then, let us possess
Our souls till he appear.
On to our mark of calling press;
Redemption draweth near.*
("Sweet Is the Peace the Gospel
Brings," *Hymns*, no. 14).

See: Find peace to my soul; Peace of
God rest upon you.

Peaceable followers of Christ
(Moroni 7:3). Those that walk
humbly and meekly after that pattern of Christ. "That we may lead a
quiet and peaceable life in all godliness and honesty" (1 Timothy 2:2).
"Receive my Spirit, the Holy Ghost,
even the Comforter, which shall
teach you the peaceable things of
the kingdom" (D&C 36:2).

Peaceable walk (Moroni 7:4). *See:*
Peaceable followers of Christ.

People of Christ (Jesus) (4 Nephi
1:34; Moroni 6:7). Meaning followers of Christ and those who lead a
Christlike life. *See also:* People of
God; People of the Lord.

People of God (Mosiah 25:24;
26:5; Alma 1:24; 2:11; 19:14; 24:4,

26; 25:13; 4 Nephi 1:40). Meaning
those that believe in the true and
living God, reverence Him, love
Him, and keep His commandments. *See also:* People of Christ
(Jesus); People of the Lord.

People of liberty (Alma 51:7, 13).
Those who seek to maintain liberty and freedom. *See also:* Defend
themselves; Title of liberty.

People of the church (Mosiah
18:27; 26:35–36; Alma 1:7, 10, 21;
2:3; 4:4, 6, 8–9; 6:1, 3–4). These
are the members of the Church who
have entered by the gate of baptism
and continue in good standing and
in faith to live the gospel.

People of the first covenant
(Mormon 7:10). *See:* Numbered
among the people of the first covenant.

People of the house of Israel
(3 Nephi 10:5; 16:5; 17:14; 29:3).
See: House of Israel.

People of the Lord (1 Nephi 14:14;
15:14; 22:14; 2 Nephi 1:19; 6:13;
30:2; Mosiah 1:13; 18:34; 19:1;
27:10; Alma 9:20; 24:29; 27:5, 14;
27:30; 54:8; Helaman 15:3; 16:23;
3 Nephi 6:29; Mormon 3:21; 8:15,
21). Those that strive to live the
commandments of the Lord their
God and are therefore favored of
the Lord. *See also:* People of Christ
(Jesus); People of God.

Perceived his (the/their) thoughts
(Alma 10:17; 18:16). *See:* Know all
my (thy) thoughts.

Perfect brightness of hope (2 Nephi 31:20). "When we have hope, we trust God's promises" (*True to the Faith*, 85). Hope is expectations born of faith because "hope cometh of faith" (Ether 12:4). A perfect brightness of hope is to have exceedingly great hope and expectations. The second verse of the hymn "We Thank Thee, O God, for a Prophet" reads, "When dark clouds of trouble hang o'er us / And threaten our peace to destroy, / *There is hope smiling brightly before us,* / And we know that deliverance is nigh. / We doubt not the Lord nor his goodness. / We've proved him in days that are past" (*Hymns*, no. 19; emphasis added). The words "We've proved him in days that are past" have reference to the faith we have nurtured and gained in life from testimony experiences. Because of that faith, we have "hope smiling brightly before us." If we strive to keep the commandments and strive to serve God and our fellowman, then we can justly hope for the promised rewards in the kingdom of heaven. Hope is of God, even a gift from God, which sheds itself abroad in the hearts of the children of men. It is universal for men and women to have hope. Like our conscience, if we seek truth and righteousness, then hope burns brighter in us. On the other hand, if our ways are wickedness, then hope begins to flicker out, and only hopelessness and despair remain (see Moroni 10:22). Thus we see that hope is carried to us by the light of Christ, and that hope, like conscience, lights every man and woman who cometh into the world. If we diligently seek God's ways, hope grows to become a perfect brightness of hope, and along with faith and charity, they light our way.

Perfect faith (2 Nephi 9:23). Meaning complete faith and faith without any doubts. As we progress in the gospel, our faith becomes more whole, more complete, and more perfect, until we have faith to do all things, faith nothing wavering, faith unshaken, even faith unto knowledge. The brother of Jared had perfect faith and therefore was able to see the finger of the Lord (see Ether 3:9, 11, 15). *See also:* Perfect knowledge.

Perfect form (frame) (Alma 11:43–44; 40:23). The Resurrection shall be to a perfect body having no defect, and which body is immortal. *See also:* Immortal body.

Perfect in Christ (Moroni 10:32–33). *See:* Sanctified in Christ (me).

Perfect knowledge (2 Nephi 9:13–14; Jacob 4:12; 7:4; Alma 32:21, 26, 29; 55:1; Ether 3:20; Moroni 7:15–17). Perfect knowledge is absolute knowledge or a certainty of things. Faith, if nurtured properly, grows to become perfect knowledge. We can have a perfect knowledge of some things during life, but still have to live by faith in regards to many other things in life. For example,

Joseph Smith believed God would answer his prayer and therefore went to the grove to pray. In the First Vision, Joseph Smith saw God the Father and His Son and thereafter had a perfect knowledge that God lives. Yet Joseph Smith still continued to live by faith in regards to many other things in the gospel after he saw God. The brother of Jared grew in faith and thereby gained knowledge concerning many things about God, thus progressing to a point that he had perfect knowledge of God. "Wherefore, having this perfect knowledge of God, he could not be kept from within the veil; therefore he saw Jesus, and [Jesus] did minister unto him" (Ether 3:20). We hear individuals say in testimonies that they know a thing is true. Either (1) they had a surety of the thing revealed unto them (see example at Alma 40:3); or (2) they have a strong faith that a thing is so because they received a spiritual impression that it was true, and when they say they know it is true, they are saying they know they had a spiritual impression, and they cannot deny that spiritual manifestation. We will always operate by faith, even after we gain a perfect knowledge of a gospel principle. For example, by inspiration we learn that a gospel law is true, yet we will still exercise faith in that knowledge by continuing to live that law after we have gained a knowledge that it is true. Thus faith and knowledge are interactive, and growth in faith and knowledge progresses hand in hand until at some future point we obtain perfect knowledge and perfect faith. *See also:* Perfect faith.

Perfect love (Moroni 8:16–17, 26). *See:* Pure love of Christ.

Perfect remembrance of all your wickedness (2 Nephi 9:46; Alma 5:18). *See:* Bright recollection of all our guilt.

Perfect understanding (Alma 48:11). *See:* Applied your hearts to understanding; Men of perfect (sound) understanding.

Perfect uprightness before God (Alma 50:37). Meaning strict and unwavering adherence to the commandments of God.

Perfected in him (Christ) (Moroni 10:32). *See:* Sanctified in Christ (me).

Perfectly honest and upright in all things (Alma 27:27). Meaning being fully virtuous. *See also:* Just and true [individuals].

Performances and ordinances (of God/the law of Moses) (2 Nephi 25:30; Mosiah 13:30; Alma 30:23; 4 Nephi 1:12). Refers to the law of Moses, which was observed strictly by the Nephites from day to day to keep them in remembrance of the Lord and their duty towards Him. This was done until the coming of Christ, when the law of Moses was fulfilled and replaced by the higher law of love and obedience taught by Jesus.

Performances of the church (Alma 31:10). *See:* Performances and ordinances (of God/the law of Moses).

Perish in the dark (2 Nephi 32:5). The destiny of those who do not keep the commandments and do not come unto Christ. *See also:* Cloud of darkness; Encircled about with everlasting darkness and destruction.

Perish not (Jacob 5:4, 11; Mosiah 4:22, 30; Alma 27:12; Ether 13:7). *See:* Not perish; Shall not perish.

Perished in their sins (Mosiah 15:26). Those who die without repenting of their sins, and more particularly, those that knew the commandments of God and rebelled, kept not the commandments and died in their sins. *See also:* Die(-th) in their sins; Moses 7:1.

Perisheth forever (Mosiah 4:18). *See:* Everlasting death.

Perisheth unto himself (Helaman 14:30). No one else makes our moral choices for us. Thus if we reap damnation in life, it is because of the choices of each individual, himself or herself.

Permitted to act for yourselves (Helaman 14:30). Meaning each of us has unfettered moral agency, for God said to Adam and Eve, and to all mankind, "Nevertheless, thou mayest choose for thyself, for it is given unto thee" (Moses 3:17).

Persecute the church of God (Mosiah 27:1–2, 13; Alma 1:19, 28; 4 Nephi 1:29). *See:* Destroy the church.

Persecute the humble (meek) (2 Nephi 9:30; 28:13; Alma 4:15; Helaman 3:34; 3 Nephi 6:13). For some reason the mean and hateful often persecute, oppress, harass, and torment the meek and humble people of the earth. Maybe they think it is sport, maybe they believe they are easy targets, and maybe they think it makes them bigger and more important. Nevertheless it is evil, and they will be judged for it.

Persecute your brethren (Jacob 2:13; Mosiah 24:8; Alma 5:54; Helaman 3:34). *See:* Persecute the humble (meek).

Persecuted for my name's sake (3 Nephi 12:10). When we covenant with God to take upon us the name of Christ, to always remember Him and to keep His commandments, then often comes the trial of faith where we are persecuted and hated for our beliefs and actions. "If thou art called to pass through tribulation; if thou art in perils among false brethren; if thou art in perils among robbers; if thou art in perils by land or by sea; if thou art accused with all manner of false accusations; if thine enemies fall upon thee; if they tear thee from the society of thy father and mother and brethren and sisters; and if with a drawn sword thine enemies tear thee from the bosom of thy wife, and of thine offspring; . . . and thou be dragged to prison, and thine enemies prowl around thee like wolves for the blood of the lamb; and if thou shouldst be cast into the pit, or into the hands of murderers, and the sentence of death passed upon thee; if thou be cast into the deep; if the billowing surge conspire against thee; if fierce winds become thine enemy; . . . if the very jaws of hell shall gape open the mouth wide after thee, know thou, my son, that all these things shall give thee experience, and shall be for thy good. The Son of Man hath descended below them all. Art thou greater than he?" (D&C 122:5–8).

Persuade all men to come unto Christ (repentance) (1 Nephi 3:21; 6:4; 19:18, 23; 2 Nephi 25:23; 26:27; Jacob 1:7–8; Mormon 3:22). It is our duty before God that because we know of the gospel, we would desire to share it with all the world. It is a measure of our belief and gratefulness that we would want others to hear it. "Behold, I sent you out to testify and warn the people, and it becometh every man who hath been warned to warn his neighbor" (D&C 88:81). *See also:* All are alike unto God; Anxiety for you.

Persuaded that Jesus is the Christ (2 Nephi 25:16; Mormon 5:14). It is here prophesied that the day will come that the Jews, who before rejected Jesus, will begin to believe that Jesus is the Christ, their Redeemer and Savior. One point

in time when this will be particularly so is at the Second Coming, when Jesus appears on the Mount of Olives and rescues the one third of the inhabitants of Jerusalem (see Zechariah 14:4; D&C 45:48–53). From that point on there shall be a great conversion of the Jews to Jesus Christ.

Pertaining to righteousness (1 Nephi 15:33; Mosiah 18:18; 23:18; Alma 5:42; 12:16, 32; 21:23; 24:30; 35:16; 40:26; Helaman 11:19; 14:18). *Pertaining* means regarding, related to, or connected to. As one progresses in the gospel, more and more wonderful things of God are revealed. D&C 11:13–14 says, "Verily, verily, I say unto you, I will impart unto you of my Spirit, which shall enlighten your mind, which shall fill your soul with joy; And then shall ye know, or by this shall you know, all things whatsoever you desire of me, which are pertaining unto things of righteousness, in faith believing in me that you shall receive." On the other hand, those that turn from God and choose wickedness shall have all things pertaining to righteousness taken away from them. *See also:* Greater things; Mysteries of God.

Perverse generation (people) (Alma 9:8; 10:17, 25; 31:24; Helaman 13:29; Mormon 8:33; Moroni 9:19). *Perverse* means evil and disobedient to the commandments.

Pervert(-ed/-ing) the right ways of the Lord God (of all righteousness) (1 Nephi 13:27; 22:14; 2 Nephi 28:15; Jacob 7:7; Mosiah 12:26; 29:7, 23; Alma 10:18; 30:22, 60; 31:1; Moroni 8:16). Meaning wicked men falsify, corrupt, distort, change from good to evil, disguise evil within, and lead astray people from the true gospel.

Pestilence of earthquakes (famine/tempest/the sword) (2 Nephi 6:15; 10:6; Mosiah 12:4, 7; Alma 10:22–23; 45:11; Helaman 10:6; 11:14–15; 12:3; 13:9; Ether 11:7). *See:* Famine(-s) and pestilence(-s); He doth visit them with death, terror, famine and pestilence.

Pierce their very soul (them to the center) (Jacob 2:9; Helaman 5:30; 3 Nephi 11:3). The word of God, and the still small voice of God, have the power to go to the very center of man and cause man to quake. Sometimes it comes as a warning and a call to repent. Other times it is given to cause one to believe or strengthen testimony.

Pierce you with one glance of his eye (Jacob 2:15). The Almighty God, by His great power, and by His all-seeing eye, can strike wicked people to the dust at His will. Yet our God allows us a time to repent, and He is extremely longsuffering towards His children's waywardness, hoping they will return unto Him. *See also:* Probationary state (time).

Piercing eye of the Almighty God (Jacob 2:10). *See:* Pierce you with one glance of his eye.

Pillar of fire (1 Nephi 1:6; Helaman 5:24, 43; 3 Nephi 19:14). God has at times used a pillar of fire as a sign of God and His power. A pillar of fire is memorable and significant to the observer. A pillar of fire led the children of Israel in the wilderness (see Exodus 13:21). When Moses went up into the mount into the midst of a cloud and fire "And the sight of the glory of the Lord was like devouring fire on the top of the mount in the eyes of the children of Israel" (Exodus 24:17).

Place at God's (my) right hand (Mosiah 26:23–24; Ether 12:4). *See:* Right hand of God.

Place of filthiness prepared for that which is filthy (1 Nephi 15:34). *See:* Depths of hell.

Place of Mormon (Mosiah 18:4–5, 7, 16, 30; Alma 21:1). The secluded place that Alma the Elder resorted to, where he taught the gospel as he heard it from Abinadi, and the place where he first baptized people who were believers. Mosiah 18 is the first appearance of the name Mormon in the verses of the Book of Mormon. Later the prophet Mormon says, "I am called Mormon, being called after the land of Mormon" (3 Nephi 5:12).

Place of my rest (Enos 1:27). *See:* Enter into his (my/the) rest (of the Lord/of God).

Place of refuge (2 Nephi 14:6; Helaman 15:2, 12). Meaning a place of safety, shelter, and protection. The Lord God promises a place of refuge for the Saints. *See also:* Glory of Zion shall be a defence.

Place prepared [heaven] (Enos 1:27; Ether 12:32, 34, 37). "In my Father's house are many mansions: if it were not so, I would have told you. I go to prepare a place for you" (John 14:2). *See also:* D&C 98:18.

Place prepared [hell] (1 Nephi 15:34–35; 2 Nephi 28:23). *See:* Depths of hell.

Plain and precious things (1 Nephi 13:26, 28–29, 32, 34–35, 40; 14:23; 19:3). Refers to the truths that were taken out, changed, or translated incorrectly in the Bible.

Plainness of prophecy (speech/the truth/the word of God) (1 Nephi 13:29; 2 Nephi 9:47; 25:4, 7; 31:2–3; 32:7; 33:5–6; Jacob 2:11; 4:14; Enos 1:23; Alma 14:2). The truth, the word of God, and the gospel is plain, straightforward, and direct. The plainness of the gospel is often sharp and hurtful to the wicked, because it reveals their sins. To the faithful the gospel has plainness because understanding is revealed by the Holy Ghost.

Plan of deliverance (2 Nephi 11:5). *See:* Eternal plan of deliverance.

Plan of happiness (2 Nephi 9:1; Alma 42:8, 16). *See:* Plan of salvation.

Plan of mercy (Alma 42:15, 31). *See:* Merciful God (Being).

Plan of redemption (Jacob 6:8; Alma 12:25–26, 30, 32–33; 17:16; 18:39; 22:13; 29:2; 34:16, 31; 39:18; 42:11, 13). It is only by the plan of salvation that man can be redeemed from the fall and from one's sins. Key to the plan is the Atonement of Christ. By no other name but by Jesus Christ can man be redeemed. *See also:* Plan of salvation.

Plan of restoration (Alma 41:2). *See:* Restoration of God.

Plan of salvation (Jarom 1:2; Alma 24:14; 42:5). The plan of salvation is real. It is God's plan to advance His spirit children to become like Him and dwell with Him eternally. It is the plan of happiness and the plan of redemption. It is also sometimes known by the names *plan of heaven, plan of life, plan of the gospel, plan of God, plan of ordinances, plan of saving His children, plan of exaltation, plan of the earth, plan of the atonement, plan of the Lord, plan of moral agency, plan of progression, plan of eternal life, plan of the Great Creator, plan of the Almighty, plan of mercy,* and *the plan of the Father.* God has provided His children the perfect plan. There is no better plan possible. "We will go down, for there is space there, and we will take of these materials, and we will make an earth whereon these may dwell; And we will prove them herewith, to see if they will do all things whatsoever the Lord their God shall command them . . . and they who keep their second estate [faithful on earth] shall have glory added upon their heads for ever and ever" (Abraham 3:24–26). Joseph Smith said, "God himself, finding he was in the midst of spirits and glory, because he was more intelligent, saw proper to institute laws whereby the rest could have a privilege to advance like himself . . . He has power to institute laws to instruct the weaker intelligences, that they may be exalted with Himself" (*History of The Church of Jesus Christ of Latter-day Saints*, 6:312). *See also:* Plan of happiness; Plan of the Eternal God; Plan of the great Creator.

Plan of the adversary (Alma 12:5). The plan of the adversary, who is Satan, is to disrupt God's plan of salvation, and to take captive as many individuals as will follow him.

Plan of the Eternal God (2 Nephi 9:13; Alma 34:9). *See:* Plan of salvation.

Plan of the evil one (thine adversary) (2 Nephi 9:28; Alma 12:5). *See:* Plan of the adversary.

Plan of the great Creator (2 Nephi 9:6). *See:* Plan of salvation.

Plates of brass (1 Nephi 3:3, 12, 24; 4:16, 24, 38; 5:10, 14, 18–19; 13:23; 19:21–22; 22:1, 30; 2 Nephi 4:2, 15; 5:12; Omni 1:14; Mosiah 1:3, 16; 10:16; 28:11, 20; Alma 37:3; 3 Nephi 1:2; 10:17). The record that Lehi was commanded by the Lord to send his sons back to Jerusalem to obtain (1 Nephi 3:2–4). The plates of brass "did contain the five books of Moses, which gave an account of the creation of the world, and also of Adam and Eve, who were our first parents; And also a record of the Jews from the beginning, even down to the commencement of the reign of Zedekiah, king of Judah; and also the prophecies of the holy prophets, from the beginning, even down to the commencement of the reign of Zedekiah; and also many prophecies which have been spoken by the mouth of Jeremiah. . . . [Also] a genealogy of his [Lehi's] fathers; wherefore he [Lehi] knew that he was a descendant of Joseph; yea, even that Joseph who was the son of Jacob, who was sold into Egypt, . . . [and thus these records] were desirable; yea even of great worth unto us, insomuch that we could preserve the commandments of the Lord unto our children" (1 Nephi 5:11–22). "They contained a record of God's dealings with men from the beginning down to that day. . . . There was more on them than there is in the Old Testament as we now have it. (1 Ne. 13:23.) The prophecies of Zenock, Neum, Zenos, Joseph the son of Jacob, and probably many other prophets were preserved by them. . . . The value of the Brass Plates to the Nephites cannot be overestimated. By means of them they were able to preserve the language (1 Ne. 3:19), most of the civilization, and the religious knowledge of the people from whence they came. . . . At some future date the Lord has promised to bring them forth, undimmed by time and retaining their original brightness, and the scriptural accounts recorded on them" (McConkie, *Mormon Doctrine*, 103).

Plates of gold (Mosiah 8:9; 28:11). The plates found by the people of Limhi, which plates were a record of the Jaredites, a portion of which is translated in the Book of Mormon as the Book of Ether. *See also:* Twenty-four plates.

Plates of Jacob (Jacob 3:14). The same as the Plates of Nephi (small plates), but renamed by Jacob. *See also:* Plates of Nephi.

Plates of Nephi (Words of Mormon 1:3, 5, 9; Mosiah 1:6, 16; 28:11; 3 Nephi 5:10; 4 Nephi 1:19, 21; Mormon 2:17–18; 6:6). These plates "contain the records of the sayings of our fathers from the time they left Jerusalem" (Mosiah 1:6). The small plates of Nephi were mostly devoted to the spiritual matters of the people and the teachings and ministry of the prophets among them. The large plates of Nephi were kept to record the secular history of the people. However, from the time of Mosiah forward, the large plates also included spiritual matters.

Plead your cause (Jacob 3:1). If one is faithful, the Lord will defend and provide blessings in that person's behalf. *See also:* Advocateth the cause of the children of men; Great Mediator.

Pleasing bar of God (the great Jehovah) (Jacob 6:13; Moroni 10:34). The judgment bar will be pleasing and pleasant to the righteous. On the other hand, it will strike awful dread and fear into the wicked, because they will know of their wickedness and that the judgments of God must come down upon them.

Pleasing unto God (1 Nephi 6:5; 2 Nephi 5:32; Jacob 2:7). Righteous humble faithfulness is pleasing unto God. Truthfulness, guilelessness, cleanliness, honesty, virtue, contriteness, submissiveness, valor, meekness, loyalty, trustworthiness, kindness, obedience, and all other good and honorable characteristics are pleasing to God.

Pleasing word of God (Jacob 2:8–9; 3:2). Refers to the gospel, meaning the good news of Jesus Christ. The word of God is pleasant to the genuine seeker of truth. *See also:* Word of God.

Pointing our souls to him (Jacob 4:5). Meaning to direct us to Christ, to remind us of Christ, and to focus us upon Christ. There is much symbolism in the gospel to help us to always remember Him, to do His will, and to follow His example.

Points of doctrine (1 Nephi 15:14; Alma 41:9; Helaman 11:22–23, 28; 3 Nephi 11:28; 21:6). The doctrine of the Church is made up of many subsets and individual items of doctrine. As we gain a testimony of various points of gospel doctrine, our testimony of the gospel of Jesus Christ as a whole grows, line upon line and precept upon precept. *See also:* Doctrine of Christ; D&C 10:62–63.

Ponder(-ing) in his (mine/your) heart (1 Nephi 11:1; 2 Nephi 4:15–16; 32:1, 8; Helaman 10:2–3; 3 Nephi 17:3; Moroni 10:3). It is commonly said in the Church, "We speak to God when we pray and God speaks to us as we read the scriptures and ponder them." We are admonished to ponder, meditate, and reflect upon the things of God and upon the scriptures. We should take the time after church meetings, after reading the scriptures, and after praying to ponder, for this is most likely when we will be inspired with testimony, comfort, direction, and understanding. *Compare:* D&C 138:1.

Poor and needy (2 Nephi 20:2; 24:30; Alma 1:27; 4:13; 5:55; Mormon 8:37). We are commanded to care for the poor and the needy. "For the poor shall never cease out of the land: therefore I command

thee, saying, Thou shalt open thine hand wide unto thy brother, to thy poor, and to thy needy, in thy land" (Deuteronomy 15:11). "And remember in all things the poor and the needy, the sick and the afflicted, for he that doeth not these things, the same is not my disciple" (D&C 52:40). King Benjamin reminds us that in order to "retain a remission of [our] sins" (Mosiah 4:12) we must "succor those that stand in need of succor; ye will administer of your substance unto him that standeth in need; and ye will not suffer that the beggar putteth up his petition to you in vain, and turn him out to perish" (Mosiah 4:16). The poor and needy are not just those who are temporally poor and needy. We must also assist those who are poor and needy in spirit, those who are poor and needy in friendship, those who are poor and needy in health, and those who are poor and needy in other ways. *See also:* Impart of their substance.

Poor in heart (2 Nephi 28:13; Alma 32:3–4). Meaning meek, humble, and contrite. *See also:* Lowly in heart; Poor in spirit.

Poor in spirit (3 Nephi 12:3). Footnote *b* in Matthew 5:3 defines poor in spirit as "poor in pride," thus meaning without pride, or "humble in spirit" and having "a contrite heart."

Popular in the eyes of the world (1 Nephi 22:23; Alma 35:3).

Worldly acclaim and popularity come about because some people are beautiful, faddish, famous, fashionable, favorite, promoted, rich, or socially prominent. It is much better to be acceptable and approved of God, than of men. "For none is acceptable before God, save the meek and lowly in heart" (Moroni 7:44).

Portion of his spirit (Alma 17:9; 18:35; 24:8; 40:13). Even a small portion or part of God's Spirit or the Holy Ghost is a great blessing and advantage to the receiver. It has the effect of enlightenment, comfort, joy, power, encouragement, and gratitude.

Possessed with a lying spirit (Alma 30:42). To allow the devil, the father of lies who speaks no truth, to take possession of one's soul, and thus become a follower of lying ways.

Potter's clay (2 Nephi 27:27). Shall the clay pot say to the potter who made it ye know not of me? Man cannot say that God our creator has no knowledge of us, for He knows all concerning each of us. "But now, O Lord, thou art our father; we are the clay, and thou our potter; and we all are the work of thy hand" (Isaiah 64:8).

Pour out their hearts to him (God) (Mosiah 24:12). *See:* Mighty prayer; Pour(-ed/-ing) out his soul in prayer unto God.

Pour(-ed/-ing) out his blessings (Alma 16:21; Helaman 3:25; Ether 9:20; 3 Nephi 10:18; 24:10). The Lord has often promised blessings upon the faithful. "Prove me now herewith, saith the Lord of Hosts, if I will not open you the windows of heaven, and pour you out a blessing that there shall not be room enough to receive it" (3 Nephi 24:10).

Pour(-ed/-ing) out his soul in prayer unto God (Enos 1:9; Mosiah 24:21; 26:14; Alma 19:14; 49:17; 58:10; Helaman 7:11, 14; Mormon 3:12). Meaning to pray with all one's might, mind and soul. *See also:* Mighty prayer.

Pour(-ed) out his Spirit upon them (into my soul) (Jacob 7:8; Mosiah 4:20; 18:10, 12, 13; 25:24; Alma 8:10; 16:16; 19:14, 36; Helaman 6:36). The blessing of the Holy Ghost's influence flowing down from heaven upon whom the Lord God wills. *Compare:* Acts 2:17–18. *See also:* Pouring out of the Holy Ghost.

Pouring out of the Holy Ghost (3 Nephi 20:27). *See:* Pour(-ed) out his Spirit upon them (into my soul).

Power according to (because of/ received by) faith (1 Nephi 1:20; 10:17; 2 Nephi 1:10; 26:13; Mosiah 21:30; Alma 14:28; 18:35; 44:5; 57:26; 3 Nephi 7:18; Mormon 8:24; Moroni 7:32–33; 10:7). "There is, however, a level of faith that not only governs our behavior but also empowers us to change what is and to make things happen that otherwise would not happen. I am speaking of faith not only as a principle of action but also as a principle of power. Paul stated that this was the faith by which prophets 'subdued kingdoms, wrought righteousness, obtained promises, stopped the mouths of lions, quenched the violence of fire, escaped the edge of the sword, out of weakness were made strong, waxed valiant in fight, turned to flight the armies of the aliens, [and] women received their dead raised to life again' (Hebrews 11:33–35). These are grand things—but in some ways similar to conquering a powerful addiction or other comparable obstacle to conversion and baptism.

"Key to our obtaining power through faith is learning, asking, and acting according to the will of God. 'Christ hath said: If ye will have faith in me ye shall have power to do whatsoever thing is expedient in me' (Moroni 7:33).

"He cautions, however, 'If ye ask anything that is not expedient for you, it shall turn unto your condemnation' (D&C 88:65).

"Your own faith in Christ will grow wonderfully as you seek day by day to know and to do the will of God. Faith, already a principle of action in you, will then become also a principle of power" (Christofferson, "Building Faith in Christ," 55). *See also:* Power by faith.

Power and authority from (of) God (Mosiah 18:17; 27:14; Alma 14:10, 24–25; 23:6; 30:51–52;

3 Nephi 12:1; Moroni 8:28). Meaning the priesthood of God. *See also:* Authority from (of) God.

Power and gift of Christ (the Lamb) (1 Nephi 13:35; Moroni 7:16). It is done by power and is a gift from above. *See also:* Gift and power of God (the Lamb); Power of God.

Power and glory of the God of Israel (1 Nephi 19:13). *See:* Power and gift of Christ (the Lamb).

Power and great glory (1 Nephi 11:28; 22:24; 2 Nephi 6:14; 33:11; Moroni 7:35). How Jesus will appear at his Second Coming. *See also:* Coming of Christ.

Power and wisdom of God (Mosiah 4:6, 9; 5:15; Alma 26:29, 35). God is all powerful (omnipotent) and all knowing (omniscient). He has the power to do all He wills to do, and there is no knowledge that He has not yet obtained. *See also:* Wisdom in (of) God (the Lord/ the Father).

Power and word of God (1 Nephi 17:29; 2 Nephi 1:26; Alma 17:17; 53:10; 62:45; 3 Nephi 28:20; 4 Nephi 1:30). The true servants of God are given great power from God to teach the word of God, which carries great power to the convincing of men of the truth and to the performing of mighty miracles.

Power by faith (1 Nephi 10:17; 2 Nephi 1:10; 26:13; Mosiah 27:14; Alma 14:28; 18:35; 37:40; 44:5;

57:26; 3 Nephi 7:18; Mormon 8:24; Moroni 7:33, 41; 10:7). Faith is power. All things are done by faith, accomplished by faith, were created by faith, and are ordered and commanded by faith. The infinite power of God is obtained in men's lives by faith, always if it be the will of God. *See also:* Power according to (because of/received by) faith.

Power given unto him (them) (2 Nephi 1:10; Mosiah 8:16; Alma 8:31; Helaman 5:11, 37; 8:13; 3 Nephi 7:15). *See:* Authority from (of) God; Power and authority from (of) God.

Power of Christ (the Lamb of God/the Lord) (1 Nephi 11:31; 13:16, 35, 39; 14:14; 17:55; 2 Nephi 3:15; 27:11; Jacob 7:15; Alma 4:14; 9:28; 15:6; 41:2; 3 Nephi 7:21; Mormon 9:26; Moroni 7:16, 41). Jesus Christ (Jehovah in the Old Testament) has great power, given to Him from the Father. He has the power to create, to show forth great power and glory, to command the elements, to perform mighty miracles, to raise Himself from the dead, to resurrect and redeem mankind, to command Satan, and to rule and reign as King of Kings. By His goodness and righteousness He has received this power, also by doing only the will of the Father. He received a fulness of power when He received the fulness of His father (all things that the Father hath). His power is endless. *Compare:* Power of the Father. *See also:* Power of God.

Power of deliverance (1 Nephi 1:20; Alma 7:13; 15:2). God has all power to deliver, save, and rescue men, women, and children, after the trial of their faith, from captivity, bondage, and tyranny. The Atonement of Jesus Christ provides power of deliverance from sin and spiritual captivity. *See also:* Deliverance by the hand of the Lord; Deliverance of Jesus Christ.

Power of God (1 Nephi 3:20; 13:18–19, 30; 14:14; 17:29, 48; 18:20; 2 Nephi 1:27; 27:10, 12; 28:5, 26; Jacob 6:8; 7:21; Enos 1:23, 26; Omni 1:20; Mosiah 8:16; 15:3; 21:30; 23:13; 27:15, 18, 20; Alma 5:4; 7:8; 12:7; 14:10, 24–25; 17:17; 19:6, 17; 23:6; 30:51–52; 37:15, 28, 40; 57:26; Helaman 9:36; 10:16; 3 Nephi 28:29; Mormon 5:22; 7:9; 8:16, 28; 9:13; Ether 5:3–4; Moroni 10:7, 32). We believe that God is omnipotent, meaning that He has all power. Both God the Father and God the Son have this great and infinite power. "Know ye not that he [God] hath all power?" (Mormon 5:23). God has all power, and there is no power that He does not have. There are few, if any, characteristics of God that are mentioned more frequently in the scriptures than the power of God. *See also:* According to the power of God; According to the power of the Father; All power; All-powerful Creator; Almighty power of the Lord; Arm of the Lord (revealed); Authority from (of) God; Believest thou in the power of

Christ unto salvation; By the hand of the Lord (God); By the power of his holy arm; By the power of his voice (word); By the power of the Father he hath risen; Do all things [God can]; Everlasting power; Filled with the power of God; Gave power; Gift and power of God (the Lamb); Give unto you power; God Almighty; God is powerful; God of miracles; God shall smite him (thee/you); Great power; He has all power to save; I am able to do mine own work; I will show unto the children of men; In his glory and in his power and in his might, majesty, and dominion; In power and great glory; In the name of the all-powerful God (Almighty); Kept and preserved; Know all my (thy) thoughts; Know that the Lord God hath power to do all things; Led by the power of his arm (the hand of God); Lifted up by the power of God; Lord hath made bare his holy arm; Lord Omnipotent; Made bare his holy arm; Make him (thee/them) mighty; Marvelous power of God; Matchless (miraculous) power; Mercy and power of God; Mightier than all the earth; Mighty God; Mighty power; Mighty to save; Mighty words; Mysterious and marvelous power of the Lord; Over all [God is]; Pierce you with one glance of his eye; Power and wisdom of God; Power of Christ (the Lamb of God/the Lord); Power of God; Power of heaven; Power of his (holy) arm; Power of his redemption; Power of his voice (word); Power of the atonement; Power of the Father; Power of the Redeemer; Power of (the) redemption (and the resurrection); Power of the resurrection; Power of the word of God; Power to make intercession; Quick and powerful; Sealed up by the power of God; See the salvation of God (the Father/the Lord); Shake the earth; Show forth his mighty power; Show forth power; Show unto you with power and great glory; Strength (and power) of God; That the Lord might show forth his power; Who can comprehend the marvelous works of God; Wrought upon by the power of God.

Power of heaven (3 Nephi 21:25). *See:* Powers of heaven.

Power of his captivity (2 Nephi 2:27, 29; Alma 12:6, 17). Refers to those who through sin give Satan the power to take their souls captive. By sinning, individuals subject themselves to Satan. *See also:* Power of Satan.

Power of his (holy) arm (Jacob 2:25; Enos 1:13; Omni 1:13; Mosiah 29:20). *See:* Arm of the Lord (revealed).

Power of his redemption (Omni 1:26; Moroni 8:20). *See:* Power of (the) redemption (and the resurrection).

Power of his voice (word) (1 Nephi 17:29, 46; 2 Nephi 1:26; Jacob 4:9; Alma 5:5; 7:8; 17:4; 26:13; Helaman 12:10–12; 4 Nephi 1:30; Mormon

8:24; 9:17; Ether 5:4). The elements instantly obey God's words (see Abraham 2:7). Thus by the omnipotent power of God's word (or in many cases by Jesus Christ who has been given all power and in John is called "the Word"), God the Father accomplishes His desires. The *Lectures on Faith* state: "It is by words [that] every being works when he works by faith. God said, 'Let there be light: and there was light.' Joshua spake, and the great lights which God had created stood still. Elijah commanded, and the heavens were stayed for the space of three years and six months, so that it did not rain. . . . All this was done by faith. . . . Faith, then, works by words; and with [words] its mightiest works have been, and will be performed" (*Lectures on Faith*, 72–73). In this sense the word of God is all powerful. Also another name for Jesus Christ, the Son of God, is "the Word" (see John 1:1–2), and the scriptures tell us Christ created the earth. *See also:* Almighty word; By his word; By the power of his voice (word); Power of the word of God.

Power of justice (Jacob 6:10). The eternal law and administration of justice is absolute. In other words, there is no power to put aside the consequences of justice except through the mercy and Atonement of Jesus Christ. If men do not have faith in Jesus, and do not repent and become baptized, they will suffer for their sins because of justice. *See also:* Works of justice.

Power of mine arm (Jacob 2:25). *See:* Arm of the Lord (revealed); Power of his (holy) arm.

Power of Satan (1 Nephi 13:29; 2 Nephi 30:18; Alma 10:25; 12:17; 3 Nephi 2:2; 6:15; 7:5; 4 Nephi 1:28; Ether 15:19). Satan also has power, but it is far inferior to the power of God. Much of Satan's power derives from people giving him power over themselves. As men and women yield to the temptations of the devil, they are giving themselves over to Satan, and by so doing people remove themselves from the protection of God and from the protection of righteousness. President James E. Faust has written, "We need not become paralyzed with fear of Satan's power. He can have no power over us unless we permit it. He is really a coward, and if we stand firm, he will retreat. The Apostle James counseled, 'Submit yourselves therefore to God. Resist the devil, and he will flee from you' (James 4:7). He cannot know our thoughts unless we speak them. And Nephi states that the devil 'hath no power over the hearts' of righteous people (see 1 Nephi 22:26). We have heard comedians and others justify or explain their misdeeds by saying, 'The devil made me do it.' I do not really think the devil can make us do anything. Certainly he can tempt and he can deceive, but he has no authority over us that we do not give him.

"The power to resist Satan may be stronger than we realize. The Prophet Joseph Smith taught; 'All beings who have bodies have power over those who have not. The devil has no power over us only as we permit him. The moment we revolt at anything which comes from God, the devil takes power" [Ehat and Cook, *Words of Joseph Smith*, 60].

"He also stated, 'Wicked spirits have their bounds, limits, and laws by which they are governed' [*History of the Church*, 4:576]." Additionally, "'The devil is not smart because he is the devil; he is smart because he is old'" ("The Forces That Will Save Us," 5–9). *See also:* Power of his captivity; Power of the devil (evil one); Powers of hell; Satan did get hold (possession) upon the hearts of the people; Satan had (hath) great power.

Power of the atonement (2 Nephi 9:25; 10:25). The Atonement of Jesus Christ provides the power to overcome both physical death and spiritual death. It is also the power to heal us of weaknesses, ignorance, sin, and doubt.

Power of the devil (evil one) (2 Nephi 2:27; Jacob 7:4, 18; Alma 28:13; Helaman 16:6; 3 Nephi 2:2; Ether 8:16; Mormon 1:19). *See:* Power of Satan.

Power of the Father (3 Nephi 21:4; 27:15; Mormon 7:5). God, our Father in Heaven, has power because of His goodness, His love, His knowledge, His glory, His perfect faith, His priesthood, to name just a few. Of particular note is D&C 29:36. It is by the power of the Father, given to Jesus from the Father, that Jesus has power (see Helaman 5:11; 3 Nephi 27:15; Mormon 7:5). Jesus received a fulness of the Father, therefore He received a fulness of the Father's power. *See also:* Power of God.

Power of the Holy Ghost (Spirit) (1 Nephi 2:14; 10:17, 19; 13:37; 2 Nephi 2:8; 26:13; 28:31; 32:3; 33:1; Jacob 7:12–13, 17; Alma 7:10; 18:35; 3 Nephi 21:2; 29:6; Moroni 3:4; 6:4, 9; 7:36, 44; 8:7; 10:4–5, 7). As God the Father and Jesus Christ have power, the Holy Ghost, the third member of the Godhead, has power. This power is so the Holy Ghost can fulfill His mission among men and women: to bestow testimony; to teach the things of God; to sanctify (purify); to inspire; and to lend to men and women the comfort and peace of God. The power of the Holy Ghost marks the path, protects the path, empowers the path, and teaches us along the path. Additionally, men can do great things by the power of the Holy Ghost when that power comes upon them by the will of God to carry out the work of the Lord (for example, speak with power or work mighty miracles). To further clarify, "The Holy Ghost is manifested to men on the earth both as the *power* of the

Holy Ghost and as the *gift* of the Holy Ghost. The power can come upon one before baptism and is the convincing witness that the gospel is true. [It gives one] a testimony of Jesus Christ and of His work and the work of His servants upon the earth. The gift can come only after proper and authorized baptism and is conferred by the laying on of hands. . . . For those who receive this gift, the Holy Ghost acts as a cleansing agent to purify them and sanctify them from all sin" (Bible Dictionary, s.v. "Holy Ghost," 704). Men speak and do righteous works by the power of the Holy Ghost, which power is received by faith on the Son of God (see 1 Nephi 10:17). *See also:* Acts 1:8; D&C 109:79.

Power of the Redeemer (Helaman 5:11). *See:* Power of Christ (the Lamb of God/the Lord); Power of the atonement.

Power of (the) redemption (and the resurrection) (Jacob 6:9; Omni 1:26; Mosiah 18:2; Alma 12:32; Mormon 9:13; Moroni 8:20, 22). Meaning the power of the Atonement to bring about the redemption of man (remission of sins) and to bring about the resurrection of man (immortal life). *See also:* Atonement of Christ (the Only Begotten Son); Power of his redemption.

Power of the resurrection (2 Nephi 9:6, 12; 10:25; Jacob 4:11; 6:9; Mosiah 15:20; 18:2; Alma 4:14;

41:2; Mormon 7:5; 9:13; Moroni 7:41). God the Father gave Jesus Christ the power to conquer physical death and resurrect Himself to immortal life. The Resurrection of Christ also opened the gates of death so that all mankind can and will also be resurrected by the power of resurrection that Christ now holds and exercises for all who have lived here on earth. *See also:* Power of the atonement.

Power of the word of God (2 Nephi 1:26; Words of Mormon 1:17; Alma 17:4; 53:10; 62:45; 3 Nephi 28:20; 4 Nephi 1:30; Mormon 8:16). *See:* Power of his voice (word).

Power of their words (Alma 17:4). The teachings of the servants of God carry great power to the convincing of men of the truth when those servants teach by the Spirit.

Power over the hearts of men (people) (1 Nephi 22:15, 26; 2 Nephi 30:18; Mosiah 27:9; Alma 10:25; 48:17; Ether 15:9). Satan and evil men can only have power over people if they yield their hearts unto them. *See also:* Power of Satan; Satan did get hold (possession) upon the hearts of the people.

Power [not given] that they could utter the things which they saw and heard (3 Nephi 28:14). *See:* Forbidden that I (they) should write (utter/preach).

Power to baptize (Alma 5:3; 3 Nephi 11:22). Meaning having the priesthood power and authorization (by one holding the keys) to baptize in the name of Jesus Christ, and thus provide a true and heaven-recognized ordinance.

Power to do all things which are according to his word (Alma 7:8). *See:* According to God's word; Power of God.

Power to do many mighty works in his name (Alma 19:4). Meaning to perform miracles in the name of Jesus Christ. The servants of God who hold the true priesthood of God have this power. *See also:* D&C 3:4.

Power to give the Holy Ghost (3 Nephi 18:37). Meaning having the priesthood power and the authority to give the gift of the Holy Ghost by the laying on of hands once one is baptized. This ordinance requires the higher, or Melchizedek, priesthood. For example, an elder has this power (see D&C 20:41; 53:3). When Joseph Smith and Oliver Cowdery received the authority to baptize from John the Baptist, "he said this Aaronic Priesthood had not the power of laying on hands for the gift of the Holy Ghost, but that this should be conferred on us hereafter" (Joseph Smith–History 1:70).

Power to make intercession (Mosiah 15:8). Christ by His Atonement has the power to intercede with mercy and forgive our sins. *See also:* Atonement of Christ (the Only Begotten Son); Great Mediator; Made intercession for the transgressions; Make intercession for the children of men.

Power to ordain (Mosiah 25:19). *See:* Authority from (of) God.

Power to save (Alma 12:15). *See:* Mighty to save.

Power was given unto them that they might know (Alma 12:7). *See:* Know all my (thy) thoughts.

Power which the Lord had given them (Alma 8:32). *See:* Authority from (of) God; Power and word of God.

Powers of heaven (3 Nephi 20:22; 28:7). Meaning the powers of Christ that shall be in the midst of the people of God. "For I, the Lord, have put forth my hand to exert the power of heaven; ye cannot see it now, yet a little while and ye shall see it, and know that I am, and that I will come and reign with my people" (D&C 84:119).

Powers of hell (Alma 37:16; 48:17). Also known as the powers of darkness. *See also:* Power of Satan.

Powers of the earth (3 Nephi 28:39). Meaning the effects of mortality no longer influence them. *See also:* Not taste of death; Three disciples of Christ; Three disciples of Jesus (who should [were to] tarry).

Praise and thanksgiving unto the Lord (Mosiah 2:20; Alma 26:8; 3 Nephi 10:10; Ether 6:9). Giving thanksgiving to God is an integral part of praising Him.

Praise him all the day long (1 Nephi 18:16; Ether 6:9). Just as we have been commanded to pray without ceasing, we should praise God without ceasing. In 3 Nephi 20:1–2, Jesus commanded the multitude to arise from prayer and stand upon their feet, yet He "commanded them that they should not cease to pray in their hearts." In like manner we should not cease to praise God in our hearts.

Praise him forever (2 Nephi 4:30; Mosiah 18:30; Alma 26:12, 14, 16; 29:17; 36:28). We should praise God always, and it will be the great opportunity of those who gain salvation to praise God forever in the eternities to come. In vision, Joseph Smith "beheld the glory of the Son, on the right hand of the Father, . . . and saw the holy angels, and them who are sanctified before his throne, worshiping God, and the Lamb, who worship [and praise] him forever and ever" (D&C 76:20–21).

Praise him through grace divine (2 Nephi 10:25). Meaning praise Him for His grace divine, which is His Atonement on behalf of mankind.

Praise his name (2 Nephi 9:49; Alma 26:8, 12). "[We] will sing praise to the name of the Lord most high" (Psalm 7:17). To praise His name is to: make His name be remembered; glorify and honor His name; give thanksgiving in His name; mention His name is exalted; make holy His name; bless His name; and take upon us His name. These are only a few of the ways we can praise His name.

Praise of the world (1 Nephi 13:9; 2 Nephi 26:29; Mormon 8:38). It is sinful to seek the praise of the world, for this is not our purpose nor our mission in life. *See also:* Seek not for power; Vain things of the world.

Praise (pray) all the day (1 Nephi 18:16; Enos 1:4; Mosiah 21:14; Mormon 3:12; Ether 6:9). *See:* Praise(-d/praising) God; Pray(-eth/-ing) continually (without ceasing).

Praise the Lord (1 Nephi 18:16; 2 Nephi 4:30; 22:1, 4; Alma 26:16; 3 Nephi 10:10; Ether 6:9). *See:* Praise(-d/praising) God; Praise his name.

Praise(-d/praising) God (1 Nephi 1:8, 15; 15:15; 18:16; 2 Nephi 4:30; 9:49; 10:25; Mosiah 2:20; Alma 24:23; 26:8, 12, 14, 16–17; 36:22; 3 Nephi 4:31). God has given us so much; everything we have is from Him. Even more, the Father gave His Only Begotten Son, and His Son, Jesus Christ, gave His life to atone for our sins. Therefore we should praise them always. To praise God is to: declare His wonderful doings; exclaim His glory is great; sing to Him praises; shout Hosanna to God; let all people praise Him; let all things praise Him; praise

Him forever; delight in Him; make an offering in remembrance of Him; expound there is no other as great; thank Him that He created us; remember that He redeemed us; and bless His holy name. These are only a few examples of how we can praise God. *See also:* Praise him all the day long; Praise him forever; Praise him through grace divine; Praise his name; Praise of the world; Praise the Lord.

Pray always (and not faint) (2 Nephi 32:9; 3 Nephi 18:15, 18–19). It is probably not possible to pray and do a math problem simultaneously. But we can pray before the math test, at short intervals during the test, and then offer a prayer of thanks after the test. However, prayer does not replace preparation and effort by ourselves. Someone has said we must pray as though the result depends on the Lord and then we must rise from our knees and work as though the result depends on our effort. To pray always means to pray often, to pray many times during the day, and to never forget our blessings from God. To pray always means to keep God and God's will foremost in our minds, rather than letting worldly things take over our minds.

Pray continually for them (1 Nephi 2:18; 2 Nephi 33:3; Enos 1:9; 3 Nephi 12:44; 17:21; 18:23; 19:23, 28; Mormon 3:12; Moroni 8:28). The prophets and all just and true men live at a higher level because the welfare of their fellowmen weighs heavily on their minds and souls. They pray for their fellowmen. The example given to us by Jesus is to pray for them His people. *See also:* Anxiety for you; Could not bear that any soul should perish; Desire for the welfare of my brethren; Weighed down with sorrow.

Pray in their hearts (3 Nephi 20:1). To pray but not out loud and not using one's physical voice. Rather, to think the words within one's mind, but so sincerely that it comes from the heart. Our real intents occur in the heart and should be offered up unto God as thanks and humble petitions. Though God knows the intentions of our hearts, we are commanded to pray for our righteous desires and to give thanks.

Pray unto God (1 Nephi 7:21; 2 Nephi 9:44, 52; 33:3; Jacob 3:1; Words of Mormon 1:11; Mosiah 27:22; Alma 30:54; 62:51; 3 Nephi 19:18; Moroni 7:48; 9:22). In Alma 34:18–27 we are commanded to pray oft concerning all our righteous needs. The Lord's Prayer in Matthew 6:9 and 3 Nephi 13:9 was introduced with the words "after this manner therefore pray ye." In Moroni 7:6 we are told that when we pray unto God, except you shall do it with real intent it profits you nothing. We must always pray in the name of Jesus Christ.

Pray(-ed) in faith (1 Nephi 15:11; 2 Nephi 33:3; Jacob 3:1; Enos 1:15;

Mosiah 4:21; Alma 22:16; 31:38; Moroni 7:26). Prayer without faith is hypocrisy. Prayer without faith avails nothing and is vain. Prayer without faith has no power or fervor and damns the soul. On the other hand, sincere prayer having faith is heard of God and answered according to God's will. There are countless examples of prayer with faith changing the course of nations, moving the elements, healing the sick and infirm, protecting individuals from harm, softening hearts, bringing souls unto repentance, and applying the Atonement of Christ to sins.

Prayed mightily (Alma 2:28; 46:13). *See:* Mighty prayer.

Pray(-ed) unto the Father in my (the) name (of Christ) (2 Nephi 32:9; 33:12; 3 Nephi 18:19–21, 23, 30; 20:31; Moroni 3:2; 4:2; 8:3). We are promised in D&C 88:64 "Whatsoever ye ask the Father in my name it shall be given unto you, that is expedient for you." *See also:* Ask the Father in my name (in the name of Christ).

Pray(-ed) unto the Lord (1 Nephi 1:5–6; 7:17, 21; 8:8–9; 18:21; Enos 1:11; Alma 2:28; 62:51; 3 Nephi 3:20; Ether 12:36). *See:* O Lord.

Prayed with many long strugglings (Enos 1:10–11). *See:* Wrestle which I had before God; Mighty prayer.

Prayer and supplication (Enos 1:4; Alma 31:10). Meaning to pray while adding supplications, which are pleadings, entreaties, sincere requests, humble appeals, and repentant petitions.

Prayers of the faithful (2 Nephi 6:11; 26:15). God is particularly attentive to the prayers of the faithful. *See also:* According to his (your) faith.

Prayers of the righteous (Alma 10:22–23; 62:40; Mormon 5:21). God is particularly attentive to the prayers of the righteous. *See also:* Obedient to the commandments (of God).

Pray(-eth/-ing) continually (without ceasing) (2 Nephi 9:52; 33:3; Enos 1:15; Mosiah 26:39; Alma 13:28; 15:17; 26:22; 34:27, 39; 62:51; 3 Nephi 19:24, 26, 30; 20:1; Moroni 6:4; 8:3). In Alma 34:27, "Yea, and when you do not cry unto the Lord, let your hearts be full, drawn out in prayer unto him continually for your welfare, and also for the welfare of those who are around you." *See also:* Cried unto God (him) continually (this long time); Pray always (and not faint).

Preach repentance (Mosiah 18:7, 20; Alma 13:18; 37:33; Helaman 13:2; 3 Nephi 7:23; Moroni 3:3). Man must repent and come unto Christ, otherwise man cannot be saved. God has commanded often that His servants are to teach faith in the Lord Jesus Christ and repentance. "Preach naught but repentance" (D&C 19:21). "Say nothing but repentance unto this generation" (D&C 6:9; 11:9).

Preach the gospel (3 Nephi 28:23; Mormon 9:22). *See:* Declare good tidings; Gospel of (Jesus) Christ.

Preach the word (of God) (Mosiah 28:6, 9; Alma 4:19; 5:13; 8:8, 24; 16:15, 21; 17:8, 14; 21:12; 22:26; 23:3–4; 29:13; 31:8, 11; 32:1; 35:2–3; 42:31; 43:2; 48:19; Helaman 5:4; 6:37; 7:2; 3 Nephi 5:4). The word and knowledge of men avails not salvation, but only the word of God. The word of God brings peace, joy, redemption, and safety. *See also:* Preaching of the word (of God); Word of God.

Preach up unto themselves their own wisdom and their own learning (2 Nephi 26:20, 29; Alma 1:12, 16). Beware of priestcrafts wherein men and women preach worldly knowledge and understanding mixed and combined with a little scripture to sound pious. These, for this cause, teach to get gain and honor of the world, but seek not the well-being of the kingdom of God.

Preach with great power and authority (Alma 23:6; Helaman 5:17–18; 6:5). To teach the gospel of Christ by the power of the Holy Ghost. This gift protects the preacher from harm and evil, and makes their words irrefutable. *See also:* Minister with power and great authority.

Preaching and prophesying (Jacob 1:4; Enos 1:23; Alma 8:24; Helaman 6:2; 16:4; 3 Nephi 2:10). Prophesying often accompanies preaching, particularly with the preaching of prophets, seers, and revelators. The word of God contains not only that which we should do (the commandments and ordinances), but also includes revelation of future events which is prophecy. See the many scriptural phrases herein beginning with the words *prophesied, prophesy,* and *prophesying.*

Preaching of the word (of God) (Mosiah 25:21; 27:32; Alma 21:11, 16; 23:1; 31:5; 43:2; Helaman 6:2). *See:* Preach the word (of God).

Precepts of men (2 Nephi 27:25; 28:14, 26, 31). Meaning the teachings or philosophies of men, and not the doctrine, principles, laws, and ordinances of Christ. The precepts of God are praised in the headnotes that introduce the separate stanzas of Psalm 119: "Ponder the precepts and ways of the Lord" (vv. 9–16). "O Lord, grant us Thy law, and make us to understand Thy precepts" (vv. 25–32). "O Lord, save us, for we have sought Thy precepts" (vv. 89–96).

Precious land(-s) (1 Nephi 17:38; 2 Nephi 1:10; 3:2). *See:* Land choice above all other lands.

Precious steel (1 Nephi 4:9). It has been suggested (see Chadwick, "Lehi's House at Jerusalem," 113–17) that Nephi and his family were workers in metals because he recognized fine steel (1 Nephi 16:18) and fine brass (1 Nephi 16:10). In 2 Nephi 5:15, Nephi says, "I did teach my people to . . . work in all manner of . . . iron, and of copper, and of brass, and of steel, and of gold, and of silver, and of precious ores, which were in great abundance" in the promised land. *See also:* Fine steel.

Precious things (1 Nephi 2:4, 11; 3:22, 24; 2 Nephi 5:16; Jarom 1:8; Mosiah 11:8–9; 19:15; 21:21; 22:12; Alma 1:29; 4:6; 15:16; 31:28; Helaman 12:2; 3 Nephi 6:2; 4 Nephi 1:41; Ether 9:17). Refers to possessions of this world which have great monetary or worldly value. The words "precious things" in the Book of Mormon are often found in company with the words *gold* and *silver*. We are cautioned by the Lord not to seek after worldly wealth but rather to seek after the spiritual. Exceeding riches most often leads to the sin of pride. *Contrast:* Plain and precious things. *See also:* Jacob 2:18–19.

Precious unto God (him) (Jacob 5:74; Alma 39:17). *See:* Souls are precious.

Preparatory redemption (Alma 13:3). Meaning the "atonement which was prepared from the foundation of the world for all mankind" (see Mosiah 4:6–7). In other words, the redemption provided by Christ as planned in the pre-earth councils. Alma 13:3 confirms that many had their holy calling ("high priests of God," Alma 13:10) prepared from the foundation of the earth because of their exceeding faith and good works in the pre-earth life. Thus they were foreordained to be high priests just as Jesus Christ was foreordained to provide the Atonement, a redemption prepared from the foundation of the world for all mankind.

Preparatory state (Alma 12:26; 42:10, 13). Meaning the probationary mortal life that is part of the plan of salvation. *See also:* Probationary state (time).

Prepare a way (1 Nephi 3:7; 22:20). God will prepare a way for His servants and His people. *See also:* Prepare the way; D&C 95:1.

Prepare quickly (Alma 5:28–29). Are you prepared to meet God? If not, prepare quickly; for the hour is near, and we know not the hour of His coming. *See also:* At hand; Judgments must speedily come unto you; Time speedily cometh.

Prepare the (their/your) minds (souls) (2 Nephi 9:46; Alma 16:16; 34:3; 39:16; 3 Nephi 17:3). *See:* Prepare their hearts.

Prepare the way (1 Nephi 17:13; Jacob 5:61, 64; 3 Nephi 21:27; 24:1; Moroni 7:31). The Lord has promised He will prepare the way for His people, leading them to safety and salvation. *See also:* Prepare a way.

Prepare their hearts (Alma 13:24; 16:16). We must prepare our hearts, minds, and souls to receive and experience the wonderful things prophesied in the future, including the coming of Christ. This preparation means looking forward with joyous expectation because one is worthy, not in fear because of unworthiness. *See also:* Prepare the (their/your) minds (souls).

Prepare to meet God (Alma 12:24; 34:32). The message of the prophets through the ages has been, "Repent and prepare to meet God, for the kingdom of heaven is nigh at hand." *See also:* At hand; Probationary state (time).

Prepare (ye) the way of the Lord (1 Nephi 10:7–8; 11:27; Alma 7:9; 9:28; Helaman 14:9; Ether 9:28). John the Baptist fulfilled his mission in preparing the way of the Lord by (1) calling people to repentance; (2) baptizing converts to the Lord; and (3) teaching the true doctrine of Christ to an apostate nation.

Additionally, prophets through the ages have warned the world to prepare the way for the coming of Jesus Christ, both at the meridian of time and for His Second Coming. We must:

- Prepare ourselves spiritually to be worthy to greet the Lord at His coming,
- Prepare others also to be worthy to greet the Lord,

- Prepare a large community of saints (the King of kings should be greeted by many, not just a small group),
- Prepare for a joyful and royal reception,
- Prepare a majestic house (temple) for His habitation,
- Prepare for great festivals and praises of song to honor Him,
- Prepare by warning and informing all the world of His expected return, and
- Prepare because He might come any day without warning.

See also: Make (making) his (my) paths straight.

Prepared a place (house) for you in the mansions of my Father (Enos 1:27; Ether 12:32–34, 37). *See:* Dwell with God (him in glory); Lifted up to dwell in the kingdom prepared for him; Mansions of my (thy) Father; Place prepared [heaven].

Prepared a place of filthiness (fire and brimstone/hell) (1 Nephi 15:34–35; 2 Nephi 28:23). *See:* Depths of hell; Place prepared [hell].

Prepared by (of) the Lord (1 Nephi 17:5, 41; 18:12; 2 Nephi 5:12; Mosiah 1:16; Alma 37:38). This earth has not been left by God to drift and exist aimlessly. Rather God has planned all concerning this world; He directs the course of nations and peoples (see D&C 117:6); He foreordains many to specific missions (see D&C 101:80); and He blesses individuals and nations who reverence Him in honest and upright living. The Lord has also prepared and directs smaller things and events in people's lives. In hindsight we can often recognize those things. *See also:* Foreknowledge of God; Prepared from the beginning (foundation of the world).

Prepared for the wicked (1 Nephi 15:29; Helaman 3:29). *See:* Prepared a place of filthiness (fire and brimstone/hell).

Prepared for them (2 Nephi 9:16, 18; 28:23; Alma 37:46). God has prepared places in the hereafter based on and graded on our actions during our earthly probation. *See also:* Prepared a place (house) for you in the mansions of my Father; Prepared for the wicked; D&C 76.

Prepared from the beginning (foundation of the world) (1 Nephi 10:18; 2 Nephi 9:18; Mosiah 4:6–7; 15:19; 18:13; 28:14; Alma 12:30; 13:3, 5, 7; 18:39; 22:13; 42:26; Ether 3:14; 4:19). In our Heavenly Father's great plan of salvation, all necessary things were prepared for from the foundation of the world, or from the time of planning and creation of the world. *See also:* Foundation of the world; From the foundation of the world; Laid from the foundation of the world; Redemption prepared from the foundation of the world.

Prepared means for the interpretation thereof (Mosiah 8:13; Alma 37:21, 24; Mormon 9:34; Ether 3:23). Meaning the interpreters or the Urim and Thummim. *See also:* Interpretation thereof; Two stones.

Preparing the minds of the people (Alma 48:7). *See:* Prepare the (their/your) minds (souls).

Preparing the way (1 Nephi 14:17; 3 Nephi 21:28). Refers in these two verses to Heavenly Father preparing to gather His covenant people to the lands of their inheritance. *See also:* Gather in the house of Israel.

Presence of God (2 Nephi 2:8, 10; 9:8–9; Alma 36:14–15; 42:23; Mormon 7:7). To be in the presence of God is a most significant thing. These verses talk about: to dwell in the presence; stand to be judged in the presence; Satan fell from the presence; being shut out from the presence; the very thought of coming into the presence; and the Resurrection bringeth men into the presence of God to be judged.

Presence of the Lord (1 Nephi 2:21; 8:36; 5:20; 2 Nephi 9:6; 26:7; Mosiah 2:38; 3:25; Alma 9:13–14; 42:7, 9, 11; 50:20; Helaman 12:25; 14:15–17; Mormon 9:13; Ether 2:15; 4:1; 10:11). These verses describe: cut off from; cast off from; nigh consumed before; brought into; bring back into; and go down from the presence of the Lord. *See also:* Presence of God.

Preserve his people in righteousness (3 Nephi 4:29). The

Lord God will protect, preserve, and maintain His righteous people. Compare Mosiah 1:13, where if the people become wicked He will no more preserve them. *See also:* Land choice above all other lands; Preserve the righteous.

Preserve our (the/these) records (1 Nephi 3:19; 5:21; Jacob 1:3; Enos 1:15–16; Omni 1:1; Mosiah 28:20). The Lord God commanded Nephi and succeeding prophets to keep a record of the people and their doings. Those things which were preserved in the records were: the commandments of God; the language of the people; a genealogy of their fathers; spiritual events; the revelations of God; a secular history of the people; the struggles and accomplishments; wars; and government. These things were important for their children and succeeding generations. They are also invaluable to us in our day for learning and direction in our lives.

Preserve the righteous (1 Nephi 22:17; 2 Nephi 9:53). *See:* Preserve his people in righteousness.

Preserve thy seed (forever) (2 Nephi 3:16; 9:53; Alma 3:8; 46:24). A promise given to Lehi and other righteous servants through the ages. The righteous remember (honor) their parents and forefathers. Also they desire a vast posterity. The spirit of family history work bears out these desires and feelings. Eventually our progenitors,

ourselves, and our posterity will all be joined together in the family of God forever and ever if we are worthy. *See also:* Remember his (your) seed; Seed as numerous as the sand of the sea.

Preserved by the hand of the Lord God (1 Nephi 5:14; Mosiah 1:5; 28:15; Alma 37:4; 46:24). The mighty hand of God is able to do all things according to the will of God, including preserving His people. *See also:* By the hand of the Lord (God).

Press forward (1 Nephi 8:24; 2 Nephi 31:20). Meaning to push ahead and accomplish much good.

Prick their hearts (Jarom 1:12). Meaning to stimulate, arouse, and cause to remember, repent, and bring to action. *Compare:* Acts 2:37.

Pride of nobility (Alma 51:17–18, 21). Some falsely believe they are better than other people because of their family of birth, their wealth, or their social and political connections. *See also:* Blood of nobility; High birth; Lifted up in (unto) pride (of their eyes/hearts/and boasting).

Pride of the world (1 Nephi 11:36; 12:18). Pride is of the world, not of heaven. Great shall be the destruction of the prideful (the great and spacious building). "Pride goeth before destruction, and an haughty spirit before a fall" (Proverbs 16:18).

Pride of their (your) eyes (2 Nephi 26:20; Alma 1:32; 4:6, 8; 62:49;

Helaman 13:27). "Of their eyes" because in their own eyes they believe they are better than others. *See also:* Lifted up in (unto) pride (of their eyes/hearts/and boasting); Pride of their (your) hearts; Puffed up in the vain things of the world; Walk after (in) the pride of your eyes (hearts).

Pride of their (your) hearts (2 Nephi 28:15; Jacob 2:13, 16, 20; Mosiah 11:5, 19; Alma 4:8, 5:53; 6:3; 7:6; 15:17; 31:25, 27; Helaman 3:33, 36; 4:12; 7:26; 13:22, 27; 3 Nephi 16:10; Mormon 8:28, 36). "Of their hearts" because in their hearts they have imagined they are better than others. *See also:* Lifted up in (unto) pride (of their eyes/hearts/and boasting); Pride of their (your) eyes; Puffed up; Puffed up in the pride of their hearts; Puffed up in the vain things of the world; Walk after (in) the pride of your eyes (hearts).

Priest and teacher ought to become popular (1 Nephi 22:23; Alma 1:3; 35:3). A concept contrary to the true ways of God, wherein priests, pastors, and ministers are elected to their positions. In essence, this is a popularity contest, which is in sharp contrast to our belief in the Fifth Article of Faith, which states, "We believe that a man must be called of God, by prophecy, and by the laying on of hands by those who are in authority, to preach the Gospel and administer in the ordinances thereof." *See also:* Priestcraft(-s).

Priestcraft(-s) (2 Nephi 10:5; 26:29; Alma 1:12, 16; 3 Nephi 16:10; 21:19; 30:2). To teach religion, not the true gospel of Jesus Christ but an altered doctrine, for the purpose of gain, money, and the honor of men. *See also:* Priest and teacher ought to become popular; D&C 33:4.

Prince of peace (2 Nephi 19:6; Alma 13:18). Jesus Christ is the Prince of Peace, and His gospel is a gospel of peace. "For unto us a child is born, unto us a son is given; and the government shall be upon his shoulder: and his name shall be called Wonderful, Counsellor, The mighty God, The everlasting Father, *The Prince of Peace*" (Isaiah 9:6; emphasis added). "Perhaps we stray from the path which leads to peace and find it necessary to pause, to ponder, and to reflect on the teachings of the Prince of Peace and determine to incorporate them in our thoughts and actions and to live a higher law, walk a more elevated road, and be a better disciple of Christ" (Monson, "Path to Peace," 60). Melchizedek was also called the prince of peace in Alma 13 because he taught the gospel of peace to his people.

Privileges of their church (religion/worship) (Alma 2:4; 50:39; 51:6; 3 Nephi 2:12). Meaning the freedom to worship as they please (without infringing on others' rights). Thus having freedom of religion not hampered by evil laws, persecution, or prejudice. *See also:* D&C 134:4.

Probationary state (time) (Alma 12:24; 42:5, 10, 13). The period of mortal life. *See also:* Days of probation; Prepare to meet God; Prolong(-ed) their days (existence) in the land; State of probation; Time to prepare to meet God; Wasteth the days of his probation.

Proceed forth out of my mouth (2 Nephi 3:21; 29:2). The promise of God to Lehi and Nephi that the word of God will come forth to their posterity, mainly through the Book of Mormon. *See also:* Word of God.

Proceed to do a marvelous work (1 Nephi 22:8; 2 Nephi 25:17; 27:26; 29:1). *See:* Marvelous work and a wonder.

Procrastinate [not] the day of your repentance (Alma 13:27; 34:33). Now is the day of our probation. We must not put off repentance and coming unto Christ. *See also:* Everlastingly too late; Probationary state (time).

Procrastinated the day of your salvation (Alma 13:21; 34:31; Helaman 13:38). *See:* Procrastinate [not] the day of your repentance.

Professed to belong to the church (Helaman 3:33; 4:11). Sometimes to hide their wickedness and deceit, people will profess to belong to the Church yet they do not abide by and believe in the full gospel.

Professed to know the Christ (4 Nephi 1:27). *See:* Know God; Matthew 7:21–23.

Profession of Nehor (Alma 14:18; 15:15; 16:11). *See:* Order and faith of (profession of) Nehor.

Profiteth not (nothing) (2 Nephi 9:28; Jacob 5:32, 35; Moroni 7:6, 9). If we heed not the counsel of God, bring forth bad fruit, or pray and give gifts without real intent, then its consequences, results, or outcome is nonexistent, as though we did nothing.

Prolong(-ed) their days (existence) in the land (2 Nephi 2:21; Alma 9:16; Helaman 15:4, 10–11). The Lord does prolong the days of men and women so that they might learn to keep the commandments of God. God blesses and prolongs the days of the righteous. Proverbs 10:27 says, "The fear of the Lord prolongeth days: but the years of the wicked shall be shortened." Consider the promise in the commandment to honor one's mother and father (Exodus 20:12). *Compare:* Days shall not be prolonged.

Promise is unto all (Mormon 9:21). The promise that prayer will be answered if we meet the criteria in this verse.

Promise of the Lord (2 Nephi 3:5; Mosiah 7:32; Alma 48:25). *See:* Promises of the Lord; Promises shall be fulfilled; Things (which are) to come.

Promised land (1 Nephi 13:12; 14:2; 17:13–14; 18:8, 22–23; Mosiah 10:15; Alma 36:28; 37:44–45; Helaman 7:7; 3 Nephi 20:29; Ether 6:5, 8, 12, 16; 7:27). *See:* Land choice above all other lands.

Promises of the Lord (2 Nephi 10:9, 21; Alma 3:17; 9:16, 24; 17:15; 28:11–12; Helaman 15:12; 4 Nephi 1:49). *See:* Great are the promises of the Lord; Promises shall be fulfilled.

Promises shall be fulfilled (2 Nephi 3:14; 10:17; 25:21; Mosiah 7:32; Alma 37:17; Mormon 8:22). The Lord does fulfill all His promises that He has made, and not one shall go unfulfilled. *See also:* According to God's word; Promise is unto all; Promise of the Lord; Promised land; Promises which I have made (the Lord had made unto them).

Promises which I have made (the Lord had made unto them) (2 Nephi 10:17; 29:2; Mosiah 1:7; 4 Nephi 1:11). *See:* Promises shall be fulfilled.

Proper frame (order) (Alma 11:43; 40:23; 41:2, 4). *See:* Perfect form (frame).

Prophecies and the promises of the Lord (2 Nephi 10:9, 21; Alma 3:17; 9:24; 17:15; 28:11–12; Helaman 15:12; 4 Nephi 1:49; Mormon 8:22). The prophecies and promises of the Lord shall all be fulfilled. *See also:*

Promises of the Lord; Prophecies of the holy prophets.

Prophecies concerning that which is to come (Alma 58:40; Helaman 6:14; Ether 13:13). A prophecy is defined as a prediction, a foretelling, and a foreshadowing. A divine prophecy comes from God and is therefore guaranteed and sure. *See also:* Prophecies of the holy prophets; Things (which are) to come.

Prophecies of Isaiah (2 Nephi 25:7; Mormon 8:23). *See:* Words of Isaiah.

Prophecies of the holy prophets (1 Nephi 5:13; 13:23; Mosiah 1:2; Alma 23:5; 30:22; 43:23; Helaman 15:7; 3 Nephi 1:4; 10:14). As well as testifying that Jesus Christ is our Savior, Redeemer, and the Son of God, all the holy prophets have by the Spirit foretold of events to come in the plan of God. *See also:* Many prophecies of the holy prophets.

Prophecies which had been spoken (1 Nephi 5:13; 2 Nephi 4:1; Mosiah 1:2; 2:34; Alma 30:6; Ether 13:21; Moroni 8:29). It is well to be aware of and be familiar with the prophecies that have been spoken by the holy prophets, so that we can be prepared and knowledgeable of God's dealings with man past, present, and future. *See also:* Many prophecies of the holy prophets.

Prophesied concerning (1 Nephi 22:5; 2 Nephi 4:2; Jacob 7:11; Words of Mormon 1:4; Mosiah

12:9, 14; 15:11; 20:21; Alma 37:4). A prophecy always has a message concerning some event or person. Otherwise it would not be a prophecy.

Prophesied many (great/ marvelous) things (1 Nephi 5:19; Mosiah 7:26; 13:33; Ether 11:20). Prophecies tend not to be ordinary and mundane. Rather they concern great and marvelous things. *See also:* Great and marvelous thing(-s).

Prophesied unto them (1 Nephi 1:16; 8:38; Alma 44:18; Helaman 13:4; 3 Nephi 11:12; Mormon 2:10; Ether 11:1, 3, 5, 12). It is the mission and calling of prophets to prophesy unto the people. *See also:* Prophesy unto him (the people/ thee/them/you).

Prophesy according to (the workings of) the Spirit (2 Nephi 1:6; 25:4). If a prophecy is from anything other than from the Holy Ghost, then it is not of God. *See:* Spirit of prophecy (and revelation).

Prophesy against (concerning/ unto) this people (Enos 1:26; Mosiah 12:1, 29; 13:26; Alma 8:25, 29, 32; 36:17; Helaman 13:3; Ether 12:2). The command of the Lord to His holy messengers to foretell by the power of the Holy Ghost what is to come to pass and what will happen to the people of the earth. *See also:* Prophecies of the holy prophets.

Prophesy concerning him (1 Nephi 1:18; 2 Nephi 25:13; 26:14; Mosiah 13:33; Alma 36:17). Revelation 19:10 says, "The testimony of Jesus is the spirit of prophecy." *See also:* Prophecies of the holy prophets; Alma 6:8; 36:17.

Prophesy of Christ (2 Nephi 25:26). *See:* Prophesy concerning him.

Prophesy unto him (the people/ thee/them/you) (1 Nephi 1:18; 2 Nephi 25:4; 26:14; Enos 1:26; Mosiah 11:20; 12:1, 8, 29; 13:26, 33; Alma 8:25, 29, 32; 36:17; 45:9; Helaman 4:14; 7:2; 13:3; 14:9; 16:7; Ether 11:12; 12:2, 5; 13:20). A prophecy is always directed toward an individual, a group, or a people. God's prophecies have a purpose, and all people should take note of them, heed them, and be instructed by them.

Prophesying among (unto) them (1 Nephi 1:4; 2 Nephi 25:1; 31:1, 2; Jacob 1:4; 4:15; Jarom 1:2; Omni 1:25; Mosiah 12:25; Helaman 6:2; 16:4; 3 Nephi 2:10). Prophesying is a true sign of a prophet among the people. *See also:* Prophesy unto him (the people/thee/them/you).

Prophesying concerning (of) things to come (1 Nephi 7:1; Enos 1:19, 23; Ether 7:23). Prophesying by its very nature is of things future. Because of God's infinite knowledge and power, He can foresee the events of the future, and by the power of the Holy Ghost, God reveals those prophecies to His prophets.

Prophet of the Lord God (2 Nephi 25:9; Jacob 5:2; Mosiah 7:26; Alma 8:20; 10:7; 19:4; Ether 12:2). *See:* Holy prophet(-s/of God).

Prophets of old (1 Nephi 1:20; 19:20–21; Jacob 4:13; Alma 33:3, 17). Biblical history (also recorded in the brass plates record) is rich with prophets that God sent to call His people to repentance and to prophesy of events to come. Yet the people often rejected the prophets, and cast them out, stoned them, and slew them.

Prophets testified (1 Nephi 10:5; Jacob 7:11; Alma 30:44; 33:17; Helaman 8:9, 16, 19–20; 13:26; 3 Nephi 1:18; 7:10; 10:16; 11:10; 15:10; 20:24; 23:5). To testify is to affirm, declare, or point. *See also:* Prophets of old; Testified (testify) unto him (the people/us/you).

Prosper exceedingly (2 Nephi 5:11, 13; Mosiah 23:19–20; 26:37; Alma 50:18; Ether 7:19; 9:16). A multi-faceted prosperity or abundance where the Lord has poured out His many blessings, including a multiplying in number, becoming exceedingly rich, Church growth and acceptance, and waxing strong in the land.

Prosper in the land (1 Nephi 2:20; 4:14; 13:15, 20; 2 Nephi 1:20; 4:4; 5:11, 13; Jarom 1:9; Omni 1:6; Mosiah 1:7; 2:22, 31; 9:9; 10:5;

12:15; 21:16; 23:19–20; 27:7; Alma 1:31; 9:13; 34:24; 36:1, 30; 37:13; 38:1; 45:8, 15, 25; 50:20; 62:48, 51; Helaman 3:20; 4:13, 15; 11:20; 12:1–2; 3 Nephi 6:4; 4 Nephi 1:7; Ether 6:28; 7:19, 26; 9:16; 10:16). Blessed abundantly with the goods of life. The Lord has promised that if the people keep the commandments they shall prosper in the land. *See also:* Land choice above all other lands; Prosper exceedingly.

Prosperity in Christ (4 Nephi 1:23). Meaning to live in united joy, love, harmony, and shared bounty. Thus all the people had exceeding plenty and to spare, which was shared universally and held in common.

Prostrate upon the earth (Alma 19:17–18; 22:17; 24:21). To prostrate oneself is to lie face down on the earth, signifying extreme humility. An example is one of the ten lepers who returned to give thanks to Jesus for healing him, "And fell down on his face at the feet [of Jesus], giving him thanks" (Luke 17:16).

Protect this people in righteousness (3 Nephi 4:30). *See:* Preserve his people in righteousness.

Proud in their (your) hearts (Jacob 2:20; Alma 45:24; 4 Nephi 1:43). *See:* Pride of their (your) hearts.

Proveth all his words (2 Nephi 11:3). God sends many witnesses to prove, verify, and confirm His words. *See also:* Testimony of many (two or three).

Providence hath smiled upon you (Jacob 2:13). Providence, meaning God hath smiled, meaning blessed and prospered you. *See also:* Prosper in the land.

Provoke him to anger (2 Nephi 13:8; Jacob 1:8; Alma 12:36; Helaman 7:18). We must not arouse, incite, or aggravate God to anger by sinning. *See also:* Anger of the Lord.

Provoke not the Lord our God (Alma 12:37). *See:* Provoke him to anger.

Publish good tidings (Mosiah 27:37). To teach the gospel of Jesus Christ. The word *gospel* means good news or good tidings. *See also:* Published (publisheth) salvation.

Publish(-ed/-ing) peace (1 Nephi 13:37; Mosiah 15:14, 16–17; 27:37). The duty of the Saints is to be peacemakers and teach the same. Particularly to teach the peace of the gospel and the message of the Savior, who is called the Prince of Peace.

Published (publisheth) salvation (Mosiah 12:21; 15:14; 3 Nephi 20:40). To preach and make known the gospel of Jesus Christ, and to make known that salvation is available through Jesus Christ.

Puffed up (2 Nephi 9:42; 28:9, 12–13, 15; Alma 5:37, 53; 31:27; Moroni 7:45). Larger or greater than they really are. In the eternity of things mortal man is nothing (Moses 1:10) and is fallen. *See also:* Puffed up in (the pride of) their hearts; Puffed up in the vain things of the world.

Puffed up in (the pride of) their hearts (2 Nephi 28:9, 15; Alma 5:53; 31:27). In our hearts there is contained the true identity of who and what we are. The "intent of our hearts" is often hidden from the world but is always completely known to God.

Puffed up in the vain things of the world (Alma 5:37; 31:27). "They grew proud, being lifted up in their hearts, because of their exceedingly great riches; therefore they grew rich in their own eyes, and would not give heed to their words, to walk uprightly before God" (Alma 45:24). In other words, Satan has deceived them and convinced them that the things of this world are more important than keeping the commandments, helping our fellowman, and seeking the kingdom of heaven. *See also:* Vain things of the world.

Pull down his wrath upon us (Alma 12:37; 54:9). Meaning to bring down or be deserving of the wrath of God because of sin. *See also:* Wrath of God (the Lord).

Pull down the (their) pride (Alma 4:19; 51:17–18; 60:36). Meaning to combat, eliminate, preach against and abolish the evil of pride. *See also:* Pride of their (your) hearts.

Punishment of the sinner (Alma 42:1). Both breaking the law and keeping the law have their consequences. The law would be null and void if there were no punishment. In other words, why should there be a law if there were no punishment? It is an eternal principle that there be law, punishment, reward, justice, and mercy. *See also:* Consequences of sin; Punishment that (which) is affixed.

Punishment that (which) is affixed (2 Nephi 2:10; Alma 42:16, 18, 22). Elder Joseph B. Wirthlin taught: "The Lord has given you the gift of agency (see Moses 7:32) and instructed you sufficiently to know good from evil (see 2 Ne. 2:5). You are free to choose (see 2 Ne. 2:27) and are permitted to act (see 2 Ne. 10:23; Hel. 14:30), but you are not free to choose the consequences. With absolute certainty, choices of good and right lead to happiness and peace, while choices of sin and evil eventually lead to unhappiness, sorrow, and misery" ("Running Your Marathon," 75). *Contrast:* Happiness which is affixed. *See also:* Punishment of the sinner.

Pure and delightsome people (2 Nephi 30:6). Joseph Smith in the third (1840) edition of the Book of Mormon changed "white and delightsome" to "pure and delightsome." Thus in the 1981 edition, which is the current edition, it is rendered "pure and delightsome." *See:* Delightsome people.

Pure and spotless before God (Alma 5:24; 13:12; Mormon 9:6). *See:* Stand spotless before me at the last day.

Pure heart(-s) and clean hands (2 Nephi 25:16; Alma 5:19). This is the kind of person that can ascend unto exaltation. "They that hath clean hands, and a pure heart; who hath not lifted up his soul unto vanity, nor sworn deceitfully. He shall receive the blessing from the Lord, and righteousness from the God of his salvation" (Psalm 24:6). Both the inner thoughts and the outward actions must obey this decree. *See also:* Pure in heart.

Pure in heart (Jacob 2:10; 3:1–3; 3 Nephi 12:8). People who have pure and undefiled intent, who strive mightily to pattern their lives after Christ. "Zion can be built up only among those who are the pure in heart, not a people torn by covetousness or greed, but a pure and selfless people. Not a people who are pure in appearance, rather a people who are pure in heart. Zion is to be in the world and not of the world, not dulled by a sense of carnal security, nor paralyzed by materialism. No, Zion is not things of the lower, but of the higher order, things that exalt the mind and sanctify the heart" (Kimball, "Becoming the Pure in Heart," 81).

Pure love of Christ (Moroni 7:47). "Charity is the pure love of Christ, and it endureth forever; and whoso is found possessed of it at the last day, it shall be well with him" (Moroni 7:47). This love is manifest in our works to God and to man. If we faithfully strive for charity it will begin to grow in us. In the end however, charity in its fulness is a gift from God to the faithful. Mortal man is incapable of developing this perfect love without the help of God.

Pure mercies of God (Moroni 8:19). *See:* Mercies of Christ (God/the Father/the Holy One of Israel/the Lord/thy Son); Merciful God (Being).

Purge them as gold and silver (3 Nephi 24:3). That is, to burn away one's impurities. A silversmith will purge silver of its impurities by heating it to melting, at which point the impurities float to the surface. As the silver is continued to be fired, the silversmith will watch the superheated silver until all the impurities are burned away and he can see clearly his reflection in the surface of the silver ["received his image in your countenances"]. *See also:* D&C 128:24.

Purified even as he is pure (Moroni 7:48). Jesus prayed, "Father, I thank thee that thou hast purified those whom I have chosen [12 disciples], because of their faith, and I pray for them, and also for them who shall believe on their words [us], that they may be purified in me, through faith on their words, even as they are purified in me" (3 Nephi 19:28). Because of Christ's Atonement, we may become purified upon our repentance, faith in Christ, and our striving to do what is right. *See also:* D&C 35:21.

Purified in me (3 Nephi 19:28–29). It is only through the Atonement of Christ that we can be purified. *See also:* Purified even as he is pure.

Purified until they are cleansed from all stain (Alma 5:21). This verse appears to indicate that the process of purification may take place over a period of time.

Purify the sons of Levi (3 Nephi 24:3). *Compare:* D&C 128:24. *See:* Offer unto the Lord an offering in righteousness.

Purifying and the sanctification of their hearts (Helaman 3:35). *See:* Hearts may be purified.

Put down the power and miracles of God (2 Nephi 26:20; 28:6; 4 Nephi 1:29, 31; Mormon 8:28; 9:20). Meaning those that deny miracles, teach against miracles, and persecute those who believe. *See also:* God of miracles.

Put on immortality (Enos 1:27; Mosiah 16:10; Alma 40:2; Mormon 6:21). Meaning to be resurrected to immortal life. *See also:* Immortal body; Put on incorruption.

Put on incorruption (2 Nephi 9:7, 13; Mosiah 16:10; Alma 5:15; 40:2; 41:4). "So when this corruptible [body] shall have put on . . . immortality, then shall be brought to pass the saying that is written, Death is swallowed up in victory" (1 Corinthians 15:54). In other words the Resurrection of Christ brings about the resurrection and immortality of all mankind. *See also:* Immortal body; Put on immortality.

Put on thy beautiful garments (2 Nephi 8:24; 3 Nephi 20:36; Moroni 10:31). D&C 82:14 says, "For Zion must increase in beauty, and in holiness; her borders must be enlarged; her stakes must be strengthened; yea, verily I say unto you, Zion must arise and put on her beautiful garments." This is an admonishment to ancient Jerusalem and to Zion today. In the millennium, after the Jews have been gathered home, Jerusalem of old will be renewed, cleansed, and beautified. Likewise, the Church today is to prosper, strive for the glory of God, and become beautiful. This includes putting on the magnifying of the priesthood and the beautiful garments of righteousness. *See also:* Put on (thy) strength O Zion; Isaiah 52:1.

Put on (thy) strength O Zion (2 Nephi 8:24; 3 Nephi 20:36). In March 1838, the Lord answered certain questions including, "Questions by Elias Higbee: What is meant by the command in Isaiah 52d chapter, 1st verse, which saith: Put on thy strength, O Zion— and what people had Isaiah reference to? He had reference to those whom God should call in the last days, who should hold the power of priesthood to bring again Zion, and the redemption of Israel; and to put on her strength is to put on the authority of the priesthood, which she, Zion, has a right to by lineage; also to return to that power which she had lost" (D&C 113:7–8).

Put their (your) trust in him (the Lord God) (Mosiah 4:6; 7:19, 33; 10:19; 23:22; 29:20; Alma 5:13; 36:3, 27; 38:5; 57:27; 58:33; 61:13; Helaman 12:1; Moroni 9:22). To exercise great faith in the goodness, wisdom, protection, and salvation of the true and living God. *See also:* Trust in God (the Lord).

Put to death (Mosiah 17:1, 8, 20; 21:23; 24:11; Alma 25:7, 12; 46:35; 62:9; 3 Nephi 1:9; 6:23, 24; Ether 10:6; 11:5; Moroni 1:2). Meaning to kill, murder, or cause to die. The laws of government can put individuals to death for certain crimes as enumerated in their laws. Also wicked men put to death those that stand in their way. The righteous abhor murder, for God has commanded, "Thou shalt not kill" (Exodus 20:13). *See also:* Temporal death.

Putteth his trust in man, or maketh flesh his arm (2 Nephi 4:34; 28:31). The might and power of man is nothing compared to the power and wisdom of God. Foolish is the person who puts his trust in man instead of in God. D&C 121:33 says, "What power shall stay the heavens? As well might man stretch forth his puny arm to stop the Missouri river in its decreed course, or to turn it up stream, as to hinder the Almighty." *See also:* Arm of flesh; Boast in their own strength; Maketh flesh his arm.

Putteth up his petition to you (Mosiah 4:16, 22). Meaning the beggar who lifts up his cup to you and asks alms or assistance. *See also:* Poor and needy.

Q

Quake and tremble (1 Nephi 1:6; 22:23; 2 Nephi 4:22; Mosiah 27:31; 28:3; Helaman 9:5; 12:9; 3 Nephi 11:3). The wicked will shudder, quiver, and shake before the Lord God because of their unrepentant evil ways. Actually, all things quake and tremble at the voice and power of God; however, having a clear conscience will allow us to stand before Him with confidence. *See also:* Fear and tremble; Shake the earth; Shrink from the presence of the Lord.

Quench the Holy Spirit (Jacob 6:8). To *quench* is to stifle, extinguish, ignore, deny, reject, or trample. Those that reject the Christ, His gospel, and the word of God also reject the influence of the Holy Ghost in their lives. *See also:* Past feeling.

Quick and dead (Moroni 10:34). *See:* Judge of both quick and dead.

Quick and powerful (Helaman 3:29). In various places in the scriptures it says that the word of God is quick and powerful. "Open ye your ears and hearken to the voice of the Lord your God, whose word is quick and powerful, sharper than a two-edged sword, to the dividing asunder of the joints and marrow, soul and spirit: and is a discerner of the thought and intents of the heart" (D&C 33:1). "The scriptures are described as 'quick and powerful' (Helaman 3:29; see also Hebrews 4:12). The word *quick* in these verses means 'living.' In other words, the scriptures are alive. Though they were written long ago, they have application today. That makes them powerful. We can profit and learn from them. Likening scriptures to our personal lives will invite inspired thoughts to help us with our modern day personal experiences" ("Likening the Scriptures," 34).

Quick to do iniquity (Mosiah 13:29; Alma 46:8; Helaman 12:4, 5). Mortal men are quick to do iniquity. It is their natural tendency because of their fallen nature and the presence of Satan and his temptations during our mortal probation. We must ever be watchful and guard against this tendency. It requires our might, mind, and strength, and our seeking the help of God.

R

Racked with a consciousness of guilt (Mormon 9:3). *See:* Bright recollection of all our guilt.

Racked with (eternal) torment (Mosiah 27:29; Alma 36:12, 16–17). *See:* Endless misery (and wo); Endless torment; Eternal torment.

Rage in the hearts of the children of men (2 Nephi 28:20). Meaning the devil has taken control of their hearts, their intents, and their desires. Thus love and kindness has been replaced with hate and anger. *See also:* Satan did get hold (possession) upon the hearts of the people.

Raise him (me/them) up at the last day (Alma 26:7; 36:28; 3 Nephi 15:1). Meaning to be raised up with the righteous at Christ's Second Coming. *See also:* Last day; Lifted up at the last day.

Raise their voices to God (Enos 1:4; Mosiah 24:12; 25:10). Meaning to pray unto God. *See also:* Cry unto God (Jesus Christ/the Lord).

Raise up a mighty nation among the Gentiles (1 Nephi 22:7). Refers to God's hand in establishing and building up the mighty nation we know as the United States of America. "And for this purpose have I established the Constitution of this land, by the hands of wise men whom I raised up unto this very purpose, and redeemed the land by the shedding of blood" (D&C 101:80).

Raise up a righteous branch (2 Nephi 3:5; 9:53; 10:1; Jacob 2:25). Refers to Lehi and his posterity, which is a branch of the seed of Joseph, that the Lord led away to preserve a righteous people unto Himself. *See also:* Branch of the house (tree) of Israel.

Raise up out of the fruit of thy loins (1 Nephi 22:20; 2 Nephi 3:6–7, 11, 18). Meaning the Lord will bring forth or send down a special descendant in one's posterity.

Raise up seed unto (me) the Lord (1 Nephi 7:1; Jacob 2:30; Ether 1:43). Means to propagate and raise up righteous followers of Christ.

Raise(-d from) the dead (Alma 22:18; 3 Nephi 7:19; 19:4; 26:15; 4 Nephi 1:5). By the priesthood and the power of God, individuals have been raised from the dead, as was Lazarus in John 11:43–44. This is being brought back to life and is not being resurrected. *See also:*

Immortal body; Resurrection of the dead; Resurrection of the body.

Raised from this mortality (temporal death) (Alma 11:42; 12:12). *See:* Raise(-d from) the dead.

Raised in (to) immortality (Alma 5:15; 11:45; 12:12; 41:4). *See:* Immortal body.

Raised unto life eternal (Mosiah 15:23; Moroni 7:41). *See:* Eternal life; D&C 29:43.

Read upon the house tops (2 Nephi 27:11). To broadcast far and wide. *See also:* Revealed upon the house tops.

Real intent (of heart) (2 Nephi 31:13; Moroni 6:8; 7:6, 9; 10:4). *See:* Intents of our hearts; Thoughts and intents of his (the) heart.

Reap destruction (2 Nephi 26:10; Mosiah 7:31). To harvest, be rewarded, and earn destruction and damnation as a result or consequence of wickedness.

Reap rewards according to their works (Alma 3:26; 9:28). *See:* According to their (your) works (deeds); Judged according to (of) their works.

Reap the rewards of your faith (Alma 32:43). *See:* According to his (my/our/the/their/thy/your) faith.

Rebel(-led/-ling/-lion) against God (1 Nephi 2:16, 23–24; Jacob 1:8; Mosiah 2:37; 3:12; 15:26; 16:5; 27:11; Alma 3:18; 9:24; 10:6; 36:13; 62:2; Helaman 8:25; 3 Nephi 6:18;

4 Nephi 1:38; Mormon 2:15). To know the will or commandments of God but willfully not obey is to sin. This is the very act of Satan in the premortal existence and is what Satan seeks to have us do. Having "known the ways of righteousness nevertheless have gone astray" (Alma 5:37). *See also:* Contrary to God; Dissented from the church; Enemy of (to/unto) God; Open rebellion against God; Spirit of the devil; Willfully rebel(-led/against God).

Receive all manner of wickedness (4 Nephi 1:27). Meaning they were willing to accept and participate in many wicked practices. *See also:* Foolish imaginations.

Receive his Spirit (the Holy Ghost) (2 Nephi 31:13; 32:5; Alma 22:15; 34:38; 3 Nephi 28:18; 4 Nephi 1:1). *See:* Receive(-d) the Holy Ghost.

Receive no witness until after the trial of your faith (Ether 12:6). Faith proceeds the miracle and the witness or testimony. If you shall ask having faith, then the truth will be manifest unto you (see Moroni 10:4). "If any of you lack wisdom, let him ask of God. . . . But let him ask in faith, nothing wavering" (James 1:5–6).

Received his image in your countenances (Alma 5:14). *See:* Image of God engraven upon your countenances.

Received into heaven (kingdom of God/state of happiness) (2 Nephi 10:25; Mosiah 2:41; Alma 7:21; 40:12; 3 Nephi 28:40; Ether 5:5). The righteous are promised to be received into heaven in the next life, a state of happiness, and eventually into the kingdom of heaven. The wicked have no such promise.

Received me (3 Nephi 9:17). Those that come unto Christ, receive the gospel and ordinances thereof, and endure to the end. *See also:* Come unto Christ.

Received me not (3 Nephi 9:16). Those that come not unto Christ, but reject Him and His redemption.

Received much strength of the Lord (1 Nephi 4:31). *See:* In the strength of our God (the Lord).

Receive(-d) the Holy Ghost (2 Nephi 31:13, 18; 32:2, 5; 3 Nephi 28:18; 4 Nephi 1:1). To receive the gift of the Holy Ghost by the laying on of hands, by those having authority in the priesthood. Once this gift is received, after baptism, the individual has the promise of the constant companionship of the Holy Ghost if they remain worthy by keeping the commandments. The Holy Ghost will tell us all things that we should do. *See also:* Gift and power of the Holy Ghost.

Receiveth wages of him whom he listeth to obey (Mosiah 2:33; Alma 3:27; 5:42). *See:* Consequences of sin; Justice of God; Restoration of God.

Reconcile yourselves to the will of God (2 Nephi 10:24). *See:* Reconciled to (unto) Christ (God).

Reconciled to (unto) Christ (God) (2 Nephi 10:24; 25:23; 33:9; Jacob 4:11). Means to become one with, to accept God and His way of life, to have no differences with, and to be approved and validated by. In other words, to be worthy and qualified to obtain the redemption of Christ.

Record is true (1 Nephi 1:3; 3 Nephi 5:18; 8:1; 17:25; 18:37). A witness that the record is true. *See also:* Testimony of many (two or three).

Record of the Jews (1 Nephi 3:3; 5:6, 12; 13:23; Omni 1:14; Mormon 7:8; Ether 1:3). The Bible or, as it is called in Ezekiel 37:19, the stick of Judah.

Record which shall come unto the Gentiles from the Jews (1 Nephi 13:23; Mormon 7:8). Refers to the Bible. *See also:* Book which doth proceed out of the mouth of the Jews; Plain and precious things.

Recover his (my) people (the Jews) (Jacob 6:2). The scattered tribes of Israel; in some verses the Jews are singled out; all are promised to be gathered in and restored to the lands of their inheritance. This will include their conversion to and reception of Jesus Christ as their Savior and Redeemer; and their acceptance of the laws, principles, and ordinances of the gospel. *See also:* Gather in the house of Israel.

Recover my people (the Jews) (2 Nephi 29:1, 5). *See:* Recover his people.

Recover them a second time (2 Nephi 6:14; 21:11; 29:1; Jacob 6:2). In the last days and at His Second Coming, the Lord God will gather in His people, which are the house of Israel, from their long dispersion and from their lost and fallen state. The Lord set His hand to gather Israel the first time when He brought them out of Egypt and when He brought them home from Babylon. *See also:* Gather in the house of Israel.

Redeem all those (mankind) who believe on his name (Alma 19:13; Helaman 14:2). The redemption provided by Jesus Christ is promised to and available to all men and women who repent and properly seek the benefits of that redemption. *See also:* All are alike unto God.

Redeem his (my) people (Mosiah 13:33; 15:1, 11; Alma 5:21, 27; 6:8; 11:40; 33:22; Helaman 5:10; Ether 3:14). Jesus Christ came to earth with the mission to redeem His people. Jesus desires to redeem His people—all those who will come unto Him.

Redeem mankind from their sins (Alma 21:7). *See:* Redeem them from their sins (transgressions);

Redemption of (for) man(-kind/the world).

Redeem my soul (2 Nephi 4:31). *See:* Redeemed my soul (from hell).

Redeem the children of men from the fall (2 Nephi 2:26). *See:* Redeemed from the fall.

Redeem the world (Helaman 5:9). Jesus Christ's redemption is universal and infinite, such that the Resurrection applies to all mankind in all the world. Redemption from sins and salvation is available to all the world on condition of repentance, baptism, proper ordinances, and faithfulness to the end. *See also:* Redeemer of all mankind (the world).

Redeem them from their sins (transgressions) (Mosiah 15:12; Helaman 5:10, 11). Jesus Christ suffered for the sins of mankind, if they will repent and follow Him. *See also:* Redeem the world.

Redeem those who will be baptized (Alma 9:27). Redemption is not possible without baptism. Baptism is the gate to the kingdom of God and the beginning of the path to the kingdom of heaven or salvation.

Redeemed by the Lord (Mosiah 15:24; Alma 46:39; Helaman 8:23). *See:* Redeemed from the fall.

Redeemed from the fall (2 Nephi 2:26; Mormon 9:13; Ether 3:13). The Lord, Jesus Christ, came into the world to redeem mankind from the fall of Adam, which introduced mortality to man and initiated man's probationary state here on earth. This was according to Heavenly Father's plan of salvation, which included the need for a Savior and Redeemer. Jesus redeems all mankind from physical death by means of the Resurrection, and redeems men and women from sin, upon their repentance and faithfulness, so that they may again dwell with God.

Redeemed from the gall of bitterness and bonds of iniquity (Mosiah 27:29). The consequences of sin are the drinking of the gall of bitterness and the bonds or chains of sin. *See also:* Chains of hell; Gall of bitterness.

Redeemed his people (Mosiah 15:18; 16:4; 18:20). Man is in a lost and fallen state: (1) because of the fall of Adam and (2) because of our own sins and transgressions. The redemption of Christ has overcome both of these. *See also:* Redeem the world; Redeemed from the fall.

Redeemed his servant Abraham (Jacob) (1 Nephi 20:20; 2 Nephi 27:33). The Lord redeemed His faithful servants Jacob and Abraham, as well as all the world. *See also:* Redeem the world.

Redeemed Jerusalem (Mosiah 12:23; 15:30; 3 Nephi 16:19; 20:34). Those of Jerusalem should be overjoyed because the Lord's redemption applies to them as well.

Redeemed my soul (from hell) (2 Nephi 1:15; 2:3; 4:31; 33:6; Mosiah 27:29). Many have prayed to have the redemption apply to them, and some have been made to know that they have been redeemed. We all hope for the same.

Redeemed none such (Mosiah 15:27; 26:26; Alma 12:18). Redemption from sin comes to none who rebel against God and who die in their sins knowing they have sinned and not repented.

Redeemed of God (by/of the Lord) (2 Nephi 8:11; Mosiah 18:9; 27:24–25; Alma 41:7). Jesus Christ, the Lord God, is the Savior and Redeemer.

Redeemed the children of men (them/us) (Mosiah 15:9, 23; Alma 1:4; 46:39; 58:41; 3 Nephi 20:13; Mormon 9:13). *See:* Redeem the world.

Redeemed without money (3 Nephi 20:38). Meaning to obtain salvation without paying money, for salvation is free to all those who repent and come unto Christ. *See also:* Buy milk and honey, without money and without price.

Redeemer cometh (2 Nephi 2:3; Alma 7:7; 19:13). Testimony given before the birth of Jesus that He would come and be the Redeemer. This knowledge was received from the Holy Ghost by vision or some other form of revelation.

Redeemer liveth (Alma 7:7). We must gain personal testimony that our Redeemer liveth. Jesus Christ our Savior and Redeemer is from all eternity to all eternity. The redemption was taught and known of before He came to earth (see Jacob 4:4). One could be redeemed of one's sins based on the coming redemption before Jesus suffered in the garden (see Mosiah 27:24). The departed spirits in paradise awaited the result of His redemptive Resurrection (see D&C 138:16–18). *See also:* Job 19:25.

Redeemer of all mankind (the world) (1 Nephi 10:5–6; 11:27; Alma 28:8). *See:* Redeem the world.

Redeemer of Israel (1 Nephi 21:7). Jesus is of Israel because His lineage is of Israel; and He is the Redeemer of the people of Israel. *See also:* Redeemer of all mankind (the world); Redeemer the Holy One (Mighty One) of Israel.

Redeemer the Holy One (Mighty One) of Israel (1 Nephi 20:17; 22:12; 2 Nephi 1:10; 3 Nephi 22:5). Jesus Christ is the Redeemer and Savior. He is the Holy One and the Mighty One of Israel. A=B, A=C, therefore B=C. *See also:* Holy One; Mighty one of Israel (Jacob).

Redemption cometh in and through Christ the Lord (the Holy Messiah/the Son of God) (2 Nephi 2:6; Mosiah 16:15; Alma 22:13; 34:7; 3 Nephi 9:17). *See:* Atonement of Christ (the Only Begotten Son).

Redemption of Christ (Jacob 6:9; Omni 1:26; Words of Mormon 1:8; Mosiah 16:15; 18:13; Alma 15:8; 21:9, 13; 34:7; 3 Nephi 6:20; 9:17; Mormon 9:12–13; Moroni 7:38; 8:20). The redemption spoken of includes the Resurrection to immortal life and the possibility of obtaining eternal life. Because of Jesus Christ we can be cleansed of our sins if we repent, are baptized, and strive to live the commandments to the end. If we do, we can be found "guiltless before him [God] at the judgment day[,] hath it given unto [us] to dwell in the presence of God in his kingdom, to sing ceaseless praises with the choirs above, . . . in a state of happiness which hath no end" (Mormon 7:7).

Redemption of God (Mosiah 13:32; Alma 5:15). *See:* Redemption of Christ.

Redemption of (for) man(-kind/ the world) (1 Nephi 1:19; Mosiah 15:19; 18:2; 21:9; Alma 13:32; 21:9; 22:13; 42:26; 3 Nephi 9:21; Mormon 7:7; 9:12–13; Moroni 7:38). *See:* Redeem the world; Redemption of Christ; Redemption of Christ.

Redemption prepared from the foundation of the world (Mosiah 15:19; 18:13; Alma 12:25, 30; 18:39; 22:13; 42:26). The plan of salvation and Christ's role therein was planned from the beginning (see Abraham 3:27). *See also:* Lamb of God; Preparatory redemption;

Prepared from the beginning (foundation of the world).

Refiner's fire and like fuller's soap (3 Nephi 24:2). Also quoted in Malachi 3:2–3 and D&C 128:24. The refiner uses the heat of fire to melt gold and silver so the impurities come to the surface and can be skimmed away. The fuller's soap is a powerful soap to whiten wool. *Compare:* 1 Nephi 20:10; Alma 34:29. *See also:* Fuller's soap; Purge them as gold and silver.

Reformed Egyptian (1 Nephi 1:2; Mosiah 1:2; Mormon 9:32). The language of reformed Egyptian "had been altered by the Nephites according to their manner of speech. Some scholars believe that reformed Egyptian was a type of shorthand. Moroni explains that if the plates had been larger they would have been written in Hebrew, and then the record would have been without imperfections (see v. 33). This suggests that reformed Egyptian must not have been as precise and accurate as Hebrew, and it must have required less space to write than Hebrew. Knowing this gives us a greater appreciation of how efficient the reformed Egyptian language must have been.

"The Hebrew language is very compact when compared to English and many other western languages. A typical English sentence of fifteen words will often translate into seven to ten Hebrew words. We have no indication of the size of the characters Mormon and Moroni used, but if they rejected Hebrew because the plates were not 'sufficiently large' (v. 33), then reformed Egyptian must have been a language remarkable for its ability to convey a lot of information with few words" (*Book of Mormon Student Manual*, 4). Striking is the statement "none other people knoweth our language" (Mormon 9:34).

Regulation should be made throughout (in) the church (Alma 45:21; 62:44). Because there had been some disruption and deviation from the true order of the Church, there needed to be made some adjustment, correction, reordering, guidance, and instruction to reestablish the gospel and word of God.

Reign in dominion (1 Nephi 22:24). *Dominion* means supreme authority and absolute power. The scripture here refers to Christ's Second Coming as King of kings and Lord of lords when He shall reign over all the earth. The words of the scriptures say, "The Son of God cometh in his glory, in his might, majesty, power, and dominion" (see Alma 5:50; 12:15).

Reign of the judges (Mosiah 29:44; Alma 1:1, 33; 3:25, 27; 4:1, 5–6, 9–10, 20; 8:2–3; 10:6; 11:4; 14:23; 15:19; 16:1, 12, 21; 28:7, 9; 30:2, 4–5, 32; 35:12–13; 43:3; 44:24; 45:2, 20; 46:37; 48:2; 49:29; 50:1, 17, 23–25, 35; 51:1, 12, 37; 52:1, 14–15, 18; 53:23; 55:35; 56:1;

57:5; 59:1; 62:11–12, 39, 52; 63:1, 3–4, 10, 16; Helaman 1:1, 13–14, 34; 2:1, 12; 3:1, 18, 22–23, 32–33, 37; 4:4, 8–10, 17–18; 6:1, 15, 32, 41; 7:1; 10:19; 11:1, 24, 29, 35; 16:9–13, 24). In Mosiah 29 we learn that none of the sons of Mosiah would be king in the stead of Mosiah. Mosiah taught that if the people could always have "just men" to be king it would be well, but that "unrighteous king[s] doth pervert the ways of all righteousness" (Mosiah 29:23). Therefore Mosiah proposed a system of judges chosen by the voice of the people, thereby the people would enjoy their liberty and rights. Also every man would share the burden of government. Alma the younger became the first chief judge in about 92 B.C., and this system continued until the coming of Jesus Christ to the American continent.

Reign(-s) of the kings (1 Nephi 9:4; Jacob 1:9, 11, 14; 3:13; Mosiah 29:47). When Nephi, son of Lehi, became old and saw that he must soon die, he anointed another to be king over the Nephites in his stead. These kings reigned from Nephi [between 544 and 421 B.C.] down until King Mosiah [about 92 B.C.], at which time Mosiah proposed and the voice of the people chose judges to rule over them (see Mosiah 29).

Reject the stone (the sure foundation) (Jacob 4:15, 17). Refers to the Jews' rejection of Christ in the meridian of time, also any

others who reject the Savior and Redeemer. *See also:* Rejected Jesus (my Redeemer/the Messiah); Rock of our Redeemer.

Rejected Jesus (my Redeemer/the Messiah) (2 Nephi 25:18; Mosiah 14:3; 27:30; Mormon 6:17). Many have rejected and will reject the Lord Jesus Christ to their damnation.

Rejected the gospel (truth/word of God) (1 Nephi 17:35; 2 Nephi 27:14; 28:29–30; Helaman 6:2; 8:25; 3 Nephi 16:10; 4 Nephi 1:38; Ether 4:3). The word of God brings salvation, joy, and peace if followed, but men have their agency, and many have rejected and will reject it.

Rejected the (words of the) prophets (1 Nephi 3:18; 7:14; 2 Nephi 27:5; Jacob 6:8; Ether 11:2, 22; 13:2). *See:* Rejected the gospel (truth/word of God).

Rejecting signs and wonders (so great a knowledge) (1 Nephi 19:13; Moroni 8:29). Great signs and miracles do not a believer make. Those who have seen miracles and had great truths made known unto them and then rejected them will have a greater condemnation.

Rejoice and exult in the hope (Alma 28:12). "Now the God of hope fill you with all joy and peace in believing, that ye may abound in hope, through the power of the Holy Ghost" (Romans 15:13).

Rejoice and glorify (in) God (2 Nephi 4:30; Alma 26:11;

Helaman 11:18). Truly we must rejoice, glorify, and praise God for all He has done, does now, and will do for mankind and for each individual. The mighty plan of salvation is for the benefit of all who accept it and their Savior. All that we have comes from God, and we must ever be grateful.

Rejoice in Christ (the Holy One of Israel/the Lord) (1 Nephi 8:3; 2 Nephi 4:30; 25:26; 27:30; Mosiah 28:2; Alma 37:9). *See:* Rejoice and glorify (in) God.

Relying upon the merits of Christ (2 Nephi 2:8; 31:19; Alma 24:10; Helaman 14:13; Moroni 6:4). Elder Gerrit W. Gong has said: "'Our Savior wants to make us whole. Our Savior wants to make us clean. He can and will mend our bodies and spirits. In due course He will remove every sickness and infirmity. In due course He will cleanse every repented sin and misdeed. As we repent, He will help us forgive others, including ourselves. . . . Believe in the mercy, merits, and grace of God'" (Gong, "Believe, Not Fear"). *See also:* D&C 3:20.

Remember his (your) seed (2 Nephi 29:2, 14). Among other promises and covenants, the Lord God promised these prophets that He would remember and bless these prophets' posterity. Any righteous persons would seek the Lord's blessing upon their children and upon their children's children throughout all time and eternity.

Remember how great things he has done (Mosiah 27:16; Alma 62:50; Ether 6:30). We must always remember and give thanks for the many blessings we receive at God's hand.

Remember me (2 Nephi 5:25; 3 Nephi 18:7, 11). *See:* Remember the Lord our (their/your) God.

Remember, remember (Mosiah 2:41; Alma 37:13; Helaman 5:9, 12; 14:30). The Lord and His prophets have often admonished us to remember. So important is it that in these instances it is emphasized by saying the word remember twice in succession.

Remember the Lord our (their/ your) God (1 Nephi 17:45; 19:18; Mosiah 9:3; 13:29; 23:27; Alma 55:31; 58:40; 62:49; Helaman 11:7; 12:5; 13:22). We must always remember the Lord God and keep His commandments. When people forget the Lord, that is when they stray and leave the path that leads to salvation. In the sacrament prayers we promise to "always remember him" (see Moroni 4:3; 5:2; D&C 20:77, 79). Concerning the Lord, we must remember His Atonement, His blessings, His promises, His commandments, His counsel, His love, His patience, His greatness, and His glory. *See also:* Always remember him (me); Remember how great things the Lord had done;

Remember me; Remember, remember; Stir them up in remembrance of the Lord.

Remember your awful guilt (2 Nephi 9:46). *See:* Bright recollection of all our guilt; Remembrance of our guilt.

Remember(-ed/-est) his (my/the) covenant(-s/promises) (1 Nephi 14:8; 17:40; 19:15; 2 Nephi 3:5; 29:1, 2; 3 Nephi 16:11–12; 20:29; 29:3; Mormon 5:20; 8:21, 23; 9:37). It is the way of the Lord to covenant with His people. The Lord has stated He will remember all the covenants and promises He has made to all the children of men. Most notably He will remember the promises to the house of Israel and to Lehi and Nephi and their posterity: that He will restore the gospel to them and gather them again. *See also:* Children of Israel; Children of the covenant; Covenant people (of the Lord); Covenant which he made with Abraham; Covenant(-ing) with God (him); Fulfilled the covenant; Gather in the house of Israel; If ye will keep my commandments ye shall prosper in the land; Know concerning the covenants of the Lord; Messenger of the covenant; Numbered among the people of the first covenant; Scattered tribes of Israel; Seed of Abraham; Tame olive tree.

Remembrance of God (2 Nephi 5:25; Mosiah 4:11; 13:30). *See:* Remember the Lord our (their/your) God.

Remembrance of our guilt (Alma 5:18). *See:* Bright recollection of all our guilt; Remember your awful guilt.

Remembrance of the Lord (their God) (Helaman 11:34; Moroni 6:6). *See:* Remember the Lord our (their/your) God.

Remembrance of their duty (Mosiah 1:17; Mosiah 13:30; Alma 4:3, 19). In these verses, meaning to remember our duty to God.

Remission of sins (2 Nephi 25:26; 31:17; Enos 1:2; Mosiah 3:13; 4:3, 11–12, 20, 26; 15:11; Alma 4:14; 7:6; 12:34; 13:16; 30:16; 38:8; Helaman 14:13; 3 Nephi 1:23; 7:16, 23, 25; 12:2; 30:2; Moroni 3:3; 8:11, 25–26; 10:33). The forgiveness of man's sins by God. O the beauty of the plan of salvation and the Atonement, that we might be forgiven of our sins. *See also:* Atonement of Christ (the Only Begotten Son); Conditions of repentance; Garments cleansed through the blood of the Lamb (made white/washed); Guilt was swept away; I will forgive.

Remnant of our (your) seed (1 Nephi 15:13–14; 2 Nephi 30:3–4; 3 Nephi 21:4). *See:* Remnant of these (this) people.

Remnant of the house (seed) of Israel (Jacob) (1 Nephi 10:14; 13:33–34; 19:24; 2 Nephi 20:20–21; 28:2; Alma 46:23; 3 Nephi 5:24; 20:10, 16; 21:2, 12, 22–23;

29:8; 4 Nephi 1:49; Mormon 5:12, 24; 7:1, 10). Most often in the Book of Mormon this refers to the seed of Lehi, who are the branch of Joseph that is over the wall. *See also:* Branch of the house (tree) of Israel; Fruit of the loins of Joseph.

Remnant of the house (seed) of Joseph (Alma 46:23–24, 27; 3 Nephi 5:23–24; 10:17; 15:12; Ether 13:6–8, 10). Remnant means a part or section from a residue of the whole. *See also:* Remnant of the house (seed) of Israel (Jacob).

Remnant of the seed of my brethren (1 Nephi 13:38–39). *See:* Remnant of these (this) people.

Remnant of these (this) people (3 Nephi 21:26; Mormon 3:19; 5:9; 7:1). Refers to the latter-day generations of the Lamanites that are descendants of the Book of Mormon people. *See also:* Remnant of our (your) seed; Remnant of the seed of my brethren.

Remorse of conscience (Alma 5:18; 29:5; 42:18). The sadness and regret of unrepented sins. A state of mind that should move us to repent. Remorse is one of the steps of repentance. *See also:* Clear conscience before God; Conditions of repentance.

Remove mountains (Jacob 4:6; Helaman 10:9; Mormon 8:24; Ether 12:30). "If ye have faith as a grain of mustard seed, ye shall say unto this mountain, Remove hence to yonder place; and it shall remove;

and nothing shall be impossible unto you" (Matthew 17:20). *See also:* If ye have faith.

Removed their hearts far from me (2 Nephi 27:25). Speaking of the professors of religion in the last days. They are corrupt because, "They draw near to me with their lips, but their hearts are far from me" (Joseph Smith–History 1:19). *See also:* Matthew 7:22–23.

Rend that veil of unbelief (Ether 4:15). Unbelief veils and covers our sight of truth and light. *See also:* Because of unbelief; Scales of darkness shall begin to fall from their eyes; Veil of unbelief.

Repair unto them the injuries (wrongs) which they had done (Mosiah 27:35; Alma 27:8; Helaman 5:17). One of the steps of repentance is to restore all that is possible; to restore to the one(s) wronged. *See also:* Conditions of repentance.

Repent all ye ends of the earth (Alma 5:50; 3 Nephi 9:22; 27:20; Mormon 3:22; Ether 4:18; Moroni 7:34). In other words, repent all ye people of the earth, for the world lies in sin and darkness.

Repent and be baptized (2 Nephi 9:23; 3 Nephi 11:37–38; 18:11, 16; 21:6; Mormon 7:8; Moroni 8:10). "We believe that the first principles and ordinances of the Gospel are: first, Faith in the Lord Jesus Christ; second, Repentance; third, Baptism by immersion for the remission of sins; fourth, Laying on of hands for the gift of the Holy Ghost" (Articles of Faith 1:4). From there, one must continue faithful to the end and receive the other ordinances of salvation.

Repent and be born again (Alma 5:49; 7:14). *See:* Born again (of God).

Repent and believe in his name (his Son/me) (2 Nephi 9:24; 30:2; Alma 19:36; 26:35; 3 Nephi 11:32). The first steps on the gospel path are faith in the Lord Jesus Christ and repentance.

Repent and come unto God (him/ me/my Beloved Son) (1 Nephi 10:18; 2 Nephi 28:32; Jacob 6:5; Alma 29:2; 3 Nephi 9:22; 12:19; 18:32; 21:6, 20; 27:20; 30:2; Mormon 3:2; Ether 4:18; 5:5; Moroni 7:34). To come unto Jesus infers to believe in Him, to repent, to be baptized, to serve Him, to keep His commandments, to build His kingdom, to preach of Him, to love Him, to follow His example, and to live His gospel to the fullest.

Repent and come with full purpose of heart (Jacob 6:5). Not halfheartedly. *See also:* Full purpose of heart; Zeal towards God.

Repent and forsake your sins (Alma 39:9). *Forsake* means abandon, leave behind, quit one's sins, desert your sins, and not return to them. *See also:* Forsake your sins.

Repent and harden not your hearts (Alma 12:33, 37; 34:31). *See:* Harden not our (their/your) hearts.

Repent and hearken unto the voice of the Lord (Helaman 12:23; 3 Nephi 21:22). *See:* Hearken to the word of God (the Lord).

Repent and I will receive you (Alma 5:33). The Savior Jesus Christ has promised He will forgive and accept the repentant. "I will be merciful unto them, saith the Lord God, if they will repent and come unto me" (2 Nephi 28:32).

Repent and observe to do my will (serve God/work righteousness) (Alma 13:10; 42:4; Helaman 15:17). *See:* Repent and serve God.

Repent and prepare the way of the Lord (to stand before judgment) (Helaman 14:9; Mormon 3:22). *See:* Judgment-seat of Christ (God); Prepare the way of the Lord.

Repent and return unto the Lord (Helaman 13:11; 3 Nephi 9:13; 10:6; 16:13; Moroni 9:22). *See:* Repent and turn from your evil ways (unto the Lord God).

Repent and serve God (Alma 42:4). Repentance is only a beginning. Once we have entered the gate of repentance and baptism, we must continue on faithfully, keeping the commandments, enduring to the end, and serving God and our fellowmen.

Repent and turn from your evil ways (unto the Lord God) (Mosiah 11:21, 23; Helaman 11:4; 13:11;

Ether 2:11; 11:1). *Repent* quite literally means to turn away from sin and turn back or return to God. *See also:* Return unto me (the Lord).

Repent in sackcloth and ashes (Mosiah 11:25; Helaman 11:9). A sign of sincere repentance. An individual puts off worldly fine clothing and dresses in a garment of coarse material, then marks themselves with black charcoal as a sign of humbleness and lowliness. Anciently, to wear sackcloth and ashes was a sign of great anguish, submissiveness, lowliness, and remorse.

Repent of all our (their/your) sins (Alma 22:16; 24:11; Helaman 14:13; 3 Nephi 3:25; Mormon 7:5). Meaning to repent of all—not just some of your sins while holding on to a few favorites. God requires our whole souls and complete allegiance to Him. "Ye must bow down before him [God], and worship him with all your might, mind, and strength, and your whole soul; and if ye do this ye shall in nowise be cast out" (2 Nephi 25:29).

Repent of his (their/your) evil (Mosiah 11:29; 3 Nephi 30:2; Mormon 2:8, 15; 5:22; 15:3). *See:* Repent of your sins.

Repent of their abominations (iniquities/wickedness) (1 Nephi 18:15; 2 Nephi 5:22; 28:17; Mosiah 11:20; 12:12; 16:12; 18:1; 26:11; Alma 3:14; 5:56; 6:3; 9:18; 10:20; 37:22, 25–26; 60:33; 62:45; Helaman 4:14; 8:26; 3 Nephi 3:15;

9:2; 30:2; Mormon 5:2; 7:5; Ether 2:11; 7:23, 26; 9:34; 11:1, 6, 12). *See:* Repent of your sins.

Repent of your sins (Jacob 3:8; Mosiah 4:10; 16:13; Alma 7:15; 3 Nephi 9:13; 12:19; Ether 8:23). The types of sins are many. We can recognize our sins by hearing the word of God from the servants of God and reading the scriptures. Once recognized, we must quickly repent of them. *See also:* All manner of abominations (iniquity).

Repent ye (repent ye) for the kingdom of heaven is (nigh) at hand (2 Nephi 31:11; Alma 7:9; 9:25; 10:20; Helaman 5:29, 32; 7:17; 14:19). The call of the Lord to all mankind. Matthew 3:2, footnote *a*, says *repent* is "the Greek word [that] denotes 'a change of heart or mind,' i.e., 'a conversion.'" *See also:* At hand; Kingdom of heaven is nigh (soon) at hand.

Repentance and faith in God (on the name of the Lord) (Mosiah 3:12, 21; 18:7, 20; 25:15, 22; Alma 7:14; 9:27; 12:30; 13:10; 22:14; 34:15–17; 37:33; Helaman 6:4; 13:6; 15:7; 3 Nephi 7:16; 27:19; Ether 12:3; Moroni 3:3; 8:25). *See:* Faith and repentance.

Repented (repenteth) of his (my/their/your) sins (2 Nephi 31:14; Mosiah 18:1; 26:29, 35; 27:24; Alma 6:2; 12:34; 20:17; 24:24; 26:22; 32:13, 15; 41:6; Helaman 11:9, 15; 3 Nephi 7:25; 9:22; Ether 2:15; 7:13; 11:12; Moroni 6:2, 8).

These verses are examples of individuals who truly repented.

Repented (repenteth) not (1 Nephi 14:5; Mosiah 2:38; 12:1; Alma 15:15; 42:28; Helaman 13:11, 33, 36; 14:18; 3 Nephi 8:24–25; Mormon 3:13, 15; 4:10; 5:2, 11; 6:22; Ether 13:17, 22; 15:6; Moroni 6:7). These verses confirm that those who do not repent shall perish.

Repenteth and is baptized (3 Nephi 11:23; 18:30; 23:5; 27:16). *See:* Repent and be baptized.

Repenting nigh unto death (Mosiah 27:28). True repentance, particularly repentance from heinous sins, is a very hard, painful, and often drawn-out process where one has to root out or tear out the sinful habit and predisposition from one's very soul. In other words, one must wrest with himself to pluck out and cast off the sin. The process may even seem like it brings one close to the jaws of death, and therefore requires constant and frequent prayer for assistance from God and for His forgiveness.

Reprove with equity (2 Nephi 21:4; 30:9). Meaning to judge fairly and rightly.

Repugnant to the commandments of God (Mosiah 29:36). *See:* Abominable in the sight of the Lord.

Requisite with the justice of God (Alma 41:2–3; Alma 61:12). Meaning mandatory or compulsory, or required and demanded by the law of justice administered by God. *See also:* Judgments are just.

Resist the Spirit of the Lord (truth) (Alma 30:46; 32:28). To resist the Holy Ghost is to draw away from God, and doing so leads to destruction. Rather we must take "the Holy Spirit for [our] guide" (D&C 45:57). *See also:* Unto them I will show no greater things.

Resist(-ing) evil (iniquity/wickedness) (Alma 48:16; 61:10, 14; 3 Nephi 12:39). It should be our every effort to resist sin. We should pray to God that we may resist evil. It is the command of God to resist evil.

Responsibility which I am under to God (Jacob 1:19; 2:2). Those that have a calling from God have a responsibility to God to carry out that calling and magnify it. *See also:* Magnify mine (our) office.

Rest from all afflictions (care/sorrow/troubles) (Alma 34:41; 40:12). *See:* Rest of the Lord (their God).

Rest in paradise (Alma 40:12; Moroni 10:34). *See:* Enter into his (my/the) rest (of the Lord/of God); Paradise of God.

Rest of the Lord (their God) (Jacob 1:7; Alma 12:36, 37; 13:6, 12, 13, 16, 29; 16:17; 57:36; 60:13; Moroni 7:3; 9:6; 10:34). A state of rest most often associated with a reward after death (i.e., rest from earthly cares), but is also a state that can be obtained while in this life (see Psalm 95:10–11; Alma 13:12–13). "Come unto me, all ye that labour and are heavy laden, and I will give you rest" (Matthew 11:28). We must seek to be worthy of the rest of the Lord. *See also:* Enter into his (my/the) rest (of the Lord/of God).

Rest to their souls (Alma 37:34; 57:36; Moroni 9:6). *See:* Rest of the Lord (their God).

Restoration of God (Alma 42:28). Refers to the judgments of God and the rewards that each of us will receive for our deeds here on earth. "The meaning of the word restoration is to bring back again evil for evil, or carnal for carnal, or devilish for devilish—good for that which is good; righteous for that which is righteous; just for that which is just; merciful for that which is merciful. . . . See that you are merciful unto your brethren; deal justly, judge righteously, and do good continually; and if ye do all these things then shall ye receive your reward; yea, ye shall have mercy restored unto you again; ye shall have justice restored unto you again; ye shall have a righteous judgment restored unto you again; and ye shall have good rewarded unto you again. For that which ye do send out shall return unto you again, and be restored" (Alma 41:13–15).

Restoration of his people (1 Nephi 21:6; 2 Nephi 30:8). *See:* Restore his people; Restored again to (unto) the land(-s) of their inheritance.

Restoration of the Jews in the latter days (1 Nephi 15:19–20). *See:* Restore his people; Restored again to (unto) the land(-s) of their inheritance.

Restoration (of those things) of which has been spoken by the mouths of the prophets (Alma 40:22, 24; 41:1). The restoration which is the Resurrection, and the restoration which is a result of the judgment of our deeds. *See also:* Restoration of God; Restored to its (their) perfect (proper) form (frame/order); Restored unto that which is good.

Restoration [resurrection] shall come to all (Alma 11:44). All who have lived on earth will be resurrected to a perfect body. This is a free gift of the Atonement of Christ. *See also:* Perfect form (frame); Restored to its proper frame; Resurrection of the body.

Restoration to the knowledge of Christ (truth) (Alma 37:19; Helaman 15:11; Mormon 9:36). Meaning the Lamanites will be restored to a knowledge of Jesus Christ and the gospel. *See also:* Restored to the true church and fold of God.

Restoration to the lands of their inheritance (3 Nephi 29:1). *See:* Restored again to (unto) the land(-s) of their inheritance.

Restoration unto the house of Israel (2 Nephi 3:24). Joseph Smith is here prophesied to bring to pass much that will contribute to the restoration of the house of Israel. This includes the Book of Mormon, the restoration of the true Church, the great missionary work, and the blessing of the land of Israel for the return of the Jews.

Restore his people (2 Nephi 25:17). *See:* Gather in the house of Israel; Lord will set his hand; Recover them a second time; Restored again to (unto) the land(-s) of their inheritance.

Restored again to (unto) the land(-s) of their inheritance (2 Nephi 10:7; 25:11). The Lord has covenanted with righteous men throughout the ages that their posterity would be restored [gathered back] to various lands. For example, the Jews will be restored or gathered back to Jerusalem. *See also:* Restore his people.

Restored one to the other [body and spirit] (2 Nephi 9:12, 13; Alma 40:23; 41:2). Refers to the Resurrection, where the body and spirit will be reunited or restored. *See also:* Restored to its (their) perfect (proper) form (frame/order).

Restored to its (their) perfect (proper) form (frame/order) (Alma 11:43–44; 40:23; 41:2, 4). Refers to the Resurrection, wherein all will be raised to an immortal body that will be perfect without

disease or deformity, and will live forever, never to die again. *See also:* Immortal body; Resurrection of the body.

Restored to that God who gave them breath (2 Nephi 9:26; Alma 42:23). Refers to the Atonement, which restores men and women back to God. Without the effects of the Atonement, they could not return, but would be lost forever.

Restored to the true church and fold of God (2 Nephi 9:2). Refers to the Jews when they accept Christ and are gathered home to the lands of their inheritance.

Restored unto grace for grace according to their works (Helaman 12:24). A gift from God to those who repent. They will then again be able to progress according to their good works.

Restored unto that which is good (Alma 41:3, 14; 42:27; Helaman 12:24; 14:31). Those that have done good will have good restored unto them as a reward, whereas those that have done evil will have evil restored unto them. *See also:* Restoration of God.

Restored unto the knowledge of their fathers and of Jesus Christ (2 Nephi 30:5). Refers to the Lamanites in the latter days who shall hear and accept the word of God, principally through the Book of Mormon. *See also:* Remnant of these (this) people.

Restoring the house of Israel (Jacob/the Jews) (2 Nephi 3:13; 3 Nephi 5:25; Mormon 5:14). *See:* Restore his people; Restored again to (unto) the land(-s) of their inheritance.

Resurrection of Christ (Holy One of Israel) (2 Nephi 9:12; Mosiah 15:21; Alma 40:16, 18–20; 41:3; Helaman 14:17; 3 Nephi 6:20). Jesus Christ has power over death. He said, "I lay down my life, that I might take it again. No man taketh it from me, but I lay it down of myself. I have power to lay it down, and I have power to take it again" (John 10:17–18). Thus Jesus, our Savior and Redeemer, provided the Resurrection for all mankind. *See also:* According to the power of the resurrection; All shall rise from the dead, both the just and the unjust; Death is (was) swallowed up in the victory of (in) Christ; Resurrection of the body; Resurrection of the dead; Rise(-n) from the dead [Jesus Christ]; Risen again [Jesus Christ].

Resurrection of damnation (Mosiah 16:11; 3 Nephi 26:5). Meaning a reward of damnation and hell. Or, in other words, being resurrected to damnation and hell.

Resurrection of the body (Alma 11:45; 40:18, 21; 41:2). The resurrection of the mortal body to immortality is a free gift to all who have lived here on earth, because of the Resurrection of Christ, who is the "first fruits of the resurrection." This resurrection is described in Alma 11:43–45: "The spirit and the body shall be reunited again in its perfect form; both limb and joint shall be restored to its proper frame. . . . This restoration shall come to all, both old and young, both bond and free, both male and female, both the wicked and the righteous; and even there shall not so much as a hair of their heads be lost; but everything shall be restored to its perfect frame. . . . This mortal body is raised to an immortal body, that they can die no more; their spirits uniting with their bodies, never to be divided." *See also:* Bringeth to pass the resurrection; Immortal body; Resurrection of Christ (Holy One of Israel); Resurrection of the dead; 2 Nephi 9:13, 15; Alma 12:20; 40:23.

Resurrection of the dead (2 Nephi 2:8; Mosiah 13:35; 15:20; 18:2; 26:2; Alma 4:14; 12:8, 24–25; 16:19; 21:9; 40:1, 3, 16; 42:23; Helaman 14:15; Mormon 7:6). Because of Jesus Christ, who brought about the Resurrection, all mankind will be resurrected and have immortality to dwell eternally in kingdoms or places prepared by God, according to their works while in the flesh. *See also:* Immortal body; Resurrection of the body; Rise from the dead [all men]; Second trump.

Retain a hope through faith (Alma 25:16). Hope and faith are closely interrelated. Because of our faith we have a hope of things promised to come. *See also:* Have hope; Hope in Christ; Hope(-s) of glory; Perfect brightness of hope.

Retain(-ing) a remission of their (your) sins (Mosiah 4:11–12, 26; Alma 4:14). These verses describe the things we must do to retain a remission of our sins. Those actions include to remember the greatness of God, humble ourselves, pray daily, continue in faith, keep the commandments of God and care for the poor. Once we are baptized and born again there is much of mortal life still ahead of us. We must be diligent in following the example of Christ and repenting whenever we err.

Return again [Jews] (1 Nephi 10:3; 2 Nephi 6:9; 25:11). Nephi was given to see that those that were in Jerusalem after Lehi and his family left were destroyed or carried away captive into Babylon. He also saw in vision that the Lord caused that they would return again to Jerusalem from Babylon. *See also:* Restore his people; Restored again to (unto) the land(-s) of their inheritance.

Return all these things upon your own heads (2 Nephi 29:5; 3 Nephi 20:28). A promise that those who hate and persecute will receive back the same hate and persecuting as a just judgment. *See also:* Restoration of God.

Return railing for railing (3 Nephi 6:13). To *rail* is to mock, revile, berate, and vilify. "And behold, it is

written, an eye for an eye, and a tooth for a tooth; but I say unto you, that ye shall not resist evil, but whosoever shall smite thee on thy right cheek, turn to him the other also" (3 Nephi 12:38–39; see Matthew 5:38–39). "If men will smite you, or your families, once, and ye bear it patiently and revile not against them, neither seek revenge, ye shall be rewarded; but if ye bear it not patiently, it shall be accounted unto you as being meted out as a just measure unto you" (D&C 98:23–24).

Return unto me (the Lord) (Helaman 13:11; 15:16; 3 Nephi 9:13; 10:6; 16:13; 18:32; 24:7). *See:* Repent and turn from your evil ways (unto the Lord God); Turn unto the Lord God.

Reveal all things (things never revealed) (2 Nephi 27:10–11, 22; Alma 26:22). After the Second Coming of our Lord and during the Millennium, all things will be revealed. "Yea, verily I say unto you, in that day when the Lord shall come, he shall reveal all things— Things which have passed, and hidden things which no man knew, things of the earth, by which it was made, and the purpose and the end thereof—Things most precious, things that are above, and things that are beneath, things that are in the earth, and upon the earth, and in heaven" (D&C 101:32–34). Thus the sealed portion of the Book of Mormon, the scriptures of the

Lost Tribes, and those marvelous things that Nephi, the brother of Jared, Moroni and others were commanded not to write, will all be revealed. *See also:* 2 Nephi 29:13.

Revealed upon the house tops (Mormon 5:8). In the end all unrepented wickedness that has transpired will be revealed for all to see. There will be no more hiding of what has gone on behind doors and in darkness. *See also:* Read upon the house tops; Luke 12:3; D&C 1:3; 88:108.

Revelations of God (2 Nephi 5:6; Jacob 4:8; Mormon 8:33; 9:7). The scriptures and the inspired words of the living prophets, seers, and revelators are the revelations and word of God. *See also:* Word of God.

Revile against (1 Nephi 17:42; 2 Nephi 9:40; 28:16; Jacob 3:9; Alma 10:24; 30:31; 34:40; Helaman 8:2, 5; 10:15; 3 Nephi 22:17; Ether 7:24). To *revile* is to belittle, berate, malign, ridicule, and vilify. "Contention is not of me," said the Lord (3 Nephi 11:29). *See also:* Spirit of contention.

Revolted from the church (4 Nephi 1:20). Meaning to apostatize, turn from, leave, disbelieve, and discredit the Church of God. *See also:* Rebel(-led/-ling/-lion) against God.

Reward thee openly (3 Nephi 13:4, 6, 18). Do your alms, pray, and fast in secret; and your Father in Heaven, who sees in secret, shall reward you openly. Hypocrites do alms, pray, and fast publicly to be seen of men. They have their reward already. If our motives and sincerity are right, then God will bless us. *See also:* Matthew 6:4, 6, 18.

Rewardeth you no good thing (Alma 34:39). Satan, the devil, gives no good gift because it is not in his nature to do so. Thus we see how utterly wicked Satan is. *Compare:* 2 Nephi 13:9; Moroni 7:10–18.

Riches and honor (Alma 1:16). *See:* Vain things of the world.

Rid my (our) garments of your (blood and) sins (2 Nephi 9:44; Jacob 2:2; Mosiah 2:27–28; Mormon 9:35). The prophets and anointed teachers have the sacred responsibility to cry repentance unto the people. If they do not fulfill their calling in this regard, the sins of the people come upon the prophets, and they would not be found spotless at the last day (see Jacob 1:19). *See also:* Blood come upon our garments; Blood should not come upon me; Garments are not spotted with your blood; Garments spotless; Shake them (my garments) before you; Shook your iniquities from my soul.

Right hand of God (1 Nephi 20:13; Mosiah 5:9; Alma 28:12; Helaman 3:30; 3 Nephi 29:9; Ether 12:4; Moroni 7:27). The faithful will sit down in heaven at the right hand of God, whereas the goats (the wicked) will be relegated to the left hand and then cast out (see Mosiah 26:24–27). *Compare:* Left hand of God. *See also:* At the right hand of God; Inheritance at my right hand; Sitteth on the right hand.

Right way(-s of the Lord) (1 Nephi 13:27; 22:14; 2 Nephi 25:28–29; 28:15; Jacob 7:7; Mormon 9:20; Moroni 6:4). The right way is to believe in Jesus Christ and follow Him. *See also:* Paths of righteousness; Strait and narrow course (path); Way of the Lord.

Righteous branch (2 Nephi 3:5; 9:53; 10:1; Jacob 2:25). It was hoped that this segment or branch of the house of Israel would remain righteous, and for a time they did. *See also:* Branch of the house (tree) of Israel.

Righteous is favored of God (1 Nephi 17:35). He that is righteous is favored of God. God reserves His choicest blessings for those that keep His commandments. The scriptures say that the wicked are cursed (not favored). *See also:* Favored of the Lord.

Righteous judgment (Mosiah 3:10; Alma 41:14; Helaman 14:29). We can be assured that God will judge each of us and all our fellowmen with a righteous judgment. Meaning a perfect, all-knowing, merciful, just, and specifically suited judgment. *See also:* Judgments are just; Judgment of God.

Righteous need not fear (1 Nephi 22:17, 22). "Fear not" is the promise of the Lord to the faithful. "Hearken unto me, ye that know righteousness, the people in whose heart is my law; fear ye not the reproach of men, neither be ye afraid of their revilings" (Isaiah 51:7).

Righteous' sake (Alma 45:15; 46:10; 62:40; Helaman 13:14). *See:* For the righteous' sake.

Righteous shall be righteous still (2 Nephi 9:16; Mormon 9:14). In the final judgment the righteous shall retain and maintain that status; the same with the wicked, who will be unchanged, for "Ye cannot say, when ye are brought to that awful crisis, that I will repent" (Alma 34:34). *See also:* Restoration of God; Restored unto that which is good.

Righteous shall not perish (1 Nephi 22:19; 2 Nephi 26:8; 30:1; Omni 1:7; Alma 21:6). *See:* Not perish; Perish not; Shall not perish.

Righteous shine forth (Alma 40:25). In the judgment the righteous shall shine forth, for the light of Christ will be found in them. This scriptural phrase also in Matthew 13:43. *See also:* Countenance did shine upon them; Image of God engraven upon your countenances; Let your light so shine; White and exceedingly fair and beautiful.

Righteous works (Alma 5:17). Works that serve others, bring about righteousness amongst the people, and build up the kingdom of God. *See also:* Abound(-ing) in good works; Good works; Judged according to (of) their works.

Righteousness shall be the girdle of his loins (2 Nephi 21:5; 30:11). *See:* Girdle of his (their) loins; Robe of righteousness.

Rights and privileges (of their religion/and liberty) (Mosiah 29:32; Alma 2:4; 30:27; 43:9, 47; 46:20; 48:13; 51:6; 55:28; 61:9; 3 Nephi 2:12; 3:10). Meaning having freedom of religion. *Compare:* D&C 98:5. *See also:* Privileges of their church (religion/worship).

Ripe for destruction (Alma 10:19; Helaman 13:14). *See:* Ripe(-ned) in iniquity.

Ripe(-ned) in iniquity (1 Nephi 17:35; 2 Nephi 28:16; Ether 2:9; 9:20). Elder Delbert L. Stapley said, "These conditions exist today, as is evidenced by the increased numbers of killings, by lawlessness, and by moral transgressions. All standards that were so sacred in the past are crumbling under the pressure of the ungodliness of agnostic, atheistic, subversive and radical groups. Evil designing people get financial gain from trafficking in drugs, alcohol, prostitution, pornography, and dishonest schemes regardless of the destruction to the moral, ethical, and spiritual values of life.

"The only way Satan can be bound is for people to forsake his temptations and enticements to do evil and to walk uprightly and circumspectly before the Lord" ("Our Responsibility," 94). *See also:* Fully ripe (in iniquity); Ripening for an everlasting destruction.

Ripening for an everlasting destruction (1 Nephi 17:35; Alma 10:19; 37:28, 31; 45:16; Helaman 5:2; 6:40; 8:26; 11:37; 13:14). *See:* Consumed as stubble; Ripe(-ned) in iniquity.

Rise from the dead [all men] (Alma 11:41; 12:8, 20; 40:5, 9; 3 Nephi 23:9). *See:* Resurrection of the dead.

Risen again [Jesus Christ] (Mormon 7:5). By the power of the Father given Him, Jesus Christ rose from the dead. *See also:* Power of the resurrection; Resurrection of Christ (Holy One of Israel).

Rise(-n) from the dead [Jesus Christ] (1 Nephi 10:11; 2 Nephi 25:13, 14; 26:1; Mosiah 3:10; 16:7; Alma 33:22; Helaman 14:20; Ether 12:7). *See:* Resurrection of Christ (Holy One of Israel).

Rising generation (Mosiah 26:1; Alma 5:49; 3 Nephi 1:30). Meaning the new or younger generation.

Rites of worship (Alma 43:45; 44:5). *Rites* meaning the practices of our religion, which we should have freedom to pursue and participate in.

Robe of righteousness (2 Nephi 4:33; 9:14). Means to be clothed with purity. Those that sincerely strive to be righteous by keeping the commandments and obtaining forgiveness through the Atonement in their own behalf will obtain this blessed state. Nephi had the brass plates, wherein he likely read Isaiah 61:10, "I will greatly rejoice in the Lord, my soul shall be joyful in my God; for he hath clothed me with the garments of salvation, he hath covered me with the robe of righteousness, as a bridegroom decketh himself with ornaments, and as a bride adorneth herself with her jewels." Job said "I put on righteousness, and it clothed me" (Job 29:14). *Contrast:* Nakedness before God. *See also:* Clothed with purity; Encircle me around in the robe of thy righteousness.

Rock and my (their) salvation (1 Nephi 13:36; 15:15). A descriptive phrase referring to Jesus Christ. *See also:* Rock of my (their/your) salvation.

Rock of my righteousness (2 Nephi 4:35). *See:* Rock of our Redeemer.

Rock of my (their/your) salvation (2 Nephi 4:30, 35; 9:45; Jacob 7:25). "The stone upon which they might build and have safe foundation" (Jacob 4:15). *See also:* Built upon my rock; My rock and my salvation; Rock of our Redeemer.

Rock of our Redeemer (Helaman 5:12). Our house will not fall if it is founded upon the rock, who is Christ. "Build the foundation of your life upon 'the rock of our Redeemer,' such that when the shafts of the evil one and the storms of the world assail you, they will, as Helaman taught, have 'no power over you to drag you down to the gulf of misery and endless wo, because of the rock upon which ye are built, which is a sure foundation, *a foundation whereon if men build they cannot fall'* (Helaman 5:12; emphasis added). Of the Lord Jesus Christ I bear my ardent witness: He is the Rock" (Nash, "Great Plan of Happiness," 50). *See also:* Built upon my rock.

Rod of his mouth and with the breath of his lips (2 Nephi 21:4; 30:9). In D&C 19:15, "therefore I command you to repent—repent, lest I smite you by the rod of my mouth, and by my wrath, and by my anger, and your sufferings be sore—how sore you know not, how exquisite you know not, yea, how hard to bear you know not." Elder Jeffrey R. Holland has written, "In that day the Word will come with power, and there will be incomparable power in his words. In those last days Christ's judgment will be the truth he speaks and an acknowledgment of that truth from all who hear him" (*Christ and the New Covenant,* 87). *See also:* Breath of his lips.

Rod of iron (1 Nephi 8:19–20, 24, 30; 11:25; 15:23). Represents the word of God, meaning the gospel and commandments of Jesus Christ. The rod of iron or iron rod leads to the tree of life in Lehi's dream. If one holds to the iron rod he may press forward through the mists of darkness and obtain the tree and its fruit.

Rolled together as a scroll (Mormon 5:23; 9:2). *See:* Earth shall be rolled together as a scroll; Wrapt together as a scroll.

Root of Jesse (2 Nephi 21:10). Joseph Smith is the Root of Jesse. "It is a descendant of Jesse, as well as of Joseph, unto whom rightly belongs the priesthood, and the keys of the kingdom, for an ensign, and for the gathering of my people in the last days" (D&C 113:6). *Compare:* Stem of Jesse; D&C 113:12.

Root out of dry ground (Mosiah 14:2). Tender and exposed, not covered up and hid. Also found once more in Isaiah 53:2.

Rooted out (Alma 22:15). To be pulled out entirely, branch, trunk, and roots, that no part or portion is left. In other words, entirely eliminated. For example, Proverbs 2:22: "The wicked shall be cut off from the earth, and the transgressors shall be rooted out of it."

Run faster than he has strength (Mosiah 4:27). Compare with D&C 10:4, in which the Lord told Joseph Smith: "Do not run faster or labor more than you have strength and means provided to enable you to translate; but be diligent unto the end."

S

Sackcloth and ashes (Mosiah 11:25). "A coarse, dark cloth made of hair of camels and goats and used anciently for making sacks and bags was called *sackcloth*. It was also used for making the rough garments worn by mourners, and so it became fixed in the prophetic mind as a symbol for sorrow and mourning. It was the custom for mourners, garbed in sackcloth, either to sprinkle *ashes* upon themselves or to sit in piles of ashes, thereby showing their joy had perished or been destroyed. (Gen. 37:34; Esther 4:1–3; Isa. 61:3; Jer. 6:26.) The use of sackcloth and ashes anciently was also a token of humility and penitence" (McConkie, *Mormon Doctrine*, 659).

Sacrifice for sin (2 Nephi 2:7). Jesus Christ is the sacrifice for sin. He was slain for the sins of mankind, which would be forgiven men and women if they would repent and come unto Christ. *See also:* Infinite atonement; Lamb of God.

Sacrifice(-s) and burnt offerings (1 Nephi 5:9; 7:22; Mosiah 2:3; 3 Nephi 9:19). Refers to the law of Moses and the rites and ordinances required thereunder.

Said (say) unto this mountain be moved (cast down/come over) (Helaman 10:9; 12:17; Ether 12:30). "If ye have faith as a grain of mustard seed, ye shall say unto this mountain, Remove hence to yonder place; and it shall remove; and nothing shall be impossible unto you" (Matthew 17:20). *See also:* If ye have faith; Remove mountains.

Saints of God (1 Nephi 13:5, 9; 14:12; 15:28). A saint is a true follower of Christ; one who lives fervently the principles of the gospel. A saint declares Christ, exemplifies the love of Christ, serves others, is tolerant, is a good citizen, is a hard worker, abhors sin, praises God, and seeks to fulfill their mission in life, along with many other good things.

Saints of the church of the Lamb (Holy One of Israel) (1 Nephi 14:14; 2 Nephi 9:18). *See:* Saints of God.

Saith our God (2 Nephi 10:18). *See:* Saith the Lamb of God (Lord [God]).

Saith the Father (3 Nephi 16:7–8, 10, 13–14; 20:20, 28–29; 21:14, 20, 29). In these verses Jesus is teaching what God the Father has instructed and said. *See also:* Thus saith the Father.

Saith the Lamb of God (Lord [God]) (1 Nephi 13:24; 17:53; 19:16; 20:15, 22; 21:5, 18; 2 Nephi 3:11–13; 13:15; 24:22–23; 26:4–6; 27:27–28; 28:15, 17, 32; Jacob 2:24–25, 29–30, 32–33; 5:8; Alma 45:19; Helaman 13:10–12, 14, 17–20, 32; 15:16–17; 3 Nephi 22:1, 8, 10, 17; 24:1, 5, 7, 10–13, 17; 25:1, 3; Mormon 8:20; Ether 4:7; 9:20). Words of importance because they are from the Lord God. *See also:* Thus saith our God (the Lord).

Salt of the earth (3 Nephi 12:13). Salt is a seasoning and a preservative for food. Likewise the Saints of God are a savor and preservative among the people of the earth. These are important functions of the Lord's faithful. "When men are called unto mine everlasting gospel, and covenant with an everlasting covenant, they are accounted as the salt of the earth and the savor of men" (D&C 101:39).

Salt that hath lost its savor (3 Nephi 12:13; 16:15). "They are called to be the savor of men; therefore, if that salt of the earth lose its savor, behold, it is thenceforth good for nothing only to be cast out and trodden under the feet of men" (D&C 101:40). Thus Saints lose their calling and place in the kingdom if they are not faithful in their duties. *See also:* Salt of the earth.

Salvation is free (2 Nephi 2:4; 26:27). *See:* Buy milk and honey, without money and without price; Redeemed without money.

Salvation of our (their) souls (Jacob 4:13; Alma 9:28; 17:11; 24:27; 26:20; 37:7–8; Helaman 5:20; 3 Nephi 5:11, 20). The salvation of our souls should be our highest priority. The word *salvation* as used in the scriptures includes the meanings: the Resurrection, forgiveness of sins, saved at the last day, obtaining rest in heaven, and gaining exaltation and eternal life. *See also:* Bring(-eth) salvation; Brought unto salvation; Partake of his salvation; Plan of redemption; Plan of salvation; Power of his redemption; Redemption of Christ; Redemption of mankind; Salvation of the Lord (our God).

Salvation of the Father (3 Nephi 20:35). Heavenly Father provides salvation through the plan of salvation and the Atonement of His son Jesus Christ. *See also:* Salvation of the Lord (our God).

Salvation of the Lord (our God) (1 Nephi 19:17; Mosiah 12:24; 15:28, 31; 16:1; 17:15; 3 Nephi 16:20; 20:35). Meaning the redemption and glory of Jesus Christ. Salvation or redemption comes only by and through our Lord Jesus Christ. *See also:* Salvation of our (their) souls; Salvation of the Father.

Salvation shall (should) be declared (Mosiah 15:24, 28; 28:3).

Meaning the gospel of Jesus Christ, the redemption through Christ, or the good news of Christ being preached and declared unto the world.

Same yesterday, today, and forever (1 Nephi 10:18; 2 Nephi 2:4; 27:23; 29:9; Alma 31:17; Mormon 9:9; Moroni 10:19). God is an unchanging God. Thus we can have faith in Him because we know He will be constant and will not change the rules. *See also:* Changeth not; Course is one eternal round.

Sanctified by (the reception of) the Holy Ghost (Alma 5:54; 13:12; 3 Nephi 27:20). After one is born of the water (baptized), then comes the baptism of fire, or being born of the Spirit. If one has truly prepared in humility and genuine repentance, then after being baptized and after having hands laid upon their head for the gift of the Holy Ghost, there will come the visitation of the Spirit and ratification of forgiveness of sins. This can happen at the time of baptism or at various times later in life. *See also:* Baptism of fire and of the Holy Ghost; Born again (of God); Mosiah 4:2–3; Moses 6:59–60.

Sanctified in Christ (me) (Ether 4:7; Moroni 10:33). To receive a remission of sins through the Atonement of Jesus Christ.

Sanctification of their hearts (Helaman 3:35). Not only to be forgiven of sins, but to have one's heart and intents purified.

Sand of the sea (1 Nephi 12:1; 2 Nephi 20:22; Mormon 1:7). Referred to because of the immense number of the grains of sand of the sea. They are innumerable to man.

Satan desireth to have you (3 Nephi 18:18). Satan strives to destroy men and women and to bind them captive. God invites us to heaven, whereas Satan tempts and entices us to hell. *See also:* Chains of hell.

Satan did get hold (possession) upon the hearts of the people (Alma 8:9; 10:25; 27:12; 40:13; Helaman 16:23; 3 Nephi 2:2; 4 Nephi 1:28; Ether 15:19). *See:* Devil has got so great hold upon your hearts; Ensnare the hearts of men; Get hold upon their hearts; Great hold upon the hearts of the people; Hold upon the (their/your) hearts; Lead(-ing/stealing) away the hearts (souls) to destruction (hell); Power of Satan; Power over the hearts of men (people); Rage in the hearts of the children of men; Satan did lead away the hearts of the people; Stir(-reth) up the hearts of men.

Satan did go about (Helaman 16:22; 3 Nephi 2:3). "Satan is abroad in the land, and he goeth forth deceiving the nations" (D&C 52:14).

Satan did lead away the hearts of the people (3 Nephi 6:16; Mormon 5:19). *See:* Satan did get hold (possession) upon the hearts of the people.

Satan did stir them up (Alma 27:12; Helaman 6:21; 16:22; Moroni 9:3). Meaning to incite, provoke, instigate, and urge to contention, anger, and sin. Thus Satan goes about to destroy peace and righteousness.

Satan had (hath) great power (1 Nephi 13:29; 3 Nephi 6:15). Satan only has power over men and women if they allow him to have power over them. To sin and rebel against God is to give oneself over to the power of Satan. *See also:* Power of Satan.

Satan has (shall have) no more power over them (1 Nephi 22:15, 26; 3 Nephi 28:39; Ether 8:26). If people are righteous and ignore the temptations of the devil he can have no power over them. *See also:* Power of Satan.

Save the world from sin (Alma 7:14; 3 Nephi 9:21). Jesus Christ came to the world to save the world from sin. He did not save the world *in* sin. The Atonement of Christ breaks the bands of death and allows men and women to have their sins remitted or forgiven if they humbly repent. There is no other name but Christ by which we may be saved.

Save them in their sins (Alma 11:34, 36–37). False doctrine. Christ will not redeem man *in* their sins, but will redeem man *from* their sins if they repent and come unto Him. We cannot remain in or cling to our sins and be saved; rather we must forsake them and turn from them. *See also:* Cannot be saved in your sins.

Saved at the last day (1 Nephi 13:37; 22:31; 2 Nephi 33:12; Alma 1:4; 22:18; 3 Nephi 27:6). Meaning being granted salvation, obtaining exaltation, and being blessed to dwell with God eternally when that great and last day comes, which is the judgment day.

Saved by faith in his name (Moroni 7:26). "And he commandeth all men that they must repent, and be baptized in his name, *having perfect faith in the Holy One of Israel*, or they cannot be saved in the kingdom of God" (2 Nephi 9:23; emphasis added).

Saved in the kingdom of God (1 Nephi 13:37; 2 Nephi 9:23; 25:13; 28:8; 31:21; 33:12; Jacob 6:4; 3 Nephi 9:22; 11:33; Ether 15:34; Moroni 10:21, 26). Meaning saved in heaven to dwell with God in the eternities. "If thou wilt do good, yea, and hold out faithful to the end, thou shalt be saved in the kingdom of God, which is the greatest of all the gifts of God; for there is no gift greater than the gift of salvation [exaltation]" (D&C 6:13). *See also:* Be saved.

Savior of the world (1 Nephi 10:4; 13:40). Jesus Christ is the Savior of the World, and He has stated that He is (see D&C 43:34). Additionally, prophets have testified of Jesus.

Apostles have the specific mission to witness that Jesus is the Christ, the Savior of the World.

Saw and bear record (1 Nephi 11:32, 36; 12:7; 3 Nephi 18:39). *See:* Bear(-eth) record.

Saw in a vision (1 Nephi 1:8; 8:36; 10:17). A vision is one type of revelation wherein one is given to see the past, present, or future with the object to bring about the purposes of God. A vision can be presented before a person or seen in one's mind. *See also:* In a vision.

Saw Jesus (2 Nephi 2:4; 11:2, 3; 31:17; Ether 3:20; 9:22; 12:39). Righteous individuals are sometimes granted to see in person or in vision the Lord Jesus Christ. Prophets and Apostles in particular are blessed with this so that they might testify of the truthfulness of His being and His mission as our Savior and Redeemer. *See also:* Saw the Son of God (Righteousness); Seen my Redeemer; Visited of the Lord; D&C 93:1.

Saw the heavens open (1 Nephi 1:8; 11:14, 30; 12:6; Helaman 5:48; 3 Nephi 17:24). Often God instructs an individual by opening the heavens before them or, in other words, allowing an individual to peer past the veil into heaven. Joseph Smith said, "Could you gaze into heaven five minutes you would know more than you would by reading all that ever was written on the subject" (*Teachings of the Prophet*

Joseph Smith, 324). The Prophet Joseph could say this because he did, in fact, peer into heaven many times.

Saw the Son of God (Righteousness) (1 Nephi 11:24, 32; Ether 9:22). These verses are examples of individuals who saw the Lord Jesus Christ. *See also:* Saw Jesus.

Scales of darkness shall begin to fall from their eyes (2 Nephi 30:6). Refers to the latter days when the Lamanites will receive and accept the gospel, and a true knowledge of Jesus Christ will be restored to their view. When one begins to sin, a darkness begins to gather around that person so that he cannot clearly see the truth. It is as though some disease afflicts the person and cloudy scales form over their eyes so they cannot see or comprehend the realities of God and the eternities as they really are. These scales of darkness are analogous to the mists of darkness in Lehi's dream. However, when one accepts the gospel and repents, the scales of false traditions and error fall away, and the light of the gospel becomes clear and discernable to their vision. In Job 41:15, the scales form because of pride. When Saul of Tarsus journeyed near Damascus and the Lord Jesus appeared unto him, Saul was then struck blind. Then when Ananias put his hands on him to heal him, Acts 9:18 states, "And immediately there fell from his eyes as it had been scales: and he received sight forthwith, and arose, and was baptized."

Scattered abroad (1 Nephi 21:1; Mosiah 28:17; Alma 13:22; 25:12; 28:2; Helaman 15:12; 3 Nephi 5:24; 20:13). The Lord has scattered many different people, mostly because of their unbelief and sin. These peoples include the Jews, the people at the Tower of Babel, the Nephites and the Lamanites. *See also:* Scattered among all nations; Scattered and confounded; Scattered before the Gentiles; Scattered to and fro upon the isles of the sea; Scattered tribes of Israel; Scattered upon all the face of the earth.

Scattered among all nations (1 Nephi 22:3, 5; 2 Nephi 6:11; 10:6; 25:15). Meaning the scattering of the Jews and the house of Israel. *See also:* Scattered tribes of Israel.

Scattered and confounded (1 Nephi 22:5, 7). When the Lord scatters a people He often confounds them also. *Confound* means to confuse, discomfort, bewilder, and mix up.

Scattered before the Gentiles (1 Nephi 13:14; 15:17; 22:7; 2 Nephi 1:11; Helaman 15:12; Mormon 5:20). Meaning the descendants of the Lamanites. It was prophesied that in the latter days the Gentiles will have "raised forts against them." Consider the forts built against the American Indians (see 2 Nephi 26:15).

Scattered to and fro upon the isles of the sea (1 Nephi 22:4). *See:* Islands (isles) of the sea; Scattered among all nations; Scattered tribes of Israel.

Scattered tribes of Israel (1 Nephi 22:4; 3 Nephi 16:4, 8; 28:29). Because Israel backslid, turned to other gods, and kept not the commandments, God has scattered Israel and afflicted them for their unrighteousness. Yet God loves His covenant people of Israel and has promised to again gather Israel. *See also:* Dispersed of my people [Judah]; Gather in the house of Israel; Hiss and a byword; Jews are (were) scattered; Led away [scattered]; Natural branches (of the olive tree); Scattered abroad; Scattered among all nations; Scattered upon all the face of the earth.

Scattered upon all the face of the earth [the Jews] (1 Nephi 10:12–13; 14:14; 22:3; 3 Nephi 5:24; 16:4; 20:13; 21:24). *See:* Scattered among all nations; Scattered tribes of Israel.

Scattered upon all the face of the earth [the people of Babel] (Mosiah 28:17; Ether 1:33). *Compare:* Genesis 11:9.

Scourge him and crucify him (1 Nephi 19:9–10; 2 Nephi 6:9; Mosiah 3:9; 15:5–7). These prophets were given to know that Jesus Christ would be whipped and crucified by wicked men.

Scourge unto the people (thy seed) (1 Nephi 2:24; 2 Nephi 5:25; Jacob 3:3; 3 Nephi 20:28). It is very likely that the Lord softened the hearts of Laman and Lemuel enough that they consented to leaving Jerusalem at Lehi's urging. The Lamanites were a necessary and important tool of the Lord to humble the Nephites and bring them to a remembrance of their God, thus praying to God to deliver them from the attacks of the Lamanites.

Scourged his skin with faggots (Mosiah 17:13). *Scourge* often means to whip, but here they tortured Abinadi's skin with faggots, or bundles of sticks set afire, that caused him to die in extreme pain.

Scourged them by other nations (all people) (1 Nephi 19:13; 2 Nephi 25:16). Because the Jews crucified their Lord, it was prophesied that they would be scourged for many generations. *Scourged* means afflicted, abused, distressed, mistreated, smitten, and otherwise punished in many ways. *See also:* Hiss and a byword; Make game of the Jews.

Scriptures fulfilled (Helaman 16:14; 3 Nephi 9:16; 10:11). All prophecies and sayings in the scriptures have been, are, or will be fulfilled (come to pass) without exception. This we can count on as being absolute. For God has said, "What I the Lord have spoken, I have spoken, and I excuse not myself; and

though the heavens and the earth pass away, my word shall not pass away, but shall all be fulfilled, whether by my own voice or by the voice of my servants, it is the same" (D&C 1:38). *See also:* According to God's word.

Seal in heaven (on earth) (2 Nephi 33:15; Helaman 10:7). Authorized servants of God who have the priesthood keys have the power to seal on earth things which will then also be sealed in heaven. "And verily, verily, I say unto you, that whatsoever you seal on earth shall be sealed in heaven; and whatsoever you bind on earth, in my name and by my word, saith the Lord, it shall be eternally bound in the heavens" (D&C 132:46).

Seal (them) up (2 Nephi 27:22; Ether 3:22–23, 27–28; 4:5; Moroni 10:2). Many scriptures and sacred items "are sealed up to come forth in their purity, according to the truth which is in the Lamb, in the own due time of the Lord" (1 Nephi 14:26). *See also:* Hid them up unto the Lord; Sealed up.

Seal you his (Mosiah 5:15). Same as calling and election made sure. Joseph Smith taught, "When the Lord has thoroughly proved [a person], and finds that the [person] is determined to serve Him at all hazards, then the [person] will find his calling and election made sure" (*Teachings of the Prophet Joseph Smith*, 150). Such an election must be sealed by the Holy Spirit of Promise. On the other hand, Amulek teaches in Alma 34:35 that the devil can seal you his also. *See also:* 2 Peter 1:3–10, 16–19; Mosiah 26:20; 28:7; D&C 76:53; 84:33–41; 88:3; 131:5; 132:19.

Sealed the truth of his words by his death (Mosiah 17:20). Many prophets throughout the ages were martyrs to the cause because of their testimony of Jesus Christ. Their words were sealed by their blood, and their blood will cry forth from the earth as a testimony against the wicked. *Compare:* D&C 135:3.

Sealed up (1 Nephi 14:26; 2 Nephi 26:17; 27:8, 22; 30:3; Ether 4:5; 5:1). *See:* Seal (them) up.

Sealed up by the power of God (2 Nephi 27:10). *See:* Seal (them) up; Sealed up; Words of the book which were sealed.

Sealed upon the earth [by man] (2 Nephi 30:17). Those things sealed or hidden by man shall all be of no effect (loosed from the sealing of man) and shall be revealed, in the Lord's due time.

Search diligently (Mosiah 1:7; 3 Nephi 23:1; Moroni 7:19). "Ask, and it shall be given unto you; seek, and ye shall find; knock, and it shall be opened unto you" (Matthew 7:7; Luke 11:9; 3 Nephi 14:7). *See also:* Search the prophets; Search(-ed) the scriptures.

Search the prophets (Jacob 4:6; 3 Nephi 20:11; 23:1, 5; Mormon 8:23). Meaning to study the words of the prophets. *See also:* Search diligently; Search(-ed) the scriptures.

Search(-ed) the scriptures (1 Nephi 5:21; Jacob 7:23; Words of Mormon 1:3; Mosiah 1:7; Alma 14:1; 17:2; 33:2–3; 3 Nephi 10:14). Meaning to study the scriptures carefully and at length. We must do more than just casually read the scriptures. Rather we must cross-reference them, examining the footnotes and the topical guide. Most of all we must fast and pray concerning their meaning. We must be like the sons of Mosiah: "They had waxed strong in the knowledge of the truth; for they were men of a sound understanding and they had searched the scriptures diligently, that they might know the word of God" (Alma 17:2). President Marion G. Romney said, "I counsel you . . . to make reading the Book of Mormon a few minutes each day a lifelong practice. All of us need the uninterrupted association with the Spirit of the Lord. We need to take the Holy Spirit for our constant guide that we be not deceived. . . . [Joseph Smith said] one can get and keep closer to the Lord by reading the Book of Mormon than by reading any other book. Don't be content with what someone else tells you about what is in it. Drink deeply from the divine fountain itself" ("The Book of Mormon," 67).

Season speedily cometh (Jacob 5:71, 76). *See:* Time speedily cometh.

Second commandments (Alma 12:37). Meaning all the commandments given to men since the first of the commandments given to Adam and Eve in the Garden of Eden not to partake of the forbidden fruit (see Alma 12:31).

Second death (Jacob 3:11; Alma 12:16, 32; 13:30; Helaman 14:18–19). Refers to spiritual death or being cut off from the presence of God. "It is very clear in Doctrine and Covenants 76:30–37, that the only persons who will be completely overcome by this dreadful fate are the sons of perdition, who go with the devil and his angels into 'outer darkness.' All the rest of mankind, even the wicked, will receive some measure of salvation after they suffer the wrath of God. However, they will of necessity be brought to repentance and the acceptance of the gospel of Jesus Christ as far as it will apply to them. They will not be given the ordinances which do not pertain in their kingdoms. From the reading of other passages we discover that there will be great multitudes embracing the vast majority of mankind, who will never be privileged to come back to dwell in the presence of the Father and the Son. These receive banishment from their presence, but not entirely do they get beyond the divine benediction. . . . All those who are permanently subject to the second death are those who have had the testimony of the Holy Ghost and who have known the truth and then have rejected it and put Christ to open shame" (Joseph Fielding Smith, *Answers to Gospel Questions*, 1:76, 78). *See also:* Spiritual death.

Second time to recover (restore) (2 Nephi 6:14; 21:11; 25:17; 29:1; Jacob 6:2). *See:* Recover them a second time; Restore his people; Set his (my) hand again the second time.

Second trump (Mosiah 26:25). Has to do with the timing of the resurrection of men. The first Resurrection shall be at Christ's Second Coming and at the beginning of the millennium. "They are Christ's, the first fruits, they who shall descend with him first, and they [the saints and they the just and true] who are on the earth and in their graves, who are first caught up to meet him; and all this by the voice of the sounding of the trump of the angel of God" (D&C 88:98). Then the final Resurrection at the end of the millennium: "Then shall they that never knew me come forth and shall stand before me. And then shall they know that I am the Lord their God, that I am their Redeemer; but they would not be redeemed" (Mosiah 26:25–26). *See also:* Resurrection of the dead; Alma 40:3–5 [know not how many times, but there are times appointed]; Mormon 9:13 [trump mentioned];

D&C 88:99 [many trumps mentioned].

Secret abominations (2 Nephi 10:15; Alma 37:22–23, 25–27, 29; 3 Nephi 16:10; 30:2; Mormon 8:40; Ether 11:22). *See:* Secret combination(-s).

Secret band (of robbers) (Helaman 2:4, 8, 10–11; 6:22; 7:25; 8:1, 28; 11:2, 10, 26). *See:* Secret combination(-s).

Secret combination(-s) (2 Nephi 9:9; 26:22; Alma 37:30–31; Helaman 3:23; 3 Nephi 4:29; 5:6; 7:6, 9; Mormon 8:27; Ether 8:18, 22, 24; 9:1; 11:15; 13:18; 14:10). "The Book of Mormon teaches that secret combinations engaged in crime present a serious challenge, not just to individuals and families but to entire civilizations. Among today's secret combinations are gangs, drug cartels, and organized crime families. The secret combinations of our day function much like the Gadianton robbers of the Book of Mormon times. They have secret signs and code words. They participate in secret rites and initiation ceremonies" (Ballard, "Standing for Truth and Right," 38). The Book of Mormon says, "Oaths which were given by them of old who also sought power, which had been handed down even from Cain, who was a murderer from the beginning. And they were kept up by the power of the devil to administer these oaths unto the people, to keep them in darkness, to help such as sought power to gain power, and to murder, and to plunder, and to lie, and to commit all manner of wickedness and whoredoms. . . . Which combination, is most abominable and wicked above all, in the sight of God; for the Lord worketh not in secret combinations, neither doth he will that man should shed blood, but in all things hath forbidden it, from the beginning of man" (Ether 8:15–16, 18–19). *See also:* Works of darkness.

Secret murder(-s) (2 Nephi 9:9; 26:22; Alma 37:22; Helaman 2:4, 8; 6:23–30, 38; 11:25; 3 Nephi 5:5; 9:9). *Compare:* Moses 5:31. *See:* Secret combination(-s).

Secret oaths (and covenants) (Alma 37:27, 29; Helaman 6:21, 25–26, 30; 4 Nephi 1:42; Ether 8:15, 20; 10:33). *See:* Secret combination(-s).

Secret plans (of wickedness) (Alma 37:29, 32; Helaman 6:30; 11:10, 26; Ether 8:9; 9:26; 13:15). In Alma 37, Alma the Younger goes to great lengths to warn his son Helaman of the danger of these evils. *See:* Secret combination(-s).

Secret society (3 Nephi 3:9; Ether 9:6; 11:22). *See:* Secret combination(-s).

Secret works (of darkness) (2 Nephi 9:9; 10:15; Alma 37:21, 23, 25; Helaman 8:4; 10:3; 3 Nephi 3:7). *See:* Secret combination(-s).

See eye to eye (Mosiah 12:22; 15:29; 16:1; Alma 36:26; 3 Nephi 16:18; 20:32). To be as one, and to agree and partake as equals of heavenly things. *See also:* Face to face.

See fit in his wisdom (2 Nephi 27:22; Mosiah 21:15; Alma 29:8; 3 Nephi 28:29; 29:1; Mormon 5:13). The Lord does His work based on His great wisdom. *See also:* Wisdom in (of) God (the Lord/the Father).

See God (2 Nephi 9:4; 3 Nephi 12:8). "Blessed are the pure in heart: for they shall see God" (Matthew 5:8). In D&C 93:1 is an expanded description of those who will be blessed to see God. It should be our desire to see God, to know that He is, and to talk to Him face to face. "Seek the Lord, and his strength: seek his face ever more" (Psalm 105:4). Many holy men have been so blessed (e.g., Lehi in 1 Nephi 1:8–9; Jacob in 2 Nephi 2:4; Emer in Ether 9:22; Moroni in Ether 12:39). *See also:* Saw Jesus.

See him as he is (Moroni 7:48). *See:* We shall see him as he is.

See his face with pleasure (Enos 1:27). The faithful look forward to returning to God, whereas the wicked shudder even at the thought. *Contrast:* Nakedness before God; Shrink from the presence of the Lord. *See also:* Great and dreadful day of the Lord; Not be ashamed; Robe of righteousness.

See out of obscurity (2 Nephi 27:29). *See:* Out of obscurity.

See the salvation of God (the Father/the Lord) (1 Nephi 19:17; Mosiah 12:24; 15:31; 16:1; Alma 24:27; 3 Nephi 16:20; 20:35). Meaning see the power, glory, might, and miraculous ability of the Lord God. The time will come when all shall hear of Christ, acknowledge His power and greatness, bow before Him as their King, and be judged of Him. *See also:* Salvation of the Lord (our God); Exodus 14:13; 2 Chronicles 20:17; Isaiah 52:10; Luke 3:6; D&C 123:17; 133:3.

Seed as numerous as the sand of the sea (1 Nephi 12:1; 20:19). Refers to one's posterity being great and without number. This was one of the promises made by the Lord to Father Abraham, and a like promise has been made to others in the scriptures. Additionally, all those who become part of the Abrahamic covenant have the same promise. *See also:* Covenant which he made with Abraham; Seed of Abraham.

Seed be scattered (1 Nephi 13:14, 39; 22:7–8; Alma 25:12; 3 Nephi 5:24; 16:4; Mormon 5:15). Through the ages it has been prophesied that the seed (meaning the descendants) of the Jews, the Lamanites, and others would be scattered, driven, and redistributed to many other lands and places. We can now look back and see that these prophecies have truly come to pass.

Seed of Abraham (1 Nephi 15:18; 22:9; 2 Nephi 29:14; 3 Nephi 20:25, 27). "The heirs of the promises and covenants made to Abraham and obtained only by obedience to the laws and ordinances of the gospel of Jesus Christ" (Bible Dictionary, s.v. "Seed of Abraham," 771). *See also:* Covenant which he made with Abraham.

Seed of Joseph (2 Nephi 25:21; Alma 46:23–24, 27; 3 Nephi 5:21, 23; 10:17; Ether 13:6–7, 10). The Lord made the same promises to Joseph that He made to Abraham concerning the blessings that would come to their seed or posterity. *See also:* Seed of Abraham.

Seed of thy loins (2 Nephi 3:11). Meaning the posterity, in this case, of Nephi the son of Lehi.

Seek deep to hide their counsels from the Lord (2 Nephi 27:27; 28:9). Meaning to hide and conceal their evil doings and secret combinations, usually done in the dark so others will not come to know their deeds of iniquity. *See also:* Secret combination(-s); Works of darkness; Isaiah 29:15.

Seek for power (1 Nephi 22:23; 3 Nephi 4:29; 6:15). It is wickedness to seek for power over men, the honor of men, and wealth greater than that of other men. Rather we should seek righteously for aid from the power of the Spirit to help bring souls unto God. *See also:* Desirous for gain (power); Get power; Seek not for power.

Seek not after riches (Jacob 2:18–19; Alma 39:14; Helaman 6:17; 3 Nephi 6:15). Seeking after riches leads to the evil of pride. "Seek not for riches but for wisdom, and behold, the mysteries of God shall be unfolded unto you, and then shall you be made rich. Behold, he that hath eternal life is rich" (D&C 6:7). *See also:* Desirous for gain (power); Get gain; Vain things of the world.

Seek not for power (Alma 60:36; 61:9). *See:* Seek for power.

Seek not to counsel the Lord (Jacob 4:10). *See:* Counsel not the Lord.

Seek revenge (Mosiah 19:19; Alma 27:2). "If men will smite you, or your families, once, and ye bear it patiently and revile not against them, neither seek revenge, ye shall be rewarded; but if ye bear it not patiently, it shall be accounted unto you as being meted out as a just measure unto you" (D&C 98:23–24). *See also:* Defend themselves; Sword of vengeance.

Seek (sought) for the glory of God (2 Nephi 1:25; Alma 60:36). This must be our utmost seeking even as our Savior Jesus sought to glorify His Father in Heaven. *See also:* Glory of God.

Seek the Lord diligently (1 Nephi 2:19; 10:17). Once one has heard of the Lord Jesus, it behooves them to seek to learn of Him and come to know Him. "Learn of me, and listen to my words; walk in the meekness of my Spirit, and you shall have peace in me. I am Jesus Christ" (D&C 19:23–24). *See also:* Know God; Know of Christ; Know their Redeemer; Seek this Jesus.

Seek this Jesus (Ether 12:41). Meaning go to, search, look for, discover, ask of, and inquire concerning Jesus Christ. The questions each must ask are: Have we sufficiently come unto Jesus, and has our seeking been what is required to gain exaltation? "And now, my beloved brethren, I would that ye should come unto Christ, who is the Holy One of Israel, and partake of his salvation, and the power of his redemption. Yea, come unto him, and offer your whole souls as an offering unto him, and continue in fasting and praying, and endure to the end; and as the Lord liveth ye will be saved" (Omni 1:26).

Seek to bring forth my Zion (1 Nephi 13:37). Meaning to establish, build up, and champion Zion, which refers to the Church of God, the community of Saints, the pure in heart. *See also:* D&C 6:6; 11:6; 12:6; 14:6.

Seek ye the kingdom of God (Jacob 2:18; 3 Nephi 13:33). This should be our highest priority. *See also:* Kingdom of God; Kingdom of heaven.

Seeker of happiness (Alma 27:18). All reasonable men and women seek happiness. Being a seeker of true happiness can only come by total acceptance of and living the gospel of Jesus Christ. *See also:* Abraham 1:2.

Seeking for power, and authority, and riches (Alma 46:4; 60:17–18; 3 Nephi 6:15). In D&C 121:34–35: "Behold, there are many called, but few are chosen. And why are they not chosen? Because their hearts are set so much upon the things of this world, and aspire to the honors of men." Rather we should be like Moroni, the chief captain of the Nephite armies, who said, "I seek not for power, but to pull it down. I seek not for honor of the world, but for the glory of my God, and the freedom and welfare of my country" (Alma 60:36). *See also:* Seek not after riches.

Seen a vision (1 Nephi 5:4; 8:2; 2 Nephi 1:4). We believe in visions (Articles of Faith 1:5). God has called prophets, seers, and revelators to guide His Saints. Additionally, visions are a gift of the Spirit, and are given at God's will to bless and guide the humble followers of God. *See also:* I have seen; In a vision; Saw in a vision.

Seen angels (Jacob 7:5; Alma 19:34; 3 Nephi 7:15). We believe in the ministering of angels to mortals here on earth. *See also:* Angels minister(-ed/appeared/declared/descending) unto him (them).

Seen Jesus (3 Nephi 19:2; Ether 12:39). *See:* Saw Jesus; Seen my Redeemer.

Seen my Redeemer (2 Nephi 11:2–3; 31:17; Alma 19:13). Various prophets and saints have been blessed to see Jesus Christ, and He has revealed Himself unto them. The scriptures teach that we should seek the face of the Lord always. Examples include 1 Chronicles 16:11; 2 Chronicles 7:14; D&C 88:68; 93:1; 101:38. *See also:* Saw Jesus.

Seer is a revelator and a prophet (Mosiah 8:16). "There have been many seers in the history of God's people on this earth but not so many as there have been prophets. 'A seer is greater than a prophet . . . and a gift which is greater can no man have . . .' (Mosiah 8:15–18). Joseph Smith is the great seer of the latter days. In addition, the First Presidency and the Council of the Twelve are sustained as prophets, seers, and revelators" (Bible Dictionary, s.v. "seer," 771).

Sell themselves for naught (2 Nephi 26:10; Mormon 8:38). Meaning to sell their souls for a mess of pottage (Genesis 25:33–34). Or using another scriptural phrase, "The wages of sin is death" (Romans 6:23). In other words they give up their righteous standing before God in exchange for the things of the world or that which has no worth and does not last.

Send his angel (Alma 39:19). *See:* Angels minister(-ed/appeared/declared/descending) unto him (them).

Sense of his (your) guilt (awful situation) (Mosiah 2:38; 4:5; Ether 8:24). *See:* Bright recollection of all our guilt.

Sent angels (2 Nephi 4:24; Alma 12:29; 27:4; Helaman 5:11; Moroni 7:22). *See:* Angels minister(-ed/ appeared/declared/descending) unto him (them).

Sent prophets (Mosiah 3:13; 3 Nephi 9:11; Ether 7:23). God sends prophets to declare His word and warn the people to repent. "Surely the Lord God will do nothing, but he revealeth his secret unto his servants the prophets" (Amos 3:7). *See also:* Came prophets.

Servant of the devil (Moroni 7:11). Those that follow the bidding of Satan. *See also:* Devil and his angels (children); Enemy to God; Workers of darkness (and secret combinations).

Serve God (Mosiah 21:35; Alma 30:9; 42:4; 3 Nephi 5:3; 13:24; 24:14; Ether 2:9–10). We must serve God with all our might, mind, and strength. *See also:* Repent and serve God.

Serve him (2 Nephi 1:7; Mosiah 2:21; 7:33; 18:10, 13; 21:31–32; Alma 30:9; Ether 2:8; 13:2; Moroni 6:3; 7:13). *See:* Serve God.

Service of God (Mosiah 2:16, 17, 18). The service of God is here defined as service to fellowmen. *See also:* Serve God.

Set at defiance the commandments of God (Alma 5:18). To oppose, resist, mock, despise, and disobey God. *See also:* Rebel(-led/-ling/-lion) against God.

Set at naught (1 Nephi 19:7; Helaman 4:21; 12:6). *See:* Thing of naught.

Set him at naught (1 Nephi 19:7). "The world, because of their iniquity, shall judge him to be a thing of naught" (1 Nephi 19:9). *See also:* Esteemed him as naught (afflicted).

Set his heart upon the glory of the world (Ether 8:7). *See:* Get power; Glory of the world.

Set his (my) hand again the second time (2 Nephi 21:11; 25:17; 29:1; Jacob 6:2). *See:* Lord will set his hand; Recover them a second time.

Set their hearts upon the vain things of the world (Alma 4:8; 5:53; 7:6; 31:27; Helaman 7:21; 12:4). *See:* Set their (your) hearts upon riches; Vain things of the world.

Set their (your) hearts upon riches (Mosiah 12:29; Alma 1:30; 4:8; 5:53; 7:6; 31:24; Helaman 6:17; 7:21; 13:20–21). "Set their hearts upon" means to desire and seek after. *See also:* Vain things of the world.

Set them up for a standard (1 Nephi 22:6; 2 Nephi 29:2). *See:* Ensign to the nations (people).

Set up my standard to the people (1 Nephi 21:22; 22:6; 2 Nephi 6:6; 29:2). "This Church is the standard which Isaiah said the Lord would set up for the people in the latter days. This Church was given to be a light to the world and to be a standard for God's people and for the Gentiles to seek to. This Church is the ensign on the mountain spoken of by the Old Testament prophets. It is the way, the truth, and the life" (Romney, in Conference Report, April 1961, 119). *See also:* Ensign to the nations (people); D&C 45:9; 115:5.

Shadow of changing (turning) (Alma 7:20; Mormon 9:9–10). With God there is no change from the holy being He now is, not even the smallest inkling, trace, or faint shadow of change or variance, for God is the same yesterday, today, and forever. He is unchangeable. *See also:* In him there is no variableness neither shadow of changing.

Shadow of his (my) hand (1 Nephi 21:2; 2 Nephi 8:16). Meaning protected by the Lord's hand or sheltered under God's almighty power.

Shadow of those things which are to come (Mosiah 13:10; 16:14). *See:* Type(-s) and shadow(-s).

Shake at the appearance of sin (2 Nephi 4:31). *See:* Abhor sin (such wickedness).

Shake off the chains (2 Nephi 1:13, 23; 9:45). *See:* Arise from the dust; Chains of hell.

Shake the earth (1 Nephi 17:45; 2 Nephi 12:19, 21; 23:13; 24:16; Mosiah 27:11, 15, 18; Alma 29:1; Helaman 5:27; 12:11; 14:21; 3 Nephi 8:6, 24; Ether 4:9). The Lord God hath all power, and at His word the earth shall shake and tremble.

Shake them (my garments) before you (2 Nephi 9:44). *See:* Rid my (our) garments of your (blood and) sins.

Shake thyself from the dust (2 Nephi 8:25; 3 Nephi 20:37). *See:* Arise from the dust.

Shall be a sign unto you (1 Nephi 11:7; Helaman 14:4–5, 20; 3 Nephi 21:7). *See:* Give unto thee (you) a sign.

Shall be damned (2 Nephi 9:24; 3 Nephi 11:34; Mormon 9:23; Ether 4:18). Meaning shall be stopped as to their progression. *See also:* Believeth not shall be damned; Damnation to the (of his/to your own/upon their) soul(-s).

Shall be made known (1 Nephi 13:41; 15:11; 2 Nephi 30:16; Mosiah 8:17; Alma 13:26; 3 Nephi 16:7; 21:2–3). *See:* Made known; Made manifest.

Shall be revealed (2 Nephi 27:11; 30:17). *See:* Made manifest; Revealed upon the house tops.

Shall be saved (1 Nephi 13:37; 22:17, 31; 2 Nephi 2:9; 6:12; 25:13; 28:8; 31:15; Jacob 6:4; Mosiah 12:33; Alma 22:6; 24:16; 32:13; Helaman 12:23; 3 Nephi 11:33; 23:5; 27:6; Mormon 9:23; Ether 4:18). *See:* Be saved.

Shall be (as) stubble (1 Nephi 22:15; 2 Nephi 26:4, 6; 3 Nephi 25:1). *See:* Consumed as stubble.

Shall be your rearward (3 Nephi 20:42; 21:29). *See:* Lord will go before you, and the God of Israel will be your rearward.

Shall come to pass (1 Nephi 14:1; 22:1, 20; 2 Nephi 3:20; 9:15; 10:8; 12:2, 11; 13:24; 14:3; 17:7, 18, 21–23; 18:21; 20:12, 20, 27; 21:11; 24:3–4, 24; 25:7, 14; 26:10, 19; 27:6, 15, 19, 24; 28:3; 29:13–14; 30:7–8; Mosiah 5:9–10; 11:22–24; 12:2–4, 6, 8, 31; 17:15; 26:25; Alma 40:12–13; Helaman 10:10; 13:18; 14:7–8; 3 Nephi 20:20–21, 23, 30; 21:8, 11, 14, 19–20; 27:16; 28:29; Mormon 5:20). *See:* According to God's word.

Shall know of greater things than these (Alma 37:4; Mormon 8:12). *See:* Greater things; Know of greater things; Mysteries of God.

Shall know that the Lord is God (1 Nephi 17:14; 21:26; 22:12; 2 Nephi 6:15, 18; Mosiah 5:9; 11:22; 12:3; 3 Nephi 20:39). The day will come that the Jews and all men will come to know that Jesus Christ is the Lord their God.

Shall know that these things are true (Ether 4:11; 5:3). By the Spirit and by the power of God you shall know it is true. *Compare:* Moroni 10:4–7.

Shall know them by their fruits (works) (3 Nephi 14:16, 20; Moroni 7:5). *See:* By their works ye shall know them.

Shall manifest himself (1 Nephi 13:42; 14:1; 2 Nephi 25:12; 32:6; Enos 1:8; Alma 45:10). Meaning Jesus Christ shall manifest Himself, show Himself, and come unto them. *See also:* Manifest himself in the flesh; Manifest himself unto them in power and great glory; Manifest himself unto them in word, and also in power, in very deed.

Shall (may/must) be fulfilled (1 Nephi 7:13; 15:18; 17:3; 2 Nephi 9:17; 10:15; 25:7, 21, 24, 30; Mosiah 21:4; Alma 5:57–58; 7:11; 13:26; 30:3; 34:13; 37:24; 45:14; Helaman 11:8; 16:13–14; 3 Nephi 1:4–5, 25; 5:1, 14, 25; 15:6; 16:17; 20:11–12, 46; 21:4; 28:7, 29; 29:1, 2; Mormon 8:22, 33; Moroni 10:31). *See:* According to God's word.

Shall not ask that which is contrary to my will (Helaman 10:6). *See:* Ask not amiss.

Shall not be confounded (1 Nephi 22:22; 2 Nephi 7:7). The righteous are promised by the Lord, "I will go before you and be your rearward

[rear guard]; and I will be in your midst, and you shall not be confounded [not be confused or baffled by men or devils]" (D&C 49:27).

Shall not perish (1 Nephi 1:14; 22:19; 2 Nephi 1:28; 4:7; 26:8, 30; Jacob 5:4, 11, 53; Omni 1:7; Mosiah 4:30; 7:19; Alma 24:14; Ether 2:20; 13:7). The righteous shall not perish but shall dwell with God. *See also:* Not perish; Perish not.

Shall perish (1 Nephi 14:5; 15:10; 2 Nephi 9:28, 31–32; 10:16; 23:22; 26:32; 28:16; 30:1; 32:4; Jacob 5:8, 65; Mosiah 4:30; 13:28; Alma 21:6; 33:21; 46:27; Moroni 8:16). The wicked shall perish, meaning die as to things spiritual. *See also:* Spiritual death.

Shall see eye to eye (Mosiah 12:22; 15:29; 16:1; 3 Nephi 16:18; 20:32). *See:* Eye to eye; See eye to eye.

Shalt not write (1 Nephi 14:25; 2 Nephi 4:25). *See:* Forbidden that I (they) should write (utter/preach).

Shed innocent blood (Mosiah 17:10; Alma 14:11; 20:19; 60:13). To shed the blood of innocent people—that is, to kill the innocent—is a most serious crime. *Compare:* Abominable above all sins save it be the shedding of innocent blood or denying the Holy Ghost. *See also:* Put to death; D&C 132:19, 26.

Shedding of blood if it were necessary (save God shall command you) (Alma 48:16; Mormon 7:4). *See:* Defend themselves.

Shedding of the blood of Christ (Moroni 10:33). *See:* Atoning blood of Jesus Christ.

Sheep having no shepherd (Alma 5:37; 25:12). *See:* Good Shepherd.

Sheep of the Good Shepherd (Alma 5:38, 39, 60). *See:* Good Shepherd.

Shine exceedingly (Helaman 5:36). *See:* Shone with exceeding luster.

Shone with exceeding luster (Mosiah 13:5). The Lord has commanded, "Arise and shine forth, that thy light may be a standard for the nations" (D&C 115:5). See the example of Moses in Exodus 34:29–35, also the examples in 1 Nephi 1:9 and 3 Nephi 19:25–28. *See also:* Luster was above that of the sun at noon-day; Shine exceedingly.

Shook the earth (Mosiah 27:18; Alma 14:27; 38:7; Helaman 5:27, 31–33). *See:* Earth shook.

Shook your iniquities from my soul (2 Nephi 9:44). *See:* Rid my (our) garments of your (blood and) sins.

Should not pass away till it should all be fulfilled (3 Nephi 1:25). *See:* Law (is) fulfilled; Law of Moses.

Should not write (1 Nephi 14:25; 2 Nephi 4:25; 3 Nephi 26:16). *See:* Forbidden that I (they) should write (utter/preach).

Shout praises unto the Holy One of Israel (2 Nephi 22:6; 31:13). It will be our great privilege to sing and shout praises to the Lord our Savior and Redeemer forever. *See also:* Hosanna to the Lord (the Most High God); Praise(-d/praising) God; Sing ceaseless praises with the choir above unto the Father and unto the Son; Sing praises unto the Lord; Sing redeeming love; Sing to his praise (forever); Singing and praising God.

Show forth good examples (Alma 17:11). Being a good example has more effect than a thousand speeches. *See also:* Abound(-ing) in good works; Give thee for a light; Let your light so shine.

Show forth his mighty power (1 Nephi 15:17; 18:11; 2 Nephi 33:11; Mosiah 23:24; Alma 8:31; 37:14, 18–19; 3 Nephi 21:6; Ether 3:5; 9:35; 12:31; Moroni 7:35). *See:* All power; Power of God; Show forth power.

Show forth power (1 Nephi 18:11; Mosiah 23:24; Alma 8:31; 17:29; 30:51; 37:14, 18–19; 3 Nephi 21:6; Ether 3:5; 9:35). To bring about His purposes, God can show forth His power, sometimes through His servants. *See also:* Show forth his mighty power.

Show it to no man (them not) (Ether 3:21, 28). *Compare:* Moses 1:42; 4:32. *See:* Seal (them) up.

Show unto me (thee/you) a sign (Jacob 7:13–14; Alma 30:43–44, 45, 48, 51; 32:17). The Lord Jesus said, "A wicked and adulterous generation seeketh after a sign; and there shall no sign be given unto it" (Matthew 16:4). *Compare:* Give unto thee (you) a sign; Be unto you a sign.

Show unto the Gentiles (1 Nephi 15:17; 3 Nephi 21:6; Ether 4:13; 12:28). Meaning to prove to, witness to, inform of, and call attention to the Gentiles things that are prophesied to happen and things which the Gentiles should do.

Show unto you all things what ye should do (2 Nephi 32:5). *See:* All things what ye should do.

Show unto you one thing which I have inquired diligently of God (Alma 40:3). A great example of how God will answer our questions if it is His will.

Show unto you with power and great glory (2 Nephi 33:11; Moroni 7:35). *See:* Show forth power.

Show(-ed) him (them/you) all things (1 Nephi 19:21; 2 Nephi 32:5; Ether 3:26; 12:21). The Lord has shown many things, even "all things," to the prophets according to His will, pleasure, and purposes. *Compare:* Moses 7:67.

Show(-ed/-n) himself (1 Nephi 12:6; 2 Nephi 9:5; 26:1; Helaman 16:18–19; 3 Nephi 11:12; 19:2–3; 26:13, 15; 27:2; Ether 3:13, 17; 4:1, 2; 12:7). It was prophesied that Jesus would show Himself unto the people, and He did in fact do so.

Show(-n) unto them (2 Nephi 27:27; 29:14; Alma 37:41; Helaman 15:15; 3 Nephi 10:18; 19:35; 21:10; Ether 12:27–28). The Lord God is able to show and has shown things unto people to prove He is God and to bring about His purposes. *See also:* Lord had (has) shown (unto) him (me/them); Show forth power.

Shrink from the presence of the Lord (2 Nephi 9:46; Jacob 2:6; Mosiah 2:38; 3:25; 27:31). Best explained in Mosiah 27:31: "Yea, every knee shall bow, and every tongue confess before him. Yea, even at the last day, when all men shall stand to be judged of him, then shall they confess that he is God; then shall they confess, who live without God in the world, that the judgment of an everlasting punishment is just upon them; and they shall quake, and tremble, and shrink beneath the glance of his all-searching eye." *See also:* Not be ashamed.

Shrink with fear (guilt/shame) (2 Nephi 9:46; Jacob 2:6; Mosiah 2:38). *See:* Shrink from the presence of the Lord; Not be ashamed.

Shut out from the presence of our God (2 Nephi 9:9). *See:* Cut off from the presence of the Lord; Spiritual death.

Sift you as chaff (wheat) before the wind (Alma 37:15; 3 Nephi 18:18; Mormon 5:16, 18). *See:* Chaff before the wind.

Signs and wonders (1 Nephi 19:13; 2 Nephi 18:18; 26:13; Mosiah 3:15; Helaman 14:6, 28; 15:3; 16:4, 13, 23; 3 Nephi 1:22; 2:1, 3). "Signs [and wonders] mark, indicate, represent, symbolize, give direction, or point to other things beyond themselves, and are sometimes miraculous or extraordinary in nature. The scriptures speak of God's 'signs and wonders' by which his work, power, and wisdom are made known or recognized by people in the earth (Ex. 7:3–5). True signs provide objective evidence that an event can reasonably be expected, such as the new star in the east being a sign of Christ's birth (Matt. 2:1, 2), or certain dark clouds heralding a storm (Matt. 16:1–4). False or counterfeit signs are deceptive and give a false hope of security if accepted (Ex. 7:11–12; 8:7; D&C 63:7–9)" (*Encyclopedia of Mormonism*, 3:1309). "For I am God, and mine arm is not shortened; and I will show miracles, signs, and wonders, unto all those who believe on my name" (D&C 35:8). "And they shall see signs and wonders, for they shall be shown forth in the heavens above, and in the earth beneath" (D&C 45:40). "Wherefore, I, the Lord, am not pleased with those among you who have sought after signs and wonders for faith, and not for the good of men unto my glory" (D&C 63:12).

Sign(-s) given (1 Nephi 11:7; 19:10; 2 Nephi 26:3, 8; Helaman 16:13; 3 Nephi 1:9, 13–14, 16, 18–19; 2:3, 7–8; 5:2; 8:3–4; 11:2; 21:2; Moroni 10:1). *See:* Signs and wonders.

Signs of his coming (Helaman 14:12). Prophesied signs preceded Jesus Christ's coming to mortality at the meridian of time, and signs that would precede Jesus's Second Coming are now being shown as foretold by Jesus and other prophets. *See also:* Coming of Christ; Things (which are) to come; Matthew 24:29–51; D&C 45:16–23.

Signs shall follow them that believe (Mormon 9:24; Ether 4:18). Refers to the miracles of God. Miracles generally are only manifest to those of faith, according to the will of God. *See also:* Signs and wonders; God of miracles.

Similitude of God and his Only Begotten Son (Jacob 4:5). Refers to the commanded sacrifice of Isaac by his father, Abraham, which was a similitude or likeness of Jesus Christ as part of Heavenly Father's plan of salvation.

Simpleness of the way (1 Nephi 17:41; Alma 37:46). Refers to the children of Israel in the wilderness, who when poisonous fiery flying serpents were sent among them, once bitten looked not upon the brazen serpent, and had not faith that it would heal them because of the simpleness of the way (see Helaman 8:14–15).

Sin appeareth (was very abominable) (Jacob 2:5; Mosiah 11:2). *See:* Abhor sin (such wickedness).

Sin which is unpardonable (Jacob 7:19; Alma 39:6). *See:* Unpardonable sin.

Sincere heart (Moroni 10:4). *See:* Pray(-ed) in faith; Real intent (of heart).

Sincere repentance (Mosiah 29:19). Meaning real repentance, not counterfeit or hypocritical. *See also:* Come(-th) unto repentance; I will forgive; Repent and come with full purpose of heart.

Sincerity of heart (Mosiah 4:10; 26:29). *See:* Sincere repentance; D&C 5:24.

Sing ceaseless praises with the choir above unto the Father and unto the Son (Mormon 7:7; Ether 6:9). *See:* Sing praises unto the Lord.

Sing praises unto the Lord (Mormon 7:7; Ether 6:9). In Psalm 47:6–7, "Sing praises to God, sing praises: sing praises unto our King, sing praises. For God is the King of all the earth." Such is the song, praise, and worship of those who have accepted Jesus as their Redeemer and those who follow after Christ's way.

In the hymn "Come, Sing to the Lord,"

Come, sing to the Lord, his name adore! . . .
Come, sing to the Lord, his praises ring! . . .

Come, sing to the Lord, his name be blessed!
(*Hymns*, no. 10).

Sing redeeming love (Alma 5:9; 26:13). Means to sing praises to God for His mercy and love in providing redemption and salvation for mankind. See the revealed words of a song of redeeming love found in D&C 84:98–102. *See also:* Revelation 15:3–4; D&C 133:56.

Sing to his praise (forever) (Mosiah 18:30; Alma 26:8). All creation sings praises to the Lord (see D&C 128:23). All Saints also sing praises to their God and Redeemer, and do so forever (see D&C 76:21). *See also:* Sing praises unto the Lord.

Singing and praising God (1 Nephi 1:8; Alma 36:22; 3 Nephi 4:31). *See:* Sing praises unto the Lord.

Sins and iniquities shall be answered upon their heads (Jacob 3:10; Mosiah 29:30–31). Because of the parents' wickedness in leading their children into sin, the sins of the children shall be heaped upon the parents in the judgment day. The same applies to kings who lead their people into sin.

Sins are forgiven (Enos 1:5; Alma 24:10). At various times the Lord has told individuals that their sins are forgiven. For this great blessing we must pray and supplicate our God. *See also:* Luke 5:20; 7:48;

D&C 25:3; 29:3; 31:5; 36:1; 50:36; 60:7; 62:3; 90:1, 6; 108:1; 110:5; 112:3.

Sins of the world (1 Nephi 10:10; 11:33; 2 Nephi 31:4; Mosiah 26:23; Alma 5:48; 7:14; 30:26; 34:8, 12; 36:17; 39:15; 42:15; 3 Nephi 11:11, 14; 28:9, 38; 4 Nephi 1:44). "And the whole world lieth in sin, and groaneth under darkness and under the bondage of sin" (D&C 84:49). *See also:* Repent all ye ends of the earth; Save the world from sin.

Sit down in peace (Alma 38:15). After they die, those who have been just and true in this earth life will rest from all earthly cares and enjoy the love and peace of God. *See also:* Find peace to my soul.

Sit down in the kingdom of God (Alma 5:24; 7:25; 29:17; 34:36; 3 Nephi 28:10). Meaning when the faithful die, they will find peace, their joy shall be full, and they will receive their reward for righteousness. *See also:* Go no more out; Right hand of God.

Sit down with Abraham, and Isaac and with Jacob (Alma 7:25; Helaman 3:30). Means to receive exaltation in the celestial kingdom and sit down on the right hand of God as do Abraham, Isaac, and Jacob. In D&C 132:37 it reads: "Abraham . . . Isaac . . . and Jacob . . . have entered into their exaltation, according to the promises, and sit upon thrones, and are not angels but are gods." *See also:* Abraham, Isaac, and Jacob.

Sitteth on the right hand (Moroni 9:26). *See:* Right hand of God.

Slain for the sins of the world (1 Nephi 11:33; Alma 30:26; 3 Nephi 11:14). Jesus suffered and was slain for the sins of all mankind, so that those who repent and come unto Him will have their sins remitted. This was the mission of Christ here on earth and was appointed to Him in the councils of heaven before the earth was formed. *See also:* Atonement of Christ (the Only Begotten Son).

Slay the wicked (2 Nephi 21:4; 30:9). God will slay and destroy the unrepentant wicked. *See also:* Hewn down and cast into the fire; Shall perish; Wicked destroyed.

Sleep of hell (2 Nephi 1:13; 27:5; Alma 5:7). The wicked are unfeeling and therefore unaware of the things of righteousness. They are surrounded by darkness and as if asleep. *See also:* Shake off the chains; Spirit of deep sleep.

Sleepeth in God (Alma 19:8). Also rendered "carried away in God" (see Alma 19:6). Same as Alma the younger, who became as dumb and could not move (see Mosiah 27:19).

Slow to remember the Lord our God (1 Nephi 17:45; Mosiah 9:3; 13:29; Alma 55:31; 62:49; Helaman 12:5). *See:* Remember, remember.

Small and simple things (Alma 37:6). "Out of small things proceedeth that which is great" (D&C 64:33). *See also:* Small means.

Small means (1 Nephi 16:29; Alma 37:6). *See:* Small and simple things; D&C 64:33; 123:15.

Small plates (Jacob 1:1; 7:27). The small plates "were more particularly devoted to the spiritual matters and the ministry and teachings of the prophets" (A Brief Explanation about the Book of Mormon; the Book of Mormon). *See also:* 1 Nephi 9:2–4.

Smite the earth (2 Nephi 21:4; 30:9; Helaman 10:6; 3 Nephi 25:6; 28:20). Meaning, depending on the context: destroy the wicked, bring famine and pestilence, and cause the people of the earth to obey. *See also:* Slay the wicked; With his rod.

Smite you to the dust (Jacob 2:15). Repent quickly, for God has power to destroy you for your wickedness. *See also:* 2 Nephi 12:10; 21:4; 30:9.

Snare of the adversary (Alma 12:6). *See:* Catch (caught) in a snare; Ensnare the hearts of men; Lay a snare; Subtlety of the devil; Wiles of the devil.

Snatch(-ed) us from our awful, sinful and polluted state (Mosiah 27:28–29; Alma 26:17). If we come unto Christ and repent of our sins, He will lift us, catch us up from, and save us from our sins. *See also:*

Atonement of Christ (the Only Begotten Son).

Soften my (our/the/their) heart(-s) (1 Nephi 2:16; 7:5, 19; 18:20; 2 Nephi 10:18; Mosiah 21:15; 23:28–29; Alma 24:8). God has power to soften our hearts and make us more willing and fit for the acceptance of righteous things. *Compare:* Harden(-ed) his (our/the/their/your) heart(-s) against the Lord.

Sold yourselves for iniquities (naught) (2 Nephi 7:1; 3 Nephi 20:38). Meaning sold, relinquished, or gave away your eternal well-being or standing in exchange for sin, which sin is nothing and worthless. *See also:* Sell themselves for naught; Thing of naught.

Solemn mockery (Moroni 8:9, 23). *See:* Mockery before God.

Son of God (1 Nephi 10:17; 11:7, 18, 24; 2 Nephi 25:16, 19; Mosiah 3:8; 4:2; 15:2; Alma 5:50; 6:8; 7:9–10, 13; 9:26; 11:32, 35, 38; 13:16; 16:19–20; 21:7; 33:14, 17–18, 22; 34:2, 5, 7, 14; 36:17–18; Helaman 5:12; 8:14–15, 20; 14:2, 8, 12; 16:18; 3 Nephi 1:17; 5:13, 26; 9:15; 20:31; Mormon 7:5; 9:22; Ether 4:7; 12:18). Jesus Christ is the Son of God. *See also:* Jesus Christ.

Son of God (shall) come(-th) (1 Nephi 10:17; 2 Nephi 25:19; Mosiah 4:2; Alma 5:48, 50; 6:8; 7:9; 9:26; 11:32, 35; 16:19–20; 21:7; 33:22; Helaman 8:14, 20; 14:2; 16:18). *See:* Coming of Christ.

Son of perdition (3 Nephi 27:32; 29:7). Satan is Perdition, and those who follow him become sons of perdition. "In LDS scripture Lucifer and Cain are called Perdition, meaning 'destruction' (D&C 76:26; Moses 5:24). The unembodied spirits who supported Lucifer in the war in heaven and were cast out, and mortals who commit the unpardonable sin against the Holy Ghost, will inherit the same condition as Lucifer and Cain, and thus are called 'sons of perdition'" (*Encyclopedia of Mormonism*, 3:1391).

Son of Righteousness (2 Nephi 26:9; 3 Nephi 25:2; Ether 9:22). Another name or title for Jesus Christ. The full rendering is Son of the Man of Righteousness, meaning the Son of the Father who is the Man of Righteousness. A similar name for Jesus Christ is Man of Holiness (Moses 7:35). God the Father is also known as Man of Holiness (Moses 6:57).

Son of the Eternal Father (1 Nephi 11:21; 13:40; Alma 11:38). Meaning Jesus Christ, even the Lamb of God, the Only Begotten Son in the Flesh, the Son of God the Heavenly Father. *See also:* Son of the living God.

Son of the living God (2 Nephi 31:16; 3 Nephi 30:1; Mormon 5:14; 9:29). A name or title for Jesus Christ. Jesus Christ is the Only Begotten of the Father in the flesh. *See also:* Son of the Eternal Father.

Song of redeeming love (Alma 5:26). *See:* Sing redeeming love.

Sons (and daughters) of Christ (God) (Mosiah 5:7; 27:25; 3 Nephi 9:17; Ether 3:14; Moroni 7:26, 48). This scriptural phrase "has reference to the relationship between [Christ] and those who accept His gospel and thereby become heirs of eternal life. . . . Salvation is attainable only through compliance with the laws and ordinances of the gospel; and all who are thus saved become sons and daughters unto God in a distinctive sense" ("The Father and the Son," 14, 15). This relationship is attested to in many places in the scriptures. For example, consider the words of King Benjamin, "And now, because of the covenant which ye have made ye shall be called the children of Christ, his sons, and daughters; for behold this day he hath spiritually begotten you; for ye say that your hearts are changed through faith on his name; therefore, ye are born of him and have become his sons and his daughters" (Mosiah 5:7). *See also:* Ether 3:14; D&C 11:30; 35:2.

Sorceries and witchcrafts and magics (Alma 1:32; 3 Nephi 21:16; 24:5; Mormon 1:19; 2:10). President James E. Faust wrote, "It is not good practice to become intrigued by Satan and his mysteries. No good can come from getting close to evil. Like playing with fire, it is too easy to get burned: 'The knowledge of sin tempteth to its commission' (Joseph F. Smith, *Gospel Doctrine* [1939], 373). The only safe course is to keep well distanced from him and any of his wicked activities or nefarious practices. The mischief of devil worship, sorcery, witchcraft, voodooism, casting spells, black magic, and all other forms of demonism should always be avoided" ("The Forces That Will Save Us," 5).

Sore repentance (Mosiah 23:10; Alma 27:23). *See:* Repenting nigh unto death.

Sorrowing of the damned (Mormon 2:13). *See:* Pains of a damned soul; Pains of hell.

Sorrows and afflictions (Alma 28:8). *See:* Bear afflictions (with patience).

Sought me diligently (1 Nephi 2:19). *See:* Seek the Lord diligently.

Sought my will (Helaman 10:4). *See:* Will of God.

Sought power and authority (2 Nephi 1:25; Alma 51:8; 60:16–17; Helaman 2:5; 3 Nephi 6:15; Ether 8:15, 16). It is the carnal nature of man to seek unrighteous power and authority over their fellowmen. Satan tempts man to this desire and action. *See also:* Usurp power and authority.

Soul began to be (was) harrowed up (Alma 14:6; 36:12; 39:7). *See:*

Harrowed up by the memory of all my (many) sins.

Soul could never die (Alma 12:20; 42:9). *See:* Eternal as the life of the soul.

Soul delight in fatness (2 Nephi 9:51). *See:* Let your soul delight in fatness.

Soul delighteth (2 Nephi 4:15–16; 11:2, 4–6; 25:4–5, 13; 31:3). *See:* My soul delighteth.

Soul did (doth/will) rejoice (1 Nephi 1:15; 2 Nephi 4:30; Alma 7:26). The righteous and just will always celebrate and exult when good, diligence, charity, revelation, faith, perseverance, and other godly attributes and events are manifest.

Soul hungered (Enos 1:4). *See:* My soul hungered.

Soul rent with anguish (1 Nephi 17:47; Mormon 6:16). Exceedingly sad because of the wickedness that exists. *See also:* Afflict my soul.

Soul was racked with eternal torment (Mosiah 27:29). *See:* Endless misery (and wo); Endless torment; Eternal torment.

Souls are precious (Alma 31:35; 39:17). "Remember the worth of souls is great in the sight of God" (D&C 18:10). *See also:* D&C 109:43.

Souls did expand (Alma 5:9; 32:34). As we strive to be faithful, our knowledge and blessings expand. "Yea, a man whose heart did swell with thanksgiving to his God, for the many privileges and blessings which he bestowed upon his people" (Alma 48:12).

Souls were illuminated (Alma 5:7). The gospel of Jesus Christ brings light into the lives of those who accept it and live it. *See also:* Illuminated by the light of the everlasting word; Light of the body; Marvelous light of God.

Sound understanding (Alma 17:2). *See:* Men of perfect (sound) understanding.

Space granted unto man in which he might repent (Alma 12:24). *See:* Probationary state (time).

Spake from the dead (2 Nephi 27:13; Mormon 8:26; 9:30). An expression meaning their words and teachings will be preserved and brought forth after the writers are dead. *See also:* Cry from the dust; Crying from the dead (dust); Speak from the dead.

Spake (speak/taught) with power and authority from God (1 Nephi 2:14; Words of Mormon 1:17; Mosiah 13:6; 18:26; Alma 17:3; 3 Nephi 7:17; Moroni 7:35). *See:* Minister with power and great authority.

Spared because ye were more righteous than they (3 Nephi 9:13). This phrase gives great hope to those who strive after righteousness and look forward to the coming of Christ. None are perfect in this

life, but if we repent, humbly try to follow Christ, and do not rebel, we then hope that we will be worthy to stand at the Second Coming of Christ. *See also:* Abide the day of his coming.

Speak by the power of the Holy Ghost (2 Nephi 32:3; 33:1). *See:* Power of the Holy Ghost (Spirit).

Speak by way of command (Alma 5:62). *See:* By way of command (-ment); Commanded to write; Thus saith our God (the Lord).

Speak forth marvelous things (words) (Helaman 5:33, 45; 3 Nephi 17:16–17; 26:14). Men touched by the Spirit of God, God, and angels speak marvelous, wonderful, and miraculous things, even heavenly things.

Speak from the dead (2 Nephi 27:13; Mormon 8:26; 9:30). *See:* Spake from the dead.

Speak from the dust (2 Nephi 3:19–20; 26:16; 33:13; Moroni 10:27). *See:* Cry from the dust.

Speak out of the ground (2 Nephi 26:16; Mormon 8:26). Elder LeGrand Richards said, "Obviously, the only way a dead people could speak 'out of the ground' or 'low out of the dust' would be by the written word, and this the people did through the Book of Mormon. Truly it has a familiar spirit, for it contains the words of the prophets of the God of Israel" (*A Marvelous*

Work and a Wonder, 67–68). *See also:* Cry from the dust.

Speak peace to our souls (Alma 58:11). Meaning God provided peace to their souls. *See also:* Peace to my soul.

Speak unto them out of the ground (2 Nephi 26:16). *See:* Speak out of the ground.

Speak with power (1 Nephi 2:14; Words of Mormon 1:17; Mosiah 13:6). *See:* Minister with power and great authority; Spake (speak/taught) with power and authority from God; Taught (teach) with power and authority of God.

Speakest hard things against us (1 Nephi 16:2, 3; 2 Nephi 9:40). *See:* Cuts you to your hearts; Taketh the truth to be hard.

Speaketh by the power of the Holy Ghost (2 Nephi 33:1). *See:* Speak by the power of the Holy Ghost.

Speaking out of the dust (Moroni 10:27). *See:* Cry from the dust.

Speaking with the Lord (1 Nephi 3:1; Mosiah 13:5). The holy prophets have spoken with the Lord. *See also:* Face to face; Saw Jesus; Seen Jesus; Seen my Redeemer.

Speaking with tongues (Omni 1:25; Alma 9:21; Mormon 9:7). The gift of tongues is one of the gifts of the Spirit. It is given so people can converse and understand. It is not useless babblings. *See also:* Gifts of God; Spiritual gifts.

Speech shall be low out of the dust (2 Nephi 26:16). *See:* Cry from the dust.

Speedily repent (Jacob 3:4; Alma 5:56; 30:57). Do not delay the day of your repentance. *See also:* Prepare quickly.

Spend their time (your strength) with harlots (Mosiah 11:14; 12:29). Do not spend your time, money, and energies with fornicators, adulterers, and prostitutes. *See also:* Consume it on your lusts.

Spirit and body shall again reunite (Alma 11:43; 40:19–21; Moroni 10:34). *See:* Resurrection of the body.

Spirit ceased (ceaseth) to strive with man (1 Nephi 7:14; 2 Nephi 26:11; Mormon 5:16; Ether 2:15; 15:19; Moroni 8:28; 9:4). "One of the most tragic experiences that can come to individuals [is] to have the Lord withdraw his Spirit. . . . When withdrawn, it becomes difficult for us to pray, to have direction and guidance, to withstand evil" (Lee, *Stand Ye in Holy Places*, 117–18).

Spirit doth not dwell in unholy temples (Mosiah 2:37; Helaman 4:24). *See:* He doth not dwell in unholy temples; Unholy temples.

Spirit hath constrained(-eth) me (1 Nephi 4:10; 7:15; Alma 14:11; 2 Nephi 28:1). Meaning the Holy Ghost directed, compelled, and required. In D&C 63:64: "Remember that that which cometh from above is sacred, and must be spoken with care and by constraint of the Spirit; and in this there is no condemnation, and ye receive the Spirit through prayer; wherefore, without this there remaineth condemnation." *See also:* According to the Spirit; Spirit said unto me (saith).

Spirit knoweth all things (1 Nephi 22:2; Words of Mormon 1:7; Mosiah 5:3; Alma 7:13; 18:18, 28; 22:10–11). As God the Father and Jesus Christ know all things, so does the Holy Ghost know all things. "By the power of the Holy Ghost ye may know the truth of all things" (Moroni 10:5). "The Holy Ghost, even the Comforter, which showeth all things" (D&C 39:6). *See also:* All things what ye should do; Things pertaining to (unto) righteousness (and) to the kingdom of God.

Spirit manifest (said) unto me (1 Nephi 2:17; 4:11–12; 11:2, 4, 8, 11; Alma 5:46–47, 51; 7:9; 38:6; 39:12; Mormon 3:20). *See:* According to the Spirit; Manifest by the Spirit; Spirit said unto me (saith).

Spirit of Christ (Moroni 7:16; 10:17). *See:* Light of Christ; Spirit of God.

Spirit of contention (3 Nephi 11:29). Jesus said, "He that hath the spirit of contention is not of me, but is of the devil, who is the father of contention, and he stirreth up the hearts of men to contend with anger, one with another" (3 Nephi 11:29). *See also:* Contend one with another; Contention(-s) among them (the people); Disputations among the people (them/you); Father of contention; No contention; Revile against; Stir(-red/-reth) the people (them) up to anger.

Spirit of deep sleep (2 Nephi 27:5). Those that reject the prophets will find themselves unconscious of and insensible to spiritual things. *See also:* Sleep of hell; Isaiah 29:10.

Spirit of freedom (Alma 60:25; 61:15). The spirit of freedom is a subset of the Spirit of God. God is a God of freedom and has given all men and women their moral agency. "Ye shall know the truth, and the truth shall make you free" (John 8:32). As we keep the commandments we become freer to enjoy more blessings and greater potential. Whereas if we sin we become bound down by the chains of the devil. *See also:* Made free.

Spirit of God (1 Nephi 13:12–13; 17:47, 52; Alma 5:46–47; 7:5; 9:21; 13:4; 18:16; 24:30; 30:42; 38:6; 61:15; Helaman 5:45; 3 Nephi 7:21–22; Moroni 10:8–9). Generally means the Holy Ghost, the third member of the Godhead, who can influence us, direct us, instruct us, comfort us, and warn us. However, in some contexts it means the Light of Christ, which indicates to us right and wrong. *See also:* Light of Christ; Spirit of Christ; Spirit of the Lord.

Spirit of God wrought upon him (them) (1 Nephi 13:12–13; 17:52; 19:12; 2 Nephi 1:27; Enos 1:26; Mosiah 5:2; 3 Nephi 7:22; Moroni 6:4). Meaning the Spirit worked a change upon them. *See also:* Wrought a mighty change in our (their) hearts.

Spirit of prophecy (and revelation) (2 Nephi 25:4; Jacob 1:6; 4:6; Mosiah 12:25; Alma 3:27; 4:13, 20; 5:47; 6:8; 8:24; 9:21; 10:12; 12:7; 13:26; 16:5; 17:3; 23:6; 25:16; 37:15; 43:2; Helaman 4:12, 23). "The 'testimony of Jesus [which comes by the power of the Holy Ghost] is the spirit of prophecy' (Revelation 19:10). The spirit of prophecy, however, is far more than just a belief that Jesus lives. It includes an understanding that Jesus is the literal Son of God. It includes a correct knowledge of His purpose in coming into mortality and the significance and nature of His mission. It includes an understanding of the gospel plan for His children, particularly those who spiritually become His sons and daughters through the covenant of baptism. All of this comes through the power of the Holy Ghost. . . .

"Righteous people who are serving the Lord and seeking to do His will can obtain the spirit of prophecy by searching the scriptures diligently and giving themselves 'to much prayer, and fasting' (Alma 17:3). The Lord will give knowledge to those who prepare themselves and sincerely seek it.

"The Prophet Joseph Smith once said, 'God hath not revealed anything to Joseph, but what He will make known unto the Twelve, and even the least Saint may know all things as fast as he is able to bear them' (*Teachings of the Prophet Joseph Smith*, p. 149)" (*Old Testament Student Manual*, 132). In Joseph Smith's history, he says, "No sooner had I baptized Oliver Cowdery, than the Holy Ghost fell upon him, and he stood up and prophesied many things which should shortly come to pass. And again, so soon as I had been baptized by him, I also had the *spirit of prophecy*, when, standing up, I prophesied concerning the rise of this Church, and many other things connected with the Church, and this generation of the children of men. We were filled with the Holy Ghost, and rejoiced in the God of our salvation. Our minds being now enlightened, we began to have the scriptures laid open to our understandings, and the true meaning and intention of their more mysterious passages revealed unto us in a manner which we never could attain to previously, nor ever before had thought of" (Joseph Smith–History 1:73–74; emphasis added). *See also:* Spirit of revelation.

Spirit of revelation (Alma 4:20; 5:46; 8:24; 9:21; 17:3; 23:6; 45:10; Helaman 4:23; 3 Nephi 3:19). When the "Lord God hath made [things] manifest unto [men] by his Holy Spirit" (Alma 5:46). In Revelation 19:10 we learn, "The testimony of Jesus is the spirit of prophecy."

President Wilford Woodruff said, "It is the privilege of every man and woman in this kingdom to enjoy the spirit of prophecy, which is the Spirit of God; and to the faithful it reveals such things as are necessary for their comfort and consolation, and to guide them in their daily duties" (*Discourses of Wilford Woodruff*, 61).

President James E. Faust said, "Personal revelation will surely come to all whose eyes are single to the glory of God, for it is promised that their bodies will be 'filled with light, and there shall be no darkness' in them (D&C 88:67)" (Faust, "The Forces That Will Save Us," 9).

An interesting insight was recorded in a meeting in Salt Lake City on January 14, 1871: "He [Elder Pratt] mentioned that as Joseph used the Urim and Thummim in the translation of the Book of Mormon, he wondered why he did not use it in the translation of the New Testament. Joseph explained to him that the experience he had acquired while translating the Book of Mormon by the use of the Urim and Thummim had rendered him so well acquainted with the Spirit of Revelation and Prophecy, that in the translating of the New Testament he did not need the aid that was necessary in the 1st instance" (Minutes of the School of the Prophets).

Spirit of the devil (2 Nephi 2:29; 33:5; Mosiah 2:32–33; Alma 30:42; 34:35; 40:13; 3 Nephi 11:29). Just as there is a spirit of freedom, a spirit of anarchy, etc.—being in and around Satan and subjecting oneself to his temptations produces in oneself a spirit of evil and rebellion. The devil and his minions work to influence people with this spirit and engulf people in this spirit so that they will be miserable like unto the devil, and be cut off from the influence of good and the presence of God. *See also:* Power of Satan; Rebel(-led/-ling/-lion) against God.

Spirit of the Lord (1 Nephi 1:12; 7:14–15; 11:1, 11; 13:15; 15:12; 2 Nephi 1:27; 4:12; 21:2; 26:11; Words of Mormon 1:7; Mosiah 2:36; 4:3; 5:2; 13:5; 18:13; 21:34; 28:4; Alma 4:15; 11:22; 19:14; 21:16; 22:4–5; 32:28; 34:35; 39:12; 40:13; Helaman 4:24; 6:35; 16:2; Mormon 2:26; 5:16; Ether 12:2; 15:19; Moroni 9:4). "The Spirit of the Lord doth not dwell in unholy temples" (Helaman 4:24). *See also:* Spirit of God.

Spirit of the Lord (prophecy) which is (was) in him (me) (2 Nephi 1:6, 27; 4:12; 25:4, 11; Jacob 4:15; Words of Mormon 1:7;

Alma 5:46–47; 7:5, 16–17, 26; 11:22; 18:35; 38:6; 45:10; Ether 12:2). Meaning speaking by the power and knowledge of the Holy Ghost. *See also:* Filled with the Spirit (of God/the Lord); Spirit of prophecy (and revelation).

Spirit of the Lord shall rest (was) upon him (2 Nephi 21:2; Mosiah 13:5; 18:13). Referring to the Holy Ghost visiting and influencing a person. *See also:* Filled with the Holy Ghost; Spirit of God wrought upon him (them); Visit them with his Spirit.

Spirit of the truth (Alma 30:46). There is a multitude of meanings here. Truth has power and even a spirit about it. The term "Spirit of Truth" is another name referring to Jesus Christ. God the Father, Jesus Christ, and the Holy Ghost deal only in truth, and that truth that goes forth from Them is the Spirit of Truth. Additionally the scriptures say, "He shall receive of my Spirit, even the Comforter, which shall manifest unto him the truth of all things" (D&C 124:97). *See also:* Spirit speaketh the truth and lieth not.

Spirit of (unto) prophesying (Jacob 4:15; Mosiah 12:25). *See:* Spirit of prophecy (and revelation); Spirit of revelation.

Spirit poured out (Alma 19:14). *See:* Pour(-ed) out his Spirit upon them (into my soul).

Spirit said unto me (saith) (1 Nephi 4:11–12; 11:2, 4, 8; Alma 5:50–51, 52; 7:14). Meaning the Spirit prompted him or instructed him of the words or message to speak. The Spirit says only the words and commands of God. *See also:* Thus saith our God (the Lord).

Spirit speaketh the truth and lieth not (Jacob 4:13). Absolute truth.

Spirit stopped (stoppeth mine) utterance (2 Nephi 32:7; Mosiah 4:20). *See:* Forbidden that I (they) should write (utter/preach).

Spirit which is in me (2 Nephi 1:6; 25:11; Jacob 4:15; Alma 7:17). *See:* Spirit of the Lord (prophecy) which is (was) in him (me).

Spirit which testifieth in me (Alma 7:16, 26). Testimony from the Holy Ghost, sometimes referred to as the Spirit of testimony. *See also:* Testify of these things.

Spirit which they listed to obey (Mosiah 2:32–33, 37; Alma 3:26–27). *Listed to obey* means to choose to obey. Each individual must choose to follow the Spirit of God or the spirit of the devil.

Spiritual death (2 Nephi 9:12; Alma 12:16; 42:9; Helaman 14:16, 18). "Spiritual death is separation from God. The scriptures teach of two sources of spiritual death. The first source is the Fall, and the second is our own disobedience.

"The Book of Mormon prophet Samuel taught, 'All mankind, by the fall of Adam being cut off from the presence of the Lord, are considered as dead, both as to things temporal and to things spiritual' (Helaman 14:16). During our life on the earth, we are separated from God's presence. Through the Atonement, Jesus Christ redeems everyone from this spiritual death. Samuel testified that the Savior's Resurrection 'redeemeth all mankind from the first death— that spiritual death. . . . Behold, the resurrection of Christ redeemeth mankind, yea, even all mankind, and bringeth them back into the presence of the Lord' (Helaman 14:16–17). The prophet Lehi taught that because of the Atonement, 'all men come unto God; wherefore, they stand in the presence of him, to be judged of him according to the truth and holiness which is in him' (2 Nephi 2:10).

"Further spiritual death comes as a result of our own disobedience. Our sins make us unclean and unable to dwell in the presence of God (see Romans 3:23; Alma 12:12–16, 32; Helaman 14:18; Moses 6:57). Through the Atonement, Jesus Christ offers redemption from this spiritual death, but only when we exercise faith in Him, repent of our sins, and obey the principles and ordinances of the gospel (see Alma 13:27–30; Helaman 14:19; Articles of Faith 1:3)" (*True to the Faith*, 48). *See also:* Death as to things pertaining unto righteousness; Death of the spirit; Everlasting death; Second death.

Spiritual gifts (Alma 9:21; 3 Nephi 29:6; Mormon 9:7; Moroni 10:8, 11, 17, 19, 24–25). *See:* Gifts of God.

Spiritual law (2 Nephi 2:5). The commandments of God are spiritual law. Spiritual law is divine law or eternal law. To keep God's laws is to progress spiritually and to become spiritually begotten of God. To break God's commandments is to experience spiritual death, which requires repentance and the Atonement to bring us back to God. *See also:* Temporal law.

Spiritually begotten (born of God) (Mosiah 5:7; Alma 5:14). *See:* Born again (of God).

Spiritually minded (2 Nephi 9:39). To be God-minded as opposed to carnally minded. "Let virtue garnish thy thoughts unceasingly" (D&C 121:45).

Spoken by the (mouth of the) angel (Mosiah 4:11; 5:5). *See:* Angel had (has/hath) spoken.

Spoken by the (mouth of the holy) prophets (1 Nephi 3:20; 5:13; 2 Nephi 9:2; 25:18; Jacob 6:8; 7:11; Mosiah 18:19; Alma 18:36; 30:6; 40:22, 24; Helaman 15:11; 3 Nephi 1:13; 2:7; 5:1–2; 10:11; 20:24; 29:2; Ether 15:3; Moroni 8:29). Those things spoken by the mouth of the prophets are contained in the scriptures and are spoken today by living prophets. Those things are to be preserved, remembered, and taught because they testify of Christ, prophesy of things to come, are a witness to the people, speak salvation to men's souls, and shall all be fulfilled.

Spotless at his judgment-seat (the last day) (2 Nephi 33:7; Jacob 1:19; Mormon 9:6). *See:* Stand spotless before me at the last day.

Spotless before God (Alma 12:14; 13:12; 14:7; 3 Nephi 27:20). Meaning being able to stand before God purified and sanctified through the Atonement of Jesus Christ. *See also:* Stand spotless before me at the last day.

Springing up unto everlasting life (Alma 32:41; 33:23). Meaning coming forth to eternal life. *See also:* Everlasting life.

Spurn(-eth) at the doings of the Lord (3 Nephi 29:4–5, 8). To rebel against and reject the works of the Lord God. *See also:* Against God; Contrary to God.

Stand as a (bright) testimony against the world (this people/ you) (2 Nephi 25:28; Mosiah 3:24; 17:10; Alma 14:11; 39:8; Ether 5:4). Sins cannot be buried or hidden, but will be revealed to all at the judgment day.

Stand as a witness (as witnesses) against them (Alma 14:11; Mormon 3:16). The blood of the innocent shall stand as a witness against the wicked who have murdered the Saints of God. Also God has

commanded certain men to witness events.

Stand as witnesses of God (Mosiah 18:9; 24:14). To teach and testify that God lives.

Stand before God (1 Nephi 15:33; 2 Nephi 9:22, 44; 28:23; Enos 1:27; Mosiah 26:25; Alma 5:15, 18; 11:41, 43; 12:8, 15; 24:15; 33:22; 40:21; 3 Nephi 26:4; 27:14; Mormon 5:22; 9:2; Ether 5:6). "And I saw the dead, small and great, stand before God; and the books were opened; and another book was opened, which is the book of life; and the dead were judged out of those things which were written in the books, according to their works" (Revelation 20:12). *See also:* Bar of God.

Stand before his (the) bar (of God) (Mosiah 16:10; Alma 5:22; Mormon 9:13). Meaning to stand before God to be judged. *See:* Bar of God; Stand before God.

Stand before the judgment-seat of Christ (3 Nephi 28:31; Mormon 3:20, 22; 6:21; 7:6). *See:* Bar of God; Stand before his (the) bar (of God).

Stand before the Lamb of God (Mormon 9:2). *See:* Stand before God.

Stand fast in that (this) liberty wherewith God hath made them free (Mosiah 23:13; Alma 58:40; 61:21). *See:* Defend themselves.

Stand fast in the faith (of Christ) (Alma 1:25; 45:17; 46:27). An admonition to remain faithful to the Lord and His commandments.

Stand forth (Alma 22:26; Helaman 5:26). Meaning to come forward and speak.

Stand spotless before me at the last day (3 Nephi 27:20). To be purified and cleansed of all sin through the Atonement of Jesus Christ by the time the judgment day arrives. *See also:* Found spotless (pure, fair, and white); Garments are spotless; Garments spotless; Holy without spot; Pure and spotless before God; Spotless at his judgment-seat (the last day); Without spot.

Stand to be judged (Mosiah 2:27; 27:31; Mormon 3:20). *See:* Stand before God.

Stand with brightness before God (him) (2 Nephi 9:44). At the judgment, to stand before God clean and bright, without stain of sin or filthiness. *See also:* Spotless before God; Stand spotless before me at the last day.

Standard of liberty (Alma 46:36; 51:20; 62:4–5). *See:* Defend themselves; Title of liberty.

Standard unto my (the) people (1 Nephi 21:22; 2 Nephi 6:6; 29:2). A standard is a flag, banner, ensign, or emblem which gives notice, calls to, and marks events of God.

Standing betwixt them and justice (Mosiah 15:9). If we have repented, come unto Christ, and merited the redemption of His Atonement, Jesus Christ our Savior and Redeemer stands between us and the demands of justice, which are the punishments for our sins. *See also:* Atonement of Christ (the Only Begotten Son); Demands of justice.

State of endless wo (Alma 28:11; Helaman 12:26). The state of the damned. *See also:* Endless misery (and wo).

State of ignorance (Alma 9:16). The state of those who are ignorant of the law or know not the commandments of God, thus they are under no condemnation. For example, the heathen nations that have not the law will be brought forth in the first Resurrection and "it will be tolerable for them" (Mosiah 15:24; Alma 9:15; D&C 45:54). They will be brought forth with the righteous, they will dwell in the millennium, and the gospel will be taught to them.

State of immortality (Alma 12:12). *See:* Immortal state.

State of innocence (2 Nephi 2:23). Referring to the condition Adam and Eve were in before they partook of the forbidden fruit. They knew no joy or sadness, no good nor evil, no sickness or health because they had not yet experienced opposites. Their existence was without these, and contrary to what many believe, life in the Garden of Eden was to them not constant bliss, because they did not know or comprehend bliss.

State of misery (Mosiah 3:25; Alma 40:14–15; 42:1). The unrepentant sinner will be assigned to a state of misery. *See also:* Endless misery (and wo).

State of (never-ending) happiness which hath no end (Mosiah 2:41; Alma 28:12; 40:12, 15; Mormon 7:7). *See:* Endless happiness.

State of probation (2 Nephi 2:21). *See:* Probationary state (time).

State of rest and peace (Alma 40:12). *See:* Enter into his (my/the) rest (of the Lord/of God); Find peace to my soul.

State of righteousness (Mosiah 27:25). Changed from a carnal state to a state of righteousness. *See also:* Born again (of God).

Statutes and judgments (1 Nephi 17:22; 2 Nephi 1:16; 5:10; Mosiah 6:6; Alma 8:17; 25:14; 58:40; Helaman 3:20; 6:34; 15:5; 3 Nephi 25:4). Meaning the commandments, decrees, laws, and ordinances of God. *Compare:* D&C 119:6; 124:39; 136:2. *See also:* Judgments and statutes.

Stay his hand (Alma 10:23; Moroni 9:14). Meaning to hold back God's hand from exercising judgment against the wicked. *Compare:* None can stay it [the hand of the Lord].

Stay themselves upon God (the Lord) (1 Nephi 20:2; 2 Nephi 20:20). Meaning to depend upon the Lord, and also to be subject to and governed by the Lord.

Stay yourselves (2 Nephi 27:4). Stand up in open-eyed surprise or stop in their tracks and be fearful of judgment.

Steadfast and immovable (in good works/in keeping the commandments of God/in the faith) (1 Nephi 2:10; Mosiah 4:11; 5:15; Alma 1:25; Helaman 15:8; 3 Nephi 6:14; Ether 12:4). *See:* Steadfastness in (unto) Christ.

Steadfastly believeth on his name (Alma 5:48). Some people say they believe on Jesus Christ but after a while do not act as if they do. *See:* Endure(-th) to the end.

Steadfastness in (unto) Christ (2 Nephi 25:24; 26:8; 31:20; Helaman 15:10). *Steadfast* means to remain firm and constant in determination or adherence. Relative to the gospel of Christ we must be steadfast in faith, in truth, in testimony, in prayer, in keeping the commandments, in service to others, and in devotion to God.

Stem of Jesse (2 Nephi 21:1). Another name for Jesus Christ the Lord (see D&C 113:1). The term refers to Christ being the Stem, Branch, and seed of King David; Jesse was the father of David. It was prophesied that the Messiah would be of the lineage of David (Isaiah 11:1–5; Jeremiah 23:5–6).

Stiff necks (2 Nephi 28:14; Jacob 2:13). This scriptural phrase is also used in the Bible in Deuteronomy

31:27; Psalm 75:5; and Jeremiah 17:23. *See:* Stiffnecked people.

Stiffen(-ed) their neck (2 Nephi 6:10; 10:5). *See:* Stiffnecked people.

Stiffnecked people (2 Nephi 25:28; Jacob 4:14; 6:4; Enos 1:22; Jarom 1:4; Omni 1:28; Mosiah 3:14; 13:29; Alma 9:5, 31; 15:15; 20:30; 26:24; 37:10; Helaman 4:21; 5:3; 9:21; 13:29; Mormon 8:22). These are people who hold their heads high in pride and will not bow their heads and humble themselves before God. These are people who are quick to do iniquity and slow to remember the Lord their God.

Stiffneckedness of men (the people) (1 Nephi 2:11; 2 Nephi 32:7; Words of Mormon 1:17; 3 Nephi 15:18). *See:* Stiffnecked people.

Stiffness of their necks (2 Nephi 25:12; Jarom 1:3). *See:* Stiffnecked people.

Still small voice (1 Nephi 17:45; Helaman 5:30; 3 Nephi 11:3). We must learn to recognize and heed the still small voice of God. Also, we must step out of the noise of the world often so that we might hear the still small voice of the Spirit. *See also:* Pierce their very soul (them to the center); Voice did pierce them to the center (very soul).

Sting of death (is swallowed up in Christ) (Mosiah 16:7–8; Alma 22:14; Mormon 7:5). *See:* Death is (was) swallowed up in the victory of (in) Christ.

Stir his people up in iniquity (rebellion) (Mosiah 10:6; 16:22; 3 Nephi 6:15). *See:* Stir(-red/-reth) the people (them) up to anger.

Stir them up in remembrance of the Lord (2 Nephi 5:25; Helaman 11:4, 34). It is imperative to remember the Lord Jesus Christ, the Redeemer and Savior, all the days of our life. *See also:* Remember the Lord our (their/your) God.

Stir up the hearts of men (Helaman 6:21; 3 Nephi 11:30; Mormon 4:5). *See:* Satan did get hold (possession) upon the hearts of the people; Spirit of contention.

Stir(-red/-reth) the people (them) up to anger (1 Nephi 16:38; 2 Nephi 28:19–20; Mosiah 9:13; 10:6; 11:28; 17:12; 18:33; 21:2, 11; Alma 2:8; 6:21; 11:20; 24:1; 25:8; 27:2, 12; 35:10; 43:8; 44:16; 46:30; 47:1; 48:3; 51:9; 63:14; Helaman 1:17; 4:3–4; 6:17, 21; 8:7; 11:24; 16:22; Ether 15:6; 3 Nephi 11:29, 30; Mormon 4:5; Moroni 9:3). To cause agitation and contention, rebellion and wickedness, riotings and disturbances. The work of the devil and his minions is to fight against and destroy all that is good. *See also:* Spirit of contention.

Stir(-red/stirring) up in (unto) remembrance (1 Nephi 2:24; 2 Nephi 28:19; Jarom 1:12; Mosiah 1:17; 6:3; Alma 4:19; 25:6). To bring the people to a remembrance of the words of the prophets, their covenants with God, and their duty before God and man. *See also:* Bring souls to repentance; Persuade all men to come unto Christ (repentance); Prick their hearts.

Stirring them up continually to keep them in the fear of the Lord (Enos 1:23). *See:* Stir them up in remembrance of the Lord; Stir(-red/stirring) up in (unto) remembrance.

Stone upon which they might build and have safe foundation (Jacob 4:15–16). *See:* Rock of our Redeemer.

Stone(-d) the prophets (1 Nephi 1:20; 2 Nephi 26:3; Helaman 13:25, 33; 3 Nephi 7:14; 8:25; 10:12; Ether 8:25). *See:* Kill the prophets.

Stood before me (my father/them) (1 Nephi 1:11; 3:29; 8:5; 11:14; Mosiah 3:2; 3 Nephi 11:20). When the Lord or angels visit men they often appear before them. In Moses 7:4 it reads, "And I saw the Lord; and he stood before my face, and he talked with me, even as a man talketh one with another, face to face." *See also:* Face to face.

Stood in a cloud (Mosiah 27:11; Ether 2:5, 14). Often the Lord or His messengers stand within a cloud and talk to the prophets. *Compare:* Exodus 14:19; 34:5; Numbers 12:5; Deuteronomy 31:15.

Stoppeth utterance (2 Nephi 32:7; Mosiah 4:20; Alma 30:49–50).

God commands that one should not speak and has the power to make one dumb of speech. *See also:* Forbidden that I (they) should write (utter/preach).

Straight course (path) to eternal bliss (2 Nephi 9:41; Alma 7:9; 37:44). Meaning to keep God's commandments strictly, and thus remaining on the straight and narrow path to God, neither turning to the right nor to the left. *See also:* Strait and narrow course (path).

Straightness of the path (2 Nephi 31:9). *See:* Straight course (path) to eternal bliss.

Strait and narrow course (path) (1 Nephi 8:20; 2 Nephi 31:18–19; Helaman 3:29). "The word *strait* should not be confused with *straight*, which is pronounced the same although spelled differently. *Strait* means 'narrow, close fitting, limited in space or time.' The strait gate leading to the kingdom of God on the earth (the Church) is narrow and restricted, meaning certain conditions must be met before the person can enter. Thus, 'few there be that find it.' Similarly, a strait gate protects all the ordinances of the gospel, including the path 'that leadeth unto the exaltation and continuation of the lives' (D&C 132:22)" (Ludlow, *Companion to Your Study of the Doctrine and Covenants,* 2:282). *See also:* Enter in (into/by) the (narrow/strait) gate (way/path); Gate by which ye should enter.

Strait is the gate (path) (2 Nephi 33:9; Jacob 6:11; 3 Nephi 14:13–14; 27:33). *See:* Strait and narrow path.

Straiten(-ed) them (1 Nephi 17:41). Meaning to correct, admonish, chasten, and discipline them.

Strangers to God (Alma 26:9). Those who know not God versus "My sheep hear my voice, and I know them, and they follow me" (John 10:27). *See:* Know God; Voice of the Good Shepherd.

Strength (and power) of God (Mosiah 21:30; Alma 56:56). God has all power. *See also:* In the strength of our God (the Lord); Power of God.

Strength in (of) the Lord (1 Nephi 4:31; Words of Mormon 1:14; Mosiah 9:17; 10:10–11; Alma 20:4; 31:38; 46:20; 60:16; 61:18; 3 Nephi 4:10; Mormon 2:26). *See:* Strength (and power) of God.

Strengthen them (us) (1 Nephi 17:3; Mosiah 23:2; 24:15; Alma 2:28; 58:10). *See:* Lord did strengthen them.

Strengthen their (your) faith (Alma 25:16; 32:30). To nourish faith by keeping the commandments and seeking God.

Strengthen thy stakes and enlarge thy borders (3 Nephi 22:2; Moroni 10:31). *See:* Bring again (forth) Zion; Lengthen thy cords and strengthen thy stakes; Isaiah 54:2.

Strengthened by the hand of the Lord (Alma 2:18, 28). *See:* Lord did strengthen them.

Strengthened him in the Lord (Alma 15:18). Meaning to teach and administer the gospel of Jesus Christ unto a person. *See also:* Zechariah 10:12; D&C 31:8.

Stretch(-ed) forth his (mine/ our/thy) hand(-s) (1 Nephi 17:53; 2 Nephi 15:25; Jacob 5:47; Mosiah 12:2; 16:1; Alma 10:25; 13:21; 14:10–11; 15:5; 19:12; 32:7; Helaman 13:4; 3 Nephi 11:9; 12:1; Ether 3:6). The Lord stretches forth His hand to nourish, direct, and act.

Stretches forth his hands unto them all the day long (Jacob 6:4). *See:* Hen gathereth her chickens (under her wings); Lengthen out mine arm.

Stricken (wounded) for our transgressions (Mosiah 14:5, 8). Jesus suffered for our sins so we would not have to suffer for them if we will repent and come unto Him. *See also:* With his stripes we are healed; Isaiah 53:5.

Strict are the commandments (ordinances) of God (Alma 30:3; 37:13). Meaning exact and that which must be obeyed. Alma 37:20 says, "Be diligent in keeping the commandments of God as they are written." Thus we cannot change or ease the commandments in the slightest way.

Strict command(-s/-ment) from (of) God (Jacob 2:9–10; Alma 12:9; 58:40; Helaman 13:1). *See:* Strict are the commandments (ordinances) of God.

Strict in the plain road (2 Nephi 4:32). This is Nephi's desire: to be true and faithful and stay on the strait and narrow path.

Strict to remember (Alma 58:40). *See:* Strict command(-s/-ment) from (of) God.

Strictness of the word (of God) (Jacob 2:35; Alma 35:15). *See:* Strict are the commandments (ordinances) of God.

Strip yourselves of all uncleanness (Mormon 9:28). "I speak after the manner of men because of the infirmity of your flesh: for as ye have yielded your members servants to uncleanness and to iniquity unto iniquity; even so now yield your members servants to righteousness unto holiness" (Romans 6:19). *See also:* Deny yourselves of all ungodliness.

Stripped of envy (pride) (Alma 5:28, 29). Eliminated envy and/ or pride from one's life. *See also:* Envyings and strifes; Pride of their (your) eyes.

Striving with unwearied diligence (Helaman 15:6). *See:* Unwearied diligence.

Struck as if he were dead (Alma 22:18). *See:* Fell to (unto) the earth (as if he were dead).

Struck dumb (Alma 30:49–50; Helaman 5:25). Made speechless or unable to talk.

Struck with fear (Alma 14:29; 36:11; Ether 3:6). The acts of God and heaven can cause great fear in the observers.

Struck with wonder and amazement (Mosiah 13:8; 25:7; Helaman 14:7). They stood in awe and were exceedingly startled. *See also:* Stay yourselves.

Struggling in the spirit (Enos 1:10; Alma 8:10; 17:5). *See:* Labor in the spirit.

Stubbornness of heart (Alma 32:16). *See:* Harden(-ed) his (our/ the/their/your) heart(-s) against the Lord; Hardness of their (your) heart(-s).

Stumbling block (1 Nephi 14:1; 2 Nephi 4:33; 26:20; Mosiah 7:29; Alma 4:10). Temptations of the devil placed by Satan to trip up man and cause him to fall (or turn) from the strait and narrow path of God. The meaning is more specific in 1 Nephi 14:1 and 2 Nephi 26:20 where the stumbling block is the loss of the plain and precious truths from the Bible which cause the Gentiles to stumble. *See also:* Snare of the adversary.

Stumbling of the Jews (Jacob 4:14–15). Because of their blindness in rebellion the Jews would stumble, fall, and be taken captive. *See also:* 2 Nephi 18:14–15.

Subject unto man in the flesh (2 Nephi 9:5). Jesus condescended, that is stooped, to the level of men, to live as mortal men and be subject to the same vicissitudes that men are. Jesus Christ even subjected Himself to the false accusations and the sentence of death passed by evil men that He might die to be resurrected as the firstfruits of the Resurrection. This, so that all men and women could also be resurrected, and if faithful be redeemed. *See also:* Mosiah 15:7.

Subjected the flesh to the will of the Father (Mosiah 15:2). To give up every worldly, personal, and physical desire, and instead do only the will of God. *See also:* Suffered the will of the Father in all things; Will of the Son being swallowed up in the will of the Father.

Subjected them according to his will (Mosiah 16:11; Alma 12:6, 17). Refers to the wicked becoming captive and subject to the will of Satan. *See also:* Chains of hell.

Subjected (subjecting) to the spirit of the devil (Mosiah 16:11, 13; Alma 34:35). *See:* Subjected them according to his will.

Subjects to the devil (Alma 5:20; 34:39). Meaning ruled over by Satan. *See also:* Subjected them according to his will.

Submit to all things which the Lord seeth fit (to all the will of the Lord) (Mosiah 3:19; 24:15). *See:* Will of God.

Subtle man (Alma 47:4). Meaning a crafty, cunning, lying, and deceiving man. In the Bible, *subtle* is spelled "subtil."

Subtle plan (Alma 12:4). Meaning a crafty, cunning, lying, and deceiving plan.

Subtlety of the devil (Alma 12:4). The very nature of Satan, the devil, is lying and deceiving to snare man and bring man under his wicked power. In the Bible, *subtlety* is spelled "subtilly" and "subtilty." *See also:* Cunning one.

Succor his (my) people (Mosiah 7:29; Alma 7:12). *Succor* means to help, aid, or provide relief. The Lord also came to earth to experience mortality so that he could fully understand the pains and sorrows of man. Thus Jesus Christ can effectively and perfectly help and minister to His people. Sometimes that succor is outright healing, other times it is comfort and understanding. Someone has said that succor is a "heavenly hug and healing love."

Succor(-ing) those who stand in need of their (your) succor (Mosiah 4:16; Alma 4:13). "Pure religion and undefiled before God and the Father is this, To visit the fatherless and widows in their affliction, and to keep himself unspotted from the world" (James 1:27). *See also:* Impart of their substance; Poor and needy.

Sucking child shall play on the hole of the asp (2 Nephi 21:8; 30:14). Parallel translations in other versions of the Bible use terms including "the infant child will play near the hole of the cobra or adder," and "the toddler will put his hand into the viper's nests and they will not be harmed." There will be no enmity found anywhere when Christ rules and is King over all (see D&C 101:26).

Suffer and die to atone for their sins (Alma 33:22; Helaman 13:6). Jesus Christ suffered and died for the sins of men, if men will repent and come unto Him. *See also:* Atonement of Christ (the Only Begotten Son).

Suffer his cross and bear the shame of the world (Jacob 1:8). Those who are judged "faithful in the testimony of Jesus while they lived in mortality," are those "who had offered sacrifice in the similitude of the great sacrifice of the Son of God, and had suffered tribulation in their Redeemer's name" (D&C 138:12–13). *See also:* Take up your cross.

Suffer [not] yourselves to be slain by the hands of your enemies (Alma 43:46). *See:* Defend themselves.

Suffer the second death (Alma 13:30). To suffer spiritual death. *See also:* Second death; Spiritual death.

Suffer with patience these afflictions (Alma 31:31; Helaman 3:34). "When you face adversity, you can be led to ask many questions. Some serve a useful purpose; others do not. To ask, Why does this have to happen to me? Why do I have to suffer this, now? What have I done to cause this? will lead you to blind alleys. It really does no good to ask questions that reflect opposition to the will of God. Rather ask, What am I to do? What am I to learn from this experience? What am I to change? Whom am I to help? How can I remember my many blessings in times of trial?" (Scott, "Trust in the Lord," 17). *See also:* Bear afflictions (with patience).

Suffered all manner of afflictions (Alma 26:30; 60:3). *See:* Suffer with patience these afflictions; Suffering all manner of afflictions for Christ's sake.

Suffered the will of the Father in all things (3 Nephi 11:11). *See:* Subjected the flesh to the will of the Father; Will of the Son being swallowed up in the will of the Father.

Suffereth himself to be led into temptation (3 Nephi 18:25). When any man or woman breaks any commandment they open themselves to more temptation of the devil. Thus it behooves us to repent quickly and return to the correct path. *See also:* Yield to no temptation.

Suffereth himself to become subject unto man in the flesh and die for all men (2 Nephi 9:5, 22; Alma 7:13; Helaman 14:15). The Lord Jesus condescended to take upon Himself mortality and allowed wicked men to murder Him, so that He could bring about the Atonement and redemption of man. *See also:* According to the flesh; Atonement of Christ (the Only Begotten Son); Subject unto man in the flesh.

Suffereth the pains of all men (2 Nephi 9:21). Jesus suffered the pains of all men so that He could take upon Him their sins if they repent and come unto Him. *See also:* Atonement of Christ (the Only Begotten Son); Alma 7:11–12; D&C 18:11.

Suffering all manner of afflictions for Christ's sake (Mosiah 26:38; Alma 4:13). "'No pain that we suffer, no trial that we experience is wasted. It ministers to our education, to the development of such qualities as patience, faith, fortitude, and humility. All that we suffer and all that we endure, especially when we endure it patiently, builds up our character, purifies our hearts, expands our souls, and makes us more tender and charitable, more worthy to be called the children of God . . . and it is through sorrow and suffering, toil and tribulation, that we

gain the education that we come here [to earth] to acquire and which will make us more like our Father and Mother in heaven'" (Orson F. Whitney, quoted in Kimball, *Faith Precedes the Miracle*, 98). *See also:* Bear afflictions (with patience).

Sunk deep into my heart (Enos 1:3). Meaning to think and ponder deeply, to consider seriously.

Sunk down with joy (Enos 1:3; Alma 19:13–14). To be physically overpowered by the joy of redemption and the love of God.

Supplicate (supplication) to God (Enos 1:4; Alma 31:10; 3 Nephi 4:10). *Supplicate* means to petition, beseech, implore, and pray most earnestly and sincerely. *See also:* Mighty prayer.

Supplicating of his grace (Alma 7:3). To humbly seek God's grace in our behalf. *See also:* By grace that we are saved after all we can do; Grace of God.

Support the cause of (their) liberty (Alma 43:9; 44:5; 48:10; 51:17). *See:* Title of liberty; Defend themselves.

Supreme Being (Creator) (Alma 11:22; 30:44). God is supreme, meaning above all, infinite, foremost, the greatest, and highest of all.

Supreme goodness of God (Alma 12:33). His goodness is supreme or above all. *See also:* Infinite goodness (of God).

Sure foundation (Jacob 4:16–17; Helaman 5:12). Jesus Christ is the sure foundation, even the cornerstone. Those that build their lives upon this foundation, that is upon His word and upon faith in His Atonement, are promised peace in this life and salvation in the next life. *See also:* Built upon my rock; My rock and my salvation; Rock of our Redeemer.

Surely as the Lord liveth (Helaman 15:17; 3 Nephi 5:24). *See:* As the Lord (God) liveth (and as we live).

Surely come to pass (2 Nephi 24:24; 28:1; 31:1; Jacob 6:1; Words of Mormon 1:4; Helaman 8:7). *See:* According to God's word; And it came to pass.

Swallowed up by the victory of (in) Christ (Mosiah 16:8; Alma 27:28; Mormon 7:5). *See:* Death is (was) swallowed up in the victory of (in) Christ.

Swallowed up in the hopes of glory (Alma 22:14). Meaning to be overcome in joy and spirit by the hopes of a glorious reward if we are faithful. *See also:* Swallowed up in the joy of Christ (his God).

Swallowed up in the joy of Christ (his God) (Alma 27:17; 31:38). The blissful lot of those who experience the happiness of redemption through Christ. The Spirit brings this joy when the Holy Ghost sanctifies us, which is the process of being born of the Spirit. *See also:* Mosiah 4:2–3.

Swallowed up in the will of the Father (Mosiah 15:7). Jesus accepted and fully encompassed Himself, without question or resentment, to the will of the Father.

Swallowed up in their pride (Alma 31:27). To be enveloped and captive by pride.

Swear before (by) the heavens (Mormon 3:9–10). The Lord Jesus said, "I say unto you, swear not at all; neither by heaven, for it is God's throne; nor by the earth, for it is his footstool; neither shalt thou swear by thy head, because thou canst not make one hair black or white; but let your communication be Yea, yea; Nay, nay; for whatsoever cometh of more than these is evil" (3 Nephi 12:34–37). *See also:* Forswear thyself (thou shalt not); Made an oath unto us; Swear not at all.

Swear in his (my) wrath (Jacob 1:7; Alma 12:35). The Lord God has sworn (promised in His anger) punishments upon the rebellious and unrepentant workers of iniquity. *See also:* Anger of the Lord; Workers of iniquity.

Swear not at all (3 Nephi 12:34, 36). Jesus's instruction not to swear by any object. *See also:* Swear before (by) the heavens.

Swear unto him by the God of heaven and also by the heavens

(Ether 8:14). *See:* Made an oath unto us; Swear before (by) the heavens.

Swear unto you with an oath (Mosiah 20:24; 3 Nephi 3:8). *See:* Made an oath unto us.

Swearing with an oath [men so swearing] (Alma 49:27; Mosiah 19:4; Helaman 1:11; Ether 15:28). Men often swear oaths. *See also:* Made an oath unto us; Swear before (by) the heavens.

Swept off (Ether 2:8–10). *See:* Cut off; Land choice above all other lands.

Swift to do iniquity (1 Nephi 17:45). *See:* Quick to do iniquity.

Sword of destruction (Alma 10:22; Helaman 11:5; 3 Nephi 2:19; 3:6). The Lord often sends the sword of destruction upon the wicked. *See also:* Pestilence of earthquakes (famine/tempest/the sword).

Sword of his almighty wrath (Alma 54:6). *See:* Sword of justice.

Sword of justice (Alma 26:19; 54:6; 60:29; Helaman 13:5; 3 Nephi 20:20; 29:4; Ether 8:23). *See:* Judgments are just; Sword of destruction; Sword of vengeance.

Sword of Laban (1 Nephi 4:9, 18–19; 2 Nephi 5:14; Jacob 1:10; Words of Mormon 1:13; Mosiah 1:16). The sword of fine steel that Nephi took from Laban when he was commanded to obtain the plates of brass. *See also:* Fine steel; D&C 17:1.

Sword of vengeance (Mormon 8:41). "Judgment is mine, saith the Lord, and vengeance is mine also" (Mormon 8:20). Of us it is required to forgive seventy times seven (Matthew 18:22). We must leave vengeance and final justice to God. *See also:* Avenge his blood (their wrongs/themselves); Seek revenge; Sword of justice; Vengeance is mine.

Swore in his wrath (Ether 1:33; 2:8). *See:* Swear in his (my) wrath.

Sworn with an oath (Alma 48:13; 49:17; Ether 9:5). *See:* Made an oath unto us.

T

Tabernacle of clay (Mosiah 3:5; Moroni 9:6). A scriptural phrase used to describe our physical earthly bodies, for from dust we are formed and to dust we shall return. Jesus also took upon Himself a tabernacle of clay when He was born of Mary.

Take happiness in iniquity (sin) (Alma 41:10–11; Helaman 13:38; Mormon 2:13). True joy is not possible from sin. *See also:* Despair cometh because of iniquity; Wickedness never was happiness.

Take heed (2 Nephi 17:4; Mosiah 5:11; 3 Nephi 13:1; Moroni 7:14). *See:* Give heed.

Take not up weapons save God shall command you (Mormon 7:2–4). *See:* Defend themselves; Take up arms; Ye shall defend your families even unto bloodshed.

Take off my garments and I shake them before you (2 Nephi 9:44). *See:* Rid my (our) garments of your (blood and) sins.

Take root in you (Alma 32:41, 42). Meaning one's faith and testimony begins to sprout and grow. See the parable of the sower (Mark 4:3–8, 14–20).

Take the name of the Lord their God in vain (2 Nephi 26:32; Mosiah 13:15). Meaning to swear obscenities using God's name. "Thou shalt not take the name of the Lord thy God in vain" (Exodus 20:7). *See also:* Taketh his name in vain.

Take up arms (Alma 2:10; 24:6; 26:25, 34; 27:23, 28; 43:11; 48:23; 51:13, 17, 20; 53:13, 16; 62:9; 3 Nephi 2:11–12). *See:* Defend themselves.

Take up your cross (Jacob 1:8; 3 Nephi 12:30). In Matthew 16:24: "Then said Jesus unto his disciples, If any man will come after me, let him deny himself, and take up his cross, and follow me." Footnote *a* in that verse refers to JST, Matthew 16:26, which says, "And now for a man to take up his cross, is to deny himself all ungodliness, and every worldly lust, and keep my commandments." Luke 14:27 says, "And whosoever doth not bear his cross, and come after me, cannot be my disciple." D&C 56:2 says, "And he that will not take up his cross and follow me, and keep my commandments, the same shall not be saved." *See also:* D&C 23:6; 112:14.

Take upon him death (Alma 7:12). Jesus suffered death that He might take up again His body and become the first to be resurrected, thus providing resurrection to all who come to live here on earth. *See also:* Atonement of Christ (the Only Begotten Son); Resurrection of the body.

Take upon him flesh and blood (Mosiah 7:27; Ether 3:9). *See:* Manifest himself in the flesh; Tabernacle of clay.

Take upon him the form (image) of man (Mosiah 7:27; 13:34). *See:* Manifest himself in the flesh; Take upon him flesh and blood.

Take upon him the pains and the sicknesses of his people (Alma 7:11). Jesus observed firsthand and experienced pains and sicknesses so that He could empathize with pains and sicknesses, and comfort his people. This was in addition to suffering for our sins. According to God's will He will minister unto our pains and sicknesses. *See also:* Take upon him their infirmities.

Take upon him the sins of his people (Alma 7:13). *See:* Take(-th) away the sins of the world; Take upon him the transgressions of his people; Take upon me the sins of the world.

Take upon me the sins of the world (3 Nephi 11:11). Jesus Christ suffered for the sins of all mankind in the Garden of Gethsemane and upon the cross. For that suffering to apply to us individually and for our sins to be forgiven, we must repent and come unto Christ.

Take upon him the transgressions of his people (Mosiah 15:9; Alma 11:40; 34:8). *See:* Atonement of Christ (the Only Begotten Son); Take upon him the sins of his people; Take upon me the sins of the world.

Take upon him their infirmities (Alma 7:12). Infirmities are debilities, feebleness, sickliness, afflictions, and disorders. Thus Christ also suffered for these types of weaknesses and afflictions so that He could understand them and comfort us in them. *See also:* Take upon him the pains and the sicknesses of his people.

Take(-n) an oath (Alma 44:8; 53:11; 56:8). *See:* Made an oath unto us.

Take(-n) away our stain (Alma 24:11–12). Though our sins be (stained) red, they shall be as white as snow (stain removed) (see Isaiah 1:18) if we come unto Christ and follow Him. "Though your sins be as scarlet, they shall be as white as snow" (Isaiah 1:18). *See also:* Garments cleansed through the blood of the Lamb (made white/washed); Take(-th) away the sins of the world.

Taken away the guilt from our hearts (2 Nephi 9:14; Enos 1:6;

Alma 24:10). The Atonement of Christ not only removes the stain of our sins but also relieves us of the pain of our guilt. *See also:* Guilt was swept away; Peace of conscience.

Taken captive by the devil (Alma 12:11; 40:13; 3 Nephi 18:15). Satan, the devil, the father of all lies, attempts to deceive and blind men and to lead them captive at his will, even as many as will not hearken to the voice of God (see Moses 4:4). *See also:* Chains of hell.

Take(-n) upon him (them/us/ you) the name of Christ (2 Nephi 31:13; Mosiah 5:8, 10; 6:2; 25:23; Alma 1:19; 23:16; 34:38; 46:15, 18, 21; 3 Nephi 27:5; Mormon 8:38; Moroni 4:3). One of the three promises made at baptism, which promises are renewed in the ordinance of the sacrament. To take upon us the name of Christ means to become true Christians, declare Christ's gospel, and strive with all our might to live as Jesus did. Or, as in Acts 11:26, become disciples of Christ. D&C 18:23–25 says, "Behold, Jesus Christ is the name which is given of the Father, and there is none other name given whereby man can be saved; wherefore, all men must take upon them the name which is given of the Father, for in that name shall they be called at the last day; wherefore, if they know not the name by which they are called, they cannot have place in the kingdom of my Father." *See also:* 3 Nephi 27:5–9.

Taken upon himself their iniquity and their transgressions (Mosiah 15:9). Iniquities and transgressions being the same as and are other words for sin. *See also:* Take(-th) away the sins of the world.

Take(-th) away the sins of the world (1 Nephi 10:10; 2 Nephi 31:4; Alma 5:48; 7:14; 24:10–11; 39:15). Jesus Christ took away the sins of the world, by means of the Atonement, on condition of our individual faith in Him, repentance, and striving to live the gospel. *See also:* Take upon him the transgressions of his people.

Taketh his name in vain (Mosiah 13:15). The second of the Ten Commandments, "Thou shalt not take the name of the Lord in vain." *Vain* meaning inappropriate, irreverent, and blasphemous. *See also:* Take the name of the Lord their God in vain.

Taketh the truth to be hard (1 Nephi 16:2). "Words of truth are hard against all uncleanness" (2 Nephi 9:40). *See also:* Speakest hard things against us.

Taketh upon him my name (3 Nephi 27:6). *See:* Take(-n) upon him (them/us/you) the name of Christ.

Taketh upon me the sins of the world (Mosiah 26:23; 3 Nephi 11:11). *See:* Take upon him the transgressions of his people.

Taking away of their stumbling blocks (1 Nephi 14:1). The Gentiles and any others who accept the gospel in the last days shall have the stumbling blocks of unbelief and false doctrine removed from before them. *See also:* Stumbling block.

Taking no thought for themselves what they should eat or what they should drink (Alma 31:37). Meaning to go forth to preach the gospel without purse or scrip. And thus relying in faith on God and fellowmen to provide food and shelter. *See also:* Mark 6:8; D&C 24:18–19.

Tame fruit (Jacob 5:18, 25). The tame or good fruit in the parable of the vineyard are the fruits of the harvest, meaning souls brought unto Christ to be saved. *See also:* Tame olive tree.

Tame olive tree (Jacob 5:3, 14; 6:1). Refers to the house of Israel. In the parable of the vineyard (2 Nephi 15:1–7), the tame olive tree and branches represent the children of Israel, and the wild trees and branches represent the Gentiles. When the Lord of the vineyard (the vineyard representing the earth) takes away many of the young and tender branches of the tame olive tree and grafts them into wild olive trees whithersoever He wills, it is referring to the scattering of the tribes of Israel and the Lord's leading away groups of believers, such as Lehi and his family. When the Lord of the vineyard brings back the tame branches and grafts them back into the tame tree, this refers to the restoration of the tribes of Israel to their promised lands. When branches and fruit become corrupted it refers to the people becoming wicked and perverted. When it talks about the servants in the vineyard it refers to the prophets and other servants of God who strive to bring souls unto Christ. The burning of wild branches and burning of the vineyard have reference to the burning of the wicked and the whole earth at His Second Coming. The Lord desires that His vineyard bring forth good and natural fruit so that He may lay up and preserve fruit unto Himself, meaning to cultivate righteousness and bring souls unto the harvest or fold of God. The Lord remembers His covenant people, both roots and branches, and He stretches forth His hands to them all the day long.

Tasted of God's love and goodness (Mosiah 4:11; Alma 36:26; Mormon 1:15). Lehi tasted of God's love when in a dream he partook of the fruit of the tree in his dream. We each can taste a little bit of God's love when we serve others, when we receive testimony from the Holy Ghost, and at other special times in our lives. For example, see 2 Nephi 4:21. The ultimate gift of God's love and goodness will be to receive exaltation and eternal life.

Taught from on high (Ether 6:17). To receive holy instruction from

God through the Holy Ghost or in other times to receive the ministering of angels who bear the message. *Compare:* D&C 43:16; 52:9. *See also:* Angels minister(-ed/appeared/declared/descending) unto him (them).

Taught to hate the children of God (of Nephi) (Mosiah 10:17; 4 Nephi 1:39). Satan is the one who teaches hate. The Lamanites taught their children to hate the Nephites. Apostates teach their children to hate the Church of God. Yet God says He will be merciful to the children wrongly taught to hate (see Alma 9:16).

Taught (teach) with power and authority of God (1 Nephi 2:14; Words of Mormon 1:17; Mosiah 13:6; 18:26; Alma 17:3; 3 Nephi 7:17). *See:* Minister with power and great authority; Spake (speak/taught) with power and authority from God; Speak with power.

Teach the word (of God) (Jacob 1:19; Mosiah 18:3, 7; 27:32; Alma 23:4; 29:8; 38:10, 15; Helaman 5:14; 16:21; Moroni 10:9–10). *See:* Preach the gospel; Preach the word (of God).

Teach your children (Enos 1:1–3; Mosiah 1:3–4; 4:14–15; Alma 56:45–48). It is the duty of parents in Zion to properly teach their children and help them gain a testimony of Jesus Christ. *See also:* Proverbs 22:6; D&C 68:25–31.

Teachers who sell yourselves for that which will canker (Mormon 8:38). False preachers who teach for money, wear fine apparel in pride, and ignore the poor and afflicted (see Mormon 8:33–41). To preach for money is priestcraft. *See also:* 2 Nephi 26:29; Alma 1:12, 16; 3 Nephi 16:10; D&C 33:4.

Teachers who were of the profession of Nehor (Alma 14:18). *See:* Order and faith of (profession of) Nehor.

Tell you concerning your thoughts (Jacob 2:5; Alma 10:17; 12:3; 18:16, 18, 20, 32; Helaman 9:41; 3 Nephi 28:6). *See:* Know all my (thy) thoughts.

Temporal body (1 Nephi 15:31, 32). The mortal or physical body. *Compare:* Immortal body. *See also:* Death of the temporal body; Flesh and blood; Living soul; Mortal body; Natural frame; No more corruption; Resurrection of the body.

Temporal death (Alma 11:42; 12:16, 24; 42:8; Mormon 9:13). The death of the mortal body, when the spirit and the body are separated. In the great plan of salvation, temporal death is co-equal in importance and rejoicing as is physical or mortal birth. We experience a temporary physical death, but then we will at a future date be resurrected because of the Resurrection of Christ. *See also:* Death of the temporal body.

Temporal law (2 Nephi 2:5). This is the one place in the scriptures that contains the scriptural phrase "temporal law." Yet, "Verily I say unto you that all things unto me are spiritual, and not at any time have I given unto you a law which was temporal; neither any man, nor the children of men; neither Adam, your father, whom I created. . . . I gave him commandment, but no temporal commandment gave I unto him, for my commandments are spiritual; they are not natural nor temporal, neither carnal nor sensual" (D&C 29:34–35). It appears temporal laws, if so called, are identified as such by man, and are in truth a subset of the spiritual laws of God. For example, the children of Israel hardened their hearts against God (see D&C 84), therefore they were given the lesser priesthood and the "carnal or temporal law." The dietary code of the law of Moses could certainly be called a temporal law. A number of God's commandments may seem temporal to us, but to God they are all spiritual laws. "Keep the commandments, though temporal or spiritual they may seem. They all have a spiritual purpose" (Joseph Fielding Smith, *Answers to Gospel Questions*, 4:211). Since we live in a "temporal existence," many things seem temporal to us. In the scriptures we find the terms: *temporal body, temporal death, temporal needs, temporal labors, temporal creation, temporal concerns, temporal things,* and *temporal*

salvation. Regardless they are all spiritual to God. *Compare:* Spiritual law.

Temporally and spiritually (1 Nephi 14:7; Mosiah 4:26; 18:29; Alma 42:7; Mormon 2:15). These verses talk of relief of the poor, captive to Satan, cut off from God, and day of grace is past—both temporally and spiritually. *See also:* Things both temporal and spiritual.

Tempt God (the Lord) (2 Nephi 17:12; Jacob 7:14; Alma 30:44; 3 Nephi 24:15). God is not tempted by the devil as mortal man is. Yet the term is used in these first three verses, in which it is said to be a mockery to tempt (or ask) God for a sign in behalf of an unbeliever, that the unbeliever may believe, for faith comes before the miracle. In the fourth verse it is said that to live wickedly and expect the same reward as the faithful receives is to tempt God, or again to ask for that which is not probable.

Temptations of the devil (1 Nephi 12:17, 19; 15:24; Alma 34:39; 3 Nephi 6:17; 18:15). "And he became Satan, yea, even the devil, the father of all lies, to deceive and to blind men, and to lead them captive at his will, even as many as would not hearken unto my voice" (Moses 4:4). *See also:* Yield to no temptation.

Tempted above that which ye can bear (Alma 13:28). God has promised, "There hath no temptation taken you but such as is common to man: but God is faithful, who will not suffer you to be tempted above that ye are able; but will with the temptation also make a way to escape, that ye may be able to bear it" (1 Corinthians 10:13). We must pray that we will escape the temptations of the devil.

Tender mercies of the Lord (1 Nephi 1:20; 8:8; Ether 6:12). At times the Savior sends the "most personal and timely message[s] of comfort and reassurance. . . . I testify that the tender mercies of the Lord are real and that they do not occur randomly or merely by coincidence. Often, the Lord's timing of His tender mercies helps us to both discern and acknowledge them. . . . The Lord's tender mercies are the very personal and individualized blessings, strength, protection, assurances, guidance, lovingkindnesses, consolation, support, and spiritual gifts which we receive from and because of and through the Lord Jesus Christ. Truly, the Lord suits 'his mercies according to the conditions of the children of men' (D&C 46:15)" (Bednar, "The Tender Mercies of the Lord," 99). *See also:* Merciful God (Being).

Terrible one (2 Nephi 27:31). A name for Satan, who is the devil.

Testified (testify) unto him (the people/us/you) (Jacob 2:6; Alma 1:4; 5:44–45; 9:7; 19:15; 34:8; 47:34; Helaman 8:8; 9:23; 3 Nephi 23:9). It is the calling of prophets to testify. "Surely the Lord God will do nothing, but he revealeth his secret unto his servants the prophets" (Amos 3:7). *See also:* Prophets testified; Prophecies of the holy prophets; Prophesy unto him (the people/ thee/them/you).

Testify of Jesus Christ (Jacob 7:11, 19; Alma 6:8; 33:17; 3 Nephi 6:23; 7:10; 15:10; 20:24). To testify of God the Father and Jesus Christ is the most important testimony. To testify of Christ's Atonement for man is exceedingly important to every man's and woman's salvation and eternal happiness. *See also:* Testimony of Jesus Christ.

Testify of these things (1 Nephi 1:19; 10:5; Enos 1:19; Mosiah 26:9; Alma 10:12; 34:30; Helaman 8:16, 20, 22; 3 Nephi 1:18; 6:21, 23; 10:15; Mormon 3:16). It is the obligation of all those who have had truth revealed unto them to testify of truth and defend truth in this world of wickedness and lies.

Testimony against the world (them/this people/you) (2 Nephi 25:28; Mosiah 3:24; 17:10; Alma 4:19; 39:8; Ether 5:4). The words of truth and testimony spoken to men and women will stand as testimony that they have heard the word and chose either to adhere to the word or reject it.

Testimony before (to/unto) God (Alma 24:15, 18; 3 Nephi 7:25; 18:7). By doing certain things we testify before and to God that we will remain faithful. For example, partaking of the sacrament is a testimony to God that we will take upon us the name of Jesus, always remember Him, and keep His commandments.

Testimony of his (the) word (2 Nephi 27:13; Alma 4:20; 7:20). Meaning the preaching of the word of God. *See also:* Word of God.

Testimony of Jesus Christ (Alma 6:8; Moroni 7:31). To gain salvation we must gain a testimony of Jesus Christ. To come unto Christ is to come to know that He truly is our Savior and Redeemer, the Son of God, and then to follow Him. *See also:* Testify of Jesus Christ.

Testimony of many (two or three) (2 Nephi 29:8; Alma 30:44; Helaman 9:39; Ether 5:4). The scriptures say in Matthew 18:16, 2 Corinthians 13:1, and D&C 6:28 that in the mouth of two or three witnesses shall every word be established. "Never does one man stand alone in establishing a new dispensation of revealed truth, or in carrying the burden of such a message and warning to the world. In every dispensation, from Adam to the present, two or more witnesses have always joined their testimonies, thus leaving their hearers without excuse in the day of judgment should the testimony be rejected" (McConkie, *Mormon Doctrine*, 436). *See also:* All these (many) witnesses; Did witness

of it; Him shall ye witness; In the mouth of three (many) witnesses; Many (more) witnesses; More than one witness; Proveth all his words; Three witnesses; Witness it.

Testimony of one man (Alma 9:2). Traditions of men and courts of law usually require more than the testimony of just one individual. *See also:* Testimony of many (two or three).

Testimony that these things are true (Mosiah 8:9; Alma 30:41). Testimony is affirmation, attestation, declaration, and confirmation by one who knows, having the truth revealed unto him. *See also:* Testify of these things; Testimony which is in me.

Testimony that they (ye) are willing (have entered into a covenant) (Mosiah 18:10, 13; 21:35; Alma 24:16; 3 Nephi 18:7). The true gospel of Jesus Christ is a gospel of covenants between man and God. The saving ordinances of the gospel, for example, are outward symbols of sacred covenants made with God.

Testimony which is in me (Alma 7:13, 16). It is our duty as saints to have a testimony and share that testimony with all who will listen. A testimony is to have remembrance of past and current inspiration from the Holy Ghost that the gospel of Jesus Christ is true. Having a testimony is having the Spirit in our lives. A testimony equals spiritual fitness.

Thank the Lord God (Mosiah 2:19, 20; Alma 24:8–10; 49:28; Helaman 13:22; Ether 6:9). *See:* Thanksgiving to God.

Thanks unto God (him) (1 Nephi 2:7; 5:9–10; 7:22; 16:32; 2 Nephi 9:52; Alma 7:23; 8:22; 26:37; 37:37; 45:1; Mormon 9:31). *See:* Thanksgiving to God.

Thanksgiving to God (Alma 19:14; 26:37; 34:38; 48:12). All that we have has been given to us by God and we must thank Him continually or risk being ungrateful recipients. "I say unto you, my brethren, that if you should render all the thanks and praise which your whole soul has power to possess, to that God who has created you, and has kept and preserved you, and has caused that ye should rejoice, and has granted that ye should live in peace one with another—I say unto you that if ye should serve him who has created you from the beginning, and is preserving you from day to day, by lending you breath, that ye may live and move and do according to your own will, and even supporting you from one moment to another—I say, if ye should serve him with all your whole souls yet ye would be unprofitable servants" (Mosiah 2:20–21).

That great day (2 Nephi 33:13; Mormon 9:2). The first verse refers to the great and last day (see 2 Nephi 33:12), which is the final judgment day. The second verse refers to the Second Coming of Christ when the earth shall burn as an oven and the Millennium will be ushered in.

That I may heal you (3 Nephi 9:13). Refers to the healing that takes place by means of the Atonement. *See also:* Atonement of Christ (the Only Begotten Son); Healing in his wings.

That old serpent (2 Nephi 2:18; Mosiah 16:3). Meaning the devil. Refer also to Revelation 20:2. *See also:* Angel fell (fallen) from heaven (from before the presence of the Eternal God); Cunning one; Enemy to God; Evil one; Father of all lies.

That the Lord might show forth his power (1 Nephi 15:17; 18:11; Mosiah 23:24; Alma 8:31; 37:14, 18; 3 Nephi 21:6). The Lord God has, many times and according to His will, shown forth His great power in signs and wonders. *See also:* Power of God; Show unto you with power and great glory.

That the word of the Lord might (shall) be fulfilled (1 Nephi 7:13; Mosiah 21:4; Alma 5:57; 7:11; 37:24; 3 Nephi 1:25; 29:2). *See:* According to God's word.

That they might cross him (Mosiah 12:19; Alma 10:16; Helaman 9:19). Meaning that they by craftiness and intrigue might "trip him up" and find reason to falsely condemn him. *See also:* Cross his words.

That we (ye) may have hope (1 Nephi 19:24; Jacob 4:4; Alma 58:11; Ether 12:8–9; Moroni 7:3, 41, 48). *See:* Have hope.

That (which has been, and which is, and) which is to come (1 Nephi 10:19; Mosiah 3:1; 4:11; 5:3; 8:17; Alma 5:48; 9:20; 21:8; 58:40; Helaman 8:23). The past, present, and future is all known to God, who has revealed a small portion of these things to man throughout the ages. *See also:* Things (which are) to come.

That which was right in the sight of God (Helaman 3:20; Ether 10:5, 16). It is good and honorable to do that which is right in the sight of God. If one does, his life, his family, and all who associate with him will be blessed.

That which will canker (Mormon 8:38). To sell your soul for that which will rust and turn to dust.

The mount (1 Nephi 18:3; Mosiah 12:33; 13:5; Ether 3:1; 4:1; 6:2). *See:* Into (unto) the mountain.

Their own will and pleasure (Alma 4:8; 17:20). When man begins to do whatever he desires according to his own will and pleasure rather than to consider the will of God, then that man is on the road to wickedness and destruction. *See also:* Walk after the desires of his (your) own heart.

Their treasure is their God (2 Nephi 9:30). Referring to the goods of this earth being where their hearts are. In other words, gold and silver and possessions of this life have become their idols and the things that they seek after to the exclusion of God. *See also:* 3 Nephi 13:21.

Their works (1 Nephi 15:32–3; 2 Nephi 9:44; 25:2; 27:27; 28:9, 23; 29:11; Mosiah 16:10; Alma 3:26; 9:28; 11:41; 12:8; 33:22; 37:23; 40:21, 26; 41:3–4; 42:23; Helaman 5:6; 6:38; 12:24; 3 Nephi 26:4; 27:11–12, 14–15, 32; Moroni 7:5). It is verified over and over in the Book of Mormon that men and women will be judged of their works. *See also:* Judged according to (of) their works.

Their works do follow them (3 Nephi 27:12). Evil will be restored for doing evil, and good will be restored unto those who have done good.

Them that sit in darkness (1 Nephi 21:9). Those that need the gospel of Jesus Christ and the light it will bring into their lives. *See also:* D&C 45:28.

Then will he (I) remember the covenant which I have made unto my people O house of Israel (1 Nephi 19:15; 3 Nephi 16:11; Mormon 5:20). *See:* Remember (-ed/-est) his (my/the) covenant(-s/ promises).

There came a voice (Enos 1:5; Helaman 5:29, 46; 3 Nephi 10:3).

The voice of God speaking to an individual or a group of people. *See also:* Hearken to the word of God (the Lord); Pierce their very soul (them to the center); Still small voice; Voice came unto him (me); Voice of the Lord; Voice of (was as) thunder.

There came many prophets (1 Nephi 1:4; Alma 37:30; Ether 7:23; 9:28; 11:1, 12, 20). The Lord God has many times sent prophets to call the people to repentance and testify of Jesus Christ. *See also:* Sent prophets; Warned of the Lord.

There has been a type (Ether 13:6). Referring to the remnant of the seed of Joseph as described in Alma 46:24. *See also:* Type(-s) and shadow.

These things are true (2 Nephi 25:20; Mosiah 2:41; Alma 30:41; 34:7–8; Helaman 7:29; Ether 4:11; 5:3; Moroni 7:35). Examples of testimony given of truth.

They have their reward (Alma 11:25; 41:5; 3 Nephi 13:2, 5, 16). They who act falsely or as hypocrites will have the reward they seek, which is to be seen of men, and have the honor of men. The reward, which is short lived rather than eternal, is no reward but is a punishment.

They know him (me) God (their Redeemer) (1 Nephi 22:25; Mosiah 26:24; 3 Nephi 5:26). *See:* Know God.

They (shall) have eternal life (Mosiah 15:23–24; 28:7; Alma 11:40). *See:* Eternal life.

They shall have peace with him (2 Nephi 26:9). "Learn of me, and listen to my words; walk in the meekness of my Spirit, and you shall have peace in me" (D&C 19:23). Also, "Peace I leave with you, my peace I give unto you: not as the world giveth, give I unto you. Let not your heart be troubled, neither let it be afraid" (John 14:27). *See also:* Find peace to my soul.

They that never knew me (Mosiah 26:25). *See:* Know God.

They were in one (3 Nephi 4:3; 4 Nephi 1:1). United as one in all things, both temporally and spiritually. *See also:* All things common.

Thing framed say of him that framed it, he had no understanding (2 Nephi 27:27). Meaning that a thing or person created by God says to God that He, God, does not understand what He has created. How absurd. God the creator understands perfectly what He has created, and the beliefs of man cannot make it otherwise. God has all power and all knowledge, and thus He can be a creator. *See also:* Isaiah 29:16.

Thing of naught (1 Nephi 19:9; 2 Nephi 2:12; 27:32; 28:16; 33:2). The word *naught* means good for nothing, worthless, and of no account. Often people think

Things both temporal and spiritual

something is a thing of naught to their own peril. *See also:* Esteem them as (things of) naught; Set at naught; Set him as naught; Trample the God of Israel (Holy One) under your feet.

Things both temporal and spiritual (1 Nephi 15:32; 22:3; Mosiah 2:41; Alma 7:23). In respective order these verses say: consequences of sin are both temporal and spiritual, the scattering and gathering of Israel is both temporal and spiritual, and the blessings of God are both temporal and spiritual. *See also:* Temporally and spiritually.

Things of God (the Lord) (1 Nephi 5:4; 6:3; 2 Nephi 4:16; 5:32; 26:17; Alma 10:8; 19:34; 3 Nephi 28:15). We must learn of and seek the things of God, meaning God's mission for us, God's commandments, God's plan of salvation, and the way of life that God desires for us.

Things of the world (1 Nephi 22:23; 2 Nephi 9:30; Alma 1:16; 4:8; 5:37, 53; 7:6; 31:27; 32:3–4; 60:32; Helaman 12:4; 3 Nephi 6:15; 4 Nephi 1:24). Meaning the physical and carnal things of the world, which are temporary, and shall all pass away. We should not seek the things of the world, but instead seek the things of God.

Things pertaining to (unto) righteousness (and) to the kingdom of God (1 Nephi 15:33; 22:3; Mosiah 18:18; 23:18; Alma 5:42; 12:16, 32; 21:23; 24:30; 35:16; 40:26;

Helaman 11:19; 14:18; 3 Nephi 6:23). D&C 11:13–14 says, "Verily, verily, I say unto you, I will impart unto you of my Spirit, which shall enlighten your mind, which shall fill your soul with joy; And then shall ye know, or by this shall you know, all things whatsoever you desire of me, which are pertaining unto things of righteousness, in faith believing in me that you shall receive." *See also:* Death as to things pertaining to righteousness.

Things that (which) are spiritual (1 Nephi 15:32–33; 22:1, 3; Mosiah 2:41; Alma 7:23; 37:43; Helaman 14:16). These include the commandments, laws, prophecies, and words of God. *See also:* Things of God (the Lord); Things pertaining to (unto) righteousness (and) to the kingdom of God.

Things that (which) are temporal (1 Nephi 15:31; 22:3, 6; Mosiah 2:41; Alma 7:23; 12:31; 37:43; Helaman 14:16). These are physical, mortal, carnal, and temporary. *See also:* Things of the world.

Things (which are) to come (1 Nephi 13:35; 14:26; 2 Nephi 6:4; 9:4; Jacob 4:12; 7:7; Enos 1:19; Words of Mormon 1:7; Mosiah 3:1; 5:3; 7:26; 8:17; 13:10, 31; 16:6, 14; Alma 5:44; 7:7; 9:20; 10:12; 21:8; 25:10, 16; 30:13–14; 31:22; Helaman 8:22; 3 Nephi 15:7; Mormon 3:16; Ether 4:1). The true spirit of prophecy tells of the things to come. *See also:* According to the prophecy (prophecies) of the Lord; At that day; Be unto you a sign; Day cometh; In that day; Know of things to come; Promises of the Lord; Prophecies concerning that which is to come; Signs of his coming; That (which has been, and which is, and) which is to come.

This is my gospel (3 Nephi 27:13, 21). The good news which is the gospel of Jesus Christ. *See also:* Doctrine of Christ; Fulness of my (the) gospel; Gospel of (Jesus) Christ; True doctrine; Word of Christ; Word of the Lord; D&C 39:6.

This is the law and the prophets (3 Nephi 14:12; 15:10). *See:* Law and the prophets.

Those that (who) stand in need (Mosiah 4:16; 18:9; Alma 34:28; Mormon 9:27). We should look out for and assist those that stand in need. If we do not, we do not follow Christ. *See also:* Poor and needy.

Those whom he hath chosen (3 Nephi 12:1; 15:11; 19:12, 28; 28:36). *See:* Lord hath chosen him (them).

Thou art merciful (1 Nephi 1:14; Alma 33:4–5, 8–9, 11; Ether 3:3). *See:* Merciful God (Being).

Thou art of the devil (Jacob 7:14; Alma 12:4; 30:42). Examples of individuals who have given themselves over to Satan and become active proponents of evil.

Thou hast been faithful (1 Nephi 2:1; 2 Nephi 1:31; Alma 8:15; Ether 12:37). If we are faithful, God will bless and direct our lives, as He did in these cases. *See also:* Faithful in keeping the commandments; Faithful unto the Lord; Hold out faithful to the end; Let us be faithful (unto the Lord); Trial of your faith.

Thou hast prepared (Ether 12:32, 34). *See:* Way is prepared.

Thou shalt not ask that which is contrary to my will (Helaman 10:5). Like Jesus, who always did the will of His Father, we should seek to do the will of the Father. *See also:* Ask not amiss; D&C 46:30.

Thoughts and intents of his (the) heart (Mosiah 4:30; 5:13; 24:12; Alma 12:7, 14; 18:32; Helaman 9:41). "Yea, I tell thee, that thou mayest know that there is none else save God that knowest thy thoughts and the intents of thy heart" (D&C 6:16). *See also:* Know all my (thy) thoughts.

Thoughts are made known (Jacob 2:5; Alma 10:17; 12:3, 7; 18:16, 18, 20; Helaman 9:41; 3 Nephi 28:6). *See:* Know all my (thy) thoughts.

Thoughts will condemn us (Mosiah 4:30; 5:13; Alma 10:17; 12:3, 14; 18:32). According to these verses, our words, our works, and even our thoughts will be judged. We must become changed and strive with our might to possess only good words, works, and thoughts. *See also:* Know all my (thy) thoughts.

Three days of darkness (1 Nephi 19:10; Helaman 14:20, 27; 3 Nephi 8:3, 23; 10:9). The sign given of the Lord's crucifixion and death.

Three disciples of Jesus (who should [were to] tarry) (3 Nephi 28:4–9, 36–40; 4 Nephi 1:14, 37; Ether 12:17). Nine of the Nephite twelve desired and were promised an inheritance in Christ's kingdom when they died. The remaining three Nephite disciples desired and were given power over death so as to remain on the earth until Jesus comes again. *See also:* Not taste of death.

Three witnesses (2 Nephi 27:12; Ether 5:4; Moroni 6:7). By the witness of two or three shall the word of God be established. God has called multiple witnesses to verify His word. An example is the "Testimony of Three Witnesses" found in the front of the Book of Mormon. *See also:* Testimony of many (two or three).

Throne is high in the heavens (1 Nephi 1:14; 17:39; 2 Nephi 16:1; Moroni 9:26). *See:* God sitting upon his throne; Throne of God.

Throne of God (1 Nephi 1:8, 14; 2 Nephi 28:23; Jacob 3:8; Alma 36:22; Mormon 3:10; Moroni 9:26). The scriptures indicate often that "[God] ruleth high in the heavens,

for it is his throne, and earth is his footstool" (1 Nephi 17:39).

Through his (mine) Only Begotten Son (Jacob 4:11; Alma 12:33–34; 13:5). Meaning that through the Atonement of Jesus Christ we may receive mercy and be redeemed.

Through the blood of the Lamb (Mosiah 3:15, 18; Alma 5:21, 27; 13:11; 21:9; 24:13; 34:36; Helaman 5:9; Ether 13:10; Moroni 10:33). Only by and through the atoning blood of Christ can we be cleansed and obtain salvation. *See also:* Atoning blood of Jesus Christ; Garments cleansed through the blood of the Lamb (made white/ washed).

Through the merits of Christ (2 Nephi 2:8; Alma 24:10; Helaman 14:13). *See:* Relying upon the merits of Christ.

Thrust down to hell (2 Nephi 9:34, 36; 28:15). *See:* Depths of hell.

Thrust in the sickle (Alma 26:5). Meaning to work with one's might. Before mechanical machines were invented to harvest grain, a hand sickle was used to cut the grain for harvest. The harvest in the scriptures refers to the bringing of converts to the gospel of Jesus Christ. "For behold the field is white already to harvest; and lo, he that thrusteth in his sickle with his might, the same layeth up in store that he perisheth not, but bringeth salvation to his soul" (D&C 4:4).

Thrust your hands into my side (3 Nephi 11:14–15). Our Lord and Savior maintains the crucifixion wounds in His side and His hands and feet as a witness of His suffering and death for all mankind. The Twelve Apostles in New Testament times (John 20:19–28), the Nephites at Christ's coming to the American continent (3 Nephi 11:14), and others have had the privilege to thus witness that Jesus is the Christ who was slain for the world. This sign or witness was testified of in Zechariah 13:6 and D&C 45:51–52.

Thunderings and lightnings (1 Nephi 12:4; 19:11; 2 Nephi 26:6; Helaman 14:21, 26; 3 Nephi 8:12, 17, 19). The prophecies of, and then the fulfilling of, the thunderings, lightnings, and tumultuous destructions among the Nephites and Lamanites at the time of Christ's crucifixion and before His appearance to them.

Thus came the voice (word) unto me (2 Nephi 31:14; Jacob 2:11). *See:* Thus saith our God (the Lord).

Thus commandeth (saith) the Father (3 Nephi 16:10, 16; 24:1). God the Father gave instructions to His Son, Jesus Christ, before coming to the Nephites, and Jesus carried out those instructions. *See also:* Saith the Father.

Thus hath the angel spoken (1 Nephi 11:34, 36; 2 Nephi 6:11; Helaman 14:9, 26). *See:* Angels minister(-ed/appeared/declared/descending) unto him (them).

Thus saith our God (the Lord) (1 Nephi 20:17; 21:7–8, 22, 25; 2 Nephi 3:7; 5:22; 6:6, 17; 7:1; 8:22; 10:7, 18; 17:7; 20:24; 26:17–18; 27:33; 28:30; 29:4; Jacob 2:23, 25, 28; 5:3; Mosiah 3:24; 11:20, 25; 12:2; 23:7; Alma 8:17, 29; 45:16; Helaman 7:23; 10:11, 14; 13:8, 11; 3 Nephi 20:38). The preface often used by holy prophets to identify when they are speaking the word of the Lord. Because it is from the Lord, we should take particular notice. *See also:* Saith the Lamb of God (Lord [God]).

Thy faith hath made thee whole (Enos 1:8). The redemption of Christ from our sins is conditional upon our belief in Jesus, our acceptance of His commandments and law, and our faithfulness. To be made whole and cleansed of sin does not come to one of unbelief. *See also:* Matthew 9:22; Mark 5:34; 10:52; Luke 8:48; 17:19.

Thy watchmen shall lift up their voices (Mosiah 12:22; 15:29; 3 Nephi 16:18; 20:32). The watchmen of the Lord are the prophets who warn the people of their sins and tell the way to salvation.

Thy ways are just (2 Nephi 26:7). God never varies from being totally just. Everything about Him is just.

His words are just, His actions are just, His thoughts are just, and His judgment is just. Yet God desires to be merciful to us His children, therefore the Atonement of Jesus Christ is provided to save us from just judgment. *See also:* Judgments are just.

Thy will (O Lord) be done (2 Nephi 1:19; Jacob 7:14; Helaman 10:5; 3 Nephi 13:10; Ether 12:29). "After this manner therefore pray ye. . . . Thy will be done" (Matthew 6:9–10). *See also:* Will of God.

Tidings of great joy (1 Nephi 13:37; Mosiah 3:3; Alma 13:22; Helaman 16:14). The gospel of Jesus Christ is defined as tidings of great joy. These tidings include peace, the life and mission of Jesus Christ, salvation, redemption, the kingdom of God, and the Second Coming of Christ.

Time cometh (1 Nephi 13:42; 14:7; 22:7, 15–16, 24; 2 Nephi 1:10; 2:3, 26; 11:7; 22:15, 23–24; 30:10; Jacob 3:4; 5:71, 77; Mosiah 3:5, 21; Alma 7:7; 13:25; 40:4, 10; 45:13; Helaman 13:14, 31; 14:3; 3 Nephi 20:30; Mormon 8:33, 41; 9:14; Ether 3:21; Moroni 10:27). *See:* At that day; Day cometh; In that day.

Time cometh that I shall glorify my name in the flesh (Ether 3:21). The Savior is speaking here and refers to the time when He will come to earth in a mortal body, carry forth His ministry, suffer for the sins of all mankind, and become the firstfruits of the Resurrection, thus providing salvation for man.

Time draweth near (Jacob 5:29, 62, 64; Alma 13:21). Referring to the fact that the coming of the Lord is near at hand or soon. *See:* Time is at hand.

Time is at hand (Mosiah 7:18; Alma 5:31, 36; 9:28; 10:23; 60:29; 3 Nephi 1:13–14; 17:1; Ether 4:16). Meaning the time is soon or about to be. *See also:* At hand; End is nigh at hand; Hour is close at hand; Kingdom of heaven is nigh (soon) at hand.

Time is not far distant (Mosiah 7:18; Alma 7:7). *See:* Hour is close at hand; Time is at hand.

Time of his coming (Alma 13:24–26; 16:16; 25:15; 39:16–17, 19; Helaman 14:3). Refers to the coming of the Lord Jesus, either in the meridian of time or in the last day. *See also:* Coming of Christ.

Time of solemnity (Alma 28:6). Referring to the many who had died in battle. It was a time of reflection, earnestness, reverence, and faith.

Time only is measured unto men (Alma 40:8). It is hard, if not impossible, for mortals to comprehend that time is only considered in this mortal sphere. After the millennium, "Time is no longer" (D&C 84:100), and "There shall be time no longer" (D&C 88:110). God "lives in a unique circumstance wherein the past, present and future blend in an 'eternal now.' Those of us who need to wear mere wristwatches should be reluctant, therefore, to insist on our timetables for Him" (Maxwell, *Whom the Lord Loveth*, 18).

Time speedily cometh (1 Nephi 22:15, 23–24; 2 Nephi 23:22; 30:10; Jacob 3:4; 5:71, 76; Moroni 10:27). Meaning the time or end draweth near suddenly and quickly. *See also:* End soon cometh; Last days.

Time to prepare to meet God (Alma 12:24; 34:32–33). *Contrast:* Unprepared to meet their God. *See:* Prepare to meet God; Probationary state (time).

Tithes of one-tenth part (Alma 13:15). Members of God's Church have the bidding and blessing of paying tithing. Tithing is one tenth of one's income (see D&C 119:4). Latter-day scripture declares who in the Church has authority to dispose of tithing funds (see D&C 120:1). Tithing monies are used to build temples and chapels, for missionary work, and for other sacred purposes.

Title of liberty (Alma 46:13, 36; 51:20). In order to rally his people to freedom, Moroni made a flag of his coat and wrote thereon, "In memory of our God, our religion, and freedom, and our peace, our wives, and our children" (Alma 46:12). *See also:* Defend themselves; Standard of liberty.

To act or to be acted upon (2 Nephi 2:13–14, 26). As part of the plan of salvation we have been given our moral agency to choose. Thus we are free to act for ourselves and not to be forced or acted upon. Yet our choices have consequences. "The Lord has given you the gift of agency (see Moses 7:32) and instructed you sufficiently to know good from evil (see 2 Ne. 2:5). You are free to choose (see 2 Ne. 2:27) and are permitted to act (see 2 Ne. 10:23; Hel. 14:30), but you are not free to choose the consequences. With absolute certainty, choices of good and right lead to happiness and peace, while choices of sin and evil eventually lead to unhappiness, sorrow, and misery" (Wirthlin, "Running Your Marathon," 75).

To get gain (1 Nephi 22:23; 2 Nephi 27:16; Alma 10:32; 11:20; 30:35; Helaman 6:8, 17; 7:21; 3 Nephi 29:7; 4 Nephi 1:26; Mormon 8:14, 33, 40). *See:* Get gain.

To go no more out (Alma 7:25; 34:36; Helaman 3:30; 3 Nephi 28:40). *See:* Go no more out.

Tongue cannot speak the words (3 Nephi 17:17; 19:32; Mormon 4:11; Moroni 9:19). *See:* Could not find utterance; Unspeakable things.

Tongue of angels (2 Nephi 31:13–14; 32:2). "And now, how could ye speak with the tongue of angels save it were by the Holy Ghost? Angels speak by the power of the Holy Ghost" (2 Nephi 32:2–3).

The angels speak by the power and authority of the Holy Ghost; for a man to speak with the tongue of angels, a man must likewise speak as prompted and inspired by the Holy Ghost.

Took an oath (Alma 49:13). *See:* Made an oath unto us.

Took upon them the name of Christ (Alma 46:15; Moroni 6:3). *See:* Take(-n) upon him (them/you/us) the name of Christ.

Torment as a lake of fire and brimstone (2 Nephi 9:16, 19, 26; 28:23; Jacob 6:10; Mosiah 3:27; Alma 12:17). There is not, nor will there be, an actual, physical place consisting of a lake of fire and brimstone, but this phrase more accurately describes the fate of the wicked, who will experience torments and anguish like the torments of a hot fever, including gnashing of teeth. *See also:* Lake of fire and brimstone.

Touch not their unclean things (Alma 5:57; 3 Nephi 20:41; Moroni 10:30). If we frequent the mud puddle, it is sure we will get mud on us. Likewise, if we frequent sinful places and sinful things, we are not likely to escape without becoming sinful ourselves. "Wherefore come out from among them, and be ye separate, saith the Lord, and touch not the unclean thing; and I will receive you, and will be a Father unto you, and ye shall be my sons and daughters, saith the Lord Almighty" (2 Corinthians 6:17–18).

Traditions of our (their/your) fathers (Enos 1:14; Mosiah 1:5; 26:1; Alma 3:11; 9:8, 16–17; 17:9, 15; 21:17; 24:6–7; 26:24; 30:16, 23; 60:32; Helaman 5:19, 51; 15:4, 15). Every society has its social, political, legal, and moral traditions, be they good or bad. Smaller groups of people also have their traditions, such as in communities, neighborhoods, clubs, gangs, religions, and families. Traditions are mentioned often in the Book of Mormon. Good traditions, correct traditions, and righteous traditions are generally attributed to the Nephites, which are the traditions of believing in Christ and the teachings of the gospel, meaning the traditions handed down beginning with Lehi and Nephi. Evil, unholy, wicked, corrupt, false, and incorrect traditions are the traditions of disbelief in Christ and hatred against the Nephites (see Mosiah 10:12–17), meaning the traditions handed down beginning with Laman and Lemuel. *See also:* Foolish traditions (things); Handed down; Incorrect traditions; Traditions of the Lamanites; Traditions of the Nephites; Wicked and abominable traditions of their fathers.

Traditions of the Lamanites (Mosiah 1:5; Alma 3:11; 9:16; 17:9; 19:14; 24:7; 25:6; 26:24; 37:9; 47:36; 60:32; Helaman 5:19; 15:4).

See: Traditions of our (their/your) fathers.

Traditions of the Nephites (Alma 23:5). *See:* Traditions of our (their/your) fathers.

Trample the God of Israel (Holy One) under your feet (1 Nephi 19:7; Alma 5:53; 60:33). To trample is to tread on or tread under one's feet, meaning to treat as naught and to walk on. *See also:* Thing of naught.

Trampled under their feet the commandments of God (the Holy One) (1 Nephi 19:7; Mosiah 29:22; Alma 5:53; 60:33; Helaman 4:22; 6:31, 39; 12:2; 3 Nephi 14:6). To reject and consider Jesus Christ and His commandments as a thing of naught. *See also:* Thing of naught; D&C 76:35; 132:27.

Transfigured the holy word of God (Mormon 8:33). Not only were plain and precious truths left out of the Bible (1 Nephi 13:28), but wicked men changed (transfigured) the meaning and words to benefit themselves. *See also:* Many plain and precious things.

Transformeth himself nigh unto an angel of light (2 Nephi 9:9). The devil can appear like an angel. *See also:* Angel of light; Form of an angel.

Transgress (and go) contrary to the light and knowledge which they do have (2 Nephi 9:27; Mosiah 2:33, 36; Alma 9:23). It is worse to have known the commandments and turn away from them, than to have never known. *See also:* Open rebellion against God; Rebel(-led/-ling/-lion) against God; Willfully rebel(-led/against God).

Transgress the commandments (laws) of God (Mosiah 4:14; 26:29; Alma 37:15; 46:21; 60:33). To transgress is to disobey, violate, break, or trespass against.

Transgression of their parents (2 Nephi 2:21; Alma 22:12). Meaning the transgression of Adam and Eve in partaking of the forbidden fruit, thus causing the fall of man, whereby man became mortal. "For as in Adam all die, even so in Christ shall all be made alive (1 Corinthians 15:22). *See also:* Beguiled our first parents.

Travail(-s) of his (the) soul (Mosiah 14:11; 29:33). *Travail* means to labor hard and long. "The spirit and the body are the soul of man" (D&C 88:15). Thus travails of the soul are the exertions, strains, toil, and drudgery while in this life.

Tread them (the wicked) down (3 Nephi 16:14–15; 25:3). Another description of the fate of the wicked. They will be as that which is thrown out and trod under the foot of man.

Treasure is their God (2 Nephi 9:30). The Ten Commandments say, "Thou shalt have no other gods before me. Thou shalt not make unto thee any graven image, or any likeness of anything that is in heaven above, or that is in the earth beneath or that is the water under the earth. Thou shalt not bow down thyself to them, nor serve them: for I the Lord thy God am a jealous God" (Exodus 20:3–5). In today's world people's false gods are more likely bank accounts, houses, boats, fine apparel (as was with some Book of Mormon people), their jobs, or finely toned and muscled bodies. *See also:* Costly apparel.

Treasure up the things which ye have seen and heard (Ether 3:21). Meaning to value and ponder the things of God. Concerning Mary, the mother of Jesus, it is recorded, "But Mary kept all these things, and pondered them in her heart" (Luke 2:19). Moses, after seeing great things was commanded, "Show them not unto any except them that believe" (Moses 1:42).

Treasure(-s) in heaven (Helaman 5:8; 8:25; 3 Nephi 13:20). In the Sermon on the Mount the Savior said, "Lay not up for yourselves treasures on earth, where moth and rust doth corrupt, and thieves break through and steal: but lay up for yourselves treasures in heaven, where neither moth nor rust doth corrupt, and where thieves do not break through nor steal: for where your treasure is, there will your heart be also" (Matthew 6:19–21). Treasures in heaven consist of approval of God, peace, pleasant

habitation, family, and heavenly work. Someone has said, "My only treasure is in Christ."

Tree of life (1 Nephi 11:25; 15:22, 28, 36; 2 Nephi 2:15; Alma 5:34, 62; 12:21, 23, 26; 32:40–41; 33:23; 42:2–3, 5–6). "[A representation of] the love of God, which sheddeth itself abroad in the hearts of the children of men; [and] it is the most desirable above all things . . . and most joyous to the soul" (1 Nephi 11:22–23). Further, the tree of life "is a representation of Jesus Christ and that the joy and happiness received by partaking of the fruit of the tree symbolizes the blessings of the Savior's Atonement (see 1 Nephi 8:10; 11:8–9, 21–24)" (Andersen, "Hold Fast to the Words of the Prophets"). Additionally, the tree of life represents the joy of the gospel and in the end represents eternal life.

Trial of your faith (Alma 1:25; Ether 12:6). The title of President Spencer W. Kimball's book *Faith Precedes the Miracle* describes the order of things. This earth life is a test of our faith to see if we will by faith keep the commandments and live Christlike lives. As we live faithfully, God begins to give us spiritual rewards that increase as we continue faithfully. *See also:* 1 Peter 1:7; D&C 105:19.

Trials and troubles and afflictions (Mosiah 29:33; Alma 36:3,

27; 38:5). *See:* Bear afflictions (with patience).

Tribulation and anguish of soul (Alma 8:14). Distress or suffering because of the wickedness of the people. *See also:* Cast down (and grieved) because of the wickedness of the people; Weighed down with sorrow.

Tribulations of his mind (Alma 15:3). Distress or suffering because of one's sins.

Tribunal of God (Alma 5:18). The word *tribunal* means court of justice. *See also:* Judgment bar; Stand before God.

Trieth their patience and their faith (Mosiah 23:21). The Lord will often test the faith of His people. Our whole life on earth is a test to see if we will in faith do the will of God. *See also:* Bear afflictions (with patience); Keep the commandments (of God).

Troubled in spirit (Mosiah 26:10, 13). Being worried, concerned, and not right within. Having troubled, distressed, and anxious feelings towards a matter.

True and faithful (2 Nephi 31:15). Meaning loyal, truthful, guileless, devoted, constant, unswerving, unwavering, firm, staunch, exact, and reliable. *See also:* Just and true [individuals].

True and living (and only) God (1 Nephi 17:30; 2 Nephi 1:10; Alma 5:13; 7:6; 11:25–27; 20:15; 43:10; Helaman 13:18; Mormon 8:10; 9:28; Ether 2:8). A scriptural phrase used in the scriptures to identify the real and only God. *See also:* Know God.

True at all times (Alma 53:20). Being loyal and exact always. *See also:* Just and true [individuals].

True believers in (of) Christ (Alma 46:14–15; 4 Nephi 1:36–37). Not only those that believe in Jesus Christ, but those that truly follow Him.

True church (of Christ) (2 Nephi 9:2; 4 Nephi 1:26, 29). There have been and are today many churches with many differing doctrines and philosophies. To find the true Church of God one would expect to find these principles: Built upon the doctrine and gospel of Christ; the correct organization; accepted of God; correct authority or priesthood; directed by revelation from God; blessed and sustained by the Spirit; correct church name (3 Nephi 27:8); hearts drawing near to God; and a unity of faith. *Contrast:* Built up churches to get gain (power/praise of men). *See also:* Belong to the church (of God); Church of Christ; Church of God; My church.

True doctrine (2 Nephi 31:21; Helaman 11:23; 3 Nephi 21:6). The doctrine as taught or revealed by Christ, which has not been changed, alloyed, or corrupted by man. *See also:* Doctrine of Christ; D&C 10:62.

True faith (in/of God) (Enos 1:14, 20; Alma 44:4; 3 Nephi 6:14). *See:* Church of Christ; Doctrine of Christ; True church (of Christ); True doctrine.

True fold of God (1 Nephi 15:15; 2 Nephi 9:2). *See:* Fold of God; True faith (in/of God).

True followers of his son, Jesus Christ (Moroni 7:48). Meaning those who in fact follow the example of Jesus and keep His commandments. Not those that draw near to Him with their lips but their hearts are far from Him. And not Mormons who are Mormons on Sunday but not during the rest of the week. By their thoughts and intents ye shall know them, and God knows our thoughts and intents. *See also:* True believers in (of) Christ.

True knowledge (2 Nephi 10:2; Helaman 15:13). Which is the knowledge of their Redeemer. *See also:* Knowledge of the truth.

True Messiah (1 Nephi 10:14; 2 Nephi 1:10; 25:18). Jesus Christ of Nazareth is the only true Messiah. He will come again and show the wounds in His hands, feet, and side to verify His identity. *See also:* Another Messiah; None other name.

True points of my doctrine (Helaman 11:23; 3 Nephi 21:6). *See:* Doctrine of Christ; True doctrine.

True vine (olive-tree) (1 Nephi 15:15; Alma 16:17). "In several places in the Book of Mormon the house of Israel is likened to an olive tree. In this analogy, some of the natural branches of the olive tree (the direct descendants of the house of Israel) are grafted or planted in other parts of the vineyard (in other words, they are led to other parts of the earth). However, Nephi prophesies that in the last days these natural branches of the house of Israel 'shall be grafted *in*, being a natural branch of the olive-tree, into the true olive-tree' (1 Nephi 15:16. Italics added.). This evidently means that the direct descendants of Israel are going to be brought to a knowledge of the true covenants that the Lord made anciently with the house of Israel.

"Essentially this same idea is expressed in 1 Nephi 10:14, where Nephi says that in the last days 'the natural branches of the olive-tree, or the remnants of the house of Israel, should be grafted in, or come to the knowledge of the true Messiah, their Lord and their Redeemer.' (1 Nephi 10:14)" (Ludlow, *Companion to Your Study of The Book of Mormon*, 113). In another context, the Savior said "I am the true vine and my Father is the husbandman" (John 15:1). *See also:* Tame olive tree.

True worshipers of Christ (4 Nephi 1:37). "If any man be a worshipper of God, and doeth his will, him he heareth" (John 9:31).

See also: Worship in spirit and truth; D&C 93:19.

Truly penitent (Alma 27:18; 29:10; 32:7; 42:24). A requirement for salvation. How does one measure the sincerity of an individual's repentance? As individuals examining the verity of our own repentance, we are often unsure. Only God can judge if a person is truly penitent. Fortunately, God our Heavenly Father often reveals to individuals that their sins have been forgiven. For the purposes of church administration and ministry the same is often revealed to priesthood leaders concerning the repentance of others.

Trump of God (Alma 29:1). As used here it is the desire of Alma to be heard by all in declaring the gospel of Jesus Christ. In ancient and historic times the sounding of trumpets heralded important events. In scripture the sounding of trumps signifies certain events that are to take place. *See also:* Second trump; Trump shall sound.

Trump shall sound (Mosiah 26:25; Mormon 9:13). The signal of the various times or levels of the Resurrection. *See also:* Second trump; Trump of God.

Trust in God (the Lord) (2 Nephi 4:34; Mosiah 4:6; 7:19, 33; 10:19; 29:20; Alma 5:13; 17:13; 36:3, 27; 38:5; 57:27; 58:33; Helaman 12:1; Moroni 9:22). *See:* Put their (your) trust in him (the Lord God).

Trusted him unto the Lord (Alma 19:23). Like many latter-day parents who trust their missionary sons and daughters to the Lord for two years.

Truth and righteousness (Alma 38:9; Helaman 6:34). The ultimate characteristics and that which should be our only goal. *See also:* Just and true [individuals].

Truth which is in (of) Christ (God) (1 Nephi 13:24–25; 2 Nephi 2:10; 28:28; Jacob 2:11; 4:13; Enos 1:26; Mosiah 13:4; 27:36; Alma 9:26; 17:2). All truth emanates from the Father and the Son. They are the source of truth and light (see D&C 88:6–13). Jesus said, "I am the light, and the life, and the truth of the world" (Ether 4:12). Additionally, "He that keepeth his commandments receiveth truth and light, until he is glorified in truth and knoweth all things" (D&C 93:28).

Try the faith of my people (3 Nephi 26:11). "And we will prove them herewith, to see if they will do all things whatsoever the Lord their God shall command them" (Abraham 3:25). *See also:* Act for themselves (yourselves); After much tribulation; Trial of your faith.

Try their faith (3 Nephi 26:9). *See:* Try the faith of my people.

Turn aside the just for a thing of naught (2 Nephi 27:32; 28:16). To reject truth and good, and choose instead evil. *See also:* Thing of naught.

Turn aside their hearts against the Holy One of Israel (1 Nephi 19:13–15). Referring to the Jews who rejected their Savior Jesus. Also a warning to all others not to turn away from Christ. *See also:* Hiss and a byword.

Turn aside to the right hand or to the left (Alma 24:23). "Ye shall observe to do therefore as the Lord your God hath commanded you: ye shall not turn aside to the right hand or to the left. Ye shall walk in all the ways which the Lord your God hath commanded you, that ye may live, and that it may be well with you" (Deuteronomy 5:32–33). *See also:* His paths are straight; Straight course (path) to eternal bliss; Walk in his paths (which are straight).

Turn away thine anger (Alma 9:12; Helaman 11:11–12, 16–17; 13:11, 37; Ether 1:36; 3:3). Words to pray to God as individuals or a people turn to God, turn away from sin, humble themselves, and repent. *See also:* Anger of the Lord.

Turn from our iniquities (your evil ways) (Mosiah 20:21; Mormon 5:22). To repent is to turn away from evil and embrace good. "Turn ye, turn ye from your evil ways" (Ezekiel 33:11). *See also:* Repent and turn from your evil ways (unto the Lord God).

Turn the heart of the fathers to the children, and the heart of the children to their fathers (3 Nephi 25:6). Refers to the spirit of Elijah or family history wherein we seek our ancestors that they may be saved though vicarious temple ordinances. Thus the whole earth will not be wasted. *See also:* Malachi 4:6; D&C 128:17.

Turn their backs upon the poor (Helaman 6:39). *See:* Clothe the naked; Esteemed by their brethren as dross; Poor and needy.

Turn to me that I may have mercy upon them (Alma 3:14). *See:* Turn unto the Lord God.

Turn unto the Lord God (Mosiah 7:33; 11:23; Alma 3:14; 39:13; Helaman 7:17; 11:4; 13:11; 3 Nephi 16:15; Mormon 9:6; Ether 11:1). Meaning to turn from sin and to the Lord. *See also:* Come unto him (me/thee); Repent and turn from your evil ways (unto the Lord God).

Turn unto their own ways (Helaman 6:31). Meaning to turn to the sinful ways of man.

Turning away every one of you from his iniquities (2 Nephi 9:45; 3 Nephi 20:26). *See:* No more desire (disposition) to do evil; Acts 3:26.

Turning from the right to the left (Alma 7:20). God does not walk crooked paths. He does not ever change from that which is correct to that which is untrue. *See also:* Shadow of changing (turning).

Turning their (your) backs upon the poor (2 Nephi 20:2; Alma 4:12;

5:55; 32:3; 34:28; Helaman 6:39).
See: Poor and needy.

Twelve apostles of the Lamb
(1 Nephi 11:35–36; 12:9; 13:24, 26,
39–41; 14:20). The twelve chosen
by Jesus in Jerusalem and seen by
Nephi in his vision. These twelve
will judge the twelve tribes of Israel.
The Twelve Apostles are special witnesses of Christ. *Compare:* Twelve
disciples of the Lamb.

Twelve disciples of the Lamb
(1 Nephi 12:8). The twelve men who
were chosen by Jesus from among
the Nephites during His appearance
in the Americas. These twelve were
to minister unto the Nephites and
shall judge them. *Compare:* Twelve
apostles of the Lamb.

Twelve others (1 Nephi 1:10; 11:29;
12:7). Refers to the Twelve Apostles
Jesus chose in Jerusalem at the
meridian of time. *See also:* Twelve
apostles of the Lamb.

Twelve tribes of Israel (1 Nephi
12:9; Mormon 3:18). The children
of Israel—the posterity of the twelve
sons of Jacob (the Lord changed his
name to Israel). *See also:* Children
of Israel; O house of Israel (Jacob);
1 Nephi 21:6.

Twenty-four plates (Mosiah 8:9;
Alma 37:21; Ether 1:2). The record of the Jaredites found by the
people of Limhi in the days of King
Mosiah. This record was abridged
by Moroni and included in the

Book of Mormon as the Book of
Ether. *See also:* Plates of gold.

Twinkling of an eye (3 Nephi
28:8). Meaning "in a moment"
(1 Corinthians 15:52). *See:* Changed
in a twinkling of an eye.

Two stones (Mosiah 8:13, 19;
28:20; Alma 37:21, 24; Mormon
9:34; Ether 3:23, 28; 4:5).
Having reference to the Urim and
Thummim, also called the interpreters, which were "two stones in silver
bows—and these bows fastened to a
breastplate" (Joseph Smith–History
1:35). "An instrument prepared
of God to assist man in obtaining
revelation from the Lord and in
translating languages. . . . Using
a Urim and Thummim is the special prerogative of a seer. . . . Joseph
Smith used it in translating the
Book of Mormon and in obtaining
other revelations" (Bible Dictionary,
s.v. "Urim and Thummim," 786–
87). *See also:* Prepared means for the
interpretation thereof.

Two thousand stripling soldiers
(Alma 53:18, 22; 56:3, 5, 9–10, 27–
28, 49–50, 52, 54, 57; 57:6, 19–20,
25). Because their parents had taken
an oath never again to take up arms,
and because of the perilous plight of
the nation caused by enemy armies,
these young men volunteered to go
and fight in the war. They were of
exceptional valor, but more importantly had great faith, because "they
had been taught by their mothers,
that if they did not doubt, God

would deliver them" (Alma 56:47). And in a miraculous way, not one lost his life in battle.

Type in this thing (of his coming) (Alma 25:15; 37:45). *See:* Type(-s) and shadow(-s).

Type of his order (Alma 13:16). *See:* Holy order (of God); Type(-s) and shadow(-s).

Type was raised up (Alma 33:19). *See:* Type(-s) and shadow(-s).

Type(-s) and shadow(-s) (2 Nephi 11:4; Mosiah 3:15; 13:10, 31; 16:14; Alma 13:16, 31; 25:10, 15; 33:19; 37:43, 45; Ether 13:6). Throughout the ages of man, God has given signs, ordinances, and analogies that help us to remember and turn us to the Savior and His mission. These types and shadows are similitudes or images of Christ, that

we might look forward to and have faith in His coming and His redemptive Atonement. "By definition a type is an intended similarity between a person, object, or event and another person, object, or event. A shadow is similar in meaning, but refers to something that will follow or come to pass. . . . Elder Bruce R. McConkie stated, 'It is wholesome and proper to look for similitudes of Christ everywhere and to use them repeatedly in keeping him and his laws uppermost in our minds" ("Types and Shadows").

Type(-s) of things to come (Mosiah 13:31; Alma 25:10). *See:* Shadow of those things which are to come; Type(-s) and shadow(-s).

Typifying of him (2 Nephi 11:4). *See:* Type(-s) and shadow(-s).

U

Unchangeable from all eternity to all eternity (Moroni 8:18). God is an "unchangeable Being" (Mormon 9:19) and is "infinite and eternal, from everlasting to everlasting the same unchangeable God" (D&C 20:17).

Uncircumcised of heart (2 Nephi 9:33; Helaman 9:21). Meaning to have a heart or intent that is not humble and that is unclean as a result of not keeping the commandments of God. To be uncircumcised is opposite to the covenant that Abraham made with God, for which circumcision was a token of obedience. "The Lord thy God will circumcise thine heart, and the heart of thy seed, to love the Lord thy God with all thine heart, and with all thy soul" (Deuteronomy 30:6). *See also:* 2 Nephi 8:24; 3 Nephi 20:36.

Unclean spirits (1 Nephi 11:31; 3 Nephi 7:19). Refers to the devils that sometimes come to inhabit and vex men and women. Christ, His Apostles, and righteous men of the priesthood have power over unclean spirits and can cast them out of individuals so vexed. *See also:* Mark 6:7; Luke 4:36; 6:18; Acts 5:16; 8:7.

Unclean thing (1 Nephi 10:21; 15:34; Alma 11:37; 40:26; 3 Nephi 27:19; Moroni 10:30). Meaning that which is tainted and stained with sin and filthiness, and no unclean thing or individual can enter into the Kingdom of heaven, for God has so declared it.

Unconquerable spirit (Alma 52:33; 3 Nephi 3:4). People of unconquerable spirit are not easily discouraged, dissuaded, derailed, or defeated.

Under condemnation (Mosiah 26:31; Helaman 14:19; 3 Nephi 18:33; Moroni 8:22, 24; 9:6). Meaning condemned, guilty of, or having violated the law of God.

Under this head ye are made free (Mosiah 5:8). Meaning "being in Christ they are free from bondage of sin—'and there is no other head [other than Christ our Head] whereby ye can be made free.' Only those who accept Christ and receive the Spirit can free themselves from the sins of the world" (McConkie, *New Witness*, 285). "People entangled in sin are not free . . . Freedom from worldly ideologies and concepts unshackles man far more than he knows. It is the truth that sets men free" (Kimball, "Second Century Address"). "Ye shall know the truth, and the truth shall make you free" (John 8:32). *See also:* Made free.

Understand (understood) not the scriptures (Jacob 2:23; 7:11; Alma 33:2; 3 Nephi 1:24; 10:14; Mormon 9:8). Concerning those that teach unsound doctrine it has been said either they have not read the scriptures or, if they have, they do not understand them. A true understanding of the scriptures can only be obtained by revelation and the Holy Ghost. "Open your mouths in proclaiming my gospel, the things of the kingdom, expounding the mysteries thereof out of the scriptures, according to that portion of the Spirit and power which shall be given unto you, even as I will" (D&C 71:1). Those who do not understand the scriptures include those who have only read a little and supposed the remainder, those who wrestle with the scriptures to prove a personal point, and those who have interpreted wrongly, or who have been deceived by Satan.

Understanding of men (1 Nephi 13:29; 2 Nephi 31:3; Jacob 4:13). The knowledge and wisdom of men is small and finite, even that of the most brilliant and gifted men and women. Whereas, God has all wisdom and understanding, and He comprehends all things (see Alma 26:35). "For what man knoweth the things of a man, save the spirit of man which is in him? even so the things of God knoweth no man, but the Spirit of God" (1 Corinthians 2:11). God in His wisdom gives or reveals only as much as can be assimilated by the understanding of men.

Understanding of their prudent shall be hid (2 Nephi 27:26). A prudent man is careful, logical, analytical, and rational. But all the wisdom and prudence of the world is insignificant when compared to the revelations and truths found in the Book of Mormon. The latter-day restoration will eclipse and overshadow the understanding of prudent men of the world. "Woe unto them that are wise in their own eyes, and prudent in their own sight" (Isaiah 5:21). *Compare:* Isaiah 29:14; 1 Corinthians 1:19; D&C 76:9.

Understanding which God has given me (Words of Mormon 1:9). Understanding is a gift from God given to the righteous who seek and pray for it (see D&C 110:1; 138:11, 29). Whereas, the wicked are confounded by God's wisdom (see Jacob 7:8; Mosiah 12:19).

Understood not the dealings of the Lord (voice they heard) (2 Nephi 16:9; Mosiah 3:15; 10:14; 13:32; 27:12; Alma 9:3; 3 Nephi 11:3–4; 15:2, 18, 22–23). "Take heed to yourselves, that your heart be not deceived" (Deuteronomy 11:16). "For my thoughts are not your thoughts, neither are your ways my ways, saith the Lord. For as the heavens are higher than the earth, so are my ways higher than your ways, and my thoughts than your thoughts" (Isaiah 55:8–9). *See also:* Understand (understood) not the scriptures.

Unfold the scriptures (this mystery) unto you (Jacob 4:18; Alma 12:1; 40:3). By the Spirit of God (Holy Ghost) the scriptures and mysteries of God can be unfolded, revealed, understood and disclosed. *Compare:* D&C 10:64; 90:14. *See also:* Mysteries of God; Unfolding unto them all my revelations (such mysteries).

Unfolding unto them all my revelations (such mysteries) (Mosiah 8:19; Ether 4:7). *See:* Greater things; Mysteries of God; Unfold the scriptures (this mystery) unto you.

Unholy temples (Mosiah 2:37; Alma 7:21; 34:36; Helaman 4:24). Our body is a temple and we are commanded not to defile it with unholy things. "Know ye not that ye are the temple of God, and that the Spirit of God dwelleth in you? If any man defile the temple of God, him shall God destroy; for the temple of God is holy, which temple ye are" (1 Corinthians 3:16–17).

Unpardonable sin (Jacob 7:19; Alma 39:6). The sin which is unpardonable is to "deny the Holy Ghost when it once has had place in you, and ye know that ye deny

it" (Alma 39:6). This unpardonable sin is "a sin for which there is no forgiveness, neither in time nor in eternity. It is blasphemy against the Holy Ghost; it is to deny Christ, to come out in open rebellion, to make open war against the Son of Man after gaining, by the power of the Holy Ghost, a sure and perfect knowledge of the truth and divinity of the Lord's work. It is to . . . assent unto the death of Christ— to crucify him afresh. . . . It is to wage open warfare, as does Lucifer, against the Lord and his Anointed, knowing that the course so pursued is evil" (McConkie, *Mortal Messiah*, 2:215). *See also:* Better for you that ye had not known me; Contend no more against the Holy Ghost; Deny the Holy Ghost; D&C 76:31–38; 132:27.

Unprepared to meet their God (Alma 5:28; 48:23). To be living in one's sins and unrepentant is to be unprepared to meet God. *See also:* Prepare to meet God.

Unquenchable fire (Jacob 6:10; Mosiah 2:38; 3:27; Alma 5:52; Mormon 9:5). *Unquenchable* means unable to put out, extinguish, suppress, or eliminate. Thus as the scriptures describe, fire whose flame ascendeth up forever and ever. This will be the experience of the unrepentant wicked. Unquenchable fire is eternally existing punishment that some will experience for a time and others will suffer forever. *See also:* Hell fire.

Unsearchable are the depths of the mysteries of him (Jacob 4:8). The many great and marvelous things of God are learned only by revelation, and it is impossible for mortal man to see or know *all* of them (thus they are unsearchable or not readily interpreted/investigated). *See also:* No man knoweth of his ways save it be revealed unto him; Job 5:9; Psalm 145:3; Romans 11:33; Ephesians 3:8.

Unshaken faith (2 Nephi 31:19; Jacob 4:6; Enos 1:11; Mormon 9:28). *See:* Faith began to be (becometh) unshaken; Perfect faith.

Unspeakable things (3 Nephi 26:18; 28:13). At various times God has revealed marvelous things which cannot be written. Because they are more wonderful than mortals have imagined, because human words are inadequate to write them, and because they are not lawful to be written, the Spirit forbids that they be written. 3 Nephi 17:16–17 describes, "The eye hath never seen, neither hath the ear heard, before, so great and marvelous things as we saw and heard Jesus speak unto the Father; and no tongue can speak, neither can there be written by any man, neither can the hearts of men conceive so great and marvelous things as we both saw and heard Jesus speak; and no one can conceive of the joy which filled our souls at the time we heard him pray for us unto the Father." Concerning what any of us experience, the Lord has revealed a little and sufficient to try our faith. 3 Nephi 26:9–10 says, "And when they shall have received this, which is expedient that they should have first, to try their faith, and if it shall so be that they shall believe these things then shall the greater things be made manifest unto them. And if it so be that they will not believe these things, then shall the greater things be withheld from them, unto their condemnation." *See also:* Forbidden that I (they) should write (utter/preach).

Until the own due time of the Lord (2 Nephi 27:10). *See:* Own due time (of the Lord).

Unto life (2 Nephi 9:15; Alma 11:45; 28:14; 29:4; 3 Nephi 14:14; Moroni 7:41). Depending on the context, this phrase means to be raised in the Resurrection unto life immortal, or it means to be saved unto life eternal or exaltation.

Unto the end [of the world] (2 Nephi 27:10–11; Mosiah 4:7). Meaning to the end of this earth's mortal existence and the end of that phase of this earth's existence. *See also:* Last day.

Unto the end [of your lives] (1 Nephi 13:37; Mosiah 4:6, 30; 5:8; 26:23; 27:27; 3 Nephi 27:17, 19). Meaning to the end of a man's mortal existence, at which time he will be judged according to his deeds.

Unto the ends of the earth (1 Nephi 21:6; 2 Nephi 24:2; 29:2; 3 Nephi 11:41; Mormon 9:21, 25; Ether 3:25). *See:* All ye ends of the earth.

Unto the fulfilling of the covenant (promises/prophecies/word) (1 Nephi 9:6; 10:13; 18:11; 22:20; 2 Nephi 31:18; Alma 37:16; 50:19; 3 Nephi 10:14; 20:12, 22; 21:7; 29:9; Mormon 1:19; 5:14; Moroni 8:29; 10:28). *See:* According to God's word.

Unto them I will show no greater things (Alma 12:10; 3 Nephi 26:10; Ether 4:7, 8, 13). Those that rebel in unbelief and contend against the things of God will have the great mysteries of Godliness withheld from them. As they continue in sin and rebellion they will know less and less of the truth until they know none of it.

Unwearied diligence (Helaman 15:6). Meaning to continue to work and serve when one would normally become weary and tired. *See also:* With unwearyingness.

Upon the wings of his Spirit (2 Nephi 4:25). Meaning carried away in the Spirit to see visions. *See also:* Carried away in the spirit (in a vision).

Usurp power and authority (Alma 25:5; 30:23; 60:27; Helaman 7:4). *Usurp* means to take away from another or to obtain wrongly. *See also:* Sought power and authority.

Utterly destroy(-ed) (1 Nephi 13:30; 2 Nephi 3:3; 4:9; 9:53; 21:15; 30:1; Mosiah 12:8; Alma 9:12, 24; Helaman 6:37; 7:24; 15:16–17; Ether 11:12). *Utterly* means completely, thoroughly, and entirely.

V

Vain and foolish doctrines (thing[-s]) (2 Nephi 28:9; Alma 1:16; 39:11; Helaman 12:4; 16:22; 3 Nephi 2:2). The philosophies of men have no foundation in truth or the revealed word of God, but they sound pleasing to the ears of worldly men and satisfy their desires for evil and lustful things. *See also:* Foolish and vain.

Vain imaginations (1 Nephi 12:18). Meaning desire and praise of vain things. *See also:* Vain things of the world.

Vain repetitions (3 Nephi 13:7). Insincere babblings, proud statements, and much speaking made in prayer to be heard of men. Rather we must secretly and humbly pray with real intent, otherwise our prayers profiteth nothing (Moroni 7:9).

Vain things of the world (Alma 1:16; 4:8; 5:37, 53; 7:6; 31:27; 39:11, 14; 60:32; Helaman 7:21; 12:4; 3 Nephi 6:15). "Vain things, which cannot profit nor deliver; for they are vain" (1 Samuel 12:21). The word *vain* means useless or meaningless. Brigham Young said, "Men are greedy for the vain things of this world. In their hearts they are covetous. It is true that the things of this world are designed to make us comfortable, and they make some people as happy as they can be here; but riches can never make the Latter-day Saints happy. Riches of themselves cannot produce permanent happiness; only the Spirit that comes from above can do that" (*Discourses of Brigham Young,* 306). *See also:* Fine things of the world; Lusts of the flesh; Precious things; Puffed up in the vain things of the world; Seek not after riches; Things of the world.

Vale of sorrow (Alma 37:45). *Vale* is another word for valley (in, for example, the saying "hill and vale"). *See also:* Valley of sorrow.

Valley of sorrow (2 Nephi 4:26). Refers to a time or an experience of sorrow, often referring to this life of sorrow in which we struggle to be faithful in our trials and tribulations. A low point in life. *See also:* Afflict my soul; Bear afflictions (with patience).

Vapor of darkness (smoke) (1 Nephi 12:5; 19:11; 22:18; 3 Nephi 8:20; 10:13). The destructions of God are often accompanied with a vapor of darkness or smoke.

For example, just before Christ's appearance to the Nephites there were tempests, fires, thunderings, earthquakes, and a thick darkness. *See also:* Mist(-s) of darkness [during the great destruction by God]; Three days of darkness.

Veil of unbelief (Alma 19:6; Ether 4:15). "The wicked one cometh and taketh away light and truth, through disobedience" (D&C 93:39). Thus sin plunges us into darkness as though a veil of darkness is drawn across us so that we no longer comprehend or enjoy light and truth. *See also:* Cloud of darkness; Scales of darkness shall begin to fall from their eyes.

Veil was taken from off the eyes (Ether 3:6). Meaning the eyes of our understanding were opened and things were revealed from beyond the veil (see D&C 110:1).

Vengeance is mine (Mormon 3:15; 8:20). "Vengeance is mine" saith the Lord (Mormon 3:15). *See also:* Avenge his blood (their wrongs/themselves); Judgment is mine, saith the Lord; Sword of vengeance.

Verified his word unto them in every particular (Alma 25:17). *See:* According to God's word; Word of God (prophets/the Lord) has been (was/were) fulfilled (verified).

Verily, verily I say unto you (Alma 48:17; 3 Nephi 11:29, 31, 35, 39; 12:13–14, 26, 32, 34; 13:1; 14:1; 16:1, 9, 16; 18:15, 18, 27; 20:12, 39,

46; 21:3; 27:4, 21). Every occurrence of this phrase in the Book of Mormon is given by the Lord Jesus Christ, except for the first one listed here in Alma. *Verily, verily* is the same as a teacher or mother saying "Pay attention, pay attention." *Verily* literally means "in very truth" or truly, certainly, for sure, and without doubt. "Verily, verily I say unto you" appears to be used to preface statements that we should pay attention to.

Victory of Christ (over death) (Mosiah 15:8; Alma 27:28). *See:* Death is (was) swallowed up in the victory of (in) Christ.

Victory over the devil (Alma 16:21). This verse refers to the influence of Satan in the land being nigh eliminated because the people are converted to Christ, live the gospel fully, and receive great blessing from God for so doing. In the future, at the end of the world, there will be a final victory over the devil, and he shall be cast out to outer darkness forever.

Victory over the grave (Mormon 7:5). *See:* Death is (was) swallowed up in the victory of (in) Christ.

Vineyard of the Lord (2 Nephi 15:7; Alma 28:14). The Lord's vineyard is the earth, and servants of God are the laborers bringing converts unto Christ. *See also:* Fruit(-s) of my (our/their) labors; Labor(-ed) in the vineyard(-s) of the Lord;

What could I have done more in my vineyard.

Virtue of the word of God (Alma 31:5). Meaning by the advantage, benefit, power and authority of the word of God. *See also:* Doctrine of Christ.

Visionary man (1 Nephi 2:11; 5:2, 4). Meaning one who has many visions. Often certain individuals, who do not believe in someone's visions, use this as a derogatory label. *See also:* Imaginations of his heart.

Visit him with fire and with the Holy Ghost (3 Nephi 11:35). *See:* Baptism of fire and of the Holy Ghost.

Visit my people in their afflictions (Mosiah 24:14). *See:* Console you in your afflictions.

Visit them in their iniquities and abominations (Mosiah 12:1; Ether 14:25). *See:* Visit them (this people) in my anger.

Visit them (this people) in my anger (Mosiah 11:20; 12:1; Alma 8:29; 9:12; 33:10; Helaman 13:10). God is a God of body, parts, and passions, including the passion of anger. He loves His children, but by rebelling against Him and breaking His commandments continually we can invoke His anger against us. In God's mercy He admonishes us to come unto Him and He provides us a window of mortal probation in which to repent (see 2 Nephi 2:21), but if we refuse to heed Him, justice must prevail. The scriptures say in many passages that God's anger will be meted out to us in consequence of our wrongful actions. *See also:* Anger of the Lord; Consequences of sin.

Visit them with a sore curse (Jacob 2:33; Enos 1:10). *See:* Visit them (this people) in my anger.

Visit them with his Spirit (Alma 17:10; Ether 4:11). To be visited by the Spirit is one of the sweetest things we can experience in life. Such a visit should be remembered always and recorded. When the Spirit of God (the Holy Ghost) visits, it bears testimony; brings peace, comfort, and hope; delivers the love of God; grants the gifts of the Spirit; and causes us to be born again. *See also:* Spirit of God; Visited by the power and Spirit of God.

Visit us by angels (Alma 9:21, 25; 24:14; 3 Nephi 7:15). *See:* Angels minister(-ed/appeared/declared/descending) unto him (them).

Visitation of the Holy Ghost (Moroni 8:26). *See:* Visit them with his Spirit.

Visited by the power and Spirit of God (Alma 9:21; 3 Nephi 7:21; 12:2). *See:* Visit them with his Spirit.

Visited of the Lord (2 Nephi 27:2; Mormon 1:15). At the Second Coming of Jesus Christ, all the earth will be visited by Him and see His glory and power together.

Additionally, through the ages righteous men have been visited of the Lord. *See also:* Beheld (behold) his glory; Great and dreadful day of the Lord; Saw Jesus; D&C 93:1.

Visiting the iniquities of the fathers upon the children unto the third and fourth generations (Mosiah 13:13). Children pattern themselves after their parents. It is automatic and a thing of human nature. There also appears to be a Godly curse when it involves sin. This is very unfortunate in the case of evil behavior, because it perpetuates itself. Fortunately some break out of the cycle, particularly if they accept the gospel. On the other hand, if people are true, faithful, and good, the Lord has promised that "inasmuch as he is faithful, I will multiply blessings upon him and his seed after him" (D&C 104:25, 42). *See also:* Generation to (another) generation.

Voice came into my mind (Enos 1:10). *See:* Voice came unto him (me); Voice of the Lord.

Voice came unto him (me) (1 Nephi 16:25–26, 39; 17:7; 18:5; 2 Nephi 31:12, 14; Enos 1:5, 10; Mosiah 24:13, 16; 26:14; Alma 20:2; Helaman 5:29, 32–33, 46, 48; 10:3; 13:3; 3 Nephi 1:12; 10:3; 11:3; Mormon 3:14). *See:* Voice of the Lord.

Voice did pierce them to the center (very soul) (Helaman 5:30; 3 Nephi 11:3). The voice of God, even if conveyed as a small whisper, penetrates the soul of man, because all the elements yield to God's voice. "Yea, thus saith the still small voice, which whispereth through and pierceth all things, and often times it maketh my bones to quake while it maketh manifest" (D&C 85:6). *Compare:* Voice of (was as) thunder.

Voice from the Father (2 Nephi 31:15). The voice from heaven can be from God the Father. *See also:* Voice of the Lord; Voice of the Spirit.

Voice of his (the) angels (1 Nephi 17:45; Mosiah 27:11, 18; Alma 9:29; 10:8, 20–21; 29:1; 36:8; 38:7). God often sends His angels to deliver messages and call men and women to repentance. "The revelations of God which shall come hereafter by the gift and power of the Holy Ghost, the voice of God, or the ministering of angels" (D&C 20:35). *See also:* Angels minister (-ed/appeared/declared/descending) unto him (them).

Voice of one crying from the dust (2 Nephi 26:16; 33:13). *See:* Cry from the dust.

Voice of the Good Shepherd (Alma 5:37–38, 41, 57, 60; Helaman 7:18; 3 Nephi 15:17, 21; 16:3). The true followers of Christ, meaning the sheep of His fold, know the Good Shepherd's voice and follow His voice. *See also:* Good Shepherd; Voice of the Lord.

Voice of the Lord (1 Nephi 16:9, 25–26, 39; 17:7; 18:5; Enos 1:10; Mosiah 16:2; 24:16; 26:14; Alma 5:16; 9:21; 20:2; Helaman 13:3; 3 Nephi 1:12; Mormon 3:14; Ether 11:7). If we worthily, diligently, and faithfully seek the word of God and desire to know His mind and will, He will of a surety reveal it unto us. Elder Neal A. Maxwell said, "Most revelation comes in the following manner: [The Lord said] 'I will tell you in your mind and in your heart, by the Holy Ghost' (D&C 8:2). Now as you and I liken that scripture to us, remember that intellect and feelings are involved. When Enos was struggling in the spirit, behold, the voice of the Lord came into his mind (see Enos 1:10). This voice need not pass through the eardrums. Instead the words go directly to our minds, and they are audible and distinct. Sometimes [instead] revelations come by means of feelings, feelings [that are often] without explanations. So whether by words or by feelings, there comes to us an accompanying and reassuring sense of peace. This confirming peace is such a reassuring blessing, to know that it is right and that the Lord directed us" (*Worldwide Leadership Training Meeting Manual, 11 January 2003* [Salt Lake City: The Church of Jesus Christ of Latter-day Saints, 2003], 5). *See also:* Voice came unto him (me).

Voice of the Son (2 Nephi 31:12, 14). The voice from heaven can be from the Father, the Son, or the Holy Ghost. *See also:* Voice from the Father; Voice of the Lord; Voice of the Spirit.

Voice of the Spirit (1 Nephi 4:18; 11:10–11; 22:2; Alma 5:51). The voice from heaven can also be from the Holy Ghost. *See also:* Voice from the Father; Voice of the Lord; Voice of the Son.

Voice of the (this) people (Mosiah 7:9; 22:1; 29:2, 25–27, 29; Alma 2:3–4, 7; 4:16; 10:19; 27:21–22; 46:34; 51:7, 15–16; Helaman 1:5–6, 8, 13; 2:2; 5:2). Meaning the vote and consensus of the people.

Voice of (was as) thunder (1 Nephi 17:45; Mosiah 27:11, 18; Alma 29:2; 36:7; 38:7; Helaman 5:30). At times God and His angel messengers speak with a voice of power and thunder, yet at other times heaven speaks with a still small voice which can pierce the very soul. When heaven speaks with thunder, the very ground shakes, men fall to the ground in fear and trembling, and they are shaken to the very core. *Compare:* Voice did pierce them to the center (very soul).

Wade (wading) through much tribulations (affliction and sorrows) (1 Nephi 17:1; Mosiah 27:28; Alma 7:5; 8:14; 53:15; Helaman 3:34). *See:* After much tribulation; Bear afflictions (with patience).

Wait for him (me) (1 Nephi 21:23; 2 Nephi 6:7, 13). Refers to the people of the Lord who wait and look for the coming of the Messiah their God. *See also:* Wait upon the Lord.

Wait upon the Lord (2 Nephi 18:17). Refers to those who faithfully serve the Lord. Also those who wait faithfully for the Lord's response and blessing, which often does not come in our time but comes in the Lord's own due time. "I waited patiently for the Lord; and he inclined unto me, and heard my cry" (Psalm 40:1). Someone has said, "The Lord's answers are never late but seldom early." *Compare:* Wait for him (me). *See also:* Own due time (of the Lord).

Walk after the commandments which they had received from their Lord (4 Nephi 1:12). *See:* Commandments of God (the Father/the Lord).

Walk after the desires of his (your) own heart (Mosiah 11:2; Helaman 13:27). To follow after one's own desires and wants rather than following the will of God. *See also:* Carnal wills and desires; Their own will and pleasure.

Walk after the holy order of God (Alma 5:54; 7:22). Meaning to walk after the ways of the gospel of Jesus Christ. *See also:* Way of the Lord.

Walk after (in) the pride of your eyes (hearts) (Helaman 13:27; Mormon 8:36). *See:* Pride of their (your) eyes; Pride of their (your) hearts.

Walk blameless before him (Alma 7:22). Meaning striving greatly to avoid sin and error, and if an error is made to repent of it immediately. *See also:* Walk guiltless before God; Walking with a clear conscience before God.

Walk circumspectly before God (Mosiah 26:37; Helaman 15:5; 16:10). *Circumspectly* means carefully, cautiously, or vigilantly. The opposite meaning is carelessly and recklessly.

Walk guiltless before God (Mosiah 4:26). *See:* Walk blameless before him; Walking with a clear conscience before God.

Walk humbly before the Lord (Ether 6:17, 30). "What doth the Lord require of thee, but to do justly, and to love mercy, and to walk humbly with thy God" (Micah 6:8).

Walk in crooked paths (Alma 7:20). God does not walk in crooked paths (see D&C 3:2).

Walk in his paths (which are straight) (2 Nephi 12:3; Alma 7:9). *See:* Strait and narrow path; Way of the Lord.

Walk in the light of the Lord (2 Nephi 12:5). *See:* Marvelous light of God.

Walk in the path of the low valley (2 Nephi 4:32). Footnote *b* to this verse points to the Topical Guide subject of "Walking with God," thus enjoying the peace and safety that God gives to those who walk humbly in righteousness.

Walk in the paths of righteousness (1 Nephi 16:5). *See:* Paths of righteousness.

Walk in the strait path which leads to life (2 Nephi 33:9). Meaning life eternal. *See also:* Strait and narrow path.

Walk in the way(-s) of the Lord (Mosiah 6:6; 29:43; Alma 25:14; 41:8; Ether 10:2). *See:* Way of the Lord.

Walk in (the ways of) truth (Mosiah 4:15; Helaman 6:34). The word of God is truth and must be followed. We must be seekers of truth, followers of truth, preachers of truth, and examples of truth always. *See also:* God of truth; I am the light and the life (and the truth) of the world; Know the truth; Knowledge of the truth; Walk in (the ways of) truth; Worship in spirit and truth.

Walk in wisdom's paths (Mosiah 2:36; Helaman 12:5). It would be foolish to stray from wisdom's paths. *See also:* Learn wisdom; Wisdom in (of) God (the Lord/the Father).

Walk through the Red Sea on dry ground (Mosiah 7:19). Note that the miracle of Moses parting the Red Sea (by the Lord) also included not walking through a muddy sea bed, but on dry ground (see Exodus 14:16, 22).

Walk uprightly before God (1 Nephi 16:3; Mosiah 18:29; Alma 1:1; 45:24; 53:21; 63:2; Helaman 6:34). To walk uprightly is to walk morally, justly, virtuously, honestly, and truthfully. *See also:* Walk blameless before him; Walk circumspectly before God.

Walk with stretched-forth necks and wanton eyes (2 Nephi 13:16). A stretched-forth neck is holding one's head above others in pride. Wanton eyes are careless, heedless, unjustified, and prideful eyes. *See also:* Walking and mincing as they go, and making a tinkling with their feet.

Walked mournfully before the Lord of Hosts (3 Nephi 24:14). Often individuals look around and see the wicked happy and faring very well in life. These same individuals see the faithful as restricted, weak, and walking through life mournfully, meaning downtrodden, cheerless, and heavyhearted. However, God promises He can discern between the righteous and the wicked, and He promises the righteous are recorded in the book of life and will enjoy eternal happiness.

Walking and mincing as they go, and making a tinkling with their feet (2 Nephi 13:16). Wealthy, haughty, prideful, and fashionable women who scorn, ignore, and persecute the poor as they strut and parade along in expensive clothing and ornaments. *See also:* Walk with stretched-forth necks and wanton eyes.

Walking circumspectly before God (Mosiah 26:37; Helaman 16:10). *See:* Walk circumspectly before God.

Walking in all diligence (Mosiah 26:38). Meaning to walk before God with fervor, determination, and devotion. *See also:* Walk blameless before him.

Walking in his ways and keeping his commandments (Mosiah 23:14). *See:* Commandments of God (the Father/the Lord); Way of the Lord.

Walking uprightly before God (Alma 1:1). *See:* Walk uprightly before God.

Walking with a clear conscience before God (Mosiah 2:27). *Compare:* Not be ashamed. *See:* Walk blameless before him; Walk guiltless before God.

Wanderers in a strange land (Jacob 7:26; Alma 13:23; Alma 26:36). Refers to the Nephites being a branch of Joseph that has grown over the wall. They live in a land far away from the main branch of Israel.

The phrase is also a metaphor describing the Saints of God who strive to live the gospel in a wicked and corrupt world (see Psalm 119:19). In other words, it refers to our life's sojourn here on earth. To the Saints of God, our life's probation takes place in a strange place very unlike the godliness for which we strive. *Compare:* 1 Nephi 8:23, 32.

Wanton eyes (2 Nephi 13:16). *See:* Walk with stretched-forth necks and wanton eyes.

Warned of the Lord (2 Nephi 5:5–6; Alma 48:15; Omni 1:12; Mosiah 16:12; 23:1; Ether 9:3). The Lord God always warns the people of impending destruction if they do not repent. "Surely the Lord God will do nothing, but he revealeth his secret unto his servants the prophets"

(Amos 3:7). One of the callings of prophets is to warn the people. The Lord also warns individuals and groups of danger.

Warnings and revelations of God (2 Nephi 5:6). *See:* Warned of the Lord.

Warred a good warfare (Alma 1:1). Similar statement to Paul's "I have fought a good fight, I have finished my course, I have kept the faith" (2 Timothy 4:7). In reality the war against Satan began in the pre-mortal existence and continues throughout our lives. We each must fight against sin and darkness to promote righteousness and stay faithful to God.

Wars and rumors of wars (1 Nephi 12:21; 14:15–16; 2 Nephi 25:12; Mormon 8:30). Many wars and the news of wars have occurred throughout the history of the earth. Those prophesies both have come to pass and are yet to come to pass as the end of the world approaches (see D&C 45:26; Joseph Smith–Matthew 1:23, 28).

Washed bright through the blood of the Son of God (Alma 24:13). *See:* Garments cleansed through the blood of the Lamb (made white/washed).

Washed from your sins (Alma 7:14). If we have truly repented, then when we are baptized our sins are washed from us (see Acts 22:16;

D&C 39:10). *See also:* Waters of baptism.

Washed their garments in my (the) blood (of the Lamb) (Alma 5:21; 13:11; 3 Nephi 27:19; Ether 13:11). *See:* Garments cleansed through the blood of the Lamb (made white/washed).

Washed white through the blood of the Lamb (Alma 5:21; 13:11). *See:* Atoning blood of Jesus Christ; Garments cleansed through the blood of the Lamb (made white/ washed).

Waste places (1 Nephi 21:19; 2 Nephi 8:3; 15:17; Mosiah 12:23; 15:30; Helaman 11:20; 3 Nephi 16:19; 20:34). The Lord has promised that the waste places, deserts, and other destroyed and unusable lands will in His own time be watered gardens and as the Garden of Eden. *See also:* Ye waste places of Jerusalem.

Wasteth the days of his probation (2 Nephi 9:27). "Nevertheless there was a space [a time] granted unto man in which he might repent; therefore this life became a probationary state; a time to prepare to meet God; a time to prepare for that endless state which has been spoken of by us, which is after the resurrection of the dead" (Alma 12:24). *See also:* Everlastingly too late; Probationary state (time).

Watch for iniquity (2 Nephi 27:31). Meaning those that seek and desire iniquity. *See also:* Imagine up foolish and vain things in their hearts.

Watch over the church (the people) (Mosiah 23:18; Alma 5:59; 6:1). To care for, protect, nourish, and foster the people. This is the calling and mandate of leaders, but it is also the responsibility of every individual in the group to care for his neighbor.

Watch(-ing) and pray(-ing) always (continually) (Alma 13:28; 15:17; 34:39; 3 Nephi 18:15, 18; Moroni 6:4). *Watch* here means to be mindful of and guard against evil and temptation. Pray also for protection and strength against Satan the devil.

Watchmen shall lift up their voice (Mosiah 12:22; 15:29; 3 Nephi 16:18; 20:32). Usually means the watchmen shall sound the alarm, but in these verses refers to servants of God, the prophets, who shall sing praises and glory at the coming of the Lord and at the culmination of the Lord's salvation for mankind.

Waters of baptism (1 Nephi 20:1; Alma 7:15). The "waters of baptism" is an ordinance that is symbolic of being washed clean. The old and sinful person is buried in the waters and then comes forth out of the waters born to a new life. Both these verses talk about "into the waters" and "out of the waters," thus confirming that immersion or submersion is the proper procedure (see 3 Nephi 11:25–26; D&C 20:73–74). *See also:* Washed from your sins.

Waters of life (Alma 5:34; 42:27). The word of God, the gospel of Jesus Christ, the saving principles and ordinances that bring salvation. *See also:* Bread and the waters of life; Fountain of living waters; Living waters.

Wax in iniquity (Jacob 2:23; Alma 8:28). Meaning to grow or increase in iniquity.

Wax proud (Alma 4:6). Meaning to grow or increase in pride. *See also:* Proud in their (your) hearts; Puffed up.

Wax strong in the Spirit (Mosiah 18:26). To increase in being influenced, instructed, and directed by the Spirit of God.

Wax strong in wickedness (Alma 21:3). Meaning to become exceedingly wicked. *See also:* Wax in iniquity.

Waxed bold (2 Nephi 4:24). Grew bold, increased in intensity.

Wax(-ed) great (in the land) (Mosiah 2:2; 24:7; 3 Nephi 6:4; Ether 7:19). The people grew or increased in size, number, strength, and prosperity.

Wax(-ed) hard (Alma 35:15; Ether 7:8). Meaning to become hardened against and no longer responsive to the things of God. *See also:* Wax in iniquity.

Waxed old (2 Nephi 4:12; Jacob 5:3; Mosiah 1:9). Became very old.

Wax(-ed) strong (Jarom 1:5; Mosiah 9:11; 18:26; 29:40; Alma 9:22; 13:17; 21:3; 50:18; 60:31; 62:48, 51; Helaman 3:35; 6:12; 11:32, 36–37; 3 Nephi 1:29; 2:3; 4 Nephi 1:10, 40; Ether 6:18; 7:8). *To wax* means to grow or increase in size, number, strength, or intensity. Sometimes we hear the expression "to wax and wane," meaning "to increase and then decrease, as the phases of the moon. As the moon waxes and wanes, so does the height of the tide change" (*Cambridge Idioms Dictionary*, s.v. "Wax and wane").

Waxed strong in the knowledge of the truth (Alma 17:2). Increase in the knowledge of truth, "for this is good and acceptable in the sight of God our Saviour; who will have all men to be saved, and to come unto the knowledge of the truth" (1 Timothy 2:3–4).

Way for man is narrow (2 Nephi 9:41; Jacob 6:11; 3 Nephi 14:14; 27:33). *Compare:* Broad roads. *See:* Enter in (into/by) the (narrow/strait) gate (way/path); Narrow is the course (path/way); Strait and narrow path.

Way is prepared (1 Nephi 10:18; 2 Nephi 2:4; Alma 37:46; 41:8). God prepares the way for all His work to be done. Man must have the faith that this is so and forge ahead to do our small part in the grand plan of things. Then we can stand back and see God accomplish all His designs and works. Most significantly is that the plan of salvation is prepared by a loving Heavenly Father and His Son so that we each may be redeemed. *See also:* Place prepared [heaven]; Prepared by (of) the Lord; Prepared from the beginning (foundation of the world); Redemption prepared from the foundation of the world; Which was prepared.

Way of all the earth (2 Nephi 1:14; Mosiah 1:9; Alma 1:1; 62:37; Helaman 1:2). Meaning to die physically. *See also:* Go the way of all the earth; Temporal death.

Way of righteousness (Mosiah 29:23; Alma 5:37; Helaman 6:31). To live the commandments is the way of righteousness. *See also:* Armor of righteousness; Paths of righteousness; Pertaining to righteousness.

Way of the Lord (1 Nephi 13:27; 16:29; 22:14; 2 Nephi 28:15; 29:7; Jarom 1:7; Mosiah 6:6; 12:26; 29:43; Alma 9:28; 10:5; 25:14; 30:22, 60; 31:1, 11; Mormon 6:17; Ether 10:2; Moroni 8:16). Meaning to live fully the gospel, keep the commandments, complete the required ordinances, and love our fellowman. *See also:* His ways; Strait and narrow path; Walk in the light of the Lord.

Way which is narrow (2 Nephi 9:41; Jacob 6:11; 3 Nephi 14:14; 27:33). *See:* Way for man is narrow.

Ways of remembrance (1 Nephi 2:24). To walk in the ways of the Lord and His gospel is to always remember Him and keep His commandments. We must always remember His blessings to us, His tender mercies to us, and His great Atonement in our behalf. *See also:* Remember, remember; Remembrance of the Lord (their God); Stir them up in remembrance of the Lord.

We shall see him as he is (Moroni 7:48). D&C 130:1 says, "We shall see that he is a man like ourselves." Yet He is a glorified man, thus we need to become more like Him. We must also become the sons and daughters of God. We must through the Atonement become pure like He is pure. We must be full of charity like He is—the example of pure love. *See also:* Image of God engraven upon your countenances; Purified even as he is pure; 1 John 3:2; D&C 130:1.

Weak like unto their brethren (Mosiah 1:13; Helaman 4:24; Mormon 2:26). Once the Nephites had fallen into wickedness they became weak like unto the Lamanites, no longer worthy of the Lord's help. *See also:* In the strength of our God (the Lord).

Weakness before thee (shown us/ which is in me) (1 Nephi 19:6; Jacob 4:7; Ether 3:2). Mortal man is full of weakness. We must never forget that because of our weaknesses we need to seek the assistance of God. *See also:* Weakness shall be made strong (mighty).

Weakness in writing (of their words) (2 Nephi 3:21; 33:4, 11; Ether 12:23, 25, 40). The writers of the Book of Mormon often expressed their weakness in putting in words what they desired to write, and the weakness of the languages they used. They therefore prayed that God would make their word mighty to the convincing of men their messages. *See also:* Mighty in writing; Mighty in word.

Weakness shall be made strong (mighty) (2 Nephi 3:13, 21; 33:4; Ether 12:23, 27, 37). *See:* Made strong.

Weakness which is in me according to the flesh (1 Nephi 19:6). Because of our mortal nature, all men on earth have weaknesses and sin, with the exception of Jesus Christ, who never sinned. It is part of the plan of God that we pass through this mortal existence to prove our faith and come to understand good versus evil. The redemption provided by the Savior can cleanse us from our earthly sins and bring us back into the presence of God.

Weaned child shall put his hand on the cockatrice's den (2 Nephi 21:8; 30:14). A cockatrice is a serpent (see Jeremiah 8:17) that is said to have deadly venom (see Bible Dictionary, s.v. "Cockatrice," 647). These two verses talk of the millennium, when there will be no enmity (hate nor hurt) in all the earth. Thus the lion and the lamb shall lie down together, and a cockatrice will not hurt a child.

Wear stiff necks and high heads (2 Nephi 28:14; Jacob 2:13). Putting on haughty and proud pretenses. *See also:* Pride of their (your) eyes; Pride of their (your) hearts; Puffed up.

Wear(-ing) of costly (very fine) apparel (Alma 1:6, 27, 32; 4:6; 5:53; 31:28; Helaman 13:28; 4 Nephi 1:24; Mormon 8:36–37). Apparently costly apparel (fine linens, expensive colors, and gold jewelry) was a marker of pride in Book of Mormon peoples. *See also:* Costly apparel.

Weeping and wailing and gnashing of teeth (Alma 40:13). The state of the wicked in the afterlife: grinding of teeth, lamenting, grief, misery, mourning, regret, and sobbing.

Weighed down with sorrow (2 Nephi 1:17; Jacob 2:3; Alma 8:14). The wickedness of the world has often made the prophets sorrowful. *See also:* Anxiety for you.

Welfare of my brethren (your souls) (2 Nephi 2:30; 6:3; 32:9; Jacob 2:3; Enos 1:9; Mosiah 25:11; Alma 6:6; 60:10; Moroni 6:5). *See:* Anxiety for you.

Welfare of Zion (2 Nephi 26:29). We should be willing to give all for the welfare of Zion and the building of the kingdom of God (the Church). *See also:* Bring again (forth) Zion.

Well Beloved (Helaman 5:47). A name given to Jesus Christ, who is the Beloved Son of the Father.

Well nigh consumeth me (2 Nephi 26:7). *See:* Consuming of my flesh.

What could I have done more in my vineyard (2 Nephi 15:4; Jacob 5:41, 47, 49). *See:* Vineyard of the Lord.

Whatsoever is good cometh from God (Alma 5:40; Ether 4:12; Moroni 10:6). All good things come from God. *See also:* Good cometh from (of) God.

Whatsoever is light is good (Alma 32:35). All light originates and emanates from God. *See also:* Light of Christ; Marvelous light of God.

Whatsoever thing ye shall ask (which is right) (Enos 1:15; Mosiah 4:21; Alma 7:23; 3 Nephi 18:20; Mormon 9:21; Moroni 7:26, 33). "Ask, and ye shall receive; knock, and it shall be opened unto you; for he that asketh, receiveth; and unto him that knocketh, it shall be opened" (3 Nephi 27:29). However, we must ask for that which is right, ask not amiss, having faith, and according to the will of God. *See also:* Believing that ye shall receive.

Whatsoever thing ye shall do ye shall do it in my name (3 Nephi 27:7, 9, 28). *See:* In his (thy) name; In my name; In the name of Jesus (Christ/the Lord God).

Whatsoever thing ye stand in need (Alma 7:23; Mormon 9:27). God is mindful of each of us and our needs. He has commanded us to ask according to our needs, and if it be according to His will, He will grant it. However, many of our wants we mistake for our needs, and thus they might not be the best thing for us.

Whatsoever things the Lord put into his heart (Helaman 13:3–4). By the Spirit, God can put into our hearts and minds those things we should teach. *See also:* Giveth utterance; Loose his (their) tongue(-s).

Whatsoever ye shall seal on earth shall be sealed in heaven (Helaman 10:7). "Verily, verily, I say unto you, that whatsoever you seal on earth shall be sealed in heaven; and whatsoever you bind on earth, in my name and by my word, saith the Lord, it shall be eternally bound in the heavens" (D&C 132:46). God has given this power to various persons at various times throughout the history of mankind. *See also:* Matthew 16:19; 18:18.

When my mortal shall put on immortality (Enos 1:27). *See:* Resurrection of the body.

When the Lord shall bring again Zion (Mosiah 12:22; 15:29; 3 Nephi 16:18). *See:* Bring again (forth) Zion.

When the Lord shall see fit in his wisdom (3 Nephi 28:29; 29:1; Mormon 5:13). *See:* Wisdom in (of) God (the Lord/the Father); Own due time (of the Lord).

When the night cometh (Alma 41:5). Meaning when we die and our physical bodies sleep in the earth for a time.

Where there is no law given (2 Nephi 9:25). *See:* No law given.

Which was prepared (1 Nephi 15:29; 2 Nephi 5:12; 9:18; Mosiah 1:16; 4:7; 15:19; Alma 13:3, 5; 18:39; 22:13; 37:39, 46; Ether 3:14). *See:* Way is prepared.

While the world shall stand (3 Nephi 28:9). Meaning until the mortal existence of the world is over and Jesus Christ comes again in His glory (see 3 Nephi 28:7, 8; John 21:23). Thus while the world shall stand is until the beginning of the millennium. *See also:* D&C 38:20.

White above all that is white (1 Nephi 8:11; 11:8; Alma 32:42; 3 Nephi 19:25). Heavenly beings are described as wearing extremely white clothing. Additionally, it is by the great gift of the Atonement that we can be made white, even exceedingly white. Jesus paid for our sins, and though our sins be as red, our garments can be made white through the blood of the Lamb. *Compare:* Isaiah 1:18; Matthew 17:2; 28:3; Mark 9:3; Luke 9:29; Revelation 1:13–14; 1 Nephi 8:10–12; 11:8; 3 Nephi 19:30; D&C 20:6; Joseph Smith–History 1:32. *See also:* Alma 5:21; 13:11–12.

White and exceedingly fair and beautiful (1 Nephi 11:13; 13:15; 2 Nephi 5:21; 3 Nephi 2:15; Mormon 9:6). Righteous people are often described with these words in the scriptures. As we repent and come unto Christ, we can be cleansed by the blood of the Lamb and our countenances become white and pure. *See also:* White above all that is white.

White as the countenance and also the garments of Jesus (3 Nephi 19:25). *See:* White above all that is white.

White robe (1 Nephi 8:5; 14:19; 3 Nephi 11:8). It appears that heavenly beings dress in white, for all descriptions in the scriptures so describe their clothing. *Compare:* John 20:12; Acts 1:10. *See also:* White above all that is white.

White to exceed all the whiteness that I had ever seen (1 Nephi 8:11). *See:* White above all that is white.

Whiteness beyond (exceeded) (1 Nephi 8:11; 11:8; 3 Nephi 19:25). *See:* White above all that is white.

Who can comprehend the marvelous works of God (Mosiah 4:9; Mormon 9:16). God has all wisdom and power. Man cannot comprehend all the infinite things the Lord can comprehend. *See also:* Job 3:5.

Who can glory too much in the Lord (Alma 26:16). A rhetorical question, for there is no such thing as too much praise and glory for the Lord Jesus Christ, our Savior and Redeemer.

Who is God (the Almighty/the Holy One of Israel/the Lord/ the very Eternal Father) (1 Nephi 20:2; 2 Nephi 30:2; Omni 1:26; Mosiah 5:15; 11:27; 16:15; Alma 9:6; Helaman 10:11; 3 Nephi 5:26). Used in two ways: (1) as a question, "Who is the Lord?" or (2) as a declaration of reality, "He who is the Lord/God!"

Who is mighty to save (2 Nephi 31:19; Alma 7:14; 34:18). *See:* Mighty to save.

Who shall declare his generation (Mosiah 14:8; 15:10). Meaning who shall proclaim and witness: (1) the generation from which He comes, the divine heritage as Son of God; (2) the generation that Jesus walked among during His earthly mission in Jerusalem; or finally (3) the generation of His redeemed followers, who are the spiritually begotten sons and daughters of Christ.

Who should come (1 Nephi 10:11, 17; Jacob 7:3; Mosiah 4:3; Alma 4:13; 5:21; 6:8; 46:15; Helaman 8:14). Meaning He, Christ, will come. *See also:* Coming of Christ.

Whore of all the earth (who sat upon many waters) (1 Nephi 14:10–12; 22:13; 2 Nephi 10:16; 28:18). Another name for the great and abominable church, because not only do they participate in wickedness, but they feign righteousness and thus are hypocrites. "They that fighteth against Zion. . . are the whore of all the earth; for they who are not for me are against me, saith our God" (2 Nephi 10:16). *See also:* Great and abominable church; Great whore.

Whoredoms are an abomination (Jacob 2:28). *See:* Commit(-ting) whoredoms.

Whose shoe's latchet I am not worthy to unloose (1 Nephi 10:8). John the Baptist's statement indicating his lowly and humble status compared to the Lord Jesus. *Compare:* Mark 1:7; Luke 3:16; John 1:27.

Whoso believeth (3 Nephi 11:33–35; Mormon 9:21; Ether 12:4). Meaning those who believe, who will be blessed in various ways.

Wicked and abominable traditions of their fathers (Alma 23:3; 24:7; 47:36; Helaman 5:19; 15:7). *See:* Traditions of our (their/your) fathers.

Wicked and perverse generation (people) (Alma 9:8; 10:17, 25; 31:24; Helaman 13:29; Mormon 8:33). *Perverse* means disobedient and wayward. This scriptural phrase is generally used as a salutation that judges an audience and calls them to repentance.

Wicked combinations (3 Nephi 5:6; Ether 11:7). *See:* Secret combination(-s).

Wicked destroyed (1 Nephi 17:43; 2 Nephi 30:10; Omni 1:5; Helaman 6:37; 11:11). The scriptures attest that at various times in the past God has destroyed the wicked, and He will again in the future destroy them. *See also:* Burn as stubble; Wicked shall perish.

Wicked shall perish (2 Nephi 13:11; 23:22; 26:3). They shall perish, for the Lord has declared it. *See also:* Wicked destroyed.

Wickedness never was happiness (Alma 41:10; Helaman 13:38; Mormon 2:13). This is an eternal law and principle stated by the prophet Alma. President Ezra Taft Benson said, "You cannot do wrong and feel right. It is impossible" ("To the Rising Generation," 5). Also he said, "Wickedness never did, never does, never will bring us happiness. Violation of the laws of God brings only misery, bondage, and darkness" (*Teachings of Ezra Taft Benson*, 71). However, the world and Satan teach that there is happiness in being wicked, edgy, rebellious, and defiant. Fun in the worldly sense is not joy or true happiness. Yet sin is often enticing; otherwise there would be no true choice. Enticing sin is how Satan ensnares people, but Satan's true design is to make us miserable like unto him (2 Nephi 2:27). *See also:* Despair cometh because of iniquity; Take happiness in iniquity (sin).

Wickedness of your hearts (Jacob 2:6; Alma 10:6). Genesis 6:5 says, "And God saw that the wickedness of man was great in the earth, and that every imagination of the thoughts of his heart was only evil continually." In Jeremiah 4:14, "Wash thine heart from wickedness, that thou mayest be saved." In Acts 8:22, "Repent therefore of this thy wickedness, and pray God, if perhaps the thought of thine heart may be forgiven thee." *See also:* Hardness of heart.

Wiles of the devil (Helaman 3:29). Clever and crafty tricks of the devil to deceive men and women, that he might ensnare them. *See also:* Deceived by the devil; Ephesians 6:11.

Will be done (2 Nephi 1:19; 3 Nephi 13:10; Ether 12:29). To do the will of God should always be our intent, our true desire, and our prayer. *See also:* Will of God.

Will of God (2 Nephi 2:21; 10:24; 27:13; Mosiah 3:11; Alma 32:19; 3 Nephi 5:14; 6:18). The will of God is perfect, is preeminent (superior over all), and is not capricious (changing and erratic). Additionally, God has the power to do all that He wills, but He honors agency. *See also:* According to God's will; According to the will of God (the Lord); His holy will; My will; Reconcile yourselves to the will of God; Subjected the flesh to the will of the Father; Will be done; Will of his Holy Spirit; Will of my (the) Father; Will of the Lord; Will of the Son being swallowed up in the will of the Father.

Will of his Holy Spirit (2 Nephi 2:28). The will of the Holy Ghost would be the same as the will of God the Father and of His Son, because they are all one and united in their will. *See also:* Will of God.

Will of my (the) Father (Mosiah 15:2, 7; 3 Nephi 11:11; 14:21; 23:4; 27:13; 28:7). Jesus always did the will of God the Father, and likewise we should always seek to do the will of our Heavenly Father. As we try to do the Father's will He changes us, and we begin to have a change of heart. *See also:* Will of God.

Will of the Lord (Mosiah 24:15; Alma 14:13; Ether 15:34; Moroni 1:4). We should equally do the will of the Lord Jesus Christ and the will of God the Father, for they are one and are not divided in their intents and desires. *See also:* Will of God.

Will of the Son being swallowed up in the will of the Father (Mosiah 15:7). Meaning the will of the Son was and is always encompassed about by, superseded by, and obedient to the will of the Father. *See also:* Subjected the flesh to the will of the Father; Suffered the will of the Father in all things.

Will remember (1 Nephi 19:15–16; 3 Nephi 16:11–12; 20:29; 29:3; Mormon 5:21; 8:23). Scriptural testimony that God will remember all that He has promised. *See also:* According to God's word.

Willfully rebel(-led/against God) (Mosiah 15:26; 3 Nephi 6:18; 4 Nephi 1:38; Mormon 1:16). A particularly heinous sin, because the person knows God's commands and has been taught the right, but chooses to ignore it and do evil. *See also:* Rebel(-led/-ling/-lion) against God.

Willing to bear my name (2 Nephi 31:13; Mosiah 26:18; Moroni 4:3). *See:* Bear my name.

Wilt thou give me strength (1 Nephi 7:17; Alma 31:30, 32). We must pray, "Dear God, give me strength to overcome the temptations of this world." Also we must ask for physical strength to endure and to accomplish His will. *See also:* Lord did strengthen them.

Wings of his Spirit (2 Nephi 4:25). *See:* Upon the wings of his Spirit.

Wisdom in (of) God (the Lord/ the Father) (1 Nephi 3:19; 5:22; 2 Nephi 2:12; 9:8; Mosiah 4:6, 9; 5:15; Alma 26:29, 35; 37:8, 12; 3 Nephi 21:4; 26:2; 28:29; Ether 5:1; 8:23; Moroni 10:3). God has all and complete wisdom and knowledge. There is no wisdom and knowledge that He does not possess. There is no being that has greater knowledge and wisdom. *See also:* All wisdom; All-wise Creator; Counsel in wisdom; For a wise purpose; In mine (my) wisdom; Learn wisdom; Lord doth (will) counsel in wisdom; Power and wisdom of God; See fit in his wisdom; Wise purpose.

Wisdom of the world (1 Nephi 11:35; Mosiah 24:7; Alma 2:1). Meaning the finite learning and craft of men. "O the vainness, and the frailties, and the foolishness of men! When they are learned they think they are wise, and they hearken not unto the counsel of God, for they set it aside, supposing they know of themselves, wherefore, their wisdom is foolishness and it profiteth them not. And they shall perish. But to be learned is good if they hearken unto the counsels of God" (2 Nephi 9:28–29). "Ofttimes the wisdom of God appears as foolishness to men, but the greatest single lesson we can learn in mortality is that, when God speaks and a man obeys, [that] man will always be right" (Monson, "The Call of Duty," 37).

Wisdom of their wise and learned shall perish (2 Nephi 9:28; 27:26). *See:* Understanding of their prudent shall be hid; Wisdom of the world.

Wisdom's paths (Mosiah 2:36; Helaman 12:5). It would be wise to walk in wisdom's paths. *See also:* In mine (my) wisdom; Learn wisdom; Lord doth (will) counsel in wisdom.

Wise purpose (1 Nephi 9:5; Words of Mormon 1:7; Alma 37:2, 12, 14, 18). Because of His all-encompassing knowledge and perfect wisdom, God causes the most correct events and circumstances to transpire. *See also:* Wisdom in (of) God (the Lord/the Father).

Wist not (Helaman 9:30; 3 Nephi 11:8). Meaning understand or understood not. For example, when Mary and Joseph found the twelve-year-old Jesus discussing with the doctors in the temple and Mary questioned why he was there, Jesus said, "Wist ye not [understand ye not] that I must be about my Father's business?" (Luke 2:49).

With all diligence (your [their] might) (1 Nephi 16:4; 2 Nephi 6:3; 25:29; Jacob 1:19; 5:74; 7:25; Enos 1:12; Words of Mormon 1:18; Mosiah 2:11; 7:33; 29:14; Alma 21:23; 39:13; 51:9; 3 Nephi 5:3; 6:14; Moroni 7:48; 10:32). *See:* All your might, mind, and strength.

With all his heart (my soul) (1 Nephi 1:5; 15:25; Mosiah 21:35; Alma 45:7; Mormon 3:12; 9:27; Moroni 7:48). With all of one's heart, might, mind, and strength; to desire greatly in one's heart; to put forth a mighty effort.

With all the energy of heart (Moroni 7:48). *See:* With all his heart (my soul).

With all the faculty which I possessed (1 Nephi 15:25; Words of Mormon 1:18). To do with all ability, talent, strength, and aptitude one has. *See also:* With all his heart (my soul).

With an oath (1 Nephi 4:33; Mosiah 20:24; Alma 44:11; 48:13; 49:13, 17, 27; 50:39; 3 Nephi 3:8). *See:* Made an oath unto us.

With exactness (Alma 57:21). Being very careful to observe and keep every word their mothers taught them, therefore they lived the word of God precisely.

With fear and trembling before God (Alma 34:37; Mormon 9:27). If we are serious about obtaining salvation, then we are very concerned about doing what is required. We should fear that we may err and leave the correct path. We surely will shudder at the thought of not reaching the goal of exaltation.

With his rod (1 Nephi 17:41). Meaning God would use methods of correction to urge us back onto the path. *See also:* Famine(-s) and pestilence(-s); Rod of his mouth and with the breath of his lips.

With his stripes we are healed (Mosiah 14:5). Jesus suffered for our sins that we might be redeemed or healed. "His stripes" are descriptive words of Christ vicariously receiving a beating or whipping for the sins of mankind. *Compare:* Isaiah 53:5; 1 Peter 2:24.

With one eye (Mosiah 18:21). Meaning believing the same in perfect unity. Same as "in one mind and in one heart" (2 Nephi 1:21).

With power and authority (Words of Mormon 1:17; Mosiah 13:6; 18:26; Alma 17:3; Helaman 5:18; 6:5; 3 Nephi 7:17). *See:* Minister with power and great authority.

With power being filled with the Spirit (1 Nephi 2:14; 2 Nephi 1:27; Mosiah 18:26; Alma 8:32; 17:3; 18:35; 23:6; Helaman 10:16; 3 Nephi 7:21; Moroni 6:9; 8:28). Being filled with the Spirit often brings great power. *See also:* Filled with the Spirit (of God/the Lord).

With unwearyingness (Helaman 10:4–5). *See:* Unwearied diligence.

Within (without) the veil (Ether 3:19–20; 12:19, 21). When we came to earth a veil was placed over our memory so that we could not see the presence of God. This is necessary for the development of our faith, for if we could always see into the heavens, there would be no need for faith in God our Father, and His Son, Jesus Christ. Some have had the opportunity to see through the veil, such as the brother of Jared in these verses from Ether. In D&C 110:1, Joseph Smith said, "The veil was taken from our minds, and the eyes of our understanding were opened." *See also:* Perfect faith.

Without any respect to persons (Alma 1:30; 16:14). Freely giving of their means to those in need without judging them as to whether or not they deserved to receive. *See also:* Liberal to all; Poor and needy.

Without beginning of days or end of years (Alma 13:7–9). Meaning to have existed from all eternity and to all eternity. Always has existed and will ever exist. *See also:* From (all) eternity to all eternity.

Without end (2 Nephi 31:21). Meaning God is infinite—without end and eternal. He will always be God, and it will be so forever.

Without faith (Mormon 3:12; Moroni 7:42). "Remember that without faith you can do nothing" (D&C 8:10). Meaning to not believe. Faith is a very important element and principle in our lives. Without faith there would be no work done, no hope, no salvation, and no joy.

Without God in the world (Mosiah 27:31; Alma 41:11; Mormon 5:16). Also in Ephesians 2:12. Living without believing in God. Thus such keep not the commandments of God, and live in carnal and wicked ways. These heed not the call to repentance, heed not the invitation to follow Christ, and heed not the chance to change their evil ways and instead do good.

Without hope (Mormon 5:2; Moroni 7:42). "And if ye have no hope ye must needs be in despair;

and despair cometh because of iniquity" (Moroni 10:22).

Without money and without price (2 Nephi 9:50; 26:25; Alma 1:20). *See:* Buy milk and honey, without money and without price.

Without spot (Moroni 10:33). *See:* Stand spotless before me at the last day.

Withstand every temptation of the devil with their faith on the Lord Jesus Christ (Alma 37:33). *See:* Yield to no temptation.

Witness it (1 Nephi 11:7; Jacob 7:21; Alma 30:44; Helaman 15:7; 3 Nephi 7:20; 10:1, 3; 18:24; 19:14; Mormon 3:16). It is important to God and to people that certain things are witnessed to establish the truth of persons, events, and things. *See also:* Testimony of many (two or three).

Witness of me and the Father (2 Nephi 31:18; 3 Nephi 16:6). The Holy Ghost testifies of the Father and the Son. *See also:* D&C 20:27; 42:17; Moses 1:24; 5:9; 7:11.

Witnessed unto God (the church) (2 Nephi 31:14; Alma 7:15; Moroni 6:2). *See:* Baptized as a witness and a testimony.

Witnesses of the Father and the Son (2 Nephi 31:18; 3 Nephi 16:6). *See:* Witness of me and the Father.

Wo unto him (me/them/this people) (1 Nephi 1:13; 14:6; 2 Nephi 9:27, 30–38; 13:9, 11; 15:8, 11, 18, 20–22; 20:1; 25:14; 27:14, 27; 28:15, 16, 24–29, 32; Jacob 3:3; Mosiah 3:12; 4:23; 11:20; 12:2, 26; Alma 5:31, 32; Helaman 7:22, 25, 26, 27; 12:22; 13:11–16; Helaman 13:24; 15:2, 3; 3 Nephi 9:2; 18:33; 21:14; 28:24; 29:5–7; Mormon 8:31; Ether 8:24; Moroni 7:37; 8:16, 21; 9:15; 10:25, 26, 28). Meaning grief, suffering, calamity, and misfortune upon those on whom God pronounces it in consequence of their sins and wickedness.

Word is in Christ unto salvation (Alma 34:6). Meaning faith in Christ unto salvation. *See also:* Salvation of our (their) souls; Salvation of the Lord (our God).

Word might be fulfilled (Alma 7:11). Meaning events took place to fulfill the word of God as delivered by the prophets. *See also:* According to God's word; John 15:25.

Word of Christ (2 Nephi 31:19–20; 32:3; 33:10–11; Jacob 6:8; Alma 37:44–45; 3 Nephi 28:23, 33–34; 29:7; 30:1; Moroni 2:1; 7:31, 38; 8:8; 10:26). "As the Liahona guided the Nephites, so the word of Christ leads men to eternal life" (Alma 37, chapter heading). Nephi said, "The words of Christ will tell you all things what you should do" (2 Nephi 32:3). The message of the gospel, the teachings of Jesus Christ, the words spoken by the holy prophets, and the written words of the scriptures (2 Nephi 25:22), all which are given for the benefit and salvation of men. "And the words which he [Christ] shall speak unto you shall be the law which ye shall do" (2 Nephi 26:1). They "that will not hearken unto the words of Jesus, and also to them whom he hath chosen and sent among them; for whoso receiveth not the words of Jesus and the words of those whom he hath sent receiveth not him; and therefore he will not receive them at the last day" (3 Nephi 28:34). *See also:* Doctrine of Christ; Word of God.

Word of God (1 Nephi 11:25; 15:24; 17:35; 2 Nephi 27:14; 28:29; Jacob 2:8; 3:9; 6:7; Jarom 1:10; Words of Mormon 1:11, 17; Mosiah 13:4; 25:20; 26:3, 38–39; 28:1; Alma 1:7, 9, 15, 20, 26; 3:14, 18; 4:19; 5:1, 11, 57–58; 6:5, 8; 8:23, 30; 12:26; 14:8; 15:16; 16:14, 21; 17:2, 4, 8, 18; 21:16; 23:1, 4; 30:32; 31:5, 8; 32:1, 16; 42:5; 44:5; 45:21; 48:19; 53:10; 60:34–35; 62:44, 45; Helaman 3:29; 5:4; 6:37; 7:2; 10:17; 3 Nephi 5:4; 28:20; Mormon 8:16, 33; Moroni 6:4; 7:5; 8:9; 9:4). The word of God consists of the scriptures and the inspired words of the living prophets. The word of God also includes the inspiration that comes to us through the Holy Ghost. It is the wisdom of God and the doctrine of Jesus Christ that we should seek and heed. The sons of Mosiah "were men of a sound understanding and they had searched the scriptures diligently, that they might know the word of God" (Alma 17:2). The Lord has commanded that His servants

"establish my [God's] word" (Alma 17:11). Alma 31:5 says, "And now, as the preaching of the word had a great tendency to lead the people to do that which is just—yea, it had had more powerful effect upon the minds of the people than the sword, or anything else, which had happened unto them—therefore Alma thought it was expedient that they should try the virtue of the word of God." Nephi said, "Whoso would hearken unto the word of God, and would hold fast unto it, they would never perish; neither could the temptations and the fiery darts of the adversary overpower them unto blindness, to lead them away to destruction" (1 Nephi 15:24). "The word of God is the doctrine taught by Jesus Christ and by His prophets. . . . [It] can open the minds of people to see spiritual things not visible to the natural eye. And [it] can open hearts to feelings of the love of God and a love for truth" (Eyring, "Teaching True Doctrine," 5). *See also:* Word of Christ; Word of the Lord.

Word of God must be fulfilled (Alma 5:58; 3 Nephi 1:25; 5:1; Mormon 8:33). *See:* According to God's word.

Word of God (prophets/the Lord) has been (was/were) fulfilled (verified) (1 Nephi 7:13; 2 Nephi 5:19–20; Jarom 1:9; Omni 1:6; Mosiah 20:21; 21:4; Alma 3:14; 5:57–58; 7:11; 9:14; 13:26; 25:12, 17; 37:24, 26; 45:9; 50:19, 21; Helaman 11:8;

16:13; 3 Nephi 1:5–6, 15, 25; 5:1; 16:17; 20:11; 23:10; 29:1–2; Mormon 8:33; Ether 15:3, 33). *See: According to God's word.*

Word of God sunk deep in my heart (Enos 1:3). The words of his father concerning the gospel of Jesus Christ were seriously considered at this time by Enos, and he prayed for confirmation, testimony, and the welfare of his soul. This experience is similar to Alma the Younger's found in Alma 36:17.

Word of the angel (1 Nephi 12:19; 14:27; 2 Nephi 25:19). Meaning according to the word of an angel this will be the case. Angels are sent by God to the prophets to inform them of events that will take place in the future. *See also:* Angels minister(-ed/appeared/declared/descending) unto him (them).

Word of the Lord (1 Nephi 2:3; 7:9, 13; 10:13; 15:25; 17:23; 18:4; 2 Nephi 5:20; 12:3; 18:1; Jacob 2:4, 27; 5:10; Jarom 1:9; Mosiah 11:29; 18:32; 20:21; 21:4; 26:34; Alma 9:14; 19:36; 43:24; Helaman 10:12, 14; 13:26, 31, 36; 4 Nephi 1:12; Mormon 9:27; Ether 1:33; 4:8; 13:20; 14:24; Moroni 8:7). The word of the Lord is supreme to all others. The word of the Lord is truth, is eternal, is always fulfilled, is pleasing to the righteous, is to be obeyed, is to be preached to all the world, is the gospel of Jesus Christ, is to be remembered and cherished, is found in the scriptures and the words of the prophets, and is to be reverenced and glorified. *See also:* Word of Christ.

Words fulfilled which he prophesied (Mosiah 20:21; Helaman 16:13; 3 Nephi 1:15; 23:10; Ether 15:3). *See: According to God's word.*

Words of Isaiah (1 Nephi 15:20; 2 Nephi 6:4–5; 11:2, 8; 25:1, 4–5; 3 Nephi 16:17; 20:11; 23:1). We are commanded of the Lord to search diligently the words of Isaiah, for great are the words of Isaiah, and they shall all be fulfilled.

Words of the book (2 Nephi 3:23; 27:6, 9, 11, 14–15, 19, 22, 29; 30:3). Prophecy concerning the coming forth of the Book of Mormon in the latter days.

Words of the book which were sealed (2 Nephi 26:17; 27:7, 8, 10–11, 15, 17, 21). *See:* Seal (them) up; Sealed up.

Words of the Lamb (1 Nephi 13:41; 2 Nephi 33:14). The Lamb of God is Jesus Christ. *See also:* Word of Christ.

Words of the prophets (1 Nephi 2:13; 3:18, 20; 2 Nephi 25:19; 26:8; Jacob 6:8; Mosiah 15:11; Helaman 16:13; 3 Nephi 1:16, 20, 26; 5:1–2; 16:17; 29:2; Ether 9:29; 11:22; 15:3). The words of the prophets have been given from God for the prophets to deliver unto men. Thus they are significant. *See also:* Word of Christ; Word of God; Word of the Lord.

Words of your Maker (2 Nephi 9:40). Meaning the words of God our Maker. *See also:* Word of God.

Words of your seed (2 Nephi 29:2). Meaning the words or writings of Nephi's posterity, which would be recorded in the Book of Mormon.

Words shall condemn you (2 Nephi 33:14). The words of the prophets, scriptures, and God that we know of and do not abide by will condemn us on the judgment day. We must not rebel against or ignore the warning words given us.

Words which cannot be uttered by man (Helaman 5:33; 3 Nephi 19:34). *See:* Unspeakable things.

Words which had (hath/have) been spoken (1 Nephi 2:16; 3:20; 15:7; 2 Nephi 3:25; 6:5; 9:51; 25:1, 28; 30:1, 3; Jacob 6:8; Mosiah 3:22–23; 4:3; 5:1–2, 6; 11:27; 17:2, 4, 8–9; 21:30; Alma 5:47, 61; 10:25; 14:6–7; 20:27; 35:4, 6; 37:32; 40:15; 45:5; Helaman 8:13; 9:2, 4; 11:8; 14:10; 3 Nephi 1:15; 11:41; 13:25; 19:8; 26:8; 29:3; Ether 15:1, 3). Meaning the holy word of God which had been spoken and/or recorded. *See also:* According to God's word; Word of Christ; Word of God; Word of the Lord.

Words which were not understood (Alma 19:32). The born-again queen either spoke in tongues or spoke of things too great to be understood by carnal men and women. *See also:* Unspeakable things.

Words will condemn us (Alma 12:14). According to this verse our words, our works, and even our thoughts will be judged. We must become changed and strive with our might to possess only good words, works and thoughts.

Work in (of) darkness (2 Nephi 30:17; Alma 37:22; Helaman 6:29). *See:* Works of darkness.

Work of destruction (Alma 27:4; 38:7; Helaman 11:2, 5–6, 28; Ether 8:23). Meaning the wholesale killing or death of large numbers of people.

Work of the Father (1 Nephi 14:17; 3 Nephi 21:7, 26; Ether 4:17). Each verse talks about the purposes, designs, and plans of God the Father commencing to take place.

Work out your salvation (Alma 34:37; Mormon 9:27). We are saved unto salvation by our good works, for it is by grace we are saved after all we can do (see 2 Nephi 25:23). *See also:* Good works; Grace of God; Judged according to (of) their works; Salvation of our (their) souls.

Work shall commence (1 Nephi 14:17; 2 Nephi 3:13; 30:8; 21:27; Mormon 3:17). *See:* Work of the Father.

Workers of darkness (and secret combinations) (Alma 37:28, 30–31). Satan and his angels and the men and women that follow evil ways. *See also:* Full of darkness; Workers of iniquity; Works of darkness.

Workers of iniquity (Alma 5:32, 37). "Draw me not away with the wicked, and with the workers of iniquity, which speak peace to their neighbours, but mischief is in their hearts" (Psalm 28:3). "Our heavenly Father is more liberal in His views, and boundless in His mercies and blessings, than we are ready to believe or receive; and, at the same time, is more terrible to the workers of iniquity, more awful in the executions of His punishments, and more ready to detect every false way, than we are apt to suppose Him to be" (Joseph Smith, *History of the Church*, 5:136).

Workest according to their (after men have) faith (Ether 12:29–30; Moroni 10:7). *See:* According to his (my/our/the/their/thy/your) faith.

Work(-ing) mighty miracles (2 Nephi 26:13; Mosiah 3:5; 8:18; 15:6; Alma 23:6; 37:41; Helaman 16:4; 4 Nephi 1:5; Mormon 1:13). One of the gifts of the spirit is the working of miracles. God is a God of miracles, and miracles are manifest to the faithful. We must not seek miracles for a sign. Rather, working miracles is a blessing and a gift to humble followers of Christ. *See also:* God of miracles.

Workings in (of) the Spirit (1 Nephi 19:20; 2 Nephi 1:6; Jacob 4:15; Words of Mormon 1:7; Moroni 6:9). Meaning those things caused or brought about by the Holy Ghost. Workings of the Spirit include but are not limited to the manifestations of the gifts of the Spirit, the revelations and inspirations of the Spirit, and the influences of and the sanctification by the power of the Spirit. *See also:* Given by the Spirit of God; Power of the Holy Ghost (Spirit).

Works are in the dark (2 Nephi 27:27; 28:9). *See:* Works of darkness.

Works of darkness (2 Nephi 9:9; 10:15; 25:2; 26:10, 22; 30:17; Alma 37:21, 23; 45:12; Helaman 6:28, 30; 8:4; 10:3; Mormon 8:27). These are the works of the devil, his minions and those that follow them. The devil "is the founder of . . . works of darkness. . . . The Lord God worketh not in darkness" (2 Nephi 26:22–23). *See also:* Full of darkness; Secret combination(-s); Work in (of) darkness; Workers of darkness (and secret combinations); Works are in the dark.

Works of God (Mormon 9:16). *See:* Work(-s) of the Lord.

Works of justice (Alma 12:32; 42:13, 22). Here the word *works* means the results or consequences brought about by justice. *See:* Demands of justice; Power of justice.

Works of righteousness (Alma 5:16–17, 35–36). Works that bring about righteousness among the people and building of the kingdom of God. *See also:* Do good; Right way(-s of the Lord); Work(-s) of the Lord.

Work(-s) of the Lord (2 Nephi 1:10; 15:12; Jacob 4:8; Mosiah 8:20; Alma 18:39; 19:36; Helaman 3:26; 3 Nephi 29:5; Mormon 8:21; 9:26). In Moses 1:39, God proclaims, "This is my work and my glory— to bring to pass the immortality and eternal life of man." Latter-day revelations declare: "great and marvelous are the works of the Lord" (D&C 76:114); the Lord's works "have no end" (D&C 29:33); and "the works . . . of God cannot be frustrated" (D&C 3:1). *See also:* Dealings of the Lord God; Doings of the Lord; Works of righteousness.

Works whether they be good or evil (Mosiah 3:24; 16:10; Alma 5:41; 9:28; 11:44; 3 Nephi 26:4; 27:14; Mormon 3:20). On this basis will our lives be judged. *See also:* Choose good (or evil); Judged according to (of) their works.

Works which are meet for repentance (Alma 5:54; 9:30). *See:* Meet for repentance.

Works will condemn us (Alma 12:14). According to this verse our words, our works, and even our thoughts will be judged. We must become changed and strive with our might to possess only good words, works, and thoughts.

Worship God (1 Nephi 11:24; 2 Nephi 25:29; Alma 15:17; 21:6; 22:7; 32:3, 10–11; 33:2; 34:38; 43:9–10; 45:1; 3 Nephi 11:17; 17:10). "It is written, Thou shalt worship the Lord thy God, and him only shalt thou serve" (Luke 4:8). It is not only a command to worship God, but we should desire to worship Him because of our reverence and gratitude to Him. Additionally, men and women have an innate characteristic to worship. It appears to be part of the eternal nature of intelligence, an inborn essence of existence, of which our understanding of the plan of salvation begins to enlighten our minds. Too many in the world, however, do not know to what or to whom that worship should be directed, making coming to know God all the more important. *See also:* Worship in spirit and truth; Know God.

Worship God according to their desires (Alma 43:9). The Eleventh Article of Faith states, "We claim the privilege of worshiping Almighty God according to the dictates of our own conscience, and allow all men the same privilege, let them worship how, where, or what they may."

Worship God before the altar (Alma 15:17). Under the law of Moses, the people made sacrifices on and worshipped before the altar of the temple. Today we privately worship within the temple before its altars and before the sacrament table in our meetinghouses. *See also:* Altar of God.

Worship God in his name (2 Nephi 25:16; Jacob 4:5). Meaning worship God the Father in the name of Jesus Christ, His Only Begotten Son. "All men must repent and believe on the name of Jesus Christ, and worship the Father in his name, and endure in faith on his name to the end, or they cannot be saved in the kingdom of God" (D&C 20:29). We are commanded to do all worthy things in the name of Christ. *See also:* Whatsoever thing ye do ye shall do it in my name.

Worship him with all your might, mind, and strength (2 Nephi 25:29). Anything less would be insincere, hypocritical, and insufficient to gain salvation.

Worship in spirit and truth (Alma 34:38; 43:10). The scriptural phrase used in the scriptures to describe true worship. It simply means to worship the true God (in truth) and do so with the assistance of the Holy Ghost (in Spirit). *See also:* John 4:22–26.

Worship me saith God (2 Nephi 10:19). The first commandment is "Thou shalt have no other gods before me" (Exodus 20:3). "Him only shalt thou serve" (Moses 1:15).

Worship the Lord (their/thy God) (1 Nephi 17:55; 18:1; Mosiah 18:25; 50:39). We worship the Lord Jesus and God the Father. *See also:* Worship God; Worship God according to their desires; Worship God before the altar; Worship God in his name; Worship him with all your might, mind, and strength; Worship in spirit and truth; Worship me saith God.

Would not hear (Alma 10:6; 19:32; 21:10–11). When men and women sin and harden their hearts, they choose not to hear the word of God, which testifies of their sin. For them the word of God is hard to bear, and they mock rather than obey. *See also:* Deaf that will not hear . . . blind that will not see, for they shall perish; Deafness of their ears; Open their (your) ears to hear; Voice of the Good Shepherd.

Would to God (Jacob 1:8; Alma 13:25; 39:7). The expression of one's wish or desire, so sincere that it is almost a request of God.

Wrapt together as a scroll (3 Nephi 26:3; Mormon 5:23; 9:2). Refers to the change that will take place in the earth's surface at the Lord's Second Coming, when the seas will be pushed to the north and the south and all the continents will come back together as they were in Adam's time (see D&C 133:22–24). In the terms of the Tenth Article of Faith, "The earth will be renewed and receive its paradisiacal glory."

Wrath of God (the Lord) (1 Nephi 13:11, 14, 18; 14:15–17; 17:35; 22:16; 2 Nephi 19:19; 23:13; Mosiah 3:26; 5:5; 7:28; Alma 10:18; 14:11; 40:14; Ether 2:11). The righteous indignation and perfect justice that is poured out upon the wicked who do not repent but rebel against God and against that which is good. *See also:* Anger of the Lord.

Wrest(-ed) the scriptures (Alma 13:20; 41:1). Many attempt to interpret the scriptures to their own liking, so as to justify themselves. "Every day they wrest my words: all their thoughts are against me for evil" (Psalm 56:5). "Satan doth stir up the hearts of the people to contention concerning the points of my doctrine; and in these things they do err, for they do wrest the scriptures and do not understand them" (D&C 10:63). *See also:* Understand (understood) not the scriptures.

Wrestle which I had before God (Enos 1:2). Elder Jeffrey R. Holland said, "Pray to your Father in Heaven for help. Pray to Him as Enos did, who wrestled before God and struggled mightily in the spirit. (See Enos 1:2–10.) Wrestle like Jacob did with the angel, *refusing to let go until a blessing had come* (see Genesis 32:24–26)" ("'Sanctify Yourselves,'" 39; emphasis added).

Wrestling with God in mighty prayer (Alma 8:10). *See:* Mighty prayer; Wrestle which I had before God.

Write the (these) things (words) (1 Nephi 6:3, 5; 13:35; 14:23–24; 2 Nephi 4:15; 25:3, 21; 26:17; 29:11; 31:1; 33:1, 11; Jacob 1:2; 4:1–2; Enos 1:23; Jarom 1:2; Omni 1:4, 9; Words of Mormon 1:5; Mosiah 29:33; Alma 45:9; 3 Nephi 5:18;

23:4; 24:1; 26:12; 27:23; Mormon 3:20; 8:1; Ether 3:27; 4:1; 8:26; Moroni 1:4; 9:24). God has commanded that a record be kept for the benefit of man. Also, when the Lord has revealed things to His prophets, He has often commanded them to record those revelations for the benefit of man, as a witness of God's works, and in some cases to be hid up until a future time. *See also:* Commanded to write; Write the (these) things (words); Write these sayings after I am gone; Written the words which were commanded me; Wrote them down.

Write these sayings after I am gone (3 Nephi 16:4). *See:* Write the (these) things (words).

Written in your hearts (Mosiah 5:12; 13:11). In our hearts lie our true intents. God knoweth our hearts (see Alma 18:32), and if His law is written in our hearts, and if our deeds are good and kept deep within our hearts, then all will be well for us in the last day.

Written the words which were commanded me (2 Nephi 29:11; 3 Nephi 24:1; Ether 5:1). *See:* Write the (these) things (words).

Wrote them down (1 Nephi 1:16; Mosiah 26:33). There are many examples in the scriptures in which, after God has spoken to men, those men have written down the words or commands of God. Often the scriptures say God has commanded that the word be written down.

Personally each of us should also write down our spiritual impressions and the whisperings of the Spirit that come to us—both for our own remembrance and for the benefit of our posterity. A very important part of studying the scriptures is the "waiting for spiritual impressions, and writing [them] down" (Christofferson, "When Thou Art Converted," 11). *See also:* Write the (these) things (words).

Wrought a mighty change in our (their) hearts (Mosiah 5:2, 12–13; Alma 5:13; Ether 12:14; Moroni 6:4). *See:* Spirit of God wrought upon him (them).

Wrought miracle(-s) (1 Nephi 17:51; 2 Nephi 10:4; 28:6; Alma 26:12; 37:40; Helaman 16:23; 3 Nephi 1:4; 4 Nephi 1:5, 13, 29; Mormon 9:17–19; Ether 12:16, 18; Moroni 7:37). The word *wrought* means brought about or accomplished. *See also:* God of miracles; Miracles wrought among them.

Wrought upon by the power of God (Enos 1:26; Alma 37:40; Mormon 7:9; 9:17; Moroni 6:4). To be affected or changed by the power of God. *See also:* Power of God; Spirit of God wrought upon him (them).

Wrought upon by the Spirit (1 Nephi 13:12–13; 17:52; 19:12; Enos 1:26; 3 Nephi 7:22; Moroni 6:4). *Wrought upon* means visited, affected, and brought about a change. *See also:* Visit them with his Spirit; Spirit of God wrought upon him (them).

Y

Ye are as dross (Alma 34:29). *Dross* is garbage, debris, and waste. Amulek states here that if we turn away the needy and are not charitable we are as dross to be cast out. *See also:* Poor and needy.

Ye are free (2 Nephi 2:27; 10:23; Helaman 14:30). Meaning we have our moral agency and are free to choose good or evil.

Ye are of the house of Israel (1 Nephi 12:9; 2 Nephi 6:5; 3 Nephi 20:25; Mormon 7:2). *See:* House of Israel; Numbered among the house of Israel.

Ye cannot hide your crimes from God (2 Nephi 13:9; 27:27; Alma 12:14–15; 39:8). God knows of all our actions, thoughts, and intents. *See also:* All-searching eye; Holiness of heart; Intents of our hearts; Know all my (thy) thoughts; Real intent (of heart); Thoughts and intents of his (the) heart.

Ye ends of the earth (3 Nephi 9:22). An invitation to all the people on the earth. *See also:* All ye ends of the earth.

Ye need not suppose (1 Nephi 22:31; 2 Nephi 29:9–10; 30:1; Alma 60:13; 3 Nephi 29:2, 3, 9). Do not make incorrect suppositions or conclusions. Instead, seek only the truth that is from God.

Ye shall defend your families even unto bloodshed (Alma 43:47). *See:* Defend themselves.

Ye shall find rest (3 Nephi 28:3). *See:* Enter into his (my/the) rest (of the Lord/of God).

Ye shall have eternal life (faith/ hope/joy/justice/mercy/my Spirit/ my words/power/righteous judgment) (2 Nephi 31:20; Jacob 5:71, 75; Alma 41:14; Helaman 5:41; 10:6; 3 Nephi 9:14; 12:12; 18:7, 11; 28:10; Mormon 9:30; Moroni 2:2; 7:33, 40–41). The various and numberless promises God makes to the faithful.

Ye shall have power (Helaman 10:6; Moroni 2:2; 7:33). *See:* Authority from (of) God; Gift and power of the Holy Ghost; Give the Holy Ghost.

Ye shall live (3 Nephi 15:9). Meaning ye shall have eternal life. In 2 Nephi 31:20, 3 Nephi 9:14, and Moroni 7:41, it is rendered, "Ye shall have eternal life." *See also:* Eternal life.

Ye shall receive (3 Nephi 27:29). The Lord assures us that if we ask in faith with real intent, then we will receive. *See also:* Believing that ye shall receive.

Ye shall wonder and perish (2 Nephi 27:4; Mormon 9:26). The wicked that rejected the word of Christ and persisted in sin when warned shall at the dreadful day of the Lord's coming stand in wonder, shock, surprise, astonishment, and stupefaction.

Ye suppose that ye are better than they (that they were [more] righteous/that God justifieth you) (1 Nephi 17:33–34; Jacob 2:13–14; Alma 5:24; 32:10–11; 33:2; 42:25; 60:11–12, 21, 23; Helaman 13:29; 3 Nephi 28:35; Mormon 9:3). No one should suppose they are better than anyone else. We are to be humble and meek and avoid all likeness of pride, for all men are privileged one like unto the other in their invitation to come unto Christ (see 2 Nephi 26:28). "I [the Lord] remember one nation like unto another[.] Wherefore, I speak the same words unto one nation like unto another" (2 Nephi 29:8).

Ye waste places of Jerusalem (Mosiah 12:23; 15:30; 3 Nephi 16:19; 20:34). This is speaking of the millennium, when Jerusalem will be lifted to great glory. "They shall build the old wastes, they shall raise up the former desolations, and they shall repair the waste cities"

(Isaiah 61:4). Through the ages, Jerusalem has been the scene of countless struggles and wars which have laid it to waste many times. All these will be reversed. Additionally, Jerusalem is a desert climate, but in the millennium it will blossom as a rose and become a watered garden. *See also:* Waste places.

Yesterday, today and forever (2 Nephi 2:4; 27:23; 29:9; Alma 31:17; Mormon 9:9; Moroni 10:19). A scriptural phrase meaning always and forever. These words testify of no beginning and no end, being in perpetuity, eternal and endless. *See also:* Same yesterday, today and forever.

Yield to no temptation (Mormon 9:28). Also found in D&C 9:13. Clearly we are not to sin, which is yielding and submitting to temptation. The Savior set the perfect example wherein "He suffered temptations but gave no heed to them" (D&C 20:22). *See also:* Devices of the devil; Enter [not] into temptations; Led away by temptation; Temptations of the devil; Withstand every temptation of the devil with their faith on the Lord Jesus Christ.

Yield up the ghost (Helaman 14:21). To die physically. *See also:* Gave up the ghost.

Yield up their dead (Helaman 14:25). Meaning the graves shall yield up, surrender, and relinquish their dead when the dead are resurrected and come forth out of their graves.

Yielding their hearts unto God (Helaman 3:35). Who do we yield our hearts and full allegiance to: God, man, or Satan? Our thoughts, our words, and our deeds are an indication of whom we yield to. A purpose of life is to prove our faithfulness by striving with our might to channel aright everything we do, say, and think. We must desire with all our heart to do only the will of God, with an eye single to God's glory.

Yield(-ing) themselves (yourselves) unto (the power of) Satan (the devil) (2 Nephi 9:39; 26:10; Alma 5:20; 10:25; 3 Nephi 7:5). To give in to the temptations of Satan and thus make Satan our master so that he may sift us as chaff, bind us down with his awful chains, and make us miserable like unto him. *See also:* Power of Satan.

Yoke of bondage (Mosiah 21:13; Alma 44:2; 49:7; 61:12). The Book of Mormon talks much about bondage: (1) It talks about the mercy and power of God in delivering His people from the yoke of bondage of wicked and oppressive kings, and (2) it talks about how temporal bondage is a similitude of how we can be delivered from the bondage of sin through faith, repentance, and reliance upon the Atonement of Jesus Christ. The Savior speaks of a better way in Matthew 11:28–30, "Come unto me, all ye that labour and are heavy laden, and I will give you rest. Take my yoke upon you, and learn of me; for I am meek and lowly in heart; and ye shall find rest unto your souls. For my yoke is easy, and my burden is light." In other words, the Lord's yoke is light, it is not oppressive, and it brings great peace unto the follower and doer of the word. *See also:* Deliver(-ed) out of bondage.

Yoke of iron (1 Nephi 13:5). D&C 123:8 says, "It is an iron yoke, it is a strong band; they are the very handcuffs, and chains, and shackles, and fetters of hell."

Your nakedness before God (2 Nephi 9:14; Mormon 9:5). *See:* Nakedness before God.

Z

Zeal towards God (Alma 27:27). Meaning passion, determination, and earnestness in doing the will of God.

Zion prospereth (2 Nephi 28:21). More than a few Saints in latter-day Zion are prophesied to become complacent, apathetic, and not watchful as to their faithfulness, so that Satan steals in and captures their souls. The often-repeated prophetic theme in the Book of Mormon is to beware of prosperity and abundance, for it was in so many such cases that the Book of Mormon people prospered, then forgot to humble themselves and forgot to remember God, who was the source of all their blessings.

BIBLIOGRAPHY

Allred, McKell W. *And It Came to Pass.* Victoria, BC, Canada: Friesen Press, 2011.

Neil L. Andersen, "Hold Fast to the Words of the Prophets," CES fireside for young adults, 4 March 2007; available at https://speeches.byu.edu /talks/neil-l-andersen_hold-fast -words-prophets/.

Ballard, M. Russell. *Our Search for Happiness.* Salt Lake City: Deseret Book, 1993.

———. "Standing for Truth and Right." *Ensign,* November 1997, 37–40.

Bednar, David A. In "'Marvelous miracle' of BYU–Idaho." *Church News,* 4 November 2006; available at http://www.ldschurchnewsarchive .com/articles/49721/Marvelous -miracle-of-BYU-Idaho.html.

———. "The Tender Mercies of the Lord." Ensign, May 2005, 99–102.

Belnap, Daniel. "'I Will Contend with Them That Contendeth with Thee': The Divine Warrior in Jacob's Speech of 2 Nephi 6–10." *Journal of the Book of Mormon and Restoration Scripture,* 17/1–2 (2008): 20–39.

Benson, Ezra Taft. "A Marvelous Work and a Wonder." *Ensign,* May 1980, 32–34.

———. *Teachings of Ezra Taft Benson.* Salt Lake City: Deseret Book, 1988.

———. "The Message: To 'the Rising Generation.'" *New Era,* June 1986, 4–8.

Book of Mormon Student Manual. Salt Lake City: The Church of Jesus Christ of Latter-day Saints, 1989.

Brough, Monte J. "Adversity, the Great Teacher." *Ensign,* August 2006, 9–11.

Cambridge Idioms Dictionary, 2nd ed. Cambridge: Cambridge University Press, 2006.

Caussé, Gérald. "'For When I Am Weak, Then Am I Strong.'" BYU devotional address, 3 December 2013. Available at https://speeches .byu.edu/talks/gerald-causse_weak -strong/.

Chadwick, Jeffrey R. "Lehi's House at Jerusalem and the Land of His Inheritance." In John W. Welch, David Seely, and JoAnn Seely, *Glimpses of Lehi's Jerusalem* (Provo, UT: FARMS, 2004), 113–17.

Christofferson, D. Todd. "Building Faith in Christ." *Ensign,* September 2012, 53–55.

———. "When Thou Art Converted." *Ensign,* May 2004, 11–13.

Cook, Quentin L. "The Lord Is My Light." *Ensign,* May 2015, 62–66.

Durant, Will and Ariel. *The Lessons of History.* New York: Simon and Schuster, 1986.

Ehat, Andrew and Cook, Lyndon, eds. *The Words of Joseph Smith.* Provo, UT: BYU Religious Studies Center, 1980.

Encyclopedia of Mormonism. 4 vols. Daniel H. Ludlow, ed. New York: Macmillan, 1992.

Eyring, Henry B. "Serve with the Spirit." *Ensign*, November 2010, 59–62.

———. "Teaching True Doctrine." *Ensign*, April 2009, 5–9.

"The Father and the Son: A Doctrinal Exposition by the First Presidency and the Quorum of the Twelve Apostles [Aug. 1916]." *Ensign*, April 2002, 13–18.

Faust, James E. "The Forces That Will Save Us." *Ensign*, January 2007, 5–9.

Gong, Gerrit. In Marianne Holman, "BYU–Hawaii Students Told to Believe, Not Fear." *Church News*, 2 October 2013; available at https://www.lds.org/church/news/print/byu-hawaii-students-told-to-believe-not-fear?lang=eng.

Gospel Principles. Salt Lake City: The Church of Jesus Christ of Latter-day Saints, 2009.

Hales, Robert D. "Out of Darkness into His Marvelous Light." *Ensign*, May 2002, 69–72.

Hamula, James J. "The Sacrament and the Atonement." *Ensign*, November 2014, 83–85.

Hinckley, Gordon B. "An Ensign to the Nations," *Ensign*, November 1989, 51–54.

———. "An Ensign to the Nations, A Light to the World." *Ensign*, November 2003, 82–84.

———. "The Healing Power of Christ." *Ensign*, November 1988, 52–54, 59.

———. "The Priesthood of Aaron." *Ensign*, November 1982, 44–47.

———. "'Upon You My Fellow Servants.'" *Liahona*, May 1989; available at https://www.lds.org/liahona/1989/05/upon-you-my-fellow-servants?lang=eng.

Holland, Jeffrey R. *Christ and the New Covenant*. Salt Lake City: Deseret Book, 1997.

———. "'Sanctify Yourselves.'" *Ensign*, November 2000, 38–40.

Hunter, Howard W. "Eternal Investments." Address to CES religious educators, 10 February 1989; available at https://www.lds.org/manual/teaching-seminary-preservice-readings-religion-370-471-and-475/eternal-investments?lang=eng.

Hymns of The Church of Jesus Christ of Latter-day Saints. Salt Lake City: The Church of Jesus Christ of Latter-day Saints, 1985.

Johnson, Paul V. "All These Gifts Come from God." BYU–Idaho devotional, 6 June 2006; available at http://www2.byui.edu/Presentations/Transcripts/Devotionals/2006_06_06_Johnson.htm.

Journal of Discourses. 26 vols. Liverpool: Latter-day Saints' Book Depot, 1854–86.

Keyte, Hugh and Parrott, Andrew, eds. *The Shorter New Oxford Book of Carols*. Cambridge: Oxford University Press, 1993.

Kimball, Spencer W. "Becoming the Pure in Heart." *Ensign*, May 1978, 79–81.

———. "An Eternal Hope in Christ." *Ensign*, November 1978, 71–73.

———. *Faith Precedes the Miracle*. Salt Lake City: Deseret Book, 1972.

———. "Second Century Address and Dedication of Carillon Tower and Bells." Available at http://fc.byu.edu/jpages/ee/w_swk75.htm.

———. *Teachings of Spencer W. Kimball.* Edward L. Kimball, ed. Salt Lake City: Bookcraft, 1982.

Lectures on Faith. Salt Lake City: Deseret Book, 1985.

Lee, Harold B. *Stand Ye in Holy Places.* Salt Lake City: Deseret Book, 1976.

Let Virtue Garnish Thy Thoughts. Salt Lake City: The Church of Jesus Christ of Latter-day Saints, 2006.

"Likening the Scriptures to Our Personal Lives." *Ensign,* March 2009, 33–34.

Ludlow, Daniel H. *A Companion to Your Study of The Book of Mormon.* Salt Lake City: Deseret Book, 1976.

———. *A Companion to Your Study of the Doctrine and Covenants.* 2 vols. Salt Lake City: Deseret Book, 1978.

Maxwell, Neal A. *Whom the Lord Loveth.* Salt Lake City: Deseret Book, 2003.

McConkie, Bruce R. "Come: Let Israel Build Zion." *Ensign,* May 1977, 115–18.

———. *Doctrinal New Testament Commentary.* 3 vols. Salt Lake City: Deseret Book, 1973.

———. "Jesus Christ and Him Crucified." BYU devotional, 5 September 1976. Available at https://speeches.byu.edu.

———. "The Lord's People Receive Revelation." *Ensign,* June 1971, 77–78.

———. *Millennial Messiah.* Salt Lake City: Deseret Book, 1982.

———. *Mormon Doctrine.* 2d. edition. Salt Lake City: Bookcraft, 1966.

———. *Mortal Messiah: From Bethlehem to Calvary.* 4 vols. Salt Lake City: Deseret Book, 1979.

———. *A New Witness for the Articles of Faith.* Salt Lake City: Deseret Book, 1985.

———. *Promised Messiah.* Salt Lake City: Deseret Book, 1978.

McConkie, Joseph F. and Millet, Robert L. *Doctrinal Commentary on the Book of Mormon.* 4 vols. Salt Lake City: Bookcraft, 2007.

McKay, David O. *Cherished Experiences from the Writings of President David O. McKay.* Clare Middlemiss, comp. Salt Lake City: Deseret Book, 1955.

Merriam-Webster's Collegiate Dictionary, Eleventh Edition. Springfield, MA: Merriam-Webster, 2003.

Millet, Robert L. *Coming to Know Christ.* Salt Lake City: Deseret Book, 2012.

Minutes of the School of the Prophets, Salt Lake City, 14 January 1871. Family and Church History Department Archives, Salt Lake City, Utah.

Monson, Thomas S. "The Call of Duty." *Ensign,* May 1986, 37–39.

———. "Joy in the Journey." In *Awake, Arise, and Come unto Christ: Talks from the 2008 BYU Women's Conference.* Salt Lake City: Deseret Book, 2009.

———. "The Path to Peace." *Ensign,* May 1994, 60–63.

———. "Priesthood Power." *Ensign,* May 2011, 66–69.

Morrison, Alexander B. "'For This Cause Came I into the World.'" *Ensign,* November 1999, 25–27.

Nash, Marcus B. "The Great Plan of Happiness." *Ensign,* November 2006, 49–50.

Nelson, Russell M. "The Atonement." *Ensign,* November 1996, 33–35.

Nibley, Hugh. *An Approach to the Book of Mormon*. Salt Lake City: Deseret Book, 1964.

Nyman, Monte S. "'I Am Jesus Christ the Son of God.'" *Ensign*, December 1999, 5–11.

Oaks, Dallin H. "The Aaronic Priesthood and the Sacrament." *Ensign*, November 1998, 37–40.

———. "'Another Testament of Jesus Christ.'" BYU fireside, 6 June 1993. Available at https://speeches.byu.edu /talks/dallin-h-oaks_another -testament-jesus-christ/.

Old Testament Student Manual: 1 Kings– Malachi (Religion 302). Salt Lake City: The Church of Jesus Christ of Latter-day Saints, 2003.

Preach My Gospel. Salt Lake City: The Church of Jesus Christ of Latter-day Saints, 2004.

Reynolds, George and Sjodahl, Janne. *Commentary on the Book of Mormon*. 7 vols. Salt Lake City: Deseret Book, 1955.

Richards, LeGrand. *A Marvelous Work and a Wonder*. Salt Lake City: Bookcraft, 1960.

Romney, Marion G. "The Book of Mormon." *Ensign*, May 1980, 65– 67.

———. In Conference Report, October 1953, 34–36.

———. In Conference Report, April 1961, 116–20.

Scott, Richard G. "The Transforming Power of Faith and Character." *Ensign*, November 2010, 43–46.

———. "Trust in the Lord." *Ensign*, November 1995, 16–18.

Skinner, Andrew C. In Holman, Marianne, "Sperry Symposium: Seeing God in His Temple," *Church News*, 17 November 2013; available at http://www.ldschurchnews archive.com/articles/64140/Sperry -Symposium-Seeing-God-in-His -Temple.html

Smith, Joseph. *History of The Church of Jesus Christ of Latter-day Saints*. 7 vols. B. H. Roberts, ed. Salt Lake City: The Church of Jesus Christ of Latter-day Saints, 1932–51.

———. *Teachings of the Prophet Joseph Smith*. Joseph Fielding Smith, comp. Salt Lake City: Deseret Book, 1972.

Smith, Joseph F. *Gospel Doctrine*. Salt Lake City: Deseret Book, 1939.

Smith, Joseph Fielding. *Answers to Gospel Questions*. 5 vols. Salt Lake City: Deseret Book, 1970.

———. *Doctrines of Salvation*. 3 vols. Salt Lake City: Deseret Book, 1962.

Sperry, Sidney B. *Answers to Book of Mormon Questions*. Salt Lake City: Bookcraft, 1967.

Stapley, Delbert L. "Our Responsibility: To Save the World." *Ensign*, December 1971, 94–97.

Talmage, James E. *Articles of Faith*. Salt Lake City: Deseret Book, 1981.

Tanner, N. Eldon. "Christ's Worldwide Church." *Ensign*, July 1974, 2–6.

Taylor, John. *The Gospel Kingdom*. G. Homer Durham, ed. Salt Lake City: Bookcraft, 1987.

———. *The Government of God*. Liverpool: S. W. Richards, 1852.

———. *Mediation and Atonement of Our Lord and Savior Jesus Christ*. Salt Lake City: Deseret News Press, 1882.

Tingey, Earl C. "The Virtue of the Word of God." BYU–Idaho devotional, 23 May 2006. Available at http://www2 .byui.edu/Presentations/Transcripts /Devotionals/2006_05_23_Tingey .htm.

True to the Faith. Salt Lake City: The Church of Jesus Christ of Latter-day Saints, 2004.

Twain, Mark. *The Adventures of Huckleberry Finn*. New York: Harper and Brothers, 1912.

"Types and Shadows: Intimations of Divinity." Exhibition, BYU Museum of Art, 17 September 2009–13 March 2010; available at http://typesandshadows.byu.edu/.

Uchtdorf, Dieter F. "Always in the Middle." *Ensign*, July 2012, 4–5.

———. "Developing Christlike Attributes." *Ensign*, October 2008, 5–9.

Valletta, Thomas R. ed. *Book of Mormon for Latter-day Saint Families*. Salt Lake City: Bookcraft, 1999.

Webster, Noah. *American Dictionary of the English Language, 1828*. Online edition available at http://webstersdictionary1828.com/.

Wirthlin, Joseph B. "It's Your Choice." *Liahona*, November 1998; available at https://www.lds.org/liahona/1998/11/its-your-choice?lang=eng.

———. "Running Your Marathon," *Ensign*, November 1989, 73–75.

Widtsoe, John A. *A Rational Theology*. Salt Lake City: Deseret Book, 1952.

Woodruff, Wilford. *Discourses of Wilford Woodruff*. G. Homer Durham, ed. Salt Lake City: Deseret Book, 1995.

Worldwide Leadership Training Meeting Manual, 11 January 2003. Salt Lake City: The Church of Jesus Christ of Latter-day Saints, 2003.

Young, Brigham. *Discourses of Brigham Young*. Sel. and arr. by John A. Widtsoe. Salt Lake City: Deseret Book, 1971.